T0305441

Operational Risk toward Basel III

Founded in 1807, John Wiley & Sons is the oldest independent publishing company in the United States. With offices in North America, Europe, Australia, and Asia, Wiley is globally committed to developing and marketing print and electronic products and services for our customers' professional and personal knowledge and understanding.

The Wiley Finance series contains books written specifically for finance and investment professionals as well as sophisticated individual investors and their financial advisors. Book topics range from portfolio management to e-commerce, risk management, financial engineering, valuation, and financial instrument analysis, as well as much more.

For a list of available titles, visit our Web site at www.WileyFinance.com.

Operational Risk toward Basel III

*Best Practices and Issues
in Modeling, Management,
and Regulation*

GREG N. GREGORIOU

WILEY

John Wiley & Sons, Inc.

Library of Congress Cataloging-in-Publication Data:

Operational risk toward Basel III : best practices and issues in modeling, management, and regulation / [edited by] Greg N. Gregoriou.
    p. cm. — (Wiley finance series)
  ISBN 978-0-470-39014-6 (cloth)
  1. Banks and banking, International—Risk management. 2. Bank capital—Mathematical models. 3. Financial risk management—Mathematical models. I. Gregoriou, Greg N., 1956–
  HG3881.O58 2009
  332.1068′1—dc22

                                                  2008038661

Contents

Foreword

This is an important book, and it is published at just the right time. I have accepted with great pleasure the invitation to write the Foreword for Greg Gregoriou's new volume on operational risk, but I had not anticipated that it would allow me to reflect on the concurrent unfolding of the disastrous September events. As one financial institution after another is failing or is subjected to an emergency sale, we start to comprehend that the basic rules of banking are in the process of being fundamentally redefined. A significant fallout for the real economy is by now more than likely, and the resulting political tremors will have a potentially decisive impact on the November elections. The reported loss figures are staggering and of almost incomprehensive magnitude for the average citizen. The rescue of the German IKB has, for instance, led to accumulated losses of 9 billion euros so far, an amount that is equivalent to an extra burden of approximately 300 euros for every taxpayer. Hundreds of billions of dollars need to be committed as part of the U.S. government's bailout program, translating into a still-unknown cost for the U.S. taxpayer.

While the crisis is clearly of a systemic nature, its ultimate source lies with the notoriously myopic behavior of the banking community and, as some commentators have argued, is the outcome of collective greed. Bankers have increasingly viewed their careers as long call options that, in the worst case, could force them into a lengthy retirement in a lavish country home. The investor community valued the extraordinary returns and forced the banking community into a prisoner's dilemma where playing the transaction game became a dominant strategy for everybody involved. Betting the bank by taking on excessive liquidity risk exposures was ultimately acceptable because the buildup of counterparty risk made a governmental bailout all the more likely. Industry insiders have warned for quite some time that credit volume growth far exceeding economic growth has historically always led to some form of a financial crisis. Without question, it is particularly worrisome that the whole problem did not appear on the radar of regulatory authorities until it was too late.

The subprime crisis and its fallout in financial markets as well as the real economy will trigger far-reaching regulatory reforms and should also lead to a toughening of the penalty structure for bankers in charge of running complex financial market operations. It, however, also requires institutional efforts by banks to reexamine and strengthen their approaches to risk management. Trading and credit risk management systems must obviously be extended to capture liquidity risk exposures. Financial institutions must, however, also reevaluate the way they are dealing with operational risks in order to impose checks and balances on the bankers' irrational ignorance of the aforementioned prisoner's dilemma problem. It will require changes in the governance structures and the development of adequate back-office systems.

We are still in the early stages of developing a sound understanding of operational risk management. Hence, there is still considerable scope for academics to make valuable contributions with their ongoing research. Greg Gregoriou's new book helps to fill this knowledge gap and does so in a very timely fashion. It provides a comprehensive coverage of this exciting field, ranging from quantitative and qualitative risk measurement approaches to risk mitigation and regulatory implications. The edited volume includes American as well as European viewpoints and brings together academics as well as practitioners. The 23 chapters in total cover a lot of ground and give readers an in-depth overview of the current state of the art in operational risk management. While the contributors could not fully predict recent events, their contributions are nevertheless strongly influenced by the financial market woes of the past 14 months. This volume will therefore shape the discussion on how to better shield financial institutions against operational breakdown in future years.

—ULRICH HOMMEL, PH.D.
Professor of Corporate Finance and Director of the Strategic Finance Institute (SFI), European Business School (EBS), International University, Oestrich-Winkel, Germany
September 2008

About the Editor

A native of Montreal, Dr. Gregoriou obtained his joint PhD at the University of Quebec at Montreal in Finance, which merges the resources of Montreal's four major universities (McGill University, Concordia University, and HEC-Montreal). He has written over 50 articles on hedge funds and managed futures in various peer-reviewed publications. His articles have appeared in the *Journal of Portfolio Management, Journal of Futures Markets, European Journal of Operational Research, Annals of Operations Research*, and others. In addition to a multitude of publications with a variety of publishers, Gregoriou is author of the Wiley books *Stock Market Liquidity; International Corporate Governance After Sarbanes-Oxley; Commodity Trading Advisors; Hedge Funds: Insights in Performance Measurement, Risk Analysis, and Portfolio Allocation*; and *Evaluating Hedge Fund and CTA Performance*.

Professor Gregoriou is hedge fund editor and editorial board member for the *Journal of Derivatives and Hedge Funds*, as well as editorial board member for the *Journal of Wealth Management*, the *Journal of Risk Management in Financial Institutions*, and the *Brazilian Business Review*. Professor Gregoriou's interests focus on hedge funds and managed futures.

Acknowledgments

I would like to thank Jennifer MacDonald, Bill Falloon, and Laura Walsh at John Wiley & Sons for their immense help. I am also deeply indebted to Dr. Georges Hübner, Deloitte Professor of Financial Management in the Department of Accounting, Finance and Law, HEC Management School–University of Liège, for his comments and valuable suggestions, and also thank Jean-Philippe Peters, manager at Deloitte Luxembourg S.A. Finally, I thank the handful of anonymous referees who assisted in the selection and review process of the chapters in this text. Neither the editor nor the publisher is responsible for the accuracy of each individual chapter.

GREG N. GREGORIOU

About the Contributors

Marco Bee is Assistant Professor in Economic Statistics at the University of Trento (Italy). After spending one year as a visiting scholar at the Department of Mathematics of the Indiana University and receiving a PhD in Mathematical Statistics from the University of Trento in 1998 he has held positions at the Risk Management department of Banca Intesa in Milan from 1999 to 2005. His current research interests focus on quantitative risk management and computational statistics.

Keith H. Black serves as an associate at Ennis Knupp + Associates. He is a member of the firm's opportunistic strategies group, which advises foundations, endowments, and pension funds on their asset allocation and manager selection strategies in the alternative investment space. His prior professional experience includes commodities derivatives trading at First Chicago Capital Markets, stock options research and CBOE market-making for Hull Trading Company, and building stock selection models for mutual funds and hedge funds for Chicago Investment Analytics. He has also served as a research consultant to an equity brokerage firm and a hedge fund marketing firm. Mr. Black contributes regularly to *The CFA Digest*, and has published in *the Journal of Global Financial Markets, the Journal of Trading, the Journal of Financial Compliance and Regulation,* and *Derivatives Use Trading and Regulation.* He is the author of *Managing a Hedge Fund,* which was named to the list of the top 10 books of 2005 by the *Financial Engineering News.* He has been quoted over 50 times on hedge fund and equity market topics in the print and broadcast media, including the *Financial Times, Chicago Tribune, CFA Magazine, Pensions and Investments*, NPR, Fox, and NBC. Mr. Black previously served as an assistant professor at the Illinois Institute of Technology, where he taught a variety of courses in portfolio management and alternative investments, including equity valuation, hedge funds, and enterprise formation and finance. Mr. Black earned a BA from Whittier College in Economics and Mathematics/Computer Science as well as an MBA in Finance and Operations Research from Carnegie Mellon University. He has earned the Chartered Financial Analyst (CFA) and the Chartered Alternative Investment Analyst (CAIA) designations. He serves as a member of the CFA Institute's Retained Speakers Bureau, where he is regularly invited to present to CFA Society members worldwide on topics related to alternative investments.

Klaus Böcker is Senior Risk Controller at UniCredit Group. In this capacity, one of his primary responsibilities is overseeing all quantitative aspects of UniCredit Group's economic capital model. He studied theoretical physics at the Munich University of Technology. His main research interest is quantitative finance with special focus on risk integration and operational risk. Mr. Böcker published several papers in *Risk Magazine* and the *Journal of Risk*, and together with his coauthor, Claudia Klüppelberg, he recently received the 2007 New Frontiers in Risk Management Award of the PRMIA Institute for their research paper entitled "Multivariate Models for Operational Risk."

Silke N. Brandts is currently head of innovation and consulting management for transaction banking at DZ BANK in Frankfurt, Germany. Previously she was Project Manager at Bain & Company, Germany, in the financial service practice. She obtained her doctorate at the graduate program Finance and Monetary Economics at the Johann Wolfgang Goethe-Universität Frankfurt, Germany, after having pursued her Master's degree in Economics at the Universities of Bonn, Germany, and University of California, Berkeley.

Nicole Branger is currently Professor for Derivatives and Financial Engineering at the Westfälische Wilhelms-Universität Münster. Previously she held positions as Associate Professor at the University of Southern Denmark, Odense, as Visiting Professor of Management at the Owen Graduate School of Management, Vanderbilt University, United States, and as Assistant Professor at the Johann Wolfgang Goethe-Universität Frankfurt, Germany. She obtained her doctorate as well as her Master's in Industrial Engineering and Management at the University of Karlsruhe, Germany.

Tyrone M. Carlin is Professor and Dean of Law at Macquarie University and holds concurrent posting as Professor of Management at Macquarie Graduate School of Management. His research is concentrated in the areas of corporate governance and corporate financial reporting. He has published more than 100 articles in his fields of interest and is coeditor of the *Journal of Law & Financial Management* and the *Journal of Applied Research in Accounting and Finance*.

Simona Cosma is Researcher of Financial Institutions and Lecturer in Financial Institutions Management at the University of Salento (Italy). She holds a PhD in Banking and Finance from the University of Rome "Tor Vergata." Her research interests and publications include risk management and bank organization and marketing. She has been also coordinator and lecturer in professional training courses for banks, and she also acted as a consultant for the Italian Bankers' Association.

Carolyn Vernita Currie is a member of the Association of Certified Practising Accountants, the Chartered Secretaries Association, and a fellow of Finsia, a merger of the Australian Institute of Banking and Finance and the Securities Institute. She has almost four decades of experience in the public and private sector, as a merchant banker, regulator, internal auditor, and financial trainer. For the last 15 years she has been a Senior Lecturer in Financial Services at the University of Technology Sydney (UTS) as well as Managing Director of her own consulting company and several private investment companies.

Magali Dubosson is Dean of the Economics and Management Department of the Geneva School of Business Administration (HEG-Genève). She is a marketing professor at HEG Genève and also lecturer at EPFL, Essec Management Education Paris and at Ecole des Ponts et Chaussées Paris (AFT-IFTIM). She got her Master's degree in International Management and her PhD at HEC, University of Lausanne. Her main research interests are the pricing of services, customer service, and business models.

Giuseppe Espa is Professor in Economic Statistics at the University of Trento (Italy). In 1995 he received a PhD in Statistics from the University of Rome "La Sapienza." From 1994 to 2001 he was assistant professor and from 2001 to 2006 associate professor in economic statistics. He has been working with the Italian National Statistical Office (Istat), the Italian National Research Council (CNR), and the College of Europe. His main research interests concern spatial econometrics and applied statistics.

John Evans holds a PhD from the University of Illinois. He is currently a Professor and Pro Vice Chancellor of Curtin University in Miri, Sarawak. He is a well-experienced academic with a corporate finance background, and he is well published in internationally refereed journals in financial economics and corporate finance.

Dean Fantazzini is a Lecturer in econometrics and finance at the Moscow School of Economics—Moscow State University. He graduated with honors from the Department of Economics at the University of Bologna (Italy) in 1999. He obtained a Master's in Financial and Insurance Investments at the Department of Statistics—University of Bologna (Italy) in 2000 and a PhD in Economics in 2006 at the Department of Economics and Quantitative Methods, University of Pavia (Italy). Before joining the Moscow School of Economics, he was a research fellow at the Chair for Economics and

Econometrics, University of Konstanz (Germany) and at the Department of Statistics and Applied Economics, University of Pavia (Italy). He is a specialist in time series analysis, financial econometrics, multivariate dependence in finance, and economics with more than 20 publications.

Nigel Finch is a lecturer in Management at the Macquarie Graduate School of Management, specializing in the areas of managerial accounting and financial management. His research interests are in the areas of accounting and management decision making, finance and investment management, and financial services management. Prior to joining Macquarie Graduate School of Management, Mr. Finch worked as a financial controller for both public and private companies operating in the manufacturing, entertainment, media, and financial services industries. Subsequently he worked as an investment manager specializing in Australian growth stocks for institutional investment funds.

Guy Ford is Associate Professor of Management at Macquarie Graduate School of Management, where he teaches in the areas of financial management, corporate acquisitions, corporate reconstructions, and financial institutions management. Formerly of the Treasury Risk Management Division of the Commonwealth Bank of Australia, he has published refereed research papers in a range of Australian and international journals and is the coauthor of two books, *Financial Markets & Institutions in Australia* and *Readings in Financial Institutions Management*. He is a founding coeditor of the *Journal of Law and Financial Management*.

Emmanuel Fragnière, CIA (Certified Internal Auditor), is a professor of service management at the Haute Ecole de Gestion of Geneva, Switzerland. He is also a lecturer at the Management School of the University of Bath, UK. He specializes in energy, environmental, and financial risk. He has published several papers in academic journals such as *Annals of Operations Research, Environmental Modeling and Assessment, Interfaces,* and *Management Science.*

Giampaolo Gabbi is Professor of Financial Markets and Risk Management at the University of Siena, Italy, and Professor SDA Bocconi Milan, where he coordinates several executive courses on financial forecasting and risk management. He coordinates the McS in Finance at the University of Siena and is also head of the Master's in Economics at the same university. Professor Gabbi holds a PhD in Banking and Corporate Management. He has published many books and articles in refereed journals, including *Managerial Finance*, the *European Journal of Finance*, and the *Journal of Economic Dynamics and Control.*

Andrea Giacomelli is Professor of Contract in Risk Management at the Ca' Foscari University of Venice, is collaborating with GRETA Consulting (a division of Ca' Foscari FR s.r.l.), and is a partner in Financial Innovations, an Italian consulting firm specialized in risk management. He holds a degree from the Ca' Foscari University of Venice (Laurea in Economics). His research interests are in risk measurement and management, pricing of assets subjected to credit risk, credit scoring models, back-testing of rating systems, statistical analysis of subjective information, Bayesian networks, and econometrics. His main advisory experiences concern the development of credit rating systems and the development of approaches for the subjective analysis of risks. He teaches risk management in the International Master's in Economics and Finance program and Market and Credit Risk in the undergraduate program, and he is one of the local organizers of the CREDIT conference in Venice.

Werner Gleissner is currently the CEO of FutureValue Group AG and a Managing Director of RMCE RiskCon GmbH. The author of more than 100 articles and more than a dozen books, his current research and development activities and projects focus on risk management, rating, strategy development, the development of methods for aggregating risks, value-based management valuation, decision making under uncertainty, and imperfect capital markets. Dr. Werner lectures at various universities in the field of rating, risk management, value-based management, and entrepreneurship. Dr. Werner is also the editor of the well-known loose-leaf series on corporate risk management ("Risikomanagement im Unternehmen"). He holds a degree as a commercial engineer equivalent to a Master's in Business Engineering and a PhD in Economics and Econometrics, both from the University of Karlsruhe, Germany.

Duc Pham-Hi, PhD, is Professor of Computational Finance at ECE Graduate School of Engineering in Paris, France, and Partner at R2M-Analytics. Formerly Senior Attaché at French Commission Bancaire, member of the European Union's CEBS Op Risk working group, and Basel Accord Implementation Group on Op risk (AIGOR), he was previously proprietary trader at Natexis Banque, then director at PriceWaterhouseCoopers.

Georges Hübner, PhD, INSEAD, is the Deloitte Professor of Financial Management and cochair of the Finance Department at HEC Management School of the University of Liège. He is Associate Professor of Finance at Maastricht University and Academic Expert at the Luxembourg School of Finance, University of Luxembourg. He is also the founder and CEO of Gambit Financial Solutions, a financial software spin-off company of the University of Liège. Dr. Hübner has taught at the executive and postgraduate levels in several countries in Europe, North America, Africa, and Asia. He regularly provides executive training seminars for the preparation of the GARP (Global Association of Risk Professionals) and CAIA (Chartered Alternative Investment Analyst) certifications. His research articles have been published in leading scientific journals, including *Journal of Banking and Finance, Journal of Empirical Finance, Review of Finance, Financial Management,* and *Journal of Portfolio Management.* Dr. Hübner was the recipient of the prestigious 2002 Iddo Sarnat Award for the best paper published in the *Journal of Banking and Finance* in 2001. He is also corecipient of the Operational Risk & Compliance Achievement Award 2006 in the best academic paper category.

Andreas A. Jobst is a midcareer economist at the Monetary and Capital Markets Department (MCM) of the International Monetary Fund (IMF) in Washington, DC. His research focuses on structured finance, risk management, sovereign debt management, financial regulation, and time series econometrics. He previously worked at the Division for Insurance and Research at the Federal Deposit Insurance Corporation (FDIC), the Deutsche Bundesbank, the Center for Financial Studies (CFS) in Frankfurt/Main, the European Central Bank (ECB), the Bank of England, the Comisión Económica para América Latina y el Caribe (CEPAL) of the United Nations, the European Securitization Group of Deutsche Bank, and the Boston Consulting Group (BCG). Mr. Jobst holds a PhD in Finance from the London School of Economics (LSE). He was also educated in Oxford, Cambridge, Leicester, and Maryland. Dr. Jobst is a regular speaker at professional and academic conferences on risk management and structured finance. His most recent research was published in *Derivatives Use, Trading & Regulation, Journal of Derivatives and Hedge Funds, Managerial Finance, International Journal of Emerging Markets, Journal of Banking Regulation, Journal of Structured Finance, International Journal of Banking Law and Regulation, Journal of Operational Risk, Journal of Financial Regulation and Compliance, The Securitization Conduit, Operational Risk & Compliance,* and *Euromoney.* He has also been one of the authors of the *Global Financial Stability Report* published by the Monetary and Capital Markets Department of the International Monetary Fund (2005–2007).

Meredith A. Jones is Director of Market Research at Strategic Financial Solutions, LLC, a software company founded in 1996 whose mission is to provide solutions relating to the technological needs of the financial industry. She is responsible for researching, speaking, and writing about alternative and traditional investments as well as developing and implementing marketing initiatives and strategic partnerships for SFS. She has written articles for a number of financial publications, including the *Journal of the Alternative*

Investment Management Association, Alternative Investment Quarterly, the Investment Management Consultants Association's *Monitor,* and the Managed Funds Association *Reporter.* Her research has appeared in the *Wall Street Journal, Bloomberg Wealth Manager, Hedge Fund Alert, Infovest 21,* and other publications. Prior to joining SFS, Ms. Jones was Vice President and Director of Research for Van Hedge Fund Advisors International, Inc., a global hedge fund consultant with $500 million under management. There she led a staff of 10 research analysts in manager selection, evaluation, and ongoing monitoring. Ms. Jones conducted quantitative and qualitative due diligence, on-site visits and portfolio construction, as well as a number of other research functions.

Claudia Klüppelberg holds the Chair of Mathematical Statistics at the Center for Mathematical Sciences of the Munich University of Technology. She has held positions at the University of Mannheim and in the Insurance Mathematics group of the Department Mathematik at ETH Zurich. Her research interests combine applied probability and statistics with special application to finance and insurance risk processes. She is an Elected Fellow of the Institute of Mathematical Statistics, a member of the Editorial Board of the Springer Finance book series, and associate editor of several scientific journals. Besides numerous publications in scientific journals, Dr. Klüppelberg coauthored the book *Modelling Extremal Events for Insurance and Finance* (Springer 1997) with P. Embrechts and T. Mikosch.

K. Ahmet Köse is Associate Professor in the Business Administration School of Istanbul University in Istanbul, Turkey. He received his PhD and Master's degree in Finance from Istanbul University and was at the University of Illinois as a visiting scholar. His main interests are corporate finance and capital markets. His papers have been published in the *Journal of Business Administration, International Journal of Business Management and Economics,* and other journals. He served as the editor of *Journal of Business* in the B-School at Istanbul University and was vice-director of the Social Sciences Institute. He is a member of the Society of Certified Public Accountants of Istanbul. He is also a part-time adviser of a leading company in the Turkish Logistics industry.

Kimberly D. Krawiec is a Professor of Law at the University of North Carolina and has taught at many other law schools, including Harvard, Virginia, and Northwestern. She teaches courses in securities, corporate, and derivatives law. Professor Krawiec's research interests span a variety of fields, including the empirical analysis of contract disputes; the choice of organizational form by professional service firms, including law firms; banned commercial exchanges; corporate compliance systems; insider trading; derivatives hedging practices; and "rogue" trading. Prior to joining academia, she was a member of the Commodity & Derivatives Group at the New York office of Sullivan & Cromwell. Professor Krawiec has served as a commentator for the Central European and Eurasian Law Initiative (CEELI) of the American Bar Association and on the faculty of the National Association of Securities Dealers Institute for Professional Development at the Wharton School of Business. Representative recent publications include: "Common-law Disclosure Duties and the Sin of Omission: Testing the Meta-theories" (with K. Zeiler), 91 VA. L. REV. 1795 (2005); "Organizational Misconduct: Beyond the Principal-Agent Model," 32 FL. ST. L. REV. 571 (2005); "The Economics of Limited Liability: An Empirical Study of New York Law Firms" (with S. Baker), 2005 U. ILL. L. REV. 107 (2005); "Cosmetic Compliance and the Failure of Negotiated Governance," 81 WASH. U. L. Q. 487 (2003); and "Accounting for Greed: Unraveling the Rogue Trader Mystery," 72 OR. L. REV. 301 (2000).

Wilhelm K. Kross is currently Senior Vice President at Marsh GmbH, Germany, with previous working experience in Africa and North America. He holds a postgraduate degree in engineering from RWTH Aachen, Germany, an executive MBA from Athabasca University, Canada, and a PhD in Finance from the European Business School (EBS) International University, Germany. He is a recognized expert in the fields of project and risk management and is the author of numerous publications, including *Organized Opportunities: Risk Management in Financial Services Operations* (Wiley, 2006).

María Dolores Martínez Miranda is Associate Professor at the Faculty of Sciences in the University of Granada (Spain). She received her PhD in Mathematics from the University of Granada in 2000. Her current research interests include nonparametric density and regression estimation, mixed-effects model, and survey sampling.

Jens Perch Nielsen is Professor of Actuarial Statistics at Cass Business School, London, and CEO of the Danish-based knowledge company Festina Lente. He holds a degree in actuarial science from Copenhagen and in statistics from UC-Berkeley. He is former research director of Royal@SunAlliance with responsibilities in life as well as in non-life insurance. He is coauthor of about 50 scientific papers in journals of actuarial science, econometrics, and statistics.

Loriana Pelizzon is Associate Professor of Economics at the Ca' Foscari University of Venice. She graduated from the London Business School with a PhD in Finance. She also holds a degree from the University of Venice (Laurea in Business Administration). She was Assistant Professor in

Economics at the University of Padova from 2000 until 2004. Her research interests are on risk measurement and management, asset allocation and household portfolios, hedge funds, financial institutions, and financial crisis. Her work includes papers published in the *Journal of Financial and Quantitative Analysis, Journal of Banking and Finance, European Journal of Finance, Journal of Economics and Business, Journal of Empirical Finance*, and presentations at the Western Finance Association and European Finance Association. Professor Pelizzon has been awarded the EFA 2005—Barclays Global Investor Award for the Best Symposium paper and FMA European Conference 2005 best conference paper. She participates in many research projects and has acted as a referee for many prestigious journals. Moreover, she is a member of the Program Committee of the European Finance Association Conferences, coordinator of the EFA Doctoral Tutorial, and a member of the Teaching Committee of the PhD in Economics, University of Venice. She teaches Financial Economics and Investments in the International Master in Economics and Finance program as well as Economics and Financial Economics in the undergraduate program. She has been awarded the Best Teacher 2006 at the Ca' Foscari University of Venice. She frequently advises banks and government agencies on risk measurement and risk management strategies through her collaboration at GRETA Consulting, a division of Ca'Foscari FR s.r.l., and she is one of the local organizers of the CREDIT conference in Venice.

Jean-Philippe Peters is Manager at Deloitte Luxembourg, working in the Enterprise Risk Services unit. His expertise focuses on risk measurement and management for financial institutions, and he was actively involved in numerous Basel II–related assignments for institutions in Luxembourg, Belgium, Norway, United Arab Emirates, and South Korea. Beside his practical experience, Mr. Peters is the author of several academic publications on operational risk modeling. He is also corecipient of the Operational Risk & Compliance Achievement Award 2006 in the best academic paper category. Mr. Peters holds a Master's in Business Management from University of Liège, and he is a certified Financial Risk Manager (FRM) by the Global Association of Risk Professionals. He is finishing his PhD in Finance at the HEC Management School of the University of Liège.

Omar Rachedi received a BA degree and a MSc in Economics from the University of Pisa (Italy). He was an assistant of Professor Carlo Bianchi, Department of Economics at the University of Pisa (Italy) and now is a consultant in quantitative risk management for Deloitte Italia S.p.A. Mr. Rachedi's research interests include practical and theoretical aspects of multivariate models for risk management, with a focus on operational risk.

Fabrice Douglas Rouah is a Vice President for State Street Corporation in Boston, Massachusetts. He received his PhD in Finance and his M.Sc. in Statistics from McGill University, and his B.Sc. in Applied Mathematics from Concordia University. Dr. Rouah is the coauthor and coeditor of five books on hedge funds and option pricing, and his research is published regularly in peer-reviewed academic journals.

Daniela Russo has been Deputy Director General of the Directorate General Payment Systems and Market Infrastructure since June 2005, having joined the European Central Bank in 1998. She is a member of the SWIFT Oversight Groups; the Clearing, the Settlement Advisory and Monitoring Expert (CESAME) Group; and the Monitoring Group on the implementation of the Code of Conduct. Ms. Russo is chairperson of various internal working groups of the Eurosystem (including the Contact Group on Euro Securities Infrastructure [COGESI]) and of the CPSS working group on cross-border collateral arrangements.

Gianfausto Salvadori holds a PhD in Applied Mathematics and is Researcher of Probability and Mathematical Statistics at the University of Salento (Lecce, Italy). His research interests and publications concern the application of the theory of extreme values to geophysical phenomena and the modeling of multivariate extreme events via copulas.

John L. Simpson has a PhD from the University of Western Australia and a Master's of Commerce from Curtin University. He is currently an Associate Professor in the School of Economics and Finance at Curtin University in Western Australia. He is well published in international refereed journals of economics and financial economics on the broad research areas of international banking and finance and international risk management.

M. Nihat Solakoğlu is Assistant Professor in the Banking and Finance Department of Bilkent University in Ankara, Turkey. Previously he was assistant professor in the Department of Management at Fatih University. Before joining Fatih University, he worked for American Express in the United States in international risk management, international information management, information and analysis, and fee services marketing departments. He received his PhD in Economics and Master's in Statistics from North Carolina State University. His main interests are applied finance and international finance. His papers have been published in *Applied Economics, Journal of International Financial Markets, Institutions & Money*, and *Journal of Economic and Social Research*, and others.

Stefan A. Sperlich is Chair of Econometrics at the Georg August University Göttingen, Faculty of Economic Sciences. He holds degrees from Göttingen and Humboldt University, Berlin. His primary research interest is in applied econometrics, econometric theory, and nonparametric inference.

Pietro Stecconi graduated in Economics at the University of Rome "La Sapienza" and postlaureate specialized in Banking and Finance. After working at a commercial bank as portfolio manager, he joined the Banca d'Italia in 1989 in the payment systems area, where he has been dealing primarily with financial markets policy issues. Currently he is responsible for the regulation and supervision of the Italian securities settlement system and central clearing counterparty. Over the last years he took part in several national and international groups in the field of financial markets posttrading systems. Currently he is member of the ECB Securities Settlement Working Group and Contact Group on Euro Securities Infrastructures (COGESI) and, at national level, represents the bank at the Monte Titoli Express Users Group. Publications: "Le procedure di liquidazione dei titoli in Italia," Banca d'Italia (1991); "Guida al prestito titoli in Italia," *Bancaria Editrice* (1996); "Mercati dei derivati, controllo monetario e stabilità finanziaria," *Il Mulino* (2000).

Maike Sundmacher is a Lecturer in Finance at the School of Economics & Finance, University of Western Sydney. She teaches in Corporate Finance, Bank Management, and Credit Risk Management. Ms. Sundmacher is enrolled in a PhD degree at the Macquarie Graduate School of Management and researches in the areas of capital markets and risk management in financial institutions.

Niklas Wagner is Professor of Finance at Passau University, Germany. Former teaching positions were at Hannover, Munich, and Dresden. After receiving his PhD in Finance from Augsburg University in 1998, Professor Wagner held postdoctoral visiting appointments at the Haas School of Business, University of California Berkeley, and Stanford GSB. Academic visits also led him to the Center of Mathematical Sciences at Munich University of Technology and to the Faculty of Economics and Politics, University of Cambridge. Professor Wagner has coauthored several international contributions, for example, articles in *Economic Notes, Quantitative Finance*, the *Journal of Banking and Finance,* and the *Journal of Empirical Finance*. He regularly serves as a referee for finance and economics journals. His research interests include empirical asset pricing, applied financial econometrics, and market microstructure as well as banking and risk management. His industry background is in quantitative asset management with HypoVereinsbank and Munich Financial Systems Consulting.

Thomas Wenger is Senior Associate in Financial Risk Management at KPMG Germany, which he joined in 2006. His experience in projects at small, medium, and large European banks is in economic capital management, regulatory issues in the Basel-II framework, and model quality assurance in derivatives pricing and rating models. Dr. Wenger earned his PhD in Mathematics from Muenster University in 2000. He was a Boas Assistant Professor of Mathematics at Northwestern University from 2001 to 2004, after visiting Northwestern with a research grant from the German Research Council in 2001. In 2005 he was awarded a EU grant and visited the University of Genoa. His research interests include the mathematical study of questions in integrated risk management and credit risk management.

Jennifer Westaway has a degree in law and a Master's in Bioethics from Monash University and a PhD from Curtin University. She is currently an academic in the School of Business Law at Curtin University. Her research interests and strong publication areas include international comparative law and banking law as well as industrial and human rights law.

Operational
Risk toward
Basel III

Operational Risk Measurement: Qualitative Approaches

CHAPTER 1

Modeling Operational Risk Based on Multiple Experts' Opinions

Jean-Philippe Peters and Georges Hübner

ABSTRACT

While the Basel II accord has now gone live in most parts of the world, many discrepancies still remain on advanced modeling techniques for operational risk among large international banks. The two major families of models include the loss distribution approaches (LDAs) that focus on observed past internal and external loss events and the scenario-based techniques that use subjective opinions from experts as the starting point to determine the regulatory capital charge to cover operational risk. A major methodological challenge is the combination of both techniques so as to fulfill Basel II requirements. In this chapter we discuss and investigate the use of various alternatives to model expert opinion in a sound statistical way so as to allow for subsequent integration with loss distributions fitted on internal and/or external data. A numerical example supports the analysis and shows that solutions exist to merge information arising from both sources.

Georges Hübner gratefully acknowledges financial support from Deloitte Luxembourg.

1.1 INTRODUCTION

The revised Framework on Capital Measurement and Capital Standards for the banking sector, commonly referred to as Basel II, has now gone live in most parts of the world. Among the major changes introduced in this new regulatory framework are specific capital requirements to cover operational risk, defined by the Accord as the "risk of loss resulting from inadequate or failed internal processes, people and systems or from external events. This definition includes legal risk, but excludes strategic and reputational risk" (BCBS 2005).

Operational risk management is not new to financial institutions: stability of information technology (IT) systems, client claims, acts of fraud, or internal controls failures have been closely monitored for years. However, these elements have historically been treated separately. Basel II combines all items into one single integrated measurement and management framework.

Three methods are proposed by Basel II to measure the capital charge required to cover operational risk. The two simplest ones—the *basic indicator approach* and the *standardized approach*—define the operational risk capital of a bank as a fraction of its gross income; the *advanced measurement approach* (AMA) allows banks to develop their own model for assessing the regulatory capital that covers their yearly operational risk exposure within a confidence interval of 99.9% (henceforth this exposure is called *operational value at risk,* or OpVaR).

To comply with regulatory requirements, a sound AMA framework combines four sources of information:

1. Internal operational risk loss data
2. Relevant external operational risk loss data
3. Scenario analysis of expert opinion
4. Bank-specific business environment and internal control factors

The relative weight of each source and the way to combine them together are up to the banks; Basel II does not provide a regulatory model.

This chapter mainly relates to the third element—operational risk quantification using experts' opinion—and how it can successfully be addressed so as to produce outcome that can be combined with other elements (i.e., internal and external loss data).

Most of the literature on operational risk modeling focuses either on methods based on actual loss data, the so-called loss distribution approach (Chapelle et al. 2008; Chavez-Demoulin, Embrechts, and Neslehova 2006; Cruz 2002; Frachot, Georges, and Roncalli 2001), or on application of

Bayesian techniques to combine loss-based models and scenario analysis (Alexander 2003; Figini et al. 2007; Lambrigger, Shevchenko, and Wüthrich 2007). To our knowledge, studies focusing on scenario analysis on a stand-alone basis are more scarce, except for Alderweireld, Garcia, and Leonard (2006); Andres and van der Brink (2004); the sbAMA Working Group (2003); and Steinhoff and Baule (2006).

On the contrary, the problems related to obtaining probability measures by experts and combination of opinions from several experts have been extensively studied by statisticians over the last decades. Good reviews of these topics can be found in Garthwaite, Kadane, and O'Hagan (2005) for statistical methods used; Daneshkhah (2004) for the psychological aspects; Clemen and Winkler (2007) and Genest and Zidek (1986) for mathematical aggregation of opinions; and Plous (1993) for behavioral aggregation of opinions.

Starting from a practical business case, our objective is to bridge scenario analysis in operational risk with the vast literature on experts' opinion modeling by studying how operational and methodological challenges can be addressed in a sound statistical way.

In Section 1.2, we present the major families of AMA models and how they can be combined. Narrowing the scope of our analysis, Section 1.3 describes a business case concerning challenges banks face in practice when they desire to rely on experts' opinion. Existing solutions and their limitations are reviewed in Section 1.4. In Section 1.5 we introduce an alternative method based on the so-called supra-Bayesian approach and provide an illustration. Finally, Section 1.6 opens the door for further research and concludes.

1.2 OVERVIEW OF THE AMA MODELS

The Basel Committee released its consultative paper on operational risk in 2001. Since then, banks have started designing and developing their own internal model to measure their exposure to operational risk just as they began implementing consistent and comprehensive operational risk loss data collection processes.

The application of AMA is in principle open to any proprietary model, but methodologies have converged over the years and standards have appeared. The result is that most AMA models can now be classified into two categories:

1. Loss distribution approaches
2. Scenario-based approaches[1]

1.2.1 Loss Distribution Approach

The loss distribution approach (LDA) is a parametric technique primarily based on past observed internal loss data (potentially enriched with external data). Based on concepts used in actuarial models, the LDA consists of separately estimating a frequency distribution for the occurrence of operational losses and a severity distribution for the economic impact of the individual losses. Both distributions are then combined through n-convolution of the severity distribution with itself, where n is a random variable that follows the frequency distribution.[2]

When applied to operational risk, LDA is subject to many methodological issues that have been extensively treated in the literature over the past few years.[3]

All these issues (and others) are specifically challenging when developing LDA models for operational risk because of a major root cause: the availability of loss data points, specifically large ones. Because conducting financial activities implies interaction with many other parties (clients, banking counterparties, other departments, etc.), operational errors are often spotted relatively fast by ex-post controls, such as monitoring reports, reconciliation procedures, or broker confirmations. As such, most of the operational errors to which financial institutions are exposed have acceptable financial impact (i.e., high-frequency/low-severity events). From time to time, however, the impact can be huge, as when fraudulent purposes are combined with a weak control environment and large underlying operations (e.g., cases in Barings, Daiwa, Allied Irish Bank or, more recently, Société Générale).

Having enough relevant data points to implement a sound LDA model can prove to be difficult in many cases, including:

- Small or midsize banks with limited and/or automated activities
- New business environment due to merger/acquisition
- Specific operational risk classes that are not related to "everyday business"

In such cases, banks often rely on experts' opinions in what is sometimes referred to as scenario-based AMA.

1.2.2 Scenario-Based AMA

The scenario-based AMA (or sbAMA) shares with LDA the idea of combining two dimensions (frequency and severity) to calculate the aggregate loss distribution (ALD) used to derive the OpVaR. It differs, however, from LDA in that estimation of both distributions builds on experts' opinion regarding various scenarios.[4]

Based on their activities and their control environment, banks build scenarios describing potential adverse events actualizing the operational risks identified as relevant. Then experts are asked to give opinions on probability of occurrence (i.e., frequency) and potential economic impact should the events occur (i.e., severity).

As human judgment of probabilistic measures is often biased, a point discussed in more detail in Section 1.3, a major challenge with sbAMA is to obtain sufficiently reliable estimates from experts. One might wonder why experts should be required to give opinions on frequency and severity distributions (or their parameters). The official reason lies in the regulatory requirement to combine four sources of information when developing an AMA model. But the usefulness of this type of independent, forward-looking information should not be overlooked, provided it is carefully integrated in an actuarial, backward-looking setup. The challenge of modeling adequately experts' opinions is thus unavoidable when quantifying operational risk and is discussed in Section 1.4.

Outcome from sbAMA shall be statistically compatible with that arising from LDA so as to enable a statistically tractable combination technique. As we show in next section, the most adequate technique to combine LDA and sbAMA is Bayesian inference, which requires experts to set the parameters of the loss distribution.

1.2.3 Integrating LDA and sbAMA

When it comes to combining sbAMA and LDA,[5] banks have adopted integration methods that greatly diverge and that can be split in two groups: *ex post* combination and *ex ante* combination:

1. *Ex post* combination consists in merging the various sources at the aggregate loss distribution (ALD) level. Typically, separate ALDs are computed independently, and they are combined on the final distribution. As stated in Section 1.2, the *n*-fold convolution of the severity distribution with itself is very difficult to derived analytically so numerical solutions, such as Monte Carlo simulations, are used in practice. As a consequence, ALD is usually discretized and combinations are applied to each of the points defining the distribution (often 10,000 to 50,000 data points).

2. *Ex ante* combination focuses on the frequency and the severity distributions, prior to the simulations leading to the ALD. More specifically, sources of information are combined to derive the parameters of both distributions.

Whichever combination approach used,[6] a widely accepted solution in the academic literature is to merge information from the various components of the AMA using Bayesian inference.

Consider a random vector of observations $X = (X_1, X_2, \ldots, X_n)$ whose density, for a given vector of parameters $\theta = (\theta_1, \theta_2, \ldots, \theta_K)$, is $\ell(X \mid \theta)$ and called the *sample likelihood*. Suppose also that θ itself has a probability distribution $\pi(\theta)$, called the *prior distribution*. Then Bayes' theorem (Bayes 1763) can be formulated as

$$\ell(X, \theta) = \ell(X \mid \theta)\pi(\theta) = \hat{\pi}(\theta \mid X)\ell(X) \tag{1.1}$$

where $\hat{\pi}(\theta \mid X) =$ density of parameters θ given observed data X and is called the *posterior* distribution

$\ell(X, \theta) =$ joint density of observed data and parameters

$\ell(X) =$ a marginal density of X

Equation 1.1 can also be expressed as

$$\hat{\pi}(\theta \mid X) = \frac{\ell(X \mid \theta)\pi(\theta)}{\ell(X)} \tag{1.2}$$

where $\ell(X) =$ a normalization constant

Thus, the posterior distribution can be viewed as a product of a prior knowledge with a likelihood function of observed data. Mathematically,

$$\hat{\pi}(\theta \mid X) \propto \pi(\theta) \times \ell(X \mid \theta) \tag{1.3}$$

In the context of operational risk we consider:

- The posterior distribution $\hat{\pi}(\theta \mid X)$ provides the input to define the distributions used in the Monte Carlo simulations to derive the OpVaR.
- The prior distribution $\pi(\theta)$ should be estimated by scenario analysis (i.e., based on expert opinions).
- The sample likelihood $\ell(X \mid \theta)$ is obtained when applying LDA on actual losses (whether internal losses only or a mixture of internal and external data).

Bayesian inference has many great features, which is why it fits well with operational risk modeling:

1. It provides a structural and sound statistical technique to combine two heterogeneous sources of information (subjective human opinions and objective collected data).
2. It provides transparency for review by internal audit and/or regulators as both sources of information can be analyzed separately.
3. Its foundations rest on assumptions that fit well with operational risk, as both observations and parameters of the distributions are considered to be random.

1.3 USING EXPERTS' OPINIONS TO MODEL OPERATIONAL RISK: A PRACTICAL BUSINESS CASE

Imagine this business case, commonly observed in the banking industry nowadays: A bank wishes to use AMA to measure its exposure to operational risk (be it for the regulatory requirements of Pillar I or within its internal capital adequacy assessment process [ICAAP], under Pillar II). It has set up a loss data collection process for several years and has enough loss events to develop an LDA model (at least for its major business lines).

To ensure compliance of its model with regulatory requirements, the bank decides to associate its LDA model with scenario-based experts' opinion, adopting the *ex ante* combination technique with Bayesian inference, as described in Section 1.2.3. The operational risk manager (ORM) faces implementation and methodological challenges.

First, the ORM should decide who should serve as "experts" to assess the various scenarios. The subjective nature of this exercise might cause the ORM to consult multiple experts in an attempt to beef up the information base and reduce the uncertainty surrounding the assessment. (Subjective information is often viewed as being "softer" than "hard scientific data" such as actual loss events.) In most banks, scenario analysis is carried out by department or business lines. The ORM would thus ask the head of each business line to provide a list of staff members having sufficient skills, experience, and expertise to take part in the scenario analysis exercise.

Internal risk governance implies that the head of a business line has the ultimate responsibility for managing operational risk in the daily activities of the unit and for ensuring that a sound and efficient control environment is in place. As a consequence, this person will probably be requested to review, validate, or approve results of the estimation process. This leads to the second challenge: How should the ORM organize the scenario analysis work sessions? Often workshops are held, with all experts including the head of business line attending. Participants discuss and debate to get a final common estimate. Such a solution has advantages: It is less time consuming than individual sessions, and participants can share information to enhance accuracy of these estimates. But workshops also present some risks: A group decision-making process implies psychological factors, such as, for instance, the emergence of leaders in the discussion who strongly influence the others, who in turn may give in for the sake of group unity even though they do not agree. This is especially true when various hierarchical levels are represented (e.g., the head of business line). Another psychological factor can be linked to game theory concepts, with some experts intentionally providing estimates that are not their real beliefs in an attempt to influence others and drive the consensus toward a particular value (Fellner 1965). To reduce these risks, we assume in our business case that the ORM decides to gather the opinions from each individual expert and from the head of business line separately.

Before opinions can be combined, they must be elicited and expressed in some quantified form, which is the root of the third challenge. Indeed, as stated by Hogarth (1975), "man is a selective, sequential information processing system with limited capacity . . . ill-suited for assessing probability distributions." Unfortunately, many of the solutions to combine opinions require that each individual's opinion to be encoded as a subjective probability distribution. Consequently, the way scenarios and related questions are built is vital, as many potential biases may happen during the extraction process.[7] These biases are reflected in the main heuristics used by experts when assessing probabilities under uncertainty:

- **Availability.** People overestimate the frequency of events similar to situations they have experienced and underestimate probabilities of less familiar events (Tversky and Kahneman 1974).
- **Anchoring.** When people are asked to provide a range for the impact of a potential uncertain, severe event or assess its frequency, they use a starting point, often the perceived expected value, and adjust upward or downward. Unfortunately, this adjustment is often not sufficient and produces systematic underestimation of the variability of the estimates (O'Hagan 1998; Winkler 1967).
- **Representativeness.** When people have to assess the probability of an event, they tend to link this event with another similar event and derive their estimate from the probability of the similar event. One of the errors produced by this heuristic is called the law of small numbers, as people

typically ignore the variability of the mathematical laws of probability in small samples (Kahnemann, Slovic, and Tversky 1982).

- **Framing.** Outcomes from questionnaires (i.e., probability estimates) are sensitive to the phrasing and the order of questions used (Pahlman and Riabacke 2005).

To avoid direct probabilistic judgments by the experts, the ORM should prepare questions that fit better with the way nonstatisticians think. A solution is to give experts a list of potential loss impacts for each scenario and to ask: How many years will we have to wait, all things being equal, to observe such a scenario happening with loss impact of x or above? Such a question focuses on the notion of duration (i.e., the mean time one should expect to wait until the occurrence of a given operational risk event exceeding a certain severity), which is easier for experts to handle in practice (Steinhoff and Baule 2006).

Assuming the frequency distribution is a Poisson distribution with parameter λ, the duration until an event of magnitude x occurs can be expressed as

$$d\,(x) = \frac{1}{\lambda\,(1 - F\,(x; \Theta))} \tag{1.4}$$

where $F(x; \Theta) = $ any parametric severity distribution

Hence, based on duration estimates provided by experts for each of the potential financial impacts, it is easy to construct the related probability measures.

Then comes the final challenge: What method should the ORM use to combine these individual opinions? The quantification method shall meet these conditions:

Condition #1. Able to combine several opinions on a parameter of interest θ[8]

Condition #2. Accounting for the assessment of the head of each business line who has the ultimate responsibility of the process

Condition #3. Building on sound and robust statistical methods to get supervisory approval

Condition #4. Producing an outcome that can be plugged in the subsequent (Bayesian) combination with LDA

The next section analyzes potential solutions proposed in the literature.

1.4   COMBINING EXPERTS' OPINIONS

In many other areas where sample data are rare or nonexisting (e.g., the nuclear industry, seismology, etc.), more than one expert is requested to provide an opinion. In other words, a decision maker (DM) relies on opinions collected from a pool of experts to assess a variable of interest θ. In operational risk, θ could be the probability P that the severity of a loss event is equal to the amount A.[9]

The problem to be considered is the combination of a number of probabilities representing their respective judgments into a single probability to be used as an input (the *prior* distribution) for the Bayesian combination with LDA, as described in Section 1.2.3. This problem is called the "consensus problem" by Winkler (1968). In this section, we provide a brief overview of existing solutions used to solve the consensus problem that could fit in an operational risk context.

Note that pure group decision-making situations (i.e., workshops where one single agreed estimate is obtained) would not fit our model as they rely on aggregation approaches that are more "behavioral" in the sense that they "attempt to generate agreement among the experts by having them interact in some way" (Clemen and Winkler 2007).

1.4.1   Weighted Opinion Pool

The problem can be tackled by relying on some weighting technique to pool all experts' opinions. Mathematically, if we consider k experts and a linear weighting scheme (called *linear opinion pool*), we have

$$P = \sum_{i=1}^{k} \lambda_i P_i \tag{1.5}$$

where P = probability of interest
$\quad\quad P_i$ = opinion of the ith expert

Of course, we have $\sum_{i=1}^{k} \lambda_i = 1$.

The most obvious solution is simply to take the equally weighted average of the opinions—that is, $\lambda_i = 1/k$—for all i. If we want to use different weights, a ranking between experts should be established based on some metrics measuring the "goodness" or "reliability" of each expert. This ranking could be set up by the line manager based on his or her level of confidence in each expert. The major drawback of this alternative is that the choice of the weights is subjective and hardly justifiable.

While meeting conditions #1 and #4 introduced in the previous section, both the equal-weight approach and the manager-based ranking approach might not fit condition #3. A more convincing method is to base the ranking on measured accuracy of previous assessments made by the experts. This can be done using the classical model of Cooke (1991) by testing the level of expertise of each expert using a questionnaire that includes questions directly related to θ (target questions) but also questions to which the assessor (in our case, the ORM) already knows the answers (seed questions). The seed questions are then used to assess the degree of expertise of each expert through a scoring rule, which combines the notions of calibration and information to estimate the weight of each expert. The scoring rule requires setting up a specific parameter called the cutoff level. As the final weighted estimates can be scored just as those from each expert, this cutoff level is chosen so that this weighted estimate's score is maximized. In the field of operational risk, this method has been applied in Bakker (2004). The major difficulty with this model is defining the scoring rule.

Alternative nonlinear methods (such as the logarithmic opinion pool) have also been proposed, but, as mentioned by Genest and McConway (1990):

> *it had been hoped initially that a careful analysis ... would point to the "better" solution, but this approach is gradually being abandoned as researchers and practitioners discover that equally compelling (but irreconcilable) sets of axioms can be found in support of different pooling recipes.*

While more advanced linear solutions, such as the classical model of Cooke (1991) or the logarithmic opinion pool, meet condition #3, they still fail to provide a satisfying answer to condition #2. In the next section, we introduce an approach that fills the gap.

1.4.2 Supra-Bayesian Approach

Relying on ideas detailed in Section 1.2.3, we could assume that each opinion is the data input to a single decision maker (the head of business line in our case) who updates his or her prior views with these opinions. Such an approach would meet condition #3. Originally introduced in Winkler (1968), this method was called "supra Bayesian" by Keeney and Raiffa (1976) and has since then been studied by, among others, Morris (1974), Lindley (1983), French (1985), Genest and Schervish (1985), and Gelfand et al. (1995).

In the supra-Bayesian approach, the pooling process is: The decision maker (called the "supra Bayesian") defines his or her prior probability P for the occurrence of E, and the collected opinions from the k experts $P_1, P_2, \ldots, P_k$ constitute the sample likelihood. Using these opinions, the supra-Bayesian beliefs can be updated using Bayes' formula:

$$P(E \mid P_1, P_2, \ldots, P_k) \propto P(E) \times \ell(P_1, P_2, \ldots, P_k \mid E) \qquad (1.6)$$

Here the posterior distribution $P(E \mid P_1, P_2, \ldots, P_k)$ (or P^* in the remainder of this chapter) can be seen as the consensus. It can then be used as *prior* distribution in the subsequent phase of the modeling processes (i.e., the combination with LDA).

The supra-Bayesian approach thus nicely fits with all four conditions listed in Section 1.3. Furthermore, it does not require much additional information technology tools or specific statistical skills from the modeler, as it relies on the same concept and calculation process as those presented in Section 1.2.3. But a major difficulty remains as Equation 1.6 implies that the likelihood function is known (i.e., the probability distribution of experts' opinion given that E occurs). The supra Bayesian (or whoever has to assess the likelihood function) shall evaluate the experts, their respective prior information sets, the interdependence of these sets, and so on. In summary, this approach requires the pooling of a very substantial number of expert opinions.

Fortunately, solutions exist to address this problem, by assuming more realistically that the likelihood function cannot be specified fully. In particular, Genest and Schervish (1985) provide a model for such situation that could be applied in an operational risk context.[10] This model is explicated in the next section.

1.5 SUPRA-BAYESIAN MODEL FOR OPERATIONAL RISK MODELING

1.5.1 Model

Suppose that θ is the severity distribution we want to model, which is a continuous univariate distribution. In scenario analysis applications for operational risk, it is often assumed that θ is a member of a standard parametric family, to which the expert need only supply its parameters. The most widely used distribution in such cases is the lognormal distribution for which experts provide the mean and standard deviation. Other solutions include the triangular distribution and the PERT distribution for which experts provide minimum, most likely (mode), and maximum values.

This assumption seems too restrictive and likely inappropriate. Severity of operational risk events indeed presents a highly leptokurtic nature, which is inadequately captured by these distributions, even the lognormal one. Many studies suggest using mixture distributions or the concepts of extreme value theory (i.e., the generalized Pareto distribution).[11] Experts are unable to provide the full specifications of such complex distributions, so we assume that each expert expresses his/her opinion on θ in a partial way. That is, probabilities are provided for a small collection of disjoint exhaustive intervals in the domain of θ. In practice, we use the duration approach of Steinhoff and Baule (2006) described in Section 1.3; experts are requested to provide duration for various financial impacts, and probabilities for the disjoint ranges are built based on these duration estimates. In this case, Equation 1.4 becomes

$$d(x) = \frac{1}{\lambda\,(F\,(y; \Theta) - F\,(x; \Theta))} \tag{1.7}$$

In statistical terms, we assume the domain of θ, Θ, is an interval in R that has lower and upper bounds, namely $a_0 = \inf\{\theta \in \Theta\}$ and $a_k = \sup\{\theta \in \Theta\}$.[12] We further assume that Θ is partitioned in n intervals determined by the points $a_0 < a_1 < \ldots < a_n$ and let $I_j = (a_{j-1}, a_j)$. Let $p_i^T = (p_{i1}, p_{i2}, \ldots, p_{in})$, where p_{ij} is the opinion of the ith expert regarding the chance that $\theta \in I_j$. If we have k experts participating, this results in a $n \times k$ matrix $P = (p_1, p_2, \ldots, p_k)$. Like the experts, the supra Bayesian is not in a position to provide the fully specified distribution for θ. Thus he or she will answer the same questions as the experts. Mathematically, the supra Bayesian provides a vector of probabilities ρ for the same sets of I's. Equation 1.6 then becomes

$$P^* \propto \rho \times \ell\,(P \mid \theta \in I_j) \tag{1.8}$$

To model the likelihood function ℓ, we rely on the method proposed by Genest and Schervish (1985), who provide a Bayesian answer requiring a minimum of a priori assessments. For each interval I_j, the supra Bayesian is required only to provide the first moment (i.e., the expected value) of the *marginal* distribution F_j for $\pi_j = (p_{1j}, p_{2j}, \ldots, p_{kj})$, the vector of experts' probabilities for the occurrence $\theta \in I_j$. This mean vector is denoted $M_j = (\mu_{1j}, \mu_{2j}, \ldots, \mu_{kj})$. Note that no specification on the *conditional* distribution is thus required.

In our operational risk business case, this is equivalent to the head of the business line having to answer this question: What duration do you think your experts will most probably associate with the given loss amount? The head of the business line should be able to identify the more conservative people on his or her team (or the opposite).

Genest and Schervish (1985) test pooling processes against a consistency condition that guarantees "it is consistent with the unspecified F, in the sense that the joint distribution for $\theta \in I_j$ and π_j that is compatible with F can always be found such that the pooling process is the posterior probability P^*."

When only M_j is specified, Genest and Schervish (1985) show that the only formula to pass this test is

$$P_j^* = \rho_j + \sum_{i=1}^{k} \lambda_{ij} \left(p_{ij} - \mu_{ij} \right) \qquad (1.9)$$

with possibly negative weights λ_{ij} that expresses the coefficients of multiple linear regressions (or the amount of correlation) between each p_{ij} and $\theta \in I_j$. These weights must satisfy $n*2^{k+1}$ inequalities when no prior restrictions on the sign of the λ_{ij}'s exist. In the most common case (i.e., λ_{ij}'s are positive), the inequalities take the form

$$\max \left\{ \sum_{i=1}^{k} \frac{\lambda_{ij} \mu_{ij}}{\rho_j} ; \sum_{i=1}^{k} \frac{\lambda_{ij} \left(1 - \mu_{ij} \right)}{\left(1 - \rho_j \right)} \right\} \leq 1, \quad \forall j = 1, \dots, n \qquad (1.10)$$

1.5.2   Illustration of the Model

To illustrate this model, consider the simple case where a head of business line H and three experts A, B, and C are required to provide frequency of occurrence of an event-type E and the duration for two severity amounts €1,000,000 and €5,000,000. We further assume that the total available owned funds of the bank is €100,000,000 and that the upper bound for severity is fixed at this level. Finally, H is requested to provide expectations in terms of the experts' answers. Knowing the staff sufficiently well, H anticipates that A would provide a more severe picture of the event but remains neutral for B and C. Table 1.1 summarizes the answers received.

Using Equation 1.7 to transform these answers into probability measures leads to the figures reported in Table 1.2 and Table 1.3. In Table 1.2, the opinion of H is equivalent to ρ in Equation 1.8.

TABLE 1.1 Experts' Opinions

Question A: What is the frequency of occurrence for event *E*?

Frequency (*F*)	H	A	B	C
(# events/year)	3	5	3	3.5

Question B: how many years will we have to wait, all things being equal, to observe the event *E* of severity higher than X?

Severity (in EUR)	Duration (in years)			
S	H	A	B	C
1,000,000 (= S_1)	5	3	6	6.5
5,000,000 (= S_2)	20	15	22	20

Question C (only for *H*): What answers do you think the experts will provide for Questions A and B?

Variable	H	A	B	C
F	—	3.5	3	3
S_1	—	4	5	5
S_2	—	18	20	20

TABLE 1.2 Probability Measures Associated with Experts' Opinions

Interval (*I*)		$P = \Pr(\theta \in I \mid E)$			
Lower Bound	Upper Bound	H	A	B	C
0	1,000,000	0.9333	0.9333	0.9444	0.9560
1,000,000	5,000,000	0.0500	0.0533	0.0404	0.0297
5,000,000	100,000,000	0.0167	0.0133	0.0152	0.0143

TABLE 1.3 Beliefs of the Supra-Bayesian

Interval (*I*)		$P = \Pr(\theta \in I \mid E)$			
Lower Bound	Upper Bound	H	A	B	C
0	1,000,000	—	0.9286	0.9333	0.9333
1,000,000	5,000,000	—	0.0556	0.0500	0.0500
5,000,000	100,000,000	—	0.0159	0:0167	0.0167

TABLE 1.4 Prior and Posterior Probability Measures

Interval (I)	ρ	$P*$
I_1	0.9333	0.9499
I_2	0.0500	0.0354
I_3	0.0167	0:0147

Inequalities of Equation 1.10 are satisfied with $\lambda_1 = \lambda_2 = \lambda_3 = 0.3$. When plugging these coefficients in Equation 1.9, we obtain the posterior probability measures $P*$ reported in Table 1.4.

1.6 CONCLUSION

Operational risk quantification using scenario analysis is a challenging task, both methodologically and organizationally. But its informative value can hardly be ignored in any sound operational risk measurement framework; in addition, regulatory requirement exist regarding the use of experts' opinions in the AMA approach.

This chapter has presented the practical business case of a banking institution wishing to adopt a scenario analysis to model operational risk based on opinions from several experts who are subject to validation or review by a single hierarchical superior. While most of the existing solutions fail to meet all constraints faced by such a situation, the supra-Bayesian model presented adequately copes with the major challenges identified in our business case by providing a sound, robust, yet tractable framework to model the consensus of experts' opinions.

NOTES

1. Some alternatives exist, but they are scarcely used in the industry. As observed by the Financial Supervisory Authority (FSA 2005) in the United Kingdom, "the institutions represented on the AMA Quantitative Expert Group currently all use either Loss Distribution or Scenario approaches."
2. See, for instance, Cruz 2002 or Frachot, Georges, and Roncalli 2001 for theoretical background; see Aue and Kalkbrener 2006 or Chapelle et al. 2008 for practical illustrations.
3. See, for instance, Crama, Hübner, and Peters 2007 on impact of the loss data collection threshold; Moscadelli 2004 on tail modeling; King 2001 on the usage

of mixed distribution to model severity; Di Clemente and Romano 2004 on dependence among operational risks.

4. See sbAMA Working Group (2003) for an introduction to the general concepts of this method.
5. Similar techniques are also applied to combine internal loss data with relevant external loss data. The *ex post* combination sometimes is applied only over a given (high) threshold.
6. In the remainder of this chapter, we consider only the *ex ante* combination.
7. See Daneshkhah (2004) for a review of the literature on the subject.
8. In our case, θ are the answers to the questions linked to a given scenario.
9. Note that the probability measure P could be substituted by a probability distribution p throughout this discussion without loss of accuracy.
10. Other alternatives have been proposed by Genest and Schervish (1985); West (1988); West and Crosse (1992); and Gelfand, Mallick, and Dey (1995).
11. See, for instance, Chavez-Demoulin, Embrechts, and Neslehova (2006) or Chapelle et al. (2008).
12. In operational risk, a_0 could be 0 and a_k could be equal to a loss so important it leads the bank to bankruptcy (e.g., a loss equal to its total own funds).

REFERENCES

Alderweireld, T., J. Garcia, and L. Leonard. 2006. A practical operational risk scenario analysis quantification. *Risk* 19, no. 2:93–95.
Alexander, C. 2003. *Operational risk: Regulation, analysis and management.* London: Prentice Hall-FT.
Andres, U., and G. J. Van Der Brink. 2004. Implementing a Basel II scenario-based AMA for operational risk. In *The Basel handbook*, ed. K. Ong. London: Risk Books.
Aue, F., and M. Kalkbrener. 2006. LDA at work: Deutsche Bank's approach to quantifying operational risk. *Journal of Operational Risk* 1, no. 4:49–93.
Bakker, M. R. A. 2004. Quantifying operational risk within banks according to Basel II. Master's thesis. Delft Institute of Applied Mathematics, Delft, Netherlands.
Bayes, T. 1783. An essay towards solving a problem in the doctrine of chances. *Philosophical Transactions of the Royal Society* 53:370–418.
Basel Committee on Banking Supervision. 2005. Basel II: International convergence of capital measurement and capital standards—A revised framework. Basel Committee Publications No. 107, Bank for International Settlements, Basel, Switzerland.
Chapelle, A., Y. Crama, G. Hübner, and J.-P. Peters. 2008. Practical methods for measuring and managing operational risk in the financial sector: A clinical study. *Journal of Banking and Finance* 32, no. 6:1049–1061.
Chavez-Demoulin, V., P. Embrechts, and J. Neslehova. 2006. Quantitative models for operational risk: Extremes, dependence and aggregation. *Journal of Banking and Finance* 30, no. 10:2635–2658.

Clemen, R. T., and R. L. Winkler. 2007. Aggregating probability distributions. In *Advances in decision analysis: From foundations to applications*, ed. R.F. Miles and D. von Winterfeldt. New York: Cambridge University Press.

Cooke, R. M. 1991. *Experts in uncertainty.* New York: Oxford University Press.

Crama, Y., G. Hübner, and J.-P. Peters. 2007. Impact of the collection threshold on the determination of the capital charge for operational risk. In *Advances in Risk Management*, ed. G. Gregoriou. London: Palgrave-MacMillan.

Cruz, M. G. 2002. *Modeling, Measuring and hedging operational risk.* Hoboken, NJ: John Wiley & Sons.

Daneshkhah, A. R. 2004. Psychological aspects influencing elicitation of subjective probability. Working paper, University of Sheffield, U.K.

Di Clemente, A., and C. Romano. 2004. A copula–extreme value theory approach for modelling operational risk, In *Operational risk modelling and analysis: Theory and practice*, ed. M. Cruz. London: Risk Books.

Fellner, W. 1965. *Probability and profits.* Homewood, IL: Irwin.

Figini, S., P. Guidici, P. Uberti, and A. Sanyal. 2007. A statistical method to optimize the combination of internal and external data in operational risk measurement. *Journal of Operational Risk* 2, no. 4:87–99.

Frachot, A., P. Georges, and T. Roncalli. 2001. Loss distribution approach for operational risk. Working paper, Groupe de Recherche Opérationnelle, Crédit Lyonnais, Paris.

French, S. 1985. Group consensus probability distributions: A critical survey. In *Bayesian statistics 2*, ed. J. M. Bernardo, M. H. DeGroot, D. V. Lindley, and A. F. M. Smith, Amsterdam: North-Holland.

Financial Supervisory Authority. 2005. AMA soundness standard. Working paper. FSA AMA Quantitative Expert Group, London.

Garthwaite, P. H., J.B. Kadane, and A. O'Hagan. 2005. Statistical methods for eliciting probability distributions. *Journal of the American Statistical Association* 100, no. 470:680–700.

Gelfand, A. E., B. K. Mallick, and D. K. Dey. 1995. Modeling expert opinion arising as a partial probabilistic specification. *Journal of the American Statistical Association* 90, no. 430:598–604.

Genest, C., and K. J. McConway. 1990. Allocating the weights in the linear opinion pool. *Journal of Forecasting* 9, no. 1:53–73.

Genest, C., and M. J. Schervish. 1985. Modeling expert judgments for Bayesian updating. *Annals of Statistics* 13, no. 3:1198–1212.

Genest, C., and J. V. Zidek. 1986. Combining probability distributions: A critique and annotated bibliography. *Statistical Science* 1, no. 1:114–148.

Hogarth, R. M. (1975) Cognitive processes and the assessment of subjective probability distributions. *Journal of the American Statistical Association* 70, no. 350:271–294.

Kahneman, D., P. Slovic, and A. Tversky. 1982. *Judgment under uncertainty: Heuristics and biases.* Cambridge: Cambridge University Press.

Keeney, D., and H. Raiffa. 1976. *Decisions with multiple objectives: Preferences and value trade-offs.* New York: John Wiley & Sons.

King, J. L. 2001. *Operational risk: Measurement and modeling.* New York: John Wiley & Sons.

Lambrigger, D., P. Shevchenko, and M. Wüthrich. 2007. The quantification of operational risk using internal data, relevant external data and expert opinions. *Journal of Operational Risk* 2, no. 3:3–27.

Lindley, D. V. 1983. Reconciliation of probability distributions. *Operations Research* 31, no. 5:866–880.

Morris, P. A. 1974. Decision analysis expert use. *Management Science* 20, no. 9:1233–1241.

Moscadelli, M. 2004. The modelling of operational risk: Experience with the analysis of the data collected by the Basel Committee. Working paper 517, Banca d'Italia, Rome.

O'Hagan, A. 1998. Eliciting expert beliefs in substantial practical applications. *The Statistician* 47, no. 1:21–35.

Pahlman, M., and A. Riabacke. 2005. A study on framing effects in risk elicitation. *Proceedings of the International Conference on computational intelligence for modelling, control and automation* 1, no. 2:689–694, Vienna, Austria.

Plous, S. 1993. *The psychology of judgment and decision making.* New York: McGraw-Hill.

sbAMA Working Group. 2003. Scenario-based AMA. Working paper, London.

Steinhoff, C., and R. Baule. 2006. How to validate OpRisk distributions. *OpRisk and Compliance* 1, no. 8:36–39.

Tversky, A., and D. Kahneman. 1974. Judgment under uncertainty: Heuristics and biases. *Science* 185, no. 4157:1124–1131.

West, M. 1988. Modelling expert opinion. In *Bayesian statistics* 3, ed. J. M. Bernardo, M. H. DeGroot, D. V. Lindley, and A. F. M. Smith. Amsterdam: North-Holland.

West, M., and J. Crosse. 1992. Modelling probabilistic agent opinion. *Journal of the Royal Statistical Society*, Series B, 545, no. 1:285–299.

Winkler, R. L. 1967. The assessment of prior distributions in Bayesian analysis. *Journal of the American Statistical Association* 62, no. 319:776–800.

Winkler, R. L. 1968. The consensus of subjective probability distributions. *Management Science* 15, no. 2:361–375.

CHAPTER 2

Consistent Quantitative Operational Risk Measurement

Andreas A. Jobst

ABSTRACT

With the increased size and complexity of the banking industry, operational risk has a greater potential to occur in more harmful ways than many other sources of risk. This chapter provides a succinct overview of the current regulatory framework of operational risk under the New Basel Capital Accord with a view to inform a critical debate about the influence of varying loss profiles and different methods of data collection, loss reporting, and model specification on the reliability of operational risk estimates and the consistency of risk-sensitive capital rules. The findings offer guidance on enhanced market practice and more effective prudent standards for operational risk measurement.

2.1 INTRODUCTION

While financial globalization has fostered higher systemic resilience due to more efficient financial intermediation and greater asset price competition, it has also complicated banking regulation and risk management in

---

The views expressed in this chapter are those of the author and should not be attributed to the International Monetary Fund, its Executive Board, or its management. Any errors and omissions are the sole responsibility of the author.

banking groups. Given the increasing sophistication of financial products, the diversity of financial institutions, and the growing interdependence of financial systems, globalization increases the potential for markets and business cycles to become highly correlated in times of stress and makes crisis resolution more intricate while banks are still lead regulated at a national level. At the same time, the deregulation of financial markets, large-scale mergers and acquisitions, as well as greater use of outsourcing arrangements have raised the susceptibility of banking activities to operational risk. The recent US$7.2 billion fraud case at Société Générale caused by a 31-year-old rogue trader, who was able to bypass internal control procedures, underscores just how critical adequate operational risk management has become to safe and sound banking business.

Operational risk has a greater potential to occur in more harmful ways than many other sources of risk, given the increased size and complexity of the banking industry. It is commonly defined as the risk of some adverse outcome resulting from acts undertaken (or neglected) in carrying out business activities, inadequate or failed internal processes and information systems, misconduct by people, or as due to external events and shocks.[1] Although operational risk has always existed as one of the core risks in the financial industry, it is becoming a more salient feature of risk management. The presence of new threats to financial stability, such as higher geopolitical risk, poor corporate governance, and systemic vulnerabilities stem from the plethora of financial derivatives. In particular, technological advances have spurred rapid financial innovation resulting in a proliferation of financial products. This proliferation has required a greater reliance of banks on services and systems susceptible to heightened operational risk, such as e-banking and automated processing.

Against this background, concerns about the soundness of traditional operational risk management (ORM) practices and techniques, and the limited capacity of regulators to address these challenges within the scope of existing regulatory provisions, have prompted the Basel Committee on Banking Supervision to introduce capital adequacy guidelines of operational risk in its recent overhaul of the existing capital rules for internationally active banks.[2] As the revised banking rules on the International Convergence of Capital Measurement and Capital Standards (or Basel II) move away from rigid controls toward enhancing efficient capital allocation through the disciplining effect of capital markets, improved prudential oversight, and risk-based capital charges, banks are facing more rigorous and comprehensive risk measurement requirements (Basel Committee 2004a, 2005a, 2006b).

The new regulatory provisions link minimum capital requirements closer to the actual riskiness of bank assets in a bid to redress shortcomings in the old system of the overly simplistic 1988 Basel Capital Accord. While the old capital standards for calculating bank capital lacked any provisions for exposures to operational risk and asset securitization, the new, more risk-sensitive regulatory capital rules include an explicit capital charge for operational risk. This charge has been defined in a separate section of the new supervisory guidelines based on previous recommendations in the *Consultative Document on the Regulatory Treatment of Operational Risk* (2001d), the *Working Paper on the Regulatory Treatment of Operational Risk* (2001c) and the *Sound Practices for the Management and Supervision of Operational Risk* (2001a, 2002, 2003b).

The implementation of New Basel Capital Accord in the United States underscores the particular role of operational risk as part of the new capital rules. On February 28, 2007, the federal bank and thrift regulatory agencies published the *Proposed Supervisory Guidance for Internal Ratings-Based Systems for Credit Risk, Advanced Measurement Approaches for Operational Risk, and the Supervisory Review Process* (Pillar 2) *Related to Basel II Implementation* (based on previous advanced notices on proposed rule making in 2003 and 2006). These supervisory implementation guidelines of the New Basel Capital Accord thus far require some and permit other qualifying banking organizations (mandatory and "opt-in")[3] to adopt advanced measurement approach (AMA) for operational risk (together, the "advanced approach") as the only acceptable method of estimating capital charges for operational risk. The proposed guidance also establishes the process for supervisory review and the implementation of the capital adequacy assessment process under Pillar 2 of the new regulatory framework. Other G-7 countries, such as Germany, Japan, and the United Kingdom, have taken similar measures regarding a qualified adoption of capital rules and supervisory standards for operational risk measurement.

This chapter first reviews the current regulatory framework of operational risk under the New Basel Capital Accord. Given the inherently elusive nature of operational risk and considerable cross-sectional diversity of methods to identify operational risk exposure, the chapter informs a critical debate about two key challenges in this area: (1) the accurate estimation of asymptotic tail convergence of extreme operational risk events, and (2) the consistent definition and implementation of loss reporting and data collection across different areas of banking activity in accordance with the New Basel Capital Accord. The chapter explains the shortcomings of existing loss distribution approach models and examines the structural and systemic effects of heterogeneous data reporting on loss characteristics, which influence the reliability and comparability of operational risk estimates for regulatory purposes. The findings offer guidance and instructive recommendations for enhanced market practice and a more effective implementation of capital rules and prudential standards for operational risk measurement.

2.2 CURRENT PRACTICES OF OPERATIONAL RISK MEASUREMENT AND REGULATORY APPROACHES

The measurement and regulation of operational risk is quite distinct from other types of banking risks. Operational risk deals mainly with tail events rather than central projections or tendencies, reflecting aberrant rather than normal behavior and situations. Thus, the exposure to operational risk is less predictable and even harder to model, because extreme losses are one-time events of large economic impact without historical precedent. While some operational risk exposure follows from very predictable stochastic patterns whose high frequency caters to quantitative measures, there are many other types of operational risk for which there is and never can be data to support anything but an exercise requiring subjective judgment and estimation. In addition, the diverse nature of operational risk from internal or external disruptions to business activities and the unpredictability of their overall financial impact complicate systematic measurement and consistent regulation.

The historical experience of operational risk events suggests a heavy-tailed loss distribution; that is, there is a higher chance of an extreme loss event (with high loss severity) than the shape of the standard limit distributions would suggest. While banks should generate enough expected revenues to support a net margin that absorbs *expected losses* (EL) from predictable internal failures, they also need to provision sufficient economic capital as risk reserves to cover the *unexpected losses* (UL) from large, one-time internal and external shocks or resort to insurance/hedging agreements. If we define the distribution of operational risk losses as an intensity process of time t, the expected conditional probability $EL(T - t) = E[P(T) - P(t) | P(T) - P(t) < 0]$ specifies EL over time horizon T, while the probability $UL(T - t) = P_\alpha(T - t) - EL(T - t)$ of UL captures losses larger than EL below a tail cutoff $E[P_\alpha(T) - P(t)]$, beyond which any residual or extreme loss ("tail risk") occurs at a probability of α or less. The asymptotic tail behavior of operational risk reflects highly predictable, small loss events left of the mean with cumulative density of EL. Higher percentiles indicate a lower probability of extreme observations with high loss severity (UL).

There are three major concepts of operational risk measurement:

1. The volume-based approach, which assumes that operational risk exposure is a function of the type and complexity of business activity, especially in cases when notoriously low margins (such as in transaction processing and payments system–activities) have the potential to magnify the impact of operational risk losses

2. The comprehensive qualitative self-assessment of operational risk with a view to evaluate the likelihood and severity of financial losses based on subjective judgment rather than historical precedent
3. Quantitative techniques, which have been developed by banks primarily for the purpose of assigning economic capital to operational risk exposures in compliance with regulatory capital requirements (see Box 2.1)

The migration of ORM toward a modern framework has invariably touched off efforts to quantify operational risk as an integral element of economic capital models. These models comprise internal capital measurement and management processes used by banks to allocate capital to different business segments based on their exposure to various risk factors (market, credit, liquidity and operational risk). Despite considerable variation of economic capital measurement techniques ranging from qualitative managerial judgments to comprehensive statistical analysis, capital allocation for operational risk tends to be driven mainly by the quantification of losses relative to explicit exposure indicators (or volume-based measures) of business activity, such as gross income, which reflect the quality and stability of earnings to support capital provisioning. As modern ORM evolves as a distinct discipline, the push for quantification techniques of operational risk within more advanced economic capital models coincides with the adoption of more risk-sensitive regulatory regime.

Regulatory efforts have contributed in large parts to the evolution of quantitative operational risk measurement as a distinct discipline. The Operational Risk Subgroup (AIGOR) of the Basel Committee Accord Implementation Group defines three different quantitative measurement approaches on a continuum of increasing sophistication and risk sensitivity for the estimation of operational risk based on eight business lines (BLs) and seven event types (ETs)[4] as units of measure (Basel Committee 2003a). Risk estimates from different units of measure must be added for purposes of calculating the regulatory minimum capital requirement for operational risk. Although provisions for supervisory review (Pillar 2 of Basel II) allow signatory countries to select approaches to operational risk that may be applied to local financial markets, such national discretion is restricted by the tenet of consistent global banking standards. The first two approaches, the basic indicator approach (BIA) and the (traditional) standardized approach (TSA),[5] define deterministic standards of regulatory capital by assuming a fixed percentage of gross income over a three-year period[6] as a volume-based metric of unexpected operational risk exposure (see Table 2.1). BIA requires banks to provision a fixed percentage (15%) of their average gross income over the previous three years for operational risk losses, whereas TSA sets regulatory capital to at least the three-year average of the summation of different

BOX 2.1 OPERATIONAL RISK MANAGEMENT (ORM)

Many banks still rely on internal control processes, audit programs, insurance protection, and other risk management methods to identify, monitor, and control operational risk based largely on qualitative assumptions and judgments. In such an environment, operational risk is managed by individual business units with little or no formality, process transparency, or standardization (silo approach).

Over the recent past, the unprecedented scale of high-profile cases of substantial unexpected operational risk losses has reverberated in mounting unease about the soundness of traditional ORM practices. Amid regulatory efforts to reexamine the industry's exposure to operational risk and its implications on efficient financial intermediation, some institutions have gone beyond traditional approaches in the effort to consolidate ORM in specialized departments or groups dedicated to the identification and control of exposures from particular aspects of operational processes and designated risk types, such as legal compliance, fraud, or vendor management/outsourcing. Notwithstanding the merits of improved overall risk awareness associated with centralized ORM, this approach classifies operational risk along functional lines and negates the comprehensive measurement of operational risk in end-to-end processes.

Modern ORM integrates ad hoc self-assessment of conventional approaches into a formal, enterprise-wide oversight function, which designs and implements the ORM framework as a structure to identify, measure, monitor, and control or mitigate operational risk based on independent evaluation and quantitative methods (Alexander 2003). An ORM framework defines common operational policies and guidelines on a corporate level concerning roles and responsibilities as well as uniform risk assessment processes, reporting protocols and quantification methodologies within an agreed range of risk tolerance (Basel Committee 2005b, 2006b).

The formal treatment of operational risk ensures the consistent application of standard risk management practices in end-to-end processes, while the self-assessment of exposures by individual business units reinforces business line risk ownership and eschews functional segmentation of risk awareness. A well-integrated ORM framework helps develop a more effective management process for the detection of potential operational risk exposures and the evaluation of adequate economic capital coverage commensurate to the overall risk profile.

TABLE 2.1 Overview of operational risk measures according to the Basel Committee on Banking Supervision (2003a, 2004a, 2005b, 2006b)

ORM[1]	Data Requirements	Regulatory Capital Charge	Remarks
BIA	A fixed percentage of average annual gross income over the previous 3 years.	$= [\Sigma_{\text{years}\,(1-n)}(GI_n * \alpha)]/N$, where GI = annual (positive) gross income[2] over the previous three years ("exposure factor"), n = number of the previous three years (N) for which gross income is positive, and $\alpha = 15\%$, which is set.	Figures for any year in which annual gross income is negative or zero should be excluded from both the numerator and denominator.
TSA	The three-year average of the summation of the regulatory capital charges across each of the BLs in each year.	$= \{\Sigma_{\text{years}\,(1-3)} * \max[\Sigma(GI_{1-8} * \beta_{1-8}),\, 0]\}/3$, where GI_{1-8} = annual gross income for each of the 8 BLs and β_{1-8} = fixed percentage relating the level of required capital to the level of the gross income for each of the 8 BLs defined by the Basel Committee.	β equals 18% for the BLs corporate finance, trading, and sales, and payment and settlement; 15% for commercial banking, agency services; and 12% for retail banking, asset management, and retail brokerage.
AMA	Generated by the bank's internal operational risk measurement system.	AMA includes *quantitative* and *qualitative* criteria for the self-assessment of operational risk, which must be satisfied to ensure adequate risk management and oversight. The *qualitative* criteria center on the administration and regular review of a sound internal operational risk measurement system. The *quantitative* aspects of AMA include the use of (i) internal data, (ii) external data, (iii) scenario analysis, and (iv) business environment and internal control factors subject to the AMA soundness standard and requirements for risk mitigation and capital adjustment.	Under the AMA soundness standard, a bank must be able to demonstrate that its operational risk measure is comparable to that of the internal ratings-based approach for credit risk (i.e., a 1-year holding period and a 99.9th percentile confidence interval). Banks are also allowed to adjust their total operational risk up to 20% of the total operational risk capital charge.

[1]The three main approaches to operational risk measurement, the basic indicator approach (BIA), the standardized approach (TSA) and the advanced measurement approaches (AMA) are defined in Basel Committee (2005b).
[2]Gross income (GI) is defined as net interest income plus net noninterest income. This measure should: (i) be gross of any provisions (e.g., for unpaid interest); (ii) be gross of operating expenses, including fees paid to outsourcing service providers; (iii) exclude realized profits/losses from the sale of securities in the banking book; and (iv) exclude extraordinary or irregular items as well as income derived from insurance.

regulatory capital charges (as a prescribed percentage of gross income that varies by business activity) across BLs in each year (Basel Committee 2003b). The New Basel Capital Accord also enlists the disciplining effect of capital markets ("market discipline," or Pillar 3) in order to enhance efficiency of operational risk regulation by encouraging the wider development of adequate management and control systems. In particular, the current regulatory framework allows banks to use their own internal risk measurement models under the standards of advanced measurement approaches (AMA) as a capital measure that is explicitly and systematically more amenable to the different risk profiles of individual banks in support of more risk-sensitive regulatory capital requirements (see Box 2.2).

BOX 2.2 EVOLUTION OF THE ADVANCED CAPITAL ADEQUACY FRAMEWORK FOR OPERATIONAL RISK

The current regulatory framework (New Advanced Capital Adequacy Framework) for operational risk is defined in the revisions on the *International Convergence of Capital Measurement and Capital Standards* (Basel Committee 2004a, 2005b, 2006b) and supplementary regulatory guidance contained in the *Consultative Document on the Regulatory Treatment of Operational Risk* (2001d), the *Working Paper on the Regulatory Treatment of Operational Risk* (2001c), and the *Sound Practices for the Management and Supervision of Operational Risk* (2001a, 2002, 2003b). As opposed to the old Basel Capital Accord, the new capital rules require banks to estimate an explicit capital charge for their operational risk exposure in keeping with the development of a more risk-sensitive capital standards.

The Basel Committee first initiated work on operational risk in September 1998 (Basel Committee 1998) (see Figure 2.1), when it published—among other findings—results of an informal industry survey on the operational risk exposure in various types of banking activities in *A New Capital Adequacy Framework* (1999). In January 2001, the Basel Committee (2001d) released its first consultative document on operational risk. It was followed by the *Working Paper on the Regulatory Treatment of Operational Risk* (2001c), prepared by the Risk Management Group, and a first draft of the implementation guidelines for *Sound Practices for the Management and Supervision of Operational Risk* (2001a) was published. These supervisory principles established the first regulatory framework for the evaluation

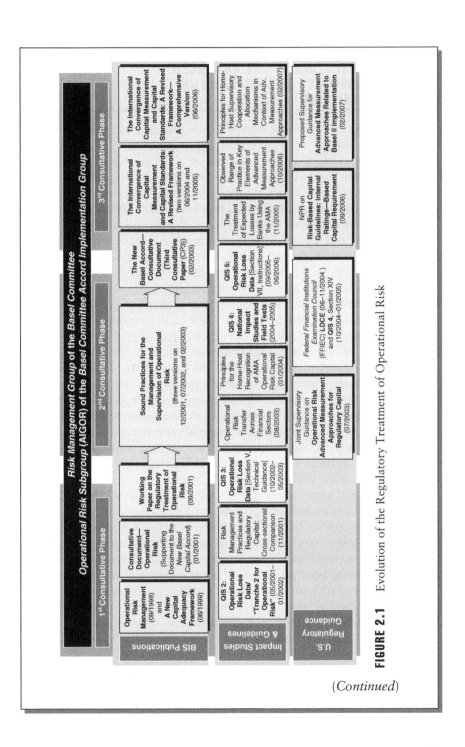

FIGURE 2.1 Evolution of the Regulatory Treatment of Operational Risk

(Continued)

BOX 2.2 EVOLUTION OF THE ADVANCED CAPITAL ADEQUACY FRAMEWORK FOR OPERATIONAL RISK (*Continued*)

of policies and practices of effective management and supervision of operational risk.

In the next round of consultations on a capital charge for operational risk, the Basel Committee examined individual operational risk loss events, the banks' quarterly aggregate operational risk loss experience, and a wider range of potential exposure indicators tied to specific BLs in order to calibrate uniform capital charges: basic indicator approach (BIA) and standardized approaches.[12] Subsequent revisions of the *Sound Practices for the Management and Supervision of Operational Risk* in July 2002 and February 2003 (Basel Committee 2002, 2003a) concluded the second consultative phase.

After the third and final round of consultations on operational risk from October 2002 to May 2003, the Basel Committee presented three methods for calculating operational risk capital charges in a continuum of increasing sophistication and risk sensitivity—BIA, (traditional) standardized approach (TSA), and AMA—to encourage banks to develop more sophisticated operational risk measurement systems and practices based on broad regulatory expectations about the development of comprehensive control processes. Banks were allowed to choose a measurement approach appropriate to the nature of banking activity, organizational structure, and business environment subject to the discretion of national banking supervisors, that is, *supervisory review* (Pillar 2 of Basel II).

The *Third Consultative Paper* (or CP 3) in April 2003 (Basel Committee 2003b) amended these provisions by introducing the *alternative standardized approach* (ASA), which was based on a measure of lending volume rather than gross income as indicator of operational risk exposure from retail and commercial banking. Additionally, compliance with the roll-out provisions for operational risk was made substantially more difficult by hardened qualifying criteria for the standardized approach, which shifted the regulatory cost benefit analysis of banks with less sophisticated ORM systems in favor of BIA.

At the same time, the ability of national regulators to exercise considerable judgment in the way they would accommodate the new capital rules in their local financial system conjured up a delicate trade-off between the flexibility and the consistency of capital rules for operational risk across signatory countries. Although national discretion could not override the fundamental precepts of the new regulatory framework, the scope of implementation varied significantly by country.[13] Some national banking supervisors selected only certain measurement approaches to operational risk for the implementation of revised risk-based capital standards. For example, in the *Joint Supervisory Guidance* on *Operational Risk Advanced Measurement Approaches for Regulatory Capital* (2003), U.S. banking and thrift regulatory agencies[14] stated that AMA would be the only permitted quantification approach for U.S.-supervised institutions to derive risk-weighted assets under the proposed revisions to the risk-based capital standards (Zamorski 2003). Eventually these provisions were endorsed in the *Notice of Proposed Rulemaking* (NPR) regarding *Risk-Based Capital Guidelines: Internal Ratings-Based Capital Requirement* (2006b).[15]

The pivotal role of *supervisory review* for consistent cross-border implementation of prudential oversight resulted also in a "hybrid approach" about how banking organizations that calculate group-wide AMA capital requirements might estimate operational risk capital requirements of their international subsidiaries. According to the guidelines of the *Home-Host Recognition of AMA Operational Risk* (Basel Committee 2004b), a significant internationally active subsidiary of a banking organization that wishes to implement AMA and is able to meet the qualifying quantitative and qualitative criteria would have to calculate its capital charge on a stand-alone basis; other internationally active subsidiaries that are not deemed significant in the context of the overall group receive an allocated portion of the group-wide AMA capital requirement.[16] Significant subsidiaries would also be allowed to utilize the resources of their parent or other appropriate entities within the banking group to derive their operational risk estimate.[17]

On February 7, 2007, the Basel Committee augmented the existing guidelines related to the information sharing and capital allocation underpinning the home-host recognition concept. The consultative document *Principles for Home-host Supervisory Cooperation and Allocation Mechanisms in the Context of Advanced Measurement Approaches (AMA)* (Basel Committee 2007) set forth two principles: first, to establish a regulatory framework for information sharing in the assessment and approval of AMA methodologies and responsibilities

(*Continued*)

BOX 2.2 EVOLUTION OF THE ADVANCED CAPITAL ADEQUACY FRAMEWORK FOR OPERATIONAL RISK (*Continued*)

of banks and second, to promote the development and assessment of allocation mechanisms incorporated as part of a hybrid AMA in terms of risk sensitivity, capital adequacy, subsidiary level management support, integration into Pillar 1, stability, implementation, documentation, internal review and validation, and supervisory assessment.

In June 2004, the Basel Committee released the first definitive rules on the regulatory treatment of operational risk as an integral part of its revised framework for the *International Convergence of Capital Measurement and Capital Standards* (2004a). In keeping with provisions published earlier in *Third Consultative Paper* (Basel Committee 2003b), the Committee stressed the importance of scenario analysis of internal loss data, business environment and exogenous control factors for operational risk exposure, and the construction of internal measurement models to estimate unexpected operational risk losses at the critical 99.9th percentile. The first comprehensive version of the New Basel Capital Accord prompted several banking regulators to conduct further national impact studies or field tests independent of the Basel Committee on Banking Supervision.

In the United States, the Federal Financial Institutions Examination Council (FFIEC),[18] the umbrella organization of U.S. bank and thrift regulatory agencies, jointly initiated the Loss Data Collection Exercise (LDCE)[19] from June to November 2004 (a repeat of earlier surveys in 2001 and 2002). The LDCE was conducted as a voluntary survey[20] that asked respondents to provide internal operational risk loss data over a long time horizon (through September 30, 2004). Such data would allow banking regulators to examine the degree to which different operational risk exposures (and the variation across banks) reported in earlier surveys were influenced by internal data or exogenous factors. These factors are considered by institutions in their quantitative methods of modeling operational risk or their qualitative risk assessments.

The general objective of the LDCE was to examine both the overall impact of the new regulatory framework on U.S. banking organizations and the cross-sectional sensitivity of capital charges to the characteristics of internal loss data and different ORM systems.

After a further round of consultations between September 2005 and June 2006, the Basel Committee defined *The Treatment of Expected Losses by Banks Using the AMA under the Basel II Framework* (Basel Committee 2005b), before it eventually released the implementation drafting guidelines for *Basel II: International Convergence of Capital Measurement and Capital Standards: A Revised Framework* (Basel Committee 2005a). These guidelines were issued again in *Basel II: International Convergence of Capital Measurement and Capital Standards: A Revised Framework—Comprehensive Version* (Basel Committee 2006b).[21] In its latest publication, *Observed Range of Practice in Key Elements of Advanced Measurement Approaches (AMA)* (Basel Committee 2006a), the Basel Committee describes emerging industry practices in relation to some of the key challenges of internal governance, data modeling, and benchmarking exercises banks face in their efforts to adopt AMA standards.

Operational risk measurement via AMA is based on the quantitative self-assessment (through internal measurement models) of the frequency and loss severity of operational risk events and represents the most flexible regulatory approach, subject to several qualitative and quantitative criteria and soundness standards.[7] While the qualitative criteria purport to ensure the integrity of a sound internal operational risk measurement system for adequate risk management and oversight, the quantitative aspects of AMA define regulatory capital as protection against both EL and UL from operational risk exposure at a soundness standard consistent with a statistical confidence at the 99.9th percentile[8] over a one-year holding period.[9] Although the Basel Committee does not mandate the use of a particular quantitative methodology, it defines the use of (1) internal data, (2) external data, (3) scenario analysis, and (4) business environment and internal control factors (BEICFs) as quantitative elements of the estimation of operational risk under AMA.[10]

The *loss distribution approach* (LDA) has emerged as one of the most expedient statistical methods to calculate the risk-based capital charge for operational risk in line with these four quantitative criteria of AMA. LDA defines operational risk as the aggregate loss distribution derived from compounding empirical and/or estimated loss severity by the estimated frequency of operational risk events under different scenarios (see Figure 2.2). The definition of UL in the context of LDA of operational risk concurs with the concept of value at risk (VaR),[11] which estimates the maximum loss exposure at a certain probability bound. However, the rare incidence of severe

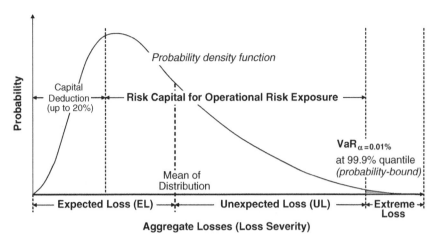

FIGURE 2.2 LDA for AMA of Operational Risk under the New Basel Capital Accord

operational risk losses defies statistical inference when measurement methods estimate maximum loss based on all data points of the empirical loss distribution. Therefore, conventional VaR is a rather ill-suited metric for operational risk and warrants adjustment so that extremes are explicitly accounted for. Therefore, generalized parametric distributions within the domain of extreme value theory (EVT) complement VaR measures.

2.3 MAIN MEASUREMENT CHALLENGES OF LDA

Since the incidence and relative magnitude of operational risk varies considerably across banks depending on the nature of business activities and the sophistication of internal risk measurement, systems and controls, the efficient ORM hinges on four issues:

1. The judicious combination of qualitative and quantitative methods of risk estimation
2. The robustness of these models, given the rare incidence of high-impact operational risk events without historical precedence
3. The sensitivity of regulatory capital charges to the varied nature of operational risk and reporting standards across different business activities
4. The risk of conflicting regulatory measures across countries as national supervisors follow different paths of supervisory review in implementing the New Basel Capital Accord

Amid a more risk-sensitive regulatory framework with broadly defined expectations of ORM and greater discretion of banks to tailor prescribed measurement standards to their specific organizational structure, business activity, and economic capital models, two main challenges emerge for the implementation of LDA and the calculation of UL risk estimates under AMA:

1. The *accurate estimation of asymptotic tail convergence of extreme losses* at the 99.9th percentile level as defined by the quantitative AMA criteria and soundness standards (i.e., shortcomings of quantitative assessments)
2. The *consistent and coherent implementation of data collection and loss reporting* across different banks and areas of banking activity (i.e., units of measure), as risk and control self-assessment (RCSA) vary in response to different BEICFs (i.e., shortcomings caused by data collection).

In their effort to adapt to the reality of an explicit capital charge for operational risk under the New Basel Capital Accord, banks have traditionally accorded more attention to optimal specification of tail dependence rather than the implications of the modes of data representation on the reliable calculation of risk estimates. Most recent research on operational risk has focused either on the quality of quantitative measurement methods of operational risk exposure (Alexander 2003; Coleman and Cruz 1999; Cruz et al. 1998; de Fontnouvelle et al. 2004; Degen et al. 2006; Grody et al. 2005; Makarov 2006; Mignola and Ugoccioni 2005 and 2006; Moscadelli 2004; Nešlehová et al. 2006) or theoretical models of economic incentives for the management and insurance of operational risk (Banerjee and Banipal 2005; Crouhy et al. 2004; Leippold and Vanini 2003). However, banking regulators are equally concerned with an even-handed implementation of operational risk measurement standards in accordance with the precepts of the supervisory review process. Yet little attention has been devoted to modeling constraints and statistical issues of operational risk reporting, modeling, and measurement, which threaten to undermine consistent regulatory framework (Currie 2004, 2005; Dutta and Perry 2006).

2.3.1 Shortcomings of Quantitative Estimation Methodologies for LDA

Although significant progress has been made in the quantification of operational risk, ongoing supervisory review and several industry studies, such as the recent publication by the Basel Committee (2006a) of the *Observed Range of Practice in Key Elements of Advanced Measurement Approaches (AMA)*, highlight significant challenges in the way banks derive risk estimates under the provisions of the New Basel Capital Accord. Quantitative risk measurement almost always involves considerable parameter uncertainty, from the application of estimation methods at high levels of statistical significance to poor data availability and few historical benchmarks to go by. Operational risk is no exception.

Effect of Loss Timing   All risk measures of extremes are inherently prone to yield unstable results, mainly because point estimates at high percentile levels hinge on only a small number of observations, far removed from the average projection. Therefore, a close examination of how the magnitude and the timing of losses qualify the classification and selection of a few extremes is crucial to reliable quantitative analysis. Loss timing matters when the relation between average and maximum loss severity of operational risk events exhibits significant cyclical variation or erratic structural change over prolonged periods. If loss timing is treated indiscriminately, periodic shifts of EL coupled with changes of periodic loss frequency would encroach on a consistent definition of what constitutes an extreme observation and causes estimation bias of UL.

Extreme outcomes from historical loss data can be selected either by *absolute* measures, if loss severity exceeds a certain time-invariant threshold value at any point in time, or by *relative* measures, if loss severity represents the maximum exposure within a certain time period. An absolute measure does not discriminate against changes in EL due to the time-varying economic impact of loss severity. In contrast, a relative measure recognizes that operational risk events whose absolute loss severity is less extreme by historical standards could in fact have a greater adverse impact on the performance of a bank than "larger extremes" when some exposure factor of operational risk, such as reported gross income, temporarily falls below some long-run average. A relative selection of extremes identifies a certain number of periodic maxima in nonoverlapping time intervals. These time intervals should be large enough to ensure that observed extremes are independent of each other but small enough so that transient extremes are not overwhelmed by a cluster of larger extremes or gradually declining EL.[22]

In addition, the consideration of relative extremes gains in importance when lower statistical power associated with risk estimates implies a greater potential of loss timing to affect the identification of extreme operational risk events—especially when the sample sizes of loss data are small. The quantitative criteria of AMA set forth risk estimates of UL to be calculated at the 99.9th percentile level, which obviously increases the chances of smaller extremes to escape an absolute measure of a time-invariant loss threshold. At the same time, depending on the sample size, very low statistical power leaves very few nonoverlapping intervals of periodic maxima for the identification of relative extremes.

Overall, the concept of flexible measure of extremes over time also raises the general question of whether individual operational risk losses should be scaled in order to account for intermittent variations of relative economic significance of operational risk for different banks or types of banking activity. In this regard, losses could be expressed as relative amounts to some average exposure over a specified time period or scaled by some fundamental data.[23] If maxima occurred with some degree of regularity and similar loss severity relative to EL and stable fundamental exposure, then absolute selection criteria yield the most reliable designation of extremes as loss timing would not influence the decision of sufficient loss severity.

EVT and GHD: The Most Common Approaches for LDA Revisited The high sensitivity of UL to higher-order effects caused by the asymptotic tail convergence of the empirical loss distribution complicates risk estimation when the level of statistical confidence extends to areas outside the historical loss experience. Given the apparent shortcomings of conventional VaR to model fat-tailed distributions under LDA in compliance with AMA standards, the development of internal risk measurement models has led to the industry consensus on the application of generalized parametric distributions, such as the *g-and-h* distribution (GHD) or various limit distributions (generalized Pareto distribution [GPD]) and the generalized extreme value (GEV)) under extreme value theory (EVT)[24] (see the appendix to this chapter). Both EVT and GHD are appealing statistical concepts, because they deliver closed form solutions for out-of-sample estimates at very high confidence levels without imposing additional modeling restrictions if certain assumptions about the underlying loss data hold. They also specify residual risk through a generalized parametric estimation of order statistics, which makes them particularly useful to study the tail behavior of heavily skewed loss data.

EVT represents an effective method to specify the limit law of extreme operational risk losses at high percentile levels over a given time horizon when the lack of sufficient empirical loss data renders back-testing impossible and consigns the specification of higher moments to simple parametric methods. GPD of EVT approximates GEV close to the endpoint of the variable of interest, where only a few or no observations are available (Vandewalle et al. 2004).[25] The popular peak-over-threshold (POT) estimation method for GPD prescribes upper-tail convergence of a locally estimated probability function for exceedances beyond a selected threshold and reparameterizes the first two raw moments to fit the entire empirical distribution (while the original tail index parameter is kept unchanged).[26] In contrast, GHD represents an alternative parametric model to estimate the residual risk of extreme losses based on a strictly monotonically increasing transformation of a standard normal variable.[27] The *g-and-h* family of distributions was first introduced by Tukey (1977) and can approximate probabilistically the shapes of a wide variety of different data and distributions (including GEV and GPD) by the choice of appropriate parameter values of skewness and kurtosis as constants or real valued (polynomial) functions (Martinez and Iglewicz 1984).

The estimation of UL beyond verifiable historical prediction entails model risk that varies by the parameter sensitivity to the identification of extreme observations and the speed of asymptotic tail decay. Faced with the scarcity of actual loss data of extreme operational risk events, however, analytical specifications of asymptotic tail behavior serve only as a rough guide of potential model risk within a restricted empirical spectrum of available loss profiles. Despite the merits of assessing competing quantitative approaches under different estimation methods and percentile ranges, even the extensive LDCE data gathered by U.S. banking regulators prove insufficient to substantiate comparability of point estimates across different loss distributions at very high percentile levels.

In general, the specification of residual risk under EVT suffers from greater parameter uncertainty than GHD, whose higher moments are not directly affected by the classification of extremes (i.e., threshold choice) and possible contamination from the timing of losses. The optimization of the threshold choice for GPD is contingent on the contemporaneous effect of estimation method and the desired level of statistical confidence. While point estimates at percentiles below a designated loss threshold are more reliable across different estimation methods and over different time horizons, they understate residual risk. Conversely, higher statistical confidence incurs higher parameter uncertainty by either (1) removing the desired percentile level of point estimates further from a prespecified loss threshold (which increases the chances of out-of-sample estimation) or (2) raising the loss threshold to a higher quantile (which limits the number of "eligible" extremes for the estimation of the asymptotic tail shape). Thus, exceedance functions of conditional mean excess (such as GPD) under EVT warrant a more careful assessment of estimation risk from different loss profiles and estimation methods at variable levels of statistical confidence (Embrechts 2000).

Recent studies indicate that EVT might not be the ultimate panacea for operational risk measurement from a comparative point of view. In their effort to derive a consistent measure of operational risk across several U.S. banks, Dutta and Perry (2006) find that GPD tends to overestimate UL in small samples, contending its adequacy as a general benchmark model.[28] Their results concur with those of Mignola and Ugoccioni (2005), who also show that the rate of upper-tail convergence to empirical quantiles can be poor, even for reasonably large samples.[29]

Nonetheless, in a recent simulation study of generic operational risk based on the aggregate statistics of operational risk exposure of U.S. banks, both GPD and GHD generate reliable and realistic AMA-compliant risk estimates of UL (Jobst 2007b). Degen et al. (2006) also caution against the unreserved use of alternative modeling by means of GHD, whose calibration entails considerable parameter risk arising from the quantile-based estimation of higher moments. The quality of the fitted GHD hinges on the specification of the selected number of percentiles and their spacing in the upper tail (contingent on log_2N of sample size N and the correlation between the order statistics of extreme observations and their corresponding quantile values). Although GHD (and its power law variant)[30] outperforms both GEV and GPD in terms of goodness and consistency of upper tail fit at low average deviation of less than 25%, it underestimates actual losses in all but the most extreme quantiles of 99.95% and higher, when GPD estimates overstate excess elongation of asymptotic tail decay,[31] suggesting a symbiotic relation between both methods contingent on the percentile level and the incidence of extreme events.

Operational Risk as a Dynamic Process and the Role of Qualitative Overlays Considerable parameter uncertainty and estimation risk of quantitative models arises in situations when the historical loss profile is a poor predictor of future exposure. LDA is static and does not capture the incidence of extremes as a dynamic process. Fluctuations of operational risk over time might defy steady-state approximation based on the central projection from historical exposure. Similar to project management, where the critical path changes in response to management action, the pattern of future losses—in particular extreme losses—might diverge from historical priors. Thus, the possibility of a dynamic transmission process of operational risk exposure curtails the validity of LDA (and related concepts) and necessitates a comparative assessment of the time-varying impact of different loss profiles under different measurement approaches. After all, EVT and GHD are only two of several concepts to measure operational risk.

The innate elusiveness of certain sources of operational risk imposes practical limitations on LDA measurability—even if operational risk exposure is examined at every level of a bank. Since extreme losses result from one-time risk events that elude purely quantitative measurement models, qualitative self-assessment can help identify the possibility and the severity of extreme operational risk events in areas where empirical observations are hard to come by—but only in general ways. This precludes existing measurement approaches that ascertain the impact of operational risk events on banking activity based on historical references without paying heed to the causality of operational risk events and the sensitivity of their financial impact across banks and over time. That said, subjective judgments are prone to historical bias and rely on rough approximations due to a lack of precise estimates of probability and loss severity. The prominence of qualitative overlays, however, needs to be carefully balanced with a considerable degree of judgment and mindful interpretation of historical precedents.[32]

It is clear that structural models based on macroeconomic factors and key risk indicators (KRIs), augmented by risk and control self-assessments (RCSAs), would help inform a better forecast of future losses from operational risk and foster a more accurate allocation of regulatory capital. In predictive factor models, macroeconomic variables can help estimate different kinds of operational risk, such as internal and external fraud, which might be more likely at times of high unemployment or organizational restructuring. Nonetheless, exogenous shocks to banking activity, such as natural disasters, continue to escape quantification and might be best addressed by ongoing monitoring of threats and qualitative assessments of the scale and scope of extreme scenarios associated with high-impact operational risk events.

2.3.2 Shortcomings of LDA Caused by Data Collection: ORM Systems and Data Characteristics

The comparative analysis of operational risk exposure reveals startling insights about the shortcomings of LDA in the presence of diverse loss data whose quantitative implications conventional measurement approaches and regulatory incentives have frequently ignored. A wide range of available (quantitative and qualitative) measurement methods and different levels of sophistication of ORM induce heterogeneous risk estimates for similar exposures, which weaken the reliable and consistent implementation of regulatory standards subject to a coherent supervisory review process.

While the current regulatory framework provides some degree of standardization of different banking activities and types of operational risk events, the efficacy of risk estimates still varies largely with the characteristics of internal loss data, which are influenced by (1) the diverse scale, scope, and complexity of different banking activities that escape uniform accountability; and (2) idiosyncratic policies and procedures of ORM systems to authenticate, identify, monitor, report, and control all aspects of operational risk BEICFs. In particular, different exposures associated with different sources of operational risk, the diversity of banks, which differ in size and sophistication of their activities (exogenous variation), and dissimilar policies and procedures to identify, process and monitor operational risk events as part of the ORM process[33] (endogenous variation) as well as considerable diversity of loss data collection (subject to different loss thresholds and interpretations of what constitutes a material operational risk event) conspire to defy consistent measurement and obscure the comparability of cross-sectional risk estimates.

These methodological difficulties are often magnified by (1) varying loss frequency and sample sizes of historical loss data as well as (2) data pooling to remedy notorious data limitations, which introduce further comparative bias in risk estimates. O'Dell (2005) reports that operational risk estimates submitted by U.S. banks as part of the LDCE in 2004 showed little convergence to common units of measure and requirements on the data collection due to different granularities of risk quantification.[34] Recent efforts by the biggest U.S. financial institutions[35] to seek simplified capital rules not only underscore the importance of consistent regulatory standards but also reveal that current implementation guidelines are still found wanting.

Data Sources and Pooling of Internal and External Loss Data The historical loss experience serves as a prime indicator of the amount of reserves banks need to hold to cover the financial impact of operational risk events. Since meaningful results from quantitative self-assessment of operational risk exposure—especially at very high levels of statistical confidence—require a large enough sample of observations under AMA soundness standards, certain BLs and/or ETs with insufficient empirical loss data might confine operational risk estimation to a certain set of "well-populated" units of measure. However, the paucity of actual loss data, the heterogeneous recording of operational risk events, and the intricate empirical characteristics of operational risk complicate consistent and reliable measurement. Even at more granular units of measurement, most banks lack the critical mass of loss data to effectively analyze, calculate, and report capital charges for operational risk.

Banks require high-quality loss event information to enhance the predictive capabilities of their quantitative operational risk models in response to new regulatory guidelines under the New Basel Capital Accord. In order to address prevailing empirical constraints on a reliable measurement of operational risk exposure, several private sector initiatives of banks and other financial institutions have investigated the merits of data collection from internal and external sources (consortium data and external data of publicly reported events). Some of the most prominent examples of proprietary external data sources of operational risk loss events are the Global Operational Loss Database (GOLD) by the British Bankers' Association (BBA), the Operational Risk Insurance Consortium (ORIC) by the Association of British Insurers (ABI), OpBase by Aon Corporation, and the operational risk database maintained by the Operational Riskdata eXchange Association (ORX). In several instances, financial services supervisors themselves have facilitated greater transparency about the historical loss experience of banks, such as the Loss Data Collection Exercise (LDCE) of U.S. commercial banks.

AMA criteria permit banks to use external data to supplement insufficient internal historical records, but the indiscriminate consolidation of loss data from different sources in proprietary databases or data consortia causes difficulties. Although external loss data in self-assessment approaches help banks overcome the scarcity of internal loss data, the pooling of loss data entails potential pitfalls from survivorship bias, the commingling of different sources of risk, and mean convergence of aggregate historical loss. While internal data (if available) serve as a valid empirical basis for the quantification of individual bank exposure, the analysis of system-wide pooled data could deliver misleading results, mainly because it aggregates individual loss profiles into a composite loss exposure, which impedes risk estimates for very granular units of measure.

The natural heterogeneity of banking activity due to different organizational structures, types of activities, and risk management capabilities belies the efficacy of aggregation. As the historical loss experience typically is germane to one bank and might not be applicable to another bank, pooled data hides cross-sectional diversity of individual risk profiles and frequently obscures estimates of actual risk exposure. Critical impediments to data pooling include divergent definitions of operational risk and control mechanisms, variable collection methods of loss data, and inconsistent data availability for different BLs and/or ETs contingent on the scale and scope of individual banks' main business activities are.

The use of pooled loss data without suitable adjustments of external data by key risk indicators and internal control factors is questionable. Cross-sectional bias would be mitigated only if different internal control systems of various-size banks were taken into account (Matz 2005) or loss data exhibited some regularity across institutions so that a viable benchmark model could be developed (Dutta and Perry 2006). Similar to the potential aggregation bias caused by data pooling, the blurred distinction of operational risk from other sources of risk (such as market and credit risk) hampers accurate empirical loss specification. Contingencies of data collection arise from the commingling of risk types in the process of loss identification, which might understate actual operational risk exposure.

Effects of Loss Frequency   Reliable quantitative risk analysis hinges on the comparability of loss profiles across different banking activities and the capacity of ORM systems to identify, report, and monitor operational risk exposures in a consistent fashion. However, different ORM processes and diverse procedures of loss data collection and reporting affect the availability and the diversity of loss data. The heterogeneity of loss frequency within and across banks as well as over time is probably the single most important but often overlooked impediment to the dependable quantification of operational risk for comparative purposes. Variations of reported event frequency can indirectly affect the volatility of losses and the estimation of EL and UL.

Effect of Loss Frequency on Expected Loss   The recent clarification on the Treatment of Expected Losses by Banks Using the AMA Under the Basel II Framework (Basel Committee 2005b) by the AIGOR of the Basel Committee Accord Implementation Group acknowledges in particular the possibility of biased estimation of EL, depending on the manner in which operational risk events are recorded over time. Loss frequency directly affects EL. A higher (lower) loss frequency decreases (increases) EL automatically in the trivial case of unchanged total exposure. The consideration of loss variation is essential to a nontrivial identification of distortions to EL caused by inconsistent loss frequency. A bank that reports a lower (higher) EL due to a higher (lower) incidence of operational risk events should not be treated the same as another bank whose operational risk losses exhibit higher (lower) variation at similar loss exposure (over the same time period). In this case, banks with more granular operational risk events would benefit from lower EL if loss volatility decreases disproportionately with each additional operational risk event. The same point applies to the more realistic case of different total exposure between banks. Higher (lower) loss frequency would decrease (increase) EL only if variation declines (rises) with higher (lower) total exposure—a contestable assumption at best. Hence, the adequate estimation of operational risk exposure entails a relative rather than an absolute concept of consistent frequency over one or multiple time periods.

Since the capital charge for operational risk under the new regulatory framework is based on the sum of operational risk estimates for different units of measure, inconsistent loss frequencies might substantially distort a true representation of EL within and across reporting banks. A systemically inconsistent frequency measure of operational risk for the same unit of measure (defined by either BL, ET, or both) of different banks arises if lower (higher) EL and a higher (lower) total loss amount is associated with lower (higher) marginal loss volatility caused by a larger (smaller) number of observations. The same concept of inconsistent frequency pertains to different units of measure within the same bank. The case of idiosyncratically inconsistent frequency is admittedly harder to argue, given the inherently heterogeneous nature of operational risk exposure of different banking activities. If the loss frequency for one BL or ET of a single bank changes considerably from one time period to another, it might also constitute a time-inconsistent frequency measure, which amplifies idiosyncratic or systemically inconsistent loss frequency of two or more different BLs or ETs within a single bank or a single BL or ET across different banks, respectively.

Regulatory guidance on operational risk measurement would need to ensure that risk estimates based on different empirical loss frequencies preserve the marginal loss variation in support of a time-consistent measurement of EL. A simple detection mechanism for possible estimation bias from idiosyncratically inconsistent loss frequency across two different units of measure in one and the same bank would compare the pairwise coefficient of variation $c_v = \sigma/\mu$ and the mean μ (EL) of total operational risk exposure $TL = EL + UL = N \times \mu$ (i.e., total losses) based on N number of losses recorded in two different BLs or ETs over time period τ. While

$$\mu_{BL_{1,\tau}} > \mu_{BL_{2,\tau}} \,\big|\, \left(c_{v_{BL_{1,\tau}}} > c_{v_{BL_{2,\tau}}}\right)$$

$$\text{if } N_{BL_{1,\tau}} < N_{BL_{2,\tau}} \wedge N_{BL_{1,\tau}}\mu_{BL_{1,\tau}} \leq N_{BL_{2,\tau}}\mu_{BL_{2,\tau}} \tag{2.1}$$

indicates "insufficient" observations for BL_1 and relative to BL_2 (i.e., few observations at high variability),

$$\mu_{BL_{1,\tau}} < \mu_{BL_{2,\tau}} \,\big|\, \left(c_{v_{BL_{1,\tau}}} < c_{v_{BL_{2,\tau}}}\right)$$

$$\text{if } N_{BL_{1,\tau}} > N_{BL_{2,\tau}} \wedge N_{BL_{1,\tau}}\mu_{BL_{1,\tau}} \geq N_{BL_{2,\tau}}\mu_{BL_{2,\tau}} \tag{2.2}$$

reverses the situation, flagging excessively granular observations of losses in BL_1 relative to BL_2 as loss volatility decreases (increases) with a higher (lower) loss frequency and larger (smaller) TL. In Equation 2.1, the unqualified treatment of loss frequency $N_{BL_{1,\tau}}$ would result in a disproportionately higher EL for BL_1, whereas in Equation 2.2, the bank could reduce EL in BL_1 to a level below a fair projection of average losses. The four remaining permutations of loss variation and EL indicate frequency consistent reporting across the two BLs under consideration. Both loss distributions in Equations 2.1 and 2.2 would result in a different capital charge under a consistent measure of loss frequency.

Extending both equations to all BLs (BL_{1-8}) or ETs (ET_{1-7}) defined by the Basel Committee (2004, 2006b) to

$$\mu_{\{BL_{x,\tau},ET_{x,\tau}\}} > m(\mu_{\{BL_{1-8,\tau},ET_{1-7,\tau}\}})|(c_{v_{\{BL_{x,\tau},ET_{x,\tau}\}}} > m(c_{v_{\{BL_{1-8,\tau},ET_{1-7,\tau}\}}}))$$

$$\text{if } N_{\{BL_{x,\tau},ET_{x,\tau}\}} < m(N_{\{BL_{1-8,\tau},ET_{1-7,\tau}\}}) \wedge N_{\{BL_{x,\tau},ET_{x,\tau}\}}\mu_{\{BL_{x,\tau},ET_{x,\tau}\}}$$

$$\leq m(N_{\{BL_{1-8,\tau},ET_{1-7,\tau}\}}\mu_{\{BL_{1-8,\tau},ET_{1-7,\tau}\}}) \tag{2.3}$$

and

$$\mu_{\{BL_{x,\tau},ET_{x,\tau}\}} < m(\mu_{\{BL_{1-8,\tau},ET_{1-7,\tau}\}})\,\big|\,(c_{v_{\{BL_{x,\tau},ET_{x,\tau}\}}} < m(c_{v_{\{BL_{1-8,\tau},ET_{1-7,\tau}\}}}))$$

$$\text{if } N_{\{BL_{x,\tau},ET_{x,\tau}\}} > m(N_{\{BL_{1-8,\tau},ET_{1-7,\tau}\}}) \wedge N_{\{BL_{x,\tau},ET_{x,\tau}\}}\mu_{\{BL_{x,\tau},ET_{x,\tau}\}}$$

$$\geq m(N_{\{BL_{1-8,\tau},ET_{1-7,\tau}\}}\mu_{\{BL_{1-8,\tau},ET_{1-7,\tau}\}}) \tag{2.4}$$

identifies idiosyncratically inconsistent loss frequency of any individual BL (BL_x) or ET (ET_x) of the same bank based on the median (m) values of variation, mean and frequency of losses across all BLs or ETs. The same detection mechanism applies to cases of systemically inconsistent loss frequency for the same BL or ET across different banks, or time inconsistent loss frequency over multiple time periods.

Effect of Loss Frequency on Unexpected Loss The reported frequency of operational risk events influences not only EL but also the estimation of UL. Irrespective of the stochastic process of extremes, higher (lower) loss frequency attributes lower (higher) probability to extreme events at the margin and increases estimation risk of UL if loss frequency is inconsistent; that is, higher (lower) loss frequency coincides with lower (higher) loss variation. Given the high sensitivity of UL to changes in the probability of extreme events, an inconsistent frequency measure could interfere with the reliable estimation of UL from both a systemic and an idiosyncratic point of view at one or multiple periods.

Banks could also employ loss frequency as a vehicle to diffuse the impact of extreme loss severity across different BLs and/or ETs (organizational diversification), if they define risk ownership and units of measure for risk estimates in a way that relegates the incidence of extreme events to even higher percentiles. Similar to the implicit truncation effect of a minimum loss threshold on the availability of loss data, loss fragmentation might arise if banks choose to either split losses between various BLs affected by the same operational risk event or spread operational risk losses among other sources of risk, such as market or credit risk.

Since the new capital rules prescribe the estimation of UL at a level of granularity that implies a loss frequency beyond actual data availability even for the largest banks, the best interest of banks lies in greater sample sizes, especially in cases of sparse internal loss data and less granular units of measure. Banks would naturally prefer higher (and inconsistent) loss frequency to substantiate regulatory capital for very predictable EL while reducing economic capital for UL. The larger the benefit of a marginal reduction of loss volatility from higher loss frequency, the greater the incentive of banks to arbitrage existing regulatory provisions and temper the probability of extreme events by means of higher reporting frequency and granularity of risk estimates.

The elusive nature of operational risk belies the general assumption of uniform frequency. While most operational risk losses comply with a static concept of loss frequency, different types of operational risk cause distinct stochastic properties of loss events, which also influence the relative incidence of extreme observations. One expedient solution to this problem is the aggregation of loss events in each unit of measure over a designated time period (weeks, months, quarters) in order to ensure the consistent econometric specification of operational risk exposure with different underlying loss frequency. Loss aggregation helps curb estimation bias from distinctive patterns of loss frequencies associated with different loss severity and units of measure of operational risk within banks. An aggregate loss measure inhibits incentives to suppress EL through many, very small losses and increases the relative incidence of extreme events without distorting the loss severity of UL. Two different series of observations with either high frequency and low average loss severity or low frequency and high average loss severity would both converge to the same aggregate expected operational risk exposure over an infinite time period (assuming the same total loss amount).

Loss aggregation also reveals time-varying loss frequency based on the relation between the mean and the median number of events in each time period of aggregation and the extent to which large fluctuations warrant adjustments to the assumption of constant loss frequency. Data limitations for robust risk estimation notwithstanding, the aggregation of operational risk losses delivers important insights about how measures of loss frequency are influenced by the type, loss severity, timing of operational risk events, as well as the degree of granularity and specificity at which operational risk events are reported (see Box 2.3).

BOX 2.3 REGULATORY INCONSISTENCIES OF THE NEW BASEL CAPITAL ACCORD

The standardized and advanced measurement approaches of operational risk under the new regulatory framework of the New Basel Capital Accord has several shortcomings concerning analytical rigor and consistent implementation of these provisions: (1) capital adjustment of operational risk estimates, (2) home-host recognition, (3) and volume-based measures of operational risk (Jobst 2007c, 2007d).

Capital Adjustment of Operational Risk Estimates under AMA

The current quantitative criteria of the AMA soundness standards allow banks to adjust the regulatory capital charge for UL by up to 20% of their operational risk exposure (capital adjustment) due to (1) *diversification benefits* from internally determined loss correlations[36] between individual operational risk estimates (units of measure) and (2) the *risk-mitigating impact* of operational risk insurance.

However, such capital adjustment is meaningful only if dependencies are measured consistently and reliably at the required level of statistical confidence that can be assessed without idiosyncratic bias. This bias is caused by the limited availability of loss data, heterogeneous loss reporting, and cross-sectional variation of the incidence and magnitude of extreme operational risk losses of the same BL or ET of different banks or across different BLs or ETs within the same bank for a fair comparative assessment of adequate capital adjustment.

Furthermore, diversification benefits negate the additive nature of operational risk and challenge the long-standing assumption of independent extremes. Even if the independence condition is relaxed, the estimation of joint asymptotic tail behavior of extreme marginals at high percentiles is not a straightforward exercise and requires a significant departure from conventional methods.

The traditional Pearson's correlation coefficient detects only linear dependence between two variables whose fixed marginals are assumed to be distributed normally, indicating an empirical relation (or the lack thereof) based on more central (and more frequent) observations at lower (and not extreme) quantiles. An expedient nonparametric method of investigating the bivariate empirical relation between two independent and identically distributed (i.i.d.) random vectors is to ascertain the incidence of shared cases of cross-classified extremes via a refined quantile-based Chi-square statistic of independence (Coles et al. 1999; Coles 2001). This measure of joint asymptotic tail dependence of marginal extreme value distributions underlies several methods (Poon et al. 2003; Stephenson 2002) to model multivariate extreme value distribution (EVD) functions. However, the implications of these models have not been sufficiently tested with regard to their impact on quantitative assumptions and regulatory incentives that underpin the proposed capital rules for operational risk. The wide dispersion of the magnitude of capital adjustment of U.S. commercial banks in a recent survey (O'Dell 2005) testifies to the significance of these considerations for sound regulatory standards.

Home-Host Recognition under AMA

The concept of home-host recognition of operational risk estimates (Basel Committee 2004b, 2007) stipulates that banking organizations that calculate group-wide capital requirements under AMA for

(Continued)

**BOX 2.3 REGULATORY INCONSISTENCIES
OF THE NEW BASEL CAPITAL ACCORD**
(*Continued*)

consolidated banking activities could use stand-alone AMA calculations for significant internationally active banking subsidiaries,
whereas other subsidiaries are assigned a relative share of the group-
wide AMA capital requirement. The flexibility of this hybrid approach
extends the opportunity of regulatory arbitrage to significant internationally active subsidiaries that perform banking activities similar to
the banking group but realize capital savings due to a favorable historical loss experience and/or a more flexible definition of units of measure.

**Volume-Based Measures of Operational Risk
in Standardized Approaches**

If banks lack the necessary risk management tools or historical information for quantitative self-assessment under AMA, the New Basel
Capital Accord stipulates standardized measurement approaches of
operational risk, which we assume volume-based dependence of operational risk (see Table 2.2). However, relating operational risk exposure to business activity fails to acknowledge that banks specialize
in a wide-ranging set of activities with a diverse nature of operational
risk exposure and maintain very different measurement methods, risk-
control procedures, and corporate governance standards, which affect
both the incidence and the level of operational risk exposure. Moreover, the tacit risk-return trade-off of volume dependence challenges
empirical evidence of operational risk exposure. In the worst case, a
highly profitable bank with ORM practices that are sound but not
sophisticated enough to meet AMA soundness standards would need
to satisfy higher fixed capital charges than a less profitable peer bank
with weaker controls. A fixed capital charge should not be defined
as a function of income but as a measure of the debilitating effect of
operational risk on income generation, which serves as a scaling factor
of loss severity. Thus, an adequate volume-based measure would need
to be constructed in a way that supports an *inverse relation* between
gross income and the capital charge for operational risk and upholds a
lower marginal rate of increase of operational risk exposure as banks
generate more income.

TABLE 2.2 Hypothetical Loss Exposure of the Largest U.S. Commercial Banks on September 11, 2001

Insured U.S.-Chartered Commercial Banks[1] (*ranked by consolidated assets, as of Dec. 31, 2001*	Major Operational Loss Event				
	(US$140 million, *Bank of New York*, Sept. 11, 2001)				
	(*In % of*)				
	Total assets[3]	Interest income	Non-Interest Income	Gross Income	Tier 1 Capital
Bank of America NA (Bank of America Corp.)[2]	0.02	1.91	3.86	1.28	0.31
JP Morgan Chase Bank (JP Morgan Chase & Co.)	0.02	3.07	4.21	1.77	0.39
Citibank NA (Citigroup)	0.02	1.51	3.06	1.01	0.32
Wachovia Bank NA (Wachovia Corp.)	0.04	3.45	9.87	2.56	0.65
First Union Bank[4]	0.06	1.86	2.05	0.98	0.78
US Bank NA	0.08	5.63	12.60	3.89	10.92
Bank One NA (Bank One Corp.)	0.05	1.60	1.94	0.88	0.64
Wells Fargo Bank NA (Wells Fargo & Co.)	0.04	3.38	6.28	2.20	0.66
Suntrust Bank	0.13	4.30	6.49	2.59	1.75
HSBC Bank USA (HSBC NA)	0.17	13.67	55.66	10.97	3.12
Bank of New York (Bank of New York Corp.)	0.18	18.87	18.60	9.37	2.58
Key Bank NA (Key Corp.)	0.18	11.79	38.67	9.04	2.42
State Street B&TC (State Street Corp.)	0.21	25.51	21.04	11.53	3.93
PNC Bank NA (PNC Financial Services Group)	0.20	6.15	5.51	2.90	3.04
LaSalle Bank NA (ABN Amro NA HC)	0.13	12.05	33.32	8.85	1.75
mean	0.10	7.65	14.88	4.65	2.22
median	0.08	4.30	6.49	2.59	1.75
std. dev.	0.07	7.24	16.01	4.01	2.68

[1]Excluded is Fleet NA Bank (Fleetboston Financial Group), which merged with Bank of America NA in 2003.

[2]"Regulatory top holder" listed in parentheses.

[3]Total assets, gross income, and Tier 1 capital represent the sum of assets, gross income, and core capital of individual banking institutions under each top holder, ignoring adjustments in consolidation at holding company level.

[4]After the merger with Wachovia, First Union did not publish financial accounts for end-2001. Fundamental information is taken from the 2000 Financial Statement.

Source: Federal Reserve Board, *Federal Reserve Statistical Release—Large Commercial Banks*, 2002. www.federalreserve.gov/releases/lbr/.

2.4 CONCLUSION

Regulatory efforts have favored the development of quantitative models of operational risk as a distinct discipline that appeals to the use of economic capital as a determinant of risk-based regulatory standards. However, the one-time nature of extreme operational risk events without historical precedent defies pure quantitative approaches and necessitates a qualitative overlay in many instances. Reliable operational risk measurement face considerable challenges regarding the accurate estimation of asymptotic tail convergence of extreme losses and the consistent definition and implementation of loss reporting across different areas of banking activity.

This chapter explained the shortcomings of existing LDA models and examined the structural and systemic effects of heterogeneous data reporting on loss characteristics, which influence the reliability of operational risk estimates for regulatory purposes. We found that cross-sectional variation of the timing and frequency of reported loss events can adversely affect the generation of consistent risk estimates. These results offer insights for enhanced market practice and a more effective implementation of capital rules and prudent standards for operational risk measurement. Although standardized approaches under the New Basel Capital Accord recognize considerable variation of relative loss severity of operational risk events within and across banks, the economic logic of volume-based measures collapses in cases when banks incur small (large) operational risk losses in BLs where an aggregate volume-based measure would indicate high (low) operational risk exposure.

Aside from the diverse characteristics of different sources of operational risk, cross-sectional variation of loss profiles (due to variable loss frequency, different minimum thresholds for recognized operational risk losses, and loss fragmentation between various BLs[37]), and the idiosyncratic organization of risk ownership prevent the consistent application of AMA. Where historical loss data are scarce, stringent regulatory standards amplify the considerable model risk of quantitative approaches and parameter instability at out-of-sample percentile levels unless available samples of loss data are sufficiently large. Normative assumptions, such as gross income as a volume-based metric, eschew such measurement bias of operational risk in favor of greater reliability, but they do so at the expense of less discriminatory power and higher capital charges.

The high percentile level of AMA appears to have been chosen deliberately to encourage better monitoring, measuring, and managing of operational risk in return for capital savings vis-à-vis simple volume-based capital charges. Evidence from U.S. commercial banks suggests significant benefits from AMA over a standardized measure of 15% of gross income, which would grossly overstate the economic impact of even the most extreme operational risk events.[38] The top 15 U.S. banks would have lost barely 5% of gross income on average if they had experienced an operational risk event comparable to the physical damage to assets suffered by the Bank of New York in the wake of the 9/11 terrorist attacks (see Table 2.2).[39] Similar analysis of LDCE data from 1999 to 2004 suggests that the worst performing bank in terms of operational risk exposure would have needed to provide capital coverage just shy of 1% of annual gross income to cover UL over a five-year time horizon (Jobst 2007a, 2007b).

The general purpose of safeguarding banking system stability is not to raise capital requirements to a point where they encumber financial activities but to encourage profitable execution of business activities within boundaries of common regulatory standards and sound market practices. Using safeguards would mutualize risk and limit externalities from individual bank failures. In this regard, effective regulation endorses policies that mitigate the loss impact on the quality and stability of earnings while ensuring adequate capitalization in order to enhance strategic decision making and reduce the probability of bankruptcy. In the context of operational risk, however, the concept of capital adequacy appears incidental to the importance of corporate governance as well as the perpetual reassessment of risk models, which consider income generation a gauge of banking soundness.

In general, the role of capital can be appreciated by considering the case of a gambler's ruin. Too little capital puts banks at risk, while too much capital prevents banks from achieving the required rate of return on capital. Although higher capital increases the general survival rate of banks, it does little to prevent bank failure unless it is paired with *ex ante* risk management and control procedures that limit the chances of fatal operational risk events whose loss severity would cause banking activities to cease altogether regardless of (economically sustainable) capitalization. Thus, monitoring risk aversion toward activities with noncurrent exposure plays a critical role in guiding the effectiveness of marginal income generation, especially when financial innovation and new risk management processes upset the established relation between risk burden and safe capital levels in the determination of overall performance. Measures to reduce risk (and systemic vulnerabilities) are effective only if banks do not respond to a perceived newfound safety by engaging in activities that might engender complacency and carry even higher (but poorly understood types of) operational risk exposure.[40] Although many banks will not be subject to a more rigorous regulatory regime of ORM under the New Basel Capital Accord, rating agencies uphold these risk management practices in their external assessment of credit quality and operational soundness of banks and, thus, motivate indirect regulatory compliance via the economic incentive of lower capital costs.

Given the elusive nature of operational risk and the absence of risk-return trade-off (unlike market and credit risk), it is incumbent on banking supervisors to institute regulatory incentives that acknowledge the effect of diverse loss profiles and data collection methods on sound internal risk measurement methods. With increasing sophistication of financial products and the diversity of financial institutions, any capital rules would need to be cast in such a way that banks may determine the approach most appropriate for their exposures and, crucially, allow for further methodological developments aimed at the expedient resolution of challenges arising from the intricate causality of operational risk. In particular, such efforts would be geared toward exploring options for (and greater flexibility in the administration of) measures that strike a balance between prescriptive and principle-based guidelines, which better reflects the economic reality of operational risk and preserves the accuracy, relevance, and comprehensiveness of regulatory provisions.

APPENDIX

Formulas

Definition and Parametric Specification of the Generalized Pareto Distribution The parametric estimation of extreme value type tail behavior under generalized Pareto distribution (GPD) requires a threshold selection that guarantees asymptotic convergence to GEV. GPD approximates GEV according to the Pickands-Balkema-de Haan limit theorem only if the sample mean excess is positive linear and satisfies the Fisher-Tippett (1928) theorem. It is commonly specified as conditional mean excess distribution $F^{[t]}(x) = \Pr(X - t \leq x \mid X > t) \equiv \Pr(Y \geq y \mid X > t)$ of an ordered sequence of exceedance values $Y = \max(X_1, \ldots, X_n)$ from independent and identically distributed (i.i.d.) random variables, which measures the residual risk beyond threshold $t \geq 0$ (Reiss and Thomas 1997). GPD with threshold $t \to \infty$ represents the (only) continuous approximation of GEV (Castillo and Hadi 1997)

$$F^{[a_n t + b_n]}(a_n(t+s) + b_n) \to W^{[t]}_{\xi,\beta}(x) = 1 + \log G_\xi(s/(1+\xi t)) \qquad (2A.1)$$

where
$$x > t \geq 0$$
$$F^{[t]}(x) = 1/n \sum_{i=1}^{n} I_{\{X_i > t\}} = k/n$$

under the assumption of stationarity and ergodicity (Falk et al. 1994), so that

$$W^{[t]}_{\xi,\beta}(x) = \begin{cases} 1 - (1 + \xi x/\beta)^{-1/\xi} & \xi \neq 0 \\ 1 - \exp(-x/\beta) & \xi = 0 \end{cases} \qquad (2A.2)$$

unifies the *exponential* (GP0), *Pareto* (GP1) and *beta* (GP2) distributions, with shape parameter $\xi = 0$ defined by continuity (Jenkinson 1955). The support of x is $x \geq 0$ when $\xi \geq 0$ and $0 \leq x \leq -\beta/\xi$ when $\xi < 0$.

It is commonplace to use the so-called peak-over-threshold (POT) method (Embrechts et al. 1997; Kotz and Nadarajah 2000; McNeil and Saladin 1997) for the GPD fit to the order statistic of fat-tailed empirical data. POT estimates the asymptotic tail behavior of nth order statistics $x_{n-k+1:n}, \ldots, x_{n:n}$ of extreme values as i.i.d. random variables beyond threshold value $t \geq 0$, whose parametric specification $W_{\xi,\mu,\sigma}^{[t]}(x) = W_{\xi,t,\sigma+\xi(t-\mu)}(x)$ is extrapolated to a region of interest for which no (i.e., out-of-sample) or only a few observations (i.e., in-sample) are available.

The threshold choice of POT involves a delicate trade-off between model accuracy and estimation bias contingent on the absolute order of magnitude of extremes. The threshold quantile must be sufficiently high to support the parametric estimation of residual risk while leaving a sufficient number of external observations to maintain linear mean excess without inducing parameter uncertainty. Although a low threshold would allow a greater number of exceedances to inform a more robust parameter estimation of asymptotic tail behavior, the declaration of more extremes implies a higher chance of dependent extremes in violation of the convergence property of GPD as a limit distribution under GEV. By the same token, an excessively restrictive threshold choice might leave too few maxima for a reliable parametric fit without increasing estimation risk.

Alternatively, a suitable threshold can also be selected by the timing of the occurrence of extremes. In order to identify extremes through a measure of relative magnitude based on a time-varying threshold, we divide the original loss data series into equivalent-size, nonoverlapping blocks and select the maximum value from each block in order to obtain a series of maxima consistent with the assumption of i.i.d. extreme observations. Block sizes need to be chosen so as to mitigate bias caused by clustered extremes during times of high volatility.[41]

The locally estimated GPD function $W_{\xi,t,\tilde{\sigma}}(x) = k/n$ for exceedance values $k = \sum_{i=1}^{n} I(x_i > t)$ over the selected threshold $t = x_{n-k+1:n}$ is then fitted to the entire empirical distribution $W_{\xi,\hat{\mu},\hat{\sigma}}(t) = (n-k)/n$ over sample size n by selecting location and scale parameters $\hat{\mu}$ and $\hat{\sigma}$ such that

$$W_{\hat{\xi},\hat{\mu},\hat{\sigma}}^{[t]}(x) = W_{\hat{\xi},t,\tilde{\sigma}}(x) \qquad (2A.3)$$

By keeping the shape parameter $\hat{\xi} = \tilde{\xi}$ constant, the first two moments are reparameterized to $\hat{\sigma} = \tilde{\sigma}(k/n)^{\tilde{\xi}}$ and $\hat{\mu} = t - (\tilde{\sigma} - \hat{\sigma})/\tilde{\mu}$. Therefore, the estimated GPD quantile function is

$$\hat{x}_p = t + \hat{\sigma}/\hat{\xi}((n/k(1-p))^{-\hat{\xi}} - 1) \equiv W_{\xi,\beta}^{[t]-1}(x) \qquad (2A.4)$$

We qualify the suitability of a certain type of GPD estimation method on its ability to align sample mean excess values to the analytical mean excess values of GPD as a binding convergence criterion of extreme observations to asymptotic tail behavior based on a given threshold choice. We distinguish among five major estimation types:

1. Moment estimator (Dekkers et al. 1989)
2. Maximum likelihood estimator
3. Pickands (Pickands 1975 and 1981) estimator
4. Drees-Pickands (Drees 1995) estimator
5. Hill (Drees et al. 1998; Hill 1975) estimator

The bivariate extreme value distribution of $G(x)$ can be expressed as

$$G(x_1, x_2) = \exp(-(y_1 + y_2)A(y_1/y_1 + y_2))) \qquad (2A.5)$$

where the jth univariate marginal distribution

$$y_j = y_j(x_j) = (1 + \xi_j(x - \mu_j)/\sigma_j)_+^{-1/\xi} \quad \text{(for } j = 1, 2) \qquad (2A.6)$$

constitutes GEV with $h_+ = \max(h, 0)$, scale parameter $\sigma > 0$, location parameter μ, and shape parameter ξ. The dependence function $A(.)$ characterizes the dependence structure of $G(x_1, x_2)$. It is a convex function on $[0, 1]$ with $A(0) = A(1) = 1$ and $\max(\omega, 1 - \omega) \leq A(\omega) \leq 1$ for all $0 \leq \omega \leq 1$. Parametric models are commonly used for inference of multivariate extreme value distributions, of which the logistic model with distribution function $G(x_1, x_2; \alpha) = \exp(-(y_1^{1/\alpha} + y_2^{1/\alpha})^\alpha)$ with dependence parameter $\alpha \in (0, 1]$ appears to be the most widely used. While $\alpha = 1$ indicates complete independence, two or more extreme value distributions reach complete dependence as α approaches zero.

Definition and Parametric Specification of the *g-and-h* Distribution   In line with Dutta and Perry (2006) and Degen et al. (2006), we also examine the *g-and-h* distribution as an alternative generalized parametric model to estimate the residual risk of extreme losses. The *g-and-h* family of distributions was first introduced by Tukey (1977) and represents a strictly increasing transformation of a standard normal variable z according to

$$F_{g,h}(z) = \mu + \sigma(\exp(gz) - 1) \times \exp(hz^2/2)g^{-1} \qquad (2A.7)$$

where $\mu, \sigma, g, h \geq 0$ are the location, scale, skewness, and kurtosis parameters of distribution $F_{g,h}(z)$

whose domain of attraction includes all real numbers. The parameters g and h can either be constants or real valued (polynomial) functions of z^2 (as long as the transformational structure $(\exp(gz) - 1)\exp(hz^2/2)g^{-1}$ is a monotonic function).[42] If $\mu = 0$, then $F_{-g,h}(z) = -F_{g,h}(-z)$, which implies that a change in the sign of g only changes the direction of the skewness but not its magnitude. When $h = 0$, GHD reduces to $F_{g,0}(z) = \mu + \sigma(\exp(gz) - 1)g^{-1}$ (g-distribution), which exhibits skewness but lacks the slow converging, asymptotic tail decay of extreme quantiles of $F_{0,h}(z) = \mu + \sigma z \exp(hz^2/2)$ ("h-distribution") for $g = 0$.

Martinez and Iglewicz (1984) show that GHD can approximate probabilistically the shapes of a wide variety of different data and distributions (including GEV and GPD) when the appropriate parameter values are chosen. Its basic structure is predicated on order statistics, which makes it particularly useful to study the tail behavior of heavily skewed loss data.[43] Since this distribution is merely a transformation of the standard normal distribution, it also provides a useful probability function for the generation of random numbers through Monte Carlo simulation. Given the transformational structure of the standard normal distribution, the quantile-based method (Hoaglin 1985; McCulloch 1996) is typically used for parametric estimation of GHD and can deliver more accurate empirical tail fit than conventional estimation methods, such as the method of moments and maximum likelihood estimation (MLE). Dutta and Babbel (2002) provide a detailed description of the estimation method.[44]

NOTES

1. This definition includes legal risk from the failure to comply with laws as well as prudent ethical standards and contractual obligations, but excludes strategic and reputational risk.
2. Besides operational risk measurement, the promotion of consistent capital adequacy requirements for credit and market risk as well as new regulatory provisions for asset securitization were further key elements of the reforms, which began in 1999. Although the revision of the old capital rules was originally set for completion in 2000, protracted negotiations and strong criticism by the banking industry of a first regulatory framework published in May 2004 delayed the release of the new guidelines for the *International Convergence of Capital Measurement and Capital Standards* (New Basel Capital Accord or Basel II) until June 2006, with an implementation expected in over 100 countries by 2008.
3. National supervisory authorities have substantial discretion (supervisory review) in determining the scope of implementation of Basel II framework. For instance, the *Advanced Notice on Proposed Rulemaking* (ANPR) on *Risk-Based*

Capital Guidelines: Internal Ratings-Based Capital Requirement (2006a) by U.S. regulators requires only large, internationally active banking organizations with total assets of US$250 million or more and total on-balance sheet foreign exposures of US$10 billion or more to adopt the Basel II guidelines on capital rules.

4. A unit of measure represents the level at which a bank's operational risk quantification system generates a separate distribution of potential operational risk losses (Seivold et al. 2006). A unit of measure could be on aggregate (i.e., enterprise-wide) or defined as a BL, a ET category, or both. The Basel Committee specifies eight BLs and seven ETs for operational risk reporting in the working paper *Sound Practices for the Management and Supervision of Operational Risk* (2003a). According to the *Operational Risk Subgroup* of the *Basel Committee Accord Implementation Group*, the eight BLs are: (i) corporate finance; (ii) trading and sales; (iii) retail banking; (iv) payment and settlement; (vi) agency services; (vi) commercial banking; (vii) asset management; and (viii) retail brokerage. The seven ETs are: (i) internal fraud; (ii) external fraud; (iii) employment practices and workplace safety; (iv) clients, products, and business practices; (v) damage to physical assets; (vi) business disruption and system failure; and (vii) execution, delivery, and process management. This categorization was instrumental in bringing about greater uniformity in data classification across financial institutions.

5. At national supervisory discretion, a bank can be permitted to apply the alternative standardized approach (ASA) if it provides an improved basis for the calculation of minimum capital requirements by, for instance, avoiding double counting of risks (Basel Committee 2004a, 2005a).

6. The three-year average of a fixed percentage of gross income (BIA) or the summation of prescribed capital charges for various BLs (TSA) exclude periods in which gross income is negative from the calculation of *risk*-weighted assets (RWAs), whose periodic aggregate determines the required capitalization of a bank, that is, the risk-based capital (RBC).

7. The quantitative criteria of AMA also offer the possibility of capital adjustment due to diversification benefits from the correlation between extreme internal operational risk losses and the risk mitigating impact of insurance.

8. Many banks typically model economic capital at a confidence level between 99.96 and 99.98%, which implies an expected default rate comparable to "AA"-rated credit exposures.

9. The AMA-based capital charge covers total operational risk exposure unless EL is already offset by eligible reserves under the generally accepted accounting principles (GAAP) (EL breakout or EL offset), such as capital-like substitutes or some other conceptually sound method to control for losses that arise from normal operating circumstances.

10. U.S. federal bank regulators also specify five years of internal operational risk loss data and permit the use of external data for the calculation of regulatory capital for operational risk in their advance notice on proposed rulemaking on *Risk-Based Capital Guidelines* (2006b). In contrast, the Basel Committee (2004a, 2005a, 2006b) requires only three years of data after initial adoption

of AMA and then five years. Moreover, for U.S.-supervised financial institutions, AMA is the only permitted quantification approach for operational risk according to the *Joint Supervisory Guidance on Operational Risk Advanced Measurement Approaches for Regulatory Capital* (2003) and the *Advanced Notice on Proposed Rulemaking* (ANPR) on *Risk-Based Capital Guidelines: Internal Ratings-Based Capital Requirement* (2006a).

11. VaR defines an extreme quantile as the maximum limit on potential losses that are unlikely to be exceeded over a given time horizon (or holding period) at a certain probability.

12. The introduction of a volume-based capital charge coincided with an alternative volume based charge developed in the *EU Regulatory Capital Directive.*

13. Concerns about this trade-off also entered into an intersectoral debate about the management and regulation of operational risk. In August 2003, the Joint Forum of banking, securities, and insurance supervisors of the Basel Committee issued a paper, *Operational Risk Transfer across Financial Sectors* (2003a), which compared approaches to operational risk management and capital regulation across the three sectors in order to gain a better understanding of current industry practices. In November 2001, a Joint Forum working group made up of supervisors from all three sectors produced the report *Risk Management Practices and Regulatory Capital: Cross-Sectoral Comparison* (2001b) on the same issues.

14. The Office of the Comptroller of the Currency, the Board of Governors of the Federal Reserve System, the Federal Deposit Insurance Corporation, and the Office of Thrift Supervision issued the NPR and the *Joint Supervisory Guidance* on an interagency basis.

15. The NPR was published as the *Proposed Supervisory Guidance for Internal Ratings-based Systems for Credit Risk, Advanced Measurement Approaches for Operational Risk, and the Supervisory Review Process (Pillar 2) Related to Basel II Implementation* (2007). It stipulated that the implementation of the new regulatory regime in the United States would require some and permit other qualifying banks to calculate their risk-based capital requirements using the internal ratings-based approach (IRB) for credit risk and AMA for operational risk (together, the advanced approaches). The guidance provided additional details on the advanced approaches and the supervisory review process to help banks satisfy the qualification requirements of the NPR. The proposed AMA guidance identifies supervisory standards for an acceptable internal measurement framework, while the guidance on the supervisory review process addresses three fundamental objectives: (i) the comprehensive supervisory assessment of capital adequacy, (ii) the compliance with regulatory capital requirements, and (iii) the implementation of an internal capital adequacy assessment process (ICAAP) ("Capital standards" 2007).

16. The stand-alone AMA capital requirements may include a well-reasoned estimate of diversification benefits of the subsidiary's own operations but may not consider group-wide diversification benefits.

17. Pursuant to this provision, the stand-alone AMA calculation of significant subsidiaries could rely on data and parameters calculated by the parent banking

group on a group-wide basis, provided that those variables were adjusted as necessary to be consistent with the subsidiary's operations.

18. The Federal Financial Institutions Examination Council (FFIEC) was established on March 10, 1979, pursuant to title X of the Financial Institutions Regulatory and Interest Rate Control Act of 1978 (FIRA), Public Law 95-630. The FFIEC is a formal interagency body empowered to prescribe uniform principles, standards, and report forms for the federal examination of financial institutions by the Board of Governors of the Federal Reserve System, the Federal Deposit Insurance Corporation, the National Credit Union Administration, the Office of the Comptroller of the Currency, and the Office of Thrift Supervision and to make recommendations to promote uniformity in the supervision of financial institutions.

19. More information about the 2004 LDCE can be found at www.ffiec.gov/ldce/. After conclusion of the LDCE, U.S. bank regulators published the *Results of the 2004 Loss Data Collection Exercise for Operational Risk* (2005). Some findings have also been published at www.bos.frb.org/bankinfo/conevent/oprisk2005/defontnouvelle.pdf and www.bos.frb.org/bankinfo/qau/pd051205.pdf by the Federal Reserve Bank of Boston. See also de Fontnouvelle (2005).

20. The LDCE asked participating banks to provide all internal loss data underlying their QIS-4 estimates (instead of one year's worth of data only) (Federal Reserve Board 2006b). A total of 23 U.S. commercial banks participated in the LDCE. Banking organizations were asked to report information about the amount of individual operational losses as well as certain descriptive information (e.g., date, internal business line (BL), event type (ET), and amount of any recoveries) regarding each loss that occurred on or before June 30, 2004, or September 30, 2004. Banks were also requested to define own mappings from internally defined BLs and ETs—as units of measure—to the categorization under the New Basel Capital Accord for reporting purposes (instead of standardized BLs and ETs).

21. This compilation included the *International Convergence of Capital Measurement and Capital Standards* (Basel Committee 2004a and 2005a), the elements of the 1988 Accord that were not revised during the Basel II process, and the November 2005 (Basel Committee 2005b) paper.

22. Alternatively, extremes could be selected from constant time intervals defined by rolling windows with daily, weekly, and monthly updating (Cruz et al. 1998; Coleman and Cruz 1999) in order to mitigate problems associated with a time-invariant qualification of extreme observations.

23. Note that our advocacy of a volume-based adjustment in this case is limited to the use of scaling for the purpose of threshold selection only. In general, the loss severity of operational risk events is independent of business volume, unless banks differ vastly in terms of balance sheet value.

24. GEV and GPD are the most prominent methods under EVT to assess parametric models for the statistical estimation of the limiting behavior of extreme observations. While GEV identifies the asymptotic tail behavior of the order statistics of i.i.d. normalized extremes, GPD is an exceedance function that measures the residual risk of these extremes (as conditional distribution of mean excess)

beyond a predefined threshold for regions of interest, where only a few or no observations are available. GPD approximates GEV if linear mean excess converges to a reliable, nondegenerate limiting distribution that satisfies the external types (Fisher-Tippett) theorem of GEV. See Coles et al. (1999), Stephenson (2002), and Vandewalle et al. (2004) for additional information on the definition of EVT.

25. The Pickands-Balkema-de Haan limit theorem (Balkema and de Haan 1974; Pickands, 1975) postulates that GPD is the only nondegenerate limit law of observations in excess of a sufficiently high threshold, whose distribution satisfies the extremal types theorem of GEV.

26. An optimal threshold value for GPD would support a stable parametric approximation of GEV and linear mean excess of extremes while allowing in-sample point estimation within a maximum range of percentiles.

27. Since this distribution is merely a transformation of the standard normal distribution, GHD is also a useful probability function for the generation of random numbers in the course of Monte Carlo simulation.

28. They also report that all operational risk loss data reported by U.S. financial institutions in the course of QIS-4 (see Box 2.2) conformed to GHD to a very high degree.

29. Compared to Mignola and Ugoccioni (2006), the model specification in Jobst (2007d) also generates markedly lower estimation error and closer upper-tail convergence of GDP, partly because higher moments of the loss-generating function approximate the average empirical loss profile of U.S. banks and maximum loss severity is left unbounded (rather than being calibrated to the standardized regulatory capital charge for operational risk).

30. In this approach, high quantiles of the aggregate loss distribution can be calculated analytically by a scaled multiplication of the largest order statistic, provided that the largest observations follow a power law.

31. GPD risk estimates in Jobst (2007a) imply capital savings of up to almost 97% compared to a uniform measure of operational risk exposure and do not corroborate the 16.79% capital-to-gross income ratio in Dutta and Perry (2006), whose high GPD risk estimates could have resulted from their choice of the Hill algorithm as the estimation method. Mittnick and Rachev (1996) found that the Hill estimation algorithm yields highly unstable estimates for samples with less than 500,000 observations and returns inaccurate results of asymptotic tail behavior for distributions for loss data with a nonzero left endpoint due to loss reporting thresholds.

32. Empirical evidence suggests that high operational risk losses occur especially when managers are grossly overconfident about the existing governance and control mechanisms (Matz 2005).

33. Banks have developed quite different methods for determining operational risk capital with varied emphasis given to the categorization of BLs and ETs as defined by the Basel Committee.

34. The Operational Risk Subgroup of the Basel Committee Accord Implementation Group also found that the measurement of operational risk is limited by the

quality of internal loss data, which tends to be based on short-term periods and includes very few, if any, high-severity losses (which can dominate the bank's historical loss experience).

35. In August 2006 representatives of Bank of America, J.P. Morgan Chase, Wachovia, and Washington Mutual attempted to convince the Federal Reserve Board that they should be allowed to adopt a simplified version of the New Basel Capital Accord (Larsen and Guha 2006), mainly because additional restrictions have raised the attendant cost of implementing more sophisticated risk measurement systems for such advanced models to a point where potential regulatory capital savings are virtually offset.

36. In general, risk measures for different operational risk estimates (by BL and/or ET) must be added for purposes of calculating the regulatory minimum capital requirement. However, banks may be permitted to use internally determined correlations in operational risk losses across individual operational risk estimates, provided they can demonstrate to the satisfaction of the national supervisor that their systems for determining correlations different units of measure are sound, implemented with integrity, and take into account the uncertainty surrounding any such correlation estimates (particularly in periods of stress). The banks must validate their correlation assumptions using appropriate quantitative and qualitative techniques.

37. These concerns are not valid for the representation of aggregate operational risk losses (without further classification by BL and/or ET) in BIA.

38. In this simplified trade-off, we do not consider any other elements of operational risk regulation, such as capital adjustment, home-host recognition, and volume-based measures, which impede the consistent calculation of regulatory capital in certain situations.

39. Large differences between capital charges under AMA and capital charge under standardized approaches hint at *prima facie* inconsistency of the current regulatory framework and call for a lower fixed capital multiplier of standardized approaches consistent with AMA risk estimates at the required level of statistical confidence.

40. Such a development of lower individual risk aversion is currently under way in credit risk transfer markets. It is in these markets that financial innovation has made banks more careless about riskier lending as derivatives continue to play a benign role to spread credit risk throughout the financial system. As long as markets remain stable and prove robust, more reliance is placed on the resilience of the financial system. The mechanism of moral hazard intensifies potential systemic vulnerabilities to credit risk across institutions and national boundaries as credit risk transfer induces less risk-averse behavior.

41. Resnick and Stărică (1997a, 1997b) propose the standardization of extreme observations to temper possible bias and inherent constraints of discrete threshold selection. For instance, time-weighted adjustments of loss frequency and the normalization of loss amounts by some fundamental data as scaling factors could be possible approaches to redress a biased threshold selection contingent on sample composition.

42. The region where the transformation function of z is not monotonic would be assigned a zero probability measure.
43. All operational risk loss data reported by U.S. financial institutions in the wake of QIS-4 conformed to GHD to a very high degree (Dutta and Perry 2006).
44. Martinez and Iglewicz (1984) and Hoaglin (1985), and most recently Degen et al. (2006), provide derivations of many other important properties of this distribution.

REFERENCES

Alexander, C. 2003. *Operational risk: Regulation, analysis and management.* London: Financial Times/Prentice-Hall.

Capital standards: Proposed interagency supervisory guidance for banks that would operate under proposed new Basel II framework. *U.S. Fed News*, February 28, 2007.

Balkema, A. A., and L. de Haan. 1974. Residual life time at great age. *Annals of Probability* 2, no. 5:792–804.

Banerjee, S., and B. Kulwinder. 2005. Managing operational risk: Framework for financial institutions. Working paper, A.B Freeman School of Business, Tulane University, New Orleans.

Basel Committee on Banking Supervision. 1998. *Operational risk management.* BCBS Publications No. 42. Bank for International Settlements (September). www.bis.org/publ/bcbs42.htm.

Basel Committee on Banking Supervision. 1999. *A new capital adequacy framework.* BCBS Publications No. 50. Bank for International Settlements (June). www.bis.org/publ/bcbs50.htm.

Basel Committee on Banking Supervision. 2001a. *Sound practices for the management and supervision of operational risk.* BCBS Publications No. 86. Bank for International Settlements (December). www.bis.org/publ/bcbs86.htm.

Basel Committee on Banking Supervision. 2001b. *Working paper on the regulatory treatment of operational risk.* BCBS Publications No. 8. Bank for International Settlements (September). www.bis.org/publ/bcbs_wp8.pdf.

Basel Committee on Banking Supervision. 2001c. *Consultative document—Operational risk (Supporting document to the New Basel Capital Accord.* BCBS Publications (Consultative Document) No. 7. Bank for International Settlements (January). www.bis.org/publ/bcbsca07.pdf.

Basel Committee on Banking Supervision. 2001d. *Consultative document—Operational risk (Supporting document to the New Basel Capital Accord).* BCBS Publications (Consultative Document) No. 7. Bank for International Settlements (January). www.bis.org/publ/bcbsca07.pdf.

Basel Committee on Banking Supervision. 2002. *Sound practices for the management and supervision of operational risk.* BCBS Publications No. 91. Bank for International Settlements (July). www.bis.org/publ/bcbs91.htm.

Basel Committee on Banking Supervision. 2003a. *operational risk transfer across financial sectors.* Joint Forum Paper, Bank for International Settlements (August). www.bis.org/publ/joint06.htm.

Basel Committee on Banking Supervision. 2003b. *Sound practices for the management and supervision of operational risk.* BCBS Publications No. 96. Bank for International Settlements (February). www.bis.org/publ/bcbs96.htm.

Basel Committee on Banking Supervision. 2004a. *International convergence of capital measurement and capital standards: A revised framework.* BCBS Publications No. 107. Bank for International Settlements (June). www.bis.org/publ/bcbs107.htm.

Basel Committee on Banking Supervision. 2004b. *Principles for the home-host recognition of AMA operational risk capital.* BCBS Publications No. 106, Bank for International Settlements (January). www.bis.org/publ/bcbs106.htm.

Basel Committee on Banking Supervision. 2005a. *Basel II: International convergence of capital measurement and capital standards: A revised framework.* BCBS Publications No. 118. Bank for International Settlements (November). www.bis.org/publ/bcbs118.htm.

Basel Committee on Banking Supervision. 2005b. *The treatment of expected losses by banks using the AMA under the Basel II framework.* Basel Committee Newsletter No. 7. Bank for International Settlements, Basel, Switzerland.

Basel Committee on Banking Supervision. 2006a. *Observed Range of Practice in Key Elements of Advanced Measurement Approaches (AMA).* BCBS Publications No. 131, Bank for International Settlements (October). www.bis.org/publ/bcbs131.htm.

Basel Committee on Banking Supervision. 2006b. *Basel II: International convergence of capital measurement and capital standards: A revised framework— Comprehensive version.* BCBS Publications No. 128. Bank for International Settlements (June). www.bis.org/publ/bcbs128.htm.

Basel Committee on Banking Supervision. 2007. *Principles for home-host supervisory cooperation and allocation mechanisms in the context of advanced measurement approaches (AMA)—Consultative document.* Bank for International Settlements, Basel, Switzerland.

Bjorn, B. J., and M. Hubert. 2004. A robust estimator of the tail index based on an exponential regression model. In *Theory and applications of recent robust methods*, eds. Hubert, M., Pison, G., Struyf, A. and S. Van Aelst, Vol. 10. Basel, Switzerland: Birkhäuser. www.wis.kuleuven.ac.be/stat/Papers/tailindexICORS2003.pdf.

Castillo, E., and S. H. Ali. 1997. Fitting the generalized Pareto distribution to data. *Journal of the American Statistical Association* 92, no. 440:1609–1620.

Coleman, R., and M. Cruz. 1999. Operational risk measurement and pricing. *Derivatives Week* 8, no. 30:5–6.

Coles, S. G., J. Heffernan, and T. A. Jonathan. 1999. Dependence measures for extreme value analyses. *Extremes* 2, No. 4:339–365.

Coles, Stuart G. 2001. *An introduction to statistical modelling in extreme values.* London: Springer-Verlag.

Crouhy, M., D. Galai, and R. M. Mark. 2004. Insuring versus self-insuring operational risk: Viewpoints of depositors and shareholders. Journal of Derivatives 12, no. 2:51–55.

Cruz, M., R. Coleman, and S. Gerry. 1998. Modeling and measuring operational risk. *Journal of Risk* 1, no. 1:63–72.

Currie, C. V. 2004. Basel II and operational risk—Overview of key concerns. Working paper 134 (March). School of Finance and Economics, University of Technology, Sydney.

Currie, C. V. 2005. A test of the strategic effect of Basel II operational risk requirements on banks. Working paper 143 (September). School of Finance and Economics, University of Technology, Sydney.

de Fontnouvelle, P. 2005. The 2004 loss data collection exercise. Presentation at the Implementing an AMA for Operational Risk conference of the Federal Reserve Bank of Boston (May 19). www.bos.frb.org/bankinfo/conevent/oprisk2005/defontnouvelle.pdf.

de Fontnouvelle, P., E. S. Rosengren, and J. S. Jordan. 2004. Implications of alternative operational risk modeling techniques. SSRN working paper (June). http://papers.ssrn.com/sol3/papers.cfm?abstract_id=556823.

Degen, M., P. Embrechts, and L. D. Dominik. 2006. The quantitative modeling of operational risk: Between *g*-and-*h* and EVT. Working paper, Swiss Institute of Technology (ETH), Zurich.

Dekkers, Arnold L. M., John H. J. Einmahl, and Laurens de Haan. 1989. A moment estimator for the index of an extreme-value distribution. *Annals of Statistics* 17:1833–1855.

Drees, Holger. 1995. Refined Pickands estimators of the extreme value index. *Annals of Statistics* 32, no. 1:2059–2080.

Drees, Holger, Laurens de Haan, and R. Sidney. 1998. How to make a hill plot. Discussion paper, Timbergen Institute, Erasmus University, Rotterdam.

Dutta, Kabir K., and J. Perry. 2006. A tale of tails: An empirical analysis of loss distribution models for estimating operational risk capital. Working paper 06–13. Federal Reserve Bank of Boston (July).

Embrechts, P. 2000. Extreme value theory: Potential and limitations as an integrated risk management tool. *Derivatives Use, Trading & Regulation* 6, no. 2:449–456.

Embrechts, P., C. Klüppelberg, and T. Mikosch. 1997. *Modelling extremal events for insurance and finance*. Heidelberg, Germany: Springer-Verlag.

Falk, M., J. Hüsler, and R. Rolf-Dieter. 1994. *Laws of small numbers: Extremes and rare events*. DMV-Seminar, Birkhäuser, Basel.

Federal Reserve Board. 2006a. *Federal Reserve statistical release—Aggregate reserves of depository institutions and the monetary base*. Washington, DC. www.federalreserve.gov/releases/h3/20050120.

Federal Reserve Board. 2006b. *Fourth quantitative impact study 2006*. Washington, DC. www.federalreserve.gov/boarddocs/bcreg/2006/20060224/.

Fisher, R. A., and L. H. C. Tippett. 1928. Limiting forms of the frequency distribution of the largest or smallest member of a sample. *Proceedings of the Cambridge Philosophical Society* 4, no. 2:180–190.

Grody, A. D., F. C. Harmantzis, and K. J. Gregory. 2005. Operational risk and reference data: Exploring costs, capital requirements and risk mitigation." Working paper (November), Stevens Institute of Technology, Hoboken, NJ.

Hill, B. M. 1975. A simple general approach to inference about the tail of a distribution. *Annals of Statistics* 3, no. 5:1163–1174.

Hoaglin, D. C. 1985. Summarizing shape numerically: The *g*-and-*h* distributions. In *Exploring data tables, trend, and shapes*, ed. D. C. Hoaglin, F. Mosteller, and J. W. Tukey. New York: John Wiley & Sons.

Jenkinson, A. F. 1955. The frequency distribution of the annual maximum (or minimum) values of meteorological elements. *Quarterly Journal of the Royal Meteorology Society* No. 87:145–158.

Jobst, A. A. 2007a. It's all in the data—Consistent operational risk measurement and regulation. *Journal of Financial Regulation and Compliance* 15, no. 4:423–449.

Jobst, A. A. 2007b. Operational risk—The sting is still in the tail but the poison depends on the dose. *Journal of Operational Risk* 2, no. 2:1–56.

Jobst, A. A. 2007c. The regulation of operational risk under the new Basel Capital Accord—Critical issues. *International Journal of Banking Law and Regulation* 21, no. 5:249–273.

Jobst, A. A. 2007d. The treatment of operational risk under the new Basel Framework—Critical issues. *Journal of Banking Regulation* 8, no. 4:316–352.

Kotz, S., and N. Saralees. 2000. *Extreme value distributions*. London: Imperial College Press.

Larsen, P. T., and G. Krishna. 2006. US banks seek looser Basel II rules. *Financial Times of London*, August 3.

Leippold, Markus, and P. Vanini. 2003. The quantification of operational risk. SSRN Working paper (November).

Makarov, M. 2006. Extreme value theory and high quantile convergence. *Journal of Operational Risk* 1, no. 2:51–57.

Martinez, J., and B. Iglewicz. 1984. Some properties of the Tukey g and h family of distributions. *Communications in Statistics—Theory and Methods* 13, no. 3:353–369.

Matz, L. 2005. Measuring operational risk: Are we taxiing down the wrong runways? *Bank Accounting and Finance* 18, no. 2–3:3–6, 47.

McCulloch, J. H. 1996. Simple consistent estimators of stable distribution parameters. *Communications in Statistics—Simulations* 15, no. 4:1109–1136.

McNeil, A. J., and S. Thomas. 1997. The peak over thresholds method for estimating high quantiles of loss distributions." Swiss Institute of Technology (ETH), Zurich.

Mignola, G., and R. Ugoccioni. 2005. Tests of extreme value theory. *Operational Risk & Compliance* 6, no. 10:32–35.

Mignola, G., and R. Ugoccioni. 2006. Sources of uncertainty in modeling operational risk losses. *Journal of Operational Risk* 1, no. 2:33–50.

Mittnick, S., and R. T. Svetlozar. 1996. Tail estimation of the stable index. *Applied Mathematic Letters* 9, no. 3:53–56.

Moscadelli, M. 2004. The modelling of operational risk: Experience with the data collected by the Basel Committee. In *Operational risk: Practical approaches to implementation*, in E. Davis. London: Risk Books, Incisive Media Ltd.

Nešlehová, J., P. Embrechts, and Valerie C-Demoulin. 2006. Infinite mean models and the LDA for operational risk. *Journal of Operational Risk* 1, no. 1:3–25.

O'Dell, Mark. 2005. Quantitative impact study 4: Preliminary results—AMA framework. Presentation at the Implementing an AMA for Operational Risk conference of the Federal Reserve Bank of Boston (May 19). www.bos.frb.org/bankinfo/conevent/oprisk2005/odell.pdf.

Office of the Comptroller of the Currency, the Board of Governors of the Federal Reserve System, the Federal Deposit Insurance Corporation, and the Office of Thrift Supervision. 2003. *Operational risk advanced measurement approaches for regulatory Capital*. Joint Supervisory Guidance (July 2). www.federalreserve.gov/BoardDocs/Press/bcreg/2006/20060206/attachment.pdf

Office of the Comptroller of the Currency, the Board of Governors of the Federal Reserve System, the Federal Deposit Insurance Corporation, and the Office of Thrift Supervision. 2005. *Results of the 2004 loss data collection exercise for operational risk* (May). http://www.bos.frb.org/bankinfo/qau/papers/pd051205.pdf

Office of the Comptroller of the Currency, the Board of Governors of the Federal Reserve System, the Federal Deposit Insurance Corporation, and the Office of Thrift Supervision. 2006a. *Risk-based capital guidelines: Internal ratings-based capital requirement*. Advance Notice of Proposed Rulemaking (August 4). www.federalreserve.gov/BoardDocs/Press/bcreg/2006/20060206/attachment.pdf and www.fdic.gov/regulations/laws/publiccomments/basel/anprriskbasedcap.pdf.

Office of the Comptroller of the Currency, the Board of Governors of the Federal Reserve System, the Federal Deposit Insurance Corporation, and the Office of Thrift Supervision. 2006b. *Risk-based capital guidelines: Internal ratings-based capital requirement*, Notice of Proposed Rulemaking (September 25). http://www.orrick.com/fileupload/1416.pdf.

Office of the Comptroller of the Currency, the Board of Governors of the Federal Reserve System, the Federal Deposit Insurance Corporation, and the Office of Thrift Supervision. 2007. *Proposed supervisory guidance for internal ratings-based systems for credit risk, advanced measurement approaches for operational risk, and the supervisory review process (Pillar 2) related to Basel II implementation—Federal Register Extract*. Federal Information & News Dispatch (February 28). www.fdic.gov/regulations/laws/publiccomments/basel/oprisk.pdf.

Pickands, J. 1975. Statistical Inference Using Extreme Order Statistics. *Annals of Statistics* 3, no. 1:119–131.

Pickands, J. 1981. *Multivariate extreme value distributions*. London: Imperial College Press.

Poon, S.-H., M. Rockinger, and T. Jonathan. 2003. Extreme Value dependence in financial markets: Diagnostics, models, and financial implications. *Review of Financial Studies* 17, no. 2:581–610.

Reiss, R.-D., and T. Michael. 1997. *Statistical analysis of extreme values*. Basel, Switzerland: Birkhäuser.

Resnick, S. I., and S. Catalin. 1997a. Asymptotic behavior of Hill's estimator for autoregressive data. *Stochastic Models* 13, no. 4:703–723.

Resnick, S. I., and S. Catalin. 1997b. Smoothing the Hill estimator. *Advances in Applied Probability* 9, no. 1:271–293.

Rootzén, H., and T. Nader. 1997. Extreme value statistics and wind storm losses: A case study. *Scandinavian Actuarial Journal* 1, no. 2:70–94.

Seivold, A., S. Leifer, and U. Scott. 2006. Operational risk management: An evolving discipline. *Supervisory Insights*. Federal Deposit Insurance Corporation. www.fdic.gov/regulations/examinations/supervisory/insights/sisum06/article01 _risk.html.

Stephenson, A. G. 2002. EVD: Extreme value distributions. *R News* 2, no. 2:31–32. http://CRAN.R-project.ortg.org/doc/Rnews/.

Tukey, J. W. 1977. *Exploratory data analysis*. Reading, MA: Addison-Wesley.

Zamorski, M. J. 2003. Joint supervisory guidance on operational risk advanced measurement approaches for regulatory capital—Board memorandum. Federal Deposit Insurance Corporation, Division of Supervision and Consumer Protection (July). www.fdic.gov/regulations/laws/publiccomments/basel/boardmem-oprisk.pdf.

CHAPTER 3

Operational Risk Based on Complementary Loss Evaluations

Andrea Giacomelli and Loriana Pelizzon

ABSTRACT

In this chapter we develop the complementary loss evaluations (CLE) framework for computing the capital charge of a bank for operational risk where CLE refers to subjective and quantitative statistical/actuarial methods for modeling the loss distribution. In this framework, the capital charge is calculated using a value-at-risk measure. First we introduce the analytical statistical/actuarial method based on the mixed frequency models or compound frequency models as a common framework where both the subjective analysis and the quantitative analysis could be integrated. Then we give a detailed description of the subjective method to evaluate losses. In particular, we show how to compute the aggregate loss distribution by compounding the loss severity distribution and the loss frequency distribution based on the self risk assessment approach. Finally, we propose a Bayesian approach to merge the qualitative and the quantitative loss distributions.

3.1 INTRODUCTION

A great deal of research has been conducted over the past few years to address issues raised by the practical implementation of Basel II Advanced Measurement Approaches (AMA). The recent breakdown of internal controls at the Société Générale has emphasized the need of a sound system for operational risk. So far, three different classes of operational risk models have been proposed by various authors. The first class is based on statistical models and historical data as the main input for calibration. The main approach, known as the loss distribution approach (LDA), is the parametric estimation of a frequency and a severity distribution for individual loss types and their subsequent aggregation that can incorporate dependencies. This general approach also includes the modeling of operational risk via extreme value theory (EVT); an alternative approach—proposed by Ebnöther, Vanini, McNeil, and Antolines (2002, 2003)—is based on common Poisson shock models, such as McNeil and Lindskog (2001). In this context, the frequencies of individual loss events are determined through underlying common and idiosyncratic shocks. Closely related are the models by Embrechts and Samorodnitsky (2002) somewhat based on ruin theory.

The second class of operational risk models also employs statistical models to quantify operational risk but uses mainly qualitative measures to calibrate the model. Key features of these models are scenario analyses and scorecards, as, for example, those proposed by Lawrence (2000).

The third class focuses on the functional modeling of operational risk processes. Functional processes and dependencies are defined and modeled via interdependence of the individual processes. While these models allow for a rather realistic, detailed and potentially forward-looking modeling of operational risk, they are very elaborate in terms of data collection and involvement of bank staff and experts to validate the model setup. Representatives are the models by Kuhn and Neu (2003), which allow for catastrophic failures, and the model by Alexander (2000) based on Bayesian belief networks.

Although all three classes have their advantages and disadvantages, we propose a model that incorporates the advantages of all three approaches: the complementary loss evaluations (CLE) framework. The CLE refers to subjective and quantitative statistical/actuarial methods for modeling the loss distribution. The main advantages of this approach are: (1) the measurement improvement of the operational risk, (2) the backward- and forward-looking characteristics, and (3) the strict link between the Basel capital charge and the operational risk management as well as between internal audit and risk management.

Section 3.2 of this chapter briefly presents the loss distribution approach. Section 3.3 describes in details the complementary loss evaluation approach. Section 3.4 shows the subjective analysis based on the self risk assessment, and Section 3.5 presents the integration of subjective and quantitative loss distributions. Section 3.6 concludes.

3.2 LOSS DISTRIBUTION APPROACH

LDA separately calculates (for each business line and risk type) separately the probability distribution function of the severity and the probability distribution function of the one-year event frequency (see Frachot, Moudolaud, and Roncalli 2004 for details). Let us define $\xi_{i,j}$ as the random variable that expresses the amount of one loss event (for an element i, j in the business line and risk type matrix) and the cumulative density function (i.e., the loss severity distribution) denoted by $F_{i,j}(\cdot)$. $N_{i,j}$ is the random variable expressing the number of loss events between times t and $t + \tau$, and it has a probability $p_{i,j}$, where $p_{i,j}(k)$ is the probability of k losses in the time interval $[t; t + \tau]$ (i.e., the frequency distribution).

The total loss in the time interval $[t; t + \tau]$ for element i, j is thus given by the random variable:

$$L_{i,j} = \sum_{n=0}^{N_{i,j}} \xi_{i,j;n} \tag{3.1}$$

The most commonly employed distributions for the severity variable are the Lognormal or the Weibull, while the frequency is assumed to be distributed as the Negative Binomial or the Poisson.

We could make different assumptions about the relations among different loss events and between the severities and the frequency of events. The easier assumption is to assume that the different $\xi_{i,j}$ are independent and that every single severity is independent of the related frequency of events. Let us call $G_{i,j}$ the cumulative distribution of $L_{i,j}$. We then know:

$$G_{i,j}(x) = \begin{cases} \sum_{n=1}^{\infty} p_{i,j}(n) F_{i,j}(x)^{[n\otimes]} & x > 0 \\ & x = 0 \end{cases} \tag{3.2}$$

Under this framework, the expected loss is:

$$EL_{i,j} = E[L_{i,j}] = \int_0^{\infty} x \, dG_{i,j} \tag{3.3}$$

and the unexpected loss at a confidence level a is:

$$UL_{i,j;\alpha} = G_{i,j}^{-1}(\alpha) - E[L_{i,j}] \tag{3.4}$$

Despite the Basel Committee's recommendation to calculate the capital charge, K, using $K_{i,j;\alpha} = UL_{i,j;\alpha}$ institutions tend to use:

$$K_{i,j;\alpha} = EL_{i,j} + UL_{i,j;\alpha} = G_{i,j}^{-1}(\alpha) \qquad (3.5)$$

This has the advantage that K is a value at risk (VaR) measure (i.e., a quantile). The determination of the expected and unexpected loss and the quantile capital charge that derives from the loss distribution is well represented in Figure 3.1.

The methods usually employed for distribution fitting are maximum likelihood and the generalized method of moments. The main problem in estimating the loss distribution is data availability. The available loss data are limited and are plagued by various sources of bias.

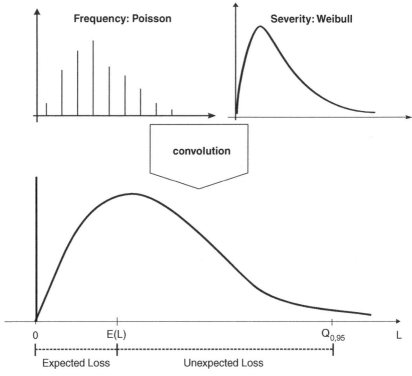

FIGURE 3.1 Relation between Severity and Frequency and the Loss Distribution

The available informative sources are:

- **Historical quantitative data.** For example, the number of frauds that occurred during one year
- **Subjective quantitative data.** For example, the number of frauds in a new operative unit
- **Historical qualitative data.** For example, loss typologies during one year
- **Subjective qualitative data.** For example, the operative unit's rating

Given that all this information is complementary and that it obviously must be integrated, the method used to merge it together is extremely important. The CLE method we present in the following sections has this aim.

3.3   COMPLEMENTARY LOSS EVALUATIONS

Vigilance and managerial aims are the reasons operational risk management systems are developed. According to Basel Regulatory, the two goals have to be achieved through the same risk management system; thus all the decision processes must be integrated inside the organs in charge of valuing and controlling the productive processes. This implies:

- Consistency between qualitative and quantitative methods
- Sharing of the valuing approaches between internal audit and risk management
- Control systems based on risk analysis

The CLE methodology is an integrated approach to measure and manage operational risk. Measuring operational risk means quantifying the unexpected losses associated with each stage of a production process, maintaining a forward-looking approach that accounts for future unexpected losses. It is extremely important to be able to aggregate the results in order to provide an overall risk measure for event type and business unit. Given that many information sources are involved in such a task, the measurement method cannot abstract from integrating all the information streams. The final step in a measurement phase is determining the capital charge consistent to the detected risk.

Managing operational risk means first of all ensuring that the managing board is committed to monitor and control the risk. Once the operational risk is considered a variable within the firm, it is important to identify an intervention priority scale able to assist managers in making decisions. Given these targets, the CLE methodology evolves through a subjective and a quantitative phase, eventually integrated together by means of a statistical framework. Therefore, such a procedure considers information of different natures, combined in an objective way.

The subjective stage (which we present in Section 3.4) aims at collecting opinions from each operative unit about key aspects of the processes and the risks it is exposed to. The tool consists of a questionnaire by which the operators state their opinions about each kind of operative loss. It is then necessary to move the operators' opinions expressed in the questionnaire into a (subjective) estimation of expected and unexpected losses.

In this manner, the procedure provides a (subjective) probability distribution function of the unexpected losses that is the prior distribution in a Bayesian approach. The quantitative stage's core part (presented in Section 3.5) lies in a Bayesian estimate that merges together the prior distribution with quantitative historical data.

3.4 SUBJECTIVE INFORMATION ANALYSIS

The use of subjective information is based on expert knowledge. More precisely, the risk of each production process is valued by the respective process owner. To achieve this, standardized forms of information need to be used. The CLE procedure is based on a collection of subjective information through questionnaires, where all entries in the questionnaire are properly defined.

If we use expert data, we usually consider that the data fully specify the risk information. The disadvantage of such data concerns their confidentiality. As Rabin (1998) demonstrates, people typically fail to apply the mathematical laws of probability correctly but instead create their own "laws," such as the so-called law of small numbers. Therefore, an expert-based database needs to be designed to circumvent the most important and prominent biases.

The CLE procedure is based on a collection of subjective information, conceived to:

- Reduce the freedom of evaluation left by ambiguous measuring scales, In order to do this, the questionnaire gathers quantitative information only.
- Contain the bias associated with subjective valuations. For this reason the questions focus on objective and easy-to-identify sizes.

Every unit manager completes the questionnaire, called Self Risk Assessment Questionnaire. The very first question examines whether a precise risk is present or not. In case of an affirmative answer, the manager is asked to provide personal valuations referring to a certain time-horizon and dealing with:

- Average frequency of the loss event
- Average severity of each individual loss
- Order of magnitude of the maximum severity of a loss event

To simplify answering, for each question the interviewee has to indicate the most suitable range of values. We never ask the experts to choose a number for a probability; rather they make a choice between different real-life situations that are more unambiguously defined. For the severity self-assessment, the experts have to indicate both the mean and the maximum severity values in their respective processes.

The questionnaire approach aims at:

- Obtaining a rating system for each operative unit indicating the risk level (unexpected losses) in a homogeneous way within the units in order to identify intervention priorities
- Getting an output that can be integrated with the results drawn from a quantitative analysis of historical loss data. To do so, we need an estimate of both expected loss (EL) and unexpected loss (UL) for each kind of loss, each risk factor, and each organizational unit.

In order to obtain useful ratings, we need to consider a normalized measure of unexpected loss so that results from different operative units can be analyzed. Such a normalization is achieved through dividing the unexpected loss by an exposure indicator (EI), which is, in line with the Basel Regulation, the gross income. The domain of the normalized unexpected loss (UL/EI) is then cut into several ranges, each of them representing a rating class.

The CLE methodology uses four rating classes presented in Figure 3.2:

Class A. 0%<UL/EI<10% OK: optimal situation, minimum operational loss risk
Class B. 10%<UL/EI<20% ALERT: this state means a first alert signal
Class C. 20%<UL/EI<40% RM CHECK: the situation is getting danger-ous and it would be better to check the processes than to consider a mitigation action
Class D. UL/EI>40% MITIGATION: the situation is critical enough to adopt a mitigation action

In such a framework, a benchmark value for the ratio UL/EI is 20% (value obtained by the Risk Management Group of the Basel Committee),

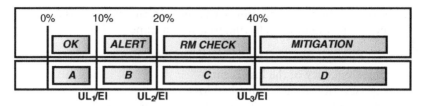

FIGURE 3.2 Rating Classes

which then represents the average systematic level. The UL values defining each single range are referred to the specific operative unit being investigated, and they aggregate all the risks the unit is exposed to. Let us assume the cutoffs are the same as reported in Figure 3.2 (0%, 10%, 20%, and 40%) and that the operative unit (OU) under analysis has a total gross income (GI) equal to 100 million and it is exposed to 20 risk typologies (questions). The UL threshold values for the entire OU will then be 0, 10, 20, 40 million. Dividing these thresholds by the number of risk typologies, we obtain an approximation of the UL threshold values for each risk typology.

The underlying hypothesis is then that each risk has the same weight within the same operative unit. These weights basically describe the impact each risk factor has on the riskiness of operative unit. The assumption of uniform weights can be relaxed, whereby a specific weight reflecting the historical loss data can be applied to each risk factor. In this way we can dynamically adjust the weight and thus are able to capture a trend, if any, in the impact of each risk factor.

3.4.1 Setting the Questions in the Self Risk Assessment Questionnaire

Here we describe the method used to set the questions to the process owners. As mentioned, the questions aim to discriminate the unexpected loss amount (and therefore the related operational rating) that better describes the analyzed production process. As the UL evaluation is based on the actuarial approach, questions have to be directly related to the frequency and severity distributions determining the UL value itself.

Let us start setting the number of questions for every questionnaire. Assuming a Poisson distribution for the frequency and a Weibull distribution for the severity, we can identify three quantities associated in a biunivocal way to these two distributions: the mean frequency fully describes the Poisson frequency distribution; the mean severity and the worst-case severity (defined as the 99.9% quantile of the severity distribution) fully describe the

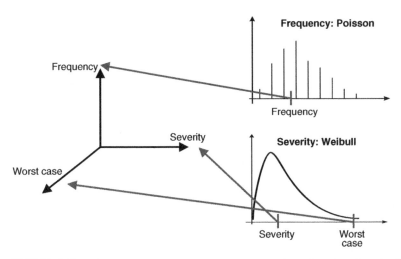

FIGURE 3.3 Three Dimensions (Mean Frequency, Mean Severity, Severity Worst Case) Characterizing the Frequency and the Severity Distribution

Weibull severity distribution (see Johnson, Kotz, and Balakrishnan 1987 for details).

The use of the Weibull distribution is justified by analytical reasons, as it allows to associate the mean and the worst-case severity values to a Weibull density function through a closed form relation. The biunivocal relation among the three dimensions and the frequency and severity distribution is presented in Figure 3.3.

As these three dimensions describing frequency and severity distributions are related to a loss distribution, we can associate to every combination of these three features a given EL and UL value, as shown in Figure 3.4.

Therefore, every questionnaire related to a single operational risk source is composed of three different sequential questions. In fact, for every single operational risk source, we can obtain both an EL and an UL evaluation answering these three questions:

1. What is the average frequency of the loss event?
2. What is the average severity characterizing each individual loss?
3. What is the order of magnitude of the maximum severity?

After defining the number and the sequence of the questions, we must set the value of ranges of UL that identify the different alternative ranges contained in the questions in every questionnaire (i.e., the operational risk rating classes). In fact, the alternative ranges have to discriminate the

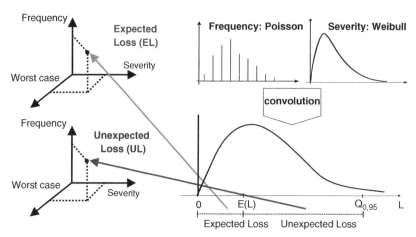

FIGURE 3.4 Relation between the Space (Mean Frequency, Mean Severity, Severity Worst Case) and the Expected and Unexpected Loss Associated with the Loss Distribution

different UL levels in order to discriminate among different operational risk rating classes.

Given that the questions refer to three-dimensional space (mean frequency, mean severity, and severity worst case), we can identify on this space the iso-UL surfaces associated with the UL values that define the operational risk rating classes, as shown in Figure 3.5.

The intersection between a given mean frequency value and the iso-UL surfaces provides a mean severity–worst-case severity plane, as illustrated in the Figure 3.6.

The projection of the iso-UL surfaces on this plane allows us to identify the critical mean and worst-case severity values that we use in the questions to set the different ranges. In particular, we consider the critical values that allow us to discriminate the different UL levels in order to determine the different operational risk rating classes. Consequently, the mean and worst-case answers provided by the process owner identify a region that contains all the different loss distributions potentially describing the operational risk profile. This region is illustrated in Figure 3.7.

3.4.2 Questionnaire Output

As a different loss distribution is associated with every point in space (mean frequency, mean severity, severity worst case), the EL and the UL

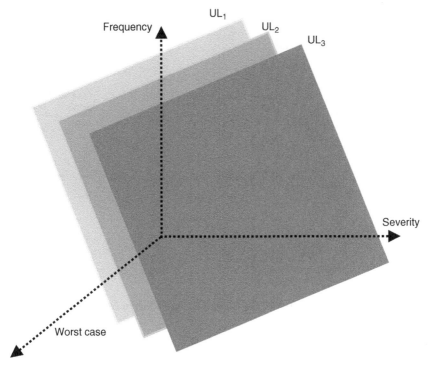

FIGURE 3.5 Iso-UL Surfaces Associated with the Space (Mean Frequency, Mean Severity, Severity Worst Case)

distributions describing the uncertainty deriving from the subjective information analysis are associated with the region identified by the process owner's answers. We obtain the EL and the UL distribution related to the region given by the answers, assuming that every point in the region has the same probability to be the true loss distribution. As we do not have any other subjective information source that would allow us to discriminate among the loss distribution contained in the region, attributing the same probability to every specific loss distribution can be considered a realistic assumption to describe the residual uncertainty that derives from the subjective information analysis. Under this assumption and considering that the UL surfaces are monotonic, the cumulative probability function for a given UL value is calculated as the area behind the iso-UL curve (on the southwest area). Figure 3.8 illustrates the estimation method of this distribution.

The questionnaire's final output is the EL and UL subjective distributions shown in the Figures 3.9 and 3.10.

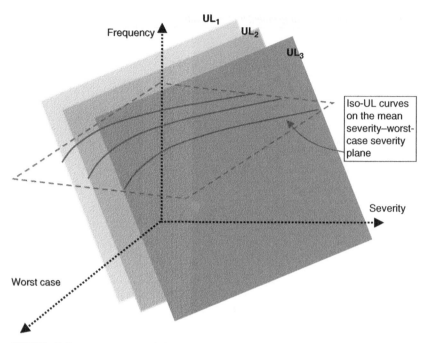

FIGURE 3.6 Intersection of the Iso-UL Surface and a Given Mean Frequency Value

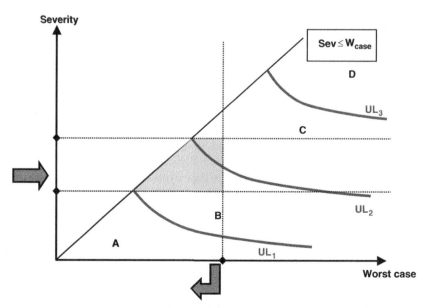

FIGURE 3.7 Critical Mean and Worst-Case Severity Values Used to Set the Ranges in the Questions and the Region Identified by the Related Answers

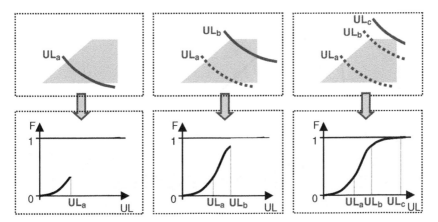

FIGURE 3.8 Estimate of the UL Distribution Associated with the Region Provided by the Answers

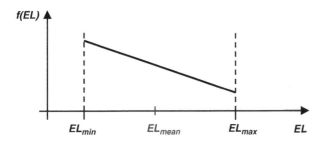

FIGURE 3.9 Density Function Associated with the EL for Each Answer

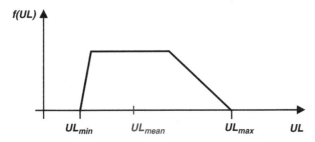

FIGURE 3.10 Density Function Associated with the UL for Each Answer

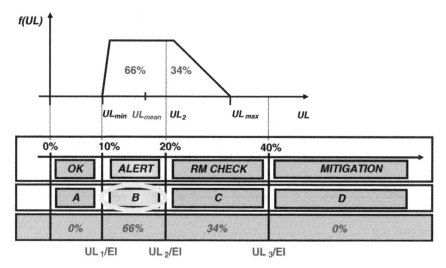

FIGURE 3.11   UL Distribution Is Mapped on the Cutoff Defining the Different Rating Classes

Finally, in order to attribute the operational rating to the production process, the UL distribution is mapped on the cutoff defining the different rating classes. We choose the rating class defined by UL ranges where the higher-probability mass of the subjective UL distribution is concentrated, as illustrated in Figure 3.11.

3.5   INTEGRATION OF THE SUBJECTIVE AND THE QUANTITATIVE ANALYSIS

Our approach has the aim to improve the loss distribution estimation by integrating the information that comes from historical quantitative data with those provided by qualitative information. The estimation of the loss distribution using historical data is well known in the literature, and many different approaches are available. In this chapter we are not addressing the issue of the best approach to estimate the loss distribution using historical quantitative data. Given this estimation we provide a simple framework to integrate the loss distribution obtained with quantitative data and the one obtained from qualitative data with the self-assessment approach presented earlier.

The need to perform this integration arises from these considerations:

- Qualitative information also captures the forward-looking dimension.
- We want to reduce the bias of quantitative information and increase the economic relevance of the analysis.
- We want to measure risks in cases where no historical data exist.

The approach we use to integrate subjective and quantitative analysis is Bayes' rule in the same spirit proposed by Alexander (2000). In fact, the output of the self-assessment questionnaire could be considered as the "prior density" for the quantitative information. We could indicate this prior density with $p(\theta|y_1)$ (i.e., the probability distribution of the model parameters given the answers we observed from the questionnaire). Let us consider then the second source of information: the quantitative data, which we indicate with y_2, where the likelihood of the sample data $p(y_2|\theta)$ is called the sample likelihood. The product of these two densities defines the posterior density that incorporates both subjective and quantitative information, that is:

$$p(\theta|y_1, y_2) \propto p(\theta|y_1)\, p(y_2|\theta) \qquad (3.6)$$

$$\propto p(\theta)\, p(y_1|\theta)\, p(y_2|\theta) \qquad (3.7)$$

The posterior distributions that include both the quantitative and qualitative information represent the best integration of the two approaches and therefore use all the information available. The gain in terms of parameter estimation of the CLE approach is represented in Figure 3.12, where the

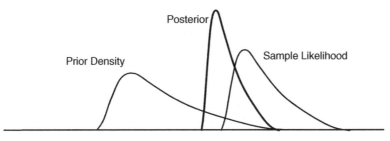

FIGURE 3.12 Posterior Density that Comes from the Integration of Subjective Distribution and the Distribution Estimated from Quantitative Data

historical quantitative information allows us to reduce the subjective uncertainty about the risk measurement of the variables of interest: the EL and the UL.

3.6 CONCLUSION

This chapter has shown how the complementary loss estimation approach could be implemented for computing a bank's capital charge for operational risk. We have described in detail the subjective method to evaluate losses. In particular, we have shown how to compute the aggregate loss distribution by compounding the loss severity distribution and the loss frequency distribution based on the self-risk assessment approach. The evaluation of the utility of the CLE approach is left to backtesting.

REFERENCES

Alexander, C. 2000. Bayesian methods for measuring operational risk. Discussion Papers in Finance, ISMA Centre, Reading, U.K.

Ebnöther, S., P. Vanini, A. McNeil, and P. Antolines. 2003. Operational risk: A practitioner's view. *Journal of Risk* 5 (3):1–18.

Ebnöther, S., P. Vanini, A. McNeil, and P. Antolines. 2002. Modelling operational risk, Zurich Cantonal Bank—corporate risk control. Zurich Cantonal Bank, Swiss Federal Institute of Technology.

Embrechts, P., and G. Samorodnitsky. 2002. Ruin theory revisited: Stochastic models for operational risk. ETH Zurich Working Paper, Zurich.

Frachot, A., O. Moudolaud, and T. Roncalli. 2004. Loss distribution approach in practice. In *The Basel handbook: A guide for financial practitioners*, ed. M. Ong. London: Risk Books.

Johnson, N. L., S. Kotz, and N. Balakrishnan. 1987. *Continuous univariate distributions*. Vol. 1, Wiley Series in Probability and Statistics. New York: John Wiley & Sons.

Kuhn, R., and P. Neu. 2003. Functional correlation approach to operational risk in banking organizations. *Physica A* 322 (2):650–666.

Lawrence, M. 2000. Marking the cards at ANZ. *Risk Magazine* operational risk supplement. London: Risk Publications.

McNeil, A., and F. Lindskog. 2001. Common Poisson shock models: Applications to insurance and credit risk modelling. Working paper, RiskLab/ETH, Zurich.

Rabin, M. 1998. Psychology and economics. *Journal of Economic Literature* XXXVI:11–46.

CHAPTER 4

Can Operational Risk Models Deal with Unprecedented Large Banking Losses?

Duc Pham-Hi

ABSTRACT

Banks calculating Basel II operational risk charge are required to include scenarios for very large losses along with internal loss data. However, apart from methodological precautions to avoid human expert bias, banks that statistically integrate quantitative scenarios—as well as the supervisor—have to keep an eye on several pitfalls. This chapter explores and illustrates a few combinations of techniques leading to situations where scenarios-based Basel II Advanced Measurement Approaches can have unexpected influences on the result of value at risk.

4.1 INTRODUCTION

One of the main characteristics of the current financial crisis is the size of losses. Asset reevaluation has shown several write-downs and write-offs in billions of dollars. According to a recent estimate, the four larger French banks, together with Credit Suisse and Deutsche Bank, lost almost US$30 billion by the first quarter 2008. Around the world, together they might total several times over the near systemic Long Term Capital Management catastrophe.

In the Advanced Measurement Approach (AMA) modeling of operational risk in the Basel II regulation context, the question is not whether it is necessary to incorporate these now not-so-unexpected losses in the regulatory capital called Pillar I calculation. It is how to do so without either losing credibility in the eyes of the supervisor because of too low estimates or pushing capital requirements to unrealistic heights.

We suggest here a new technique for general AMA modeling that specifically addresses the difficulty of incorporating catastrophe scenarios into the classic loss distribution approach (LDA). While this chapter does not claim rigorous statistical methodology, it aims at exposing a rational and desubjectivized approach to integrate extreme scenarios into distributions found with classic LDA in a satisfactory manner for both banks and the supervisor.

4.2 WHY SOME UNEXPECTED LOSSES CANNOT BE STUDIED IN SCENARIO GROUPS

AMA criteria explicitly require banks to take into account four mandatory elements: (1) internal data, (2) external data, (3) extreme scenarios, and (4) business environment and internal control factors. The two latter types of input have been most difficult to integrate quantitatively into a calculation that banks sometimes push to hair-splitting nuances. In most cases, a statistical methodology, LDA, is used, on the one hand, and a qualitative experts-based guesstimate of catastrophic loss, the scenario-based approach (SBA), is collected, on the other hand. Then the two are merged together, either using a simple but robust 25% to 75% or 50% to 50% dosage, or some arcane and mystifying methodology.

In both branches of the process, modelers run into some well-known problems in forecasting large unprecedented types of loss. Two issues have to be addressed:

1. The rather precise circumstances that trigger these broad categories of catastrophes
2. The loss amount, if possible calculated in a probabilistic way: what are the chances it will happen, and how much could be lost, at each level of confidence

Before January 17, 2008, few would have put in operational risk scenarios a single loss of US$7 billion; the previous record had been somewhat over GB$1 billion. On their own, trading desk managers or their internal controllers and auditors probably would never have suggested such a massive loss, or they would envisage it only in a scaled-down figure, as shown by a widely observed motivation to scale down external loss databases.

Having seen a new record set does not make things any easier for modelers. Should they now start considering that single losses in the US$10 billion range are possible? Definitely yes. But will this loss amount be more probable, due to the increasing interdependencies of trading places and deeper financial markets, or will it be less probable, because managers and controllers, not to mention supervisors, have grown more wary of this category of loss? In fact, quantitatively considering this order of magnitude in operational risk model demands approaches that banking authorities consider credible. Conversely, supervisors, who wish to see such prudential measures taken, may need to hint that there exist some approaches that appear as both feasible and based on technical common sense. Let us now examine the methodology-building requirements for such a need.

Today's common practice of finding scenarios is not satisfactory due to the unnatural merge method with its LDA counterpart. Even when panels of business experts elaborate a set of loss events leading up to a catastrophic loss and then estimate the financial consequences of each case, integrating these elements into the building blocks of LDA remains. One indisputable fact is some Monte Carlo methods are required. However, banks often use these methods not for real simulations but as a substitute tool to calculate a proxy convolution of frequency and severity distributions.

Banks merge scenarios with LDA in several ways, each with its own problems.

If an external loss is simply added as another data point to the internal loss database, implicitly its category's frequency does not change much, but the severity distribution has one more point, for which it is difficult to estimate the probability. By its presence in a set of losses collected over three to five years—the regulatory required depth for loss database history in Basel II—it can unwittingly be attributed an occurrence of one in three to five years. Doing separate LDA runs for scenarios-generated data, either by bootstrapping on specific samples or by chosen parametric Monte Carlo methods, introduces a dose of suspicious modeling compromise.

If the external loss is added to a separate collection of catastrophic scenarios, it will follow the general treatment of merging the scenario losses with the LDA losses. This is often done by grouping together all the scenarios of one homogenous category, calculating their financial impact through simulations according to expert panels' estimates, then adding them via a set of weighting coefficients to the LDA data. The coefficients are supposed to reflect the respective credibility of the scarce statistical observations versus the estimates of subjective, qualitative experts.

This crude method separates the heuristic estimates from the statistical treatment and makes it easier for the supervisor to detect regulatory arbitrage, if any. A refined countermeasure can be brought to the system by building a process whereby observations can automatically modify parameters of credibility to enhance its reality, according to Bayesian rules.

However, the problem is still to get the elements that will lead an educated guess into uncharted territories and reveal yet-unobserved types of losses or frauds. There are two issues here:

1. The scenarios cannot be proven to have covered all the important risks. In-bank experts in panels usually think in the context of their own bank. Modelers sometimes must cite external loss databases to make experts think outside the box and get a sense of the order of magnitude of parameters: frequencies, severity means, scatter, and so on. If we want a systematic methodology for uncovered risks, we need a feature to generate all the results of the combinations of circumstances. Even if that yields too many scenarios, it is better to sieve through this generated mass and eliminate irrelevant cases than to missed out on relevant, unexplored loss scenarios.
2. Modelers often are too conscious of the need to make economies on regulatory capital. The AMA is sometimes "sold" to senior management as a means to cut back on regulatory capital, when compared to the Standardised Approach (TSA). Bank management should keep in mind that the better a measurement instrument is, the more flaws it will reveal. Therefore, if the internal situation is truly riskier, an AMA model will surely detect more, not less, need for operational risk capital.

Experts' panels are demonstrably a necessary condition to build scenarios for the tail behavior of risk distributions. Yet unfortunately, their contribution alone is not sufficient. What then is missing?

4.3 REQUIRED FEATURES FOR A NEW METHODOLOGY TO EXPLORE UNPRECEDENTED CATASTROPHES

A new methodology to explore unprecedented catastrophes has four required features:

1. The approach must allow a common computation of both the scenarios-based part and the LDA part in a homogenous and predetermined way.

Monte Carlo iterations should apply so that subjective estimates of the results (e.g., value at risk) become by design more difficult to guess.

2. The approach must resolve the ambiguity facing business experts who are asked to build scenarios. Nonstatisticians are confused when they are asked to give an estimate of frequency, on the one hand, and a spectrum of severity values according to their likelihood, on the other hand. Most of the time, in their minds, the likelihood at each severity level will be given by the frequency of occurrence itself, thus destroying the assumed independence between the two distribution laws.

3. Truncated severity laws pose another problem. In some models, beyond some subjectively determined very large threshold, losses are simply assumed not to exist. In some cases, modelers have decided to drop off those absurdly great numbers; in other cases, they use random draws from observations where the finite sample can provide only finite theoretical loss values.

4. The generated scenarios from this new approach must have the capacity to explicitly expose the mechanism of *how* losses may happen, not just that such or such loss *amount* is possible. We suggest that a business process management approach be a main tool to lay out the events chain leading to catastrophic loss. Self-explanation will then be a built-in feature.

4.4 USING STOCHASTIC DYNAMICS TO DRIVE EVENTS IN A NETWORK COMBINING ACTORS

Creating a combination of circumstances through assembling in different order places, people, and actions liable to produce errors or frauds can yield both unexpected results through massive simulations and an explanation afterward as well. We can start with two angles of attack:

1. Locate risk zones in the firm (trading floor, server rooms, etc.) then elaborate data and value flows that transport risks.

2. Analyze chains of sequential actions and their associated actors, then draw up a flow diagram.

These two kinds of mapping should lead to the same end result if analyses are conducted fully. In the first case, all geographic operational unit mapping should be extended with a causality search in mind. In the second case, temporal analyses should take into account the proximity of factors and their role in propagating the loss risks.

Risk mapping as generally conducted in banks in Basel II operational risk projects do not provide readily useful information as far as looking for hidden potential losses are concerned. These "heat maps" are useful as they can raise the risk awareness of operatives on the field, thereby eliciting spontaneous scenarios formulation on some catastrophes that the central operational risk management is not aware of. But they do not give objective or systematic quantification of combinations of probabilities that can lead to a major breakdown or fraud. The products of these risk-mapping projects can be compared to infrared satellite snapshots of vehicles circulating in the dark around a city at night: The density of cars as detected by the heat emission of their engines is indicative of the probability of potential collisions. But without a lighted map of the streets and intersections, and without an understanding of the logic of the flows (e.g., commuting cars entering the city in the morning and exiting at the end of the workday), forecasting is largely cut off from its dynamic and logical dimensions.

4.5 OBTAINING RISK-GENERATING NODES IN A NETWORK GRAPH

With this in mind, it is easy to see that Business Process Management (BPM) has many tools to offer to help with risk analysis. One such conceptual tool is event-driven process chain (EPC) analysis. It can help map singular events happening in a banking operation with a granularity and a scope determined by the experienced modeler, depending on the operational units being considered. EPC representations have some drawbacks: They do not incorporate a timeline, and they do not naturally help find causality. That is why EPC analysis must be used in conjunction with other representation tools, in particular from the field of Unified Modeling Language (UML). Other concepts from BPM that may also help are workflow management (WFM) and, less relevant here, business process reengineering (BPR).

An EPC necessarily begins and ends with an event, although not always a loss event: It should be understood in UML semantics, "events" are passive elements because they do not transform or change the state of organizational units. That is the role of active elements and the "functions" (controller, manager, producer, etc.) or events such as triggers or outputs resulting from active elements. Three types of connectors, AND, OR, and XOR, link events to active elements. In operational risk modeling, the modeler would consider bank employees and bank clients, or even a whole department, such as front or middle office, as active elements. These organizational units generate errors—or frauds—and connectors serve as vectors for their diffusion and propagation.

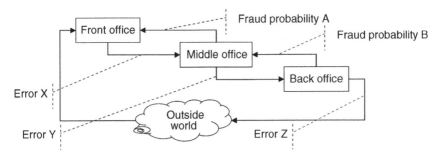

FIGURE 4.1 Simplified Model of a Group of Interacting Operational Units

With this organic modeling done, the operational risk manager now has a set of active nodes that can generate risks, interconnected with each other through causal links that show flows of information or money. By adding the time dimension, the manager can represent time lags in the flows from node to node (see Figure 4.1).

The next step is to place controls. These are materialized by human or software active nodes, which either let pass or detect and correct an error. This occurrence will be made dependent on the outcome of a random process, whose parameters can be modeled in the classic way from expert panel interviews or from data analysis. The complexity of the modeling process is largely paid back because the estimates of internal control efficiency and its impact on loss reduction are more objective and acceptable to supervisors.

The semantics and the syntax with which EPC are built are usually human orientated and therefore do not allow an automatic, formal verification of the node and flow consistency. These graphs of active and passive nodes along with connectors must be transformed into Petri nets. This is time consuming but not too difficult to achieve with a little modeling experience and at the cost of some simplification into stylized schematics. Nevertheless, this method explicitly performs one immense task regarding regulatory requirements that has always been challenging: Internal control factors are taken into account in a rigorous and parametric manner, which paves the way for easier adjustments between expert panel interviews and dialogue with supervisors on accepted values of capital reduction.

In the same manner, the modeler can also tentatively reflect business environment factors, such as in the parameters of a regime switching, error-generating random process to describe changes in levels of activity (e.g., overheat or slow periods). The model is then ready to run in simulation mode.

4.6 GENERATING LOSSES IN A STOCHASTIC MULTISTEP DYNAMIC

With inspiration from the field of ordinary differential equations, the modeler next uses the Petri nets obtained through BPM analysis to simulate losses incurred by an operational unit without the expert panel bias on the prevalence of such risks in scenarios. The step-by-step dynamic generation of random states for each node with its own storage in short-term memory will free the model from the strong hypothesis of Markovian behaviors. Assumptions that today's evolution is independent of history are philosophically unsatisfactory with the widespread practice of using regression of past observations to forecast the future.

In particular, time-step–based evolution modeling avoids the early practice observed in the AMA models, which simulate all the operational losses in the year as happening as instantaneous loss events on exercise closing day, for example, December 31—or, at best, at the end of each quarterly reporting period, according to Common Solvency Ratio Reporting (COREP) regulation. In this crude representation, the number N of operational risk loss events for a year is drawn from a Poisson or negative binomial law, then a loss amount for each of these N events is drawn randomly in the proposed severity law (e.g., a lognormal or Pareto distribution). Many operational risk managers believe that this process, which constitutes the core of a Monte Carlo analysis, is a simulation. In fact, it is fundamentally only a way to circumvent calculating a convolution product between the laws of severity and frequency for the loss process. This "December 31 loss flash" is still used in many models.

This mode of "simulation" has two other drawbacks besides its unrealistic representation:

1. It negates any possible correlation—not to speak of causal links—between events that are consecutive in time and space.
2. It diminishes the reliability of the estimation of the annual frequency parameter, because banks generally have only three to five years of loss history.

By reproducing an event-driven stochastic process on a daily time step, the operational risk modeler can incorporate autocorrelated phenomena that simulate chains of errors or amplification of fraud. Examples are internal fraud such as taking advantage of a virus attack or an information technology department being damaged by firewall failure by allowing hackers inside a private database. The right EPC representation will also depict self-sustaining perturbations, as can be observed in market rumors and trader herding behavior.

Here lies the reward for a thorough and realistic representation of real-world processes going on in banks: This network of causal links and interconnected workflows, with its time-based node switching states, can produce unexpected losses, thanks to its capacity to exploit a combination of risk factors. By running Monte Carlo iterations in sufficient number, all possible consequences of chains of events flowing through the net will be explored as nodes fire successively in complex combinations. This will also explain how things occurred after a large loss is uncovered and show how they could be prevented, unlike the flash simulation mode of scenarios.

4.7 VERIFICATION REQUIREMENTS FOR MODEL DYNAMICS

Even though the model may be based on a Petri net, thus allowing a formal syntactic verification of its internal consistency, the numerous layers of modeling motivates an independent verification process of the whole architecture. Following the many hypotheses concerning the operations of each of the EPC components and their interactions and correlations, the operational risk modeler can selectively choose to privilege some trajectories more than others in the routes taken in the Monte Carlo process. Software quality techniques may give ideas on how to force a random sampling to go through certain nodes rather than others. They will also help the modeler devise benchmarks for simple testing and stress testing the model.

Verification plays a crucial role, not only as a debugging tool, but also because, in a very productive way, it participates in the explore-and-research effort. Among the Committee of European Bank Supervisors, as reflected in their "Guideline No.10" on AMA projects in banks, the consensus is that an important part of the building effort should go into EDA (exploratory data analysis). As for all model construction that looks for realistic representation, it is probable that many prototypes will have to be built before a satisfactory result can be achieved.

4.8 REQUIREMENTS OF MODEL EVOLUTION BY LEARNING

After determination of the model parameters, rules to govern the firing and the interaction between nodes, and their quantification in terms of probability, the dynamic model can now run in the set of extreme conditions designed to qualify catastrophes. Monte Carlo *simulation* here is at its most semantically justified meaning. The output of some of the runs will reveal very large losses as a combination of a number of very rare events that all involve very large amounts of money. Thus, both the large loss and the very small probability can be presented convincingly to the supervisor, thanks to the objective, self-explanatory, detailed chain of events. The modeler is not at fault for not having envisioned such a large catastrophe. However, at the same time, the bank may be justified in not allocating additional capital since its probability has been satisfactorily demonstrated to stand beyond the value-at-risk threshold.

From a risk management point of view, this result is also very useful, as it shows which mechanisms and which routes the chain of events leading to catastrophe has taken. It helps management take proactive, preventive actions. Nonetheless, even this fine model should not be considered perfect as time goes by. Two sets of corrective actions may be put to work simultaneously to maintain high model reliability and robustness:

1. Each risk-generating node should have a built-in parameters revision process. The parameters involve at least the probability laws producing the errors. They could be pure Bayesian revision formulas, or they could be some reinforced learning-based parameters, such as the temporal difference algorithm.
2. Sensitivity measures should be made around the median scenarios in Monte Carlo iterations, with the evolving values parameters around the general model in order to determine whether some resonances or unsuspected instabilities might have been installed at lower regimes.

The process itself of creating this dynamic model should be organized as a learning process. The knowledge in the quantification of nodes and links, EPC representation, must be preserved not only as knowledge capital but also because of the regulatory obligations to document, communicate, and archive all AMA modeling efforts.

4.9 CONCLUSION

The main idea in adopting this dynamic stochastic event-driven simulation is the introduction of time-based interactions between operational units and the generation of errors at different nodes to create previously nonexistent combinations of conditions for a very large loss, unimagined by expert panels. By explicitly reproducing the causal chain and putting parameters on the model, the simulation allows business experts, modelers, and supervisors to really know where the focus is.

- Experts can get feedback on their different estimates and arrive at a better grasp of the nonlinear relationships between variables. These estimates are a cause of bad representation because the experts will extrapolate linearly some phenomena that are not linear.
- Modelers can better express the complex interactions by having more variables and parameters at their disposal.
- Risk managers can surely gain better insights on what can be done. A faithful representation enables managers to get a feel for the relative efficiencies of various actions of operational risk reduction. This is of paramount importance to the new science of quantitative risk management.
- Supervisors will be able to voice objections and challenge parts of the model more rationally. Sometimes, by their standards and experience, supervisors might feel the loss amount that a bank has computed is too small. Since they cannot put their finger on where the calculation went wrong, they only have recourse to Pillar II and to demanding additional capital requirements. In this kind of detailed model, the supervisor and the bank—which includes the modeler, the expert, and the risk manager—can agree on which phenomena, represented by which parameters, are under- or overdimensioned.

This is a radical departure from the spirit of classic LDA, where modelers use past data to adjust a picture of the present. In that "regression mode," modelers cannot invent new schemes and should not introduce new variables and parameters, as they are considered spurious quantities. They should not attempt to reproduce any psychology or behavior of the actors of fraud or errors.

This new kind of model, by presenting a more detailed representation of reality, tries to quantify losses by exploration. By being more specific regarding circumstances, it can do much more than merely demonstrate to the satisfaction of supervisors that capital requirements are met. Supervisors may allow securitizing certain specific operational risks and appeal to investors looking at a way to buy in precisely delimited, precisely scripted, but very large, risks. As such, the model is a way to measure a kind of capital on demand, or Tier 4 capital, which can be contractually and automatically raised when catastrophes happen after certain scripted scenarios. More precise than generic catastrophe bonds, more focused on exploration than statistical LDA models, the model may bring in a new method of funding some recently exposed operational risk whose necessity for cover now probably surpasses usual market capacities.

REFERENCES

Accord Implementation Group for Operational Risk. 2006. Observed range of practice in key elements of advanced measurement approaches (AMA). Basel, Switzerland.

Committee of European Bank Supervisors. 2006. Guidelines on the implementation, validation and assessment of advanced measurement (AMA) and internal ratings based (IRB) approaches. www.bundesbank.de/download/bankenaufsicht/pdf/cebs/GL10.pdf.

Condamin, L., J.-P. Louisot, and P. Naim. 2006. Risk quantification: Management, diagnosis and hedging. London: John Wiley & Sons.

Cruz, M. 2004. Operational risk modelling and analysis: Theory and practice. London: Incisive Media Investments.

Da Silva Carvalho, R., H. S. Migon, and M. S. Paez. 2008. Dynamic Bayesian models as an alternative to the estimation of operational risk measures. *Journal of Operational Risk* 3 (1):25–49.

Fontnouvelle, P., et al. 2003. Capital and risk: New evidence on implications of large operational losses. Working paper, Federal Reserve, Boston.

CHAPTER 5

Identifying and Mitigating Perceived Risks in the Bank Service Chain: A New Formalization Effort to Address the Intangible and Heterogeneous Natures of Knowledge-Based Services

Magali Dubosson and Emmanuel Fragnière

ABSTRACT

Due to the intangible and heterogeneous natures of services, classical control approaches might not provide the relevant safeguards to enable a typical bank to reach its objectives. Knowledge-based services result from diagnoses and evaluation performances whose value and quality levels are complex to measure as they are essentially based on perceptions and subjective opinions. Consequently, services cannot benefit from supply-chain risk approaches such as automation, statistical control process, and system reliability techniques in order to avoid any kind of disruption and quality lowering. To tackle these specific service-type risks, we suggest a new way of formalizing the risk management process adapted to the service chain of banks. To illustrate a

(Continued)

default of risk management, we have opted for the bank industry and the Société Générale case. Based on secondary sources, we related the chain of events that led to the enormous loss of money for the Société Générale in 2008.

5.1 INTRODUCTION

Due to the intangible and heterogeneous natures of services, classical control approaches might not provide the relevant safeguards to enable the service company to reach its objectives. Typically, knowledge-based services result from diagnoses and evaluation tasks whose value and quality levels are complex to measure as they are essentially based on perceptions and subjective opinions. Consequently, services cannot benefit from supply-chain risk approaches such as automation, statistical control process, and system reliability techniques in order to avoid any kind of disruption and quality lowering. To tackle these specific service-type risks, we believed that a new framework and formalization effort was needed in order to contribute to a risk management process adapted to the service chain. To illustrate a default of risk management, we have opted for the bank industry and the Société Générale (SocGén) case study. Based on secondary sources, we related the chain of events that led to the enormous loss of money for the SocGén in 2008.

We define a knowledge-based service as services that are delivered by highly educated and informed employees responding to specific diagnosed customer demands by offering and delivering customized value-added solutions and relations (Debely et al. 2007). Based on semistructured in-depth interviews with service providers and their customers, we identified risks as they are perceived by customers (Debely et al. 2006). These risks have to be handled and solutions have to be offered to the customers. Before that can be done, these risks have to be identified and classified according to the way that they would be managed.

Service industries that were chosen encompass the characteristics of typical service activities, which are traditionally described with the help of the IHIP paradigm (*i*ntangibility, *h*eterogeneity, *i*nstantaneity, and *p*erishability). Research has shown that intangibility is positively correlated with perceived risk (Finn 1985; Zeithaml and Bitner 2000). According to the literature, consumers perceive services as riskier than products (Guseman 1981; Mitchell and Greatorex 1993; Murray and Schlacter 1990). As stated by Mitchell and Greatorex (1993): "Intangibility greatly increases the degree of perceived risk in the purchase of services by decreasing the certainty with which services can be made." Mitchell (1999) affirms that the properties of services may lower consumer confidence and increase perceived risk, mainly by augmenting the degree of uncertainty in the decision. As fairly intangible services, bank services need to be experienced before they can truly be assessed (Parasuraman et al. 1985; Zeithaml et al. 2006). They are usually sold without guarantees.

In a bank, the broker purchases stocks and options either on behalf of a client or on behalf of the bank. Neither the bank nor the broker control all the risks associated to the various "ingredients." The broker's adequate counseling may help the customer to minimize the risk and investment annoyances. For instance, broker expertise could be crucial when dealing with margin calls or picking the right hedge fund. When participating in the design and delivery process (especially when outsourcing part of the process on the Internet), customers may increase their level of risk if they do not behave appropriately (e.g., do not have the right stock code).

Nowadays, a typical client can "assemble" for free a portfolio using tools available on the Internet, which puts cost pressure on banks and financial service companies. In such an environment, we questioned the nature of financial service companies acting as retailers of predesigned services. We suggested that they should change the nature of service delivered to the customer by focusing on the risk side associated with service delivery.

We propose a methodology to design risk management services that banks could provide to clients. Our methodology combines approaches borrowed from the risk management and audit professions as well as research from the services marketing and service operations management. We put forward a qualitative control system in order to address the operational risks encountered all the way through the travel service chain.

According to the Institute of Internal Auditors glossary (www.theIIA. org) the term *control* means: "Any action taken by management, the board and other parties to enhance risk management and increase the likelihood that established objectives and goals will be achieved." Control is thus an important part of managerial activities. However, the design of controls dedicated to services is particularly tedious. In particular, the intangibility of the service makes the identification of risks difficult.

We suggest hereafter a new type of control (Dubosson et al. 2006) whose design makes a distinction among these states of "risk attributes": threat, event(s), ignorance, and damage. In classical approaches to control, we tend to focus solely on the expected damage. Our control design involves three types of tests:

1. Whether the threat is associated with a preventive system
2. Whether the event is associated with a detection system
3. Whether ignorance of the problem is associated with a protection system

Due to the instantaneity, heterogeneity, and intangibility characteristics of services, there is little evidence of a service problem. Moreover, perception of the problem (quality) is subjective, and individual perception often cannot be related to what was actually delivered. The most patent clue of a service problem is a customer complaint. In order to avoid waiting for customer complaints to recover from a service problem, our approach favors a more integrated approach. Risk management should be designed to take into account potential problems and applied all the way down the supply chain in real time. Moreover, our approach focuses on the risks as they are perceived by customers. We suggest emphasizing an ex-ante treatment of risk as opposed to an ex-post methodology.

The chapter is organized in this way. In Section 5.2, we present the difficulties faced by the bank business. In Section 5.3, we present a brief overview of the literature on perceived risk in the context of services. In Section 5.4, we model the bank service chain and explain its particular links with risk events. In Section 5.5, we present a qualitative control system that takes into account the intangible and heterogeneous nature of knowledge-based services. We believe that it could represent a way to improve the perception of risks in the general context of services. In Section 5.6, we apply this new framework of control and design to a banking business case. In conclusion, we indicate further research directions.

5.2 BANKS IN THE POST–SUBPRIME ERA: AN IMPORTANT SECTOR IN TURMOIL

In this section, we focus on the UBS, as it is the world's biggest manager of other people's money. According to the *Economist* (July 2007) "its mixture of financial expertise and prudent risk management seemed to be a winning formula."

UBS created a hedge fund venture, the Dillon Read unit, in 2005 run by John Costas, which invested in American mortgages. This fund dealt at least $80 billion (some say $600 billion), nearly all of which came from UBS's own capital. It brought $1.2 billion in revenues in 2006, returning $700 million to the bank. In April 2007, UBS discovered losses in a $4.5 billion portfolio of subprime securities. Peter Wuffli, the investment banking chief executive, shut it down in May 2007 at a cost of at least $425 million. In July 2007, UBS announced the abrupt dismissal of Wuffli and recognized that it had failed to become best in class in investment banking. That fact could be attributed to justifiable risk aversion in business, such as structured products and leveraged finance but not in Mr. Marcel Ospel's eyes (*The Economist* 2007). In July 2007, the *Economist* concluded its article with these words: "The risk for UBS is that it may stick its neck out at exactly the wrong time in the credit cycle. It may not be long before Mr. Wuffli's cautious strategy about debt may start looking prescient."

Other trading desks in UBS were also aggressively trading in subprime and securities, and traders were generally less experienced thanks to the Dillon Read's talent raids. They did the same trades on a far bigger scale. UBS continued to hold large positions in mortgage-backed securities until well after the market collapsed in mid-2007. Traders loaded up on AAA-rated mortgage-backed debt because it was considered to have little risk or even be risk free (*BusinessWeek* 2008).

In November 2007, Credit Suisse and UBS revealed that their results were in line with the predictions they had made at the start of October. UBS announced a loss of $622 million, which it attributed to a poor performance in its fixed income, currencies, and commodities business. Its chairman, Marcel Ospel, said that while the figure was unacceptable, it was vital to be open with shareholders and the market as quickly as possible. He said that substantial losses had occurred in the company's position related to the U.S. subprime residential mortgage market inherited from the now-closed Dillon Read Capital Management business. Since then, banks have shocked investors by repeatedly reevaluating billions of write-downs and announcing billions of losses.

There was a time when the "quants" were the stars of the finance show. Some experts say the complex models of risk mislead banks about the safety of subprime securities. Some others say that managers and "quants" do not speak the same language, and managers no longer are able to understand what quants do; they should catch up and learn. And if both of them learn? According to Raj Singh (*The Economist* 2008):

> *Banks' risk models, which try to put a value on how much they should realistically expect to lose in the 99% of the time that passes for normality, draw on reams of historical data. But this can produce a false sense of security.... In insurance we have to think the unthinkable all the time, pointing out that the industry came up with a scenario of a multiple plane crash above a metropolitan area well before the attacks on New York's World Trade Centre in 2001. In banks, different teams often track different risks, masking potentially catastrophic correlations between them. Smart insurers are aware of the way in which life, property, business interruption, and risks interact.*

In February 2008, Credit Suisse surprised all the industry by announcing that at least part of its $2.85 billion in subprime-related write-downs were linked to "mismarking" and pricing errors by a number of its traders. It is unclear whether these mismarkings and errors were on purpose or by mistake. This leads us to question the internal control system, risk management and the appropriateness of valuation methods.... Credit Suisse requires its traders to value their trades on a daily basis, a process that is supervised by their managers. These evaluations are cross-checked on a weekly, monthly, or ad-hoc basis by independent controllers. The mismarkings were detected during such a cross-check. At most banks, assessment models are created by teams of quantitative analysts and a separate risk-control group has to sign off the use of specific models for certain instruments. Traders bear primary responsibility for using reasonable price estimates, but the heads of trading desks and bank's relevant product control group are also tasked with making sure those valuations aren't wildly out of line with market indicators. Banks might also use third-party valuation services which aggregate prices on illiquid instruments from a range of banks (Mijuk and Bradbery 2008).

In March 2008, Bear Stearns & Co. was sold to JPMorgan Chase & Co. at a $2-a-share price because of a lack of liquidity when it had traded a week earlier around $70 per share. The Securities and Exchange Commission is looking into how financial firms priced mortgage-backed securities such as collateralized debt obligations (CDOs) and whether they should have told investors earlier about the declining value of the securities. The banking industry may face a wave of lawsuits from institutions that bought these investments. Due to the inherent complexity of the investments, it is said that many bought into the loans without fully understanding the underlying risk. U.S. law firm Coughlin Stoia Geller has launched a class action against UBS for all purchases of shares in the bank between March 13 and December 11, 2007, accusing UBS of keeping its share price artificially high by not writing down its CDO positions sooner. The Federal Banking Commission is putting pressure on the banking industry to overcome the crisis quickly and strengthen its capital base. And in a second step, it will investigate how these enormous write-downs could arise.

In order to fight back and recover shareholder confidence, banks are raising capital (e.g., $4 billion for Lehman Brothers, $30 billion for Citigroup, $13 billion for Merrill Lynch, according to W. F. Tanona, a Goldman Sachs analyst), trying to get rid of toxic assets and reduce leverage, and are announcing jobs cutting. The Fed announced that it would lend directly to securities dealers, for the first time since the 1930s. But in the case of UBS, for instance, what seems the worst is the fact that the crisis is spreading to bank's cash cow: private banking. Bank officials claim that the effect is not so damaging as the departing funds are compensated for by the flows of new money. Customers are also leaving retail banking in Switzerland as they do not feel confident anymore in banks. They feel as if they are returning to the nightmare of the Swissair grounding, which marked the fall of another Swiss symbol that was also associated with UBS.

After each bad news announcement, financiers hope that the turmoil might end. That was the case in February 2008, as auditors forced banks to come clean on their exposures regarding subprime mortgage securities, and so it was at the beginning of April (the time of this writing). Now the crisis might move into derivative investments or the oil crisis, or something else. Will hope triumph over experience every few weeks?

5.3 NOTION OF PERCEIVED RISK: LITERATURE REVIEW

Perceived risk has been extensively studied in the field of marketing services. Perceived risk is believed to have a greater effect on the consumer for services (Guseman 1981; Mitchell and Greatorex 1993; Murray and Schlacter 1990). Perceived risk is a two-dimensional construct comprising the uncertainty involved in a purchase decision and the consequences of taking an unfavorable action (Bettman 1973). The perception of risk has been found to be totally subjective (Havlena and DeSarbo 1990; Ross 1975). Perceived risk was considered as a subjective expectation of loss (Mitchell and Greatorex 1993; Peter and Ryan 1976).

Mitchell (1998) revealed that consumers judging low-probability/high-consequences risks (e.g. purchasing an airline ticket) are affected more by the consequence size than by the probability, and many appear to disregard the probability altogether. An example often used is that car accidents kill many more people per year than airplane crashes. However, people tend to fear airplanes more than cars. Slovic and Lichtenstein (1968) and Horton (1976) also found that the degree of negative consequences is much more important in determining risk than the probability of their occurrence. For this reason, risk perception is the result of the probability plus the consequence as opposed to the definition of risk, which is the result of the occurrence multiplied by the consequences:

Risk Perception = occurrence of risk + seriousness of loss

Jacoby and Kaplan (1972) have identified five independent types of risk: financial, performance, physical, psychological, and social. Some authors recommend combining social and psychological types of risk, as consumers find it difficult to differentiate between them and use instead the psychosocial type of risk. Roselius (1971) have added a sixth type of risk: time loss.

Product intangibility greatly increases the degree of perceived risk (Finn 1985; McDougall and Snetsinger 1990; Mitchell and Greatorex 1993; Murray and Schlacter 1990). Intangibility is composed of three dimensions: physical intangibility, mental intangibility, generality (Laroche et al. 2001). Laroche et al. observed that there is a strong relationship between mental intangibility and perceived risk and an association between physical intangibility and perceived risk, but generality has either little or no direct impact on perceived risk. Laroche et al. (2003 and 2004) studied the impact of intangibility on perceived risk and the moderating roles of involvement and knowledge. As they expected, involvement has a positive moderating effect and knowledge has a negative moderating effect (i.e., the more respondents were knowledgeable, the less intangibility exerted a significant impact on perceived risk). As the authors assumed, people perceive potential risks in the unknown.

Knowledge is recognized as a characteristic that influences how consumers evaluate the risk inherent to their purchase (Murray and Schlacter 1990). As cited by Laroche et al., Engel et al. (1993) have defined knowledge as "the information stored within memory." Park et al. (1994) have defined knowledge assessment as a judgment process in which consumers scan memory for cues in order to help them evaluate their product-related experiences. Knowledge is often conceptualized with two related dimensions: experience and expertise. Expertise is potential, latent, and virtually realizable by the consumer. Experience differentiates itself from expertise by the fact that it is concrete, operational, and actualized by the consumer. Experience is a much less useful way of reducing risk for services than for goods because of the heterogeneity involved in producing and consuming services (Mitchell and Prince 1993).

Tan (1999) and Cunningham et al. (2004) claim that the Internet is perceived to be riskier than traditional services. They explain this risk premium for Internet airline reservations by the high probability of users making unintentional mistakes, such as double booking, poor seating choices, failure to obtain electronic receipts or timely ticket delivery, or paying too much for a nontransferable, nonrefundable ticket. Moreover, mistakes can be blamed solely on the consumer, who has very limited recourse for correcting errors. For Internet shoppers, information plays a key role, since information search is more effective at reducing perceived risk levels. In favor of the Internet, it has been shown that Internet shopping technologies offer a reduction in the anxiety caused by judgmental service representatives (Meuter et al. 2000).

"Mistakes are an unavoidable feature of all human endeavor and thus also of service delivery" (Boshoff 1997). Nevertheless, Bitner et al. (1990) have shown that it is not necessarily the failure itself that leads to customer dissatisfaction. What is more likely to cause dissatisfaction is an inadequate response or a lack of response from the company. Mayer et al. (2003) have shown that customers feel how they were treated during the process is as important as what they actually experienced. They recognize what Grönross (1984) identified as the technical dimension (what actually happened during service delivery) and as the functional component (how the service was delivered). Failure in either dimension is likely to lead to low perceived service quality.

5.4 BANK SERVICE CHAIN: CHAIN OF SERVICES AND OF RISK EVENTS

The methodology used in this chapter is based on previous research on the travel agency industry (Debely et al. 2006). The aim was to sketch the service chain as experienced and felt by consumers. We take as an example private banking. We first describe the buying/designing process and the decisions to be made at the assembling stage of the process and its consequences in terms of intermediaries involved in the delivery of the service. Then we draw an example of uncertainty management (i.e., risks) to be managed.

5.4.1 Consumer Buying Process: Designing Investment Strategies

Most of the consumer buying process could be handled by the bank, which would help customers make or would make on behalf of customers the "right" choice in terms of investment. Customers mostly ignore the service chain that would be designed and somehow experienced by them. When acting on behalf of customers, banks have to be sure that they have a clear understanding of customer needs and expectations.

On the continuum of evaluation for different types of products (Zeithaml et al. 2006), banks are considered credence-based services, the attributes of which can be evaluated only after purchase and consumption, and include characteristics that consumers may find impossible to evaluate even after having consumed. These kinds of services are associated with a higher degree of customization and require the personal intervention of a service expert (Guiltinan 1987). As cited by Mitra et al. (1999), the variability and the nonstandardized nature of credence services lead to uncertainty about the actual cost and product performance (Murray and Schlater 1990) and make it difficult for consumers to evaluate alternatives before purchase (Guiltinan 1987). Mitra et al. claim that high-risk credence services are associated with greater information search and greater reliance on personal information sources.

Therefore, bank professionals could play a key role in reducing uncertainty and risk during the information search, alternative evaluation, and purchase decision phases. These professionals are a good way of obtaining reliable information, getting access to a broad choice, designing complex portfolio and investment strategies, getting expert insight about the alternatives, and making professional choices.

Throughout the buying process, bank professionals can play the role of discussion partner and can make customers more willing to accept greater risk (Woodside 1972). This tendency to accept greater risk after discussion is called the "risky-shift" phenomenon (Pruitt 1971). This tendency is controversial; some researchers claim that customers accept less risk after group discussion for high-risk products (Johnson and Andrews 1971; Woodside 1974).

5.4.2 Assembling Investment Vehicles: Choosing Intermediaries

When diversifying investment on portfolios, one has to make a series of decisions. For instance, when you buy a hedge fund, you buy a venture, a team of traders that will make decisions to buy other securities. By buying these securities, you buy particular ventures, levels of risks, currencies, and so on. Therefore, a few decisions made in the buying process imply a myriad of activities involving various companies/organizations and many subcontractors.

When mobilizing unique expertise, a banker could design a customized offer that meets or even exceeds customers' expectations. But what if anything goes wrong? The portfolio might have been designed properly; nevertheless, the customer or one of the chosen business partners (or an implied partner, such as the hedge fund chosen by the banker), or some uncontrollable factors (such as a hurricane) might cause the customer some trouble. Consumers will have to handle either a "product-category risk" (i.e., bank services) or a "product-specific risk" (Dowling and Staelin 1994).

Bank professionals who advise customers cannot assure that everything will go perfectly fine. Through the partnering and considering all the uncontrollable factors, there is a high probability that the investment will not turn out as planned and expected. The banker's postpurchase behavior is very important for services, as customers will actively discuss the process and the decisions made.

5.4.3 Uncertainty Management

According to Heskett et al. (1990), perceived risks arise in large part from customer insecurity about a lack of control of the process and the absence of

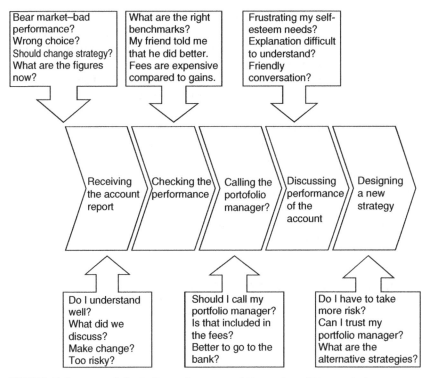

FIGURE 5.1   Part of the Delivery Process and Examples of Uncertainties

tangible clues to the quality of the complex service being purchased. When investing their money, customers may feel insecure, as many questions arise as they go through the delivery process (Figure 5.1). Moreover, the lack of information available in making service decisions and the lack of knowledge increase the risk (Bebko 2000; Mitra et al. 1999). By not having the knowledge or the correct answer, customers feel insecure about the outcome of the process. Therefore, they are forced to deal with uncertainty. To the extent that consumers realize that they may not attain all of their buying goals (i.e., fulfill their needs and wants), they perceive risk (Mitchell 1998).

Going through the activities described in Figure 5.1, we realize that many factors or behaviors can induce uncertainties and discomfort or even hinder customers carrying out the activities as expected. The human factor—the expert—is sometimes not considered as a way to reduce the risk or minimize the negative consequences; on the contrary, the expert may bring about more uncertainty.

According to Laroche et al. (2003), by developing relevant strategies to reduce perceived risks, service agents could augment purchase probabilities.

Therefore, if service companies want to be perceived as delivering good value, they have to adopt strategies to reduce uncertainties and perceived risk at the purchase stage. To reduce consumer risk, service companies should implement initiatives that directly address the risk (or reduce the adverse consequences of the adverse outcome, by giving a refund or helping to solve a problem) or the factors that contribute to the risk (or the level of uncertainty, e.g., receiving correct information or increasing tangibility) (Laroche et al. 2004; Mitchell and Boustani 1994). Indeed, it has been found (Mitchell 1998) that each product has a set of risks associated with its purchase, and each consumer has an individual risk tolerance. If that risk tolerance is exceeded, the consumer will employ one or more risk-reduction strategies to reduce the amount of perceived risk to a tolerable level. The literature cites these as the most used risk-reducing strategies: sales staff knowledge, tangibilization of services, free trials and samples, money-back guarantees, celebrity endorsements, favorable press reports, company and brand reputation.

5.5 CONTROL SYSTEM DESIGNED TO ADDRESS THE INTANGIBLE NATURE OF SERVICE RISKS

We propose to decompose the risk sequence into the following steps (TEID model) (Dubosson et al. 2006):

Threat (a potential risk that might endanger a bank; e.g., an inflammable Persian carpet is installed in a customer salon)

Event (an event related to the threat happens; e.g., cigar ashes fall on the Persian carpet and ignite a fire)

Ignorance (or unawareness of the event; e.g., the client and the client advisor have already left the salon and are unaware that a fire has started)

Damage (e.g., fire has time to spread throughout the building)

In Figure 5.2, we attempt to describe the importance of controls in order to avoid the contagion of major risks. Based on professional experience (Fragnière and Sullivan 2007), we learn that very often major risks result from a sequence of minor events. Handling trivial risks will then prevent a catastrophe to occur. Risk identification should thus be accompanied by analysis of the dynamic linkages that exist among risks. Therefore, these event-risk chains constitute the framework of the risk management process.

We thus establish a relationship between a threat and its potential resulting damage. If the internal control system (ICS) shows a lack of measures

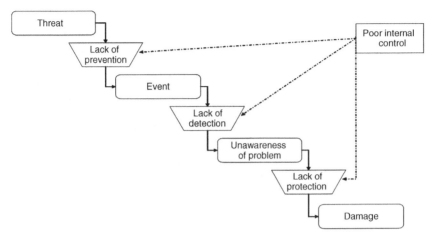

FIGURE 5.2 Illustration of a Poor ICS

of prevention, an undesirable event might happen (e.g., lack of due diligence processes). Defective or inexistent detection systems might propagate within the company (e.g., no accurate management information system to perform the reconciliation of assets). Ultimately, if no one is aware of the problem and no protective measures are in place (e.g., no insurance policy), the "expanding" damage might badly hurt the company, which consequently will not be able to reach its objectives.

5.6 APPLICATION OF THE TEID MODEL: THE SOCGÉN CASE

In this section, we do not investigate specifically and in detail the fraud perpetuated by Jérôme Kerviel at Société Générale. Rather, we explain the fraud and how such trading activities, usually implemented in any bank, could be handled by using the TEID model. Kerviel's strategy consisted in exploiting small price discrepancies between futures traded on electronic exchange platforms (e.g., EUREX) and OTC (Over the Counter) futures contracts. For instance, he might sell a futures contract through an exchange platform, involving 100 units, with a settlement date in three months, priced at 1.01. Then he might cover his (short) position by buying an OTC futures contract to a counterpart, again involving 100 units, with a settlement date in three months, priced at 1.00. This operation enabled him to net his positions and at the same time to generate a profit of 1 (i.e., $100*(1.01-1)$). These kinds of trading strategies are considered to be "plain vanilla," since their essence is simple and based on the logic of "Buy low, sell high." However, the volumes traded (a function of the number of contracts traded) must be huge in order to be profitable for a bank.

Kerviel was not able to cover his huge fraudulent futures contract positions, totaling nearly 50 billion euros. His strategy was then directional and his positions were fully exposed to market risk. To comply with the trading rules imposed on him by the bank, he created false confirmations of OTC trades, showing that his positions were properly netted. He was thus actually exposing the bank book to immense market risk. Ultimately, the bank discovered his huge positions and closed them, leading to a loss of roughly €5 billion.

Next we develop a series of controls according to the TEID model that could protect against this specific type of scam. The main goal of our approach is to deal with the risk of fraud in an upstream as well as a downstream manner in order to limit the contagion along the chain of risk leading to the main damage (e.g., a big financial loss).

1. Management first designs a preventive control. Preventive controls typically require discipline to be effective. We can imagine these controls.
   - Any new junior trader should be under the supervision of a senior trader and integrated in a team. In the SocGén case, Kerviel was isolated from the rest of the trading desk.
   - A simple prevention control consists of rigorous enforcement of two consecutive weeks of vacation per year. Kerviel was never really away from his desk.
   - All trades should be made through authorized and secured phone lines. Traders are not allowed to trade using their cell phones or Internet messenger systems.
   - Stringent procedures should be established for OTC trades. Kerviel had no way to modify contract confirmations sent by EUREX. However, he managed quite easily to falsify OTC contracts.
2. Management will then design a detective control. It is crucial to emphasize the role of back offices in the detective control phase. Usually back-office employees dare not challenge "quants" (i.e., traders with quantitative skills). Moreover, due to their "management by exception" approach, no further investigation was conducted to understand what happened each time an abnormal figure was detected. Articles in the press confirm that over the last two years, several abnormal signals (e.g., Eurex margin calls) popped up that should have raised management attention to Kerviel's illicit trades. Controllers should conduct systematic and rigorous reviews of each book to ensure their true accountability.

Especially rigorous protocols should be established to verify OTC contracts, the correctness of netting positions, and the respects of risk limits.
3. Management will finally design a protective (or recovery) control. If the first two controls (preventive and detective) are not effective in preventing the contagion of events, this control step will mitigate the main damage (e.g., financial loss). These are last-resort controls. Senior traders and controllers must have the full emergency power to close problematic trading books. Provisions must be set up to sustain large unexpected losses. If the problem is tackled too late, then the financial loss leads to a reputational risk. This is what happened to Société Générale. We can assume that the reputational damage is far bigger than financial loss.

5.7 CONCLUSION

Our experience tells us that in practice, banks focus essentially on curative controls and too little on preventive controls. The main reason for this is related to the difficulty in handling risks associated with intangible services. We suggest that companies disaggregate the service chains into single steps. For each step, after having identified the potential perceived risks, companies should define measures to be taken as preventive, detective, and curative controls. Indeed simpler, though very effective, controls can be set up upstream. This approach could be applied to all service activities in banks and extended to the management of perceived risks as experienced by customers. To illustrate the need to take into account the whole chain of risk when designing an effective control system, we have described the Société Générale fraud that led to the enormous loss of money in 2008.

REFERENCES

Bebko, C. P. 2000. Service intangibility and its impact on consumer expectations of service quality. *Journal of Services Marketing* 14, no. 1:9–26.

Bettman, J. R. 1973. Perceived risk and its components: A model and empirical test. *Journal of Marketing Research* 10, no. 2:184–190.

Bitner, M. J., B. H. Booms, and M. S. Tetreault. 1990. The service encounter: Diagnosing favorable and unfavorable incidents. *Journal of Marketing* 54, no. 1:71–84.

Booms, B., and M. Bitner. 1981. Marketing strategies and organization structures for service firms. In *Marketing of services*, ed. J. Donnelly and W. George. Chicago, IL: American Marketing Association.

Boshoff, C. R. 1997. An experimental study of service recovery options. *International Journal of Service Industry Management* 8, no. 2:110–130.

Cunningham, L. F., J. Gerlach, and M. D. Harper. 2004. Assessing perceived risk of consumers in internet airline reservations services, *Journal of Air Transportation* 9, no. 1:21–35.

Debely, J., M. Dubosson, and E. Fragnière. 2006. The travel agent: Delivering more value by becoming an operational risk manager. Proceedings of the La Londe 9th International Research Seminar in Service Management, June, 178–203.

Debely, J., M. Dubosson, and E. Fragnière. 2007. The pricing of knowledge-based services: Insights from the environmental sciences. New Delhi 2nd International Conference on Services Management, June. Available at SSRN: http://ssrn.com/abstract=951651. To appear in the *Journal of Services Research*.

Debely, J., M. Dubosson, and E. Fragniere. 2007. The consequences of information overload in knowledge based service economies. ESSHRA Conference proceedings, June 12–13, Berne, Switzerland. Available at SSRN: http://ssrn.com/abstract=999525.

Denton, D. K. 2001. Better decisions with less information. *Industrial Management* 43, no. 4:21–25.

Dowling, G. R., and R. Staelin. 1994. A model of perceived risk and risk-handling activities. *Journal of Consumer Research* 21, no. 1:119–134.

Dubosson, M., E. Fragnière, and B. Millet. 2006. A control system designed to address the intangible nature of service risks. Proceedings of the Shangai IEEE International Conference on Service Operations and Logistics, and Informatics, Shanghai. June.

Eavis, P., and D. Enrich. 2008. Skunk at the bank party; Danger still lurks in balance sheets while stocks soar. *Wall Street Journal* (Eastern Edition), April 2, 2.

Engel, J. F., R. D. Blackwell, and P. W. Miniard. 1993. *Consumer behavior*. Chicago: Dryden Press.

Finance and economics: Down the Matterhorn; Investment Banking. 2007. *The Economist.* July 14, 83.

Finn, A. 1985. A theory of the consumer evaluation process for new product concepts. *Research in Consumer Behavior* 1, no. 2:35–65.

Fragnière, E. and G. Sullivan. 2007. *Risk management*. Boston: Thomson Publishers.

Grönroos, C. 1984. A service quality model and its marketing implications. *European Journal of Marketing* 18, 40:36–44.

Guiltinan, J. P. 1987. The price bundling of services: A normative framework. *Journal of Marketing* 51, no. 2:74–85.

Guseman, D. S. 1981. Risk perception and risk reduction in consumer services. In *Marketing of services*, ed. J. H. Donnelly. et al. (Chicago: American Marketing Association.

Havelena, W. J., and W. S. DeSarbo. 1990. On the measurement of perceived consumer risk. *Decision Sciences* 22, no. 4:927–939.

Heylighen, F. 2002. Complexity and information overload in society: Why increasing efficiency leads to decreasing control. Draft paper, April 12. Brussels: CLEA, Free University of Brussels.

Heskett, J., W. Sasser, and C. Hart. 1990. *Service breakthroughs: Changing the rules of the game*. New York: Free Press.

Horton, R. L. 1976. The structure of decision risk: Some further progress. *Journal of the Academy of Marketing Science* 4, no. 4:694–706.

Jacoby, J., and L. Kaplan. 1972. The components of perceived risk. In *Proceedings 3rd Annual Conference Association for Consumer Research*, ed. M. Venkatesan. Chicago: Association for Consumer Research.

Johnson, D. L., and I. R. Andrews. 1971. Risky-shift phenomenon as tested with consumer products as stimuli. *Journal of Personality and Social Psychology* 20, no. 3:328–385.

Karmarkar, U. S., and R. Pitbladdo. 1995. Service markets and competition. *Journal of Operations Management* 12, no. 4:397–412.

Laroche, M., J. Bergeron, and C. Goutaland. 2001. A three-dimensional scale of intangibility. *Journal of Service Research* 4, no. 1:26–38.

Laroche, M., J. Bergeron, and C. Goutaland. 2003. How intangibility affects perceived risk: The moderating role of knowledge and involvement. *Journal of Services Marketing* 17, no. 2:122–140.

Laroche, M., G. H. G. McDougall, J. Bergeron, and Z. Yang. 2004. Exploring how intangibility affects perceived risk. *Journal of Service Research* 6, no. 4: 373–389.

Mayer, K. J., J. T. Bowen, and M. R. Moulton. 2003 A proposed model of the descriptors of service process. *Journal of Services Marketing* 17, no. 6:621–639.

McDougall, G. H. G., and D. W. Snetsinger. 1990. The intangibility of services: Measurement and competitive perspectives. *Journal of Services Marketing* 4, no. 4:27–40.

Meuter, M. L., A. L. Ostorm, R. I. Roundtree, and M. J. Bitner. 2000. Self-service technologies: Understanding customer satisfaction with technology-based service encounters. *Journal of Marketing* 64, no. 3:50–64.

Mijuk, G., and A. Bradbery. 2008. Credit Suisse move hikes sector pricing concerns. Dow Jones Newswires, February 19.

Mitchell, V. W. 1998. A role for consumer risk perceptions in grocery retailing. *British Food Journal* 100, no. 4:171–183.

Mitchell, V. W. 1999. Consumer perceived risk: Conceptualizations and models. *European Journal of Marketing* 33, nos. 1–2:163–195.

Mitchell, V. W., and P. Boustani. 1994. A preliminary investigation into pre- and post-purchase risk perception and reduction. *European Journal of Marketing* 28, no. 1:56–71.

Mitchell, V. W., and M. Greatorex. 1993. Risk perception and reduction in the purchase of consumer services. *Service Industries Journal* 13, no. 4:179–200.

Mitchell, V. W. and G. S. Prince. 1993. Retailing to experienced and inexperienced consumers: A perceived risk approach. *International Journal of Retail & Distribution Management* 12, no. 5:10–21.

Mitra, K., M. Reiss, and L. Capella. 1999. An examination of perceived risk, information search and behavioral intentions in search, experience and credence services. *Journal of Services Marketing* 13, no. 3:208–228.

Mollenkamp, C., and M. Whitehouse. 2008. Banks fear a deepening of turmoil. *Wall Street Journal* (Eastern Edition), March 17, A1.

Murray, K. B., and J. L. Schlacter. 1990. The impact of services versus goods on consumers' assessment of perceived risk. *Journal of the Academy of Marketing Science* 8, no. 1:51–65.

Next year's model? Risk management. 2008. *The Economist*, March 1, 15.

Parasuraman, A., V. A. Zeithaml, and L. L. Berry. 1985. A conceptual model of service quality and its implications for future research. *Journal of Marketing* 49, no. 4:41–50.

Park, W. C., D. L. Mothersbaugh, and L. Feick. 1994. Consumer knowledge assessment. *Journal of Consumer Research* 21, no. 1:71–82.

Peter, J. P., and M. J. Ryan. 1976. An investigation of perceived risk at the brand level. *Journal of Marketing Research* 13, no. 2:184–188.

Pruitt, D. G. 1971. Conclusions: Towards an understanding of choice shifts in group discussion. *Journal of Personality and Social Psychology* 20, no. 3:495–510.

Roselius, T. 1971. Consumer rankings of risk reduction methods. *Journal of Marketing* 35, no. 1:56–61.

Ross, I. 1975. Perceived risk and consumer behavior: A critical review. *Conference of the American Marketing Association* 1, no. 1:19–23.

Slovic, P., and S. Lichtenstein. 1986. Relative importance of probabilities and payoff in risk taking. *Journal of Experimental Psychology Monograph* 78, no. 3:1–18.

Stanley, R. 2008. Behind the mess at UBS. *BusinessWeek*, March 3, 30–31.

Tan, S. J. 1999. Strategies for reducing consumers' risk aversion in Internet shopping. *Journal of Consumer Marketing* 16, no. 2:163–180.

Woodside, A.G. 1972. Informal group influences on risk taking. *Journal of Marketing Research* 9, no. 3:223–225.

Woodside, A. G. 1974. Is there a generalised risky shift phenomenon in consumer behavior? *Journal of Marketing Research* 11, no. 2:225–226.

Wurman, R. S. 1990. *Information anxiety*. New York: Bantam Books.

Zeithaml V. A., and M. J. Bitner. 2000. *Services marketing: Integrating customer focus across the firms*, 2nd ed. New York: McGraw-Hill.

Zeithaml V. A., M. J. Bitner, and D. D. Gremler. 2006. *Services marketing: Integrating customer focus across the firms*. New York: McGraw-Hill.

CHAPTER **6**

Operational Risk and Stock Market Returns: Evidence from Turkey

M. Nihat Solakoğlu and K. Ahmet Köse

ABSTRACT

Following several high-severity, low-frequency events in the financial sector, operational risk has gained importance both for regulators and managers of financial sector firms during the last decade. The banking sector in Turkey also experienced a severe crisis, due not only to economic conditions but also to events directly related to operational risk. However, it was only by mid-2007 that banks in Turkey were required to have necessary capital for operational risk. This study investigates the banking sector in Turkey in relation to operational risk. In addition, the study analyzes the reaction of stock market return to operational risk events between 1998 and 2007 using event study analysis. We find that returns show a negative reaction starting right before the event date. Moreover, this negative reaction appears to be significant for pre-2002 events but not for events after 2002.

6.1 INTRODUCTION

For risk management departments in financial institutions, four types of risks need to be managed to minimize the loss of a portfolio or even the firm itself. These risk types are market risk, credit risk, liquidity risk, and operational risk. Market risk is created by the unexpected changes in market prices. Credit risk is the risk financial institutions face when there is a complete or partial loss related to default. Liquidity risk exists if there is a possibility that an asset or a position in a portfolio cannot be converted quickly to liquid assets or the conversion occurs quickly but at a lower price than fair market price (Jarrow 2008).

Operational risk is not new for financial institutions; they face many such losses in the past. However, the focus on the management of operational risk, by institutions and regulatory agencies, has increased recently following highly publicized and costly operational losses in the financial sector. Some examples of these costly losses are: the loss of about $1.3 billion due to a rogue trader, which led the Barings bank to bankruptcy in 1995; a $2 billion settlement paid by Prudential Insurance in 1990s; the $1.2 billion payment to auto insurance policyholders by State Farm Insurance because of a breach-of-contract lawsuit (see Cummins et al. 2006). A more current example is the loss of about $7.2 billion due to unauthorized derivatives trading in January 2008[1] at Société Générale. This is the largest operational loss event so far caused by a rogue trader. Along with high cost and publicity of operational losses, higher financial transparency and complex production technologies used in the financial sector have contributed to increasing attention on the management of operational risk (Cummins et al. 2006).[2]

Operational risk is defined as "the risk of loss resulting from inadequate or failed internal processes, people and systems or from external events. This definition includes legal risk, but excludes strategic and reputational risk" by the revised Basel Committee report (Basel Committee [BCBS] 2006, 144). Legal risk in the definition includes "exposure to fines, penalties, or punitive damages resulting from supervisory actions, as well as private settlements." As clear from the definitions, institutions can face operational risk because of internal or external events. The other three types of risks—market, credit, and liquidity risks—occur only under specific external events. Furthermore, operational risk is asymmetric. That is, institutions do not expect any gains but face loss of a portfolio or the firm under an operational risk event (Cummins et al. 2006).[3]

The Basel Committee breaks operational losses into eight standard business lines for banks and seven event types. The business lines are:

1. Corporate finance
2. Trading and sales
3. Retail banking
4. Commercial banking
5. Payment and settlement
6. Agency services
7. Asset management
8. Retail brokerage

Operational losses can be caused by any of these event types:

1. Employment practices and workplace safety
2. Internal fraud
3. External fraud
4. Clients, products, and business practices
5. Damage to physical assets
6. Business disruption and system failures
7. Execution, delivery and process management (BCBS 2006)

The work on operational risk mostly concentrates on the estimation of operational risk processes and the determination of the economic capital (Jarrow 2008). Empirical works have paid little attention to modeling of operational risk, which caused banks to allocate operational risk capital via a top-down approach. One reason was the lack of operational loss data. Several vendors, such as OpRisk and OpVantage, have constructed databases recently using mostly public information. Another reason is the availability of the information; not all operational losses are publicly reported (Fontnouvelle et al. 2003).

It appears that operational losses are concentrated in retail and commercial banking and retail brokerage mostly within the United States. For losses outside the United States, retail brokerage seems to have a lower weight, but retail and commercial banking still has the lead. Furthermore, while "clients, products, and business practices" is the leading event, followed by internal and external fraud events, within the United States, the internal fraud event is the leading cause of operational losses outside the United States (Fontnouvelle et al. 2003).[4]

Given the importance of operational risk in the financial sector and the role it played on Turkish banks in the 2001 financial crisis, we first examine the Turkish banking sector briefly to identify the importance of operational risk there. Then we analyze the reaction of stock returns to operational risk events. Finally we present our main conclusions and suggestions for further research.

6.2 OPERATIONAL LOSSES AND THE BANKING SECTOR IN TURKEY

The financial crisis of 2000–2001 had severe consequences on the banking sector in Turkey. The reasons for the crisis have been discussed many times in the past, but one fact has not been forgotten by bank customers and employees: the control of 15 banks was transferred to the Saving Deposits Insurance Fund (SDIF). In addition, owners of five banks were arrested (see Table 1 in Özatay and Sak 2003). It is now clear that many of the problems in the banking sector at that time were related to operational loss events, including internal and external fraud.

Despite the dreadful experience the sector went through in the late 1990s and early 2000s, operational loss capital was not required until the middle of 2007 by the Banking Regulation and Supervision Agency (BRSA). Based on the second survey results on the banking sector (BRSA 2005), about 69% of the banks planned to use the standardized approach, about 45% of the banks planned to use the basic indicator approach, about 45% planned to use the alternative standardized approach, and the rest planned to use advanced measurement approaches.[5] In addition, about 50% of the banks in the survey state that they do not classify operational losses into operational loss events.

Table 6.1 reports some banking statistics for Turkey. Except for the capital requirements for operational risk data, which is as of mid-2007, the rest of the data used in the table are as of the end of 2006. For all banks, the ratio of capital requirements for operational risk to total bank assets was 1.7%. For market risk, this ratio was 0.5%; for credit risk, it was 9.1%. As discussed in the literature (e.g., Jarrow 2008), the estimates for the necessary capital to cover operational risk are at least as large as the necessary capital to cover market risk. There is no surprise in Turkey: The estimate for operational risk, on average, is larger than the estimate for market risk.

It is no surprise that the ratio of operational risk capital to total assets is very small for development and investment banks. For deposit banks, however, the operational risk ratio increases significantly. Specifically, for state banks, this ratio is 7.3%, much larger than the ratios of domestic private banks and foreign banks. Moreover, the ratio of necessary capital for operational risk to market risk is about 18, much larger than the average of about 3 for all banks or for other depository bank classifications. This, of course, raises the question of the determination of operational risk capital amount and its effect on the firm value. Note also that total credits extended to total assets and total deposits are smaller for state banks, and their average number of branches and average number of employees are much larger.

TABLE 6.1 Descriptive Statistics for Banking Sector in Turkey

	Assets[a]	Average # of Branches	Average # of Employees	Credits/ Assets	Credits/ Deposits	Credit Risk Ratio	Market Risk Ratio	Operational Risk Ratio
All Banks	10387035	147	3070	39.9%	91.2%	9.1%	0.5%	1.7%
Deposit Banks[b]	14069822	204	4158	40.1%	91.2%	12.4%	0.7%	2.2%
State Banks	47787474	716	13074	35.6%	48.2%	25.2%	0.4%	7.3%
Domestic Private Banks	18972500	256	5230	47.8%	79.1%	18.7%	1.2%	2.9%
Foreign Banks	3954907	71	1720	36.1%	113.7%	4.7%	0.3%	0.7%
Development and Investment Banks	1180068	3	352	39.3%	—	0.9%	0.1%	0.2%

[a]1000 YTL
[b]Includes banks under the control of Savings Deposit Insurance Fund.
Except for capital requirements, 2006 year-end values are used. For capital requirements, 2007 midyear values are used.
Source: Banking Regulation and Supervision Agency; Banks Association of Turkey[6]

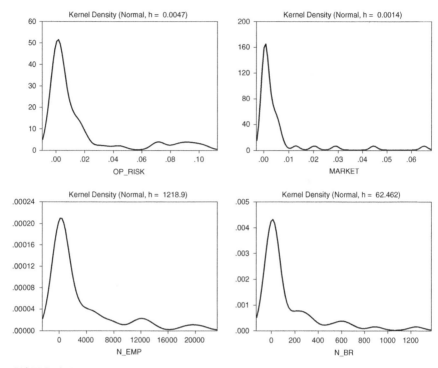

FIGURE 6.1 Empirical Distributions

Empirical distributions for operational and market risk capital, number of employees, and number of branches are presented in Figure 6.1. It is clear that all the variables selected have long right tails, indicating that few of the banks have a large number of employees, a large number of branches, and larger ratios of necessary capital for operational and market risk to total assets. It should also not be surprising that banks that are represented in the right long tail of the distribution in the four graphs are mostly the same ones.

6.3 REACTION OF STOCK RETURNS TO OPERATIONAL RISK EVENTS

The market value impact of operational loss events has not been investigated extensively in the literature. There are two reasons for this: the recent focus on the importance of operational losses and the lack of operational loss data, except for high-severity, low-frequency events (see Cummins et al. 2006 for an event study on U.S. financial institutions). Here we conduct an event study analysis for the banking sector in Turkey. Given the availability of market price data, we focus only on a smaller segment of banks that are/were traded on the Istanbul Stock Exchange (ISE) since 1998.

We obtained the daily data of securities traded at the Istanbul Stock Exchange and the market index[7] from the web site www.analiz.com for the banks with at least one operational loss event. Since no operational loss database exists, we obtained event data by exploiting two different sources. The main source of the event data is the company news archive provided by the Istanbul Stock Exchange. This source includes mostly the legal events and events related to processes and systems. We also used newspaper archives in Turkey[8] and observed several small to large operational loss events due to mostly internal fraud. Unfortunately, in many cases, the name of the financial institution is withheld, even for the recent incidents, a fact that creates transparency issues regarding the public availability of the financial news.[9] Overall, we have identified 22 events since 1998. The events themselves indicate that banks in Turkey do not face high-severity events in general. Most of the events, in particular the fraud events, can be classified as low- to medium-severity events.

For the analysis, we employ the standard event study methodology to identify the response of stock returns to operational risk events. The abnormal returns (AR) are calculated to determine the unexpected change in the returns before or following the announcement. For the cumulative effect on returns, we use cumulative abnormal stock returns (CAR) around the specific events related to operational risk.

The following specification of the market model is used to determine the expected returns in our analysis:

$$R_{it} = \alpha_i + \beta_i R_{mt} + \varepsilon_{it} \qquad (6.1)$$

where R_{it} = daily return of security i at time t
          R_{mt} = market return at time t

where all returns are calculated as the log differences.

As always, we assume ε_{it} is the disturbance term satisfying the classical assumptions. We estimate the model specified with Equation 6.1 with 80 observations dating over $[-100, -20]$ days before the event date, where a negative sign indicates the number of days before the event. Given the existence of events that fall under the legal definition of events, we keep the event window wider than usual and include 20 days before and after the event date. However, in calculating the cumulative abnormal returns, we examine three alternative event windows: event window of 7 days ($t = -3$ to $t = +3$), event window of 21 days ($t = -10$ to $t = +10$), and finally the event window of 41 days ($t = -20$ to $t = +20$). We estimate abnormal stock returns (AR_{it}) for security i at time t as the ordinary least squares (OLS) residuals defined by Equation 6.2:

$$AR_{it} = R_{it} - (\hat{\alpha}_i + \hat{\beta}_i R_{mt}) \qquad (6.2)$$

The average abnormal returns for each day of the event window are reported in Table 6.2. To save space, only the event window 10 days prior and 10 days after the event is included in the table. The means of abnormal returns, as reported in the table, are oscillating around zero throughout the event window, but there does not seem to be a negative trend as we expect after an event related to operational risk. However, there does seem to be a higher dispersion at the day of the event as indicated by the standard deviation. As indicated by the kurtosis and skewness, the abnormal returns follow a leptokurtic and mostly skewed distributions across unit of observations.

TABLE 6.2 Average Abnormal Returns

Day	Average	Median	Std. Dev	Kurtosis	Skewness	Range
−10	0.083	−0.004	0.336	13.016	3.552	1.548
−9	−0.011	−0.007	0.080	2.459	−0.586	0.371
−8	0.105	−0.004	0.376	17.386	4.059	1.774
−7	−0.001	0.001	0.139	10.049	−0.397	0.891
−6	−0.050	−0.005	0.277	8.734	−2.244	1.558
−5	0.018	0.008	0.072	6.948	2.084	0.358
−4	−0.019	−0.005	0.275	11.341	−2.367	1.557
−3	−0.084	−0.005	0.472	21.048	−4.536	2.421
−2	−0.385	0.012	1.791	21.352	−4.595	8.798
−1	0.071	0.007	0.232	8.639	3.058	0.951
0	−0.239	0.006	1.296	21.365	−4.585	6.679
1	−0.085	−0.002	0.281	16.284	−3.920	1.321
2	0.002	−0.005	0.398	11.130	1.989	2.437
3	−0.089	−0.002	0.372	12.891	−3.402	1.931
4	−0.078	−0.004	0.190	3.391	−2.205	0.646
5	−0.086	−0.009	0.273	10.732	−3.320	1.162
6	0.297	0.005	1.466	21.390	4.591	7.502
7	0.033	0.005	0.084	4.359	2.101	0.353
8	−0.068	−0.012	0.320	19.786	−4.308	1.738
9	−0.032	−0.006	0.115	16.762	−3.870	0.601
10	−0.046	−0.003	0.183	16.313	−3.922	0.873

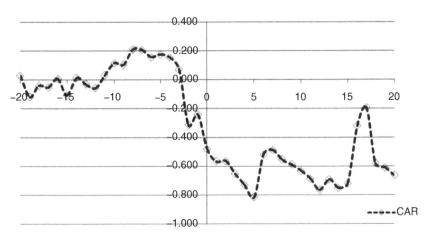

FIGURE 6.2 Cumulative Abnormal Returns (41-day event window)

The cumulative abnormal returns (CAR) for a 41-day event window—20 days before and 20 days after the event date[10]—are presented in Figure 6.2. The CAR$_t$ for any day t inside the event window is defined as the sum of average abnormal returns (AAR$_t$) up to that day as $\text{CAR}(t) = \sum_{i=-t_1}^{t} \text{AAR}_i$ where t_1 represents the starting day of the event window.

As it is clear from Figure 6.2, CAR shows a declining trend starting about 4 days before the event date and continues to fall for another 5 days after the event date. Similarly, we present the calculated CAR values for 21-day and 7-day event windows in Figure 6.3. It is clear that the negative reaction of stock returns to events related to operational risk is clear with all event windows. That is, the market reacts negatively to the events related to operational risk by lowering the stock return in the short run.

It is interesting to note the market reaction to the event before the event occurs. This finding may indicate the existence of information leakage to investors before the event date. Or this finding might be caused by the late reporting of the events either by the ISE or by the newspapers. In addition, there might be other relevant information that affects investor expectations before the date of the event.

The event dates we consider for the analysis start from 1998 and end in 2007. Nevertheless, the Turkish economy, particularly the financial sector, went through a severe crisis in 2000–2001; many banks went bankrupt or were taken over by the SDIF (see Özatay and Sak 2003). Hence, it may be important to identify breakpoints and examine the behavior of CAR for subperiods. One approach is to use experience or educated guess; the

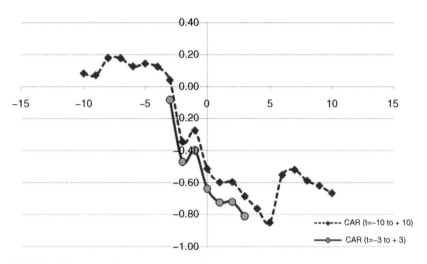

FIGURE 6.3   CAR for 21-Days and for 7-Days Event Windows

alternative is to let the data determine the breakpoints. We choose to follow the second approach and use the Iterative Cumulative Sums of Squares (ICSS) algorithm introduced by Inclan and Chao (1994). The ICSS algorithm can be used to detect multiple breakpoints in a time series by testing for volatility shifts.

To introduce the algorithm, let us assume ε_t is the series in question with zero mean and $\sigma^2{}_t$ as the unconditional variance. Inclan and Chao (1994) define cumulative sum of squares between time 1 and k as:

$$C_k = \sum_{t=1}^{k} \varepsilon_t^2, \qquad \text{where } t = 1, \ldots, T \quad \text{and} \quad k = 1, \ldots, T$$

The centered and normalized cumulative sum of squares until time k is represented by the D_k statistics.

$$D_k = \frac{C_k}{C_T} - \frac{k}{T}, \quad \text{with } D_0 = D_T = 0$$

If there is no volatility shift in the series, the plot of D_k against k will oscillate around zero. With a volatility shift, however, we will observe D_k statistics drifting away from zero. Based on Inclan and Chao's (1994) study, an asymptotic critical value of 1.358 can be used to create boundaries to identify the point in time with a volatility shift.[11]

We used monthly returns for the market portfolio, namely ISE100, to identify the sudden changes in volatility. The source of data was the ISE.[12] The breaks predicted by the ICSS algorithm are consistent with our expectation.[13] The ICSS algorithm identified one breakpoint. Thus, the first period, January 1995 to October 2001, corresponds to the pre-2001 financial crisis in Turkey, and the second subperiod, post-October 2001, corresponds to the stable and growth environment with the banking sector closely monitored by BRSA and regulations updated in accordance with the standards. Although not reported here, the first subperiod corresponds to a higher return and standard error than the second subperiod, indicating a higher-risk, higher-return environment.

Based on the outcome of volatility shifts, we recalculated CARs for pre- and post-2002 events. Out of 22 events, 12 belong to the first subperiod and the rest to the second subperiod. The CARs for 21-days event window for both subperiods are displayed in Figure 6.4.[14] Given the high-risk environment with loose regulations in the banking sector, we expect stock return reaction to operational risk events to be more significant and negative in the first subperiod.

As expected, we observe a declining trend in CAR_t values for the pre-2002 period several days before the announcements. However, the values of CAR_t at time t for the post-2001 period appear to be quite small, and there does not seem to be a trend in either the positive or the negative direction. We believe we can argue that the reaction of stock returns to operational risk events is weaker, though not with strong evidence, for the post-2001

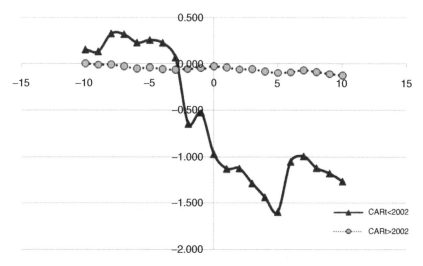

FIGURE 6.4 CARs and Pre-2002 and Post-2001 Events

period mostly due to effective regulation of the banking sector. In addition, other high-severity events that were not included in the data could cause a multiplier effect on the market response before the 2001 period.[15]

6.4 CONCLUSION

The importance of operational risk for the financial sector has increased dramatically following several costly and public events, with the latest high-severity event being the unauthorized trading loss at the Société Générale bank. The banking sector in Turkey experienced a severe crisis in the early 2000s. The crisis was due in part to economic conditions at that time and in part due to events that fall under the definition of operational risk. As a result of the problems, ownership for many banks was transferred to SDIF. The estimation of capital requirements for operational risk, however, did not start until the middle of 2007, with most banks using the standardized or basic indicator approach for the estimation. Consistent with the findings in this specific literature, the capital requirements are higher for operational risk than the market risk.

We also investigated the reaction of stock returns to operational risk events through a classical event study analysis. Since there was no database of operational risk events, we scanned through news archive for the banks that are/were trading at the Istanbul Stock Exchange. We also analyzed the archives of major newspapers with respect to fraud-related events. Overall, we identified 22 events. We believe the low number of events was caused by two factors: not all events are revealed to the public and, if the event is revealed to the public, the institution name is kept confidential. In addition, many of the events in Turkey are low-severity events that limit public focus on that area, particularly after 2002.

We find negative stock return reaction to operational risk events, with the reaction starting several days earlier than the event date. However, when we take into account the structural breaks, identified through the ICSS algorithm, we observe that the reaction loses its significance for the current period. That is, for the pre-2002 period, returns react negatively to events, but this finding does not hold for the post-2001 period.

NOTES

1. Some other examples are: Allied Irish Bank's loss of $740 million (Cummins, Lewis, and Wei 2006), the loss of $691 million due to rogue trading in Allfirst Financial, the Household Finance settlement charge of $484 million, the estimated loss of $140 million because of the September 11 attack on the Bank

of New York (Fontnouvelle et al. 2003). The blackout in New York City on August 14, 2003, is also an example of operational risk for institutions there due to "business disruption and system failures." Similarly, the August 1999 major earthquake in Turkey can fall under the same event definition.
2. Fontnouvelle et al. (2003) indicate that there were more than 100 events with operational losses exceeding $100 million in the last decade. In addition, many operational losses were not publicly announced, and many low-severity, high-frequency events do not get public attention.
3. For a clear discussion on other gains and problems, see Wahlström (2006).
4. For Japan, the leading events are "external fraud" and "execution, delivery and process management" events in terms of the number of losses. In addition, the concentration of losses is under the retail banking business line (Bank of Japan 2007).
5. For details on the measurement approaches, see BCBS (2006).
6. Both organizations provide bank-level data through their web pages: www.bddk.org.tr and www.tbb.org.tr, respectively.
7. The market index is called ISE100 and includes 100 firms traded on the Istanbul Stock Exchange.
8. The newspapers we used are *Hürriyet*, *Milliyet*, and *Sabah*. In terms of market share, these three papers have the lion's share. They can be accessed freely through these web addresses: www.hurriyet.com.tr, www.milliyet.com.tr, and www.sabah.com.tr.
9. An example is the internal fraud loss of about $13 million from a bank branch in Turkey in March 2008. Although the loss was publicly announced, the name of the financial institution name was not.
10. Note: We use the public announcement date as the event date.
11. Critical values are calculated from the distribution of D_k under the null hypothesis of homogeneous variance. One can use the critical values to obtain upper and lower boundaries to detect volatility shifts. For details on the ICSS algorithm and some uses, please see: Inclan and Chao (1994), Ewing and Malik (2005), Marcelo et al. (2008).
12. www.imkb.gov.tr.
13. We could say our experience or educated guess would be correct, and it could save a lot of time in this special case.
14. Since the 21-day window was sufficient to produce required information in earlier figures, we present CARs only for that specific event window.
15. The bankruptcies in the banking sector and the transfer of control to SDIF led investors and customers to view banks as having lower credibility around that time, and any information available became important.

REFERENCES

Bank of Japan. 2007. Results of the 2007 Operational Risk Data Collection Exercise. Planning and Coordination Bureau of the Financial Service Agency and Financial Systems and Bank Examination Department of the Bank of Japan.

Banking Regulation and Supervision Agency. 2005. *Türk Bankacılık Sistemi Basel II 2. Anket Çalışması Sonuçları* (Basel II second survey study results on the Turkish Banking System). Ankara, Turkey: BRSA.

Basel Committee on Banking Supervision (BCBS). 2006. *International Convergence of Capital Measurement and Capital Standards*, Bank for International Settlements.

Cummins J. D., C. M. Lewis, and R. Wei. 2006. The market value impact of operational loss events for U.S. banks and insurers. *Journal of Banking and Finance* 30, no. 10:2605–2634.

Ewing, B. T., and F. Malik. 2005. Re-examining the asymmetric predictability of conditional variances: The role of sudden changes in variance. *Journal of Banking and Finance* 29, no. 10:2655–2673.

Fontnouvelle, P., V. DeJesus-Rueff, J. Jordan, and E. Rosengren. 2003. Capital and risk: New evidence on implications of large operational losses. Working paper, Federal Reserve Bank of Boston.

Inclan, C., and G. C. Tiao. 1994. Use of cumulative sums of squares for retrospective detection of changes of variance. *Journal of the American Statistical Association* 89, no. 427:913–923.

Jarrow, R. A. 2008. Operational risk. *Journal of Banking and Finance* 32, no. 5: 870–879.

Marcelo, J. L. M., J. L. M., Quiros, and M. M. M. Quiros. 2008. Asymmetric variance and spillover effects: Regime shifts in the Spanish stock market. *Journal of International Financial Markets, Institutions and Money* 18, no. 1:1–15.

Özatay, F., and G. Sak. 2003. Banking sector fragility and Turkey's 2000–01 financial crisis. Discussion paper, Central Bank of the Republic of Turkey.

Wahlström, G. 2006. Worrying but accepting new measurements: The case of Swedish bankers and operational risk. *Critical Perspectives on Accounting* 17, no. 4:493–522.

Operational Risk Measurement: Quantitative Approaches

Integrating Op Risk into Total VaR

Niklas Wagner and Thomas Wenger

ABSTRACT

Operational risk (OpR) is the risk of losses at financial institutions due to the failure of internal processes, such as fraud, information technology failures, and lawsuits. The measurement of such risks poses several challenges in its own right: the scarcity of data and the skewness and kurtosis of typical loss distributions. In this chapter we focus on challenges and problems arising in the task of integrating a measure for OpR into an institution's total value at risk (VaR), along with measures for other risks such as market risk and credit risk. It turns out that many of the aspects that make the measurement of OpR difficult on a stand-alone basis also leave a trace in integrated risk measurement. We provide an approximation method for total VaR based on the Cornish-Fisher expansion. The proposed method of simulated higher moments (MSHM) approach continues to perform reasonably well in cases when the quality of the commonly used variance-covariance method deteriorates. In stylized examples, we also address the question of whether the diversification effect between risks can be expected to hold in the presence of OpR losses.

7.1   INTRODUCTION

To clarify the nature of the challenge in calculating an integrated VaR of a portfolio of loss variables $X_1, \ldots, X_N$, let us take as a starting point the square root (or variance-covariance) formula and consider the levels of knowledge with respect to the full multivariate loss distribution, the dependence structure, and the marginals. The square root formula proceeds as follows, based on the quantiles of the marginal loss distributions $VaR_\alpha(X_i)$, and the pairwise linear Pearson correlations between the marginals ρ_{ij}.[1] We fix a common confidence level α, for example 99%. The VaR of a loss variable, whether stand-alone or aggregate at a portfolio level, will then always refer to the quantile of the distribution of the loss variable at that confidence level.

In analogy to the variance-covariance formula for multivariate normal assets (or losses), the quantity $VaR(X_1 + X_2 + X_3)^2$ is calculated as

$$VaR(X_1)^2 + VaR(X_2)^2 + VaR(X_3)^2 + 2\rho_{12}\, VaR(X_1)\, VaR(X_2)$$
$$+ 2\rho_{13}\, VaR(X_1)\, VaR(X_3) + 2\rho_{23}\, VaR(X_2)\, VaR(X_3)$$

from which the total VaR itself is obtained by taking the square root. This approach is strictly valid in the case of multivariate normal risks. Note the following implications of this formula:

Implication 1. The total VaR in the case of independent risks is bounded above by the total VaR in the case of risks with a pairwise correlation of 1.

Implication 2. The total VaR is an increasing function in each of the pairwise correlations.

Implication 3. The total VaR is a function depending on the marginal VaRs and the pairwise correlations alone.

Implication 4. The total VaR is some function of marginal VaRs and the pairwise correlations, where the latter range freely in the interval $[-1;1]$ with no further restrictions between them.[2]

From a practical point of view, none of these implications seems strong or surprising; rather, they all seem intuitive. Clearly we are reluctant even to question them unless the need were to arise. However, the next example (Example 7 in Embrechts, McNeil, and Straumann 1999) shows that the implications are by no means valid for general classes of loss distributions.

Example (Pareto losses with tail coefficient <1):
Consider two copies X, Y of loss variables whose distribution is Pareto, given for $x \geq 1$ by $1 - x^{-1/2}$. This distribution is heavy tailed (already the first moment fails to be finite). In this case

$$VaR(X + Y) > VaR(X) + VaR(Y)$$

Since independence and comonotonicity are extreme cases of the dependence structure in any family connected by the bivariate Gaussian copula, this example provides a case where the aggregate VaR based on a Gaussian copula is not an increasing function of the Gaussian copula parameter.[3]

While the violation of I1 or I2 certainly feels wrong in the context of integrated risk management, where marginals can be reasonably assumed to have finite first moments, the possible violation of I3 or I4 is more remote.

We address the validity of implications I1 to I4 in the setup of integrated risk management for market, operational, and credit risk. We employ stylized forms of marginal loss distribution types and consider Gaussian and student-t copulas as dependence structures.

Widely shared common belief suggests the following.

Belief 1. Under practically relevant circumstances, the extreme behavior in the example does not occur; independence is always preferable to comonotonicity even with VaR as a risk measure.

Belief 2. In the tested range of parametrizations of the multivariate risk and the resulting aggregate loss, total VaR is indeed higher if pairwise correlations are higher.[4]

Belief 3. Total VaR is not in general a function of marginal VaRs and pairwise correlations alone. In particular, this fails in the presence of tail dependence between marginals.

Belief 4. The theoretical question of the existence of a functional form of total VaR in terms of marginal VaR, pairwise correlation, plus some extra set of variables—but with no imposed relations on the pairwise correlations—is not subject to intense debate. In practice, either the square root formula is applied or a simulation is run.

Our first contribution in this chapter is to provide distinct sets of circumstances where the beliefs can be validated; we find that in a certain minimalistic model setup for integrated risk management, which combines plausible marginals and dependence structure, interrisk diversification indeed holds in the sense that VaR increases when dependence gets stronger.

The second contribution is to provide an approximate method for the determination of the total VaR that requires less computational effort than a full Monte Carlo simulation but still produces results more reliable than the square root formula precisely when that formula tends to fail. The failure occurs mainly in the case where there is no functional expression for total VaR purely in terms of marginal VaR and linear correlation, for example, in the presence of tail dependence. We view this approximation as a first step toward functional expressions for total VaR on a semianalytical basis. The proposed approximation method consists of a

Cornish-Fisher expansion based on simulated higher cumulants of the aggregate loss distribution.

In Section 7.2, we review results from the literature and describe the basic problems in the definition and determination of total risk measures including OpR. In Section 7.3, we specify the MSHM approach to the approximation of the quantile of total loss. In Section 7.4, we provide simulation results, and Section 7.5 concludes.

7.2 A BRIEF REVIEW OF INTEGRATED RISK MANAGEMENT IN THE PRESENCE OF OPR

7.2.1 Stylized Facts on Typical Loss Distributions for OpR

The total loss distribution in a typical advanced measurement approach (AMA) model exhibits high skewness and kurtosis. In fact, fitting such distributions by means of translated Gamma distributions does not perform well at high quantiles (see, e.g., Embrechts, Frey, and McNeil 2005, 478). A better fit is obtained by distributions from the class of generalized Pareto distributions (GPD) (see Böcker and Klüppelberg 2007). These have heavy tails in the sense that only a finite number of moments exist. And it does happen in practice that the variance is no longer finite.

7.2.2 Subadditivity and Methods for the Calculation of a Total Risk Measure

We assume that models for marginal risk contributions are chosen in a way that satisfies basic compatibility requirements, such as calibration to a common risk horizon (e.g., one year).[5] It is known that counterintuitive consequences like those in the introductory fat-tailed example can be systematically avoided only if a coherent risk measure, such as expected shortfall, is employed. Specifically, VaR as a risk measure is generally not sub-additive when applied to a portfolio of risks, (i.e., a diversification benefit need not result when separate risks are aggregated into one). Also, the solutions for the problem of reallocation of risk capital are smooth mainly in the framework of expected shortfall.[6] However, financial institutions do not always employ such measures. Economic capital based on these measures would be higher than VaR-based capital. Hence, in particular, possibilities for the growth of business would be more severely limited. In practice, stand-alone market risk and credit risk are often measured on a VaR basis for risks. More recently, operational risk also is measured on a VaR basis in AMA models.

Counterexamples to subadditivity are limited in their severity. For loss variables X and Y and confidence levels $\alpha \leq u \leq 1$, there is the estimate (see Kiesel, Liebman, and Stahl 2007, 11):

$$\mathrm{VaR}_{\alpha}(X + Y) \leq \mathrm{VaR}_{u}(X) + \mathrm{VaR}_{1 + \alpha - u}(Y)$$

In case the marginals are not normal and/or the dependence structure is given by some (not necessarily Gaussian) copula, the square root formula from the introduction is not justified by theory. Its use is based mostly on its simplicity and the empirically observed fact that the formula tends to produce a value often not too far from the result of a full Monte Carlo simulation (see Böcker and Hillebrand 2007, Rosenberg and Schuermann 2005, as well as Morone, Cornaglia, and Mignola 2007).[7] When relying on the formula, Morone et al. point out that it is important to employ the correct quantity for the interrisk correlations. Assuming the validity of an estimated Gaussian or student-t copula as determinant of the dependence structure, it is not true that the interrisk correlations must coincide with the entries of the matrix specifying the copula, since there is a noneligible impact of the marginals on the pairwise Pearson correlations. In a simulation approach, we can eliminate this problem by calculating the correlation to be employed in the formula from the simulated joint losses. This allows for a consistent comparison of the various methods. Böcker and Hillebrand (2007) provide a method to calculate the correlation between market and credit risk directly (without simulation), assuming a joint normal factor model.[8]

7.2.3 Problems Arising for an Integrated Measurement

The failure of subadditivity applies to operational risks at various levels, for example, in an AMA model: in individual loss cells, across business lines, and across event types. The problem has been studied in detail, and upper bounds for aggregate risk have been obtained that are more conservative than the sum of VaRs across a portfolio of losses (see Embrechts and Puccetti 2006).

7.2.4 Marginal Increase of Risk Due to Extra Risk in General and OpR in Particular

In the case of comonotonic risks, it is known (see, e.g., Prop. 6.15 in Embrechts, Frey, and McNeil 2005) that VaR is strictly additive for all continuous and strictly increasing loss distributions. But as the introductory example shows, part of the problem is that the comonotonic case is not necessarily the worst case. We will be interested in finding sufficient conditions that rule out this kind of behavior. An optimistic guess is presented next.

7.2.5 Hypothesis

Assuming Gaussian dependence, the existence of the first moments for both marginals suffices to guarantee that the aggregate VaR is an increasing function of the copula parameter and in particular subadditivity of VaR holds. When restricted to marginal loss distributions that play a role for practical purposes, this guess does not seem to be in conflict with the available evidence—the notorious example from the introduction can be ruled out ad hoc. A modest goal is to provide classes of examples relevant for practical purposes that demonstrably are in the subadditive range.[9] We now review some cases of such conditions as well as numerical evidence from simulations.

Morone, Cornaglia and Mignola (2007) and Rosenberg and Schuermann (2005) put into practice a general framework of risk integration, proceeding by means of joining the typical marginals for OpR, market risk, credit risk, and others into a joint distribution with a Gaussian or student-t dependence structure. The authors arrive at aggregate losses in terms of VaR (and other measures) and calculate re-allocations of economic capital to the various sources of risk.[10] In all calculations in these papers, there arises a diversification benefit in the process of aggregating via VaR. Hence subadditivity is not violated in the numerical examples arising in these works. Many practitioners have confirmed these conclusions in various other settings and parametrizations. Going beyond mere numerical evidence, Danielsson, Jorgensen, Sarma, and deVries (2005) provide a class of examples where subadditivity can indeed be proved, both for independent and for dependent risks. Recall that the main example challenges even the monotonicity of the VaR as a function of the copula parameter in a Gaussian dependence structure. Hence, even the independent case is nontrivial for the question of subadditivity. However, Danielsson et al. consider only the situation of marginals with equal tail indices. In particular, these results do not apply in the case of risk integration involving, say, market risk modeled as normal and operational risk modeled as fat-tailed.

The problem of lack of subadditivity is particularly virulent in the modeling of OpR, even for stand-alone risk. This subject has been dealt with on a very comprehensive basis, and Embrechts, Neshlehova, and Wüthrich (2008) and Klüppelberg and Resnick (2008) prove subadditivity in a large class of models typical for OpR and in fact even characterize some classes of models by the subadditivity property. In Embrechts et al. (2008), under the assumption of Archimedean dependence structure and marginals regularly varying at infinity, a necessary condition for subadditivity is derived in terms of the index of variation at infinity. However, again the background assumption in both references is that marginals have the same tail indices.

The works mentioned so far do not provide proofs of subadditivity (in the sense of the hypothesis presented) in the case of marginals with different tail indices. This may be because the philosophy of producing models for aggregate risk based on Gaussian or other copula approaches is not distinguished by theoretical criteria[11] but only by practical considerations. Indeed, to actually prove subadditivity for unequal marginals, even in the case of Gaussian dependence structure, requires the marginals to be at least somewhat related to Gaussians, for formal manipulations and estimations to gain ground. This is indeed what happens in the theory of portfolio VaR with modified Weibull margins as presented by Malevergne and Sornette (2003), which we review in the next section.

7.2.6 Portfolio VaR with Modified Weibull Margins and Gaussian Dependence Structure

Malevergne and Sornette define a random variable X to have a modified Weibull distribution with parameters c, χ—denoted by $W(c, \chi)$ if the density is given by

$$p(x) = \frac{1}{2\sqrt{\pi}} \frac{c}{\chi^{c/2}} |x|^{c/2-1} \exp\left(-\frac{|x|^c}{\chi}\right)$$

In this two-parameter family of distributions, we find among others the Gaussian for $c = 2$ and distributions fatter than the exponential for $c < 1$.[12] Malevergne and Sornette prove this key fact about the family of modified Weibull distributions:

Theorem 7.1 Weighted sums of independent or comonotonic or (Gaussian copula) dependent modified Weibull distributions (equal or unequal) are equivalent in the tail to another modified Weibull distribution.

From this theorem it follows that VaR for a portfolio of modified Weibull assets (or losses) with Gaussian dependence is asymptotically subadditive (Malevergne and Sornette 2003). The proof of the theorem is far from immediate and requires extensive calculations with Gaussian integrals. A direct application of the theorem to the case of integration of risks is possible only for those margins that can reasonably be modeled as modified Weibull distributions. This includes market risk and all other risks that can be assumed to be normal. Including subexponential margins, also OpR can be reasonably modeled. The situation is less favorable for credit risk. It seems that the typical credit loss distributions do not lend themselves easily to an analytical treatment via those types of margins that interact well with Gaussian dependence structures. However, in their preliminary version, Rosenberg and Schuermann (2005) have employed a Weibull fit to represent the marginal credit risk (Rosenberg and Schuermann 2005) and found that "standard goodness of fit tests cannot reject the specification." From such a perspective, the observed fact that subadditivity of VaR holds in empirical models appears closer to being a demonstrable consequence of the theory of Malevergne and Sornette (2003): Within the limits of achievable adequacy of estimation of parameters, it is.[13]

7.3 CLOSED-FORM APPROXIMATION BASED ON MSHM IN THE MODERATELY HEAVY-TAILED CASE

7.3.1 Setup for OpR modeling

The questions raised by fat tails of loss distributions in single risk cells and potential lack of subadditivity of OpR-VaR also enter the topic of risk aggregation and the determination of total economic capital, across all risk types. From a different point of view, the problem is to quantify (or at least bound) the marginal increase of total VaR due to OpR.[14]

For the purpose of estimating integrated risk, it is reasonable to separate some of the risk cells making up OpR before obtaining an integrated OpR measure and to deal with the dependence structure of individual risk cells (or aggregates of some subset of all cells) with the other risk types separately. The reason is that wildly different types of dependencies are expected, depending on the nature of the OpR cell. For some cells, independence with all other risks is highly plausible; for other cells, there is a rationale to expect high correlation and even strong tail dependence. Some illustrative examples of this intuition result from considering typical OpR cases:

- Information technology failures in the event of crash events
- Lawsuits brought about by clients in the face of nonfavorable market movements
- External fraud

From such examples, it is plausible to assume that correlations between certain cells comprising OpR and other risks exist. They are pronounced in the case of market risk but rather negligible when it comes to credit risk.

In this chapter, we stop at this high-level observation and do not go into a higher resolution of the integrated risk measure.[15] We focus on presenting the effects of the functional dependence of total VaR on abstract model parameters. We do not aim at building a realistic joint risk model.

7.3.2 Setup for Aggregation

We deal with three types of stylized marginals that are distributed according to normal, generalized Pareto distributions (GPD) and the Vasicek large-portfolio limiting formula. And we take the dependence to be given by a student-t copula of arbitrary degree of freedom, d (hence including the Gaussian case for very large d). We chose the overall student-t dependence structure to demonstrate sensitivities in the presence of tail dependence. Strictly speaking, it is realistic only for pairs of risk types, not in total. In fact, none of the phenomena we discuss pertains to integrating three or more marginals in a critical way.[16]

The setup is chosen minimalistically to allow for our two contributions:

1. An approximation of total VaR that is sensitive to tail dependence—contrary to the square root formula
2. A (minimal) model specification in which total VaR can be expected to behave subadditively in the presence of non-normal margins

We consider an AMA model for OpR in which the tails are well approximated by a distribution that does have at least a sufficiently large number of finite higher moments—such as an appropriately chosen GPD. Operating under this assumption, and also assuming that we have described the dependence structure involving all risks by a suitable copula,[17] we can apply the Cornish-Fisher expansion to arrive at a closed-form approximation for the quantiles of the total loss distribution. To approximate the terms in the expansion (which are explicit functions of the cumulants or moments of the total loss distribution), we employ our copula model, which allows us to simulate arbitrary higher moments of the aggregate loss variable.

Recall that X is the aggregate loss variable with its quantile $q_\alpha(X)$ at confidence level α:[18]

$$X = X_1 + X_2 + X_3$$

based on marginal loss variables X_i whose distribution is known and whose dependence structure is described by a copula C—which we will in fact take to be a student-t copula. We denote the expectation and standard deviation of X by μ and σ respectively, and we assume them to be finite. We are interested in approximate closed formulas for $q_\alpha(X)$. Starting from the formal identity

$$\exp\left(\sum_{j=1}^{\infty} \frac{\kappa_j t^j}{j!}\right) = \sum_{j=0}^{\infty} \frac{E(X^j)t^j}{j!}$$

and putting $\mu_j := E((X - \mu)^j)$, we have the series of equations for the first three cumulants $\kappa_1 = \mu, \kappa_2 = \mu_2, \kappa_3 = \mu_3$, and then

$$\kappa_4 = \mu_4 - 3\mu_2^2, \kappa_5 = \mu_5 - 10\mu_3\mu_2$$

We may assume without loss of generality that X is normalized.[19] The terms of the Cornish-Fisher expansion for $q_\alpha(X)$ are explicitly known functions of the quantile $q = q_\alpha(\Phi)$ of the cumulative Gaussian distribution. We refer to Abramowitz and Stegun (1972) for more details on the facts discussed next.[20] In each step, one further cumulant enters, but the previous ones also produce various new contributions.

$$q + \frac{q^2 - 1}{6}\kappa_3 + \frac{q^3 - 3q}{24}\kappa_4 - \frac{2q^3 - 5q}{36}\kappa_3^2 + \frac{q^4 - 6q^2 + 3}{120}\kappa_5$$

$$-\frac{q^4 - 5q^2 + 2}{24}\kappa_3\kappa_4 + \frac{12q^4 - 53q^2 + 17}{324}\kappa_3^3$$

And the first term of the expansion involving κ_6 is

$$\frac{q^5 - 10q^3 + 15q}{720}\kappa_6 - \frac{3q^5 - 24q^3 + 29q}{384}\kappa_4^2 - \frac{2q^5 - 17q^3 + 21q}{180}\kappa_3\kappa_5$$

$$+\frac{14q^5 - 103q^3 + 107q}{288}\kappa_3^2\kappa_4 - \frac{252q^5 - 1688q^3 + 1511q}{7776}\kappa_3^4$$

The polynomials in q result from collecting terms in various sums of Hermite polynomials in q.

We then proceed to approximate the individual terms in this truncated expansion, which means we need to estimate the cumulants κ_j. By the list of formulas just given, this amounts to approximating the higher-centered moments μ_j of the aggregate loss, which in turn is accomplished by simulating from the copula, applying the marginals, and taking averages.[21]

There are numerous sources of error in this chain of approximations and estimations. But the method is explicit, and the number of simulations needed for a stable calculation of the higher moments is often smaller than the number of simulations required for the stable calculation of the quantile itself. In this chapter we deliberately invoke a modest target level of precision: We do not seek to reach the precision that is common in market risk, for example. If we did, the Cornish-Fisher expansion would be a doubtful choice, since its error margin and stability properties often are deemed unsuitable for the measurement of market VaR (see Jaschke 2001). But in our setting, the individual contributions of OpR and credit risk already are subject to a level of model risk, which by itself can exceed the error margins of the Cornish-Fisher expansion by orders of magnitude. We certainly do not recommend the expansion for practical use without further scrutiny; rather we employ it to provide a simple closed formula, which allows us to detect the sensitivity of total VaR with respect to the degree of tail dependence in the copula.

To the extent that we trust the result of the expansion (at a chosen given order), we have also answered the question of the existence of a functional form for total VaR. From the abstract perspective of Sklar's theorem, it follows that the sets of parameters that determine the marginals together with the correlation matrix and the degree of freedom of the student-t copula do determine uniquely the numerical value of the total VaR (at any confidence level), hence presenting total VaR as a function of these parameters. However, from this line of thought alone, it is not evident that such a (set-theoretic) function would even be continuous. While this is almost certainly the case in practice, the argument leaves open another, more important issue: Can such a function be cast in a form that contains the pairwise linear correlations, so that the question of monotonicity of total VaR in linear correlations can be meaningfully raised? Note that for this to hold, more is needed than for the (technically much simpler) question of whether total VaR is a monotone function of the copula parameters. And even the Cornish-Fisher expansion only suggests such a functional form without actually providing one, since the cumulants are not generally known to be expressible as functions of a set of variables containing pairwise correlations.

There is an "implicit" function issue here, whose clarification or explicit solution would be of practical use, even in special cases. The difficulty lies in finding a functional expression that would contain linear correlations as free parameters, not subject to relations with other parameters determining the copula or the marginals. While explicit expressions are always going to be difficult to obtain here, in the case of copulas richer than Gaussian, such functional expressions may even fail to exist altogether—at least this appears to be an open problem.

7.3.3 Sensitivity to Tail Dependence: When the Square Root Formula Performs Poorly

Going back to the square root formula, we recall one of its basic systematic weaknesses: Linear correlations are the only information it picks up about the dependence structure, but linear correlations are known to be insufficient to fully determine the dependence structure. Hence, there is an a priori element of necessary oversimplification when the square root formula is used. Thus, the question of whether the approximation it provides happens to be good enough is a practical question.

While there may be various sources of inaccuracy of the square root formula from a theoretical point of view, one way to produce an example of its shortcoming is to link marginals by means of a copula with explicitly built-in tail dependence, such as a student-t copula with relatively small degree of freedom and hence high coefficient of tail dependence.[22] It has been verified in simulations (see, e.g., Böcker and Spielberg 2005; Rosenberg and Schuermann 2005; Morone, Cornaglia, and Mignola 2007) that in the presence of tail dependence (small, "finite" degree of freedom of the student-t copula, as opposed to the infinite degrees of freedom of the Gaussian copula), the square root formula no longer performs well. It is very plausible that this happens because the quantiles of the total loss are influenced not only by linear correlations but are also increasing in the level of tail dependence. In fact, it seems highly plausible that this holds generally;[23] in this case, it is clear that aggregate VaR is a set-theoretic function of the degree of freedom, when a correlation matrix underlying the student-t copula is held fixed. The issue of separating free and dependent variables still exists in this case, but we are not trying to hold linear correlations of marginals fixed; in fact, they are slightly affected by a change of degree of freedom (even when the matrix specifying the copula is held constant), but this variation is very small.[24]

The a priori reason why the Cornish-Fisher expansion has a chance to sidestep these shortcomings is because it is explicitly sensitive to the mixed terms in the expectations of the binomial expansion of powers of the random variables representing total loss $X = X_1 + \cdots + X_N$.

It is the expectations of these mixed monomials that generalize the terms defining linear correlation and that are hence in excellent position to pick up more of the tail dependence introduced by the copula. Short of an analytic derivation of the precise sensitivity, we establish numerically that the higher moments of the total loss, and hence the cumulants, and hence the terms in the Cornish-Fisher expansion, are strongly sensitive to the level of tail dependence.

This is done[25] by varying the degree of freedom of a student-t copula while keeping its underlying matrix fixed. In the next section we describe a particular parametrization in which the phenomenon is highly visible and which is practically reasonable.

7.4 SIMULATION RESULTS

7.4.1 Specification of the Stylized Models for Marginal Risks

We model market risk by a Gaussian, credit risk by the Vasicek distribution, and OpR by a GPD. The first question to consider is the range of parameters for these marginals to choose from. Since we are not interested in an overall sensitivity analysis, only in the study of the impact of assumptions about the correlation structure and the impact of the numerical or analytical method to estimate aggregate quantiles, we only need to make sure that the parametrization is in line with conditions of practical relevance. To achieve this, we reason in this way: We put relative weights on the marginal risks to ensure that the proportion is realistic. We take this to mean that stand-alone credit risk covers half of the sum of the stand-alone VaRs. The remaining half is split evenly between market risk and OpR. As a second assumption, we ignore the choice of mean of the Gaussian, leaving only its variance as a free parameter, or equivalently (since market risk is modeled as normal), its VaR itself. The scale parameter of the GPD has the same impact as the weight assigned to the GPD in the portfolio of losses, so there is only the shape parameter to be chosen freely for the GPD. In line with practical estimates in the fitting to loss distributions in actual AMA models, it is taken as low as possible, leading to highly skewed and leptokurtic distributions. In examples where we need to gain some numerical stability with the estimation of moments, however, we take it high enough to ensure the existence of the first few moments of the GPD. From these assumptions, it follows that fixing the parameters for the credit loss distribution is in fact enough to fix the others. We choose the parameters PD and asset correlation for the Vasicek distribution to be in the midrange of the Basel II calibration of models, with a PD of 1% and asset correlations of 5%. From the relative weighting of credit VaR to the stand-alone VaR for market risk we solve for the variance for market risk. The shape parameter and the weight of the GPD are adjusted so that the stand-alone OpR for VaR remains fixed at half of the credit VaR and equal to the market VaR.

The result of this "stylization" of parameters leaves us with altering only the correlation matrix and the degree of freedom of the student-t copula by linking the marginals. All other choices of parameters are set in a range that does not contradict practical experience. We do not introduce any explicit calibration to loss amounts in a given currency, since none of the questions we address is sensitive to the total size of the losses, but only to their relative size with respect to the marginal losses. We do not study the sensitivity with respect to the parametrization of the marginals in this chapter.

7.4.2 Simulation Method

The numerical approximation is performed by means of the quasi–Monte Carlo (qMC) method, (see, e.g., Glasserman 2004) instead of ordinary Monte Carlo. This is feasible since there are a priori grounds to expect the qMC method to perform well, due to the low problem dimension: In our simulation or numerical integration procedure, we encounter only a few loss variables and a copula depending on a small number of parameters. Instead of drawing points in $[0,1]^D$ according to a product of uniform distributions and then applying the inverse transform method, we fill the unit hypercube—of prespecified, fixed, low-dimension D (unrelated to the degree of freedom of our student-t copula)—with a deterministic set of points of low discrepancy. We pick a Halton sequence. We do not determine the size or validity of error bounds for the qMC method; instead we observe that the result of the qMC calculation of the total loss stabilizes within small relative errors for a wide range of parametrizations, with a point set of at least 5,000 members, and a significant portion of a Gaussian margin in the total loss.[26] This speed of convergence exceeds by far the straightforward Monte Carlo approach.

To ensure that the qMC results stabilize in the range between 5,000 and 10,000 evaluations, with a GPD present among the marginals, it is necessary to take the shape parameter of the GPD high enough, thus ensuring the existence of the first few moments of the GPD. Without this assumption, there is no hope (not even a theoretical possibility) to attain stable results for the first higher moments or cumulants of the stand-alone GPD itself, although the cumulants of the total loss may still (and do) stabilize (and even quickly) due to a smoothening effect of the Gaussian representing market risk.

7.4.3 Description of Numerical Results

In the simulations, we compare the results for the quantiles of the aggregate loss at the fixed confidence level $\alpha=99\%$[27] for the three methods:

1. We calculate the result of the square root formula.

2. We look at the various truncations of the expansion (i.e., we truncate into the first few partial sums that contain the first occurrences of the cumulants).
3. We calculate the quantile of the qMC simulation of the total loss. The result of this computation serves as a benchmark, at least for a high enough number of evaluation points.

We distinguish the different approximation methods as different curves in the plots Figures 7.1 to 7.4; the plots show the dependence of the total VaR on one isolated quantity, with all others fixed.
We investigate these parameters:

■ In Figure 7.1, the entries of the correlation matrix are increased from 0 to 1.
■ In Figure 7.2, the number of degrees of freedom is increased from 2 (high level of tail dependence) to 200 (almost Gaussian copula).
■ In Figure 7.3, the shape parameter of the OpR distribution is varied between 4 and 12 while keeping the fraction of stand-alone OpR-VaR and stand-alone credit-VaR at $^1/_4$.
■ Figure 7.4 the number of points in the qMC method is increased from 5,000 to 10,000.

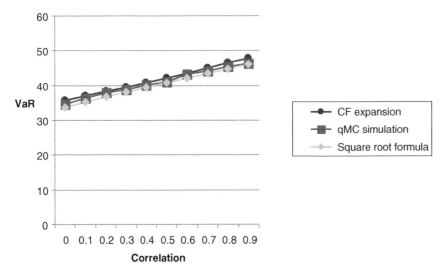

FIGURE 7.1 Impact of Correlation on Total VaR

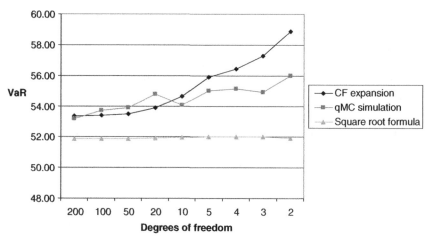

FIGURE 7.2 Impact of Tail Dependence on VaR

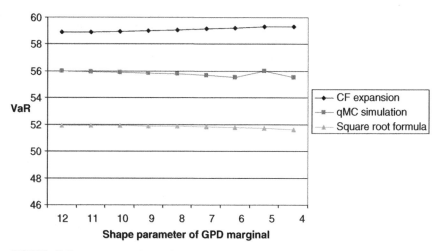

FIGURE 7.3 Fattening the Tail

The interpretation of the plots follows.

When varying the correlation matrix in Figure 7.1, we fix the degrees of freedom at 200, hence we are dealing basically with a Gaussian copula. We increase the matrix entries uniformly from 0 to 1. Independent of the calculation method chosen, the measured total VaR strictly increases (even roughly linearly) when the matrix entries increase. This is in line with results

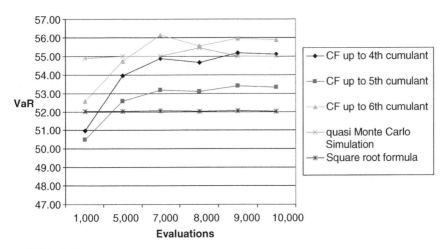

FIGURE 7.4 Stability of qMC Simulation

in the literature (Morone, Cornaglia and Mignola 2007; Rosenberg and Schuermann 2005), and it nicely confirms Implications 1 and 2 and Beliefs 1 and 2. In Figures 7.2 to 7.4, we fix the correlation matrix to have pairwise entries of 50%.

The main point of the chapter can be seen in Figure 7.2. The square root formula is blind with respect to the possible presence of tail dependence between marginals. The Cornish-Fisher expansion, on the contrary, "sees" the impact of the tail dependence via the increased higher moments of the total loss that are forced by extreme comovements of the marginals. In this simulation, we set the shape parameter equal to 12.

In Figure 7.3, changing the shape parameter of the GPD describing OpR amounts to amplifying the source for potentially severe high-impact losses. In our examples, we leave the stand-alone VaR for OpR unchanged. Hence, the change of parameter amounts to fattening the tails of the OpR marginal loss. Consequently, we expect little or no impact in the square root formula approximation. For the Cornish-Fisher expansion or simulation, we might expect an impact in the presence of tail dependence: with the same stand-alone OpR for VaR, total VaR might be higher when the OpR margin has a fatter tail, because then the effect of the comoving tail events could get amplified. However, as Figure 7.3 shows, we do not quite find this. Instead, we find that the shape parameter has little impact on VaR, while there is a clear difference in VaRs calculated according to the three different methods. We have fixed the degree of freedom at 2 here, so that a pronounced tail dependence is present. The significance of the choice of calculation method is evident: The square root formula consistently underestimates the simulated VaR, for a wide range of shape parameters. So far we have no systematic reason for the smallness of the impact of fat OpR tails on total VaR. As the stability of the qMC simulation and the Cornish-Fisher expansion deteriorates for small shape parameters (since then the OpR marginal does not strictly speaking have any well-defined Cornish-Fisher expansion at all), there may be a wealth of nontrivial interaction or cancellation taking place in the limiting process, visible only at a much higher level of resolution.

In Figure 7.4, even when calculating the total VaR by means of the square root formula, we need the simulation output to a small extent. The linear correlation of the marginals is obtained only after the simulation. It is not equal to the respective copula matrix parameter, not even in the Gaussian case. However, the correct estimate is obtained already at a very small number of evaluations (even less than 1,000 would easily suffice). The stability of the Cornish-Fisher expansion as well as the direct simulation of the quantile itself is satisfactory when at least 5,000 evaluations are made, in the sense that relative errors diminish rapidly. This is shown in Figure 7.4 for the degree of freedom equal to 5.

There is no guarantee that the expansion will track the simulation more closely than the square root formula for all possible parametrizations. And in fact, this is not the case. But our main point is that the square root formula cannot pick up any information about tail dependence and hence fails miserably when tail dependence is present. This is demonstrated by the numerical example in Figure 7.2 and again in Figure 7.3, where the tails of the marginals are fattened in addition to tail dependence. Furthermore, there is also no guarantee that a later truncation of the Cornish-Fisher expansion will always track the simulated quantile more closely than an earlier truncation. There are parametrizations where the shorter formula (which requires less computation) provides a better approximation. This happens in fact in Figure 7.4, where the simplest truncation of the expansion happens to be closest to the qMC result. The precise study of the accuracy and speed of (or even lack of) convergence in relation to parametrizations is beyond the scope of this chapter and is dealt with elsewhere. It strongly depends on the range and relative size of the parameter values.

7.5 CONCLUSION

We conclude by pointing out questions and problems that have not been addressed here but that should be borne in mind in applications. We plan to deal with some of these issues in more detail in future work.

The possible failure of subadditivity of VaR is known to disappear as soon as we choose to measure integrated risk by expected shortfall instead of value at risk.[28] However, not all financial institutions favor expected shortfall (or any coherent risk measure) in their integrated approach to risk measurement. Nor does the regulator always encourage such risk measures. For the individual risk measure in market and credit risk, the capital charges are based on VaR, not on a coherent risk measure. Our analysis shows that subadditivity of VaR is a subtle property exhibiting a rich interaction with the whole multivariate risk profile. While it may be true that the property holds for most practically relevant risk models, it does so by virtue of facts that result from the actual structure of risk models (most favorably normal or student-*t* factor models), and it is not easily deducible in a copula-building block approach. For this reason, to have valid upper bounds for aggregate risk remains an important and nontrivial feature of a risk model. Coherent risk measures provide a fallback solution.

One should also bear in mind that the calculation of quantiles of integrated loss distributions is subject to considerable model risk, as is the quantity to balance such quantiles: the various tiers of capital and risk-taking capacities. When it comes to matching high quantiles of total loss with equity and its surrogates, we are not strictly speaking in a situation where reference to balance sheet data makes good sense: Reasons include the risk horizon and its possible lack of synchronicity with reporting frequencies and, more importantly, because it is a very bold idealization to view balance sheet (or other) specifications of risk-taking capacities as independent from loss events. They clearly are not. It suffices to include matters of liquidity in the assessment to find the illusory nature of such an idealization.[29] The task of matching risk-taking capacity dynamically to a measure of integrated risk—which would crucially also have to contain business risk and liquidity risk—is highly nontrivial, while at the same time clearly necessary, in particular in light of recent market events (see International Institute of Finance 2008). This fact stresses the need to arrive at integrated models for the total loss distribution that allow for scenario-specific or conditional approaches. And if such scenario-specific and conditional measurements are possible with the chosen model, they may contain even more information and be more reliable than an approach based on an abstractly computed expected shortfall. The main goal of risk management is the calculation of conditional total VaR even under exogenously specified scenarios—employing an econometric model. The value of such calculation, if it succeeds, even exceeds the value of knowledge of expected shortfall, because the scenario-based calculation works through a more profound wealth of information. Also, in a scenario-based approach that includes various different choices of confidence levels, the shortcomings arising from possible extra modes in (local, desk-wise) loss densities disappear. The problem is that such an approach relies on econometric models whose reliability is well founded only for market risk.

It would be helpful to have a theoretical reasoning behind the close fit that the square root formula often provides as well as a fully conceptual characterization of when it fails. Part of the answer may be contained in a systematic study of the conditions under which the Cornish-Fisher expansion performs well in a distributional setup such as the one under study here.

NOTES

1. In this chapter, we will take $i = 1, 2, 3$ corresponding to market, operational and credit risk, respectively.
2. In particular: Their individual range of values is unrestricted, the range of pairs of values is unrestricted, and, finally, all possible triples of pairs of values are allowed. None of these "freedoms" is trivial (or even true) from a theoretical perspective.
3. When forming a multivariate distribution by linking marginals with a Gaussian copula, the linear correlation of the marginals is not in general equal to the copula parameter, but it can still be reasonably expected to be an increasing function of the copula parameter. While, in general, comonotonic risks need not have correlation 1, they do if their distribution is additionally assumed to be of the same type. Since in the text example we take two copies of the same distribution, it would seem that we have in particular a case where total VaR is not an increasing function of linear correlation. This, however, is a statement that we cannot even meaningfully make, because correlations are not well defined due to the infinite moments of the distribution in the example.
4. However, not the full range of correlation matrices is obtainable.
5. This common calibration forces a considerable amount of model risk, since it implies that market and credit risk must be dealt with on the same time scale, which clearly impedes the quality of their respective parametrizations.
6. In fact, if VaR is used for the allocation of risk capital on the level of business lines or trading desks—as opposed to preaggregated types of risks as in this chapter—then it is known that incentive schemes do not work as desired: The possibility of multimodal loss distributions "hiding" high-but-unlikely losses below the threshold of the confidence level cannot be counteracted effectively when VaR is used as a risk measure. However, this difficulty is related to the generation of deliberately influenced loss densities. For the purpose of aggregating across risk types—remote from incentive schemes for purposefully acting business lines—worrying about such difficulties with VaR may be unnecessary.
7. To be sure, to know the quality of this formula as an approximation, one has to first carry out the simulation.

8. In our approach based on the Cornish-Fisher expansion, another option is to rely directly on historical loss series to estimate the moments of the aggregate loss distribution and thereby do entirely without estimation of the dependence structure as specified by a parametric copula.

9. This is a much weaker goal than trying to make specific claims about the worst-case upper bound in the terminology of the Frechet problem as in Embrechts, Frey, and McNeil (2005), because we freely allow assumptions to be made on the copula, even that it be Gaussian.

10. The dependence structure is estimated by maximum likelihood techniques based on dependence measures like Kendall's τ, similar to the procedure described in Embrechts, Frey, and McNeil (2005), Example 5.59.

11. See Mikosch (2005) for arguments showing that theoretical considerations can sometimes even work against copula models and Shaw (2007) for arguments why dependence modeling is ideally carried out with a universe of stochastic differential equations (SDEs) in the background—which are not always easy to come up with in practice.

12. There are further modifications that lead to nonzero means. But the focus of the theory is on the asymptotic tail behavior, so the means are of minor importance.

13. Also, the difficulty on an analytical level may diminish at a closer look, and a feasible approach for an analytical proof of diversification results emerges even without the strength of the theory of modified Weibull margins when we look at the structure of joint (normal) factor models, as in Böcker and Hillebrand (2007), instead of sticking to the (a priori questionable) quick fix of separating marginals and dependence by one overall copula. In fact, in Böcker and Hillebrand, it turns out naturally that in a joint normal factor model for market and credit risk (where credit risk is modeled by the Vasicek distribution, e.g.), the copula describing the dependence structure is automatically Gaussian. In such a model setup, there is a much better chance that subadditivity strictly results from the axioms. We return to this in future work, but for the moment we just note that simulation in the range of practically relevant parametrizations suggests even a linear dependence of VaR on correlation (see Figure 7.1 plot P1), so that the analytical proof is mainly of theoretical interest—and highly supported by evidence.

14. Rosenberg and Schuermann (2005) assert that the sensitivity with respect to copula choice (in a Gaussian or student-t model) is small, whereas the sensitivity with respect to the a priori weight of a loss category is high. Morone, Cornaglia, and Mignola (2007) fix the degree of freedom (and hence the level of tail dependence) in the student-t copula, taking 3 degrees of freedom throughout. Rosenberg and Schuermann (2005) consider a range between 3 and 10 of possible degrees of freedom; however, the assumption of one global degree of freedom (and one overall student-t copula) is implausible, since the level of tail dependence varies considerably among pairs of risk types, thus leading to a distortion in the estimation of the remaining copula parameters if uniformity of the degree of freedom is taken for granted. We do not deal with the theoretically and practically difficult problem of parametrization of the dependence structure in this chapter.

15. If we were to split up the specification of the total dependence structure according to all cells making up OpR, this would quickly lead to a scarcity of data, hence adding to the difficulty of parametrization of multivariate modeling efforts.

16. For the purpose of building an overall risk model, one has to pass to a nested structure of copulas, because a student-t copula admits only one global degree of freedom governing tail dependences, whereas in practice, not all pairs of marginal risks can be expected to have tail dependence to the same degree. The study of nested copulas leads to a set of questions and problems quite different from what we study here; parametrization is very difficult, and questions of gluing copulas consistently are nontrivial even theoretically. We will not touch on this subject any further, mentioning only that both problems are (trivially) absent in the case of adding an independent marginal.

17. "Suitable" means in particular that we have a means available to simulate from it; this makes it difficult to use the empirical copula itself, since it will generally be highly impractical to simulate from it: Already the errors introduced by discretization and/or interpolation based on historical time series of losses are likely to be so large that the advantage of empirical adequacy may be more than offset. To be sure, this is a general difficulty in building integrated models for total risk. It exists whether we proceed by means of a copula or with a joint factor model; only the way we deal with it technically changes with the chosen approach. This inevitability is a practical consequence of Sklar's theorem: We may not like the problem of estimating parameters in a copula, but even if we had built a factor model, the truth is—by Sklar's theorem—that we are estimating some copula, namely the empirical one.

18. If F denotes the cumulative distribution of X, then $q_\alpha(X) = F^{-1}(\alpha)$.

19. This means we may assume $\mu = 0$ and $\sigma = 1$, after transforming X into a normalized variable by passage to $X' := (X - \mu)/\sigma$ which leads to $\mu'_j = \frac{\mu_j}{\sigma_j}$ and using the equation $q_\alpha(X) = q_\alpha(X')\sigma + \mu$ to transform back to the searched quantile.

20. The iterative structure and in particular the counting of the order of the expansion is transparent only in the context of its application to the estimation of quantiles of a sample of independent and identically distributed (i.i.d.) random variables, since the order in the expansion is related to the sample size (unequal to N above in our context). Nevertheless, we keep the truncation pattern of the expansion, in order to maintain the best possible chance that the approximation will improve on inclusion of more terms.

21. The proposed procedure can be carried out even without first specifying a copula, by estimating the moments or cumulants directly from historical loss data. While this would be a much faster method, in most cases it is not to be expected that joint time series of losses are available that would lead to a sufficiently conservative dependence structure. To put it another way: In the process of estimating a copula from data, it is advisable to emphasize extremal comovements (this is part of the rationale for the choice of student-t copula) and possibly accept a lesser quality of overall fit to the data. If the first priority

is given to fitting the (possibly very short-length) data, a very mild correlation structure may result, suggesting a misleading level of diversification effects. In the practical parametrization of the dependence structure, this consideration is only one out of several trade-offs that require resolution.

22. We do not need the explicit relation between tail dependence coefficient and degree of freedom in the case of a student-t copula. See Embrechts, Frey, and McNeil (2005) Example 5.33, p. 211.

23. At the same time, again, even in the (analytically most manageable) case of modified Weibull distributions, to analytically derive such sensitivities is far from simple, and it is not in the literature, to our knowledge.

24. This variation is an interesting subject for study in its own right, because it appears in numerical examples that the linear correlation of marginals may even slightly decrease with increasing level of tail dependence and everything else held fixed. We have not found systematic reasons for this phenomenon yet, but it clearly casts doubt on the square root formula of an even more basic kind than failure to capture the quantile: The quantile according to the square-root formula is not even guaranteed to qualitatively behave well with respect to tail dependence.

25. Employing Embrechts, Frey, and McNeil (2005) Example 5.33, p. 211.

26. This has a considerable smoothening effect and stabilizes the calculation of the moments of the aggregate loss. The stand-alone approximation of nonnormal marginals like GPDs or Vasicek distributions requires much more points, even though the required number of points generally increases with problem dimension for qMC. We do not study this interplay in any quantitative way here.

27. At a different confidence level, the interpretation of the speed of convergence has to be adjusted.

28. Unfortunately, for that to be feasible, we need to know finiteness of expected shortfall first, and the example from the introduction is problematic in that case as well.

29. An example is provided by large losses from defaults. The assumption that, in the worst case, these eat into equity may not be conservative. Even within the risk horizon, the worst case may be worse than that, if funding costs increase as liquidity dries up.

REFERENCES

Abramowitz, M., and I. A. Stegun. 1972. *Handbook of mathematical functions.* New York: Dover Publications.

Boecker, K., and M. Hillebrand. 2007. Interaction of market and credit risk: An analysis of inter risk correlation and risk aggregation. www-m4.ma.tum.de/Papers/.

Boecker, K., and C. Klueppelberg. 2007. Economic capital modeling and Basel II: Compliance in the banking industry. www-m4.ma.tum.de/Papers/.

Boecker, K., and H. Spielberg. 2005. Risikoaggregation mit Kopulas. *Die Bank* 8, no. 3:56–69.

Danielsson, J., B. N. Jorgensen, B. Sarma, and C. G. deVries. 2005. Sub-additivity re-examined: The case for value at risk. Preprint EURANDOM, Eindhoven, Netherlands.

Embrechts, P., and G. Puccetti. 2006. Bounds for functions of dependent risks. *Finance and Stochastics* 10, no. 3:341–352.

Embrechts, P., A. McNeil, and D. Straumann. 1999. Correlation and dependence in risk management: Properties and pitfalls. Working paper, Swiss Federal Institute of Technology, Zürich (ETH), Zurich.

Embrechts, P., J. Neshlehova, and M. V. Wuethrich. 2008. Additivity properties of value at risk under Archimedean dependence and heavy tailedness. Working paper, Swiss Federal Institute of Technology, Zürich (ETH), Zurich.

Glasserman, P. 2004. *Monte Carlo methods in financial engineering*. New York: Springer.

Jaschke, S. 2001. The Cornish-Fisher approximation in the context of delta-gamma-normal approximations. Working paper, Humboldt University, Berlin.

International Institute of Finance. 2008. Interim report of the IIF committee on market best practices. www.iasplus.com/crunch/0804iifbestpractices.pdf.

Klueppelberg, C., and S. I. Resnick. 2008. The Pareto copula, aggregation of risks and the emperor's socks. *Journal of Applied Probability* 45, no. 1:67–84.

Kiesel, R., T. Liebmann, and G. Stahl. 2007. Mathematical framework for integrating credit and market risk. University of Ulm, Germany.

Malevergne, Y., and D. Sornette. 2003. "VaR efficient portfolios for a class of super- and sub-exponentially decaying asset return distribution." http://arxiv.org/abs/physics/0301009.

McNeil, A., R. Frey, and P. Embrechts. 2005. *Quantitative risk management: Concepts, techniques, tools*. Princeton, NJ: Princeton University Press.

Mikosch, T. 2005. Copulas: Tales and facts. www.defaultrisk.com.

Morone, M., A. Cornaglia, and G. Mignola. 2007. Economic capital assessment via copulas: Aggregation and allocation of different risk types. www.defaultrisk.com.

Rosenberg, J. V., and T. Schuermann. 2005. A general approach to risk management with skewed, fat tailed risks. www.defaultrisk.com. Working paper version 5.

Rosenberg, J. V., and T. Schuermann. 2005. A general approach to risk management with skewed, fat tailed risks. Staff report No. 185, Federal Reserve Bank of New York. Working paper version 2004.

Shaw, W. T. 2007. *Dependency without copulas or ellipticity*. London: King's College.

CHAPTER 8

Importance Sampling Techniques for Large Quantile Estimation in the Advanced Measurement Approach

Marco Bee and Giuseppe Espa

ABSTRACT

In most cases, in the advanced measurement approach, the loss distribution cannot be obtained in closed form, so that probabilities of losses exceeding a given monetary amount have to be computed by means of simulation techniques. If this probability is small, importance sampling is the most efficient method. In this chapter we show how to choose optimally the importance sampling density in the compound Poisson setup under different hypotheses for the severity distribution.

8.1   INTRODUCTION

The measurement and management of operational risk have experienced a rapid growth in the last few years. The main reason probably has been increased regulatory pressure, witnessed by the explicit introduction of this type of risk in the New Basel Capital Accord (Basel 2005). The most sophisticated approach listed by the Basel II Accord is the so-called Advanced Measurement Approach (AMA), which is typically adopted by the largest banks. Roughly speaking, it allows banks to build their own internal models, similar to what happens for the measurement of market and credit risk. From the methodological point of view, however, operational risk is based on different techniques, mainly because losses are not related to financial grounds.

The actuarial methodology, with particular reference to the techniques of the non–life insurance field, plays a key role for the measurement of operational risk. The reason is twofold:

1. It has been observed empirically that the distribution of operational losses is similar to the distribution of claims.
2. As will be seen later, both types of losses are caused by the joint impact of two random sources, respectively called *frequency* and *severity*.

Although the methodology used for the estimation of loss distributions in non–life insurance has a long tradition (see, e.g., Mikosch 2004 for a review), the aims pursued in the two fields of applications are substantially different. Insurance companies need to predict the amount of losses in order to determine the premium to be charged to customers, which is usually modeled as a function of the expected value of the loss distribution (see Mikosch 2004, section 3.1.3). Operational risk managers are interested in risk measures, which in turn are related mostly to tail events.

The most commonly used risk measure is the Value at Risk (VaR). Referring the reader to the next section for precise definitions and references, let us recall that the VaR at confidence level α is the smallest number l such that the probability that the loss Y exceeds y is no larger than $(1 - \alpha)$; in other words, the VaR is the α quantile of the loss distribution Y. One possible way of estimating VaR is Crude Monte Carlo (CMC) simulation. This approach requires the simulation of a large number (say, B) of random numbers from the distribution of Y; the CMC estimator of the α quantile is simply the α quantile of the simulated distribution. The law of large numbers ensures that this estimator is consistent, but its variance increases dramatically as α gets small. Some analytical details concerning this problem are given in the next section; for the moment, to get a hint of what happens, consider the next simulation experiment.

Example 8.1   Let the severity be denoted by the random variable $W \sim$ Logn (1.5, 3), where Logn (μ, σ^2) denotes the Lognormal distribution with parameters μ and σ^2. Figure 8.1a shows VaR figures, for confidence levels between 99 and 99.995%, obtained by means of CMC simulation. As in this simplified example the functional form of the density is indeed known,

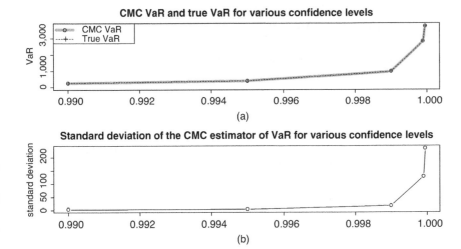

FIGURE 8.1 Crude Monte Carlo VaR Estimates and Standard Deviations

the quantile can also be computed integrating numerically the density: in the graph, the result of the latter approach is termed "true VaR." Figure 8.1b shows an estimate of the standard error of the CMC estimator, obtained by repeating 500 times the simulation procedure just above and computing the standard deviation of the results of the 500 replications.

From the graphs it can be seen that the estimator remains essentially unbiased as α increases, but its standard deviation quickly becomes unacceptably large. The preceding example was purposely kept simple enough to allow a comparison between the "true" VaR and the CMC VaR; it should be clear that simulation would not be needed at all. In the following section we will move to the standard Poisson mixture setup used in operational risk management, where the density of the loss distribution is almost invariably unknown and simulation techniques are often the only possibility of computing risk measures.

Section 8.2 of the chapter formalizes the Poisson mixture model commonly used in the AMA and introduces some basic results concerning importance sampling and MC simulation for heavy-tailed distributions. Sections 8.3 and 8.4 develop importance sampling techniques for the estimation of tail probabilities respectively for the Poisson-Lognormal and the Poisson-Pareto mixtures. In Section 8.5 we give, for both distributional assumptions, examples based on simulated data. Section 8.6 concludes and outlines possible directions for future research.

8.2 PRELIMINARIES: POISSON MIXTURES AND IMPORTANCE SAMPLING

8.2.1 Loss Distributions in the Advanced Measurement Approach

In any field of risk management, a precise identification of the most appropriate techniques for VaR estimation can be performed only after defining the loss distribution. Thus, the main object of interest to the risk manager is the loss distribution; in the AMA, similarly to the actuarial approach, it usually belongs to the family of *compound distributions*.

Definition 8.1 The total loss Y over a predetermined time horizon is given by the random sum

$$Y = \sum_{i=1}^{K} W_i \tag{8.1}$$

where K = random variable with a counting distribution
          $W_1, \ldots, W_k = i.i.d.$ continuous positive random variables, also independent from K

The corresponding cumulative distribution function (cdf) is

$$F_Y(x) = P(Y \le x)$$
$$= \sum_{k=0}^{\infty} p_k P(Y \le x | K = k)$$
$$= \sum_{k=0}^{\infty} p_k F_W^{*k}(x)$$

where $p_k = P(K = k)$
     $F_W^{*k}(x) = k$-fold convolution of the cdf of W (McNeil, Frey, and Embrechts, 2005, section 10.2.2)

The two random variables K and W have an easy interpretation: K represents the *frequency* of losses (i.e., the number of losses during the time period under analysis), whereas W is the *severity* of the losses (the *magnitude*, measured by the monetary amount, of the losses).

The joint distribution of K and W is usually analytically intractable. Often even the conditional distribution of $(Y|K = k)$, which is just a deterministic sum of k random variables, does not admit a simple form; for example, the density of the sum is unknown both when the W_i's are Lognormal and when they are Pareto.

Fortunately, however, simulating Equation 8.1 is straightforward as long as we are able to simulate K and W. The procedure for simulating a value from Y consists of two steps:

1. Simulate a random number from the distribution of K, and call k^* the value obtained.
2. Simulate k^* random numbers from the distribution of W and sum them up.

Repeating a large number of times B these two steps, one obtains a Monte Carlo approximation of the loss distribution. The VaR is just given by the α quantile of the simulated distribution: $VaR_\alpha = \inf\{y \in \mathbb{R} : P(Y > y) \leq 1 - \alpha\}$, with $\alpha \in (0, 1)$.

8.2.2 Importance Sampling and Cross-Entropy

The procedure outlined in the preceding subsection always allows one to obtain a consistent estimator of the VaR, but for small α, the instability problems pointed out in Example 1 become serious, unless the sample size is huge.

The Basel II Accord prescribes a 99.9% confidence level for the VaR, but many banks use a level as large as 99.95 or even 99.99%. For these values, the aforementioned difficulties become very relevant. To deal with these types of issues, several variance reduction techniques are available in the literature; among them, importance sampling is one of the most effective.

To begin with, consider that most of the applications where stochastic simulation is used can be expressed as a definite integral. Let X be a random variable defined on some probability space $(\Omega, \Im, P)$, and assume that it is absolutely continuous with density f; moreover, let h be a known function. In such a setup, we evaluate the following integral:

$$\eta = E(h(X)) = \int_{\mathbb{R}} h(x) f(x) dx \qquad (8.2)$$

For example, if we take $h(x) = 1_{\{x \geq d\}}$, where 1_A is the indicator function of the set A, η is the so-called *tail probability*, defined as $P(X \geq d)$. If we take $h(x) = x1_{\{x \geq d\}}$, η is the *tail conditional expectation* $E(X|X \geq d)$, also known as *expected shortfall* in the risk management literature.

In many cases of practical interest, the analytical evaluation of Equation 8.2 is impossible; a solution is CMC, which consists in simulating B observations from the density f and estimating Equation 8.2 by means of its empirical counterpart:

$$\hat{\eta} = \frac{1}{B} \sum_{i=1}^{B} h(x_i)$$

Although the law of large numbers guarantees the consistency of this estimator, its variability becomes very large when dealing with rare events.

The method of importance sampling (IS) is ideally suited for the solution of such difficulties. To introduce it, notice that Equation 8.2 can be rewritten as

$$\eta = E_f(h(X)) = \int_{\mathbb{R}} h(x)\frac{f(x)}{g(x)}g(x)dx = E_g\left(h(x)\frac{f(x)}{g(x)}\right) = E_g(h(x)r(x))$$

where $g =$ is a density (usually called IS, or instrumental, density) the subscript indicates with respect to which distribution the expectation is taken

$r(x) = f(x)/g(x) = $ likelihood ratio

Although the only condition to be imposed on g is that its support includes the support of f, the choice of g is of crucial importance for the properties (in particular, the rate of convergence to the true value and the variance) of the resulting estimator.

It should now be clear how IS works; algorithm 1 summarizes the steps.

Algorithm 8.1 (importance sampling). For the estimation of Equation 8.2, perform these two steps:

1. Simulate B observations from the density g.
2. Compute $\hat{\eta}^{IS} = \frac{1}{B} \sum_{i=1}^{B} h(x_i)r(x_i)$.

Looking at the algorithm, it can be seen that we have to seek a density g whose tails are thicker than those of f, or the likelihood ratio would be unbounded. But apart from these intuitive remarks, are there any precise mathematical conditions that can guide us in the search for a good (possibly optimal) IS density? Some conditions ensuring the existence of the variance of $\hat{\eta}^{IS}$ have been derived by Geweke (1989); see Casella and Robert (2004, section 3.3.2) for details. More important, the density g that minimizes the variance of the estimator was found by Rubinstein (1981; see Casella and Robert 2004, p. 95, for a proof):

Theorem 8.1 The choice of g that minimizes the variance of the importance sampling estimator is

$$g^*(x) = \frac{|h(x)\,f(x)|}{\int\limits_{\mathbb{R}} |h(z)|\,f(z)dz}$$

This result cannot be used directly in practical applications, because it requires the knowledge of the integral of $h(x)f(x)$ (i.e., the quantity we are interested in); however, it implies that the optimal IS density should be as similar as possible to the original probability measure conditioned on the event of interest; as we will see, this idea is the basis of the minimum cross-entropy approach to IS.

In this chapter we are interested in applying IS to an r.v. $Y_k = \sum_{i=1}^{k} W_i$, where the W_i's are i.i.d. continuous positive r.v.'s and, for now, k is a positive integer; we will see later on how to extend the results to the setup where K is an r.v. Defining $h_k(y) = 1_{\{Y_k > c\}}(y)$, the probability $p_k = P(Y_k > c)$ is given by

$$p_k = E_{f_k}(h_k(x)) = \int\limits_{\mathbb{R}^k} h_k(x)\,f_k(x)dx$$

where f_k = joint density of $X_1, \ldots, X_k$, which by virtue of the hypothesis of independence is equal to $f_k(x_1, \ldots, x_k) = \prod_{i=1}^{k} f(x_i)$

The IS approach is based on the fact that

$$p_k = E_f(h_k(x)) = E_g(h_k(x)r_k(x))$$

where $r_k(x) = f_k(x)/g_k(x)$
   $g_k = k$-variate density

The most obvious solution consists in taking $g_k(x_1, \ldots, x_k) = \prod_{i=1}^{k} g(x_i)$. Under these hypotheses, the likelihood ratio is equal to

$$r_k(x) = \frac{\prod_{i=1}^{k} f(x_i)}{\prod_{i=1}^{k} g(x_i)}$$

With these definitions, we can now go back to the operational risk setup.

8.2.3 Heavy-Tailed Distributions and Importance Sampling

In view of the implementation of an IS algorithm, an important distinction to be made concerns light- and heavy-tailed distributions; for the current purposes, a distribution is defined light-tailed if its moment generating function exists (Rubinstein and Kroese 2004, p. 4); see Embrechts, Klüppelberg, and Mikosch (1997) for a more thorough discussion.

Another concept that will be needed is that of subexponential distributions (Embrechts et al. section 1.3.2): a distribution with density f on $(0, \infty)$ is said to be subexponential if, given a random sample $X_1, \ldots, X_n$ from f, we have:

$$\lim_{x \to \infty} \frac{P(X_1 + \cdots + X_n > x)}{P(X_1 > x)} = n$$

for all $n \in \mathbb{N}$. The intuitive description of the concept is simple: a necessary condition for the sum of k i.i.d. heavy-tailed random variables $X_1, \ldots, X_k$ to be large is that one summand is large.

When modeling operational losses, it is clear that a major decision consists in choosing the distributions of the r.v.'s K and W. As for the first one, there are theoretical and empirical reasons (see McNeil et al. 2005, p. 475) which make the Poisson distribution the most common choice. The choice of the severity is less straightforward; the main issue to be considered is the "degree of heaviness" of the tail of the loss distribution. In general, the amount of most operational losses is rather small, but occasionally very large losses are observed (De Koker 2006; McNeil et al. 2005, section 10.1.4). Such a behavior is indeed typical of the so-called heavy-tailed distributions. This restricts the set of possible distributions, but still does not identify a single member of the class of heavy-tailed distributions; without entering into details, we summarize the state of the art by saying that the two most frequent choices are the Pareto distribution, when the data are very heavy-tailed (see the discussion in McNeil et al. 2005, section 10.1.4) and the Lognormal distribution when the data are moderately heavy-tailed

(Bee 2006; Mignola and Ugoccioni 2006; see Buchmüller et al. 2006, p. 311, for a survey of the most common industry choices). Thus, in the following we will apply IS to the compound-Poisson and compound-Pareto models.

For the implementation of the cross-entropy approach with subexponential distributions, we also need this result (see Asmussen 2000, lemma 5.6 for a formal statement): let $A(d) = \{X_1 + \cdots + X_k > d\}$, where the X_i's are subexponential with distribution function F. The event $A(d)$ occurs if $k - 1$ of the X_i's have distribution F and one has the conditional distribution of X given $X > d$. For our purposes, it will be enough to recall that both the Lognormal and the Pareto belong to the class of subexponential distributions; in the next sections we show how the last result is used for the determination of the optimal IS density.

8.2.4 Choosing the Instrumental Density

Determining the density g is clearly of crucial importance for a successful implementation of IS. In general, this problem consists of two steps: the choice of the parametric family and the choice of the optimal member of the family (i.e., the choice of the parameter(s) of the IS density).

As for the parametric form of the IS density, the most obvious solution (which we call the standard approach) consists in choosing g in the same family of the original density f: for example, if $X \sim Logn\ (\mu, \sigma^2)$, one would put g equal to the density of $X \sim Logn\ (\mu_1, \sigma_1^2)$, possibly with either $\mu_1 = \mu$ or $\sigma_1^2 = \sigma^2$.

This approach is in principle the easiest one; so one might ask why one would need to look for a different technique. To answer this question, recall that we are interested in simulating (1) for some fixed k. It can be shown that, as k gets large, this methodology suffers a drawback: The distribution of $r_k(X)$ becomes more and more skewed, with most weights close to zero in the limit; a huge sample size is needed to get a single nonzero weight. The consequence of this drawback, known as *weight degeneracy* (Casella and Robert 2004), is that the variance is obviously minimized, but the estimator is useless because it is essentially computed with only one observation; for intermediate values of k, the estimator is downward biased unless the sample size is very large.

A possible remedy consists in using an IS density belonging to the class of defensive mixtures (DM; from now on DM approach); the idea, first proposed by Hesterberg (1995), consists in building the IS density g as a two-population mixture of the original density f and another density f_2 of the same family but with different parameters:

$$g(x) = \pi f(x) + (1 - \pi) f_2(x) \quad \pi \in (0, 1)$$

It is not difficult to show that $r_k(X)$ is unbounded when $\pi = 1$ (i.e., when the IS density belongs to the same parametric family of the original density f), but when $\pi < 1$, the maximum of $r_k(X)$ is equal to $(1/\pi)^k$.

In both approaches, the final step consists in choosing the parameter(s) of g according to some optimality criterion. A tool commonly employed for light-tailed distributions is the so-called tilted density, defined as $g_t(x) = e^{tX} f(x)/M_X(t)$, where f is the original density and $M_X(t)$ is its moment-generating function. However, as the severity distributions used in operational risk are in most cases moderately to heavy-tailed, we do not give additional details here; interested readers are referred to McNeil et al. (2005, section 8.5.1).

When the moment-generating function does not exist, the problem becomes more intricate. In this setup, minimizing the variance of the resulting estimator with respect to the parameters is in general unfeasible. However, a different way of reasoning provides us with a useful technique; from theorem 1, and assuming without loss of generality that X is a continuous r.v., it follows that the optimal IS density g should be as similar as possible to the original density conditioned on the event of interest, which we define as $f^{(c)}$. How can we measure the discrepancy? The Kullback-Leibler distance or Cross-Entropy (CE) between the two distributions is a frequently used measure enjoying several desirable properties. It is defined as:

$$D(f^{(d)}(x), g(x)) = E^{(d)} \log \frac{f^{(d)}(x)}{g(x)} \tag{8.3}$$

Thus, the goal consists in minimizing Equation 8.3. As concerns this issue, a very interesting feature of this technique is that minimizing CE is strictly related to maximum likelihood estimation. It can indeed be shown that

$$\min D(f^{(d)}(x), g(x)) = \max_\theta E^{(d)} \left(\sum_{i=1}^{k} \log f_\theta(x_i) \right)$$

where f_θ = original density
        θ = vector of parameters

Now note that $\sum_{i=1}^{k} \log f_\theta(x_i) = k \int \log(f_\theta(x)) f_k(x) dx$, where f_k is the empirical distribution, which assigns probability $1/k$ to each observation. Thus, maximum likelihood results can be translated into minimum CE results by replacing f_k with $f^{(d)}$.

A detailed comparison of the properties of the standard and DM approach has been performed by Bee (2007), whose results show that, when the severity has the Lognormal distribution, the properties of the DM approach are more desirable than those of the standard one.

Next we apply the standard and DM approach to the setups of Lognormal and Pareto severity; in all cases the optimal values of the parameters will be found by minimizing the cross-entropy.

8.3 MODERATELY HEAVY-TAILED CASE: LOGNORMAL SEVERITY

8.3.1 Defensive Mixture Approach

The results just presented provide a method for determining the optimal parameters of the IS density. Consider first the case where the severity W has the Lognormal distribution: $W \sim \mathrm{Logn}(\mu, \sigma^2)$, where as usual $\mu = E(\log(W))$ and $\sigma^2 = \mathrm{var}(\log(W))$. Recalling that maximum likelihood estimation of the parameters of a Lognormal mixture is equivalent to maximum likelihood estimation of the parameters of a normal mixture, we can just consider the maximum likelihood estimations (MLEs) of the parameters π and $\mu_2 =: \mu + t$ of a normal mixture (see, e.g., Flury 1997, section 9.2):

$$\hat{\pi} = \frac{1}{k} \sum_{i=1}^{k} \pi_{1x_i} = \int_{\mathbb{R}} \pi_{1x_i} F_k(dx) \tag{8.4}$$

$$\hat{\mu}_2 = \frac{1}{k(1-\hat{\pi})} \sum_{i=1}^{k} \pi_{2x_i} x_i = \frac{1}{(1-\hat{\pi})} \int_{\mathbb{R}} x \pi_{2x_i} F_k(dx) \tag{8.5}$$

where F_k = empirical distribution function
π_{jx_i} = so called posterior probability that x_i belongs to the jth population ($j = 1, 2$)

Denoting with ϕ_{μ, σ^2} the $N(\mu, \sigma^2)$ density, π_{1x} and π_{2x} are respectively given by

$$\pi_{1x} = \frac{\pi \phi_{\mu, \sigma^2}(x)}{\pi \phi_{\mu, \sigma^2}(x) + (1 - \pi) \phi_{\mu_2, \sigma^2}(x)}, \quad \pi_{2x} = 1 - \pi_{1x} \tag{8.6}$$

Putting $d^* = \log(d)$, the conditional density of $(\log(W)|\log(W) > d^*)$ is equal to

$$\phi_{\mu,\sigma^2}^{(d^*)}(x) = \frac{\phi_{\mu,\sigma^2}(x)}{1 - \phi_{\mu,\sigma^2}(d^*)} 1_{\{x > d^*\}}$$

where $\phi_{\mu,\sigma^2} = N(\mu, \sigma^2)$ distribution function

As seen in the preceding section, the values of π and μ_2, which minimize entropy (π^* and μ_2^*, say), are given by (4) and (5) with F_k replaced by $\phi_{\mu,\sigma^2}^{(d)}$. More precisely, we know that the event of interest occurs if $(k-1)$ observations have density ϕ_{μ,σ^2} and one has density $\phi_{\mu,\sigma^2}^{(d^*)}$, so that

$$\hat{\pi} = \frac{k-1}{k} \int_{-\infty}^{\infty} \pi_{1x}\phi_{\mu,\sigma^2}(x)\,dx + \frac{1}{k}\frac{1}{1 - \phi_{\mu,\sigma^2}(d^*)} \int_{d^*}^{\infty} \pi_{1x}\phi_{\mu,\sigma^2}(x)dx \quad (8.7)$$

$$\hat{\mu}_2 = \frac{k-1}{k} \int_{-\infty}^{\infty} x\pi_{2x}\phi_{\mu,\sigma^2}(x)\,dx + \frac{1}{k}\frac{1}{1 - \phi_{\mu,\sigma^2}(d^*)} \int_{d^*}^{\infty} x\pi_{2x}\phi_{\mu,\sigma^2}(x)dx \quad (8.8)$$

Now the key to the solution of the system formed by (7) and (8) consists in noting that Equations 8.6, 8.7, and 8.8 are the equations of the EM algorithm (Dempster, Laird, and Rubin 1977; McLachlan and Krishnan 1996) for maximum likelihood estimation of the parameters of a random variable V distributed as a two-population normal mixture with parameters (μ, σ^2) and (μ_2, σ^2) respectively, where $(k-1)$ observations are from the mixture itself and one observation is from the distribution of $V|V > d^*$. In particular, Equation 8.6 implements the E-step, Equations 8.7 and 8.8 the M-step. Hence, in order to get the optimal values π^* and μ_2^*, we just have to iterate Equations 8.6, 8.7, and 8.8 until convergence; note that the integrals in Equations 8.7 and 8.8 have to be solved numerically at each iteration.

8.3.2 Standard Cross-Entropy Approach

When the IS density has the same parametric form of the original density, the standard CE approach consists in choosing the optimal tilting parameter

t (t^*, say) by minimizing the CE between the original density conditioned to the event of interest and the IS density. Rubinstein and Kroese (2004) show that the best algorithm for finding t^*, in particular when the probability of the event is very rare, is the so-called adaptive cross-entropy approach. Due to space limitations, here we will apply the algorithm without giving any detail; interested readers are referred to Rubinstein and Kroese (2004, chap. 3).

8.4 HEAVY-TAILED CASE: PARETO SEVERITY

The so-called Poisson-GPD approach, where GPD stands for Generalized Pareto Distribution, is typically used when the distribution is strongly heavy-tailed. For details on this model, which is frequently used in environmental, actuarial, and financial applications, see Smith (2003).

8.4.1 Defensive Mixture Approach

Let X be a Pareto r.v. with density

$$f(x) = \frac{ca^c}{x^{c+1}} 1_{\{x \geq a\}}(x) \quad a, c \in \mathbb{R}^+$$

The defensive mixture could in principle be constructed as a mixture of two Pareto distributions with parameters (a_1, c_1) and (a_2, c_2). However, maximum likelihood estimation of the parameter a_2 of a Pareto mixture with $a_1 \neq a_2$ breaks down because some requirements for the EM algorithm to converge to a local maximum are not satisfied (in particular, theorem 7.2 in Little and Rubin 1987, does not apply). Thus, we have to impose the restriction $a_1 = a_2 = a$. It follows that the density of the defensive mixture is defined as

$$g(x) = \pi \frac{c_1 a^{c_1}}{x^{c_1+1}} 1_{\{x \geq a\}}(x) + (1 - \pi) \frac{c_2 a^{c_2}}{x^{c_2+1}} 1_{\{x \geq a\}}(x) \quad a, c_1, c_2 \in \mathbb{R}^+, c_1 > c_2$$

where the last inequality ensures that the second population has a heavier tail. Given a random sample of k observations from the mixture, the complete likelihood and log-likelihood functions are given by

$$L_c(c_1, c_2, a; x) = \prod_{i=1}^{k} \left\{ \left(\frac{c_1 a^{c_1}}{x_i^{c_1+1}} 1_{\{x \geq a\}}(x_i) \right)^{z_i} + \left(\frac{c_2 a^{c_2}}{x_i^{c_2+1}} 1_{\{x \geq a\}}(x_i) \right)^{1-z_i} \right\}$$

$$l_c(c_1, c_2, a; x) = \sum_{i=1}^{k} \left\{ z_i \log \left(\frac{c_1 a^{c_1}}{x_i^{c_1+1}} 1_{\{x \geq a\}}(x_i) \right) \right.$$

$$\left. + (1 - z_i) \log \left(\frac{c_2 a^{c_2}}{x_i^{c_2+1}} 1_{\{x \geq a\}}(x_i) \right) \right\} \qquad a, c_1, c_2 \in \mathbb{R}^+, c_1 > c_2$$

The complete-data maximum likelihood estimators are given by

$$\hat{\pi} = \frac{k_1}{k} \qquad\qquad \hat{a} = \min_{1 \leq i \leq k} x_i$$

$$\hat{c}_1 = \frac{k_1}{\sum\limits_{i=1}^{k_1} z_i \log (x_i/\hat{a})}, \qquad\qquad \hat{c}_2 = \frac{k_2}{\sum\limits_{i=1}^{k_2} (1 - z_i) \log (x_i/\hat{a})}$$

where $k_1 =$ number of observations in the first population

Given the linearity of the complete log-likelihood function l_c, the EM algorithm is implemented in this way:

E-step. Compute

$$\pi_{1x_i} = \frac{\pi f(x_i; a, c_1)}{\pi f(x_i; a, c_1) + (1 - \pi) f_2(x_i; a, c_2)} \qquad i = 1, \ldots, k \qquad (8.9)$$

M-step. Compute

$$\hat{\pi} = \frac{1}{n} \sum_{i=1}^{k} \pi_{1x_i}$$

$$\hat{c}_2 = \frac{k(1 - \hat{\pi})}{\sum\limits_{i=1}^{k} \pi_{2x_i} \log (x_i/\hat{a})}$$

where $\hat{a} = \min_{1 \leq i \leq k} x_i$.

The E and M steps are then iterated until convergence.

In the entropy minimization setup, the determination of the optimal numerical values π^* and c^* proceeds exactly as in the preceding case: We have to substitute to the empirical distribution function the conditional Pareto distribution function $F^{(d)}(x; a, c_1)$. However, analogously to the lognormal case, we know that, when summing k subexponential r.v.'s, the rare event occurs if $k - 1$ of the X_is have distribution F and one has the conditional distribution of X given $X > d$. Thus the equations to be implemented are

$$\hat{\pi} = \frac{k-1}{k} \int_a^\infty \pi_{1x} f(x; a, c_1) dx + \frac{1}{k} \frac{1}{1 - F(d; a, c_1)} \int_d^\infty \pi_{1x} f(x; a, c_1) dx$$

$$\hat{c}_2 = \frac{k-1}{k} \frac{(1 - \hat{\pi})k}{\int_a^\infty \pi_{2x} \log(x_i/\hat{a}) f(x; a, c_1) dx}$$

$$+ \frac{1}{k} \frac{(1 - \hat{\pi}) k}{\frac{1}{1-F(d;a,c_1)} \int_d^\infty \pi_{2x} \log(x_i/\hat{a}) f(x; a, c_1) dx}$$

where π_{1x} is defined in (9).

8.4.2 Cross-Entropy Approach

The standard cross-entropy approach in the Pareto case has been thoroughly investigated by several authors; see Asmussen et al. (2005, section 3.1) and the references therein. In particular, Asmussen et al. propose to keep fixed the parameter a and decrease c (recall that the tail of the Pareto distribution gets heavier as c gets small); by exploiting the connection between minimum cross-entropy and maximum likelihood, they find that the optimal value of c is given by $1/J_d$, where

$$J_d = \frac{\log(1 + d)}{n} + \frac{1}{c}$$

so that, for large d, the optimal value is $c^* \approx n/\log(1 + d)$. The same authors show, by means of simulations, that the performance of the IS estimator is approximately constant in a large interval of the optimal value c^*. So we will just use this value to perform our experiments, whose aim consists mainly in comparing the standard CE approach with the DM approach.

8.5 SIMULATION RESULTS

In Sections 8.3 and 8.4, we developed two IS methodologies for the estimation of tail probabilities of the distribution $Y = \sum_{i=1}^{k} W_i$ where k is a positive integer. However the loss distribution typically used in the AMA is the random sum (1); therefore, we have to find a way of estimating tail probabilities in this more general setup. Fortunately, the solution is rather easy: put $P(K = k) = q_k$. We have

$$P(Y > d) = \sum_{i=1}^{\infty} q_i \int_{d}^{\infty} f_{W_i}(w)dw$$

Thus, the IS procedure developed earlier can be applied to each summand. The only problem is that we have to truncate the series; however, given the properties of the Poisson distribution, it can usually be truncated after a few terms. The decision concerning the truncation point has to be made on the basis of the value of λ; for example, with $\lambda = 1$, $P(K \geq 7) \approx 8.3 \cdot 10^{-5}$, implying that, if we simulate 10,000 observations, we can stop when $k = 6$ or when $k = 7$, so that 5 (respectively 6) terms are summed (the first term, corresponding to $k = 0$, can also be discarded because the loss is zero).

8.5.1 Lognormal Severity

We consider estimation of the tail probability of the distribution (1) for $K \sim Pois\,(5)$ and $W_i \sim Logn\,(1.5, 3)$ for $d \in \{1,000, 3,000, 5,000, 7,500, 10,000\}$. The first step consists in finding the parameters of the optimal density both in the DM and in the ST approach. We have estimated the optimal parameters for $k \in \{2, \ldots, 20\}$ and for all the values of d introduced above (with $\lambda = 5$, the probability of a value larger than 20 is approximately equal to $8 \cdot 10^{-8}$, so that truncating the series at $k = 20$ is definitely enough); due to space constraints, here we summarize the results of this step. In the DM approach, the estimated value of π is an increasing function of both k and d, but k has a more pronounced impact: for example, for $k = 2$ and $d = 10,000$, $\pi = 0.49$, whereas for $k = 20$ and $d = 10,000$, $\pi = 0.95$. However, the parameter μ_2 has only a slight decrease, from $\mu_2 = 11.07$ when $k = 2$ to $\mu_2 = 10.84$ when $k = 20$. As for the ST approach, the parameter μ_2 is again a decreasing function of k and d: for example, for $k = 2$ and $d = 10,000$, $\mu_2 = 4.07$, for $k = 20$ and $d = 10,000$, $\mu_2 = 0.99$.

Next we examine the performances of the estimators of the tail probabilities $p_k = P(Y_k > d)$ for the values of d listed earlier. To assess the stability of the estimators, we repeated the simulation $B = 1,000$ times and computed the MC estimate of the standard error of the estimators, defined as $\widehat{se}(\hat{\pi}) = \sqrt{\text{var}(\hat{\pi}^{(i)})}$, where $\hat{\pi}^{(i)}$ is the estimate obtained at the ith replication. A typical measure of the stability of an estimator used in the literature concerning rare events is the relative error (see Rubinstein and Kroese 2004, p. 8), defined as $\tau = \sqrt{\text{var}(1_{\{X \geq c\}})}/E(1_{\{X \geq c\}})$. However, if an estimator is biased, the relative error, being based on the variance, is not a good measure of performance; as a consequence, we estimated a version of the relative error (we call it "MSE relative error") based on the mean squared error (MSE) instead of the variance: $\tau_{MSE} = \sqrt{MSE(1_{\{X \geq c\}})}/E(1_{\{X \geq c\}})$. Although we do not know the true value of π and therefore, in principle, we cannot compute the MSE, there is a way out consisting in estimating π with the DM approach (which guarantees a high level of precision: see Figure 8.2) with a very large sample size; the resulting value $\hat{\pi}^{DM}$ will then be used to compute τ_{MSE}, as if it were the true value.

Table 8.1 displays the results; notice that the two IS estimators are computed with 1,000 replications, whereas the CMC estimator is based on 10,000 replications. Although all the estimators are approximately unbiased, the DM estimator is much more stable, and therefore definitely preferable.

To conclude the analysis, it is interesting to look at the convergence of the IS estimators. Figure 8.2 shows the values of $\hat{\pi}^{DM}$ and $\hat{\pi}^{ST}$ as a function of the sample size for $d = 3,000$ and $d = 10,000$. Before commenting on the graphs, notice that N is on a logarithmic scale and that we used different ranges for the sample sizes in the two cases ($10 \leq N \leq 500,000$ for DM and $500 \leq N \leq 10,000,000$ for ST). Despite of the smaller values of N, the DM approach displays a much quicker convergence, in particular for $d = 10,000$.

TABLE 8.1 Estimates and MSE Relative Errors in the DM, ST, and CMC Approaches with Lognormal Severity

	$\hat{\pi}_{DM}$	$\hat{\pi}_{ST}$	$\hat{\pi}_{CMC}$	$\tau_{MSE,\hat{\pi}_{DM}}$	$\tau_{MSE,\hat{\pi}_{ST}}$	$\tau_{MSE,\hat{\pi}_{ST}}$
$d = 1,000$	0.00560	0.00559	0.00564	$8.57 * 10^{-7}$	0.00220	0.00655
$d = 2,500$	0.00047	0.00047	0.00048	$9.82 * 10^{-8}$	0.00294	0.01148
$d = 5,000$	0.00014	0.00012	0.00014	$2.97 * 10^{-8}$	0.00958	0.01965
$d = 7,500$	$4.73 * 10^{-5}$	$4.18 * 10^{-5}$	$5.17 * 10^{-5}$	$1.18 * 10^{-8}$	0.04303	0.0853
$d = 10,000$	$2.19 * 10^{-5}$	$2.20 * 10^{-5}$	$2.5 * 10^{-5}$	$5.72 * 10^{-9}$	0.0671	0.1241

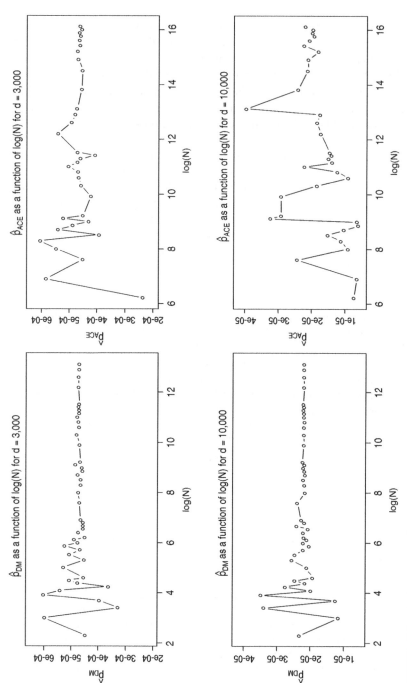

FIGURE 8.2 Estimators in the Poisson-Lognormal Setup as Functions of the Sample Size

TABLE 8.2   Estimates and MSE Relative Errors in the DM, ST, and CMC Approaches with Pareto Severity

	$\hat{\pi}_{DM}$	$\hat{\pi}_{ST}$	$\hat{\pi}_{CMC}$	$\tau_{MSE,\hat{\pi}_{DM}}$	$\tau_{MSE,\hat{\pi}_{ST}}$	$\tau_{MSE,\hat{\pi}_{ST}}$
$d = 1{,}500$	$8.73 * 10^{-5}$	$8.75 * 10^{-5}$	$8.1 * 10^{-5}$	0.02146	0.06812	1.07658
$d = 5{,}000$	$1.42 * 10^{-5}$	$1.43 * 10^{-5}$	$1.8 * 10^{-5}$	0.02624	0.09005	2.37646
$d = 10{,}000$	$5.02 * 10^{-6}$	$5.04 * 10^{-6}$	$4.67 * 10^{-6}$	0.03257	0.10237	4.52800
$d = 20{,}000$	$1.76 * 10^{-6}$	$1.77 * 10^{-6}$	$3.67 * 10^{-6}$	0.05000	0.12512	5.16046
$d = 30{,}000$	$9.67 * 10^{-7}$	$9.67 * 10^{-7}$	$1.67 * 10^{-6}$	0.05274	0.13814	7.70419

8.5.2 Pareto Severity

In this section we perform the same analysis of the preceding section, under the hypothesis that the distribution has the Pareto distribution with parameters $a = 1$ and $c = 1.5$. The choice of the numerical value of c is motivated by the fact that the $Par(a, c)$ distribution with $c \in (1, 2)$ has finite mean and infinite variance, which is typically considered the relevant case in the operational risk literature.

Table 8.2 shows point estimates and MSE relative errors for the three approaches with $d \in \{1{,}500, 5{,}000, 10{,}000, 20{,}000, 30{,}000\}$.

Similar to the Lognormal case, the *DM* approach is the most stable one, although the difference between $\tau_{MSE,\hat{\pi}_{DM}}$ and $\tau_{MSE,\hat{\pi}_{ST}}$ is less relevant with respect to the Lognormal case. Figure 8.3 shows the convergence of the estimators, from which it can again be seen the quicker convergence of the DM estimator.

8.6 CONCLUSION

In this chapter we have proposed some importance sampling techniques for VaR estimation in the AMA. The motivation comes from the well-known fact that standard Monte Carlo is very inefficient when the goal is the estimation of tail probabilities; this problem, combined with the practice of using very large confidence levels for VaR estimation in operational risk, makes variance reduction techniques absolutely necessary. In the Poisson-Lognormal and Poisson-Pareto setups, we propose the use of two different importance sampling strategies. In the first one, the instrumental density is a mixture of the severity and of a density belonging to the same parametric family of the severity but with different parameters; the second one is based on an instrumental distribution belonging to the same parametric family of

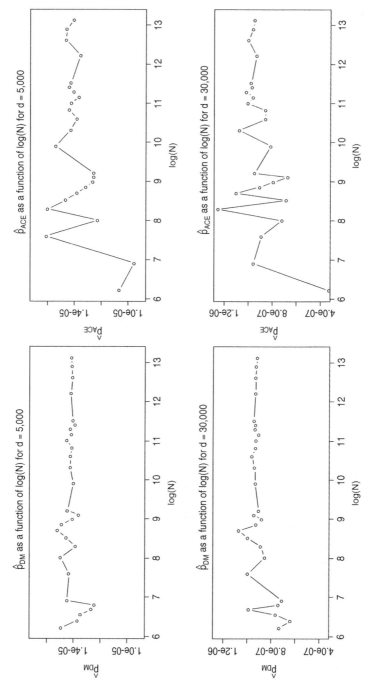

FIGURE 8.3 Estimators in the Poisson-Pareto Setup as Functions of the Sample Size

the severity. In both cases, the optimal importance sampling densities are found by means of the minimum cross-entropy criterion.

The results show that both IS approaches solve satisfactorily the problem. Moreover, the first one converges more quickly, in particular when the severity is Lognormal.

The methods presented here work well for the estimation of VaR in the Poisson-Lognormal and Poisson-Pareto setups; it would be of obvious interest to extend these results in two directions. First, whereas the frequency is almost invariably modeled by means of the Poisson distribution, several other models have been proposed for the severity; the algorithms proposed here should therefore be adapted to these setups. Second, VaR is not the only risk measure of interest; for example, expected shortfall has better properties and is often employed. Unfortunately, developing IS for the estimation of expected shortfall in a compound distribution does not seem obvious, and this topic requires some further research.

REFERENCES

Asmussen, S. 2000. *Ruin probabilities*. London: World Scientific.

Asmussen, S., D. P. Kroese, and R. Y. Rubinstein. 2005. Heavy tails, importance sampling and cross-entropy. *Stochastic Models* 21, no. 1:57–76.

Basel Committee on Banking Supervision. 2005. *Basel II: International convergence of capital measurement and capital standards: A revised framework*, www.bis.org. Basel, Switzerland.

Bee, M. 2006. Estimating the parameters in the loss distribution approach: How can we deal with truncated data? In *The advanced measurement approach to operational risk*, ed. E. Davis. London: Risk Books.

Bee, M. 2007. Importance sampling for sums of lognormal distributions, with applications to operational risk. Discussion paper, Department of Economics, University of Trento.

Buchmüller, P., M. Haas, B. Rummel, and K. Stickelmann. 2006. AMA implementation in Germany: Results of BaFin's and Bundesbank's industry survey. In *The advanced measurement approach to operational risk*, ed. E. Davis. London: Risk Books.

Casella, G., and C. P. Robert. 2004. *Monte Carlo statistical methods*. New York: Springer.

De Koker, R. 2006. Operational risk modeling: Where do we go from here? In *E The advanced measurement approach to operational risk*, ed. E. Davis. London: Risk Books.

Dempster, A. P., N. M. Laird, and D. B. Rubin 1977. Maximum likelihood from incomplete data via the *EM* algorithm (with discussion). *Journal of the Royal Statistical Society B* 39, no. 1:1–38.

Embrechts, P., C. Klüppelberg, and T. Mikosch. 1997. *Modeling extremal events for insurance and finance.* New York: Springer.

Flury, B. 1997. *A first course in multivariate statistics.* New York: Springer.

Geweke, J. 1989. Bayesian inference in econometric models using Monte Carlo integration. *Econometrica* 57, no. 6:1317–1340.

Hesterberg, T. 1995. Weighted average importance sampling and defensive mixture distributions. *Technometrics* 37, no. 2:185–194.

McLachlan, G. J., and T. Krishnan. 1996. *The EM algorithm and extensions.* New York: John Wiley & Sons.

McNeil, A. J., R. Frey, and P. Embrechts. 2005. *Quantitative risk management: Concepts, techniques and tools.* Princeton, NJ: Princeton University Press.

Mignola, G., and R. Ugoccioni. 2006. Tests of extreme-value theory applied to operational risk data. In *The advanced measurement approach to operational risk*, ed. E. Davis. London: Risk Books.

Mikosch, T. 2004. *Non–life insurance mathematics.* New York: Springer.

Rubinstein, R. Y. 1981. *Simulation and the Monte Carlo method.* New York: John Wiley & Sons.

Rubinstein, R. Y., and D. P. Kroese. 2004. *The cross-entropy method.* New York: Springer.

Smith, R. L. 2003. Statistics of extremes, with applications in environment, insurance and finance. In *Extreme values in finance, telecommunications and the environment*, ed. B. Finkenstadt and H. Rootzen. London: Chapman and Hall/CRC Press.

CHAPTER 9

One-Sided Cross-Validation for Density Estimation with an Application to Operational Risk

María Dolores Martínez Miranda, Jens Perch Nielsen, and Stefan A. Sperlich

ABSTRACT

We introduce one-sided cross-validation to nonparametric kernel density estimation. The method is more stable than classical cross-validation, and it has a better overall performance compared to what we see in plug-in methods. One-sided cross-validation is a more direct data-driven method than plug-in methods with weaker assumptions of smoothness since it does not require a smooth pilot with consistent second derivatives. Our conclusions for one-sided kernel density cross-validation are similar to the conclusions obtained by Hart and Yi (1998) when they introduced one-sided cross-validation in the regression context, except that in our context of density estimation, the superiority of this new method is even much stronger. An extensive simulation study confirms that our one-sided cross-validation clearly outperforms the simple cross-validation. We conclude with real data applications.

This research was financially supported by knowledge company Festina Lente and the Dirección General de Investigación del Ministerio de Ciencia y Tecnología under research grant SEJ2004-04583/ECON.

9.1   INTRODUCTION

Suppose we have observed data $X_1, X_2, \ldots, X_n$ that are assumed to be independent and identically distributed with common density function, $f(\cdot)$. We want to estimate this common density nonparametrically using the standard kernel estimator:

$$\hat{f}_h(x) = \frac{1}{nh} \sum_{i=1}^{n} K\left(\frac{x - X_i}{h}\right) \tag{9.1}$$

where K = kernel function
       h = bandwidth parameter

Our problem is to find a reliable data-driven estimator of the bandwidth. We would like to use the popular and widely used least squares cross-validation proposed by Rudemo (1982) and Bowman (1984). We do, however, worry about the well-known lack of stability of this method (see, e.g., Wand and Jones 1995, and Chiu 1996). Many alternatives have been proposed to the intuitively appealing method of cross-validation; for example, consider the wide range of so-called plug-in methods that aim at estimating the minimizer of the integrated squared error. However, all these plug-in methods require a pilot estimator to be plugged in. We prefer a direct and immediate method like cross-validation without the extra complications of pilot estimators and without the extra smoothing assumptions required to ensure that the pilot estimator works well. In regression, an appealing improvement of standard cross-validation exists—the so-called one-sided cross-validation—which simply is the cross-validation procedure based on the one-sided kernel version of the original kernel $K(\cdot)$. However, to do this correctly, one has to correct for the bias induced by using only one-sided kernels. This correction is obtained when applying local linear kernels, as discussed in Section 9.2.2 of this chapter. Notice that this has nothing to do with bandwidth selection in local linear regression (Fan, Gijbels, Hu, and Huang 1996). Furthermore, the estimated bandwidth coming from this procedure is then readjusted by a simple constant only depending on the kernel.[1]

The surprising fact is that this one-sided procedure is much more stable than the original cross-validation procedure and that in many ways it behaves similarly to the plug-in method without its vices: the complicated pilot estimator and the added smoothness assumptions.

In this chapter we introduce one-sided cross-validation for kernel density estimation and show through simulations that one-sided cross-validation is performing much better, is more stable, and to some extent has a similar performance to the plug-in and also the kernel density cases. We show the method's performance and superiority via simulation studies and real data applications.

9.2 ONE-SIDED CROSS-VALIDATION METHOD FOR DENSITY ESTIMATION

One commonly used measure of the performance of $\hat{f}_h$ is the mean integrated squared error (MISE), defined by

$$\text{MISE}(h) = \int E[\{\hat{f}_h(x) - f(x)\}^2]dx$$

Let us denote by h_0 the minimizer of $MISE(\cdot)$. This is the optimal bandwidth that plug-in methods aim at estimating. Another performance measure to consider is the data-dependent integrated squared error, defined by

$$\text{ISE}(h) = \int \left(\hat{f}_h(x) - f(x)\right)^2 dx$$

with the optimal (random) bandwidth, $\hat{h}_0$ as minimizer.

This is the optimal bandwidth that cross-validation aims at estimating. However, theoretical studies have shown that standard cross-validation is so unstable that plug-in methods do better at estimating $\hat{h}_0$ than cross-validation does, even though plug-in methods really aim at estimating h_0.

9.2.1 Ordinary Least Squares Cross-Validation

Cross-validation is probably still the most popular automatic bandwidth selection method. Its intuitive definition and its practical data-driven characteristics make up for its lack of stability in the eyes of many practitioners. Also, cross-validation immediately generalizes to most statistical smoothing problems. Plug-in methods are well defined only for a narrow range of statistical problems. Even there, the debate over which pilot estimator to use makes practitioners turn to cross-validation.[2]

Least squares cross-validation was proposed by Rudemo (1982) and Bowman (1984), who estimated $\hat{h}_0$ by minimizing the criterion

$$CV(h) = \int \hat{f}_h^2(x)dx - 2n^{-1}\sum_{i=1}^{n} \hat{f}_{h,-i}(X_i) \tag{9.2}$$

where $\hat{f}_{h,-i}$ = density estimator obtained by leaving out the observation X_i

Let $\hat{\hat{h}}$ be this classical cross-validation bandwidth estimator.

Hall (1983) showed that the cross-validation bandwidth is a consistent estimate of the optimal bandwidth $\hat{h}_0$, and its asymptotic normality was established in Hall and Marron (1987). They pointed out the lack of stability of classical cross-validation. Härdle, Hall, and Marron (1988) showed the equivalent result for the regression context. The cross-validation bandwidth also tends to be undersmoothing in many practical applications. There has therefore been a number of studies on more stable bandwidth selectors.[3] Most of them are related to the plug-in method: for example, the plug-in method of Sheather and Jones (1991), biased cross-validation by Scott and Terrell (1987); smoothed cross-validation by Hall, Marron, and Park (1992); and the stabilized bandwidth selector rule by Chiu (1991).

9.2.2 One-Sided Cross-Validation

Hart and Yi (1998) used local linear regression when introducing one-sided cross-validation in the regression context. They did this for two reasons: One-sided weighting clearly yields biased estimates for local constant estimation, and a good boundary correction method is crucial for the one-sided procedure. We therefore combine our one-sided cross-validation method with the local linear density estimator of Jones (1993). In density estimation, the local linear density estimator is identical to the standard kernel density estimator (not one-sided kernels) away from boundaries.

Let $K(\cdot)$ be any common symmetric kernel function and let us consider its (left) one-sided version,

$$\overline{K}(u) = \begin{cases} 2K(u) & \text{if } u < 0, \\ 0 & \text{otherwise} \end{cases} \tag{9.3}$$

Now consider the one-sided density estimator, $\hat{f}_{left,b}$ based on the one-sided kernel $\overline{K}$ and bandwidth b. We define the one-sided versions of the error measures ISE and MISE calling them OISE and MOISE. Call $\hat{b}_0$ and b_0 their minimizers (respectively).

We also have these assumptions on the kernel: $\mu_0(K) = 1, \mu_1(K) = 0$ and $\mu_2(K) < \infty$, where $\mu_l(K) = \int u^l K(u) du (l = 0, 1, 2)$.

The one-sided cross-validation criterion is defined as

$$\text{OSCV(b)} = \int \hat{f}_{left,b}^2(x)\, dx - 2n^{-1} \sum_{i=1}^{n} \hat{f}_{left,b}(X_i) \tag{9.4}$$

with $\hat{\hat{b}}$ as its minimizer. However, in Equation 9.4 we will use a kernel $\overline{K}^*$ for $f_{left,b}$ which will be derived in the following equations.

With these definitions, the one-sided cross-validation bandwidth is based on $\hat{b}$, but it has to be adjusted by a constant to become an estimator of the bandwidth for the original kernel density estimator. Let us define

$$\hat{b}_{OSCV} := C\hat{b} \qquad (9.5)$$

where the constant, C, will be the ratio of the optimal bandwidth (in MISE sense) of the density estimator ($\hat{f}_h$) to the optimal bandwidth (in MOISE sense) of the one-sided density estimator $\tilde{f}_{left,b}$, that is,

$$C = \frac{h_0}{b_0}$$

Asymptotically, our C constant will not depend on the underlying density. In order to get this to correct the bias of the one-sided kernel, we use local linear density estimators throughout.[4] Consider the minimization problem:

$$\min_{\beta_0, \beta_1} \left[\int \{ f_n(u) - \beta_0 - \beta_1(u-x) \}^2 \, K\left(\frac{u-x}{b}\right) du \right]$$

where $f_n(u) = n^{-1} \sum_{i=1}^{n} 1_{\{u = X_i\}}$ is the empirical density function. Then the local linear estimator is defined by the equivalent-kernel expression

$$\hat{f}_h(x) = \frac{1}{nb} \sum_{i=1}^{n} K^*\left(\frac{X_i - x}{b}\right) \qquad (9.6)$$

with the equivalent-kernel

$$
\begin{aligned}
K^*(u) &= e_1^T S^{-1}(1, \, u)^T K(u) \\
&= \frac{\mu_2(K) - \mu_1(K)u}{\mu_0(K)\mu_2(K) - (\mu_1(K))^2} K(u)
\end{aligned}
\qquad (9.7)
$$

being $e_1 = (1, 0)^T$ and $S = (\mu_{i+j-2})_{0 \le i, j \le 2}$. Neglecting boundary-correcting issues, for most of the commonly used kernels we get $K^* = K$, but not if we consider $\overline{K}$.

We define the operator $R(g) = \int \{g(x)\}^2 dx$, for a generic squared integrable function g. Then the optimal bandwidth for the local linear estimator is given by

$$h_0 = \left(\frac{R(K^*)}{(\mu_2(K^*))^2 R(f'')} \right)^{1/5} n^{-1/5} \qquad (9.8)$$

for the ordinary local linear estimator, and

$$h_0 = \left(\frac{R(\overline{K}^*)}{(\mu_2(\overline{K}^*))^2 R(f'')} \right)^{1/5} n^{-1/5} \qquad (9.9)$$

for the one-sided version, where $\overline{K}^* := (\overline{K})^*$ is the one-sided equivalent kernel (Equation 9.7), that is,

$$\overline{K}^*(u) = \frac{\mu_2(K) - u \left(2 \int_{-\infty}^{0} t K(t)dt \right)}{\mu_2(K) - \left(2 \int_{-\infty}^{0} t K(t)dt \right)^2} 2 K(u) 1_{\{u < 0\}} \qquad (9.10)$$

The adjusting constant becomes then

$$C = \left(\frac{R(K^*) \, \mu_2(\overline{K}^*)^2}{R(\overline{K}^*) \, \mu_2(K^*)^2} \right)^{1/5} \qquad (9.11)$$

which is a feasible number.

9.3 ASYMPTOTIC THEORY

The theoretical justification for the stability of one-sided cross-validation seems to come from the fact that its variation around the optimal bandwidth it aims to estimate is much smaller than the variation of ordinary cross-validation around its optimal bandwidth. We carry out the details of this argument next following Hall and Marron (1987). For the ease of notation, we will set $K = K^*$ and just write K in the text.

9.3.1 Assumptions

Assumption A1. The density, f, is bounded and twice differentiable, f' and f'' are bounded and integrable, and f'' is uniformly continuous.

Assumption A2. The kernel K is a compactly supported, symmetric density function on $\mathfrak{R}$ with Hölder-continuous derivative, K', and satisfies $\mu_2(K) \neq 0$.

Note that A2 refers to kernel K, not to its derivatives $\overline{K}$ or $\overline{K}^*$. Consider these additional definitions and notation, assuming that A1 and A2 hold:
Set $W(u) = -zK'(u)$ and the one-sided version, $\overline{W}^*(u) = -u\overline{K}^{*\prime}(u)1_{\{u < 0\}}$. Under assumption A2, these functions are kernels that integrate to 1 and verify that $\mu_1(W) = \mu_1(\overline{W}^*) = 0$.

Define the constants:

$$c_0 = \left[\frac{R(K)}{\{\mu_2(K)^2 R(f'')\}} \right]^{1/5}$$

and

$$c_1 = 2c_0^{-3} R(K) + 3\{\mu_2(K)\}^2 R\left(f''\right) c_0^2$$

and the one-sided versions:

$$c_0 = \left[\frac{R(\overline{K}^*)}{\{\mu_2(\overline{K}^*)^2 R(f'')\}} \right]^{1/5}$$

$$\overline{c}_1 = 2\overline{c}_0^{-3} R(\overline{K}^*) + 3\{\mu_2(\overline{K}^*)\}^2 R(f'')\overline{c}_0^2$$

Next, let us define the variance terms:

$$\sigma_c^2 = \left(\frac{2}{c_0}\right)^3 R(f)R(W) + (2\mu_2(K)c_0)^2 \left\{ \int (f'')^2 f - \left(\int f'' f\right)^2 \right\} \tag{9.12}$$

and

$$\overline{\sigma}_{oc}^2 = \left(\frac{2}{\overline{c}_0}\right)^3 R(f)R(\overline{W}^*) + (2\mu_2(\overline{K}^*)\overline{c}_0)^2 \left\{ \int (f'')^2 f - \left(\int f'' f\right)^2 \right\} \tag{9.13}$$

Observe that the difference $\int (f'')^2 f - \left(\int f'' f\right)^2$ is the variance of $f''(X)$. It will be denoted by $V(f'')$ in the text that follows.

Under conditions A1 and A2, Hall and Marron (1987) demonstrated that

$$n^{3/10}(\hat{h} - \hat{h}_0) \rightarrow N(0, \sigma_c^2 c_1^{-2}) \tag{9.14}$$

An application of Hall and Marron (1987) gives this result, which allows us to compare the variation of one-sided cross-validation to the variation of standard cross-validation:

Theorem 9.1   Under conditions (A1) and (A2),

$$n^{3/10}(\hat{h}_{OSCV} - C\hat{b}_0) \to N(0, C^2\overline{\sigma}_{oc}^2\overline{c}_1^{-2}) \qquad (9.15)$$

Then the gain in reduction of the variation can be approximated as shown next.

Remark 9.1   The ratio of the asymptotic variance of one-sided cross-validation to standard cross-validation is given by the ratio of the asymptotic variance from Equation 9.14 and the asymptotic variance of Equation 9.15:

$$G_{oc} = C^2 \left(\frac{c_1}{\overline{c}_1}\right)^2 \frac{\overline{\sigma}_{oc}^2}{\sigma_c^2} \qquad (9.16)$$

The reductions of variance for the Epanechnikov kernel and the Gaussian kernel are given by

$$G_{oc}^{Ep} = \frac{0.530605928\,R(f)R(f'') + 0.117383673\,V(f'')}{1.418004931\,R(f)R(f'') + 0.47266831\,V(f'')} \qquad (9.17)$$

and

$$G_{oc}^{Ga} = \frac{0.6913873\,R(f)R(f'') + 0.6173955\,V(f'')}{17.094364\,R(f)R(f'') + 1.363272\,V(f'')} \qquad (9.18)$$

So the variance reduction is at least 35% for the Epanechnikov kernel and at least 50% for the Gaussian kernel.

9.4   FINITE SAMPLE PERFORMANCE

The small sample performance of one-sided kernel density estimation is compared to its most immediate competitors, classical cross-validation and plug-in. The chosen plug-in method is also called refined plug-in and often referred to as Sheather-Jones bandwidth; details are given later. The performance is compared by integrated squared error (ISE) of which we derive several measures: the classical measure, where the ISE($\hat{h}$)s are calculated for all samples and then averaged (our measure m_3); a new—and perhaps better—measure where the $L2$-distance of the ISE($\hat{h}$)s from ISE($\hat{h}_0$)s is calculated (our measure m_1); and the $L1$-distance (our m_2) respectively. The new measures take variability of the ISEs into account and penalize bandwidth selectors that often do well but occasionally fail completely. We also calculate the bias of the bandwidth selectors (our m_5) and the volatility of the ISEs (our measure m_4). These numbers will help us to explain why one-sided cross-validation does better than classical cross-validation. Concretely, given a bandwidth estimate $\hat{h}$, the considered criteria are:

$$m_1 = mean(\{\text{ISE}(\hat{h}) - \text{ISE}(\hat{h}_0)\}^2)$$

$$m_2 = mean(|\text{ISE}(\hat{h}) - \text{ISE}(\hat{h}_0)|)$$

$$m_3 = mean(\text{ISE}(\hat{h}))$$

$$m_4 = std(\text{ISE}(\hat{h}))$$

and

$$m_5 = mean(\hat{h} - \hat{h}_0)$$

For brevity, we will concentrate on kernel density estimation with the local linear Epanechnikov kernel.

The plug-in bandwidth h_0 is estimated, from Equation 9.8. Here, $R(K)$ and $\mu_2(K)$ are known whereas $R(f'')$ has to be estimated with a prior bandwidth g_p. To do this, take Silverman's rule of thumb bandwidth g_p for Gaussian kernels,[5] where the standard deviation of X is estimated by the minimum of two methods: the moment estimate s_n and the interquartile range IR_X divided by 1.34, that is, $g_S = 1.06 \, min\{IR_X 1.34^{-1}, s_n\}n^{-1/5}$. Then, as the Quartic kernel K_Q comes close to the Epanechnikov but allows for estimating the second derivative, we normalize g_S by the factors of the canonical kernel (Gaussian to Quartic) and adjust for the slower rate $(n^{-1/9})$ needed to estimate second derivatives, that is,

$$g_p = g_S \frac{2.0362}{0.7764} n^{1/5 - 1/9}$$

Next, we calculate

$$\hat{R}(f'') = R(\hat{f}'') - \frac{1}{n g_p^5} R(K_Q'')$$

to correct for the bias inherited by

$$\hat{f}''(x) = \frac{1}{n g_p^3} \sum_{i=1}^{n} K_Q'' \left(\frac{x - X_i}{g_p} \right)$$

In simulation studies not shown here, the prior choice turned out to perform better than any modification we have tried, at least for the estimation problems discussed here.

9.4.1 Data Generating Processes and Numerical Results

We considered a large number of normal, gamma, and mixed densities as data generating processes (DGP). We will concentrate on these six:

1. A simple normal distribution, $N(0.5, 0.2^2)$
2. A mixture of two normals, which were $N(0.35, 0.1^2)$ and $N(0.65, 0.1^2)$
3. A gamma distribution, $Gamma(a, b)$ with $b = 1.5$, $a = b^2$ applied on $5x$ with $x \in \Re_+$, that is,

$$f(x) = 5 \frac{b^a}{\Gamma(a)} (5x)^{a-1} e^{-5xb}$$

4. A mixture of two gamma distributions, $Gamma(a_j, b_j), a_j = b_j^2, b_1 = 1.5, b_2 = 3$, applied on $6x$, that is,

$$f(x) = \frac{6}{2} \sum_{j=1}^{2} \frac{b_j^{a_j}}{\Gamma(a_j)} (6x)^{a_j-1} e^{-6xb_j}$$

   giving one mode and a plateau
5. A mixture of three gamma distributions, $Gamma(a_j, b_j), a_j = b_j^2, b_1 = 1.5, b_2 = 3, b_3 = 6$ applied on $8x$ giving two bumps and one plateau.
6. A mixture of three normals, $N(0.25, 0.075^2)$, $N(0.5, 0.075^2)$, and $N(0.75, 0.075^2)$, giving three clear modes.

As you can see in Figure 9.1, all six models have the main mass in $[0, 1]$. You can see also that we have mostly densities with exponentially decreasing tails. In this simulation study we will disregard the possible use of boundary-correcting kernels. Moreover, we assume that the empirical researcher has no knowledge of possible boundaries. For the six models, we considered sample sizes: $n = 50$, 100 and 200, and 250 repetitions (simulation runs) for each model and each sample size.

The results of the six densities are collected in Tables 9.1 to 9.3. We see that one-sided cross-validation does better and is much more stable than classical cross-validation on most of our performance measures (see

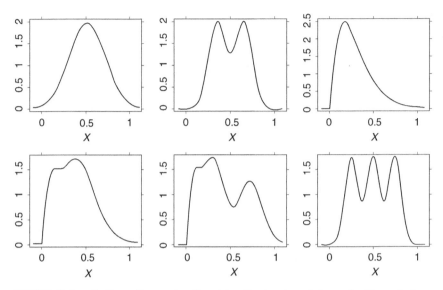

FIGURE 9.1 Six Data Generating Densities: Design 1 to 6, from the Upper Left to the Lower Right

TABLE 9.1 Criteria Values for Designs 1 and 2

		Design 1			Design 2		
n	Criteria	CV	OSCV	Plug-in	CV	OSCV	Plug-in
	m_1	.0112	.0004	3e-05	.0171	.0012	.0016
	m_2	.0407	.0064	.0029	.0552	.0263	.0357
50	m_3	.0781	.0438	.0403	.1112	.0823	.0917
	m_4	.1028	.0372	.0305	.1214	.0351	.0197
	m_5	−.0225	.0136	.0193	.0071	.0500	.0803
	m_1	.0028	8e-05	1e-05	.0019	.0004	.0009
	m_2	.0234	.0039	.0014	.0246	.0142	.0288
100	m_3	.0479	.0285	.0260	.0590	.0486	.0633
	m_4	.0530	.0209	.0185	.0450	.0241	.0137
	m_5	−.0234	.0088	.0160	.0067	.0308	.0763
	m_1	.0017	3e-05	1e-06	.0021	.0007	.0005
	m_2	.0110	.0024	.0007	.0159	.0084	.0213
200	m_3	.0255	.0170	.0152	.0384	.0309	.0438
	m_4	.0417	.0125	.0108	.0448	.0287	.0116
	m_5	−.0136	.0034	.0127	.0003	.0145	.0671

TABLE 9.2   Criteria Values for Designs 3 and 4

		Design 3			Design 4		
n	Criteria	CV	OSCV	Plug-in	CV	OSCV	Plug-in
	m_1	.0164	.0026	.0019	.0062	.0009	6e-05
	m_2	.0564	.0339	.0342	.0343	.0096	.0053
50	m_3	.1316	.1092	.1095	.0823	.0576	.0534
	m_4	.1206	.0557	.0457	.0756	.0353	.0215
	m_5	−5e-05	.0456	.0669	−.0081	.0335	.0398
	m_1	.0018	.0006	.0010	.0007	8e-05	4e-05
	m_2	.0227	.0196	.0269	.0126	.0056	.0047
100	m_3	.0698	.0667	.0741	.0466	.0397	.0387
	m_4	.0480	.0329	.0306	.0276	.0158	.0134
	m_5	−.0008	.0388	.0666	−.0035	.0327	.0395
	m_1	.0030	.0008	.0005	.0022	.0008	3e-05
	m_2	.0168	.0126	.0193	.0130	.0061	.0040
200	m_3	.0495	.0453	.0520	.0365	.0296	.0275
	m_4	.0559	.0318	.0200	.0460	.0292	.0070
	m_5	−.0038	.0245	.0593	−.0056	.0302	.0393

TABLE 9.3   Criteria Values for Designs 5 and 6

		Design 5			Design 6		
n	Criteria	CV	OSCV	Plug-in	CV	OSCV	Plug-in
	m_1	.0034	.0042	.0001	.0095	.0055	.0055
	m_2	.0283	.0239	.0088	.0455	.0659	.0669
50	m_3	.0810	.0765	.0615	.1173	.1377	.1387
	m_4	.0591	.0664	.0222	.0896	.0159	.0126
	m_5	.0023	.0860	.0518	.0211	.0989	.1057
	m_1	.0006	.0001	.0001	.0034	.0020	.0046
	m_2	.0123	.0090	.0086	.0240	.0325	.0655
100	m_3	.0480	.0447	.0442	.0687	.0771	.1101
	m_4	.0272	.0158	.0146	.0600	.0358	.0080
	m_5	.0041	.0397	.0521	.0102	.0500	.0977
	m_1	.0012	7e-05	7e-05	.0008	.0002	.0034
	m_2	.0114	.0065	.0070	.0125	.0084	.0577
200	m_3	.0359	.0310	.0315	.0403	.0362	.0855
	m_4	.0352	.0108	.0094	.0293	.0186	.0069
	m_5	−.0009	.0342	.0506	.0015	.0152	.0878

especially m_1 and m_2). Therefore, the relative improvement in performance is even bigger with our main performance measure m_1; compare Remark 9.1. One can see that the price for stability (compare, e.g., m_4) of both the one-sided cross-validation and the plug-in method is a tendency to overestimate the bandwidth a little bit; see m_5. However, the stability easily makes up for this bias, and the overall performance of both methods tends to be better than the performance of classical cross-validation. To see this, recall that the measures of interest for the practitioner are usually m_1 to m_3. The conclusion is that one-sided cross-validation performs similar to—sometimes worse than, sometimes better than—the plug-in method. Our results therefore parallel the results of Hart and Yi (1998) in the regression context.

9.5 PRACTICAL REMARKS AND DATA APPLICATIONS

9.5.1 Data Transformation and Boundary Correction

In our application we estimate densities of data belonging to the interval (0,1) because we want to apply the transformation approach of Buch-Larsen et al. (2005) to estimate some loss distributions of operational risk. While the transformation methodology of Buch-Larsen et al. (2005) has proven to be extremely efficient and beat its direct competitors in their extensive simulation study, their bandwidth selection is not very sophisticated. It is just the simplest possible bandwidth selector: Silverman's rule of thumb. Recall that if the prior information of facing a one-mode distribution is available, Silverman's rule of thumb may give nice plots but is generally much too coarse for a detailed data analysis. So, while the transformation method of Buch-Larsen et al. already has shown its usefulness, it clearly needs to be updated by a better bandwidth selection method. We use cross-validation, refined plug-in, Silverman's rule of thumb, and our new one-sided cross-validation estimator as our selection rules. We conclude that while the other estimators grossly oversmooth or undersmooth to what seems to be appropriate, the one-sided cross-validation seems to work very well in practice.

First a few words on the actual transformation. In our two cases, the modified Champernowne distribution of Buch-Larsen et al. (2005) actually simplifies since their parameter c is estimated to zero. This implies that the transformation is a special case of the original Champernowne distribution[6] and from a transformation point of view is identical to the Möbius transformation used for the same purpose by Clements, Hurd, and Lindsay (2003).

The simple Champernowne distribution has a cumulated distribution function

$$T(x) = x^\alpha (x^\alpha + M^\alpha)^{-1}$$

with density

$$t(x) = \alpha x^{\alpha-1} M^\alpha (x^\alpha + M^\alpha)^{-2}$$

where M and α will be estimated via maximum likelihood on the original data.

We will apply our method with boundary correcting kernels on the transformed data $y_i = \hat{T}(x_i)$, $(i = 1, \ldots, n)$, where $\hat{T}(\cdot)$ refers to $T(\cdot)$ with estimated α and M. We define $\hat{t}(\cdot)$ in the same way. The resulting kernel density estimate we call $\hat{f}_{transf}(y)$. Then the final density estimate for the original data is $\hat{f}(x_i) = \hat{f}_{transf}(y_i) \cdot \hat{t}(x_i)$.

Note that $\{y_i\}_{i=1}^n \in (0, 1)$. So we have to define a local linear estimator on the interval $(0, 1)$. As long as all bandwidths considered (i.e., the bandwidth of the original kernel estimator and the bandwidth of the one-sided kernel estimator) are smaller than one-half, we can continue to use the local linear estimator defined above, which takes care of only one boundary. The reason for this is that, as long as all bandwidths are smaller than one-half, we can modify our approach of one-sided kernel estimation in this way: taking weights only from the right when estimating in the interval $(0, 1/2)$ and taking weights from the left when estimating in the interval $(1/2, 1)$. The asymptotic theory that our one-sided kernel bandwidth approach is based on is of course unchanged by this, and we can proceed as described. Since in our specific applications we need bandwidths only smaller than 0.5, we do not need to generalize our procedure further to take care of two boundaries. It is enough to replace Equation 9.3 by

$$\overline{K}(u) = \begin{cases} 2K(u) & \text{if } u < 0 \text{ and } 0 < x \le 1/2 \\ 2K(u) & \text{if } u > 0 \text{ and } 1/2 < x < 1 \\ 0 & \text{otherwise} \end{cases}$$

Then calculate our one-sided bandwidth and rescale to our final bandwidth.

9.5.2 Operational Risks: Execution, Delivery, and Process Management

We first apply our method to a small data set with sample size $n = 75$. It has been taken from a major publicly available financial loss database on operational risk data. We consider the loss line "execution, delivery, and process management" with relatively few reported claims.

First we have transformed the data along the lines described earlier in text. For this transformation $\hat{T}$, we got from a maximum likelihood estimation $\hat{\alpha} = 1.1129968$ and $\hat{M} = 3.2357247$. Then we searched for the optimal bandwidths on an equispaced grid of 50 bandwidths from $h_{\min} = 1/75$ to $h_{\max} = 0.5$, respectively, $0.27 \approx C/2$ for the one-sided cross-validation (such that $b_{\max} = h_{\max}C^{-1} \approx 0.5$ and we can avoid the necessity of doing boundary correction for the OSCV density estimates). For kernel K we again used the Epanechnikov kernel, as we did in the simulations. The results were $\hat{h}_{CV} = 0.05$ for the classical cross-validation, $\hat{h}_{OSCV} = 0.24$ for the one-sided cross-validation, $\hat{h}_S = 0.29$ for Silverman's bandwidth, and $\hat{h}_{PI} = 0.43$ for the refined plug-in method. Silverman's bandwidth has been calculated as described in Section 9.4 as g_S but corrected for Epanechnikov kernels. Compared to the other bandwidth estimates, $\hat{h}_{PI}$ is much too big. A closer look at the calculation revealed that for this (small) data set, the refined plug-in method has serious problems with the estimation of the second derivative f''.

Figure 9.2 gives the resulting density plots for both the original and the transformed data except for $\hat{h}_{PI}$, as this was ridiculously oversmoothed.

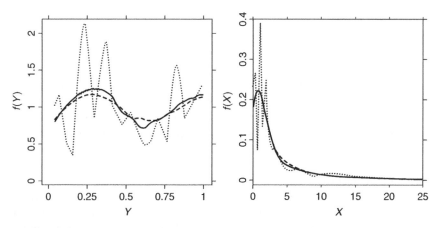

FIGURE 9.2 Density Estimates for Transformed (left) and Original Data (right): solid for $\hat{h}_{OSCV}$, dots for $\hat{h}_{CV}$, and dash for $\hat{h}_S$. The graph on the right is cut off at $x = 25$.

It can be seen clearly that CV tends to under- and plug-in to oversmooth whereas our one-sided cross-validation method lies in between. While the difference between the three curves might seem negligible to the untrained eye, the difference in the heaviness of the three tails is actually enormous, and economic judgments would be very different for these three curve estimators. Note that the transformation approach allows us to compare the entire tail and that we therefore are able to get a visual impression of the relationship between tails for different estimators. This visual comparison is more complicated on the original scale; we cannot capture the entire positive axis in one picture.

In the second example we consider external fraud taken from the same financial data base as our first data set was taken from. Here the number of observations is $n = 538$.

For this data set, the transformation $\hat{T}$ has been performed with the maximum likelihood estimates $\hat{\alpha} = 1.113242$ and $\hat{M} = 4.0$. According to the sample size, we have searched for the optimal bandwidths on an equispaced grid of 50 bandwidths from $h_{min} = 1/538$ to $h_{max} = 0.25 < C/2$. Here, we also tried with larger h_{min} for reasons we discuss later. For kernel K we again have applied the Epanechnikov kernel. The results were that $\hat{h}_{CV}$ (using the classical cross-validation) always converged to zero whatever our h_{min} was. It is well known that for increasing n, cross-validation suffers from this problem. As a remedy, Feluch and Koronacki (1992) propose to omit from the cross-validation not just observation x_i (y_i in our application) but x_i and its neighbors, in other words an ε-environment $U_\varepsilon(x_i)$. However, in practice, it is not clear how large this environment has to be; it certainly depends on sample size n. Moreover, often $\hat{h}_{CV}$ varies a lot with the size of $U_\varepsilon(x_i)$. Summarizing, in this application we failed to find a reasonable $\hat{h}_{CV}$. Other results have been $\hat{h}_{OSCV} = 0.100$ for the one-sided cross validation, $\hat{h}_S = 0.190$ for Silverman's bandwidths, and $\hat{h}_{PI} = 0.214$ for the refined plug-in method.

In Figure 9.3 are given the resulting density plots for both the original and the transformed data. Again, obviously CV tends to strongly undersmooth (not plotted as $\hat{h}_{CV} \approx 0.0$) and plug-in to oversmooth whereas our one-sided cross validation method lies in between although with the tendency to undersmooth. Also here the difference of the shown curves might seem slight, but the difference in the heaviness is so big that it is very important on which of these curves economic judgments are based.

We conclude that our one-sided method clearly beats classic cross-validation and refined plug-in in both the simulations and the real data examples. We have seen one example in which refined plug-in breaks down and one in which classic cross-validation breaks down whereas our method does reasonably well throughout.

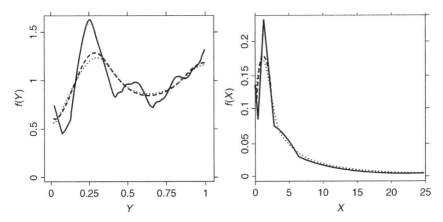

FIGURE 9.3 Density Estimates for Transformed (left) and Original Data (right): solid for $\hat{h}_{OSCV}$, dash for $\hat{h}_S$, and dots for $\hat{h}_{PI}$. The graph on the right is cut off at $x = 25$.

9.6 CONCLUSION

The challenge of estimating the loss distribution in operational risk has been analyzed. One major problem in this effort is that operational risk losses almost never fit a parametric distribution. A parametric distribution might fit most of the observed data well while having a terrible fit in the tail. However, the tail is the really important part of any operational risk loss distribution. Therefore, we consider a more flexible methodology combining a parametric outlook with a nonparametric adjustment. When very little data are available, our method is close to the standard parametric approach. When more data are available, we adjust the parametric distribution locally using a standard kernel-smoothing methodology. In this chapter we analyze the problem of choosing the level of adjustment: How much weight should one put to the locally available information? In our approach, the question corresponds to choosing bandwidth in our kernel-smoothing procedure. Standard bandwidth choosing procedures do not seem to work too well in our case; either a procedure is not sufficiency robust (cross-validation), or it depends too heavily on unrealistic estimates of derivatives of the unknown distribution (plug-in). In this chapter we present for the first time one-sided cross-validation. This procedure is as automatic and simple to implement as standard cross-validation while at the same time it is as robust and stable as standard plug-in methods. We have shown through an extensive simulation study that our bandwidth selection procedure works on a number of different distributions, and we have applied the method on a real-life operational risk data set. The results are highly satisfactory.

NOTES

1. See Hart and Yi (1998); Yi (1996, 2001, 2004).
2. See Chiu (1996) and Loader (1999) for discussions of these issues.
3. See Härdle, Müller, Sperlich, and Werwatz (2004).
4. See Jones (1993) and Cheng (1997a, 1997b).
5. See Silverman (1986).
6. See Champernowne (1936, 1952).

REFERENCES

Bowman, A. 1984. An alternative method of cross-validation for the smoothing of density estimates. *Biometrika* 71, no. 2:353–360.

Buch-Larsen, T., J. P. Nielsen, M. Guillén, and C. Bolancé. 2005. Kernel density estimation for heavy-tailed distributions using the Champernowne transformation. *Statistics* 39, no. 6:503–518.

Champernowne, D. G. 1936. The Oxford meeting, September 25–29, 1936. *Econometrica* 5, no. 2:198.

Champernowne, D. G. 1952. The graduation of income distributions. *Econometrica* 20, no. 4: 591–615.

Cheng, M. Y. 1997a. A bandwidth selector for local linear density estimators. *Annals of Statistics* 25, no. 3:1001–1013.

Cheng, M. Y. 1997b. Boundary-aware estimators of integrated squared density derivatives. *Journal of the Royal Statistical Society*, Ser. B 59, no. 1:191203.

Chiu, S. T. 1991. Bandwidth selection for kernel density estimation. *Annals of Statistics* 19, no. 4:1883–1905.

Chiu, S. T. 1996. A comparative review of bandwidth selection for kernel density estimation. *Statistica Sinica* 6, no. 1:129–145.

Clements, A. E., A. S. Hurn, and K. A. Lindsay. 2003. Möbius-like mappings and their use in kernel density estimation. *Journal of the American Statistical Association* 98, no. 464:993–1000.

Fan, J., I. Gijbels, T. C. Hu, and L. S. Huang. 1996. A study of variable bandwidth selection for local polynomial regression. *Statistica Sinica* 6, no. 1:113–127.

Feluch, W., and J. Koronacki. 1992. A note on modified cross-validation in density estimation. *Computational Statistics & Data Analysis* 13, no. 2:143–151.

Hall, P. 1983. Large sample optimality of least squares cross-validation in density estimation. *Annals of Statistics* 11, no. 4:1156–1174.

Hall, P., and J. S. Marron. 1987. Extent to which least-squares cross-validation minimises integrated square error in nonparametric density estimation. *Probability Theory and Related Fields* 74, no. 4:567–581.

Hall, P., J. S. Marron, and B. Park. 1992. Smoothed cross-validation. *Probability Theory and Related Fields* 92, no. 1:1–20.

Härdle, W., P. Hall, and J. S. Marron. 1988. How far are automatically chosen regression smoothing parameters from their optimum? *Journal of the American Statistical Association* 83, no. 401:86–99.

Härdle, W., M. Müller, S. Sperlich, and A. Werwatz. 2004. *Non- and semiparametric models*. New York: Springer.

Hart, J. D., and S. Yi. 1998. One-sided cross-validation. *Journal of the American Statistical Association* 93, no. 442:620–631.

Jones, M. C. 1993. Simple boundary correction in kernel density estimation. *Statistics and Computing* 3, no. 3:135–146.

Loader, C. R. 1999. Bandwidth selection: Classical or plug-in? *Annals of Statistics* 27, no. 2:415–438.

Rudemo, M. 1982. Empirical choice of histograms and kernel density estimators. *Scandinavian Journal of Statistics* 9, no. 2:65–78.

Scoot, D. W., and G. R. Terrell. 1987. Biased and unbiased cross-validation in density estimation. *Journal of the American Statistical Association* 82, no. 400:1131–1146.

Sheather, S. J., and M. C. Jones. 1991. A reliable data-based bandwidth selection method for kernel density estimation. *Journal of the Royal Statistical Society*, Ser. B, 53, no. 3:683–690.

Silverman, B. 1986. *Density estimation for statistics and data analysis*. London: Chapman and Hall.

Wand, M. P., and M. C. Jones. 1995. *Kernel smoothing*, vol. 60, Monographs on Statistics and Applied Probability. London: Chapman and Hall.

Yi, S. 1996. On one-sided cross-validation in nonparametric regression. Ph.D. diss., Texas A&M University, Department of Statistics.

Yi, S. 2001. Asymptotic stability of the OSCV smoothing parameter selection. *Communications in Statistics. Theory and Methods*, 30 (3): 2033–2044.

Yi, S. 2004. A comparison of two bandwidth selectors OSCV and AICc in nonparametric regression. *Communications in Statistics. Simulation and Computation* 34, no. 3:585–594.

CHAPTER 10

Multivariate Models for Operational Risk: A Copula Approach Using Extreme Value Theory and Poisson Shock Models

Omar Rachedi and Dean Fantazzini

ABSTRACT

The aggregation of event types (ETs) is a crucial step for operational risk management techniques. Basel II requires the computation of a 99.9% VaR for each ET, and their aggregation via a simple sum if the dependence among ETs is not specified. Such a procedure assumes perfect positive dependence and therefore involves the implementation of the most conservative aggregation model. We propose a methodology that uses extreme-value theory to model the loss severities, copulas to model their dependence, and a general Poisson shock model to capture the dependencies among ETs. We show that this approach allows the allocation of capital and hedge operational risk in a more efficient way than the standard approach.

Omar Rachedi thanks Professor Carlo Bianchi, Dr. Giorgio Aprile, and Francesca Fabbri for their comments and suggestions.

10.1 INTRODUCTION

The quantitative analysis of operational risk is a relative recent field of study within the more general quantitative risk management framework (see King 2001 and Cruz 2002). The operational risk issue has arisen when both market risk management and credit risk management have been found unable to hedge all possible events affecting the economic and financial results of financial institutions.

The development of this subject is a direct consequence of the New Capital Adequacy Framework, also called Basel II. This chapter proposes a new methodology to compute the capital charge needed for operational risk management.

The Basel II Agreement defines operational risk as "the risk of losses resulting from inadequate or failed internal processes, people systems or from external events." Basel II first defines seven ETs and eight business lines (BLs) in order to classify all possible operational risks (see BIS 2003). See Table 10.1.

However, Basel II has not introduced a precise advanced model for analyzing and aggregating ETs and BLs. It only describes some basic rules every financial institution has to follow: the confidence level, the time horizon, and some considerations about dependencies. Particularly, Basel II requires a one-year horizon and a 99.9% confidence level, but a robust analysis of dependencies is not developed, since every bank has to follow the more conservative aggregation model: ETs are supposed to be perfectly comonotonic (i.e., perfectly dependent) and aggregation is applied using a mere sum of the value at risk (VaR) of each ET or BL.

In this chapter, we consider only the seven ETs (their extension to BLs is straightforward) and analyze the issue of their aggregation via copulas,

TABLE 10.1 Event Types and Business Lines Mapping According to Basel II

Event Types (ETs)	Business Lines (BLs)
1. Internal Fraud	1. Corporate Finance
2. External Fraud	2. Trading and Sales
3. Employment Practices and Workplace Safety	3. Retail Banking
4. Clients, Product and Business Practices	4. Commercial Banking
5. Damage to Physical Assets	5. Payment and Settlement
6. Business Disruption, System Failures, and Execution	6. Agency Services
7. Delivery and Process Management	7. Asset Management
	8. Retail Brokerage

suggesting a new model to incorporate dependence not only among severities but also among frequencies. We then compare this new methodology with the conservative aggregation model suggested by Basel II and with the canonical aggregation model via copula proposed by Di Clemente and Romano (2004) and Fantazzini et al. (2007, 2008), to show the higher efficiency of our new approach.

Section 10.2 of the chapter is devoted to describing the standard Local Density Approximation (LDA) approach to assess operational risk. Section 10.3 discusses the aggregation across event types, with a focus on copula functions, and we present the Poisson shock model, describing the procedure to analyze dependence among frequencies and severities. Section 10.4 presents some empirical results showing how it is possible to improve efficiency in the Op-VaR computation by using our methodology. Section 10.5 serves as a conclusion.

10.2 STANDARD LDA APPROACH

As previously discussed, operational risk is directly connected with the activities implemented by a financial institution. Although there is a clear linkage with market and credit risk activities, the analysis of operational risk has many similarities with the analysis of claims in the insurance framework (see Panjer and Willmot 1992).

The standard LDA methodology analyzes frequencies and severities separately. Only in a second step are the two components integrated by means of compounding. In this way, it is possible to assess the distribution of the aggregate losses and to compute the required risk measure. In this chapter we consider the VaR and the expected shortfall (ES), also known as conditional value at risk (CVaR).

To present the LDA approach, we consider the random loss $L(i)$ over a one-year horizon for the event type $I = 1, \ldots, d$, defined as:

$$L(i) = \sum_{k=0}^{N(i)} X_k(i) \tag{10.1}$$

where $N(i) =$ number of loss events in one year for the ith ET
$X_k(i) =$ loss magnitude (i.e., the severity observed in the kth loss event in the ith ET)

Frequencies are modeled using homogeneous Poisson processes and severities are modeled using the lognormal distribution for the body of the loss distribution and an extreme value theory (EVT) distribution for the tail.

In this way we can focus on extreme loss behavior, assessing a capital charge robust to highly unexpected losses: A recent example of such losses is the €4.9 billion loss reported by Société Générale due to fraudulent derivatives trading in January 2008.

Once frequencies and severities are estimated, they are compounded using Monte Carlo sampling routines, and the required capital charge is then calculated, using the VaR at the 99.9% level:

$$VaR_t^i = F_L^{-1}(0.999) \tag{10.2}$$

where L = aggregate loss distribution for the ith ET
           F^{-1} = inverse function of the cumulative distribution L

Following the more conservative approach suggested by Basel II, the aggregation of VaRs for each ET is computed in this way:

$$K_{TOT} = \sum_{i=1}^{7} VaR_L^i \tag{10.3}$$

We also considered the ES as an alternative risk measure, given the lack of subadditivity of the VaR shown in Artzner et al. (1999). In this sense, the VaR is not a coherent risk measure. The ES can be defined as:

$$ES_i^{.999} = E\left[X_i \mid X_i > VaR_i^{.999} \right] \tag{10.4}$$

We assume here that losses are stationary and independent and identically distributed (i.i.d.), even though in practice it is possible to observe some forms of serial dependence. However, Roher (2002) shows that this kind of behavior, where it is observed, is quite marginal. Besides, we do not consider the issue of truncated data: Operational losses are usually collected above a given threshold that could vary across banks. Those missing data may cause some biases if we apply the canonical estimation procedures, thus underestimating the final capital charge. It is possible to solve this problem using a truncated extension of estimation routines or using the EM algorithm (see Bee 2005).

Another problem is the aggregation of internal and external data, in order to improve the estimation robustness. In our study this topic is not covered because this kind of aggregation would have a relatively small impact on the final estimation of the capital charge, given our large data set. However, we consider it an avenue of further research.

10.2.1 Frequency Model

The analysis of operational risk losses is split into a frequency model and a severity model. Given that losses are observed at irregular times, we use discrete distributions. The standard LDA approach models the frequency using either the homogeneous Poisson distribution or the negative binomial distribution.

The Poisson distribution expresses the probability of a number of events occurring in a fixed period of time, given that these events occur with a known average rate and independently of the time passed since the last event. If the expected number of occurrence in a given time interval is λ, then the probability that there are exactly x occurrences (x being a nonnegative integer, $x = 0, 1, 2, \ldots$) is equal to

$$f(x, \lambda) = \frac{\lambda^x e^{-\lambda}}{x!} \tag{10.5}$$

The Poisson distribution has $E(x) = V(x) = \lambda$. Thus, the number of observed occurrences fluctuates about its mean λ with a standard deviation $\sigma_x = \sqrt{\lambda}$. These fluctuations are usually known as Poisson noise. An alternative distribution to model the frequency is the negative binomial. One very common parameterization of this distribution employs two real-valued parameters p and r with $0 < p < 1$ and $r > 0$. Under this parameterization, the probability mass function of a random variable with a $neg\,Bin(r, p)$ distribution takes this form:

$$f(x; r, p) = \binom{x + r - 1}{x} \cdot p^r \cdot (1 - p)^x \quad \text{for} \quad x = 0, 1, \ldots \tag{10.6}$$

where

$$\binom{x + r - 1}{x} = \frac{\Gamma(x + r)}{x! \cdot \Gamma(r)} = (-1)^x \cdot \binom{-r}{x} \tag{10.7}$$

and $\Gamma(x) = (x - 1)!$.

The negative binomial distribution converges to the Poisson distribution when:

$$Poisson\,(\lambda) = \lim_{r \to \infty} negBin\left(\frac{r, r}{(\lambda + r)}\right) \tag{10.8}$$

In this parameterization, r controls the deviation from the Poisson. This makes the negative binomial distribution a suitable and interesting

TABLE 10.2 Number of Loss Events, Mean and Variance for Each Event Type

	ET 1	ET 2	ET 3	ET 4	ET 5	ET 6	ET 7
Number	6,001	322	405	16,779	1,704	10,832	724
Mean	28.04	39.80	15.45	27.39	48.38	18.85	282.93
Var	33.57	47.89	21.00	25.35	43.47	17.57	292.93

alternative to the Poisson, which approaches the Poisson for large r but which has larger variance than the Poisson for small r.

Since our data set shows variances very close to the means for each ETs (see Table 10.2), we employ here the Poisson distribution only.

We would like to stress that we make this choice because our loss data shows this peculiar feature. However, the negative binomial can be a better choice with different data sets, particularly when they are small.

10.2.2 Severity Model

If modeling of severity distributions is of concern, a very large variety of distributions can be considered, such as the lognormal, Burr, Gamma, and generalized Pareto distribution (GPD). Given the extreme behavior of operational risk losses, we decided to analyze the tail of the severity distributions using extreme value theory (EVT). EVT deals with the analysis of rare events, and it has been passed from the field of hydrology to finance and insurance to predict the occurrence of such events or, at least, to build more robust models for unexpected extreme events. The interested reader is referred to Embrechts et al. (1997) and McNeil et al. (2005).

EVT allows us to reject the paradigm of the Gaussian distribution for operational risk losses, with a special focus on the tail of its distribution. It becomes even more important when calculating a risk measure as the VaR or the ES at high confidence levels, such as the case of operational risk, 99.9%. For further details on the applications of EVT within operational risk management, see Chavez-Demoulin et al. (2006).

In short, EVT affirms that the losses exceeding a given high threshold u converge asymptotically to the GPD, whose cumulative function is usually expressed as:

$$GPD_{\xi\beta} = \begin{cases} 1 - \left(1 + \xi\dfrac{y}{\beta}\right)^{-1/\xi} & \xi \neq 0 \\ 1 - \exp\left(-\dfrac{y}{\beta}\right) & \xi = 0 \end{cases} \quad (10.9)$$

where $y = x - u$, $y \geq 0$ if $\xi \geq 0$ and $0 \leq y \leq -\beta/\xi$ if $\xi \leq 0$

ys are called *excesses* whereas xs are called *exceedances*

It is possible to determine the conditional distribution function of the excesses (i.e., ys) as a function of x:

$$F_u(y) = P(X - u \leq y | X > u) = \frac{F_x(x) - F_x(u)}{1 - F_x(u)} \tag{10.10}$$

In these representations the parameter ξ is crucial: when $\xi = 0$, we have an exponential distribution; when $\xi < 0$, we have a Pareto distribution—II Type and when $\xi > 0$, we have a Pareto distribution—I Type. Moreover, this parameter has a direct connection with the existence of finite moments of the losses distributions. We have the following equation:

$$E\left(x^k\right) = \infty \text{ if } k \geq 1/\xi \tag{10.11}$$

Hence, in the case of a GPD as a Pareto—I Type, when $\xi \geq 1$, we have infinite mean models, as also shown by Moscadelli (2004) and Neslehova et al. (2006).

Following Di Clemente-Romano (2004), we suggest to model the loss severity using the lognormal for the body of the distribution and EVT for the tail in this way:

$$F_i(x) = \begin{cases} \Phi\left(\dfrac{\ln x - \mu(i)}{\sigma(i)}\right) & 0 < x < u(i) \\ 1 - \dfrac{N_u(i)}{N_i}\left(1 + \xi(i)\dfrac{x - u(i)}{\beta(i)}\right)^{-1/\xi(i)} & u(i) \leq x \end{cases} \tag{10.12}$$

where Φ = standardized normal cumulative distribution functions

$N_u(i)$ = number of losses exceeding the threshold $u(i)$

$N(i)$ = number of the loss data observed in the ith ET

$\beta(i)$ = scale parameters of a GPD

$\xi(i)$ = shape parameters of a GPD

The graphical analysis for our ET3 data set reported in Figures 10.1 and 10.2 clearly shows that operational risk losses are characterized by high-frequency–low-severity and low-frequency–high-severity losses. Hence the behavior of losses is twofold: One process underlies small and frequent losses and another underlies jumbo losses. Splitting the model in two parts allows us to estimate the impact of such extreme losses in a more robust way.

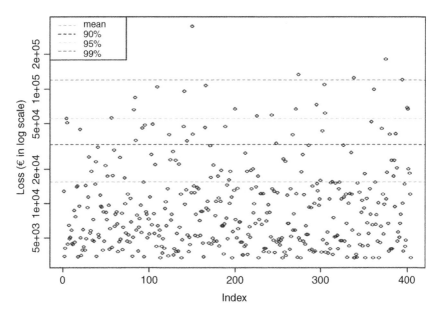

FIGURE 10.1 Scatter Plot of ET3 Losses. The dotted lines represent, respectively, mean, 90%, 95%, and 99.9% empirical quantiles

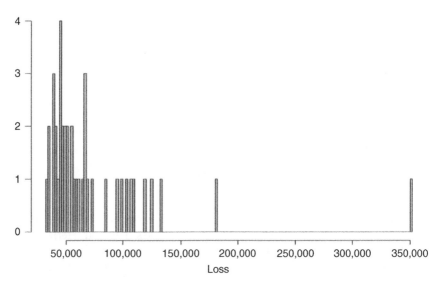

FIGURE 10.2 Histogram of ET3 Losses

An important issue to consider is the estimation of the severity distribution parameters. While the estimation via maximum likelihood (ML) in the lognormal case is straightforward, in the EVT case, it is extremely important to consider whether ML or the alternative probability weighted moment (PWM) routines are able to capture the dynamics underlying losses severities. Concerning ML, the log-likelihood function equals

$$l\left((\xi, \beta)\,; X\right) = -n\ln\beta - \left(\frac{1}{\xi} + 1\right)\sum_{i=1}^{n}\ln\left(1 + \frac{\xi}{\beta}X_i\right) \qquad (10.13)$$

This method works fine if $\xi > -1/2$. In this case, it is possible to show that

$$n^{1/2}\left(\hat{\xi}_n - \xi, \frac{\hat{\beta}_n}{\beta} - 1\right) \xrightarrow{d} N\left(0, M^{-1}\right), \quad n \to \infty$$

where

$$M^{-1} = (1 + \xi)\begin{pmatrix} 1 + \xi & -1 \\ -1 & 2 \end{pmatrix}$$

Instead, the PWM consists of equating model moments based on a certain parametric distribution function to the corresponding empirical moments based on the data. Estimates based on PWM are often considered to be superior to standard moment-based estimates. In our case, this approach is based on these quantities:

$$w_r = E\left[Z\left(G\bar{P}D_{\xi,\beta}\left(Z\right)\right)^r\right] = \frac{\beta}{(r+1)(r+1-\xi)}, \quad r = 0, 1, \ldots \quad (10.14)$$

where $G\bar{P}D_{\xi,\beta} = 1 - GPD_{\xi,\beta}$,
$\quad$ Z follows a $GPD_{\xi,\beta}$

From the previous equations, it is possible to show that

$$\beta = \frac{2w_0w_1}{w_0 - 2w_1} \quad \text{and} \quad \xi = 2 - \frac{w_0}{w_0 - 2w_1}$$

Hosking and Wallis (1987) show that PWM is a viable alternative to ML when $\xi \geq 0$.

In our empirical analysis, we estimated the GPD parameters using the previous approaches together with the standard Hill estimator. To highlight the best procedure able to guarantee stability in parameters estimates, we

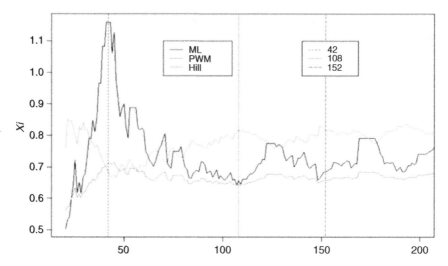

FIGURE 10.3 Comparison among ML, PWM, and Hill Estimates. Note the stability of PWM.

considered recursive estimates with different sample sizes. As Figure 10.3 shows, the empirical analysis suggests we adopt the PMW method.

10.2.3 Compounding via Monte Carlo Methods

Once frequency and severity distributions have been estimated, it is necessary to compound them via Monte Carlo methods to get a new data series of aggregate losses, so that we can then compute the desired risk measures, such as the VaR and ES.

The random sum $L = X_1 + \cdots + X_n$ (where N follows a Poisson distribution) has distribution function:

$$
\begin{aligned}
F_L(x) &= \Pr(L \leq x) \\
&= \sum_{n=0}^{\infty} p_n \Pr(L \leq x \mid N = n) \\
&= \sum_{n=0}^{\infty} p_n F_X^{*n}(x)
\end{aligned}
\tag{10.15}
$$

where $F_X(x) = \Pr(X \leq x) =$ distribution function of the severities X_i

$\qquad\qquad F_X^{*n} = n$-fold convolution of the cumulative distribution function of X

Hence, the aggregation of frequencies and severities is performed as a sum of severities distribution function convolutions, thus determining a compound distribution, whose density function can be obtained by:

$$f_L(x) = \sum_{n=0}^{\infty} p_n f_X^{*n}(x) \qquad (10.16)$$

We compute this aggregation via convolution using Monte Carlo methods. Following our approach, we must be aware that the convolution is a bit more complex because we have split the severity distribution in two parts: the body of the distribution, which follows a lognormal distribution, and the tail, which follows a GPD. As a consequence we have two different severity levels. Hence, the probability associated at each severity (i.e., the number of observations obtained by the Poisson distribution) has to be congruent with the fact that losses may belong to the body or to the tail. Therefore, it is crucial to consider $F(u)$, where u is the GPD threshold and F is the distribution function associated to this point. After having sampled from the two severity distributions, every single loss X_i whose $F(X_i) < F(u)$ will be modeled as a lognormal variable, otherwise it will be a GPD random draw.

10.3 AGGREGATION VIA COPULA

Basel II requires the most conservative aggregation approach in case a financial institution is not able to analyze the dependence among ETs in a robust way. However, ETs are far from being linked by a perfect positive dependence relationship. This fact gives us a huge opportunity to diversify and calculate a smaller and more efficient capital charge value.

We develop the analysis of dependence through the copula function, considering it a "dependence function" (Deheuvels 1978).

The Sklar's Theorem states that a n-dimensional copula (or n-copula) is a function C from the unit n-cube $[0,1]^n$ to the unit interval $[0,1]$, which satisfies three conditions:

1. $C(1, \ldots, 1, a_m, \ldots, 1) = a_m$ for every $m \leq n$ and all a_m in $[0,1]$.
2. $C(a_1, \ldots, a_n) = 0$ if $a_k = 0$ for any $m \leq k$.
3. C in n-increasing.

It is obvious from the definition that if $F_1, \ldots, F_n$ are univariate cumulative distribution functions, $C(F_1(x_1), \ldots, F_n(x_n))$ is a multivariate cumulative distribution function with margins $F_1, \ldots, F_n$, because $U_i = F_i(X_i), i = 1, \ldots, n$, is a uniform random variable.

Moreover, from Sklar's Theorem we get

$$F(x_1, \ldots, x_n) = C(F_1(x_1), \ldots, F_n(x_n)) \qquad (10.17)$$

Hence using copulas, joint distribution functions can be rewritten in terms of the margins and a unique copula (provided the marginals are continuous). Therefore, copulas separate marginal behavior, as represented by F_i, from the association.

In addition, let F be a n-dimensional cumulative distribution function with continuous margins $F_1, \ldots, F_n$ and copula C. Then, from Sklar's Theorem, for any $u = (u_1, \ldots, u_n)$ in $[0,1]^n$ we get:

$$C(u_1, \ldots, u_n) = F\left(F_1^{-1}(u_1), \ldots, F_n^{-1}(u_n)\right) \qquad (10.18)$$

where $F^{-1} =$ generalized inverse of F defined in the usual way
$F^{-1}(t) = \inf\{x \in \Re \mid F(x) \geq t\}$ for all t in $[0,1]$

In our analysis we focus on a specific class of copulas, the class of t-copulas. The reason for this choice is that Archimedean copulas can be extended to the multivariate case $(n > 2)$ with great difficulty, whereas Gaussian copulas do not allow for tail dependence and are a special case of t-copulas when the degree of freedom goes to infinity. Only when $\upsilon > 2$ is the covariance matrix of a t-copula defined.

Suppose X has this stochastic representation:

$$X = \mu + \frac{\sqrt{\upsilon}}{\sqrt{S}} Z \qquad (10.19)$$

where $\mu \in \Re^n, S \approx \chi_\upsilon^2$
$Z \approx N_d(0, \Sigma)$ are independent

Then X has a n-variate t_υ-distribution with mean μ (for $\upsilon \leq 1$ even the mean is not determinable) and covariance matrix $\frac{\upsilon}{\upsilon-2}\Sigma$.

By using Sklar's Theorem, the copula of X (i.e., the t-copula) can be written as

$$C_{\upsilon,R}^t(u) = t_{\upsilon,R}^n\left(t_\upsilon^{-1}(u_1), \ldots, t_\upsilon^{-1}(u_n)\right) \qquad (10.20)$$

where $R_{ij} = \Sigma_{ij}/\sqrt{\Sigma_{ii}}\Sigma_{jj}$ for $i, j \in \{1, \ldots, n\}$
$t_{\upsilon,R}^n =$ distribution function of $\sqrt{\upsilon}Y/\sqrt{S}$,
$S \approx \chi_\upsilon^2$ and $Y \approx N_n(0,R)$ are independent

Here t_v denotes the margins of $t_{v,R}^n$ (i.e., the distribution function of $\sqrt{v}Y/\sqrt{S}$). Instead, the density of the t-copula is

$$c\left(u_1, \ldots, u_n; R, v\right) = \frac{\Gamma\left((v+n)/2\right)\left[\Gamma\left(v/2\right)\right]^n \left(1 + \omega^T R^{-1}\omega\right)^{-(v+n)/2}}{|R|^{1/2}\,\Gamma\left(v/2\right)\left[\Gamma\left((v+1)/2\right)\right]^n \prod_{i=1}^{n}\left(1 + \omega_i^2/v\right)^{-(v+n)/2}}$$

(10.21)

where $\quad \omega = (\omega_1, \ldots, \omega_n)^T = \left(t_v^{-1}(u_1), \ldots, t_v^{-1}(u_n)\right)$

See Chapter 6 in Cherubini et al. (2004) for details about t-copula simulation. It is possible to estimate the parameters of $C_{v,R}^t$, v, and R, following two different estimation procedures, the canonical maximum likelihood (CML) and the inference of margins (IFM). The interested reader is also referred to Embrechts et al. (2002).

If the CML is used, the estimation is performed without specifying the margins. It consists of transforming the sample data $\{x_{1,t}, \ldots, x_{n,t}\}_{t=1,\ldots,T}$ into uniform variates $\{u_{1,t}, \ldots, u_{n,t}\}_{t=1,\ldots,T}$ using order statistics and then estimating the copula parameters. While the CML is the ideal estimation method for the copula parameters if we are unsure about the marginals, nevertheless it is not feasible for high-dimensional settings. This is why we consider here a second estimation procedure, the IFM suggested by Joe and Xu (1996). According to the IFM method, the parameters of the marginal distributions are estimated separately from the parameters of the copula. This procedure is built on two steps:

1. First the margins' parameters θ_1 are estimated by estimating the univariate marginal distributions:

$$\hat{\theta}_1 = \arg\max_{\theta_1} \sum_{t=1}^{T}\sum_{j=1}^{n} \ln f_j\left(x_{j,t}; \theta_1\right)$$

(10.22)

2. Then, given $\hat{\theta}_1$, the copula parameter θ_2 is estimated:

$$\hat{\theta}_2 = \arg\max_{\theta_2} \sum_{t=1}^{T} \ln c\left(F_1\left(x_{1,t}\right), \ldots, F_d\left(x_{d,t}\right); \theta_2; \hat{\theta}_1\right)$$

(10.23)

The IFM estimator is defined as the vector:

$$\hat{\theta}_{IFM} = \left(\hat{\theta}_1, \hat{\theta}_2\right)^T \tag{10.24}$$

This method exploits an attractive feature of copulas where the dependence structure is separated from the marginal distributions. Moreover, it has additional variants depending on whether the first step is implemented parametrically or nonparametrically.

However, the standard IFM procedures are not applicable here, since ET series data are not homogeneous in length: that is, for ET4 we have 16,779 loss observations and for ET2, only 332. In this case, the standard IFM approach would generate biases that cannot be disregarded.

This is why we follow the multistep approach proposed by Patton (2006). The standard two-step approach is split into a multistep approach, where each margin's likelihood is penalized by its number of loss events:

$$\hat{l}_1 = \arg\max_{l_1 \in L_1} n_1^{-1} \sum_{t=1}^{n_1} \log f_{t,1}\left(X; l_1\right)$$

$$\vdots$$

$$\hat{l}_7 = \arg\max_{l_7 \in L_7} n_7^{-1} \sum_{t=1}^{n_1} \log f_{t,7}\left(X; l_7\right)$$

$$\hat{\kappa}_c = \arg\max_{\kappa \in K} n_c^{-1} \sum_{t=1}^{n_1} \log c_t\left(X; \hat{l}_1, \ldots, \hat{l}_7, \kappa\right)$$

$$\hat{\theta}_n = \left[\hat{l}_1^T, \ldots, \hat{l}_7^T, \hat{\kappa}_c^T\right]^T$$

where $X = (X_1, \ldots, X_7)$, n_i, $i = 1, \ldots 7$, denotes the number of loss observations for the ith ET

$n_c =$ number of loss observations that all ETs share in common

10.3.1   Estimating Copulas with Discrete Distributions

According to Sklar (1959), in the case where certain components of the joint density are discrete (as in our case), the copula function is not uniquely defined on $[0,1]^n$, but on the Cartesian product of the ranges of the n

marginal distribution functions. Two approaches have been proposed to overcome this problem. The first method has been proposed by Cameron et al. (2004) and is based on finite difference approximations of the derivatives of the copula function,

$$f(x_1, \ldots, x_n) = \Delta_n \ldots \Delta_1 C(F(x_1), \ldots, F(x_n)) \qquad (10.25)$$

where Δ_k, for $k = 1, \ldots, n$, denotes the kth component first-order differencing operator being defined through

$$\Delta_k C[F(x_1), \ldots, F(x_k), \ldots F(x_n)] = C[F(x_1), \ldots, F(x_k), \ldots F(x_n)]$$
$$-C[F(x_1), \ldots, F(x_k - 1), \ldots F(x_n)]$$
$$(10.26)$$

The second method is the continuation method suggested by Stevens (1950), Denuit and Lambert (2005), and Trivedi and Zimmer (2007), which is based on generating artificially continued variables $x_1^*, \ldots, x_n^*$ by adding independent random variables $u_1, \ldots, u_n$ (each of which is uniformly distributed on the set [0,1] to the discrete count variables $x_1, \ldots, x_n$ and do not change the concordance measure between the variables).

The empirical literature clearly shows that maximization of likelihood with discrete margins often runs into computational difficulties, reflected in the failure of the algorithm to converge. In such cases, it may be helpful to first apply the continuation transformation and then estimate a model based on copulas for continuous variables. This is why we relied on the second method for our empirical analysis. For further details on discrete copulas we refer to Genest and Neslehova (2007).

10.3.2 Canonical Aggregation Procedure Using Copulas

So far, aggregation via copulas has been developed in a single direction, focusing on the dependence relationship among aggregate losses, as described in Di Clemente and Romano (2004) and Fantazzini et al. (2007, 2008).

In this approach, severities of each ET are aggregated on a temporal basis and dependence is assessed by estimating the copula function on the aggregate losses. Hence, given an operational risk data set, we can get weekly, monthly, or yearly aggregate losses. Therefore, if the ith ET has 1,450 observations, one per day, it is possible to determine 4 yearly or 48 monthly aggregate losses. Once the copula and the margins parameters have been estimated, the aggregation is assessed by following three steps:

1. Generate a multivariate random matrix $u = (u_1, \ldots, u_7)$ with margins uniformly distributed in $[0,1]$ from the copula C_θ.
2. Invert the ith determination of the previous step u_i with the distribution function of the ith margin, $\hat{F}_i$.
3. Repeat those two steps a great number of times (i.e., 10^6).

In this way, a new aggregate loss matrix is determined. The main feature of this new data set is that it is simulated with a given dependence structure, as estimated by data, but each margin keeps holding its distribution function, thanks to the inversion procedure. The 99.9% VaR and ES are then computed row by row and the total capital charge K is calculated in the usual way, summing the VaR for each ET.

10.3.3 Poisson Shock Model

We present here the aggregation model suggested by Lindskog and McNeil (2003) and Embrechts and Puccetti (2007). In contrast to those two papers, however, we employ the Poisson shock model on real data, comparing its results with the ones obtained by the canonical aggregation via copula model presented in Section 10.3.1 and the comonotonic approach suggested by Basel II.

In this model, the dependence is modeled among severities and among frequencies, using Poisson processes. Let $(\tau_i)_{i \geq 1}$ be a sequence of independent exponential random variables with parameter λ and $T_n = \sum_{i=1}^{n} \tau_i$. The process $(N_t)_{t \geq 0}$ defined by

$$N_t = \sum_{n \geq 1} I_{t \geq T_n} \tag{10.27}$$

is called a Poisson process with intensity λ. The Poisson process is therefore defined as a counting process: It counts the number of random times (T_n) that occur between 0 and t, where $(T_n - T_{n-1})_{n \geq 1}$ is an i.i.d. sequence of exponential variables.

Hence, in a given time horizon, we observe a certain number of shocks, $(N_t^e) e = 1, \ldots, m$, that is a collection of Poisson processes, randomly causing losses in the seven ETs. It follows that the total number of losses is not itself a Poisson process but rather a compound Poisson process:

$$N_t = \sum_{e=1}^{m} \sum_{r=1}^{N_t^e} \sum_{j=1}^{7} I_{j,r}^e \tag{10.28}$$

These shocks cause a certain number of losses in the ith ET, whose severity is $(X_i^k) k = 1, \ldots, N_i$, where (X_i^k) are i.i.d. with distribution function F_i and independent with respect to N_i.

Therefore, we get a certain number of shocks, driven by Poisson processes, generating losses randomly on the seven ETs. The dependence is allowed among shocks (N_t^e) (i.e., among Poisson processes) and also among loss severities (X_i^k), but the number of shocks and loss severities is independent of each other.

The operative procedure of this approach consists of eight steps:

1. Fit a copula C_θ^f to the frequency distributions.
2. Fit a copula C_θ^S to the severity distributions.
3. Generate a random vector $u^f = (u_1^f, \ldots, u_7^f)$ from the copula C_θ^f.
4. Invert each component u_i^f with the respective inverse distribution function $F^{-1}(u_i^f)$, to determine a random vector $(N_1, \ldots, N_7)$ describing the number of loss observations.
5. Generate a random vector $u^s = (u_1^s, \ldots, u_7^s)$ from the copula C_θ^S.
6. Invert each component u_i^s with the respective inverse distribution function $F^{-1}(u_i^s)$, to determine a random vector $(X_1, \ldots, X_7)$ describing the loss severities.
7. Convolve the frequencies' vector $(N_1, \ldots, N_7)$ with the one of the severities $(X_1, \ldots, X_7)$.
8. Repeat the previous step a great number of times (i.e., 10^6 times).

In this way it is possible to obtain a new matrix of aggregate losses that can then be used to compute the usual risk measures, such as the VaR and ES.

10.4 EMPIRICAL ANALYSIS

The data set consists of six years of loss observations from 2002 to 2007, containing the data of the seven ETs. The loss severities are recorded in

TABLE 10.3 Frequency and Severity Parameters
Estimates for Each ET

	λ (*Poisson*)	β (*GPD*)	ξ (*GPD*)
ET1	21.62	187.68	0.71
ET2	3.90	45.00	0.71
ET3	7.67	30.24	0.36
ET4	201.14	191.02	0.79
ET5	29.27	157.68	0.34
ET6	190.39	104.92	0.64
ET7	23.56	621.15	0.62

euros. The order of ETs is reversed to guarantee the privacy of the bank losses referred to: for example, ET4 will not necessarily refer to clients, product, and business practices.

The frequency (Poisson) and EVT estimates for each ET are reported in Table 10.3.

Note that ET1, ET2, and ET4 show fat tails, as described by the high ξ parameter; this is consistent with our model assumptions, and it suggests the use of EVT to model jumbo loss behavior.

After having estimated the marginal parameters for each ET, we fitted a student t-copula on the aggregate losses, following the canonical aggregation model proposed by DiClemente and Romano (2004) and Fantazzini et al. (2007, 2008). The estimated correlation matrix R and degrees of freedom υ were equal to

T-copula (Aggregate Losses):

$$\hat{R} = \begin{bmatrix} 1 & 0.21 & 0.37 & 0.35 & 0.23 & 0.18 & 0.65 \\ 0.21 & 1 & 0.66 & 0.62 & 0.40 & 0.27 & 0.25 \\ 0.37 & 0.66 & 1 & 0.71 & 0.37 & 0.35 & 0.31 \\ 0.35 & 0.62 & 0.71 & 1 & 0.23 & 0.41 & 0.33 \\ 0.23 & 0.40 & 0.37 & 0.23 & 1 & 0.84 & 0.21 \\ 0.18 & 0.27 & 0.35 & 0.41 & 0.84 & 1 & 0.21 \\ 0.65 & 0.25 & 0.31 & 0.33 & 0.21 & 0.21 & 1 \end{bmatrix}, \quad \hat{\upsilon} = 4.15$$

Instead, following the Poisson shock model, we estimated a t-copula for the frequency distributions and another one for the severity distributions.

The estimated parameters are reported next:

$$\hat{R}^{frequency} = \begin{bmatrix} 1 & 0.15 & 0.16 & 0.23 & 0.31 & 0.27 & 0.27 \\ 0.15 & 1 & 0.33 & 0.36 & 0.18 & 0.21 & 0.13 \\ 0.16 & 0.33 & 1 & 0.21 & 0.28 & 0.36 & 0.23 \\ 0.23 & 0.36 & 0.21 & 1 & 0.33 & 0.30 & 0.12 \\ 0.31 & 0.18 & 0.28 & 0.33 & 1 & 0.27 & 0.24 \\ 0.27 & 0.21 & 0.36 & 0.30 & 0.27 & 1 & 0.17 \\ 0.27 & 0.13 & 0.23 & 0.12 & 0.24 & 0.17 & 1 \end{bmatrix}, \; \hat{v}^f = 8.01$$

$$\hat{R}^{severities} = \begin{bmatrix} 1 & 0.23 & 0.31 & 0.27 & 0.25 & 0.17 & 0.43 \\ 0.23 & 1 & 0.59 & 0.57 & 0.42 & 0.26 & 0.25 \\ 0.31 & 0.59 & 1 & 0.58 & 0.31 & 0.39 & 0.33 \\ 0.27 & 0.57 & 0.58 & 1 & 0.20 & 0.32 & 0.30 \\ 0.25 & 0.42 & 0.31 & 0.20 & 1 & 0.76 & 0.18 \\ 0.17 & 0.26 & 0.39 & 0.32 & 0.76 & 1 & 0.22 \\ 0.43 & 0.25 & 0.33 & 0.30 & 0.18 & 0.22 & 1 \end{bmatrix}, \; \hat{v}^s = 4.32$$

Note that frequencies are not independent; this fact is highly important because it has always been disregarded by previous aggregation models.

The usefulness of implementing the Poisson shock model is well described by Table 10.4, showing the estimates of the total operational risk capital charge.

First of all, note how penalizing it could be if one had to follow the most conservative approach prescribed by Basel II, which assumes perfect comonotonic variables and completely disregards the dependence analysis. The canonical aggregation model via copula represents a first major improvement in Op-risk modeling, and the capital charge is approximately equal to 82% of the one computed following the comonotonic hypothesis, thus allowing for efficiency gains. Furthermore, the diversification is even higher when using Poisson shock model: In this case, the capital charge is approximately the 75% of the comonotonic case. Hence, these results support

TABLE 10.4 VaR and ES Final Estimates (Euro)

	VaR	ES
Comonotonic	308.861.500	819.325.756
Copula (Canonical aggregation)	273.451.379	671.577.312
Shock Model	231.790.767	655.460.604

the development of Poisson shock models to aggregate ET losses, since they allow us to perform a more accurate dependence analysis and to proceed to more efficient capital allocations.

10.5 CONCLUSION

The quantification of operational risk is a challenging task. It is often not clear how the management of operational risk differs from the management of market or credit risk, or how it can add value to a financial institution. The most conservative aggregation model suggested by Basel II hinders the ability to diversify among ETs or BLs due to the complete lack of any analysis of the dependence relationship among losses. As a consequence, not only is the capital charge conservative, but also it is overestimated, thus determining an inefficient capital allocation.

In this chapter, we presented a model of aggregation via copula, using Poisson shock models and Extreme Value Theory. This methodology allows us to consider the dependence relationship among both loss frequencies and severities and to compute a capital charge more efficiently than the standard comonotonic case. The analysis of the dependence structure cannot be achieved in a simple mechanical way. However, even if we cannot map the complex processes observed in the real world into a straightforward statistical model, it is possible to achieve mixed constructions of copulas and Poisson-related processes. These processes can provide valuable information in calculating capital charges in a more efficient way than standard approaches.

REFERENCES

Artzner, P., F. Delbaen, J. M. Eber, and D. Heath. 1999. Coherent measures of risk. *Mathematical Finance* 9, no. 3:203–228.

Bee, M. 2005. On maximum likelihood estimation of operational loss distributions. Discussion paper no. 3. University of Trento, Italy.

Basel Committee on Banking Supervision. 2003. The 2002 loss data collection exercise for operational risk: Summary of the data collected. Bank for International Settlement document, Basel, Switzerland.

Cameron, C., T. Li, P. Trivedi, and D. Zimmer. 2004. Modelling the differences in counted outcomes using bivariate copula models with application to mismeasured counts. *Econometrics Journal* 7, no. 2:566–584.

Chavez-Demoulin, V., P. Embrechts, and J. Neslehova. 2006. Quantitative models for operational risk: Extremes, dependence and aggregation. *Journal of Banking and Finance* 30, no. 10:2635–2658.

Cherubini, U., E. Luciano, and W. Vecchiato. 2004. *Copula methods in finance.* Hoboken, NJ: John Wiley & Sons.

Cruz, M. G. 2002. *Modeling, measuring and hedging operational risk.* Hoboken, NJ: John Wiley & Sons.

Deheuvels, P. 1978. Caractérisation compléte des lois extrèmes multivariées et de la convergence des types extrémes. *Publications de L'Institut de statistique de l'Université de Paris* 23, no. 3:1–36.

Denuit, M., and P. Lambert. 2005. Constraints on concordance measures in bivariate discrete data. *Journal of Multivariate Analysis* 93, no. 1:40–57.

DiClemente, A., and C. Romano. 2004. A copula-extreme value theory approach for modelling operational risk. In *Operational risk modelling and analysis: Theory and practice*, ed. M. G. Cruz. London: Risk Books.

Embrechts, P., C. Kluppelberg, and T. Mikosch. 1997. *Modeling extremal events for insurance and finance.* Berlin: Springer-Verlag.

Embrechts, P., F. Lindskog, and A. McNeil. 2002. Modelling dependence with copulas and applications to risk management. In *Handbook of heavy tailed distributions in finance*, ed. S.T. Rachev. Amsterdam: Elsevier.

Embrechts, P., and G. Puccetti. 2007. Aggregating risk across matrix structures loss data: The case of operational risk. Working paper, ETH, Zurich.

Fantazzini, D., L. Dallavalle, and P. Giudici. 2008, in press. Copulae and operational risks. International Journal of Risk Assessment and Management.

Fantazzini, D., L. Dallavalle, and P. Giudici. 2007. Empirical studies with operational loss data. In *Operational risk: A Guide to Basel II capital requirements, models, and analysis*, ed. F. Fabozzi. Hoboken, NJ: John Wiley & Sons.

Genest, C., and J. Neslehova. 2007. A primer on discrete copulas. *ASTIN Bulletin* 37, no. 2:475–515.

Hosking, J. R. M., and J. R. Wallis. 1987. Parameter and quantile estimation for the generalized pareto distribution. *Technometrics* 29, no. 3:339–349.

Joe, H., and J. Xu. 1996. The estimation method of inference functions for margins for multivariate models. Working paper, Department of Statistics University of British Columbia, Vancouver, British Columbia.

King, J. L. 2001. *Operational risk: Measurement and modeling.* Hoboken, NJ: John Wiley & Sons.

Lindskog, F., and A. McNeil. 2003. Common Poisson shock models: Applications to insurance and credit risk modeling. *ASTIN Bulletin* 33, no. 2:209–238.

Moscadelli, M. 2004.The modelling of operational risk: Experiences with the analysis with the analysis of the data collected by the Basel Committee." Working paper, Temi di Discussione del Servizio Studi, No. 517, Banca d'Italia, Roma.

McNeil, A., P. Embrechts, and R. Frey. 2005.*Quantitative risk management: Concepts, techniques and tools.* Boston: Springer.

Neslehova, J., P. Embrechts, and V. Chavez-Demoulin. 2006. Infinite mean models and the LDA for operational risk. *Journal of Operational Risk* 1, no. 1:3–25.

Panjer, H. H., and G. Willmot. 1992. *Insurance risk models.* Schaumburg, IL: Society of Actuaries.

Patton, A. 2006. Estimation of multivariate models for time series of possibly different lengths. *Journal of Econometrics* 132, no. 1:43–57.

Pfeifer, D., and J. Neslehova. 2004. Modeling and generating dependent risk processes for IRM and DFA. *ASTIN Bulletin* 34, no. 2:333–360.

Roehr, A. 2002. Modelling operational losses. *Algo Research Quarterly 5*, no. 2:53–64.

Stevens, W. L. 1950. Fiducial limits of the parameter of a discontinuous distribution. *Biometrika*, 37, no. 1/2:117–129.

Trivedi, P. K., and D. M. Zimmer. 2007.Copula modeling: An introduction for practitioners. *Foundation and Trends in Econometrics* 1, nos. 1:1–111.

CHAPTER 11

First-Order Approximations to Operational Risk: Dependence and Consequences

Klaus Böcker and Claudia Klüppelberg

ABSTRACT

We investigate the problem of modeling and measuring multidimensional operational risk. Based on the very popular univariate loss distribution approach, we suggest an "invariance principle" that should be satisfied by any multidimensional operational risk model and which is naturally fulfilled by our modeling technique based on the new concept of Pareto Lévy copulas. Our approach allows for a fully dynamic modeling of operational risk at any future point in time. We exploit the fact that operational loss data are typically heavy-tailed, and, therefore, we intensively discuss the concept of multivariate regular variation, which is considered as a very useful tool for various multivariate heavy-tailed phenomena. Moreover, for important examples of the Pareto Lévy copulas and appropriate severity distributions, we derive first order approximations for multivariate operational value at risk.

The opinions expressed in this chapter are those of the authors and do not necessarily reflect the views of UniCredit Group. Moreover, measurement concepts presented are not necessarily used by UniCredit Group or any affiliates.

11.1 INTRODUCTION

Three years ago, in Böcker and Klüppelberg (2005), we argued that operational risk could be a long-term killer. At that time, perhaps the most spectacular example for a bank failure caused by operational risk losses was Barings Bank after the rogue trader Nick Leeson had been hiding loss-making positions in financial derivatives. Meanwhile other examples achieved doubtful fame, most recently Société Générale's loss of €4.9 billion due to trader fraud and Bear Stearns' near death since it was not able to price its mortgage portfolios. Such examples clearly show the increased importance of sound and reliable operational risk management, which consists of risk identification, monitoring and reporting, risk mitigation, risk controlling, and last but not least risk quantification. Needless to say, such catastrophic losses would have never been prevented just by measuring an operational value at risk (OpVaR). Often risk mitigation is primarily a matter of highly effective management and control processes. In the case of Société Générale, for instance, the question is how Jérôme Kerviel was able to hide his massive speculative positions to the Dow Jones Eurostoxx 50 just by offsetting them with fictitious trades into the banking system.

Having said this, let us briefly—not only for a motivation to read this chapter—consider the question regarding the relevance of operational risk modeling. Perhaps the simplest answer would be a reference to the regulatory requirements. Indeed, with the new framework of Basel II, the quantification of operational risk has become a condition sine qua non for every financial institution. In this respect, the main intention for the so-called advanced measurement approaches (AMA) is to calculate a capital charge as a buffer against potential operational risk losses.

Another reason for building models, besides to make predictions, is that models can help us to gain a deeper understanding of a subject matter. This is one of our intentions in writing this chapter. We present a relatively simple model with only a few parameters, which allows us to gain interesting insight into the general behavior of multivariate operational risk. Furthermore, our approach is appealing from a purely model-theoretic point of view because, as we will show in more detail, it essentially is a straightforward generalization of the very popular loss distribution approach (LDA) to any dimension. The key feature of the one-dimensional, standard LDA model is splitting up the total loss amount over a certain time period into a frequency component (i.e., the number of losses) and a severity component (i.e., the individual loss amounts). In doing so, we assume the total aggregate operational loss of a bank up to a time horizon $t \geq 0$

to be represented by a compound Poisson process $(X_t^+)_{t \geq 0}$, which can be represented as

$$X_t^+ = \sum_{i=1}^{N_t^+} \Delta X_i^+, \quad t \geq 0 \tag{11.1}$$

Let us denote the distribution function of X_t^+ by $G_t^+(\cdot) = P(X_t^+ \leq \cdot)$. As risk measure we use total OpVaR up to time t at confidence level κ, which is defined as the quantile

$$\text{OpVaR}_t^+(\kappa) = G_t^{+ \leftarrow}(\kappa) = \inf\{z \in \mathbb{R} : G_t^+(z) \geq \kappa\}, \quad \kappa \in (0,1) \tag{11.2}$$

for κ near 1, for example, 0.999 for regulatory purposes or, in the context of a bank's internal economic capital, even higher, such as 0.9995.

That operational loss data are heavy-tailed is accepted without question among experts and statistically justified by Moscadelli (2004). Therefore, we concentrate on Pareto-like severity distributions. In general, a severity distribution function F is said to be regularly varying with index $-\alpha$ for $\alpha > 0$ ($F \in \mathbb{R}_{-\alpha}$), if

$$\lim_{t \to \infty} \frac{\overline{F}(xt)}{\overline{F}(t)} = x^{-\alpha}, \quad x > 0$$

For such heavy-tailed losses—and actually also for the more general class with subexponential distribution functions—it is now well known and a consequence of Theorem 1.3.9 of Embrechts et al. (1997) (see Böcker and Klüppelberg 2005; Böcker and Sprittulla 2006) that OpVaR at high confidence levels can be approximated by Equation 11.3 (see Figure 11.1):

$$\text{OpVaR}_t^+(\kappa) := G^{+ \leftarrow}(\kappa) \sim F^{+ \leftarrow}\left(1 - \frac{1-\kappa}{\lambda^+}\right), \quad \kappa \uparrow 1 \tag{11.3}$$

with $\lambda^+ = E[N_1^+]$ in a unit time interval.

Usually, however, total operational risk is not modeled by Equation 11.1 directly; instead, operational risk is classified in different loss types and business lines. For instance, Basel II distinguishes seven loss types and eight business lines, yielding a matrix of 56 operational risk cells. Then, for each cell $i = 1, \ldots, d$ operational loss is modeled by a compound Poisson process

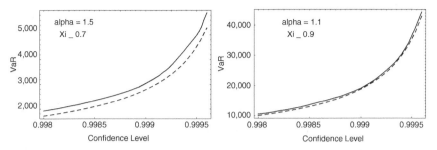

FIGURE 11.1 Comparison of the Total OpVaR Approximation (dashed line) with a Simulated Result (solid line) for a Compound Poisson Model with Pareto Loss Distribution

model $(X_t^i)_{t \geq 0}$, and the bank's total aggregate operational loss is given as the sum

$$X_t^+ = X_t^1 + X_t^2 + \cdots + X_t^d, \quad t \geq 0$$

The core problem of multivariate operational risk modeling here is how to account for the dependence structure between the marginal processes. Several proposals have been made; see, for example, Chavez-Demoulin et al. (2005); Frachot et al. (2004); and Powojowski et al. (2002), just to mention a few. In general, however, all these approaches lead to a total aggregate loss process $(X_t^+)_{t \geq 0}$, which is not compound Poisson anymore and thus does not fit into the framework of Equation 11.1. More generally, it is reasonable to demand that $(X_t^+)_{t \geq 0}$ does not depend on the design of the cell matrix; that is, whether the bank is using 56 or 20 cells within its operational risk model should in principal (i.e., abstracting from statistical estimation and data issues) not affect the bank's total OpVaR. In other words, a natural requirement of a multivariate operational risk model is that it is invariant under a redesign of the cell matrix and, thus, also under possible business reorganizations. Hence, we demand that every model should be closed with respect to the compound Poisson property, that is, that every additive composition of different cells must again constitute a univariate compound Poisson process with severity distribution function $F_{i+j}(\cdot)$ and frequency parameter λ_{i+j} for $i \neq j$:

$$X_t^i + X_t^j =: X_t^{i+j} \quad \in \text{ compound Poisson processes} \tag{11.4}$$

The invariance principle formulated in Equation 11.4 holds true whenever the vector of all cell processes $(X_t^1, \ldots, X_t^d)_{t \geq 0}$ constitutes a

d-dimensional compound Poisson process. The dependence structure between the marginal processes is then described by a so-called Lévy copula, or, as we will call it in this chapter, by means of a Pareto Lévy copula.

11.2 FROM PARETO COPULAS TO PARETO LÉVY COPULAS

Marginal transformations have been utilized in various fields. Certainly the most prominent one in the financial area is the victory march of the copula, invoking marginal transformations resulting in a multivariate distribution function with uniform marginals. Whereas it is certainly convenient to automize certain procedures, such as the normalization to uniform marginals, this transformation is not always the best possible choice.

It was pointed out by Klüppelberg and Resnick (2008) and others that, when asymptotic limit distributions and heavy-tail behavior of data is to be investigated, a transformation to standardized Pareto distributed marginals is much more natural than the transformation to uniform marginals. The analog technique, however applied to the Lévy measure, will prove to be useful also for our purpose, namely the examination of multivariate operational risk. Before we do this in some detail, let us briefly recap some of the arguments given in Klüppelberg and Resnick (2008).

Let $X = (X^1, \ldots, X^d)$ be a random vector in $\mathbb{R}^d$ with distribution function F and one-dimensional marginal distribution functions $F_i(\cdot) = P(X^i \leq \cdot)$ and assume throughout that they are continuous. Define for $d \in \mathbb{N}$

$$\mathcal{P} = (\mathcal{P}^1, \ldots, \mathcal{P}^d) = \left(\frac{1}{\overline{F^1}(X^1)} \right), \ldots, \left(\frac{1}{\overline{F^d}(X^d)} \right) \tag{11.5}$$

with $\overline{F}_i(\cdot) = 1 - F_i(\cdot)$. Note that $\mathcal{P}^i$ is standard Pareto distributed; that is, for $i = 1, \ldots, d$ holds

$$P\left(\mathcal{P}^i > x \right) = x^{-1}, \quad x \geq 1$$

Definition 11.1 Suppose the random vector X has distribution function F with continuous marginals. Define $\mathcal{P}$ as in Equation 11.5. Then we call the distribution C of $\mathcal{P}$ a Pareto copula.

Analogously to the standard distributional copula, the Pareto copula can be used to describe the dependence structure between different random variables.

Here we do not use distributional copulas directly to model the dependence structure between the cells' aggregate loss processes $(X^i_t)_{t\geq 0}$. One reason is that, as described in the introduction, we are looking for a natural extension of the single-cell LDA model (i.e., we require that $(X^+_t)_{t\geq 0}$ also is compound Poisson). This can be achieved by exploiting the fact that a compound Poisson process is a specific Lévy process, which allows us to invoke some Lévy structure analysis to derive OpVaR results. Our approach is similar to that of Böcker and Klüppelberg (2006, 2008), where we used standard Lévy copulas to derive analytic approximations for OpVaR. In this chapter, however, we use a transformation similar to Equation 11.5, which leads us to the concept of *Pareto Lévy copulas.*

For a Lévy process, the jump behavior is governed by the so-called Lévy measure Π, which has a very intuitive interpretation, in particular in the context of operational risk. The Lévy measure of a single operational risk cell measures the expected number of losses per unit time with a loss amount in a prespecified interval. Moreover, for our compound Poisson model, the Lévy measure Π_i of the cell process X^i is completely determined by the frequency parameter $\lambda_i > 0$ and the distribution function of the cell's severity, namely $\Pi_i([0, x]) := \lambda_i P(\Delta X^i \leq x) = \lambda_i F_i(x)$ for $x \in [0, \infty)$. Because we are only modeling losses, all Lévy measures Π_i are concentrated on $[0, \infty)$, and such Lévy measures are called *spectrally positive.* Moreover, since here we are mainly interested in large operational losses, it is convenient to introduce the concept of a *tail measure,* sometimes also referred to as *tail integral.* A one-dimensional tail measure is simply the expected number of losses per unit time that are above a given threshold, which is in the case of a compound Poisson model given by:

$$\overline{\Pi}_i(x) := \Pi_i([x, \infty)) = \lambda_i P(\Delta X^i > x) = \lambda_i \overline{F}_i(x), \quad x \in [0, \infty) \qquad (11.6)$$

In particular, there is only a finite number of jumps per unit time, that is, $\lim_{x\downarrow 0} \overline{\Pi}_i(x) = \lambda_i$.

Analogously, for a multivariate Lévy process, the multivariate Lévy measure controls the jump behavior (per unit time) of all univariate components and contains all information of dependence between the components. Hence, in this framework, dependence modeling between different operational risk cells is reduced to choosing appropriate multivariate Lévy measures. Since jumps are created by positive loss severities, the Lévy measure Π is concentrated on the punctured positive cone in $\mathbb{R}^d$ (the value 0 is taken out since Lévy measures can have a singularity in 0):

$$\mathbb{E} := [0, \infty] / \{0\}$$

Now, like the fact that a multivariate distribution can be built from marginal distributions via a distributional (Pareto) copula, a multivariate tail measure (see also Böcker and Klüppelberg 2006, Definition 2.1)

$$\overline{\Pi}(x) = \overline{\Pi}(x_1, \ldots, x_d) = \Pi\left([x_1, \infty) \times \cdots \times [x_d, \infty)\right), \quad x \in \mathbb{E} \qquad (11.7)$$

can be constructed from the marginal tail measures (11.2) by means of a Pareto Lévy copula. The marginal tail measures are found from Equation 11.7 as expected by

$$\overline{\Pi}_i(x) = \overline{\Pi}(0, \ldots, x_i, \ldots, 0), \quad x \in [0, \infty)$$

Definition 11.2 Let $(X_t)_{t \geq 0}$ be a Lévy process with Lévy measure Γ that has standard one-stable one-dimensional marginals. Then we call Γ a Pareto Lévy measure, and the associated tail measure

$$\overline{\Gamma}(x) = \Gamma([x_1, \infty) \times \cdots \times [x_d, \infty)) =: \hat{C}(x_1, \ldots, x_d), \quad x \in \mathbb{E}$$

is referred to as a Pareto Lévy copula $\hat{C}$.

We now can transform the marginal Lévy measures of a Lévy process analogously to Equation 11.5, yielding standard one-stable marginal Lévy processes with Lévy measures $\overline{\Gamma}_i(x) = x^{-1}$ for $x > 0$. Note that one-stable Lévy processes are *not* compound Poisson anymore; instead, they are of infinite variation and have an infinite number of small jumps per unit time expressed by $\lim_{x \downarrow 0} \overline{\Gamma}_i(x) = \infty$. For definitions and references of stable Lévy processes, see Cont and Tankov (2004).

Lemma 11.1 Let $(X_t)_{t \geq 0}$ be a spectrally positive Lévy process (i.e., a Lévy process admitting only positive jumps) with Lévy measure Π on $\mathbb{E}$ and continuous marginal tail measures $\overline{\Pi}_1, \ldots, \overline{\Pi}_d$. Then

$$\overline{\Pi}(x) = \Pi\left([x_1, \infty] \times \cdots \times [x_d, \infty]\right) = \hat{C}\left(\frac{1}{\overline{\Pi}_1(x_1)}, \ldots, \frac{1}{\overline{\Pi}_d(x_d)}\right), \quad x \in \mathbb{E},$$

and $\hat{C}$ is a Pareto Lévy copula.

Proof. Note that for all $x \in \mathbb{E}$,

$$\hat{C}(x_1, \ldots, x_d) = \overline{\Pi} \left(\left(\frac{1}{\overline{\Pi}_1} \right)^{\leftarrow} (x_1), \ldots, \left(\frac{1}{\overline{\Pi}_d} \right)^{\leftarrow} (x_d) \right)$$

This implies for the one-dimensional marginal tail measures

$$\hat{C}(0, \ldots, x, \ldots, 0) = \overline{\Pi}_i \circ \left(\frac{1}{\overline{\Pi}_i} \right)^{\leftarrow} (x) = \frac{1}{x} \qquad x \in [0, \infty) \qquad (11.8)$$

The next theorem is Sklar's Theorem for spectrally positive Lévy processes in the context of Lévy Pareto copulas. The proof is similar to the one of Theorem 5.6 of Cont and Tankov (2004).

Theorem 11.1 (Sklar's Theorem for Pareto Lévy copulas). Let $\overline{\Pi}$ be the tail measure of a d-dimensional spectrally positive Lévy process with marginal tail measures $\overline{\Pi}_1, \ldots, \overline{\Pi}_d$. Then there exists a Pareto Lévy copula $\hat{C} : \mathbb{E} \to [0, \infty]$ such that for all $x_1, \ldots, x_d \in \mathbb{E}$

$$\overline{\Pi}(x_1, \ldots, x_d) = \hat{C} \left(\frac{1}{\overline{\Pi}_1(x_1)}, \ldots, \frac{1}{\overline{\Pi}_d(x_d)} \right) \qquad (11.9)$$

If the marginal tail measures are continuous on $[0, \infty]$, then $\hat{C}$ is unique. Otherwise, it is unique on $\mathrm{Ran}(\frac{1}{\overline{\Pi}_1}) \times \cdots \times \mathrm{Ran}(\frac{1}{\overline{\Pi}_d})$. Conversely, if $\hat{C}$ is a Pareto Lévy copula and $\overline{\Pi}_1, \ldots, \overline{\Pi}_d$ are marginal tail measures, then $\overline{\Pi}$ defined in Equation 11.9 is a joint tail measure with marginals $\overline{\Pi}_1, \ldots, \overline{\Pi}_d$.

So-called Lévy copulas, as introduced in Cont and Tankov (2004) and also used in Böcker and Klüppelberg (2006, 2008), have one-dimensional marginal Lebesgue measures. As a consequence thereof, they do not have an interpretation as the Lévy measure of a one-dimensional Lévy process, because a Lévy measure is, for instance, finite on $[1, \infty)$.

From the construction above, it is also clear that, if $\tilde{C}(x_1, \ldots, x_d)$ is a Lévy copula, then the associated Pareto Lévy copula $\hat{C}$ can be constructed by $\hat{C}(x_1, \ldots, x_d) = \tilde{C}(1/x_1, \ldots, 1/x_d)$. Hence, the next examples follow immediately from those given in Böcker and Klüppelberg (2006).

Example 11.1 (independence Pareto Lévy-copula). Let $X_t = (X_t^1, \ldots, X_t^d)$, $t \geq 0$, be a spectrally positive Lévy process with marginal tail measures

$\overline{\Pi}_1, \ldots, \overline{\Pi}_d$. The components of $(X_t)_{t \geq 0}$ are independent if and only if

$$\Pi(A) = \sum_{i=1}^{d} \Pi_i(A_i) \quad A \in \mathfrak{B}(\mathbb{E})$$

where $A_i = \{x \in \mathbb{R} : (0, \ldots, 0, x, 0, \ldots, 0) \in A\}$ stands at the ith component $\mathfrak{B}(\mathbb{E})$ denotes the Borel sets of $\mathbb{E}$. This implies for the tail measure of $(X_t)_{t \geq 0}$

$$\overline{\Pi}(x_1, \ldots, x_d) = \overline{\Pi}_1(x_1) \, I_{\{x_2 = \cdots = x_d = 0\}} + \cdots + \overline{\Pi}_d(x_d) \, I_{\{x_1 = \cdots = x_{d-1} = 0\}},$$

giving a Pareto Lévy copula of

$$\hat{C}_\perp(x) = x_1^{-1} I_{\{x_2 = \cdots = x_d = 0\}} + \cdots + x_d^{-1} I_{\{x_1 = \cdots = x_{d-1} = 0\}}.$$

The resulting Lévy process with Pareto Lévy copula $\hat{C}_\perp$ is a standard one-stable process with independent components.

Example 11.2 (complete [positive] dependence Pareto Lévy copula). Let $X_t = (X_t^1, \ldots, X_t^d)$, $t \geq 0$, be a spectrally positive Lévy process with Lévy measure Π, which is concentrated on an increasing subset of $\mathbb{E}$. Then

$$\overline{\Pi}(x) = \min(\overline{\Pi}^1(x_1), \ldots, \overline{\Pi}^d(x_d)).$$

The corresponding Lévy copula is given by $\hat{C}_\parallel(x) = \min(x_1^{-1}, \ldots, x_d^{-1})$.

Example 11.3 (Archimedian Pareto Lévy copula). Let $\phi : [0, \infty] \to [0, \infty]$ be strictly decreasing with $\phi(0) = \infty$ and $\phi(\infty) = 0$. Assume that $\phi^{\leftarrow}$ has derivatives up to order d with $(-1)^k \frac{d^k \phi^{\leftarrow}(t)}{dt^k} > 0$ for $k = 1, \ldots, d$. Then the next is a Pareto Lévy copula: $\hat{C}(x) = \phi^{\leftarrow}(\phi(x_1^{-1}) + \cdots + \phi(x_d^{-1}))$.

Example 11.4 (Clayton Pareto Lévy copula). Take $\phi(t) = t^{-\theta}$ for $\theta > 0$. Then the Archimedian Pareto Lévy copula $\hat{C}_\theta(x) = (x_1^\theta + \cdots + x_d^\theta)^{-1/\theta}$ is called Clayton Pareto Lévy copula. Note that $\lim_{\theta \to \infty} \hat{C}_\theta(x) = \hat{C}_\parallel(x)$ and $\lim_{\theta \to 0} \hat{C}_\theta(x) = \hat{C}_\perp(x)$; that is, this model covers the whole range of dependence.

11.3 UNDERSTANDING THE DEPENDENCE STRUCTURE

Recall our multivariate operational risk model, in which total aggregate loss is modeled by a compound Poisson process with representation (11.1), where $(N_t^+)_{t \geq 0}$ is the Poisson process counting the total number of losses and $\Delta X_1^+, \ldots, \Delta X_d^+$ denote all severities in the time interval $(0, t]$. In this model, losses can occur either in one of the component processes or result from multiple simultaneous losses in different components. In the latter situation, ΔX_i^+ is the sum of all losses, which happen at the same time.

Based on a decomposition of the marginal Lévy measures, one can show (see, e.g., Böcker and Klüppelberg 2008, Section 3) that the component processes can be decomposed into compound Poisson processes of single jumps and joint jumps. For $d = 2$, the cell's loss processes have the representation (the time parameter t is dropped for simplicity):

$$X^1 = X_\perp^1 + X_\|^1 = \sum_{k=1}^{N_\perp^1} \Delta X_{\perp k}^1 + \sum_{l=1}^{N_\|} \Delta X_{\| l}^1$$

$$X^2 = X_\perp^2 + X_\|^1 = \sum_{m=1}^{N_\perp^2} \Delta X_{\perp m}^2 + \sum_{l=1}^{N_\|} \Delta X_{\| l}^2$$

(11.10)

where $X_{\|1}$ and $X_{\|2}$ describe the aggregate losses of cell 1 and 2, respectively, generated by "common shocks"
$X_\perp^1$ and $X_\perp^2$ are independent loss processes

Note that apart from $X_{\|1}$ and $X_{\|2}$, all compound Poisson processes on the right-hand side of Equation 11.10 are mutually independent.

If we compare the left-hand and right-hand representation, we can identify the parameters of the processes on the right-hand side. The parameters on the left-hand side are $\lambda_1, \lambda_2 > 0$ for the frequencies of the Poisson processes, which count the number of losses, and the severity distribution functions F_1, F_2; for details, we refer to Böcker and Klüppelberg (2008) (see Figure 11.2).

The frequency of simultaneous losses can be calculated from the bivariate tail measure $\overline{\Pi}(x_1, x_2)$ as the limit of arbitrarily small, simultaneous losses; that is:

$$\lim_{x_1, x_2 \downarrow 0} \overline{\Pi}(x_1, x_2) = \hat{C}(\lambda_1^{-1}, \lambda_2^{-1}) = \lim_{x \downarrow 0} \overline{\Pi}_{\|2}(x)$$

$$= \lim_{x \downarrow 0} \overline{\Pi}_{\|1}(x) = \lambda_\| \in [0, \min(\lambda_1, \lambda_2)]$$

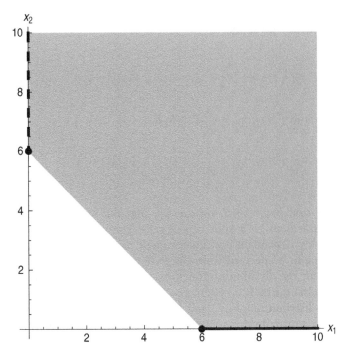

FIGURE 11.2 Decomposition of the domain of the tail measure $\overline{\Pi}^+(z)$ for $z = 6$ into a simultaneous loss part $\overline{\Pi}_\parallel(z)$ (gray) and independent parts $\overline{\Pi}_{\perp 1}(z)$ (solid black line) and $\overline{\Pi}_{\perp 2}(z)$ (dashed black line).

Consequently, the frequency of independent losses must be

$$\lambda_{\perp 1} = \lim_{x \downarrow 0} \overline{\Pi}_{\perp 1}(x) = \lambda_1 - \lambda_\parallel \quad \text{and} \quad \lambda_{\perp 2} = \lambda_2 - \lambda_\parallel$$

By comparison of the Lévy measures we obtain further for the distribution functions of the independent losses

$$\overline{F}_{\perp 1}(x_1) = \frac{\lambda_1}{\lambda_{1\perp}} \overline{F}_1(x_1) - \frac{1}{\lambda_{1\perp}} \hat{C} \left((\lambda_1 \overline{F}_1(x_1))^{-1}, \lambda_2^{-1} \right)$$

$$\overline{F}_{\perp 2}(x_2) = \frac{\lambda_2}{\lambda_{2\perp}} \overline{F}_2(x_2) - \frac{1}{\lambda_{2\perp}} \hat{C} \left(\lambda_1^{-1}, (\lambda_2 \overline{F}_2(x_2))^{-1} \right)$$

And, finally, the joint distribution functions of coincident losses and their marginals are given by

$$\overline{F}_{\parallel}(x_1, x_2) = P\left(X_{\parallel}^1 > x_1, X_{\parallel}^2 > x_2\right) = \frac{1}{\lambda_{\parallel}}\hat{C}\left(\left(\lambda_1\overline{F}_1(x_1)\right)^{-1}, \left(\lambda_2\overline{F}_2(x_2)\right)^{-1}\right)$$

$$\overline{F}_{\parallel 1}(x_1) = \lim_{x_2\downarrow 0}\overline{F}_{\parallel}(x_1, x_2) = \frac{1}{\lambda_{\parallel}}\hat{C}\left(\left(\lambda_1\overline{F}_1(x_1)\right)^{-1}, \lambda_2^{-1}\right)$$

$$\overline{F}_{\parallel 2}(x_2) = \lim_{x_1\downarrow 0}\overline{F}_{\parallel}(x_1, x_2) = \frac{1}{\lambda_{\parallel}}\hat{C}\left(\lambda_1^{-1}, \left(\lambda_2\overline{F}_2(x_2)\right)^{-1}\right) \qquad (11.11)$$

Summarizing our results, we can say that the Pareto Lévy copula approach is equivalent to a split of the cells' compound Poisson processes into completely dependent and independent parts. All parameters of these subprocesses can be derived from the Pareto Lévy copula, which we have shown here for the distribution functions and frequencies of the dependent and independent parts. Moreover, we would like to mention that the simultaneous loss distributions $F_{\parallel 1}(\cdot)$ and $F_{\parallel 2}(\cdot)$ are not independent; instead they are linked by a distributional copula, which can be derived from (11.11); see again Böcker and Klüppelberg (2008) for more details.

11.4 APPROXIMATING TOTAL OpVaR

In our model, OpVaR encompassing all risk cells is given by Equation 11.2, which can asymptotically be approximated by Equation 11.2. Needless to say, the parameters $\overline{F}^+$ and λ^+, which describe the bank's total OpVaR at aggregated level, depend on the dependence structure between different risk cells and thus on the Pareto Lévy copula. We now investigate various dependence scenarios, for which first-order approximations like (11.3) are available. Our results yield valuable insight into the nature of multivariate operational risk.

11.4.1 One Dominating Cell Severity

Although the first scenario is rather simple, assuming that high-severity losses mainly occur in one single risk cell, it is yet relevant in many practical situations. Note that the assumptions that follow results are very weak, so no process structure is needed here.

Theorem 11.2 (Böcker and Klüppelberg (2006), Theorem 3.4, Corollary 3.5). For fixed $t > 0$ let X_t^i for $i = 1, \ldots, d$ have compound Poisson distributions. Assume that $\overline{F}_1 \in \mathcal{R}_{-\alpha}$ for $\alpha > 0$. Let $\rho > \alpha$ and suppose that $E[(\Delta X^i)^\rho] < \infty$ for $i = 2, \ldots, d$. Then, regardless of the dependence structure between $X_t^1, \ldots, X_t^d$, $P(X_t^+ > x) \sim E N_t^1 P(\Delta X^1 > x)$, $x \to \infty$, and

$$
\mathrm{VaR}_t^+ (\kappa) \sim F_1^{\leftarrow} \left(1 - \frac{1 - \kappa}{E N_t^1} \right) = \mathrm{OpVaR}_t^1 (\kappa), \quad \kappa \uparrow 1
$$

This is a quite important result. It means that total operational risk measured at high confidence levels is dominated by the stand-alone OpVaR of that cell, where losses have Pareto tails that are heavier than losses of other cells. Note that the assumptions of this theorem are also satisfied if the loss severity distribution is a mixture distribution, in which only the tail is explicitly assumed to be Pareto-like, whereas the body is modeled by any arbitrary distribution class. We have elaborated this in more detail in Böcker and Klüppelberg (2008), Section 5.

11.4.2 Multivariate Compound Poisson Model with Completely Dependent Cells

Complete dependence for Lévy processes means that all cell processes jump together, that is, losses always occur at the same time, necessarily implying that all frequencies must be equal: $\lambda := \lambda_1 = \cdots = \lambda_d$. It also implies that the mass of the multivariate Lévy measure Π is concentrated on

$$
\left\{ (x_1, \ldots, x_d) \in \mathbb{E} : \overline{\Pi}_1(x_1) = \cdots = \overline{\Pi}_d(x_d) \right\}
$$
$$
= \left\{ (x_1, \ldots, x_d) \in \mathbb{E} : F_1(x_1) = \cdots = F_d(x_d) \right\}
$$

Let F_i be strictly increasing and continuous such that $F_i^{-1}(q)$ exists for all $q \in [0, 1)$. Then

$$
\overline{\Pi}^+(z) = \Pi \left(\left\{ (x_1, \ldots, x_d) \in \mathbb{E} : \sum_{i=1}^{d} x_i \geq z \right\} \right)
$$
$$
= \Pi_1 \left(\left\{ x_1 \in (0, \infty) : x_1 + \sum_{i=2}^{d} F_i^{-1}(F_1(x_1)) \geq z \right\} \right), \quad z > 0
$$

This representation yields the next result.

Theorem 11.3 (Böcker and Klüppelberg (2006), Theorem 3.6). Consider a multivariate compound Poisson process $X_t = (X_t^1, \ldots, X_t^d)$, $t \geq 0$, with completely dependent cell processes and strictly increasing and continuous severity distributions F_i. Then $(X_t^+)_{t \geq 0}$ is a compound Poisson process with parameters

$$\lambda^+ = \lambda \text{ and } \overline{F}^+(z) = \overline{F}_1(H^{-1}(z)), \quad z > 0$$

where $H(z) := z + \sum_{i=2}^{d} F_i^{-1}(F_1(z))$. If $F^+ \in \mathcal{R}_{-\alpha}$ for $\alpha \in (0, \infty)$, then

$$\text{OpVaR}_t^+(\kappa) \sim \sum_{i=1}^{d} \text{OpVaR}_t^1(\kappa), \quad \kappa \uparrow 1$$

where $\text{OpVaR}_t^i(\cdot)$ denotes the stand-alone OpVaR of cell i.

Corollary 11.1 Assume that the conditions of Theorem 11.10 hold and that $F_1 \in \mathcal{R}_{-\alpha}$ for $\alpha \in (0, \infty)$ and $\lim_{x \to \infty} \frac{\overline{F}_i(x)}{\overline{F}_1(x)} = c_i \in [0, \infty)$. Assume further that $c_i \neq 0$ for $i = 1, \ldots, b \leq d$ and $c_i = 0$ for $i = b+1, \ldots, d$. Then

$$\text{OpVaR}_t^+(\kappa) \sim \sum_{i=1}^{b} c_i^{1/\alpha} \text{OpVaR}_t^1(\kappa), \quad \kappa \uparrow 1$$

Note how the result of Theorem 11.3 resembles the proposals of the Basel Committee on Banking Supervision (2006), in which a bank's total capital charge for operational risk measured as OpVaR at confidence level of 99.9 % is usually the sum of the risk capital charges attributed to the different risk type/business line cells. Hence, following our model, regulators implicitly assume that losses in different categories always occur simultaneously as a worst-case scenario.

11.4.3 Multivariate Compound Poisson Model with Independent Cells

The other extreme case we want to consider is independence between different cells. For a general Lévy process, independence means that no two cell processes ever jump together. Consequently, the mass of the Lévy measure is concentrated on the axes, as in Example 11.1, so that we have

$$\overline{\Pi}^+(z) = \overline{\Pi}_1(z_1) + \cdots + \overline{\Pi}_d(z_d) \quad z \geq 0$$

Theorem 11.4   Assume that $X_t = (X_t^1, \ldots, X_t^d), t \geq 0$, has independent cell processes. Then $(X_t^+)_{t \geq 0}$ is a compound Poisson process with parameters $\lambda^+ = \lambda_1 + \cdots + \lambda_d$ and $\overline{F}^+(z) = \frac{1}{\lambda^+}\left[\lambda_1 \overline{F}_1(z) + \cdots + \lambda_d \overline{F}_d(z)\right], z \geq 0$.
   If $F_1 \in \mathcal{R}_{-\alpha}$ for $\alpha \in (0, \infty)$ and for all $i = 2, \ldots, d$,

$$\lim_{x \to \infty} \frac{\overline{F}_i(x)}{\overline{F}_1(x)} = c_i \in [0, \infty)$$

then

$$\mathrm{OpVaR}_t^+(\kappa) \sim F_1^{\leftarrow}\left(1 - \frac{1 - \kappa}{(\lambda_1 + c_2\lambda_2 + \cdots + c_d\lambda_d)t}\right), \quad \kappa \uparrow 1 \qquad (11.12)$$

If we compare Equation 11.12 to the formula for the single-cell OpVaR (Equation 11.3), we see that multivariate OpVaR in the case of independent cells can be expressed by the stand-alone OpVaR of the first cell with adjusted frequency parameter $\lambda := \lambda_1 + c_2\lambda_2 + \cdots + c_d\lambda_d$. Actually, we will see in the next section that this is possible for much more general dependence structures, namely those belonging to the class of multivariate regular variation.

11.4.4   Multivariate Regularly Varying Lévy Measure

Multivariate regular variation is an appropriate mathematical tool for discussing heavy-tail phenomena as they occur for instance in operational risk. We begin with regular variation of random vectors or, equivalently, of multivariate distribution functions.
   The idea is to have regular variation not only in some (or all) marginals, but along every ray starting in 0 and going through the positive cone to infinity. Clearly, this limits the possible dependence structures between the marginals; however, such models are still flexible enough to be broadly applied to various fields such as telecommunication, insurance, and last but not least VaR analysis in the banking industry. Furthermore, many of the dependence models implying multivariate regular variation can still be solved and analyzed analytically.

Let us consider a positive random vector X with distribution function F that is—as our Lévy measure Π— concentrated on $\mathbb{E}$. Moreover, we introduce for $x \in \mathbb{E}$ the next sets (for any Borel set $A \subset \mathbb{E}$ its complement in $\mathbb{E}$ is denoted by A^c):

$$[0, x]^c = \mathbb{E}\setminus[0, x] = \left\{ y \in \mathbb{E} : \max_{1 \le i \le d} \frac{y_i}{x_i} > 1 \right\}$$

Assume there exists a Radon measure ν on $\mathbb{E}$ (i.e., a Borel measure that is finite on compact sets) such that

$$\lim_{t \to \infty} \frac{1 - F(tx)}{1 - F(t1)} = \lim_{t \to \infty} \frac{P(t^{-1}X \in [0, x]^c)}{P(t^{-1}X \in [0, 1]^c)} = \nu([0, x]^c) \qquad (11.13)$$

holds for all $x \in \mathbb{E}$, which are continuity points of the function $\nu([0, \cdot]^c)$. One can show that the above definition (11.13) implies that ν has a homogeneity property; that is, there exists some $\alpha > 0$ such that

$$\nu([0, sx]^c) = s^{-\alpha}\nu([0, x]^c), \quad s > 0 \qquad (11.14)$$

and we say that F is multivariate regularly varying with index $-\alpha$ ($F \in \mathcal{R}_{-\alpha}$). Condition 11.13 also says that $F(t1)$ as a function of t is in $\mathcal{R}_{-\alpha}$. Define now $b(t)$ to satisfy $\overline{F}(b(t)1) \sim t^{-1}$ as $t \to \infty$. Then, replacing t by $b(t)$ in Equation 11.13 yields

$$\lim_{t \to \infty} tP\left(\frac{X}{b(t)} \in [0, x]^c \right) = \nu([0, x]^c) \qquad (11.15)$$

In Equation 11.15, the random variable X is normalized by the function $b(\cdot)$. As explained in Resnick (2007, Section 6.5.6), normalization of all components by the same function $b(\cdot)$ implies that the marginal tails of X satisfy for $i, j \in \{1, \ldots, d\}$

$$\lim_{x \to \infty} \frac{\overline{F}_i(x)}{\overline{F}_j(x)} = \frac{c_i}{c_j}$$

where $c_i, c_j \in [0, \infty)$

Assuming $c_1 > 0$ we set without loss of generality (w.l.o.g.) $c_1 = 1$. Then we can also choose $b(t)$ such that for $t \to \infty$

$$\overline{F}_1(b(t)) \sim t^{-1} \Leftrightarrow b(t) \sim \left(\frac{1}{\overline{F}_1}\right)^{\leftarrow}(t) \qquad (11.16)$$

and, by substituting in Equation 11.15, we obtain a limit on the left-hand side of Equation 11.15 with the same scaling structure as before.

To formulate analogous definitions for Lévy measures, note first that we can rewrite Equation 11.13 by means of the distribution of X as:

$$\lim_{t \to \infty} \frac{P_X(t[0, x]^c)}{P_X(t[0, 1]^c)} = \nu([0, x]^c)$$

and, similarly, Equation 11.15 as

$$\lim_{t \to \infty} t P_X(b(t)[0, x]^c) = \lim_{t \to \infty} t P_X([0, b(t)x]^c) = \nu([0, x]^c) \qquad (11.17)$$

Then the analog expression to Equation 11.13 for a Lévy measure Π is simply

$$\lim_{t \to \infty} \frac{\Pi(t[0, x]^c)}{\Pi(t[0, 1]^c)} = \lim_{t \to \infty} \frac{\Pi(\{y \in \mathbb{E} : y_1 > tx_1 \text{ or } \cdots \text{ or } y_d > tx_d\})}{\Pi(\{y \in \mathbb{E} : y_1 > t \text{ or } \cdots \text{ or } y_d > t\})} = \nu([0, x]^c)$$
$$(11.18)$$

for all $x \in \mathbb{E}$, which are continuity points of the function $\nu([0, \cdot]^c)$. Summarizing what we have so far yields the next definition of multivariate regular variation for Lévy measures, now formulated in analogy to Equations 11.15 or 11.17, respectively:

Definition 11.3 (multivariate regular variation for spectrally positive Lévy processes). Let Π be a Lévy measure of a spectrally positive Lévy process on $\mathbb{E}$. Assume that there exists a function $b : (0, \infty) \to (0, \infty)$ satisfying $b(t) \to \infty$ as $t \to \infty$ and a Radon measure ν on $\mathbb{E}$ such that

$$\lim_{t \to \infty} t\Pi([0, b(t)x]^c) = \nu([0, x]^c) \qquad (11.19)$$

holds for all $x \in \mathbb{E}$ which are continuity points of the function $\nu([0, \cdot]^c)$. Then ν satisfies the homogeneity property

$$\nu([0, sx]^c) = s^{-\alpha}\nu([0, x]^c), \quad s > 0$$

for some $\alpha > 0$ and the Lévy measure Π is called multivariate regularly varying with index $-\alpha$ ($\Pi \in \mathcal{R}_{-\alpha}$).

As before in the case of a regularly varying random vector X, we assume that in Equation 11.19 we can choose one single scaling function $b(\cdot)$, which applies to all marginal tail measures. In analogy to Equation 11.16, we can therefore set

$$\overline{\Pi}_1(b(t)) \sim t^{-1} \Leftrightarrow b(t) \sim \left(\frac{1}{\overline{\Pi}_1}\right)^{\leftarrow}(t), \quad t \to \infty \tag{11.20}$$

As explained, normalization of all components by the same function $b(\cdot)$ implies that the marginal tail measures satisfy for $i, j \in \{1, \ldots, d\}$

$$\lim_{x \to \infty} \frac{\overline{\Pi}_i(x)}{\overline{\Pi}_j(x)} = \frac{c_i}{c_j}, \quad c_i, c_j \in [0, \infty) \tag{11.21}$$

As we have already said, multivariate regular variation is just a special way of describing dependence between multivariate heavy-tailed measures. Therefore it is natural to ask under which conditions a given Pareto Lévy copula is in line with multivariate regular variation. Starting with a multivariate tail measure $\overline{\Pi}$, we know from Lemma 11.3 that we can derive its Pareto Lévy copula $\hat{C}$ by normalizing the marginal Lévy measures to standard one-stable marginal Lévy processes, that is:

$$\overline{\Pi}_i(x) \to \overline{\Gamma}_i(x) = \overline{\Pi}_i \circ \left(\frac{1}{\overline{\Pi}_i}\right)^{\leftarrow}(x) = \frac{1}{x}, \quad x \in [0, \infty) \tag{11.22}$$

We now consider the question under which conditions the resulting multivariate tail measure $\overline{\Gamma}$ of a standardized one-stable Lévy process corresponds to a multivariate regularly varying Lévy measure Γ (automatically with index -1).

Example 11.5 (Pareto Lévy copula and multivariate regular variation). Let $X_t = (X_t^1, X_t^2)$, $t \geq 0$, be a spectrally positive Lévy process with Lévy measure Π on $[0, \infty)^d$. Transforming the marginal Lévy measure by $(1/\overline{\Pi}_i)^{\leftarrow}(x)$, we obtain the Pareto Lévy copula $\hat{C}(x_1, x_2) = \Gamma([x_1, \infty) \times [x_2, \infty))$ of $(X_t)_{t \geq 0}$.

From Equation 11.22 we know that, if Γ is regularly varying, then with index -1, we set $b(t) = t$. Obviously, for $b(t) = t$ we are in the standard case and all marginals are standard Pareto distributed with $\alpha = 1$. Then, because in general we have

$$\Pi([0, (x_1, x_2)^\top]^c) = \overline{\Pi}_1(x_1) + \overline{\Pi}_2(x_2) - \overline{\Pi}(x_1, x_2), \quad (x_1, x_2) \in \mathbb{E} \tag{11.23}$$

we immediately get for the left-hand side of (11.19) for the transformed Lévy measure Γ

$$t\Gamma([0, (tx_1, tx_2)^\top]^c) = \frac{1}{x_1} + \frac{1}{x_2} - t\,\hat{C}(tx_1, tx_2)$$

For bivariate regular variation with index -1, the right-hand side must converge for $t \to \infty$ to a Radon measure ν on $\mathbb{E}$, more precisely:

$$\frac{1}{x_1} + \frac{1}{x_2} - t\hat{C}(tx_1, tx_2) \to \nu([0, (x_1, x_2)^\top]^c)$$

with

$$\nu([0, (sx_1, sx_2)^\top]^c) = s^{-1}\nu([0, (x_1, x_2)^\top]^c), \quad s > 0$$

This is clearly the case if the Lévy Pareto copula $\hat{C}$ is homogenous of order -1 and, more generally, if there is a Radon measure μ such that

$$\lim_{t \to \infty} t\hat{C}(tx_1, tx_2) = \mu([0, (x_1, x_2)^\top]^c), \quad (x_1, x_2) \in \mathbb{E}$$

A more general result follows, which links multivariate regular variation to the dependence concept of a Pareto Lévy copula.

Theorem 11.5 (Böcker and Klüppelberg (2006), Theorem 3.16). Let $\overline{\Pi}$ be a multivariate tail measure of a spectrally positive Lévy process on $\mathbb{E}$. Assume that the marginal tail measures $\overline{\Pi}_i$ are regularly varying with index $-\alpha$ for some $\alpha > 0$. Then the following holds.

1. The Lévy measure Π is multivariate regularly varying with index $-\alpha$ if and only if the standardized Lévy measure Γ is regularly varying with index -1.
2. If the Pareto Lévy copula $\hat{C}$ is homogeneous of order -1 and $0 < \alpha < 2$, then $\hat{C}$ is the Lévy measure of a multivariate α-stable process.

Example 11.6 (visualization of the Clayton Pareto Lévy copula). Recall the Clayton Lévy copula $\hat{C}(x_1, x_2) = (x_1^\theta + x_2^\theta)^{-1/\theta}$ for $x_1, x_2 > 0$. From Definition 11.2 we know that

$$\hat{C}(x_1, x_2) = \Gamma([x_1, \infty) \times [x_2, \infty)), \quad (x_1, x_2) \in \mathbb{E}$$

and the corresponding marginal processes have been standardized to be one-stable Lévy processes. Since $\hat{C}$ is homogeneous of order -1, we know from Theorem 11.5 that the bivariate Lévy process is a one-stable process. We can also conclude that, if the marginal Lévy tail measures $\overline{\Pi}_1$ and $\overline{\Pi}_2$ before standardizing the marginals were regularly varying with some index $-\alpha$, then the Lévy measure Π was a bivariate regularly varying tail with index $-\alpha$.

Note also that

$$\Gamma([0, x]^c) = \overline{\Gamma}_1(x_1) + \overline{\Gamma}_2(x_2) - \hat{C}(x_1, x_2)$$

$$= \frac{1}{x_1} + \frac{1}{x_2} - \left(\left(\frac{1}{x_1}\right)^{-\theta} + \left(\frac{1}{x_2}\right)^{-\theta} \right)^{-1/\theta}$$

The homogeneity can be used as follows to allow for some visualization of the dependence.

We transform to polar coordinates by setting $x_1 = r \cos\varphi$ and $x_2 = r \sin\varphi$ for $r = |x| = \sqrt{x_1^2 + x_2^2}$ and $\varphi \in [0, \pi/2]$. From the homogeneity property it follows

$$\Gamma([0, x]^c) = r^{-1} \Gamma([0, (\cos\varphi, \sin\varphi)^\top]^c) =: \Gamma(r, \varphi)$$

This is depicted in Figure 11.3, where $\Gamma(r, \varphi)$ is plotted for $r = 1$ as a function of φ, and thus the Clayton dependence structure is plotted as a measure on the quarter circle.

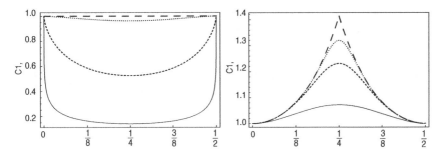

FIGURE 11.3 Plot of the Pareto Lévy copula in polar coordinates $\hat{C}(r, \varphi) = \overline{\Gamma}(r, \varphi)$ as a function of the angle $\varphi \in (0, \pi/2)$ for $r = 1$ and different values for the dependence parameter. Left Plot: $\theta = 1, 8$ (dotted line), $\theta = 0, 7$ (dashed line), $\theta = 0, 3$ (solid line). Right Plot: $\theta = 2, 5$ (solid line), $\theta = 5$ (dashed line), $\theta = 10$ (dotted line), and $\theta = \infty$ (complete positive dependence, long-dashed line).

It is worth mentioning that all we have said so far about multivariate regular variation of Lévy measures holds true for general spectrally positive Lévy processes. We now turn back again to the problem of calculating total OpVaR and consider a multivariate compound Poisson process, whose Lévy measure Π is multivariate regularly varying according to Equation 11.19. In particular, this implies tail equivalence of the marginal Lévy measures, and we can write Equation 11.21 with some $\tilde{c}_i \in (0, \infty)$ as

$$\tilde{c}_i := \lim_{x \to \infty} \frac{\overline{\Pi}_i(x)}{\overline{\Pi}_1(x)} = \lim_{x \to \infty} \frac{\lambda_i \overline{F}_i(x)}{\lambda_1 \overline{F}_1(x)} =: \frac{\lambda_i}{\lambda_1} c_i \qquad (11.24)$$

that is, $\lim_{x \to \infty} \overline{F}_i(x)/\overline{F}_1(x) = c_i$. We avoid situations where for some i we have $\tilde{c}_i = 0$, corresponding to cases in which for $x \to \infty$ the tail measure $\overline{\Pi}_i(x)$ decays faster than $x^{-\alpha}$; that is, in Equation 11.24 we only consider the heaviest tail measures, all of tail index $-\alpha$. This makes sense, because we know from our discussion at the beginning of this section that only the heaviest-tailed risk cells contribute to total OpVaR. (See Theorem 11.2.)

When calculating total aggregated OpVaR, we are interested in the sum of these tail-equivalent, regularly varying marginals (i.e., we have to calculate the tail measure)

$$\overline{\Pi}^+(z) = \Pi\left(\left\{x \in \mathbb{E} : \sum_{i=1}^{d} x_i > z\right\}\right), \quad z > 0$$

Analogously to Resnick (2007, Proposition 7.3, p. 227), the tail measure $\overline{\Pi}^+$ is also regularly varying with index $-\alpha$. More precisely, we have

$$\lim_{t \to \infty} t \overline{\Pi}^+(b(t)z) = \nu \left\{ x \in \mathbb{E} : \sum_{i=1}^d x_i > z \right\} = z^{-\alpha} \nu \left\{ x \in \mathbb{E} : \sum_{i=1}^d x_i > 1 \right\}$$

$$= : z^{-\alpha} \nu^+(1, \infty] \tag{11.25}$$

Now let us choose the scaling function $b(t)$ so that $\overline{\Pi}_1(b(t)) \sim t^{-1}$. Then we have

$$\lim_{z \to \infty} \frac{\overline{\Pi}^+(z)}{\overline{\Pi}_1(z)} = \lim_{t \to \infty} \frac{t \overline{\Pi}^+(b(t))}{t \overline{\Pi}_1(b(t))} = \nu^+(1, \infty]$$

This implies the next result for aggregated OpVaR.

Theorem 11.6 (Böcker and Klüppelberg (2006), Theorem 3.18). Consider a multivariate compound Poisson model $X_t = (X_t^1, \ldots, X_t^d)$, $t \geq 0$, with multivariate regularly varying Lévy measure Π with index $-\alpha$ and limit measure ν in Equation 11.19. Assume further that the severity distributions F_i for $i = 1, \ldots, d$ are strictly increasing and continuous. Then $(X_t^+)_{t \geq 0}$ is a compound Poisson process with parameters satisfying for $z \to \infty$

$$\lambda^+ \overline{F}^+(z) \sim \nu^+(1, \infty] \lambda_1 \overline{F}_1(z) \in \mathcal{R}_{-\alpha} \tag{11.26}$$

where $\nu^+(1, \infty] = \nu\{x \in \mathbb{E} : \sum_{i=1}^d x_i > 1\}$. Furthermore, total OpVaR is asymptotically given by

$$\text{OpVaR}_t(\kappa) \sim F_1^{\leftarrow} \left(1 - \frac{1 - \kappa}{t \lambda_1 \nu^+(1, \infty]} \right), \quad \kappa \uparrow 1 \tag{11.27}$$

We notice that for the wide class of regularly varying distributions, total OpVaR can effectively be written in terms of the severity distribution of the first cell. Specifically, the right-hand side of Equation 11.27 can be understood as the stand-alone, asymptotic OpVaR of the first cell with an adjusted frequency parameter, namely $\lambda_1 \nu^+(1, \infty]$. What remains is to find examples where $\nu^+(1, \infty]$ can be calculated analytically or numerically to understand better the influence of certain dependence parameters.

11.4.5 Revisiting the Case of Independent Operational Risk Cells

Before we present some explicit results for the Clayton Pareto Lévy copula, let us consider again the particularly easy case with independent cells. Since then all mass is on the positive axes, we obtain

$$\nu^+(1, \infty] = \nu_1(1, \infty] + \cdots + \nu_d(1, \infty] \tag{11.28}$$

From $\overline{\Pi}_1(b(t)) \sim t^{-1}$ as $t \to \infty$ it follows for the tail measure of the first cell

$$\lim_{t \to \infty} t\overline{\Pi}_1(b(t)z) = z^{-\alpha} = \nu_1(z, \infty] \tag{11.29}$$

For $i = 2, \ldots, d$ we obtain by using (11.24)

$$\lim_{t \to \infty} t\overline{\Pi}_i(b(t)) = \lim_{t \to \infty} \frac{\overline{\Pi}_i(b(t)z)}{\overline{\Pi}_1(b(t))} = \lim_{u \to \infty} \frac{\overline{\Pi}_i(uz)}{\overline{\Pi}_i(u)} \frac{\overline{\Pi}_i(u)}{\overline{\Pi}_1(u)} = \tilde{c}_i \, z^{-\alpha} = \nu_i(z, \infty] \tag{11.30}$$

and, therefore, altogether $\nu^+(1, \infty] = 1 + \sum_{i=2}^{d} \tilde{c}_i$. By (11.26) together with $\lambda_1 \tilde{c}_i = \lambda_i c_i$ we finally recover the result of Theorem 11.4.

11.4.6 Two Explicit Results for the Clayton Lévy Copula

Let us consider a bivariate example where the marginal Lévy measures are not independent and thus the limit measure $\nu^+(z, \infty]$ is not just the sum of the marginal limit measures as in Equation 11.28. Instead, $\nu^+(z, \infty]$ has to be calculated by taking also mass between the positive axes into account, which can be done by representing $\nu^+(z, \infty]$ as an integral over a density.

First, note that from Equation 11.23 together with Equations 11.29 and 11.30, it follows in the case of a Pareto Lévy copula that for all $(x_1, x_2) \in \mathbb{E}$

$$\nu([0, (x_1, x_2)^\top]^c) = x_1^{-\alpha} + \tilde{c}_2 \, x_2^{-\alpha} - \left(x_1^{\alpha\theta} + \tilde{c}_2^{-\theta} x_2^{\alpha\theta} \right)^{-1/\theta}$$

which after differentiating yields

$$\nu'(x_1, x_2) = \tilde{c}_2^{-\theta} \, \alpha^2 (1 + \theta) x_1^{-\alpha(1+\theta)-1} x_2^{\alpha\theta-1} (1 + \tilde{c}^{-\theta}(x_2/x_1)^{\alpha\theta})^{-1/\theta-2}.$$

Hence, we can calculate

$$\nu^+(1,\infty] = \nu((1,\infty] \times [0,\infty]) + \int_0^1 \int_{1-x_1}^\infty \nu'(x_1, x_2) dx_1 \, dx_2$$

$$= 1 + \alpha \int_0^1 \left(1 + \tilde{c}_2^{-\theta}(x_1^{-1} - 1)^{\alpha\theta}\right)^{-1/\theta-1} x_1^{-1-\alpha} dx_1$$

and, by substitution $u = x_1^{-1} - 1$, we obtain

$$\nu^+(1,\infty] = 1 + \alpha \int_0^\infty (1 + \tilde{c}_2^{-\theta} u^{\alpha\theta})^{-1/\theta-1} (1+u)^{\alpha-1} du$$

$$= 1 + \tilde{c}_2^{1/\alpha} \int_0^\infty (1 + s^\theta)^{-1/\theta-1} (s^{-1/\alpha} + \tilde{c}_2^{1/\alpha})^{\alpha-1} ds$$

$$= 1 + \tilde{c}_2^{1/\alpha} E\left[(\tilde{c}_2^{1/\alpha} + Y_\theta^{-1/\alpha})^{\alpha-1}\right] \qquad (11.31)$$

where Y_θ is a positive random variable with density $g(s) = (1 + s^\theta)^{-1/\theta-1}$, independent of all parameters but the Pareto copula parameter θ.

Example 11.7

(a) For $\alpha = 1$ we have $\nu^+(1,\infty] = 1 + \tilde{c}_2$, which implies that, regardless of the dependence parameter θ, total OpVaR for all $0 < \theta < \infty$ is asymptotically equal to the independent OpVaR.

(b) If $\alpha\theta = 1$, then

$$\nu^+(1,\infty] = \frac{\tilde{c}_2^{1+1/\alpha} - 1}{\tilde{c}_2^{1/\alpha} - 1}$$

with $\tilde{c}_2 = (\lambda_2/\lambda_1)c_2$ as defined in Equation 11.24.

Figure 11.4 illustrates the tail measure $\nu^+(1,\infty]$ as given in Equation 11.31 for different values of θ and α. Note that according to Equation 11.27, OpVaR increases with $\nu^+(1,\infty]$. Hence, Figure 11.4 shows that in the case of $\alpha > 1$, a higher dependence (i.e., a higher number of joint losses in the components) leads to a higher OpVaR, whereas for $\alpha < 1$, it is the other way around: A lower dependence (i.e., a lower number of joint losses in the components) leads to a higher OpVaR. This again shows how things can go awry for extremely heavy-tailed distributions. Due to the

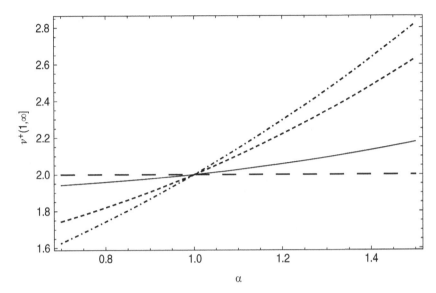

FIGURE 11.4 Illustration of the tail measure $v^+(1, \infty]$ as a function of α for different values of θ. We have chosen $\theta = 0.3$ (light dependence, solid line), $\theta = 1$ (medium dependence, dashed line), and $\theta = 10$ (strong dependence, dotted-dashed line). Moreover, the long-dashed line corresponds to the independent case.

nonconvexity of the OpVaR for $\alpha < 1$, diversification is not only not present, but the opposite effect occurs. Finally, note that for $\theta \to \infty$, independence occurs and $v^+(1, \infty] = 1 + \tilde{c}_2$ is constant, as indicated by the horizontal long-dashed line in Figure 11.4.

11.5 CONCLUSION

In this chapter we investigated a natural multivariate extension of the standard single-cell LDA by modeling dependence between different risk cells with a Pareto Lévy copula. This has the advantage that total aggregate operational loss of a bank up to time $t \geq 0$ is a compound Poisson and, in particular, does not depend on the size of the loss type/business line matrix.

Since we explicitly model the dependence of joint losses occurring at the same time, our model has a very intuitive interpretation: The total loss of two risk cells is due to the overlap of four compound Poisson processes, namely two independent ones (with different frequencies and independent severity distributions) and two completely dependent ones (with the same frequency parameter but in general different, dependent severity distributions).

Several conclusions can be drawn from our model. One important result is that frequency correlation only has a very restricted impact on the aggregated total OpVaR of a bank. Another finding is that in a multivariate problem, only the heaviest-tailed cells that have Pareto distributed severities contribute to total operational risk at high confidence level. Moreover, assuming the rich class of multivariate varying dependence structures, the asymptotic OpVaR resulting from those heaviest-tailed Pareto cells can be attributed to the stand-alone OpVaR of one cell by rescaling its loss frequency; see Equation 11.27.

There is a management cliché which says "What cannot be measured cannot be managed"; we may continue it by adding "and what cannot be managed cannot be improved." Having said that, we believe that the development of multivariate operational risk measurement models plays an important role in the improvement of an institution's overall risk management framework.

REFERENCES

Basel Committee on Banking Supervision. 2006. Observed range of practice in key elements of advanced measurement approaches AMA. Basel, Switzerland.

Böcker, K. 2006. Operational risk: Analytical results when high severity losses follow a generalized Pareto distribution (GPD)—A note. *Journal of Risk* 8, no. 4: 117–120.

Böcker, K., and C. Klüppelberg. 2005. Operational VAR: A closed-form approximation. *RISK Magazine* December, 90–93.

Böcker, K., and C. Klüppelberg. 2006. Multivariate models for operational risk. Working paper, Technical University of Munich. Available at www.ma.tum.de/stat/.

Böcker, K., and C. Klüppelberg. 2006. Modelling and measuring multivariate operational risk with Lévy copulas. *Journal of Operational Risk* 3, no. 2:3–27.

Chavez-Demoulin, V., P. Embrechts, and J. Nešlehová. 2005. Quantitative models for operational risk: Extremes, dependence and aggregation. *Journal of Banking and Finance* 30, no. 10:2635–2658.

Cont, R., and P. Tankov. 2004. *Financial modelling with jump processes.* Boca Raton, FL: Chapman & Hall/CRC.

Embrechts, P., C. Klüppelberg, and T. Mikosch. 1997. *Modelling extremal events for insurance and finance.* Berlin: Springer.

Frachot, A., T. Roncalli, and E. Salomon. 2005. Correlation and diversification effects in operational risk modeling. In *Operation risk: Practical approaches to implementation,* ed. E. Davis. London: Risk Books.

Klüppelberg, C., and S. I. Resnick. 2008. The Pareto copula, aggregation of risks and the emperor's socks. *Journal of Applied Probability* 45, no. 1:67–84.

Moscadelli, M. 2004. The modelling of operational risk: Experience with the analysis of the data collected by the Basel Committee. Working paper, Banca D'Italia, Termini di discussione, Rome, Italy.

Powojowski, M. R., D. Reynolds, and J. H. Tuenter. 2002. Dependent events and operational risk. *Algo Research Quarterly 5*, no. 2:65–73.

Resnick, S. I. 2007. *Heavy-tail phenomena.* New York: Springer.

Three

Operational Risk Management and Mitigation

CHAPTER 12

Integrating "Management" into "OpRisk Management"

Wilhelm K. Kross

ABSTRACT

Historically, financial institutions initiated their Basel II operational risk initiatives with a predominant controlling, accounting, and regulatory reporting focus. Carved in stone and prematurely transferred into largely automated information technology solutions, however, incoherent real-life implementation soon resembled a tail wagging the dog. Fairly significant efforts are now required to add a governance framework and to enable corporate leadership teams to truly live up to their responsibilities. In part this requires a rather ineffective relaunch of activities, while other features can simply be refocused or used as they are. To provide a better understanding of a sensible overall direction, this chapter demonstrates how management decision making, operations and change management, strategy development and net value generation perspectives are best integrated into ongoing OpRisk initiatives throughout their respective stages of maturity.

12.1 INTRODUCTION

For good reasons financial institutions historically initiated their Basel II operational risk (OpRisk) initiatives with a predominant controlling, accounting, and regulatory reporting and regulatory capital calculation focus. As a result, however, the second and third pillars of the Basel II framework have been somewhat neglected. Incoherent real-life implementation in some cases resembled a tail wagging the dog (see, e.g., Kross 2005). This can become problematic given that a risk-controlling department that becomes overly proactive in managing the risk managers, actually can violate the principle of functional segregation or what is commonly referred to as the four-eyes-principle. Fairly significant efforts are now required in those financial institutions to add a corporate governance framework and to enable corporate leadership teams to truly live up to their new responsibilities.

12.2 LIMITED SCOPE OPERATIONAL RISK MANAGEMENT UNDER BASEL II

In the last decade, operational risk management frameworks in financial institutions have been dominated by the advantages and the inherent shortfalls of the framework put forward by the Bank for International Settlements (BIS), commonly referred to as Basel II (see www.bis.org). Operational risk (OpRisk), defined in the context of Basel II as "the risk of loss resulting from inadequate or failed internal processes, people and systems or from external events," introduces a challenge to financial services providers and financial institutions that have to date predominantly controlled their organization's exposure to market and credit risk. Besides introducing operational risk as a new category and requiring that certain minimum regulatory capital be allocated in lieu of operational risk factors, Basel II intensifies the working relationship between financial institutions and the regulatory agencies on the basis of the so-called second pillar (see Figure 12.1). Furthermore, some degree of market discipline is fostered through transparency in regulatory and financial reporting frameworks.

For two of the three permissible approaches to calculate operational risk regulatory capital, it is not necessary to develop an appreciation of the true orders of magnitude of operational risk in the respective financial institution (see Figure 12.2). The basic indicator and the standard approaches merely use a factor, alpha or beta respectively, determined by the regulatory authority and then multiplied with the gross turnover (per business line) of the financial institution.

An inherent difficulty even for these approaches relates to the fact that operational risk under Basel II is addressed in a structure of seven risk factor categories and eight business lines. Any losses resulting from risk factors are booked to the category in which the initial event incurred. Hence, any observable correlations between the individual silos in the $8 * 7$ matrix are undesired—whether immediately after a risk event or after some delay. However, real-life facts, such as process interdependencies, internal cost

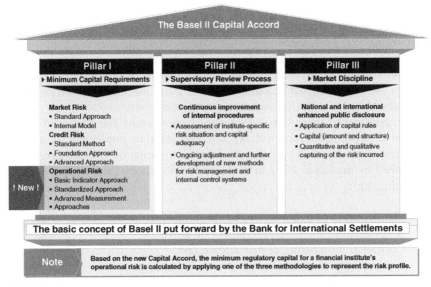

FIGURE 12.1　Basel II Capital Accord

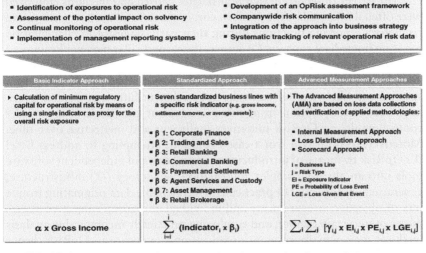

FIGURE 12.2　Calculation of Operational Risk Capital under Basel II

accounting procedures and systems, internal transfer pricing arrangements, personnel reward and recognition schemes, and various laws and regulations that are to be considered in external financial reporting may not support of this logic. Moreover, Basel II's business line orientation is not always compatible with the means and ways in which projects and project-related risk factors are managed and accounted for—in particular, when these projects are rather large in duration and scope, and interdepartmental.

In contrast to these two earlier approaches, under the advanced measurement approaches for OpRisk, it is necessary to implement as a prerequisite most if not all of those qualitative and quantitative requirements published by the BIS in 2003 in its operational risk best practices guide (see www.bis.org):

- Identification of exposures to operational risk
- Assessment of the potential impact on solvency
- Continual monitoring of operational risk
- Implementation of management reporting systems
- Development of an operational risk assessment framework
- Company-wide risk communication
- Integration of the operational risk assessment and management approach into the business strategy
- Systematic tracking of all relevant operational risk data[1]

The earlier observation that approaches chosen and methods employed were often dominated by the needs of corporate controlling, accounting, and regulatory reporting functions during their early stages of implementation raises no immediate concern. Of course, the second pillar may not be ignored altogether, a fact that many financial institutions understand. However, it is likely that starting OpRisk initiatives from a controlling or accounting perspective will likely not suffice in the not so distant future, given that a lack of proactive cooperation from risk management counterparts can render controlling-driven OpRisk initiatives inefficient and ineffective over time. Moreover, to portray a worst-case evolution, attempting to address Basel II's OpRisk by means of introducing yet another set of independent software tools into an already complex information technology (IT) infrastructure, generating another pool of practically irreconcilable data originating from a mix of objective measurements and individual and group subjective assessments of uncertain quality, and employing practically incompatible analysis methods may actually raise an organization's exposure to OpRisk, hence in some ways defeating the objective (see Figure 12.3). Luckily, modern approaches (Kross 2007) to operational risk management seem to focus to an increasing extent on the effectiveness and efficiency of risk management

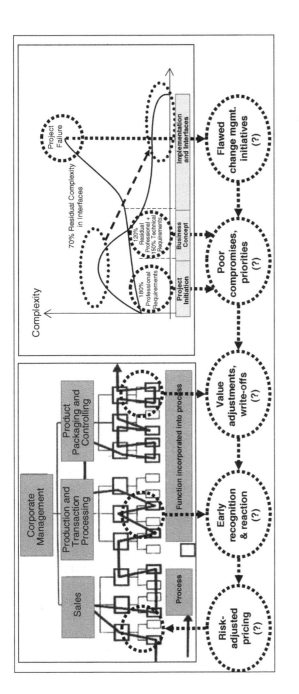

FIGURE 12.3 Dysfunctional IT Mega-Projects Endangering Operational Risk Management

253

at the board level. It is hence appropriate to conclude that with respect to management decision making, the Basel II framework for the incorporation of operational risk factors leaves a lot to be desired and promotes activities that have the potential to become counterproductive.

12.3 MANAGEMENT PERSPECTIVE IN OPERATIONAL RISK MANAGEMENT

Various authors believe that beyond reactively addressing stakeholders' and managers' requirements, appropriately implemented OpRisk management infrastructure, process, and people investments can be business enablers, turning risk management into an opportunity and addressing the requirements of advanced measurement approaches (AMA) as a desirable side effect (see Kross 2006, Chapters 4–7). Little related scientific evidence has been published and the underlying assumptions have been poorly recorded, which renders it difficult to justify the potential benefits of intensified OpRisk investments to deductive thinkers. This situation is worsened by some of the traditional financial valuation approaches, including in particular the Capital Asset Pricing Model (CAPM), according to which, in a large enough portfolio in a perfect capital market, operational factors are considered diversifiable, which in turn implies that any investment to improve operational risk performance will by definition add zero net value to the organization.

As was discussed elsewhere (Kross 2005), an in-depth analysis of approaches and methodologies chosen in real-life implementation demonstrates that most organizations that have engaged in an explicit analysis and control of OpRisk have started collecting internal loss data and have developed an appreciation of future loss scenarios in moderated and checklist-aided self-assessments. Approaches chosen seem to have been supported by IT applications; however, the make-or-buy decision and the coverage of and inherent assumptions made in commercially available and self-developed IT applications are heterogeneous. Fewer organizations are currently tracking key risk indicators in addition to other key performance indicators commonly analyzed by their accounting, controlling, and reporting functions. The use of generic risk maps and external loss databases appears to be relatively common. Advanced formalized hazard assessments are employed by a select number of organizations perceived to be first movers. And the degree of cross-industry information exchange on OpRisk aspects has increased, as indicated by the growing number of related conferences and workshops. It may hence be argued that it is a question of time until common knowledge converges within financial institutions and to a lesser extent with stakeholder groups, auditors, and regulatory authorities. Typically, when reviewing the scope of a financial institution's OpRisk initiatives today, one would expect to encounter at least these features:

- An operational framework and a policy for OpRisk, including operational guidance on consistent measurement and evaluation approaches.
- The capturing of operational risk factors through questionnaires and/or key indicators (drill-down, cause-consequence, and trend sensitivity) analyses, as well as the systematic collection of and statistical and sensitivity analyses of OpRisk indicators.
- An internal loss database, which may be merged with external loss data and with internal risk assessment data to derive an overall loss distribution.
- Interfaces to some other operational and risk control systems, and in particular to the software used for minimum regulatory capital calculations.
- Interfaces between the OpRisk system and internal and external reporting (i.e., financial accounting, management accounting, regulatory reporting) mechanisms and structures.
- Participation in data pooling and external loss data collection initiatives.
- A framework of systematic data collection coupled with regular data collection and evaluation review initiatives, and in some cases with an analysis of the organizational OpRisk management effectiveness and related costs.

The earlier notion that corporate governance and top management attention have in part been lacking, render it appropriate to submit that some elements of OpRisk frameworks seem to enable the easy and effective upgrade toward an integrated, risk-conscious corporate governance framework. However, others are almost exclusively focused on the quantification and the minimum regulatory capital provision that has become mandatory under the first pillar of Basel II.

12.4 RENDERING OPERATIONAL RISK MANAGEMENT OPERATIONALLY MANAGEABLE

Adding the "management perspective" and rendering OpRisk initiatives operationally manageable—to generate, if possible, net value and competitive advantages from successfully implemented OpRisk management investments—is not a trivial undertaking, particularly when the initiative was originally conceived for regulatory compliance or risk-controlling purposes only. Numerous interlayered aspects need to be considered and a rather complex overall master plan needs to be followed. OpRisk management initiatives must ultimately cope with what is commonly referred to as major-scale cultural change in an organization. At least these topics should be addressed:

- Scope, target, and the generic approach to methodology, limits, and risk retention.
- Responsibility allocation (i.e., the definition of risk owners/managers versus risk controlling, and process models for the line/project organization.
- Implementation of a temporary central risk management function to enhance envisaged/planned/targeted/anticipated cultural change.
- Setting up an OpRisk management implementation project, coping with known and unknown implementation challenges, and raising management effectiveness priorities above documentation priorities.
- Moderated interviews to identify the delta between responsibilities and capabilities and functional authority, to define and negotiate escalation triggers, to provide training as needed, and to design reporting and escalation mechanisms.
- A documented conclusion that risk owner responsibilities can (once trained and integrated into a reporting and escalation process structure) from now on be "lived."

Efficient and effective risk management, with an independent risk-controlling function, needs to be manageable over the short, medium, and long term with respect to the explicit efforts undertaken by each individual and the team, in addition to the data and key indicators that are collected and analyzed to support risk-based decision making. Each of these topics warrants some further discussion, which follows.

12.4.1 Implementing OpRisk Management in a Real-Life Environment

Identifying the scope and target of an OpRisk initiative that will be operationally manageable and ideally add net value to the organization does not need to be reinvented. Numerous organizations have implemented OpRisk initiatives successfully, inside and outside the financial services sector. A real-life organization faced with the need to define or modify the OpRisk policy at short notice may consider some or all of the next points. Note that the points were intentionally not defined narrowly, in order to foster an appreciation of how broad an OpRisk function can be and how closely the scope can relate to the functions and duties of top management.

- Recognize, in time, any risk factors related to processes, systems, models, the environment, or humans (including potential catastrophes).
- Develop an improved understanding of operational dependencies and weaknesses.
- Improve the performance measurement of processes, systems, and related human factors.
- Develop appropriate models to improve the evaluation of (risk) performance.
- Integrate methodologies for key risk indicator measurement, reporting, and loss databases.
- Improve the framework for risk-based decision making and prioritization under resource constraints, thereby reducing potential losses in time to an acceptable level while demonstrating the (cost) effectiveness and efficiency of risk reduction initiatives.
- Develop budgets for short-/long-term improvement of business processes/systems/transactions, allocate responsibilities, optimize processes, perform benchmarking with competitors and cross-industry best practice, and implement appropriate control measures.
- Improve the level of risk consciousness throughout the corporate value chain and promote individuals' desire to manage risk appropriately (i.e., gradually and stepwise migrating toward a strategy-supportive risk culture).
- Make contributions toward improved business leadership and sustainable strategic direction of the operation and the organization at large by improving the effectiveness of management approaches to managing operational risk factors, and optimizing business processes.

While some if not most of these topics are easily understandable at first sight, remember that the overall topic is "operational risk management," with its inherent limitations. Currently, scientists and practitioners have a relatively good understanding of hazard potentials, causes, events, technical interdependencies and so on, particularly when sufficient data is available. A good understanding of conditional probability of occurrence (derived from indicators, objectively measured, and/or subjectively estimated) prevails too in most situations. Furthermore, several promising insular and specialist discipline solutions have evolved to rather high levels of sophistication and automation. This follows the overall trend of the risk management sciences,

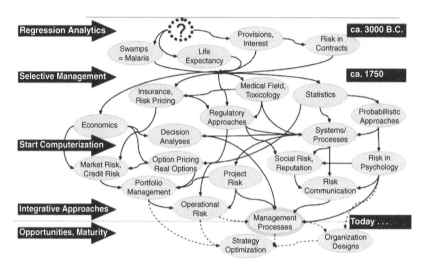

FIGURE 12.4 Evolution of Risk Analysis and Risk Management Techniques

which have evolved from initially unsystematic observation of risk, to insular solutions, to a reflection in regulatory approaches, and ultimately to an increasingly advanced set of quantitative analysis techniques, up to the current trend of reflecting risk in management decision making and management processes and in corporate planning (see Figure 12.4).

More explicitly, some important aspects reach beyond current accepted knowledge. For example:

- There is no common definition for risk that includes all facets that need to be dealt with; the risk management sciences remain inherently imprecise.
- There is no common, generic approach to risk management, no robust information on consequences and consequence chain capture, no guidance for the employment of suitable methods and their respective combinations, or the choice of a "sensible" level of detail.
- There is no guidance for integration of bottom-up versus top-down versus process- oriented approaches to risk management.
- The so-called acceptable residual risk is not appropriately defined. Neither are the appropriate rating and weighting of and sensible trade-offs between risk factors and consequence dimensions. Commercial aspects need to be reproduced, possibly using a modified definition for some sensitive fields—and subjective factors and stakeholders' value judgements play a major role, too.

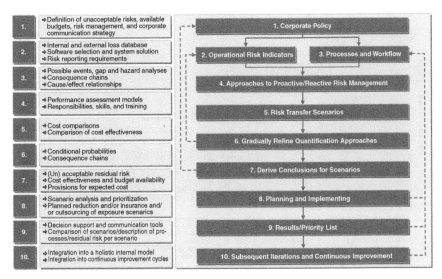

FIGURE 12.5 Exemplary OpRisk Management Implementation Process
Source: Earlier versions of the figure were introduced in Kross (2004).

■ Significant gaps remain in the current status of the risk management sciences and in the predominant research focuses: for example, consequences, trade-offs/comparison of different performance dimensions and risks remain an issue, as does the integration of risk analysis/ management, and its translation into operations management.

Hence the target and the objectives of an OpRisk management implementation initiative will invariably remain vague, even if practically tested standard frameworks (see Figure 12.5) were introduced in related literature years ago.

Once the generic policy framework has been compiled, a few facets need to be looked at more closely to achieve the ultimate objective of reducing residual operational risk from its current level to the "acceptable" level. This can be done by employing a combination of risk transfer, operational change, strategic change mechanisms and approaches by covering any losses through a combination of reserves, income, and financing (see Figure 12.6). Of course, with the choice of one or several of the preceding individual approaches and methodologies comes the requirements for risk limit setting and controlling and risk retention in terms of each of the performance dimensions, whether it is time, money, reputation, human health, managers' personal liabilities, or whatever is important to an organization.

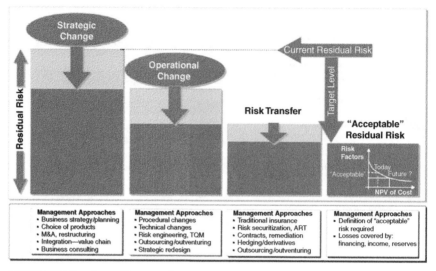

FIGURE 12.6   Overall Scope of OpRisk Management

12.4.2   Compensating the Potential Shortfalls of Real-Life OpRisk Management

Once the overall scope and the objectives of an OpRisk management initiative have been specified for the organization's needs and desires, the next step is to develop and implement a framework of risk ownership and related workflows and escalation or delegation mechanisms. Again, this sounds easier than it truly is, given that a number of typical leadership and management issues must be dealt with.

At the meta-level, the interplay of the various parts of an overall risk management functional framework must be defined. This involves defining risk management and risk ownership responsibilities in conjunction with the definition of independent risk-controlling responsibilities. In so doing, the relevance of corporate functions versus risk has to be defined in addition to the emphasis and responsibilities at the board level. Of course, some degree of redundancy (e.g., triggered through quality management approaches) may be intentional and warranted; however, too much quality is counterproductive, inter alia because it reduces management flexibility, a net value driver that is commonly quantified using real options techniques. Furthermore, literature and software tools in the field of complexity analysis indicate that operational risk correlates positively with the level of complexity; that is, the more sophisticated the management and controlling processes are, the higher the level of operational risk will be.

The organization-specific fine-tuning of OpRisk initiatives can become a challenge during both conceptual and implementation phases. Potentially conflicting objectives need to be identified and eliminated, and the different data requirements of the respective functions and their (selective and focused) perspectives need to be specified and integrated into both workflows and the coverage of IT solutions. In this context, notice that risk-related functions are typically not well integrated with straight-through processes.

Furthermore, the capture, analysis, and integration of risk and cost management data can become problematic. In particular, the organization must decide whether the reflection of risk-related costs remains as is, which implies that costs are reflected simply where they pop up in the organization. Tracing them back to their origin can be an alternative; this choice is mandated under Basel II. As mentioned earlier, some of the inherent assumptions will need to be filtered out for this approach, including in particular the various internal transfer pricing mechanisms and the way in which projects and products are accounted for and managed.

A third alternative encompasses the reflection of risk-related costs in team and personnel reward and recognition systems and the coupling of these with incentives. This latter framework needs to be extended to systematically trace opportunity costs, which has not been the case in many real-life OpRisk initiatives to date. Risk management in this context can no longer be treated as a corporate overhead; rather, risk management initiatives are looked at as part of the organization's investment portfolio. The impact of the traditionally poor integration of historic loss-oriented view with a future view on the implications of potential risk factors is elevated in its importance rather drastically.

An additional factor in some countries and cultures can be the fact that the approach that had been the rule was domineering and oriented to quality/security/safety/reliability. At their worst, these regimes pretended that everything was under control, provided that all of the restrictive guidelines were followed. For organizations under these regimes, a gradual ongoing harmonization with the more pragmatic and improvement-related Anglophile and Japanese approaches (i.e., six-sigma, continuous improvement cycles, etc.) is warranted. Incidentally, the historically quality-driven approaches are partially overwritten by recent regulatory standards anyway, in particular the second pillar of Basel II. For those more traditional and classical organizations, a quantum leap is required in which the evolutionary approach becomes the driving force and philosophy in OpRisk management initiatives (see Figure 12.7).

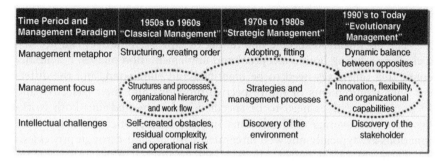

Time Period and Management Paradigm	1950s to 1960s "Classical Management"	1970s to 1980s "Strategic Management"	1990's to Today "Evolutionary Management"
Management metaphor	Structuring, creating order	Adopting, fitting	Dynamic balance between opposites
Management focus	Structures and processes, organizational hierarchy, and work flow	Strategies and management processes	Innovation, flexibility, and organizational capabilities
Intellectual challenges	Self-created obstacles, residual complexity, and operational risk	Discovery of the environment	Discovery of the stakeholder

FIGURE 12.7   Quantum Leap Required to Manage Today's OpRisk Challenges

Related literature provides an insight into further inherent leadership and governance issues at the macro- and micromanagement levels, some of which seem to bear particular relevance:

- Strategies are not clearly articulated or integrated with overall business strategies.
- Senior management "talks the talk" but does not "walk the walk."
- An organization's culture is not compatible with the strategy and there are low internal adoption rates.
- Management communicates grandiose but unachievable expectations.
- There is no champion and/or paralysis by analysis prevails.
- Priorities are not clearly articulated and frequently change, perhaps combined with slow decision-making/approval processes.
- Metrics to determine progress towards goals are soft and immeasurable.
- Iterative approaches are poorly planned, managed, and measured
- The not-invented-here syndrome permeates through the organization and slows execution.
- The pressure to implement too quickly drives solutions that are not fully functional.
- Prioritization issues (business/technical) remain unresolved and prohibit phased approaches.
- Available products inhibit the adoption of more mature technologies in the future.
- Knowledgeable technical resources are unavailable; they are available in competing initiatives/focuses.
- Some technology solutions are not scalable and are slow to grow.
- Point solutions without overall strategy prevail; pilot projects become the final solutions.

Any of these factors has the potential to substantially diminish the effectiveness and the efficiency of OpRisk initiatives.

12.4.3　Allocating Responsibilities for OpRisk Management

Once the obstacles to a robust implementation of OpRisk initiatives are recognized and some compensatory measures are implemented, the next step is to look at the current and future allocation of OpRisk management responsibilities: that is, the definition of risk owners/managers versus risk-controlling responsibilities, and the development of process models for the line and project structures and processes within the organization. A procedure that is considered suitable for this purpose, involves the following.

Develop a meta plan and measurable targets, following, for example, the logic of the framework portrayed in Figure 12.5.

By means of moderated interviews, identify the true scope and extent of risk that risk owners and risk managers are currently assigned for. One may start at the line manager level or at the project manager level, and gradually extend and iteratively expand the scope of analyses and the range of employees involved in the implementation of the OpRisk management framework—as long as there remains an overall master plan.

In the same interviews, identify with the risk owners which portions of their risk ownership responsibilities they can truly manage at this point. Some risk-related training may be lacking, which inherently inhibits the respective risk owners' ability to cope. Also, there may be some organizational and structural issues, as with the frequently experienced issue in project management that too much responsibility and too little authority is delegated to the project manager.

For any and all risk factors with which the respective risk owner cannot cope, a pragmatic and feasible solution has to be found. This may require that some specific training programs be conducted within an agreed-on time frame; but more important, it may involve the escalation or the delegation of responsibilities to a higher or a more appropriate level. The solution is that the person (or function) takes on the responsibility of managing effectively the respective risk factor in the best interest of the overall organization.

Courses and individual training programs could be bundled and coordinated, given that many risk owners may lack the same knowledge and skills—in particular in the fields of cost and risk analytics, formalized hazard assessments, advanced decision analysis techniques, and the development and implementation of related management measures. Of course, it is not sensible to attempt to make every employee a risk expert, but at a minimum, everyone should have the required skills for day-to-day risk management and be in a position to understand which risk and hazard factors need to be escalated or which ones can be ignored.

The escalation or delegation of specific risk factors to higher- or lower-level authorities (or backward or forward in the process chains and workflows) requires setting up a moderated interview with these new owners of risk responsibilities, informing them and providing them with the same input and support as was provided to their colleagues. Ultimately, this procedure is taken to the point at which all success-critical and all but the cosmetic and negligible operational risk factors are addressed and assigned somewhere and somehow. Incidentally, the situation should not be misunderstood: Risk management requires a fair amount of actual work to be done.

After training and mentoring have been provided to the risk owners and a set of flexible service levels has been defined that regulates the response time of higher-level authorities in the case of new escalations, among other things, a second interview is set up to ensure that risk owners are fully aware of their responsibilities and are capable of living up to the management responsibility. A feasible option is to link this to incentive schemes.

The central risk-controlling function is advised of any and all risk factors that were identified by means of a protocol as well as the specific allocation and escalation mechanisms that were negotiated throughout the organization. It is the duty of the central risk-controlling function to control and monitor both the allocation of these risk owner responsibilities and the efficiency and effectiveness of the respective risk management measures and related investments. Incidentally, it is sensible to assign the responsibility for risk quantification algorithms and risk modeling standards to the risk-controlling function too; doing so helps to reduce the overall controlling efforts (i.e., the model and modeling assumptions are verified just once, there are consistent data pools, etc.). A caveat is that risk owners and managers must determine the required level of detail of risk management information. This required level implies that risk aggregation at the portfolio level can be performed by the risk-controlling function as deemed appropriate, without limiting the needs of the risk managers.

Should an IT solution be available or anticipated to address OpRisk? It would need to be enhanced and customized to reflect the logic of risk owner responsibilities, related work, information flows, and the control mechanisms provided by the independent risk-controlling function.

As stated earlier, an OpRisk management implementation initiative is a major-scale cultural change and an organizational development initiative. Depending on the organizational specifics that need to be addressed, it may be appropriate to further discuss several issues that may or may not be essential.

Many if not most change initiatives today are set up and implemented as projects. This is positive in that some rather robust tools and techniques are available that render the performance of change initiatives predictable and easy to manage. However, some inherent assumptions can stifle cultural change initiatives. For example, projects by definition have a definite beginning and a definite end; however, one usually would not favor ending a cultural change initiative just because the project ends. Also, quite importantly, project managers usually do not have the authority of top-level corporate managers, whose authority may be required for the successful implementation of larger-scale change initiatives. Hence project managers and their change initiatives may be systematically set up for failure unless explicitly supported and adequately promoted by top management.

Given that OpRisk management initiatives usually confront the lack of adequately trained, available resources and insufficient time devoted by decision makers, it is an operational necessity to live with short- to medium-term compromises. Setting up an OpRisk implementation project simply as a compromise because of a lack of senior management time may be problematic; and furthermore, the priorities must be reconciled between the project and line function business on a day-to-day basis. Coping with known and unknown implementation challenges is part of what project managers do; and getting the right project manager and equipping him or her with the right tools and the right level of management support is a fundamental issue to be resolved for almost any project. However, over the short to medium term, it may be warranted to temporarily abandon some of the more traditional management paradigms in financial institutions, including but not limited to raising the priority of risk management effectiveness above the one of documentation. This latter issue may be controversial, of course, and even partially in conflict with minimum regulatory requirements.

As a temporary measure, the implementation of a central risk management function may be warranted to enhance the implementation speed of envisioned, planned, targeted, and anticipated cultural change. If such a mechanism were to be chosen, a few lessons learned should be taken into consideration.

1. The central risk management (as opposed to risk-controlling) function when compared to risk managers would never be permitted to take on a risk ownership role. Rather the function would consist of a few specialists under the leadership of a senior manager exclusively remaining in an advisory and facilitating capacity. This would provide risk owners the risk-controlling function with operational support in terms of knowledge and resources.

2. The central risk management function should never tell risk owners what to do or how to act as an internal police function. The latter falls into the scope and the responsibilities of the central risk-controlling function, which may escalate information to senior-level management and require appropriate steps to be undertaken by the respective risk owners, as deemed appropriate. For a central risk management function to be successfully accepted within the organization's structure and culture, the group must be perceived as being the "good guys." The group's contributions could be published and promoted internally once a few success stories have been generated.

3. Develop internal standards on how to conduct moderated interviews to identify the delta between responsibilities and capabilities as well as functional authority. Not forgetting to define and negotiate escalation triggers, to provide training, and to design reporting. A wealth of related information is available.[2] Although such information is readily available, given its inherent complexity, this issue is best approached by requesting short-term assistance from specialized service providers that have a proven track record in this field.

12.5 RECOMMENDATIONS AND OUTLOOK

As described in this chapter, initiating an OpRisk management initiative without reinventing the wheel is a complex undertaking with numerous inherent challenges. However, a rather large body of knowledge and experience has evolved in recent years, which renders most of the key steps manageable predictably. Lessons learned have been published, and generic frameworks and fairly capable standard software solutions are starting to make risk managers' lives easier.

To provide some further insight into the reasons why one would engage in such initiatives in the first place, an analogy is appropriate. Professor Harold Kerzner, one of the leading thinkers and practitioners in the field of project management, put forth a model that observed that knowledge workers' intensive drive for increasing levels of maturity cannot be the ultimate solution. In the context of products introduced into a market, maturity may be the point from which everything goes downhill. Rather, Kerzner submitted, top management should start to recognize their knowledge workers' willingness to change and provide further direction to develop their project management competencies beyond maturity, to excellence. Figure 12.8 was modified to replace Kerzner's expression "project" by the word "risk," which follows the inherent feeling (in the absence of tangible scientific evidence) that the same reference model is valid for the evolution

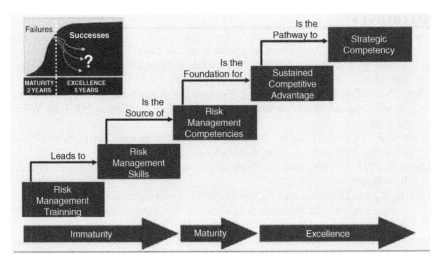

FIGURE 12.8 Migrating from Maturity to OpRisk Management Excellence

of risk management maturity and the further net benefits and competitive advantages if risk management excellence were to be established.

Kerzner was able to substantiate in his publications and presentations that working toward project management maturity helps to reduce the likelihood of failure, usually achieved within a time period of one to two years. The link to strategy crafting and to the development of competitive advantages through excellent project management would introduce a more complex set of opportunities that may not be as easy to capture. A possible research project could assess how far Kerzner's model is truly convertible to the field of operational risk management. This project could track key indicators that would best help to substantiate that advanced levels of operational risk management, beyond regulatory compliance, have the potential to add substantial levels of net value to an organization.

NOTES

1. For a formal treatment, see Alexander (2005) and Chernobai (2007).
2. For further information, please refer to Clemen and Reilly (2001), Döbeli et al. (1993), Howson and Urbach (1989), Kahnemann et al. (1982), Keeney (1992), Keeney and Raiffa (1993), Kross (2000, 2006), Kross et al. (2002), Morgan and Henrion (1990), or von Winterfeld and Edwards (1986).

REFERENCES

Alexander, C. 2005. Assessment of operational risk capital. In *Risk management: Challenge and opportunity*, eds. M. Frenkel, U. Hommel, and M. Rudolf. Berlin: Springer.

Chernobai, A., S. T. Rachev, and F. J. Fabozzi. 2007. *Operational risk: A guide to Basel II capital requirements, models and analysis*. Hoboken, NJ: John Wiley & Sons.

Clemen, R. T., and T. Reilly. 2001. *Making hard decisions*. Pacific Grove, CA: Duxbury Thomson Learning, Brooks/Cole.

Davis, E. 2005. *Operational risk: Practical approaches to implementation*. London: Risk Books.

Döbeli, B., M. Leippold, and P. Vanini. 2003. From operational risks to operational excellence, In *Advances in operational risk: Firm-wide issues for financial institutions*, ed. P. Mestchian, 2nd ed. London: Risk Books.

Dobiéy, M., W. Kross, and M. Müller-Reichart. 2003. Auch Management statt nur Controlling (Management too instead of just Controlling). *Marktplatz Energie* (Frankfurt) 6:4–5.

Hommel, U., M. Scholich, and P. Baecker. 2003. *Reale Optionen—Konzepte, Praxis und Perspektiven strategischer Unternehmensfinanzierung*. Heidelberg: Springer.

Hommel, U., M. Scholich, and R. Vollrath. 2001. *Realoptionen in der Unternehmenspraxis—Wert schaffen durch Flexibilität*. Heidelberg: Springer.

Howson, C., and P. Urbach. 1989. *Scientific reasoning: The Bayesian approach*. La Salle, IL: Open Court Publishing Company.

Kahneman, D., P. Slovic, and A. Tversky. 1982. *Judgement under uncertainty: Heuristics and biases*. Cambridge, MA: Cambridge University Press.

Keeney, R. L. 1992. *Value-focused thinking—A Path to creative decision making*. Cambridge, MA: Harvard University Press.

Keeney, R. L., and H. Raiffa. 1993. Decisions with multiple objectives: Preferences and Value trade-offs. Cambridge, MA: Cambridge University Press.

Kross, W. 2000. Pricing risk: Probabilistic approaches and case studies. Workshop proceedings, Current Perspectives on Risk Management, June 18–19, Financial Stability Institute, Bank for International Settlements, Basel, Switzerland.

Kross, W. 2002. Holes in holistic risk management—Financial institutions' approaches to operational risk. Proceedings, Society for Risk Analysis (SRA-Europe) annual meeting, July 21–24. Humboldt University, Berlin, Germany.

Kross, W. 2004. Operational risk: The management perspective. In *Risk management: Challenge and opportunity*, ed. M. Frenkel, U. Hommel, and M. Rudolf. Berlin: Springer.

Kross, W. 2006. *Organized opportunities: Risk management in financial services organizations*. Weinheim, Germany: John Wiley & Sons.

Kross, W. 2007. Kulturwandel durch MARisk (Cultural change through MARisk) (interview), *Compliance Manager 9*, no. 11:5.

Morgan, M. G., and M. Henrion. 1990. *Uncertainty: A guide to dealing with uncertainty in quantitative risk and policy analysis*. Cambridge, MA: Cambridge University Press.

Shapira, Z. 1995. *Risk taking—A managerial perspective*. New York: Russell Sage.

Von Winterfeldt, D. and W. Edwards. 1986. *Decision analysis and behavioral research*. Cambridge, MA: Cambridge University Press.

CHAPTER 13

Operational Risk Management: An Emergent Industry

Kimberly D. Krawiec

ABSTRACT

Financial institutions have always been exposed to operational risk—the risk of loss from faulty internal controls, human error or misconduct, external events, or legal liability. Only in the past decade, however, has operational risk risen to claim a central role in risk management within financial institutions, taking its place alongside market and credit risk as a hazard that financial institutions, regulators, and academics seriously study, model, and attempt to control and quantify. This chapter situates operational risk management—particularly those components of operational risk related to legal risk and the risk of loss from employee misconduct—within the broader literature on enforced self-regulation, internal controls, and compliance, arguing that the increased focus on operational risk management portends both positive and negative effects.

13.1 INTRODUCTION

Financial institutions have always been exposed to operational risk—the risk of loss from faulty internal controls, human error or misconduct, external events, or legal liability. Only in the past decade, however, has operational risk risen to claim a central role in risk management within financial institutions, taking its place alongside market and credit risk as a hazard that financial institutions, regulators, and academics seriously study, model, and

271

attempt to control and quantify. This newfound prominence is reflected in the Basel II capital accord, in numerous books and articles on operational risk, and in the emergence of a rapidly expanding operational risk management profession that is expected to grow at a compound annual rate of 5.5%, from US$992 million in 2006 to US$1.16 billion in 2009 (Celent 2006).

This increased emphasis on operational risk management corresponds to a much wider trend of "enforced self-regulation," both in the United States and internationally, that attaches significant importance to the internal control and compliance mechanisms of business and financial institutions. Driven by legal changes and well-organized compliance industries that include lawyers, accountants, consultants, in-house compliance and human resources personnel, risk management experts, and workplace diversity trainers (hereafter, legal intermediaries), internal compliance expenditures have increased substantially throughout the past decade, assuming an ever-greater role in legal liability determinations and organizational decision making, and consuming an ever-greater portion of corporate and financial institution budgets (Krawiec 2003, 2005).

This chapter situates operational risk management—particularly those components of operational risk related to legal risk and the risk of loss from employee misconduct—within the broader literature on enforced self-regulation, internal controls, and compliance, arguing that the increased focus on operational risk management portends both positive and negative effects. On the one hand, business and financial institutions that are law abiding and avoid unforeseen and unaccounted for disasters are an obvious positive. At the same time, however, all operational risk management is not created equally. Some operational risk expenditures may prove more effective at enhancing the profits or positions of particular firm constituencies and legal intermediaries, or luring regulators and firm stakeholders into a false confidence regarding operational risk management, than at significantly reducing operational risk losses. Indeed, recent rogue trading losses such as those at Société Générale and MF Global Ltd. demonstrate that operational risk measures such as those embraced in Basel II are no substitute for sound firm management and regulatory oversight.

13.2 OPERATIONAL RISK MANAGEMENT AS ENFORCED SELF-REGULATION

13.2.1 Basel II Accord

The Basel Accord of 1988 defined a set of risk-based capital requirements for financial institutions, but did not even mention operational risk

(Basel Committee 1988). Due to a number of objections to, and perceived problems with, the original accord, however, the Bank for International Settlements (BIS) began the processes of revising the accord in 2001 (Basel Committee 2001). At that time, the Basel Committee determined that operational risk levels at banks had increased in the intervening years since the first accord was reached (Basel Committee 2001).

In part, operational risk had become a more salient issue in the wake of high-profile operational risk losses, such as the Nick Leeson rogue trading scandal at Barings Bank and the World Trade Center bombing. But the concern was also prompted by business developments, such as large-scale combinations of financial institutions that stressed newly integrated systems; the growth of banks as high-volume service providers; and the increasing use of automated technology, e-commerce, outsourcing, and financial products designed to reduce market or credit risk that often increased operational risk (Basel Committee 2001). Indeed, the committee recognized that financial institutions had already begun to treat operational risk as a serious category of potential risk, integrating the concept into their internal capital assessment and allocation decisions (Basel Committee 2001).

Including an operational risk measure in banks' capital charges was not without challenges, however. Unlike market and credit risk, which had been measured and quantified for some time, and for which sophisticated models and relatively extensive data had been developed, operational risk measurement was—and, indeed, still is—in its infancy. As stated by the Basel Committee:

> 43. *Approaches to the measurement of operational risk continue to evolve rapidly, but are unlikely to attain the precision with which market and credit risk can be quantified. This poses obvious challenges to the incorporation of a measure of operational risk within the minimum capital requirement. . . .*

> 44. *On the other hand, the Committee is prepared to allow an unprecedented amount of flexibility to banks in choosing how to measure operational risk and the resulting capital requirement. Under the advanced measurement approaches (AMA), banks will be permitted to choose their own methodology for assessing operational risk, so long as it is sufficiently comprehensive and systematic. The extent of detailed standards and criteria for use of the AMA are minimal in an effort to spur the development of innovative approaches, although the Committee intends to review progress in regard to operational risk approaches on an ongoing basis. (Basel Committee 2002, 7–8)*

Under the advanced measurement approach (AMA), therefore, banks are allowed to use their own risk metrics for calculating the operational risk capital requirement, including loss data, scenario analysis, and risk mitigation measures (Netter and Poulsen 2003). Providing less flexibility is the standardized approach, under which different business lines are assigned individual gross activity measures and then are multiplied by a fixed multiple determined by the regulator. Finally, under the basic indicator approach, which is the simplest but least sensitive of the measures, the required capital is equal to a fixed multiple of a single activity measure, such as gross income (Netter and Poulsen 2003).

There have been many critics of the Basel II operational risk provisions. Some argue, for example, that operational risk models are not predictive in nature, but instead are primarily descriptive or backward looking, and that they have not been validated for many crucial operational risk events (Holmes 2003). Further, many point to the lack of meaningful data regarding operational risk, especially the low-frequency, high-impact events that may be the greatest source of operational risk losses. Finally, some argue that regulators' attention would be better focused on supervision or internal controls rather than capital requirements and that the Basel rules are likely to be unworkable and lead to distorted incentives (Netter and Poulsen 2003).

Enforced Self-Regulation Overview   With the Basel II accord (and, particularly, with the AMA), the Basel Committee moved operational risk management squarely into the growing ranks of "enforced self-regulation" (Power 2005). Also sometimes referred to as "negotiated governance," "collaborative governance," or "responsive regulation," enforced self-regulation seeks to improve the regulatory process by providing a greater governance role to the regulated group and, sometimes, other interested parties (Ayres and Braithwaite 1992; Kagan 2001). As described by Ayres and Braithwaite:

> [E]nforced self-regulation envisions that in particular contexts it will be more efficacious for the regulated firms to take on some or all of the legislative, executive, and judicial regulatory functions. As self-regulating legislators, firms would devise their own regulatory rules; as self-regulating executives, firms would monitor themselves for noncompliance; and as self-regulating judges, firms would punish and correct episodes of noncompliance. (103)

The goal of this more collaborative, less authoritative regulatory approach is to foster more efficient, effective regulation through greater involvement in the governance process by a variety of interested groups, including the regulated group. Theories of enforced self-regulation have been influential across a wide range of U.S. legal regimes in recent decades, including environmental, tort, securities, employment discrimination, corporate, organizational sentencing, and healthcare law (Krawiec 2003).

These attempts at enforced self-regulation—at least as they have been operationalized to date—are not without critics, however. Some empirical research, for example, casts doubt on the effectiveness of some enforced self-regulatory regimes (Kalev et al. 2006; King and Lenox 2000; Krawiec 2005). Moreover, analogizing to the literature on incomplete contracts, some observers warn that, whereas advocates of enforced self-regulation see only an opportunity for the negotiation of creative solutions to governance problems, the open-ended law characteristic of enforced self-regulation presents a potentially dangerous opportunity for strategic renegotiation by those with the greatest stake in the contested meaning of law: the regulated group and various legal intermediaries within and without it (Krawiec 2003).

To illustrate, the governance process can be usefully analyzed as a multistage reciprocal interaction among policymakers, the regulated group, and important private actors, namely the various legal intermediaries within and without the regulated firm with an interest in the contested meaning of law and who serve as the first-line interpreters of legal policy. For example, when business or financial institutions become subject to a new regulation, such as the operational risk requirements of Basel II, that regulation is subjected to an internal and external process by which the new law gains content. Although this is true with nearly all laws (which frequently are ambiguous, poorly articulated, or subject to differing interpretations), it is particularly true with respect to enforced self-regulatory regimes, such as Basel II, which are left purposely open-ended in an effort to provide latitude and encourage innovation in interpretation and implementation (Krawiec 2003).

The role of legal intermediaries in this process is extremely important, as senior decision makers in the regulated group (in this case senior executives at banking institutions) rarely learn of or interpret new legal mandates on their own. Instead, they learn of new laws from a variety of unofficial sources: the above-mentioned legal intermediaries and their professional networks, the media, and similarly situated regulated entities. Each of these has an incentive to interpret regulatory terms and gaps in a manner that influences their own influence and importance—constrained, of course, by the regulated group's self-interest in its own welfare-enhancing interpretation (Krawiec 2003).

Although policymakers retain the authority to reject these gap-filling interpretations as inconsistent with the initial regulatory contract, policymakers have limited time, expertise, and incentives to differentiate *ex post* a self-serving or inefficient interpretation from one that best serves the public interest. As a result, self-interested private actors with a stake in the interpretation of regulatory policy may influence policy and implementation substantially, appropriating more than their fair share of the social benefits of legal policy and undermining its efficacy and efficiency in the process (Krawiec 2003).

Legal Intermediaries and Regulatory Indeterminacy To illustrate, researchers have noted the role played by various legal intermediaries, including accountants, lawyers, human resources personnel, and psychiatrists, in pressing interpretations of ambiguous statutes or legal rulings that both overstate legal risk and the intermediary's ability to contain and control it. Presumably, such overstatement—and the development of creative containment strategies—is easier in the face of ambiguous or open-ended policy, such as that exemplified by enforced self-regulation, than is the case when law is explicit, mandatory, and unambiguous.

It has been argued, for example, that psychiatric professional associations may have interpreted *Tarasoff v. Regents of the Univ. of Calif.*, a 1976 case holding that psychotherapists owe a duty of care to third parties whom their patients have threatened to harm, in a manner that reflects the concerns of mental health care professionals. Moreover, evidence suggests that most therapists learned of the obligations considered to be imposed by *Tarasoff* through these professional organizations rather than through lawyers or primary legal sources (Givelber et al. 1984; *Tarasoff v. Regents of the Univ. of Calif.* 1976).

Similarly, there is some evidence that lawyers systematically overstate legal risks and exploit legal ambiguity when advising clients. Furthermore, they tend to recommend means of containing that risk or ambiguity that require substantial involvement by legal professionals and fall squarely within their realm of expertise. Popular containment strategies include: drafting contracts, employee manuals, or other documents in a particular manner; observing certain hiring, firing, and promotion practices; engaging in particular types and methods of disclosure; and requiring certain types of employee training (Krawiec 2003).

Whether such maneuvering derives from conscious, self-interested behavior, from self-serving bias, or from bias in the sources from which many legal intermediaries gain their knowledge is a subject for debate. Whereas some emphasize legal intermediaries' self-interest in fostering unclear legal rules in order to enhance the amount of advice and containment necessary (Macey and Miller 1987), others argue that self-serving bias may render truly objective professional advice, such as accounting audits, impossible (Bazerman 2002; Langevoort and Rasmussen 1997).

Finally, researchers have documented substantial evidence of both overstatement of legal risk and the availability of containment strategies in secondary legal materials. One study, for example, analyzed articles on the topic of wrongful discharge suits in personnel journals, practitioner-oriented legal journals, and academic law reviews (Edelman et al. 1992). The study found that personnel and practitioner-oriented legal journals significantly inflated the risk of wrongful discharge lawsuits, often through the use of alarmist or extreme language that overstated both the frequency of such suits and the rates at which plaintiffs prevailed. In contrast to the interpretation offered by these journals, the researchers' own statistics and a RAND study concluded that the cost to employers from wrongful discharge suits was slight (Dertouzos 1988; Edelman et al. 1992). As might be expected, the solutions to these threats posed by legal intermediaries are often within their field of expertise and could generate substantial revenues (Edelman et al. 1992). Similar results have been found with regard to internal grievance procedures and federal securities law (Edelman et al. 1999; Langevoort and Rasmussen 1997).

The Regulated Group   Members of the regulated group, as the subjects of new legal policy, also play an important role in constructing the meaning of new legal mandates. As previously discussed, senior executives at business and financial institutions are unlikely to learn of new laws directly from primary sources; instead they gather their information from legal intermediaries, the media, or other secondary sources. This does not mean, however, that they are uninvolved in constructing the legal regime by which their actions will be governed. Senior management, for example, may seek to minimize disruptions to current business practices while still assuring regulators that they have met the goals of new regulatory policies. They may, for example, press an interpretation of law that signals compliance but fails to fulfill the normative goals of new regulation. Similarly, they may resist interpretations of new policies offered by third parties, such as legal intermediaries or regulators, that they believe overly constrain management discretion or disrupt current business practices.

To illustrate, researchers have argued that organizational management may have resisted legal interpretations of equal employment opportunity (EEO) laws that require affirmative action or that treat the implied contract theory of wrongful discharge as requiring that employees be fired only for cause, because such interpretations overly restrict management's hiring and firing authority. They may have been more receptive, however, to interpretations holding that equal employment policies and diversity training can shield employers from liability, or that the implied contract theory of wrongful discharge requires employers to include "employment at will" clauses in employee manuals, both of which preserve management discretion (Edelman 1992).

Finally, the role of interdepartmental rivalry as various units and subunits within the regulated group struggle for position, prestige, and access to limited resources should not be overlooked. If one interpretation will enhance the power of a unit—say legal compliance, audit, or risk management—relative to other units, then it is likely that members of that unit will advance an interpretation of a new policy that most benefits their department. For example, some empirical studies trace a proliferation of certain personnel practices, such as job evaluation and promotion testing, to attempts by personnel professionals to establish and maintain their strategic position within firms during the 1940s, a time when union activity was on the rise and personnel professionals marketed themselves as having the ability to constrain union power (Baron et al. 1986).

Diffusion and Institutionalization Even acknowledging the incentives of various groups affected by legal policy to fill any gaps in incomplete law with terms that further their own interests, one might still question why their interpretations are so similar. Surely there is more than one interpretation of an indeterminate legal mandate that would further the interests of legal intermediaries and the business or financial community. How then does a consensus arise regarding the meaning of new legal policy?

As recognized by many researchers, professional networks play an extremely important role in the standardization and diffusion of a legal interpretation across the relevant community. These networks include professional associations and their regular gatherings and newsletters, commercial workshops and education courses, professional communications via the Internet, and professional publications such as periodicals, books, treatises, memoranda to clients, and articles in professional and academic journals (Edelman et al. 1999; Langevoort and Rasmussen 1997). For example, researchers have documented the role of accountants in the diffusion and institutionalization of certain financial reporting practices across Fortune 200 corporations (Mezias 1990), the role of legal professionals in the diffusion of grievance procedures as a response to Title VII litigation, (Edelman et al. 1999), and the role played by Silicon Valley lawyers in constructing norms of venture capital practice, many of which became institutionalized in the national legal regime (Suchman and Cahill 1996).

Section Summary As elaborated in this section, the Basel II operational risk requirements represent a significant embrace by the international banking community of responsive or enforced self-regulation. Although critics have leveled a number of objections to the requirements, including that they are unnecessary and that the quantitative elements of the field are insufficiently developed, few have examined the Basel II operational risk requirements as a species of enforced self-regulation, with the attendant costs and benefits. As is discussed in Section 13.3, the flexibility and indeterminacy embodied in the Basel II operational risk provisions provide opportunities for numerous legal intermediaries—particularly legal and compliance professionals, accountants, and risk management experts—to construct both an interpretation of the rules and containment strategies that enhance their position and well-being vis-à-vis the banking community.

I do not mean to suggest, of course, that enforced self-regulation such as that embodied in Basel II can never provide meaningful benefits. In theory, at least, enforced self-regulation provides an opportunity for innovation and creativity in establishing workable and cost-effective solutions to the problem of operational risk management. Moreover, under certain conditions, this goal appears to have been achieved in practice by some enforced self-regulatory regimes (Lenox 2008). At the same time, however, numerous legal intermediaries and firm constituencies have an incentive to emphasize (or overemphasize) both the extent to which operational risk falls within the domain of their expertise and their ability to contain it. Meanwhile, senior management of the regulated group have incentives to signal compliance with new legal rules while containing costs and disrupting existing business practice as little as possible. As a result, enforced self-regulation—including the enforced self-regulation of operational risk management under Basel II—presents a danger of becoming more cosmetic than real, while consuming more resources than necessary for subpar compliance. Indeed, as will be elaborated, one can already observe such jockeying over the meaning and implementation of Basel II's operational risk provisions.

13.3 OPERATIONAL RISK: BIRTH OF AN INDUSTRY

13.3.1 OpRisk Intermediaries

Basel II, of course, was not the first foray by the international banking community into enforced self-regulation. In 1996, the Basel Committee made a significant break with prior practice by permitting regulatory minimum capital requirements covering market risk exposures arising from banks' trading activities to be based on banks' own internal risk measurement models (Hirtle et al. 2001). This move was widely supported by both regulators and the banking community, but is considered by many to be fundamentally different from the operational risk requirements of Basel II.

First, by 1996, market risk modeling was in a fairly advanced state, and many financial institutions had devoted considerable resources toward developing value-at-risk models to measure potential losses in their trading portfolios (Hirtle et al. 2001). As previously discussed, operational risk models have not yet reached this level of precision or sophistication. Moreover, market risk models are considered more amenable to back-testing than are operational risk models. As a result, market risk may be more suitable than is operational risk to a regulatory approach of delegation of authority to financial institutions followed by oversight as a substitute for top-down regulation (Power 2005). Finally, operational risk is significantly more context dependent than either market or credit risk, being driven largely by complex human factors that vary from scenario to scenario and that are subject to influence by bank management (Holmes 2003).

This lack of general consensus regarding operational risk definition, modeling, measurement, and control methods means that the Basel II Accord leaves room for definition and negotiation among internal and external agents, particularly lawyers, accountants, and risk management experts, each of whom can credibly assert some expertise on the topic. As stated by Michael Power (2005, 585), "[o]perational risk as a broadly defined boundary object provides opportunities for internal agents, such as lawyers and accountants, to redefine and reposition their work in terms of risk management."

Accountants, for example, may seek to define operational risk as primarily related to internal controls and auditing functions, whereas lawyers may package operational risk management in terms of organizational governance and compliance issues. The comments of one industry observer are illustrative: "I do not think that BIS or any other regulatory authority can come up with any rules for how much capital banks can hold against operational risk. The first line of defense for such risk is internal controls" (Netter and Poulsen 2003, 21). As stated by another, "So operational risk management, in this case, is about internal controls, not about quantification and capitalization" (Cagan 2001, 2). Both this internal control conception and the organizational governance conception of operational risk management are in contrast to the view of operational risk embraced by most risk management specialists. Such specialists, trained in financial economics and possessing quantitative and modeling skills and training, tend to view operational risk as a poor cousin to market and credit risk, amenable someday—with sufficient attention and effort—to measuring, modeling, and testing (Power 2005).

The Regulated Group and "Business as Usual"   As discussed in Section 13.2, senior decision makers of the regulated group are unlikely to learn of or interpret new legal mandates on their own, instead relying to a significant degree on legal intermediaries and their professional networks and secondary sources. Consequently, lawyers, accountants, and risk management experts all have been influential in constructing the meaning of, and the terms of compliance with, the operational risk elements of Basel II. This does not mean, however, that banking institutions are uninvolved in constructing the meaning of operational risk under Basel II, bringing their own interests to bear in the interpretation. Those interests include defining operational risk and its management under Basel II in a manner that minimizes costs, especially the costs of any alterations to a profitable trading environment.

Understanding the significance of this interest requires some analysis of the conundrum faced by financial institutions with respect to operational risk losses, particularly the high-frequency, low-impact events related to employee misconduct (i.e., "rogue trading"). For example, a wide array of state and federal laws, regulatory rules, and SRO (self-regulatory organization) guidelines mandate that financial institutions adequately supervise their employees. Most financial institutions have implemented elaborate compliance procedures and programs in an apparent attempt to meet these requirements. Many firms spend millions of dollars each year on expensive computer and reporting systems and on supervisory personnel designed to control abusive trading practices (Krawiec 2000).

The continued existence of rogue trading in the face of these extensive legal and institutional disincentives presents a mystery for many scholars and industry observers. Why would management permit its employees to behave in a manner that jeopardizes not only the continued existence of the firm (and hence, of management employment) but that also risks the integrity of the markets in which the firm operates? Are financial institutions incapable of understanding the forces that give rise to rogue trading? Is rogue trading simply impossible to eliminate?

Financial institutions, of course, are not helpless or stupid in the face of employee attempts to evade the firm's trading limits. Instead, it is more likely that the costs of deterring rogue trading are commonly underestimated. As a result, attempts at the enforced self-regulation of operational risk must be viewed with the recognition that banking institutions likely have determined to tolerate at least some evasion of their trading limits, because to reduce the risk of rogue trading to zero is prohibitively costly. A similar analysis has been applied to crime, torts, and pollution (Stigler 1970).

To begin with, it is easy to see that in any trading environment there is a risk that, if left unchecked, employees will attempt to hide losses and fabricate profits. Because larger trading profits result in a larger bonus, traders can enhance their own wealth and welfare by fabricating profits. Similarly, when trades go sour, traders have an incentive to hide losses from superiors, hoping to recoup the loss later, perhaps by engaging in riskier trades (Krawiec 2000).

Proprietary traders have at their disposal a large amount of the firm's resources that they can use to maximize their own bonus compensation. If they leverage those resources and take large risks, their reward is potentially greater. Of course, if their trades are unsuccessful, this leverage and risk mean that their losses will be greater, resulting in reduced compensation and/or job loss. However, reduced compensation, job loss, and loss of esteem and status inevitably result for insufficiently profitable traders, even if low levels of leverage and risk are pursued. Accordingly, there are asymmetric costs and benefits to exceeding the firm's trading limits: Except in the most extreme cases, such as a Nick Leeson or a Jérôme Kerviel, when international notoriety and criminal sanctions result, the downside of trading loss is limited to employment termination or reduced compensation, whereas traders' upside gain can be improved substantially through greater risk and leverage.

The incentives for employees to engage in rogue trading, therefore, are pervasive, and management's attempts to control such conduct are likely subject to three countervailing forces. First, at least some supervisory and management personnel likely make a conscious decision to tolerate or turn a blind eye to some evasions of the firm's trading limits, particularly for successful traders (Krawiec 2000; Shapira 2006). This is because, to the extent that higher risks and larger positions translate into higher trading profits, the tolerance of trading limit evasions by talented traders may enhance the success of others within the firm, including some with supervisory power with respect to the firms' trading limits. In the cases of Joseph Jett and Nick Leeson, for example, the evidence raises at least a colorable claim that others within the firm were, or should have been, aware of the trading violations (*In re Kidder Peabody* 1995; Price Waterhouse 1995). As stated in the Price Waterhouse report (1995) prepared for the Singapore Minister of Finance:

> *[Baring's] claim that it was unaware that account 88888 existed, and also that the sum of S$1.7 billion which the Baring Group had remitted to BFS, was to meet the margins required for trades transacted through this account, if true, gives rise to a strong inference that key individuals of the Baring Group's management were grossly negligent, or willfully blind and reckless to the truth.*

Second, because the events that lead to rogue trading often involve serial decision making and substantial sunk costs, supervisors and others within the firm may be prone to an irrational escalation of commitment. Escalation theory stems from research indicating that people and groups are more prone to a particular type of bias—a tendency to escalate commitment—when faced with a series of decisions rather than with an isolated decision. Studies have shown that the likely response to such situations is an escalation of commitment to the previously selected course of action beyond that predicted by rational decision-making models (Bazerman 1998). The tendency to escalate is especially pronounced when an explanation for failure that is unpredictable and outside the control of the decision maker can be identified, such as a market downturn or economic shock (Staw and Ross 1978).

Third, because the same factors that facilitate rogue trading also promote profitable trading strategies, many financial institutions purposely foster a firm culture that is likely to breed some employee rogue trading. Although financial institutions could implement compliance and oversight systems so flawless that every trade was closely monitored and any unauthorized trading would be quickly detected, such a system would be extraordinarily expensive.

The expense stems not only from the costs of software, reporting systems, and supervisory personnel but also from the fact that fully rendering the trading floor accountable to management would entail an alteration of the carefully crafted institutional norms that encourage traders to maximize the firm's profits (Clark 1997; Zaheer 2000). To illustrate, many firms have purposely fashioned an incentive structure and firm culture that fosters three general norms conducive to rogue trading: materialism, risk-taking, and independence. Financial institutions foster these traits, not for the purpose of encouraging rogue trading, but because these same norms give rise to successful and profitable traders (Krawiec 2000).

This is not to suggest that traders arrive on the trading floor a psychological and cultural blank slate. Indeed, prospective traders likely do not represent a random cross-section of the population, but instead enter the firm with a predefined set of preferences, which are then sharpened and intensified through the firm's incentive structure and socialization networks. Only individuals with a particular psychological and personality makeup are attracted to, and survive in, trading institutions. Those individuals tend to be relatively comfortable with taking large risks and must have the ability to think and act quickly and to prosper under stressful conditions (Abolafia 1996). In addition, successful traders are attracted to trading by a desire for income and continue to be motivated by that desire throughout their trading career. Finally, those attracted to a career in trading are typically independent and entrepreneurial. They often reject the hierarchy and lack of autonomy that characterizes other corporate jobs (Abolafia 1996).

Once traders are hired, the institutional environment operates to reinforce those characteristics. The socialization of new traders begins with the training program, which typically includes a short period of classroom training and then a longer period as an intern on the trading floor. During this period, the institutional norms of materialism, risk-taking, and independence are solidified and reinforced (Krawiec 2000).

For example, traders have a heightened sense of materialism because the firm's incentive structure is designed specifically to foster such an attitude.

Unlike jobs in most other fields, there is no real career ladder on the trading floor. Instead, the trading hierarchy tends to consist primarily of traders who earn higher trading profits versus those who earn less. Rather than rewarding superior performance with titles and promotions, successful traders tend to be rewarded primarily with larger bonuses and, perhaps, less oversight (Abolafia 1996).

The compensation structure on the trading floor at most financial institutions, typically based almost exclusively on trading profits earned in the current fiscal year, also encourages risk-taking, by sending a message that short-term profits will be rewarded, even if incurred at the expense of greater risk. This message may be far stronger and more persuasive than the countervailing message embodied in the firm's written codes of conduct.

It has long been recognized that the firm's compensation structure is perhaps the most powerful tool at management's disposal for shaping firm culture (DeMott 1997). Moreover, the ability of compensation plans to create perverse employee incentives is neither a new discovery, nor one limited to financial institutions. Many consulting companies specialize in creating compensation policies that mirror or transform firm culture and reduce the incentives for conduct that does not further the firm's best interests (Flannery et al. 1995).

Not only financial institutions, but also regulatory bodies such as the Securities and Exchange Commission, are well aware of the moral hazard problem posed by the compensation structures at most financial institutions. The unsuccessful attempts over the years by financial institutions to revise employee compensation packages indicate that firms are aware of the costs associated with such compensation schemes but have not yet discovered a compensation system that successfully discourages rogue trading while at the same time fostering incentives and preferences that lead to the most profitable traders.

The unsuccessful struggles of Salomon Brothers to revise its compensation system provide a good example. After the firm's trading losses in 1994, Salomon overhauled its compensation system in an attempt to more closely align the interests of employees and managers with those of shareholders. Among other reforms, the plan provided for investment bankers, traders, and other employees to receive as much as half their pay in Salomon Brothers stock at a 15% discount. The shares could not be sold for five years. After announcing the plan, Salomon lost 20 of its 200 managing directors, including several top traders. The plan was later discontinued ("Bonus points" 1995; Siconalfi 1995).

Finally, traders are expected to be self-reliant and entrepreneurial, traits not always conducive to mutual monitoring. As one trader stated: "It's a very entrepreneurial business. No one is going to help you make money.

They're too busy helping themselves" (Abolafia 1996). As a result, traders operate in an independent and often uncooperative environment in which they may perceive their primary obligation as maximizing the value of their own account and feel little duty to oversee those around them for potential violations of the firm's trading rules.

13.4 CONCLUSION

The Basel II operational risk requirements represent part of a new breed of "responsive" or "enforced self-" regulation, under which the regulated group is allowed substantial involvement in its own oversight in an attempt to encourage more effective, efficient regulatory solutions. Although enforced self-regulation provides the hope of more workable regulation, the open-ended rules characteristic of enforced self-regulation also present opportunities for private actors with a stake in the interpretation of legal rules to press, not an interpretation of law most consistent with regulatory efficiency and the public interest, but an interpretation that enhances their own position and welfare vis-à-vis the regulated group. In the case of operational risk, those private actors include the accounting profession (with an existing expertise in internal controls), legal professionals (with an existing expertise in organizational governance and compliance), and risk management experts (with an existing expertise in measurement and modeling). These interests are tempered by financial institution management's interest in an interpretation of Basel II that minimizes the costs of compliance and disrupts existing business practice as little as possible. In particular, management is likely to resist any measures that could undermine the carefully crafted institutional norms of materialism, risk-taking, and independence on which many successful trading environments thrive.

What then are the specific dangers posed by the operational risk provisions of Basel II? One might argue that some regulation of operational risk is better than none at all and that perhaps now banks will at least be forced to focus on operational risk dangers and keep more capital on hand. Surely such measures, even if imperfect, can only make banks safer. Although it is too early to fully evaluate the effects of Basel II, there is reason to be skeptical of such a conclusion.

First, some enforced self-regulation, including the operational risk provisions of Basel II, may present a convenient but largely cosmetic fix. Such fixes can be costly, potentially luring regulators and firm stakeholders (and perhaps even firm management) into a false sense of confidence. Moreover, as with other types of enforced self-regulation, the Basel II operational risk provisions may displace resources that could be better and more meaningfully spent on more effective risk measures. For example, Basel II may create a perverse incentive to "manage the model rather than reality" (Holmes 2003), diverting resources toward reducing the estimates of operational risk levels rather than reducing operational risk itself. Finally, the incentives fostered by Basel II to create a numerical measure of operational risk may cause a focus on those aspects of operational risk most easily quantified—the high-frequency, low-impact events, such as routine employee errors—rather than on the more challenging and elusive aspects of operational risk, such as rogue trading, that may pose the greatest threat to financial institutions.

REFERENCES

Abolafia, M. 1996. *Making markets: Opportunism and restraint on Wall Street.* Cambridge, MA: Harvard University Press.

Ayres, I., and J. Braithwaite. 1992. *Responsive regulation: Transcending the deregulation debate.* New York: Oxford University Press.

Baron, J., F. Dobbin, and P. Jennings. 1986. War and peace: The evolution of modern personnel administration in U.S. industry. *American Journal of Sociology* 92, no. 2:350–383.

Basel Committee on Banking Supervision. 1988 *International convergence of capital measurement and capital standards.* Basel, Switzerland.

Basel Committee on Banking Supervision. 2001. Working paper on the regulatory treatment of operational risk. Basel, Switzerland.

Basel Committee on Banking Supervision. 2002. Overview paper for the impact study." Basel, Switzerland.

Bazerman, M. 1998. *Judgment in managerial decision making.* New York: John Wiley & Sons.

Bazerman, M., G. Loewenstein, and D. Moore. 2002. Why good accountants do bad audits. *Harvard Business Review* 80, no. 11:96–102.

Bonus points. 1995. *The Economist.* 335, no. 7910:71–72.

Cagan, P. 2001. Standard operating procedures. http://www.erisk.com.

Celent. 2006. *Operational risk management: Three, two, one . . . liftoff?* www.celent.com/reports/opriskmgmt2006/operationalriskmarket.pdf

Clark, G. 1997. Rogues and regulation in global finance: Maxwell, Leeson, and the City of London. *Regional Studies* 31, no. 3:221–236.

DeMott, D. 1997. Organizational incentives to care about the law. *Law and Contemporary Problems* 60, no. 4:39–66.

Dertouzos, J., E. Holland, and P. Ebener. 1988 *The legal and economic consequences of wrongful termination.* Santa Monica, CA: Rand, Institute for Civil Justice.

Edelman, L., C. Uggen, and S. Abraham. 1999. The endogeneity of legal regulation: Grievance procedures as rational myth. *American Journal of Sociology* 105, no. 2:406–454.

Edelman, L., S. Abraham, and H. Erlanger. 1992. Professional construction of law: The inflated threat of wrongful discharge. *Law and Society Review* 26, no. 1:47–83.

Flannery, T., D. Hofrichter, and P. Platten. 1995. *People, performance, and pay.* New York: Free Press.

Givelber, D., W. J. Bowers, and C. L. Blitch. 1984. Tarasoff: Myth and reality—An empirical study of private law in action. *Wisconsin Law Review* 2:443–497.

Hirtle, B., et al. 2001. Using credit risk models for regulatory capital: Issues and options. *Economic Policy Review* 7, no. 1:19–36.

Holmes, M. 2003. Measuring operational risk: A reality check. *Risk Magazine* 16, no. 8:84–87.

In re Kidder Peabody Securities Litigation, 10 F. Supp. 2d 398 (1995).

Kagan, R. 2001. *Adversarial legalism.* Cambridge, MA: Harvard University Press.

Kalev, A., F. Dobbin, and E. Kelly. 2006. Best practices or best guesses? Diversity management and the remediation of inequality. *American Sociological Review* 71, no. 4:589–617.

King, A., and M. Lenox. 2000. Industry self-regulation without sanctions: The chemical industry's responsible care program. *Academy of Management Journal* 43, no. 4:698–716.

Krawiec, K. 2000. Accounting for greed: Unraveling the rogue trader mystery. *Oregon Law Review*, 79, no. 2:301–338.

Krawiec, K. 2003. Cosmetic compliance and the failure of negotiated governance. *Washington University Law Quarterly* 81, no. 2:487–544.

Krawiec, K. 2005. Organizational misconduct: Beyond the principal-agent model. *Florida State University Law Review* 32, no. 2:571–615.

Langevoort, D., and R. Rasmussen. 1997.Skewing the results: The role of lawyers in transmitting legal rules. *Southern California Interdisciplinary Law Journal* 5, no. 3:375–440.

Lenox, M. 2008. The prospects for industry self-regulation of environmental externalities. In *Making global regulation effective: What role for self-regulation?* ed. N. Woods. Oxford: Oxford University Press.

Macey, J., and G. Miller. 1987. Toward an interest-group theory of Delaware corporate law. *Texas Law Review* 65, no. 3:469–523.

Mezias, S. 1990. An institutional model of organizational practice: Financial reporting at the Fortune 200. *Administrative Science Quarterly* 35, no. 3:431–457.

Netter, J., and A. Poulsen. 2003. Operational risk in financial service providers and the proposed Basel Capital Accord: An overview. *Advances in Financial Economics* 8, no. 1:47–171.

Power, M. 2005. The invention of operational risk. *Review of International Political Economy* 12, no. 4:577–599.

San, M. L. C., and N. T. N. Kuang. 1995. Baring futures (Singapore) Pte Ltd., The Report of the inspectors appointed by the Minister for Finance, Singapore. Investigation pursuant to Section 231 of the Companies Act, Chapter 50.

Shapira, Z. 2006. Organizations' control of their market actors: Managing the risk of government bond traders. Working Paper, New York University, New York.

Siconalfi, M. 1995. Salomon looks at backing out of pay plan." *Wall Street Journal*, C1.

Staw, B. 1976. Knee-deep in the Big Muddy: A study of escalating commitment to a chosen course of action. *Organizational Behavior and Human Performance* 16, no. 1:27–44.

Stigler, G. 1970. The optimum enforcement of laws. *Journal of Political Economy* 78, no. 3:526–536.

Suchman, M., and M. Cahill. 1996.The hired gun as facilitator: Lawyers and the suppression of business disputes in Silicon Valley. *Law and Social Inquiry* 21, no. 3:679–712.

Tarasoff v. Regents of the University of California, 13 Cal.3d 177, 529 P.2d 553, 1974. *Withdrawn and replaced by* 17 Cal. 3d 425, 551 P.2d 334, 1976.

Zaheer, S. 2000. Acceptable risk: A Study of global currency trading rooms in the United States and Japan. In *The performance of financial institutions*, ed. P. Harker and S. Zenios. Cambridge: Cambridge University Press.

CHAPTER 14

OpRisk Insurance as a Net Value Generator

Wilhelm K. Kross and Werner Gleissner

ABSTRACT

Insurance coverage has historically been somewhat neglected in real-life OpRisk initiatives, partially due to the fact that the early versions of the Basel II framework did not accept insurance as a permissible means of minimum regulatory capital reduction. Moreover, proponents of the Capital Asset Pricing Model (CAPM) to date believe that insurance implies no net value generation, given that only capital market–related aspects captured in the beta factor truly count in the description of the risk position of an enterprise.

Change is happening, however, for good reasons. This chapter presents why and how the understanding of and the traditional approaches to OpRisk management can and should be enhanced to better reflect what truly counts in operational and enterprise risk management; and in how far insurance can play a role. In presenting the findings, we also demonstrate that in the real world, with a limited risk-bearing capacity, the reduction of risk-adjusted capital and the consequential decrease of the cost of capital through operational risk transfer mechanisms cannot be explained with the CAPM.

14.1 INTRODUCTION

Historically, the integration of insurance solutions into enterprise-wide or beyond-enterprise risk management frameworks left a lot to be desired. The introduction of operational risk (OpRisk) as a new set of risk factors to be addressed under the new Basel Capital Accord, commonly referred to as Basel II, did not help either, at least during the early stages. This was largely due to the fact that the early versions of the Basel II framework did not permit insurance solutions as a means of regulatory capital reduction for OpRisk. However, during the same period the corporate risk controlling, accounting and regulatory reporting functions (i.e., usually not the risk owners or risk managers) within financial institutions spearheaded Basel II compliance initiatives.

The framework has changed however since its early versions were published more than half a dozen years ago. It is hence warranted to look at the (potential) role of insurance solutions again, this time with a broader perspective, and at the same time to eliminate some of the remaining conceptual obstacles. This chapter serves as an initiative that, it is hoped, will trigger much further discussion between researchers and practitioners in the rather complex and all-encompassing field of OpRisk management.

14.2 TREATMENT OF INSURANCE CONCEPTS UNDER BASEL II'S OPRISK CATEGORY

Early versions of the Basel II framework reflected a rather rudimentary understanding of what operational risk (OpRisk) can entail and what OpRisk management could or should encompass.[1] In a nutshell, early versions merely mentioned that minimum regulatory capital in lieu of OpRisk has to be calculated using one of several possible approaches, that OpRisk regulatory capital will be added to the amount provided in lieu of market and credit risk, and that market discipline and the involvement of regulatory authorities will be enhanced. Subsequent iterations of the Basel II framework gradually enhanced the coverage of OpRisk management facets in terms of permissible choices and related prerequisites (e.g., minimum standards to be addressed in order to be permitted to use one of the more advanced measurement approaches), temporary compromises (e.g., partial use, or staged recognition over time of regulatory capital reduction hair cuts through the employment of the more advanced approaches), and permissible risk transfer mechanisms. The latter has remained somewhat restrictive, as becomes apparent in the current wording of Basel II, which for the ease of understanding is quoted:

> 677. *Under the AMA [i.e., the advanced measurement approaches], a bank will be allowed to recognise the risk mitigating impact of insurance in the measures of operational risk used for regulatory minimum capital requirements. The recognition of insurance mitigation will be limited to 20% of the total operational risk capital charge calculated under the AMA.*

> 678. *A bank's ability to take advantage of such risk mitigation will depend on compliance with the following criteria:*

- *The insurance provider has a minimum claims paying ability rating of A (or equivalent).*
- *The insurance policy must have an initial term of no less than one year. For policies with a residual term of less than one year, the bank must make appropriate haircuts reflecting the declining residual term of the policy, up to a full 100% haircut for policies with a residual term of 90 days or less.*
- *The insurance policy has a minimum notice period for cancellation of 90 days.*
- *The insurance policy has no exclusions or limitations triggered by supervisory actions or, in the case of a failed bank, that preclude the bank, receiver or liquidator from recovering for damages suffered or expenses incurred by the bank, except in respect of events occurring after the initiation of receivership or liquidation proceedings in respect of the bank, provided that the insurance policy may exclude any fine, penalty, or punitive damages resulting from supervisory actions.*
- *The risk mitigation calculations must reflect the bank's insurance coverage in a manner that is transparent in its relationship to, and consistent with, the actual likelihood and impact of loss used in the bank's overall determination of its operational risk capital.*
- *The insurance is provided by a third-party entity. In the case of insurance through captives and affiliates, the exposure has to be laid off to an independent third-party entity, for example through re-insurance, that meets the eligibility criteria.*
- *The framework for recognising insurance is well reasoned and documented.*
- *The bank discloses a description of its use of insurance for the purpose of mitigating operational risk.*

679. A bank's methodology for recognising insurance under the AMA also needs to capture the following elements through appropriate discounts or haircuts in the amount of insurance recognition:

- *The residual term of a policy, where less than one year, as noted above;*
- *A policy's cancellation terms, where less than one year; and*
- *The uncertainty of payment as well as mismatches in coverage of insurance policies.*

Strangely enough, several truly sensitive aspects of insurance concepts and insurance products, in particular the extent of the coverage and implicit or explicit exclusions based on the specific wording, and risk retention mechanisms (e.g., business interruption insurance kicks in after 30 days and not instantly, or the insurance only kicks in after the first $1 million in losses is exceeded) are not explicitly addressed here. Neither are the insurance coverage mechanisms of suppliers and services providers, which in today's business environment can play a rather significant impact on a financial institution's sustainable success and on the survival in critical situations. Last but not least, the Basel II framework does not explicitly address the typical inherent differences between the risk quantification and risk pricing approaches typically chosen by a financial institution that would be regulated under Basel II and the risk pricing and coverage structuring approaches of an insurance company. Even a layman will recognize that these conceptual gaps are not trivial and that some further modifications, adjustments, and additions are warranted. These in turn might help to adjust the detailed conceptual design and wording of forthcoming regulatory standards, such as Solvency II.

When reflecting on insurance as a distinct case example, it is hence appropriate to conclude that Basel II considers just fragments of what is a more or less encompassing and integral operational risk management framework (see Figure 14.1).

14.3 A MORE ENCOMPASSING VIEW ON INSURANCE CONCEPTS FOR OPRISK MANAGEMENT

The rather constrained perspective of Basel II seems to have contributed to the poor understanding of what insurance concepts can address in OpRisk management and which issues and problems can be solved with risk transfer mechanisms such as insurance. An important prerequisite to the

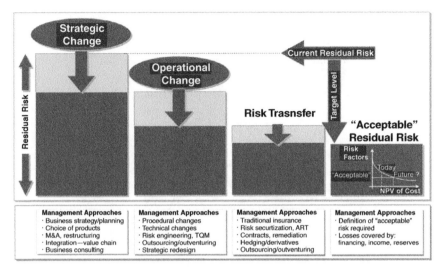

FIGURE 14.1 Overall Scope of OpRisk Management

improvement of the current status is the understanding that contrary to what Figure 14.1 shows, a risk position is not static. Michael Porter's famous five forces model provides a good generic understanding of what can happen to the competitive position of an organization unless appropriate steps are taken. Today's economic climate in the financial services sector is furthermore known to be rather significantly affected by corporate workforce downsizing initiatives, which, as some authors have submitted, has in some cases evolved to becoming a replacement for strategy (see Kross 2006). In particular, the risk position of a financial institution will change significantly if the current level of the so-called economic value added is elevated. Whether it is done as a systematic boost of the current business's profitability (e.g., marketing campaigns, cost-cutting), a reduction of the total cost of risk (e.g., risk management optimization efforts), and/or increases in turnover, for example, a result of an intensified core business or diversification (e.g., by means of mergers and acquisitions).

Moreover, the problem at hand usually entails that risk factors are interrelated and positively or negatively correlated. Figure 14.2 fosters a better understanding of risk factors in a networked world. Needless to say, the Basel II approach can be considered somewhat naive when looking at the resulting implications. A tremendous breadth and depth of risk transfer solutions is conceivable and needed. The only problem is that only a limited number of standardized risk transfer solutions have evolved to date.

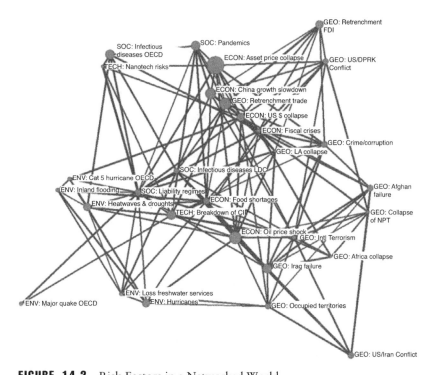

FIGURE 14.2 Risk Factors in a Networked World
Note: The sizes of the nodes in the social networking diagram indicate the assessment of the risk itself. The thickness of lines represent strength of correlation, while proximity of the nodes represents similarity of correlations.
Source: Witold Henisz, Associate Professor of Management, The Wharton School, University of Pennsylvania, USA, based on expert assessments of correlation (October 2007).

Hence in most cases a combination of operational management approaches with risk transfer mechanisms is a suitable choice for a risk manager (see Figure 14.3 for an exemplary reflection).

A further remaining challenge for the proponents of insurance concepts has been the misunderstanding that based on the Capital Asset Pricing Model (CAPM), operational risk can be considered diversifiable in a perfectly functioning capital market. Hence due to their inherent costs, insurance concepts cannot possibly add net value to an organization. Perhaps the next discussion will help to compensate for or possibly eliminate this argument.

According to the well-known approach of Modigliani and Miller (1958), there is no necessity for operational risk management, because this—like changes of the debt ratio—does not have any effect on the enterprise

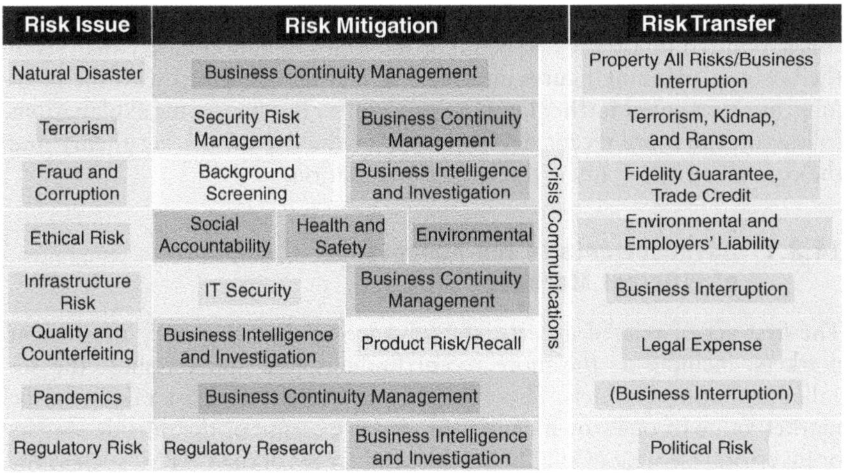

Risk Issue	Risk Mitigation			Risk Transfer
Natural Disaster	Business Continuity Management			Property All Risks/Business Interruption
Terrorism	Security Risk Management	Business Continuity Management		Terrorism, Kidnap, and Ransom
Fraud and Corruption	Background Screening	Business Intelligence and Investigation		Fidelity Guarantee, Trade Credit
Ethical Risk	Social Accountability	Health and Safety	Environmental	Environmental and Employers' Liability
Infrastructure Risk	IT Security	Business Continuity Management		Business Interruption
Quality and Counterfeiting	Business Intelligence and Investigation	Product Risk/Recall		Legal Expense
Pandemics	Business Continuity Management			(Business Interruption)
Regulatory Risk	Regulatory Research	Business Intelligence and Investigation		Political Risk

(Crisis Communications shown as a vertical band between Risk Mitigation and Risk Transfer)

FIGURE 14.3 Typical Insurance Solution Covering Individual/Combined Risk Factors

value. Both in the Capital Asset Pricing Model (see Sharpe 1964; Lintner 1965; Mossin 1966) and in the Arbitrage Pricing Theory (see Ross 1976), the expected net yields (capital-cost-rates) are described only in their dependence on systematic risks, derived from diversification and arbitrage considerations.

But to the contrary, when reflecting market imperfections like information asymmetries or bankruptcy costs, the added value of corporate risk management can be distinctly identified. For a better understanding, these topics need to be looked at:

- Costs of transaction (see, e.g., Fite and Pfleiderer 1995)
- Costs of financial distress (see, e.g., Warner 1977; Levi and Serçu 1991)
- Agency costs (see, e.g., Fite and Pfleiderer 1995; Schnabel and Roumi 1989)
- Equilibrium of investment demand and available liquidity (see Froot, Scharfstein, and Stein 1994)

These various models and conceptual approaches deliver good reasons for the relevance and the potential value contribution of risk management initiatives. However, they offer no comprehensive, full-fledged approach with whose support the gap between individual risk factors and risk mastering procedures, on the one hand, and the capital cost rates and the enterprise value, on the other hand, can be eliminated. What is needed is a solution representing risk-oriented mechanisms for the determination of capital costs. It is submitted that these can be predicted in a simulation-based analysis of the business planning figures and the risk factors connected with the planning, as represented further later in this chapter. But first, some explanations follow on the more recent developments of the capital market theory and the core elements of a new theoretical foundation.

14.3.1 Advancements to the Acceptance of Efficient Markets

The first set of related aspects, the advance to the acceptance of efficient markets, includes as the more recent findings first and foremost the so-called real option models. These show a positive effect of risk taking on the market value of one's own capital funds (at expense of the outside lenders or investors) (see, e.g., Culp 2002). Also, advances of the CAPM, such as the M CAPM, which is based on an option-theoretical basis and uses a Black-Scholes option pricing approach (see Black/Scholes 1973; Sharpe 1977), are relevant here.

Both of these advances consider both systematic and unsystematic risks. This applies similarly to the rating prognosis, which has a close relationship with risk management, as can be seen by reflecting on the Merton approach (1974), which also considers the total risk position (asset volatility). Further research results show that the expected net yield can be explained by the dependence of other risk metrics than the beta factor. Here the work of Fama and French (1992), according to which the expected net yield is dependent on business size and the ratio of book value and market price, is relevant.

14.3.2 Explanation of Approaches under the Hypothesis of Inefficient Markets

Inefficient markets may provide a justification for risk management initiatives. The behavioral finance theory gained some special publicity in this context, as it offers an understanding of the reasons for deviations of share prices from their fundamental values (see, e.g., Barberis, Shleifer, and Vishny 1989; Shefrin 2000; Shleifer 2000).

Contrary to the behavioral finance theory, which is based on methodological individualism, is the "New Finance" approach (Haugen 2002, 2004). New Finance proceeds from an appreciation of the implications of inefficient capital markets and looks for indicators that can help quantify prognoses on future share yields. Here market inefficiencies are used as perspectives for a net worth increasing enterprises risk management given that risk-reducing activities of an enterprise cannot similarly be copied by their shareholders. Besides, management can learn something from an analysis of capital market information (as a derivative of the beta factor) as opposed to the risk profile of its own enterprise. This approach rejects a microeconomic or psychological basis, which would have encompassed an appreciation of the uniqueness of individuals as well as the dynamics of the interactions that are indicated as reasons for this procedure (see, e.g., Haugen 2004).

Empirical research that has focused on systematic errors in analysts' forecasts is an additional indication of the necessity to collect the relevant information internally and to consider the potential impacts of risks (see La Porta 1996).

14.3.3 Approaches on the Basis of Internal Risk Information

Under efficient and inefficient approaches, the expected net yields are derived from capital market information, which is however interpreted just partially (as with Fama and French) as a set of risk factors. The expected net yields are the basis for the calculation of capital cost rates, which in turn affect investment decisions. A direct effect of risk management activities on capital cost rates and enterprise value is hence not immediately recognizable in either case, simply because there is no reference to proprietary enterprise risk factors.

A third approach for the justification of an inherent value contribution through risk management, which is more precisely described in a chapter paper, aims at the direct derivative of capital cost rates from proprietary information on the company's own risk factors and current and likely future risk positions. The total extent of risk relevant in inefficient markets for the enterprise value is determined by means of an aggregation of respective impacts of individual risk factors in the context of the business planning (see Gleißner 2002). Moreover, it is suggested that capital market information is not needed for the determination of the risk position (e.g., in the sense of a beta factor), but only for the regulation of risk premiums for certain risks or factors of risk.

14.4 RISK, COST OF CAPITAL, AND SHAREHOLDER VALUE

On the stock exchange, the entire expected future earnings of a company are expressed in its stock price or the so-called goodwill. It seems sensible to use shareholder value, which comprises the company's entire future prospects, rather than its latest profits as per the published financial accounting data as a yardstick for assessing a company's success and the gross or net contribution of individual entrepreneurial activities. This approach, which is commonly known as the shareholder value concept (see Rappaport 1986) involves looking at a company from the perspective of an investor who is merely interested in increasing the value of his or her capital investment—the "enterprise"—similar to a shareholder expecting an increase in stock prices. The shareholder value of an enterprise depends on two company-specific factors: the expected earnings and risks. As capital investors are generally risk-averse, they are only prepared to give a higher rating to a high-risk enterprise than to a low-risk enterprise if the earnings are disproportionally higher.

It is useful to base the valuation of an enterprise on its so-called free cash flow, the funds that can be distributed to equity suppliers and third-party lenders. It can be calculated as a corporate key indicator (i.e., before the deduction of interest expenses), as the operating result after any taxes that are due payable by the company, plus adjustments for noncash items (particularly depreciation), minus investments in tangible assets and working capital (accounts receivable from product and service delivery and performance, and stock). This takes account of the fact that a certain portion of profits has to stay within the company for investment purposes, in order to ensure sustainable earnings over the medium to long term.

Mathematically, the shareholder value of a company is defined as the present value of all future free cash flows less the value of debt (see Figure 14.4). Given that, the value of a company can be increased through the reduction of risks that affect the cost of capital (i.e., risk-adjusted rate of interest).

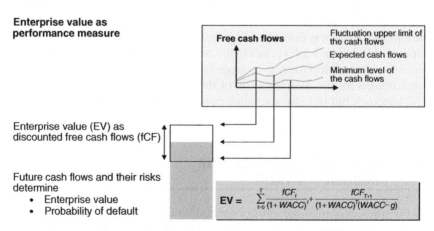

Enterprise value as performance measure

Free cash flows

Fluctuation upper limit of the cash flows

Expected cash flows

Minimum level of the cash flows

Enterprise value (EV) as discounted free cash flows (fCF)

Future cash flows and their risks determine
- Enterprise value
- Probability of default

$$EV = \sum_{t=0}^{T} \frac{fCF_t}{(1+WACC)^t} + \frac{fCF_{T+1}}{(1+WACC)^T(WACC-g)}$$

Clear success measurement, comprehensiveness, future orientation, and the inclusion of risks are the advantages of a value-based management

FIGURE 14.4 Enterprise Value

14.4.1 Enterprise Value and Capital Costs in Efficient Markets

A business segment or an investment can make a positive contribution to the goodwill of a company only if its returns are greater than its risk-adjusted cost of capital. The contribution of a corporate activity to the company's value can be described through the economic value added (EVA), which depends on the difference between returns and cost of capital:

$$EVA = \text{capital employed}^* (\text{yield} - \text{capital cost rate})$$

An investment or a business segment is financed through either equity capital (EC) or loan capital (LC). Consequentially, the cost of capital is the weighted average value of cost of loan capital CL (loan interest) and the cost of equity capital CE, whereby the tax rate T expresses the tax benefits of the loaned capital. Instead of the cost of capital, practitioners and academics generally refer to the weighted average cost of capital (WACC):

$$WACC = (1 - T)^* LC^* CL + EC^* CE$$

Of course, the equity requirements of a business segment—and thus the cost of capital and the EVA—depend on the inherent risk. If a company has several business segments that are exposed to differing risk factors over time, it is possible to determine the required equity capital (EC) (i.e., the risk-covering potential) of each business segment with the extent of the risk (RAC), and then derive its cost of capital and value contribution (EVA). One way of determining the cost of equity capital CE is through Sharpe's Capital Asset Pricing Model (CAPM):

$$CE = E_O + (E_m - E_O)^* \beta$$

where β = systematic risk—the effects of all non–company-specific influences on profitability (such as economic and interest developments)

ß   arises from the quotient of the covariance between the net yield of a share and the variance of the market net yield

E_O = risk-free interest rate

E_m = average market interest for a risk-prone capital investment, such as shares

This approach is amplified and enhanced next.

Here, only systematic risk is regarded as relevant for the cost of capital, as it cannot be removed through diversification (i.e., the consolidation of different projects or investments in a portfolio) thus resulting in counter-active and compensatory effects of certain individual risk factors. Bowman (1979) provided a theoretical basis for empirical research into the relation-ship between risk and financial (accounting) variables. He demonstrated that there is a theoretical relationship between systematic risk (beta) and a firm's leverage and accounting beta. He furthermore submitted that systematic risk is not a function of earnings volatility, growth, size, or dividend policy.

However, the existence of bankruptcy costs, agency costs, the asym-metric distribution of information, and the limited access of individual companies to capital markets data show that even idiosyncratic risk fac-tors are relevant to a company's value (see Froot et al. 1994; Pritsch and Hommel 1997). Also, equity capital and loan capital are used at market val-ues; however, we do not have perfect efficient markets (see Haugen 2002; Shleifer 2000).

14.4.2 Model Criticism

Obviously, the risk-dependent capital cost rates (WACC) rely on the true extent of risk in a company and therefore on the level of planning security with respect to the future yield of the cash flows that are consolidated into the assessment of a company's value.[2] A risk analysis should provide at least this tangible information. The frequent detour of specifying the capital cost rates by means of using primarily information from capital markets (like beta factors) instead of internal enterprise data simply because these are readily available is hardly convincing. Among the theoretical and em-pirical criticisms of the Capital Asset Pricing Model (CAPM)[3] and similar approaches for the derivation of capital cost rates, one assumption stands out: The CAPM assumes efficient capital markets, which implies most im-portantly that all capital market participants can estimate the risk position of the enterprise just like management can. This assumption surely is not stable at all. Moreover, it is considered appropriate to assume that an en-terprise can estimate its risk position and the possible changes of its risk position by means of planned activities much better than other capital mar-ket participants or analysts can (i.e., information asymmetry).[4]

Therefore, enterprises should derive the capital cost rates for their worth-oriented control systems based on an explicit reflection of the im-pact of risk management. This would solve two problems: enterprise value (i.e., discounted free cash flow) or EVA[5] is calculated on the basis of the capital cost rates, which reflect the actual risk position of the firm; and through the capital cost rates the insights of risk management activities or mechanisms are directly integrated into business decisions. This actually enables the weighting of expected yields and associated risks as they are truly inherent in important decisions.

Thus, the logical chain becomes directly apparent: A reduction of the level of risk (e.g., by means of an insurance contract) affects the level of equity capital required for the coverage of losses. Thus the capital cost rate is reduced. Proprietary capital is of course expensive. Following this approach, each action step can be judged either by means of quantifying its respective effects on the expected yields or on the basis of the effects on the inherent level of risk and thus (via the capital cost rates) the effects on the enterprise value. For the reasons specified earlier (e.g., insufficient diversification), unsystematic risks are hence relevant too.

14.4.3 Deriving Realistic Cost of Capital Rates

As reality hence shows,[6] there is a need to employ methods that take into account the idiosyncratic risks and the impacts of inefficient markets. Whatever a company's individual (nonsystematic) risk factors and risk positions are, capital markets data only reflect systematic risks and not the value of a company's policy of coping with or reducing risks.[7] Obviously, the risk-adjusted cost of capital rates must be dependent on the risk exposure of a company (i.e., idiosyncratic risk); otherwise the cost of capital rates are incorrectly calculated (see, e.g., Amit and Wernerfelt 1990). But how can the required base information be gathered?

As stated, the risk aggregation at the portfolio or enterprise-wide level reflects the capital requirements of a company to cover at least the possible losses that follow as a consequence of the aggregated risks. As a result of the aggregation, using a capable system, one is able to estimate the capital requirements, expressed as risk-adjusted capital (RAC), for any given confidence level (i.e., commonly the 95% or 99% quantiles). These capital requirements can be seen as an expression of the risk position of a company. This figure can in turn be used to obtain the cost of capital rate, by inserting the data into the WACC formula. However, one can also replace Equity Capital with the Risk Adjusted Capital (as the equity capital needed to cover the risks). The known formula with EC being replaced by RAC looks like this:

$$\text{WACC} = \frac{(1 - T) * (\text{LC} + \text{EL} - \text{RAC}) * \text{CL} + \text{RAC} * \text{CE}}{\text{LC} + \text{EC}}$$

This formula clearly shows that the cost of capital rate is determined from the equity capital needed (RAC) to cover the risks. It can thus be said that—ceteris paribus—a company can reduce its cost of capital rate by reducing its risk exposure (e.g., by transferring risks). This is due to the fact that a company with higher risks needs more equity capital to cover possible losses than a more risk-averse company would. The former also reflects a higher cost of capital rate, given that equity capital is more expensive than loan capital.

With the EVA concept, it is possible to assess the value of a company based on realistic cost of capital rates. This allows analysts and managers to better determine the goodwill of a company, by taking into account the current risk position. As higher risks will lead to a higher level of the RAC—and to an increase of the cost of capital rate (WACC)— these risks inherently require a higher profit rate in order to yield a positive impact on the goodwill of a company. Using this approach, both components are integrated to compensate the inefficiency of markets: the systematic (market) risk and the idiosyncratic (individual) risk.

14.4.4　Further Consequences of Inefficient Capital Markets

So which consequences and future challenges result from the considerations reflected on earlier in this chapter? The management of an enterprise should consider at least the next points if and when it operates in inefficient capital markets.

Because of asymmetrically distributed information, bankruptcy costs and psychological anomalies in the stock markets data as they reflect inherent risk levels, and the calculation mechanisms to derive the proprietary capital needed, the capital cost rates and the enterprise value (apart from the enterprise-independent risk premiums) should be calculated exclusively on the basis of proprietary data. Both systematic and unsystematic risk factors are relevant.

Investment decisions and financing conditions are dependent on each other. A reduction of the available cash flows limits the investment capabilities of an enterprise. A stabilization of the future cash flows through appropriately designed and implemented risk management initiatives helps management to realize more if not all lucrative investment choices (see Fazzari, Hubbard, and Petersen 1988; Froot et al. 1994).

The likelihood of an over- or an underestimation of capital market–share values when compared with their respective underlying values triggers the option of skillfully determining an appropriate timing for capital increases or share buy-back initiatives, to further enhance net enterprise value.

A performance measurement with EVA (or similar key performance indicators) must always consider the change in the capital costs as determined by the risk position of the enterprise. A risk-adjusted modification of the WACC calculation or the deviation from models like the CAPM will lead to less distorted results regarding the true creation of net enterprise value.

14.5 OPTIMIZATION OF THE TOTAL COST OF RISK

A near-optimum solution for the risk management of an enterprise can be developed only when all relevant enterprise risk factors are considered in the development of a financial forecast. Only in so doing can all diversification and hedging effects be reflected. Any other approach would tend to neglect optionalities, lead to an over- or underestimation of the risk position, and hence cause inherently poor management decisions on the basis of distorted and incomplete information. When considering the net value generation potential of risk transfer and in particular insurance solutions, it is hence sensible to perform risk aggregation scenario simulations at the enterprise-wide level (i.e., with and without the impact of insurance).

In spite of the known advantages of such enterprise-wide approaches, it is commonly observable that, in practice, fragmented solutions are used to assess the impact of separated partial solutions. A predominant argument that can easily be understood as a killer phrase has been that this helps to reduce complexity. A rather common approach, which is suboptimal though, has been to attempt to optimize the so-called costs of risk or at least those portions that have already been quantified. This approach and a few modern enhancements are discussed next.

Fundamental to these approaches is the thought that only a discrete, defined portion of risk factors is looked at and optimized for the risk compensation solution that is implemented. This is a similar perspective to the one that a person might expect to see at an insurance company that considers insuring certain operational risk factors of an enterprise. In so doing, the enterprise conceives a "virtual captive" that is structured to cover the risk factors under consideration, thereby employing the required amount of capital that would be provided for the setup and implementation of such a virtual captive. The risk costs, commonly referred to as the total cost of risk (TCOR), which are calculated taking into consideration the required cost of capital, are the target of optimization and hence cost reduction initiatives. These risk costs can be understood as the (negative) value contribution of the considered risk factors. A TCOR optimization hence attempts to reduce the net cost of risks and related management measures in an enterprise in a transparent, comprehensible, and defensible manner—and to render the risk position of an enterprise more manageable. Employing this approach, it is possible to derive the optimum balance between risk retention and risk transfer within an overall risk management strategy. The result is an integrated, economically plausible insurance management strategy that delivers a net value contribution to the enterprise at large.

14.5.1 Assessing the Total Cost of Risk

The calculation of the total cost of risk (TCOR) encompasses:

- A decision of which risk factors to include in the assessment
- An assessment of the respective cost factors that shall be reflected in the analysis

For the optimization of the value contribution of a risk transfer, it is then sensible to first consider those risk factors that are generally dispositive (i.e., that can be transferred to third parties). These may include inter alia the risks relating to physical assets and business interruptions, third-party liabilities, product recalls, technical processes and systems, and transport. If appropriate and warranted in the specific analysis, this list can be increased to include other relevant factors, such as interest risk, currency risk, and commodity price risk.

With respect to the cost factors, it is conceivable that the analysis would reflect the cost of internal control systems and organizational risk management measures (in particular preventive steps) as well as the costs of risk transfer, related external and internal services, the cost of administration and contract management, the costs of capital, any taxes and fees, implementation and maintenance costs, the cost of damage settlement if certain risk factors were to become reality, and the costs of those portions of the overall risk that are retained within the enterprise—including of course their respective marginal contribution to the overall cost of capital.

14.5.2 Managing the Total Cost of Risk

Once the TCOR is calculated, a variety of decisions and risk management measures are conceivable, including but not limited to these:

- The decision not to cover or to abolish coverage of certain risk factors in lieu of risk retention and hence proprietary coverage and/or the employment of operational or strategic risk management approaches (see Figure 14.1)
- Changes in the risk retention strategy (i.e., those portions of the various risk factors that the enterprise covers from its own reserves, operating cash flows, and financing if appropriate and necessary)

- The negotiation of insurance policies for the coverage of individual or combined risks
- Changes in insurance policies including but not limited to the change of the insurer or of insurance products and policy wordings
- Combinations of risk factors into packages and portfolios that are more easily negotiated with an insurance company (e.g., multiyear and multi-line coverage, all risk policies, etc.) due to their inherent diversification effects
- Substitution of more traditional insurance concepts with alternative risk transfer solutions
- Changes in the contractual relationships with the outside world, perhaps in combination with flexible service-level agreements
- Investments into operational control systems to demonstrate the early recognition of risk factors becoming reality and to train effective responses to incurred risk
- Outsourcing or outventuring concepts, whether operational or simply related to the development and administration of insurance solutions

14.5.3 Optimizing Total Cost of Risk: A Phased Approach

The next generic procedure may be considered useful by practitioners who desire to optimize the approach to risk transfer for an enterprise.

Phase 1. **Perform risk analysis and risk aggregation.** The risk analysis serves to identify and quantify all relevant risk factors, whether on the basis of available data and/or moderated individual or group subjective assessments. With these data, the risk aggregation is performed through simulation, to describe the extent of residual risk and the required capital coverage as well as the uncertainty bandwidth of planning figures over time.

Phase 2. **Capture the risk inventory and risk management instruments.** In this phase, all risk management measures are systematically captured and assessed. For risk transfer mechanisms, it is necessary to capture specifically which risk factors are transferred for which respective costs and which level of risk retention has been assumed.

Phase 3. **Identify the risk response policy structuring.** Once all relevant risk factors are captured in the inventory and assessed, the enterprise needs to decide at the policy level which core risk factors definitely have to be carried from proprietary funds. For all other risk factors, possible transfer mechanisms and risk transfer strategies are identified.

Phase 4. **Identify a valuation framework.** To be able to assess alternative strategies and the performance of risk transfer instruments, it is necessary to define an objective decision and performance analysis framework. This framework should be designed such that it explicitly emphasizes both the cost of risk transfer mechanisms and the different features, including of course any exclusions and the extent of risk retention.

Phase 5. **Decide on a suitable mix of instruments.** Once all alternatives and their respective performance and risk profiles are identified, it is possible to derive sensible near-optimum decisions on the structuring of risk transfer mechanisms. This implies that the enterprise does not choose simply the cheapest alternative(s) but rather the mix that best supports the enterprise's strategy and the net value generation. Of course, short-term compromises can be considered too. The TCOR is then calculated as the sum of individual net contributions to the overall risk position that is retained by the enterprise and the cost of risk transfer as indicated earlier.

Phase 6. **Implement the risk transfer strategy.** This final phase requires the details to be worked out, and the negotiation with interested risk bearers (i.e., insurers, banks, investors, contractual partners) with respect to the specific wording, and the time horizons of the respective risk transfer mechanisms. As indicated earlier, the "packaging" of risk factors and the specific definition of retained portions of risk, are the predominant factors which can yield rather lucrative commercial conditions in risk transfer contracts.

14.6 CONCLUSIONS, RECOMMENDATIONS, AND OUTLOOK FOR FURTHER RESEARCH

This chapter presents why the understanding of and the traditional approaches to OpRisk management can and should be enhanced to better reflect what truly counts in operational and enterprise risk management, and in how far insurance can play a role. In presenting our findings, we demonstrate why and how both the shortcomings of traditional valuation models such as the CAPM need to be compensated and why insurance concepts can be designed and how they can be analyzed and optimized to serve as an opportunity enabler and to truly add net value to an enterprise.

In particular, higher exposures to risk generally reduce the enterprise value, as was demonstrated in this chapter. Hence it is sensible to specifically work on risk transfer strategies that reduce the overall risk position efficiently and effectively. Insurance and other risk transfer mechanisms should not be understood simply as cost factors that add no conceivable value to the value of an enterprise, but rather as a set of suitable instruments that can (through a reduction of the proprietary capital required) deliver a positive net contribution to the enterprise value. In turn, the optimization of the residual risk position of an enterprise through appropriately designed and implemented risk transfer mechanisms permits the focusing on the true core business of the enterprise and the devotion of proprietary capital to those initiatives that best enforce the core strategy and the sustained competitive advantages of the enterprise.

NOTES

1. The web site of the Bank for International Settlements (www.bis.org) contains numerous related documents, ready to be downloaded. Sequencing them by time order shows fairly well how the understanding of operational risk and related transfer and management mechanisms have evolved over time.
2. Apart from the systematic (cross-firm) risks, there are quite good reasons and empirical vouchers for the importance of the idiosyncratic (company individual) risks in imperfect markets; see Amit and Wernerfeldt (1990).
3. For the CAPM approach and related model criticism, see Haugen (2002); Shleifer (2000); and Ulschmid (1994). For findings on the analysis of CAPM and of APT for the German stock market, see Fama and French (1992) Steiner and Uhlir (2000).
4. For value-oriented control systems, see Gleißner (2004) and the criticism of Hering (1999).
5. With respect to the economic value added concept, see Stern, Shiely, and Ross (2001).
6. For an overview of different forms of the derivation of capital rates, see Gleißner (2004), pp. 111–116; for an example of a concrete derivation of the capital costs for a company, see Gleißner and Berger (2004).
7. With respect to supplements for the meaning of unsystematic risks, see, for example, Goyal and Santa-Clara (2003). Considering partial rational reasons for a limited diversification in private portfolios too, this is more intuitively comprehensible in Hubbert (1998).

REFERENCES

Alexander, C. 2005. Assessment of operational risk capital. In *Risk management: Challenge and opportunity*, eds. M. Frenkel, U. Hommel, and M. Rudolf. Berlin: Springer.
Amit, R., and B. Wernerfelt. 1990. Why do firms reduce risk? *Academy of Management Journal* 3, no. 3:520–533.

Barberis, N., A. Shleifer, and R. Vishny. 1989. A model of investor sentiment. *Journal of Financial Economics* 49, no. 3:307–343.

Black, F., and M. Scholes. 1973. Simplifying portfolio insurance. *Journal of Portfolio Management* 14, no. 1:48–51.

Bowman, R. 1979. The theoretical relationship between systematic risk and financial (accounting) variables. *Journal of Finance* 34, no. 3:617–630.

Chernobai, A., S. T. Rachev, and F. J. Fabozzi. 2007. *Operational risk: A guide to Basel II capital requirements, models and analysis.* Hoboken, NJ: John Wiley & Sons.

Clemen, R. T., and T. Reilly. 2001. *Making hard decisions.* Pacific Grove, CA: Duxbury Thomson Learning, Brooks/Cole.

Culp, C. 2002. *The art of risk management.* Hoboken, NJ: John Wiley & Sons.

Davis, E. 2005. *Operational risk: Practical approaches to implementation.* London: Risk Books.

Döbeli, B., M. Leippold, and P. Vanini. 2003. From operational risks to operational excellence. In *Advances in operational risk: Firm-wide issues for financial institutions,* ed. P. Mestchian. London: Risk Books.

Fama, E., and French, K. R. 1992. The cross-section of expected security returns. *Journal of Finance* 47, no. 2:427–465.

Fama, E., and K. R. French. 1993. Common risk factors in the returns on stocks and bonds. *Journal of Financial Economics* 47, no. 3–56.

Fazzari, S. M., B. C. Petersen, and R. G. Hubbard. 1988. Financing constraints and corporate investment, Working paper, National Bureau of Economic Research, Cambridge, MA.

Fite, D., and P. Pfleiderer. 1995. Should firms use derivates to manage risk? In *Risk management: Problems and solutions,* ed. W. Beaver and G. Parker. New York: McGraw-Hill.

Froot, K., D. Scharfstein, and J. Stein. 1994. A framework for risk management. *Harvard Business Review* 72, no. 6:91–102.

Gleißner, W. 2001. Identifikation, Messung und Aggregation von Risiken. In *Wertorientiertes Risikomanagement für Industrie und Handel,* ed. W. Gleißner and G. Meier. Wiesbaden, Germany: Gabler.

Gleißner, W. 2002. Wertorientierte Analyse der Unternehmensplanung auf Basis des Risikomanagements. *Finanz Betrieb* 7/8:417–427.

Gleißner, W. 2004. *FutureValue-12 Module für eine strategische wertorientierte Unternehmensführung.* Wiesbaden, Germany: Gabler.

Gleißner, W. 2005. Kapitalkosten—der Schwachpunkt bei der Unternehmensbewertung und im wertorientierten Management. *Finanz Betrieb* 4:217–229.

Gleißner, W., and T. Berger. 2004. Die Ableitung von Kapitalkostensätzen aus dem Risikoinventar eines Unternehmens. *UM-Unternehmensbewertung & Management.* Frankfurt, Germany.

Gleißner, W., and M. Wolfrum. 2008. Eigenkapitalkosten und die Bewertung nicht börsennotierter Unternehmen: Relevanz von Diversifizierbarkeit und Risikomaß. *Finanz Betrieb* 9:602–614.

Gleißner, W., and M. Wolfrum. 2008. Simulationsbasierte Bewertung von Akquisitionszielen und Beteiligungen: Schätzung und Bewertung unsicherer Exit-Preise. www.finexpert.info. Nov. 2008.

Goyal, A., and P. Santa-Clara. 2003. Idiosyncratic risk matters! *Journal of Finance* 58, no. 3:975–1008.

Haugen, R. 2002. *The inefficient stock market.* Upper Saddle River, NJ: Prentice Hall.

Haugen, R. 2004. *The new finance.* New York: Pearson Education.

Hering, T. 1999 *Finanzwirtschaftliche Unternehmensbewertung.* Deutscher Universitätsverlag, Wiesbaden, Germany.

Hubbert, R. 1998. Capital-market imperfections and investment. *Journal of Economic Literature* 36, no. 2:193–225.

Keeney, R. L. 1992. *Value-focused thinking—A path to creative decisionmaking.* Cambridge, MA: Harvard University Press.

Kross, W. 2004. Operational risk: The management perspective. In *Risk management: Challenge and opportunity*, eds. M. Frenkel, U. Hommel, and M. Rudolf. Berlin: Springer.

Kross, W. 2006. *Organized opportunities: Risk management in financial services organizations.* Weinheim, Germany: John Wiley & Sons.

Kross, W. 2007. Kulturwandel durch MARisk (Cultural change through MARisk). Interview, *Compliance Manager* 9, no. 1:5.

Kürsten, W. 2006. Corporate hedging, Stakeholderinteresse und shareholder value. *JfB Journal für Betriebswirtschaft* 5, no. 6:3–31.

La Porta, R. 1996. Expectations and the cross-section of stock returns. *Journal of Finance* 51, no. 5:1715–1742.

Levi, M., and P. Serçu. 1991. Erroneous and valid reasons for hedging exchange rate exposure. *Journal of Multinational Financial Management* 1, no. 2:25–37.

Lintner, J. 1965. The valuation of risk assets and the selection of risky investments. In Stock portfolios and capital budgets. *Review of Economics and Statistics* 47, no. 1:13–37.

Merton, R. C. 1974. On the pricing of corporate debt: The risk structure of interest rates. *Journal of Finance* 29, no. 2:449–470.

Modigliani, F., and M. H. Miller. 1958. The cost of capital, corporate finance, and the theory of investment. *American Economic Review* 48, no. 3:261–297.

Morgan, M. G., and M. Henrion. 1990. *Uncertainty: A guide to dealing with uncertainty in quantitative risk and policy analysis.* Cambridge, MA: Cambridge University Press.

Mossin, J. 1966. Equilibrium in a capital asset market. *Econometrica* 34, no. 4:768–783.

Pritsch, G., and U. Hommel. 1997. Hedging im Sinne des Aktionärs. *DBW Die Betriebswirtschaft* 57, no. 5:672–693.

Rappaport, A. 1986. *Creating shareholder value.* New York: The Free Press.

Ross, S. 1976. The arbitrage theory of capital asset pricing. *Journal of Economic Theory* 13, no. 3:1051–1069.

Schnabel, J., and E. Roumi. 1989. Corporate insurance and the underinvestment problem: An extension. *Journal of Risk and Insurance* 56, no. 1:155–159.

Shapira, Z. 1995. *Risk taking—A managerial perspective*. New York: Russell Sage Foundation.

Sharpe, W. F. 1964. Capital asset prices: A theory of equilibrium under conditions of risk. *Journal of Finance* 19, no. 3:425–442.

Sharpe, W. F. 1977. The CAPM: A "multi-beta" interpretation. In *Financial decision making under uncertainty*, ed. H. Levy and M. Sarnat. Burlington, MA: Academic Press.

Shefrin, H. 2000. *Beyond greed and fear—Finance and the psychology of investing*. Cambridge, MA: Harvard Business School Press.

Shleifer, A. 2000. *Inefficient markets—An introduction to behavioral finance*. New York: Oxford University Press.

Stern, J. M., J. S. Shiely, and I. Ross. 2001. *The EVA challenge*. Hoboken, NJ: John Wiley & Sons.

Ulschmid, C. 1994. *Empirische Validierung von Kapitalmarktmodellen*. Berlin: Peter Lang Verlagsgruppe.

Volkart, R. 1999. Risikobehaftetes Fremdkapital und WACC-Handhabung aus theoretischer und praktischer Sicht. Working paper, Swiss Banking Institute, Zürich.

Warner, J. 1977. Bankruptcy costs: Some evidence. *Journal of Finance* 32, no. 2:337–347.

CHAPTER 15

Operational Risk Versus Capital Requirements under New Italian Banking Capital Regulation: Are Small Banks Penalized?

A Clinical Study

Simona Cosma, Giampaolo Gabbi, and Gianfausto Salvadori

ABSTRACT

Our research finds out the potential competitive impact of the new Italian Banking capital regulation for operational risks. Unlike the approach underlying the new discipline of the United States and many European countries, the Italian regulation allows access to the advanced measurement approaches (AMA) only to banks and financial intermediaries whose size or specialization requirements meet predefined levels. In our research we compare the capital at risk (estimated with a one-year holding period and a 99.9% confidence interval) and the capital charge calculated by basic indicator methodology. Using operational loss data of one bank that does not meet regulation constraints, we show how the new supervisory regulations on capital requirements unfairly could penalize a large group of intermediaries.

15.1 INTRODUCTION

The new regulation for Italian banks rely on a number of methodologies
to compute capital requirements regarding operational risk. The main purposes of the regulations are to: (1) make the methods accurate in terms of
having a proportional risk exposure for each bank; (2) maintain regulation
efforts, especially for small intermediaries; and (3) enhance operational risk
management in the regulatory fashion.

Since the rationale should be to pursue more successfully the regulation purposes (safe and sound behavior and efficiency) of encouraging
competitiveness and leveling the playing field, one could wonder why a
size and a functional threshold has been introduced to implement approaches different from the basic one. Basically, regulators believe that
small banks do not handle enough resources to be compliant with the
minimal regulation needs. Moreover, for small banks that concentrate in
retail activities, which are less exposed to operational risk, the assumption
is that they should not benefit from advanced models to estimate capital
requirements.

In this chapter we apply the clinical case methodology to determine the
exposure to operational risk of a small bank with unsophisticated activity.
According to the actual Italian regulations, this bank cannot implement an
advanced approach. We would like to demonstrate capital saving in the case
of advanced estimation of operational risk requirements. We compare the
basic capital requirement to the operational value at risk (VaR) estimated
with the internal losses as a proxy of the advanced approaches suggested by
the Basel II Accord. Finally, the expected loss is divided by the VaR, in order
to estimate the contribution of the numerator to the capital absorption. If
this ratio were large, it would indicate that preventing the bank from de-
ducing the expected loss from the capital requirement would be a significant
penalization factor.

In order to estimate the OpVar of the bank, we apply a methodology
to break the ties (i.e., multiple observations present in the sample). If the
theoretical model adopted to describe the observations is *continuous*, then
the presence of ties may raise some problems concerning both model validity
and fitting. We treat ties using a *mixed approach*, where suitable *point
masses* are introduced, in order to take care of the anomalous presence of
multiple observations.

The competitive puzzle in the banking system generated by regulation
has been studied especially with credit risk. Altman and Sabato (2005) and
Berger (2004) found out the impact of Basel II for small and medium busi-
nesses (SMEs), proving the advantage for large and diversified banks implementing advanced internal ratings-based (AIRB) methods and managing

SME loans on a pooled basis. Moreover, small and specialized banks could reduce the competitive advantage based on relationship lending. Berger concludes that the lower costs for this group of banks should not damage the competitive position of community banks (banks with under $1 billion in assets), because such banks have a strong comparative advantage in making relationship loans to informationally opaque SMEs.

Hancock, Lehnert, Passmore, and Sherlund (2005) analyze the "cross-eye" approach of the U.S. regulation for the mortgage market, which imposes the use of the capital standards (AIRB and Advanced Measurement Approaches [AMA]) only to core banks (large, internationally active U.S. banks with more than $250 billion in total assets or with foreign exposures greater than $10 billion) whereas the United States does not impose capital standards on the remaining banks. Their conclusion is that banks should face no competitive impact.

Calem and Follain (2007) show a shift that could affect the market share of large banks in the same market.

Hannan and Piloff (2004) determine whether lower capital requirements would favor the acquisition of smaller banks by core ones because they could be less expensive. The authors "do not find convincing evidence either that past changes in excess regulatory capital or that past changes in capital standards had substantial effects on merger activity."

Lang et al. (2005) first considered whether the adoption of AIRB is likely to have an adverse competitive impact on community and regional banks and then considered whether it may adversely affect the competitive position of nonbank issuers of credit cards. The authors concluded that core banks are likely to experience sizable increases in risk-based minimum capital requirements for their credit card portfolios, but that the increase is unlikely to affect their competitive position because the capital market already requires banks to hold levels of capital for credit card portfolios that are far above the Basel I–based regulatory capital minimum. They are skeptical that the change in regulatory requirements will alter the competitive landscape in which credit card issuance is already highly concentrated among a few large banks and is not an important activity for community or most regional banks.

Finally, they argue that nonbank companies that are large credit card issuers will be in a similar competitive position to large bank issuers that do not adopt the AIRB. Although the greater responsiveness of regulatory capital to risk under AIRB would appear to place core banks at a competitive disadvantage in times of stress, the authors argue that supervisory oversight would similarly constrain banks that do not adopt AIRB. Moreover, under such circumstances, capital markets are likely to constrain core and noncore banks equally.

Taking into account the operational risk, the literature focused the development of quantitative models Basel compliant and the evaluation of risk coefficients for the basic and the standardized approaches. Various views have been developed regarding operational risks (see Cruz 2002 and Marshall 2001 for a global analysis), such as the correlation implementation or the losses and OpVar dependence (Embrechts et al. 2002; Le Chavez-Demoulin et al. 2006; Mc Neil et al. 2005), external database scaling (De Fontnouvelle et al. 2005; Hartung 2004; Na 2004, 2006; Shih, Samad-Khan, and Medapa 2000), and the best stochastic approach to model low-frequency data (Moscadelli 2004).

Few studies investigate the competitive impact of the operational risk capital requirements. De Fontnouvelle, Garrity, Chu, and Rosengren (2005) find the Basel II impact over the capital requirements of the U.S. processing banks play a role in asset management, custody, trading, and sales, characterized by a higher operational risk intensity and a lower credit risk. The authors show that the risk to increase the capital requirement should be fairly small.

The authors concluded that in most of these markets, the key competitors were foreign banks or large investment banks that would be subject to Basel II. The key exceptions were mutual funds management and some kinds of general processing activities where nonbank competitors have dominant market shares. These nonbank firms were so well capitalized that they would be unlikely to need to raise additional capital even if they were subject to Basel II.

In this chapter, first we describe the way single regulators implemented the computational method in order to comply with operational risk capital. Section 15.2 describes the bank studied and the operational losses sample data, while Section 15.3 shows the basic empirical methodology used in the analysis. We suggest an estimation of the severity distribution in case of ties. The exposure of the bank to the operational risk is estimated via value at risk. Section 15.4 illustrates the main results of the study, and Section 25.5 concludes.

15.2 OPERATIONAL RISK CAPITAL REQUIREMENTS UNDER ITALIAN INSTRUCTIONS FOR BANKS

Supervisory instructions for banks (Banca d'Italia 2006) let intermediaries choose among three different methods to comply with the minimum capital requirement: (1) the basic indicator approach; (2) the standardized approach; and (3) advanced measurement approaches (AMA).

Banks using the basic indicator approach must hold capital for operational risk equal to the average over the previous three years of a fixed level of 15% of positive annual gross income. Gross income is defined as net interest income plus net noninterest income. This measure should: (1) be gross of any provisions; (2) be gross of operating costs; (3) rule out realized profits/losses from the sale of securities in the banking book; and (4) exclude unexpected or irregular items as well as income derived from insurance.

In the standardized approach, banks' activities are split into eight business lines: corporate finance, trading and sales, retail banking, commercial banking, payment and settlement, agency services, asset management, and retail brokerage. The capital charge for each business line is calculated by multiplying gross income by a factor (beta) assigned to that business line. Beta values range from 12% to 18% and serve as a proxy for the industry-wide relationship between the operational risk loss experience for a given business line and the aggregate level of gross income for that business line. The total capital charge is calculated as the three-year average of the simple summation of the regulatory capital charges across each of the business lines in each year.

The Italian regulation choice (differently from the United States and most European countries) is to authorize the use of the standardized approach (as well as the advanced ones) only to banks either with a regulatory capital higher than €200 million or with a regulatory capital higher than €25 million and a gross income generated by business lines different from retail and commercial banking higher than 60% of the total gross margin.

Banks complying with the qualitative and quantitative standards and the balance sheets' thresholds will be allowed to put into action the AMA. Under the AMA, the regulatory capital requirement will equal the risk measure generated by the bank's internal operational risk measurement system based on objective data (internal and shared) and subjective data (scenario and internal control within the bank). This way operational risk management (ORM) is able to fit the risk of the bank. In any case, the use of the AMA is subject to supervisory approval.

AMA methodologies should theoretically provide a reduction of the capital requirement for these reasons:

- They measure dependence between risk level of different *business lines*.
- They can reduce the cost discounting the insurance premium.
- Particular operational risk accrual can be deduced from the regulated capital.

Even though regulation does not specify the distributional assumptions used to generate the operational risk measure for regulatory capital purposes, the statistic approach should be appropriate to estimate frequency and severity, so the capital requirement would hedge both the expected and the unexpected operational loss. However, a bank must demonstrate that its approach captures potentially severe tail loss events. Whatever approach is used, a bank will give a demonstration that its operational risk measure meets a soundness standard under a one-year holding period and a 99.9th percentile confidence interval.

15.3 DATA

This study is based on the case of a bank located in northern Italy; it is a cooperative bank, with roughly 4,500 partners and 25 offices. The net income was in 2007 about €13.7 million; deposits were €904 million; and loans were around €602 million.

The bank does not respect the Italian regulation constraints. In particular its capital in 2007 is lower than €200 million (€147,274,000). Nevertheless, the bank estimates operational losses.

Data of operational losses were collected from 2000, but data from 2000 to 2002 were considered incomplete. Each loss is linked to an event type (level 1), the process where it was experienced, the nature of credit risk boundary loss, date, amount, and business line where the loss was recorded.

The event type is consistent with the first level suggested by the Basel Committee:

- Clients, Products, and Business Practice (414 losses)
- Execution, Delivery, and Process Management (333 losses)
- Business Disruption and Systems Failures (41 losses)
- External Fraud (18 losses)
- Damage to Physical Assets (17 losses)
- Other event types (3 losses)

Three business lines are mapped by the bank: retail banking, trading, and sales, as well as payment and settlement.

The database does not include credit boundary losses, near misses, potential losses, sequential, or even multieffect losses.

Table 15.1 shows data, frequency, and amount per year.

15.4 METHODOLOGY

The estimation of the exposure to the operational risk is based on the VaR that is the maximum loss not exceeded with a given probability defined as

TABLE 15.1 Database, 2003–2007

Year	Number of Losses	Amount of Losses
2003	104	38,390.54
2004	112	31,890.30
2005	123	123,976.77
2006	260	78,951.97
2007	226	309,868.62
Total	825	583,078.20

Source: Our elaboration from the bank database

the confidence level of 99.9%, over a given period of one year, as required by the Italian Supervisory instructions for banks.

Two different measures of VaR were estimated:

1. Over the complete database (ALL)
2. As the sum of three VaRs computed for three databases (subsamples of the database ALL), depending on the nature of the event types:
   - Clients, Products, and Business Practice (CPP)
   - Execution, Delivery, and Process Management (ECG)
   - Other events

Since the risk measure should be subadditive, the additive VaR is a prudent way to determine the exposure, since it does not take into consideration correlations among risks.

Afterward, we compare the VaR estimations with the basic capital requirement obtained, applying the 15% to the average of the last three years' gross margin (in our case from 2005 to 2007).

In case of a VaR estimation much lower than the basic approach capital requirement, we can conclude the capital saving could compensate organizational costs necessary to act in accordance with the conformity constraints required by the supervisor.

The expected loss is computed as the product of the expected values of severity and frequency distributions that fit the body of our data. Finally, the expected losses will be divided by the VaR, in order to estimate the contribution of the numerator to the capital absorption. Lower is the ratio, lower is the penalization since the bank cannot diminish expected losses from the capital requirement.

15.4.1 Severity Estimation

The methodology to estimate operational risk severity is the same for all the databases.[1]

We assume the stationarity of the time series, due to their shortness. The mathematical function to fit the severity distribution will be fixed through the parametric inference. The goodness-of-fit tests and the asymptotic behavior of the survival function in a bi-logarithmic plane (with a fat tail) persuade us to reject all the selected standard distributions in order to employ extreme value theory (EVT) models (Embrecht et al. 1997; Salvadori et al. 2007), in particular the POT (peaks over threshold) model.

This approach effectively estimates the distribution tail of operational losses only with data exceeding a threshold, not regarding the timing of the events. POTs are based on the fact that peaks are generalized Pareto distributed (GPD), according to the Balkema–De Haan (1974) Pickands (1975) theorem.

The quantile analysis of higher-order severity using the POT-GPD method requires:

■ The threshold definition (lower censoring threshold), driven by the mean excess plot (MEP), based on the sample mean excess function (SMEF) (see Figure 15.1 and Table 15.2).

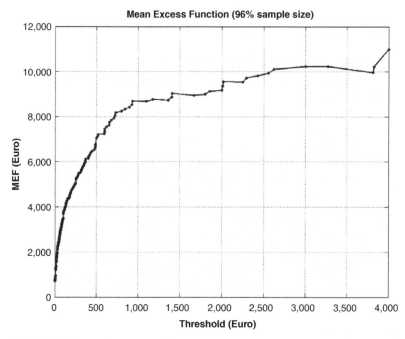

FIGURE 15.1 Calculation of the Mean Excess Function (marked line) as a Function of the Threshold: The latter is increased up to the percentile indicated in the title.

TABLE 15.2 Features of the Upper-Tail Subsample

Sample size = 825
Num. Zero values = 0
Lower-Censoring threshold = 700
Upper-Censoring threshold = ∞
Upper-Tail Subsample size = 64
Upper-Tail Subsample Percentage = 7.7576
Upper-Tail Subsample Min Value = 709.5
Upper-Tail Subsample Max Value = 82187.26

- The computation of the peaks.
- The approximation of form and scale parameters of the "excess GPD" using the maximum likelihood estimation (Table 15.3).
- The robustness assessment of the parameters choosing suitable averages of the values plotted (from left to right) (Figures 15.2 and 15.3).
- Testing the goodness of fit (K-S and A-D, Table 15.4), the excess residuals over the threshold (Davison 1984; Table 15.5 and Figure 15.4), and the performance analysis (Table 15.6), useful to check the ability of the GPD to embody the highest percentiles of losses.

The 99.9th percentile GPD value is a time-unconditional VaR. The extreme losses will be estimated by applying the extreme value theory techniques to the tail's area data (Figures 15.5 and 15.6). The "ordinary" losses aimed at computing the "expected loss" and the VaR with a Monte Carlo simulation will be taken from the sample data below the threshold selected for the GPD.

The investigation of the available data shows that some values are observed several times (i.e., multiple observations of the same realization are present in the sample). These are called "ties" in statistics. If the theoretical model adopted to describe the observations is *continuous*, then the presence of ties may raise some problems concerning both model validity and fitting.

When the sequence of ties is not "too" long, the presence of repeated values is statistically tolerated in continuous modeling. However, sometimes

TABLE 15.3 GPD-POT Estimates

Estimated Position parameter = 700
Estimated Scale parameter = 4020.5194
Estimated Shape parameter = 0.53322

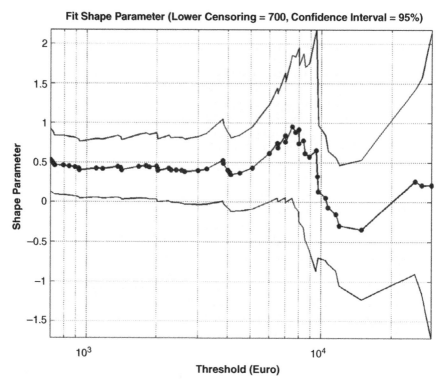

FIGURE 15.2 Maximum Likelihood Estimates of the Shape Parameter of the Exceedance GP Distribution (marked line) and Corresponding Confidence Band (continuous line), Using Sample Data Larger than the Threshold. The lowest threshold value is indicated in the title (Lower Censoring) as well as the level of the band (confidence interval).

it may be necessary to deal with ties using a *mixed approach*, where suitable *point masses* (i.e., *degenerate* laws that concentrate a positive probability onto a single point) are introduced, in order to take care of the anomalous presence of multiple observations.

Our target is twofold. On the one hand, we aim to provide a correct estimation of the probabilities of occurrence of any event, even in the presence of "long" sequences of ties. On the other hand, we wish to keep the overall parametrization at a minimum level: that is, to introduce the least possible number of free parameters in the global distribution fitting the whole data set. For these reasons, we take into consideration only the tie that is observed with the highest frequency. However, no theoretical

Fit Scale Parameter (Lower Censoring = 700, Confidence Interval = 95%)

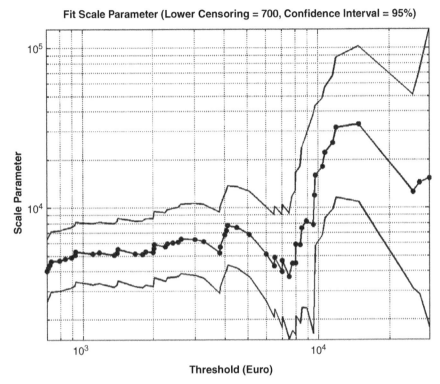

FIGURE 15.3 Maximum Likelihood Estimates of the Scale Parameter of the Exceedance GP Distribution (marked line) and Corresponding Confidence Band (continuous line), Using Sample Data Larger than the Threshold. The lowest threshold value is indicated in the title (Lower Censoring) as well as the level of the band (confidence interval).

TABLE 15.4 Goodness of Fit

Modified K.-S. Test
K.-S. critical value 90% = 1.224
K.-S. critical value 95% = 1.358
K.-S. critical value 99% = 1.628
K.-S. observed test statistics = 0.63385
Anderson-Darling Test
A.-D. critical value 90% = 1.933
A.-D. critical value 95% = 2.492
A.-D. critical value 99% = 3.857
A.-D. observed test statistics = 0.59969

TABLE 15.5   QQ-plot GP-POT Residuals

Estimated Regression slope $= 0.94107$

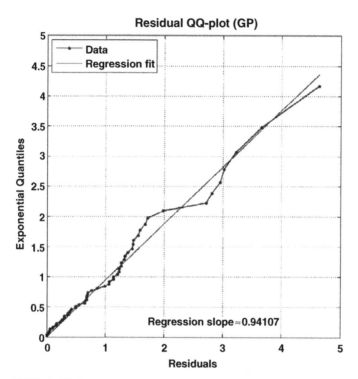

FIGURE 15.4   QQ-plot of Exponential Quantiles versus GP Residuals (marked line). The interpolating line through 0 (continuous line) is calculated via a linear regression. Also indicated is the least squares estimate of the regression slope.

TABLE 15.6   OpVaR and Violations

Expected Number of Violations Above	Theoretical	Observed
92% quantile	66.000	65
95% quantile	41.250	40
99% quantile	8.250	7
99.9% quantile	0.825	1

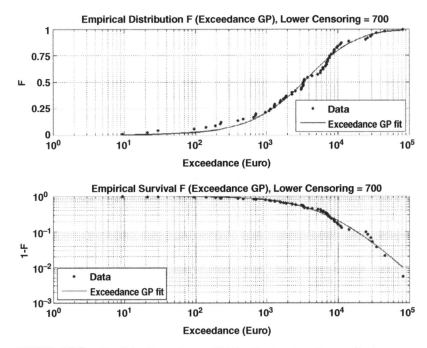

FIGURE 15.5 Fit of the Exceedance GP Distribution (continuous line), Considering the Sample Data (Markers) Larger than the Threshold Indicated in the Title (Lower Censoring). (Top) distribution function in a semilog plane; (bottom) survival function in a log-log plane.

restrictions exist on modeling *all* the ties present in the sample, but the resulting global probability distribution would take on a complicated expression, and too many parameters would be necessary (generally without really improving the overall modeling). For this purpose, a natural strategy is used, as described next.

- Identify the value t^*, that is, the tie that is observed with the highest frequency (in this investigation, $t^* = €10$).
- Split the whole domain (i.e., the range of observed values) into suitable subsets, one of which is represented by the singleton $\{t^*\}$.
- Fit (possibly different) probability distributions in each subdomain, bearing in mind that the mixture of such laws should be "invertible" in some sense (i.e., usable for simulation purposes; see next section). In particular, the occurrence of the longest tie can be modeled via a suitable *degenerate* law at t^*.

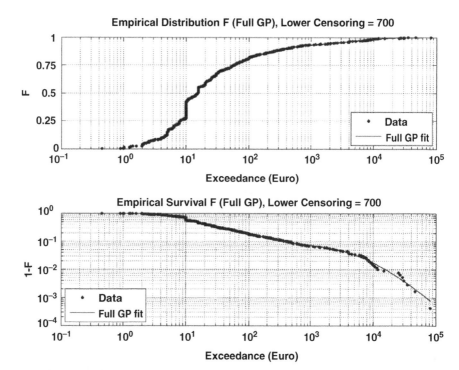

FIGURE 15.6 Fit of the Full GP Distribution (Continuous Line), Considering the Sample Data (Markers) Larger than the Threshold Indicated in the Title (Lower Censoring). (Top) distribution function in a semilog plane; (bottom) survival function in a log-log plane.

Now let u^* denote the (lower-censoring) threshold above which the GP-POT analysis is carried out (Table 15.7). In this investigation, the following four subdomains D_i's of the positive real line $\mathbf{R}_+ \equiv (0, +\infty)$ are used (see Table 15.7). In turn, each subdomain provides the support of a "local" probability distribution F_i.

$D_1 : 0 < x < t^*$ (see the "*Sub-Ties component" field, where the domain is indicated). The corresponding law F_1 is a Gamma distribution right truncated at $x = t^*$; the shape and scale parameters are reported in the "Gamma par.s" field.

$D_2 : x \equiv t^*$ (see the "*Longest-Tie component" field, where t^* is indicated). The corresponding law F_2 is a singular distribution (point mass) at $x = t^*$.

TABLE 15.7 Features of the Mixture Fit

---

*Sub-Ties component on (0,10):
Mixing par.: 0.27394
Scaling par.: 0.95386
Gamma par.s (shape, scale) = 3.4881, 1.4023

*Longest-Tie component on [10]:
Mixing par.: 0.1503
Scaling par.: 1

*Sup-Ties component on [10,700]:
Mixing par.: 0.49818
Scaling par.: 0.97475
GP par.s (shape, scale) = 0.883884, 24.561

*Upper-Tail component on (700,+∞):
Mixing par.: 0.077576
Scaling par.: 1

$D_3 : t^* < x \le u^*$ (see the "*Sup-Ties component" field, where the domain is indicated). The corresponding law F_3 is a GP distribution right truncated at $x = u^*$; the shape and scale parameters are reported in the "GP par.s" field, while the position parameter is equal to t^*. According to the software used, the fit of this GP distribution may first require that the constant t^* is subtracted from the sample data in D_3.

$D_4 : u^* < x < +\infty$ (see the "*Upper-Tail component" field, where the domain is indicated). The corresponding law F_4 is the Exceedance GP-POT distribution fitted above the threshold $x = u^*$. According to the software used, the fit of this GP distribution may first require that the constant u^* is subtracted from the sample data in D_4.

Here the idea is to fit the probability law F_i in each subdomain D_i, and construct an overall global distribution F via a suitable mixture of $F_1, \ldots . F_4$.

In a very general form, the global distribution F can be written as, for $x \in \mathbf{R}$:

$$F(x) = \{p_1 [F_1(x)/s_1]\} I_{D_1}(x) + \{p_1 + p_2 [F_2(x)/s_2]\} I_{D_2}(x)$$
$$+ \{p_1 + p_2 + p_3 [F_3(x)/s_3]\} I_{D_3}(x)$$
$$+ \{p_1 + p_2 + p_3 + p_4 [F_4(x)/s_4]\} I_{D_4}(x),$$

where I_{D_i} represents the indicator function of the domain D_i .

The *mixing coefficients* p_i's and the *scaling coefficients* s_i's are described as follows (see Table 15.7).

The p_i's satisfy the constraints $0 \leq p_i \leq 1$ for all i's, and $\sum_{i=1}^4 p_i = 1$. These parameters are estimated via a maximum likelihood technique as

$$p_i = \frac{N_i}{N}, \quad i = 1, 2, 3, 4$$

where N_i = number of sample data belonging to the set D_i
           N = total sample size

The s_i's must be introduced since some distributions are upper and truncated (namely, F_1 and F_3, respectively, at $x = t^*$ and $x = u^*$). Let $w_i = \sup\{x : x \in D_i\}$ be the largest element in D_i. Then

$$s_i = F_i(w_i)$$

In this case, these estimates are obtained:

1. $s_1 = F_1(t^*)$
2. $s_2 = 1$
3. $s_3 = F_3(u^*)$
4. $s_4 = 1$

The mixing and scaling coefficients already outlined provide suitable normalization constants, in order to derive a consistent and correct expression for the global probability distribution F. The global fit is shown in Figure 15.7; the corresponding K.-S. test statistics is 1.2295 (i.e., it can be accepted at least at a 90% level).

15.4.2 Frequency Estimation

Our estimation of the losses' frequency distribution through the classic parametric inference is based on the loss events experienced each year of the time series. Since it is five years long, we should work with five observations only. The low significance of the outcomes persuaded us to choose a frequency distribution based on a parametric hypothesis.

Distributions frequently handled to model the operational losses frequency are the Poisson and the negative binomial. Quantitative Impact Studies QIS 4 (2005) and Basel Committee's Accord Implementation Group for Operational Risk AIGOR (2006) demonstrate that most of the

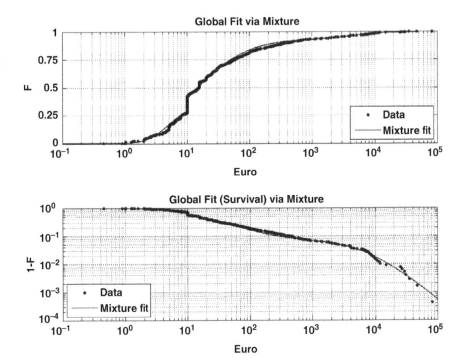

FIGURE 15.7 Global Fit (Continuous Line) of the Whole Data Set (Markers) via a Mixture Of Different Distributions. (Top) distribution function in a semilog plane; (bottom) survival function in a log-log plane.

intermediaries prefer to exploit the Poisson, whose parameter is the yearly average of losses (see Table 15.8).

15.4.3 OpVaR Methodology

The actuarial approach was applied to estimate the operational risk value at risk of the database "ALL." The VaR is the 99.9th percentile of the aggregate distribution of the operational losses, that is, the distribution that merges frequency and severity. This distribution is generated by the convolution of severity and frequency with a Monte Carlo simulation.

For the subsamples of event types, convolution is produced by the severity distribution (as a mixture of the distributions that better approximate the data body and the full GPD based on data of the tail area) and the frequency Poisson distribution, whose parameter is the yearly average losses.

TABLE 15.8 Number of Yearly Losses and Average Frequency (Poisson Parameter)

Year	All	CPP	ECG	AR
2003	104	58	38	8
2004	112	43	55	14
2005	123	45	68	10
2006	260	122	119	19
2007	226	146	52	28
Average	165	82.8	66.4	15.8

The simulation of a sample X extracted from the mixture F requires some care, as shown next. Here the idea is to use the Probability Integral Transform in order to properly "invert" the distribution function F.

Let $Y \sim U(0, 1)$, that is, a random variable with uniform distribution on $(0,1)$ and denote by y a realization (simulation) of Y, where $y \in (0,1)$. Then split the interval $(0,1)$ into four subdomains:

$$Y_1 : 0 < y < q_1 \quad \text{where} \quad q_1 = p_1$$

$$Y_2 : q_1 \leq y < q_2 \quad \text{where} \quad q_2 = p_1 + p_2$$

$$Y_3 : q_2 \leq y < q_3 \quad \text{where} \quad q_3 = p_1 + p_2 + p_3$$

$$Y_4 : q_3 \leq y < 1$$

Clearly, Y may belong to one, and only one, of the subdomains Y_i's. Given a simulated value y of Y, the first step consists in identifying the subdomain Y_i it belongs to. Then four different strategies must be adopted, as outlined next.

1. $0 < y < q_1$. In this case X must be extracted from a Gamma law with shape and scale parameters given in the section "*Sub-Ties." However, the Gamma law is right truncated at $x = t^*$. This means that y must be rescaled into the range $(0, s_1)$, as $r = s_1 y / p_1$. Then the MATLAB command x = gaminv(r, Shape, Scale) can be used.
2. $q_1 \leq y < q_2$. In this case X must be extracted from a degenerate law at $x = t^*$. This simply means that $x = t^*$, the value of the tie.
3. $q_2 \leq y < q_3$. In this case X must be extracted from a GP law with shape and scale parameters given in the section "*Sup-Ties" and position

parameter equal to t^*. However, the GP law is right truncated at $x = u^*$. This means that y must be rescaled into the range $(0, s_3)$, as $r = s_3(y - q_2)/p_3$. Then the MATLAB command $x = $ gpinv(r, Shape, Scale, Position) can be used.

4. $q_3 \leq y < 1$. In this case X must be extracted from a GP law with shape, scale, and position parameters given in Table 15.3. However, y must be rescaled into the range $(0,1)$, as $r = (y - q_3)/p_4$. Then the MATLAB command $x = $ gpinv(r, Shape, Scale, Position) can be used.

The values x of X, generated as described, provide a sample extracted from the global distribution F. An example of simulation is shown in Figure 15.8.

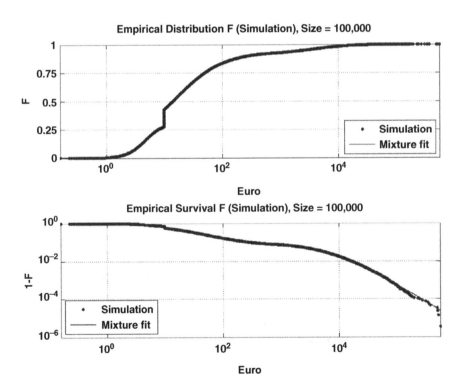

FIGURE 15.8 Simulation (Markers) of a Sample Extracted from the Mixture Probability Distribution (Continuous Line) Fitted on the Available Data. The simulation size is indicated in the title.

TABLE 15.9   OpVaR (Monte Carlo Estimation)

Poisson law par. = 165
Simulation size = 24999
Minimum number of Poisson events = 119
Maximum number of Poisson events = 219
Average number of Poisson events = 164.889
Total number of Poisson events = 4122225
Maximum simulated Loss = 4417835.8496
Maximum simulated OpVaR = 4554310.0822
OpVaR [99.9%] = 1339015.0845

Our choice to measure the VaR with the described methodology is encouraged by the literature evidence:

- The ETV application to the operational risk could lead to a relevant overestimation of the risk measures (Mignola and Ugoccioni 2006).
- The actuarial approach separately estimates frequency and severity, passing up the frequency reduction when their amount would increase. Generally speaking, this approach overestimates highest quantiles of the aggregate distribution, delivering a VaR extra estimation (Moscadelli 2004).

Our estimation of OpVaR (Table 15.9) could be an overapproximation of the risk exposure of the bank. If so, this conclusion would confirm the hypothesis of an unfair negative impact for the bank capital allocation.

15.4.4   Expected Loss Impact on the OpVaR

Our computation of the expected loss is established on probability distributions suitably fitting the database of bank losses. The same holds for severity and frequency distributions generated by data below the GPD threshold. The mean under threshold (MUT) of the severity distribution (Table 15.10) and

TABLE 15.10   Mean under GP-POT Threshold

Simulation size = 100,000
Minimum simulated value = 0.15665
Maximum simulated value = 556,674.576
MUT (estimated via simulation) = 39.5973

TABLE 15.11 Number of Yearly Losses and Average Frequency under Threshold (Poisson Parameter)

Year	All	CPP	ECG	AR
2003	95	54	37	4
2004	101	43	47	11
2005	113	44	60	10
2006	250	118	118	15
2007	202	126	51	26
Average	152.2	77	62.6	13.2

Poisson distribution of the frequency (Table 15.11) could be considered respectively as the expected severity and the expected frequency. The expected loss is simply the outcome of these average values.

A simple way to estimate the MUT is to simulate a sample of suitable size extracted from the distribution providing the global (overall) fit, and then calculate the sample average of all the simulated values smaller than the lower censoring threshold. Such an empirical approach bypasses all the complicated theoretical calculations due to the fact that the global fit is a mixture of continuous and degenerate distributions. Since the calculation of the MUT involves a distribution defined on the positive real axis, and upper truncated at the lower censoring threshold, the existence of the mean is guaranteed. Also, since the sample size is large, the convergence of the estimate to the actual value is safe.

Once we obtain the expected loss we compute the ratio with the OpVar.

15.5 RESULTS

In case OpVaR were lower than the capital requirement computed with the basic approach and a high expected loss OpVar ratio, the regulatory treatment would penalize small banks, unleveling the playing field. In our clinic study we determined the OpVaR first for the ALL database (produced by the whole records) and then summing the three OpVaR computed for the subsamples (additive OpVaR). In both cases, the financial literature gives a demonstration the outcome overestimates the risk exposure, generating prudent OpVaR values.

Two reasons justify our choice to work out two OpVaRs, the first over the ALL database and the second as the sum of the OpVaRs of the three subsamples: We want (1) to verify how robust are the OpVaR estimates and

TABLE 15.12 Basic Capital Requirement and OpVaRs

Risk Exposure	Value in Euros
Basic capital requirement	5,944,500
ALL OpVaR	1,339,015
Additive OpVaR	282,973 + 578,149 + 104,409 = 965,532

(2) to provide the best operational risk exposure for our bank. This way we can compare our two OpVaR with the basic capital requirement: If they were respectively higher and lower, no definite finding could be given about the regulatory consequence for the bank we are considering.

To state it another way, our results show that the ALL OpVaR is 22.5% of the basic capital requirement and the additive OpVaR is 15.7%. In absolute terms, the difference is respectively €4.605.485 and €5.011.168 (Table 15.12).

Our second outcome is the expected loss–OpVaR ratio. Table 15.13 shows that the value is particularly low. This confirms our hypothesis of a negative impact for small banks due to the impracticable implementation of AMA approaches in the Italian regulation.

Even though the OpVaR measures applied here are based entirely on internal data they should be compared with other data, such as external and simulated data. The amount of the difference of the OpVaRs and the capital requirement computed with the basic approach is so extraordinary that we must accept the robustness of our hypothesis, still in case of correction introduced in computational methodology. In other words, our result introduces the question about the fairness of a regulatory system that prevents advanced approaches to estimate and discover operational risk exposure of small banks.

In fact, the capital saving a bank would record applying an advanced model could be enough to compensate for the organizational fine-tuning necessary to reach the regulatory requirement.

TABLE 15.13 Expected Loss–OpVaR Ratio

Database	Expected Loss	Expected Loss–OpVaR Ratio
CPP	4,056	
ECG	2,210	(4,056 + 2,214 + 288)/965,532 = 0.70%
AR	288	
ALL	6,019	6,019 ÷ 1,339,015 = 0.45%

15.6 CONCLUSION

Our research looks into the impact of a restrictive regulation that involves the playing field where banks of different sizes compete with each other.

The Italian case is particularly interesting, since AMA and standardized approaches are forbidden to banking intermediaries that do not comply with one of these constraints: (1) the size threshold of a minimum regulatory capital of €200 million; (2) a business threshold of a minimum regulatory capital of €25 million and a gross margin generated by the retail e-commercial banking business line higher than 60% of the total gross margin of the bank.

Implicitly, regulators believe that small and unsophisticated banks do not possess the minimum resources to reengineer the organization and that their portfolio of activities is scarcely diversified in terms of business lines. Since the activity of these banks is more concentrated in business areas whose exposure to operational risks is generally low, the reasoning is that they should not obtain any benefit from the more sophisticated approaches, particularly in terms of risk mitigation.

First, the prohibition to apply advanced methodologies could be costly in terms of capital absorption, risk knowledge, and control efficacy. Second, such a regulatory decision could negatively affect the competitive position of small banks. Moreover, this point is made worse since most of the European countries did not fix any kind of structural entry to apply the advanced approaches. On the contrary, they required utilization of advanced models when the bank size is higher than specified thresholds.

In the United States, small banks can also opt to maintain the Basel I regime. *The Economist* (2006) wrote: "Smaller European banks are annoyed because their American equivalents do not have to spend time and money with Basel 2 at all." This is the reason why small Italian banks could be penalized.

The thesis we want to prove is that, according to the meritocratic logic of Basel II, all banks should be allowed to implement the advanced methodologies, without any a priori bans generating competitive distortions and discouraging improved techniques and best practices to measure and manage operational risks.

The study we present determines the exposure to the operational risk of a bank that could not put into practice any AMA method since it does not comply with the size and business thresholds defined by the Bank of Italy. Its regulatory capital is only €147,274,000 (2007 year value) and its activities basically are concentrated in retail banking.

We demonstrated that if the bank could exploit the OpVaR, its capital saving would likely balance the organizational and managing costs required by the advanced models. Our results verify that the capital absorption was, in the worst case, roughly 22% of the basic capital requirement.

Our research also suggests a method to face the ties problem usually met when estimating the global distribution of loss severity. The available data show that some values are observed several times (i.e., multiple observations of the same realization are present in the sample): these are the *ties*. If the theoretical model adopted to describe the observations is *continuous*, then the presence of ties may raise some problems concerning both model validity and fit. Our approach is to deal with ties using a *mixed approach*, where suitable *point masses* are introduced, in order to take care of the anomalous presence of multiple observations.

NOTE

1. The three subsample outcomes can be found in www.disas.unisi.it/mat_did/ gabbi/appendice_subdataset.pdf.

REFERENCES

A battle over Basel II. 2006. *Economist*, November 2, 3.

Altman, E. I., and G. Sabato. 2005. Effect of the new Basel Capital Accord on bank capital requirements for SMEs. *Journal of Financial Services Research* 28, nos. 1–3:15–42.

Balkema, A. A., and L. De Haan. 1974. Residual life time at great age. *Annual Probability* 2, no. 2:792–804.

Banca d'Italia. 2006 Working paper, Rome.

Berger A. N. 2004. Potential competitive effects of Basel II on banks in SME credit markets in the United States. www.federalreserve.org.

Calem, P. S., and J. R. Follain. 2007. Regulatory capital arbitrage and the potential competitive impact of Basel II in the market for residential mortgages. *Journal of Real Estate Financial Economics* 35, no. 3:197–219.

Cruz, M. 2002. *Modeling, measuring and hedging operational risk*. Chichester, UK: John Wiley & Sons.

Davison, A. C. 1984. In *Statistical extremes and applications*, ed. J. deOliveira. Dordrecht, Netherlands: D. Reidel.

De Fontanouvelle, P., V. Garrity, S. Chu, and E. Rosengren. 2005. The potential impact of explicit Basel II operational risk capital charges on the competitive environment of processing banks in the United States. Working paper, Federal Reserve Bank of Boston.

Embrechts, P., A. J. McNeil, and D. Straumann. 2002. In Risk management: Value at risk and beyond, ed. M. A. H. Dempster. Cambridge: Cambridge University Press.

Hancock, D., A. Lehnert, W. Passmore, and S. M. Sherlund. 2005. An analysis of the potential competitive impacts of Basel II capital standards on U.S. mortgage rates and mortgage securitization. Basel II white paper, Board of Governors of the Federal Reserve System.

Hannan T. H., and S. J. Pilloff. 2004. Will the proposed application of Basel II in the United States encourage increased bank merger activity? Evidence from past merger activity. Working Paper Federal Reserve Board, Boston, MA.

Hartung T. 2004. Operational risks: Modeling and quantifying the impact of insurance solutions. Working Paper, Institute of Risk Management and Insurance Industry, Ludwig-Maximilians, University of Munich, Germany.

Lang W. W., L. J. Mester, and T. A. Vermilyea. 2005. Potential competitive effects on U.S. bank credit card lending from the proposed bifurcated application of Basel II. Working paper, Federal Reserve Bank of Philadelphia.

Le Chavez-Demoulin, V., A. C. Davison, and A. J. McNeil. 2003. A point process approach to value-at-risk estimation. Working paper, National Centre of Competence in Research Financial Valuation and Risk Management Zurich, Switzerland.

Marshall, C. L. 2001. *Measuring and managing operational risk in financial institutions.* Chichester, UK: John Wiley & Sons.

Moscadelli, M. 2004. The modeling of operational risk: Experience with the analysis of the data collected by the Basel Committee. Temi di discussione del Servizio Studi di Banca d'Italia.

Na, H. S. 2004. Analysing and scaling operational risk. Master's thesis, Erasmus University Rotterdam, Netherlands.

Na, H. S., J. Van Den Berg, L. C. Miranda, and M. Leipoldt. 2006. An econometric model to scale operational losses. *Journal of Operational Risk* 4, nos. 1–2:11–31.

Pickands, J. 1975. Statistical inference using extreme order statistics. *Annals of Statistics* 3, no. 1:119–131.

Salvadori, G., C. De Michele, N. T. Kottegoda, and R. Rosso. 2007. *Extremes in nature. An approach using copulas.* WST Library Series, Volume 56. Dordrecht: Netherlands: Springer.

Schwizer, P., S. Cosma, and G. Salvadori. 2007. Il rischio operativo nel settore del factoring: prime verifiche empiriche, CREDIFact, Discussion Paper Series n. 1/2007, in addition to Fact & News, Year 9, n. 4, September–October, 1–37.

Shih, J., S. J. A. Samad-Khan, and P. Medapa. Is the size of an operational loss related to firm size? *Operational Risk Magazine* 1, no. 2:22–25.

CHAPTER 16

Simple Measures for Operational Risk Reduction? An Assessment of Implications and Drawbacks

Silke N. Brandts and Nicole Branger

ABSTRACT

The chapter evaluates whether simple measures for the risk mitigation achieved by operational risk insurance, such as the "premium" and "limit" approaches, can serve as appropriate proxies for the true risk reduction. We demonstrate that the risk reduction implied by the simple measures can deviate substantially from the true regulatory risk reduction. Additionally, most of the simple measures incite regulatory capital arbitrage.

16.1 INTRODUCTION

Insurance is an important instrument for the risk mitigation of infrequent but severe losses due to operational risk. Given an appropriate methodology to quantify the risk-mitigating impact of operational risk insurance, financial institutions can reduce their regulatory capital requirements if they use such

The authors would like to thank Christian Laux, Christian Schlag, and Anton Wakolbinger for helpful comments and discussions. Responsibility for any errors, omissions, and all views lies solely with the authors.

an insurance. As long as the value created by the lower capital requirement is positive, the use of operational risk insurance creates value for the financial institution.[1]

The reduction in the regulatory capital requirement is supposed to reflect the degree of the actual risk reduction achieved by the use of operational risk insurance. The main prerequisite is the existence of an appropriate measure for this true risk reduction. For a given regulatory risk measure—which in the context of most operational risk models is the value at risk (VaR) of the loss distribution—the correct way to account for the impact of operational risk insurance is to explicitly calculate the difference between the regulatory measure (VaR) based on the gross loss distribution and the regulatory measure (VaR) based on the net loss distribution after the application of the insurance contract.

Reductions of the regulatory capital requirements through the use of operational risk insurance have currently been considered for the advanced measurement approach (AMA) only, since it is the only model in which the impact of an insurance contract on the loss distribution can be explicitly calculated and in which a direct quantitative connection among the impact of insurance, the regulatory risk measure, and the capital requirement exists (see Joint Forum 2003; Risk Management Group 2001, 2006). Due to the early stage of operational risk measurement and management, however, only a limited number of financial institutions possess sufficient data and modeling expertise to model their operational risk exposure on an individual loss basis and to correctly calculate the impact of operational risk insurance.

For the more basic approaches, a capital relief due to operational risk insurance has not been officially considered yet by the Basel Committee. To potentially fill this gap, the European Commission and the Working Group of the Insurance Companies have made suggestions for so-called simple measures (see European Commission 2002; Working Group 2001). These measures are meant to allow the reduction of capital requirements within the basic approaches or to serve as proxies for the risk mitigation in more sophisticated approaches. These simple measures, known in the regulatory literature as premium and limit approaches, take simple functions of the premium or limit of an insurance contract as a proxy for the risk reduction obtained by an insurance contract.

Our chapter evaluates whether these simple measures can serve as appropriate proxies for the true risk reduction achieved by operational risk insurance and derives appropriate policy recommendations. To assess the usability of the simple measures from a regulatory point of view, two questions have to be answered: The first question is how well the simple measures reflect the true regulatory risk reduction as measured by the difference in the

VaR of the gross loss distribution and the net loss distribution after application of the insurance contract and whether structural differences exist. While an underestimation of the true risk reduction penalizes the financial institutions through lower capital reliefs, an overestimation dilutes the objective of the regulatory capital requirements for operational risk. The permission to assess the risk-mitigating impact of insurance via simple measures should consequently depend on the condition that the simple measures do not overestimate the true risk reduction. In our analysis, we compare the structural differences between the true regulatory risk reduction as measured by the changes in VaR with the risk reduction implied by the simple measure and show that none of the simple measures correctly reflects the true regulatory risk reduction for arbitrary contract choices. Furthermore, almost all simple measures overestimate the true regulatory risk reduction for at least some contract choices. Scaling factors, which bring the simple measures closer to the true risk reduction, are a potential solution to this problem. As we show, there are no simple industry-wide scaling factors that depend solely on the contract characteristics and on the specific loss distribution. If we nevertheless want to apply simple measures in a regulatory context, we have to use the measure that deviates as little as possible from the true risk reduction and shows the lowest degree of overestimation given a constant scaling factor.

The second question to be analyzed is the degree to which the simple measures allow or even incite regulatory capital arbitrage, which in our context is defined as the reduction in an institution's regulatory capital requirements with little or no corresponding reduction in the true regulatory risk measure (see, e.g., Jones 2000; Matten 2000). Regulatory capital arbitrage arises if the contract that offers the highest risk reduction according to the simple measure offers no or less risk reduction as measured by the true regulatory measure. This is a critical point from the regulatory point of view, since wrong incentives due to the introduction of simple measures can actually increase the risk-taking behavior of a financial institution compared to the status quo. As we will see, most of the simple measures suffer from this caveat, since the insurance contracts offering the highest risk reduction according to the simple measures offer no reduction in the true regulatory risk measure.

The two questions just discussed can be summarized in two formal criteria for the assessment of simple measures when it comes to the regulatory treatment of operational risk insurance:

1. Good approximation of the correct risk reduction as measured by the regulatory benchmark measure VaR
2. No or only limited incentives for regulatory capital arbitrage

To assess the performance of the measures along these criteria, we show analytically as well as by simulation which simple measures perform best in terms of fulfilling both criteria. As a policy recommendation, we propose to use an advanced cover approach, which is an extension of one of the simple measures. It minimizes the deviation between the risk reduction implied by the simple measures and the reduction in the VaR for a constant scaling factor, and it limits the incentives for regulatory capital arbitrage inherent in the remaining simple measures.[2]

16.2 LOSS PROCESS AND CONTRACTS

We assume that the general loss process X_T is given by a compound Poisson process

$$X_T = \sum_{\tau=1}^{N_T} Y_\tau \qquad (16.1)$$

where N_T = number of losses up to time T
       Y_τ = size of the τth individual loss

The intensity of the Poisson process is λ. The loss sizes Y_τ are assumed to be lognormally distributed with parameters μ and σ. This setup is considered one of the standard models for operational risk.[3] In our analysis, we will set T = 1 as we only consider a time horizon of one year. To ease notation, we set $X_T = X$ and $N_T = N$.

The insurance contracts considered are aggregate insurance contracts, which are applied to the aggregate loss X rather than to the individual losses Y_τ. This is in line with so-called all-risk insurances. The contracts are characterized by a deductible (D) that the insured has to finance by him- or herself and a limit (L) which denotes the maximum insured loss. The cover—the maximum payout of the insurance—is given by L−D. The payoff function respectively the compensation (C) is given by

$$C(X) = \max\{\min[X, L] - D, 0\} \qquad (16.2)$$

We will consider different contracts that will be defined in Section 16.3. We fix the cost of the insurance, so that the contracts differ only with respect to D and L.

16.3 PRICING OF INSURANCE CONTRACTS

There are basically two different approaches to value an insurance contract:

1. Risk-neutral pricing commonly used in the finance literature
2. Premium calculation principles frequently used in the insurance literature

For simplicity, we ignore any additional components, such as commission and expenses, and we set the interest rate r equal to zero.

16.3.1 Risk-Neutral Pricing

In case of risk-neutral pricing, the price P of an insurance contract with payoff C is

$$P = E^Q[C] \qquad (16.3)$$

where Q is the risk-neutral probability measure. The relation between the physical measure P and the risk-neutral measure Q depends on the market prices of risk for the different risk factors, in our case the frequency and the magnitude of jumps. We assume that only jump size risk is priced, that is, that the mean jump size μ is increased by a factor $\kappa > 1$, while jump intensity risk and jump volatility risk are not priced.[4]

16.3.2 Premium Calculation Principles

Premium calculation principles in actuarial mathematics are based on the distribution of the claims process under the physical measure.[5] For the expected value principle, the price of an insurance contract is

$$P = (1 + \delta)E^P[C] \qquad (16.4)$$

which is the expected compensation under the physical measure, inflated with a safety loading $\delta \geq 0$. The variance principle gives a price of

$$P = E^P[C] + \beta \text{VaR}^P[C] \qquad (16.5)$$

It equals the expected compensation under the physical measure plus a markup due to risk, which is measured by the variance of the contract and multiplied by $\beta \geq 0.$[6] For the Esscher principle, the price is

$$P = E^P \left[C \frac{e^{\theta X}}{E^P[e^{\theta X}]} \right] \tag{16.6}$$

where $\theta \geq 0$. The pricing equation can be explained by an exponential utility function with constant absolute risk aversion θ.[7]

16.4 RISK REDUCTION

The key question of this chapter is whether simple measures for risk reduction can be used as proxies for the true risk reduction achieved by operational risk insurance in a regulatory framework. In this context, we define the true risk reduction as the difference in a statistical risk measure before and after application of an insurance contract. The risk measure we consider is the value at risk.[8] Note that the initial premium paid for the contract increases the loss at time T since it denotes a payout.

First, we analyze the relation and the structural differences between the true risk reduction and the risk reduction implied by the simple measures. As we will see, all of the simple measures proposed so far overestimate the reduction in the VaR for at least some contract characteristics. Furthermore, the relation between the different approaches depends not only on the contract characteristics but also on the characteristics of the loss distribution under the physical measure and on the way in which the insurance premium is calculated. There are thus no simple scaling factors that equate the risk reduction implied by the simple measures to the true risk reduction.

The second question is how far the simple measures incite regulatory capital arbitrage. To answer this question, we derive the optimal characteristics of the insurance contracts for the different approaches. It turns out that most simple measures favor contracts that will only reduce the regulatory capital requirement as determined by the simple measures but not the VaR of the resulting net loss distribution. Hence, the true regulatory risk exposure is underestimated.[9]

16.4.1 VaR

The VaR of a loss process X is defined as $VaR(X) \equiv \inf\{x : \Pr(X \leq x) \geq q\}$ for some predetermined quantile q. For ease of notation, we denote the value at risk of the gross loss history, VaR_{gross}, by V. For an insurance contract with deductible D and limit L, the risk reduction $RR_{VaR} = V - VaR_{net}$ is given by

$$RR_{VaR} = \max\{\min[L, V] - D, 0\} - P \qquad (16.7)$$

The risk reduction depends on the characteristics of the contract and on the q-quantile V of the gross loss distribution, but not on any further characteristics of this distribution. For contracts with a high deductible $D > V - P$, the risk reduction becomes negative.

The optimal contract for reduction of the VaR is given in Proposition 16.1.[10]

Proposition 16.1. For a fixed premium P, the optimal contract which maximizes the reduction of the VaR is given by $L = V$.

16.4.2 Simple Measures

Simple measures for the risk reduction rely on the contract characteristics D and L and on the premium paid for the insurance as well as on scaling factors γ, which are meant to bring the risk reduction as calculated by the simple measures closer to the true risk reduction.[11]

According to the European Commission and the Working Group of the Insurance Companies, these factors should ideally be calibrated industry-wide.

In the literature, two different premium-based measures are proposed, which we denote by premium approach A and premium approach B. The risk reductions implied by the simple measures, RR_A and RR_B, are given by

$$
\begin{aligned}
RR_A(P) &= \gamma_A \cdot P \\
RR_B(D, L) &= \gamma_B \cdot P \cdot \left(1 - \frac{P}{L}\right)
\end{aligned}
\qquad (16.8)
$$

Premium approach A. The general problem inherent in the approach is that contracts with different combinations of D and L can have the same premium while achieving very different degrees of risk reduction as measured by the VaR. For $\gamma_A = 1$, the relationship between the simple measure and RR_{VaR} is given by,

$$RR_A(P) = \begin{cases} \leq RR_{VaR} & \text{for} \quad D \leq \min\{L, V\} - 2P \\ > RR_{VaR} & \text{for} \quad D > \min\{L, V\} - 2P \end{cases} \qquad (16.9)$$

The premium approach overestimates the risk reduction for high deductibles D. In particular, it predicts that the risk reduction is always positive, while the true risk reduction even becomes negative for $D > V - P$.

The optimal contract is not unique, since all contracts with different (D, L)-combinations but identical price give exactly the same risk reduction. While there is no incentive to choose contracts that are optimal for the reduction of the VaR, there is also no reward in choosing any contract different from the one characterized by $L = V$, either. Thus, there exists no incentive for regulatory capital arbitrage.

Premium approach B. For $\gamma_A = \gamma_B$, the premium approach B always implies a smaller risk reduction than the first approach. It overestimates the risk reduction RR_{VaR} for high values of the deductible $D > \min\{V, L\} - 2P + \frac{P^2}{L}$ and underestimates it for values below. The range of overestimation is smaller than for the premium approach A.

The most fundamental difference between the two premium approaches are the characteristics of the optimal contracts. Given a certain cost of insurance, the optimal contract is now given by the lowest possible ratio of $\frac{P}{L}$ and hence by $L = L_{max}$, where L_{max} is the maximum limit that is possible.[12] This does not necessarily ensure a risk reduction of the VaR and almost never coincides with the optimal contract.

Limit approach. In the limit approach, the limit of the insurance contract is taken as proxy for the risk reduction[13]

$$RR_L(D, L) = L - P \qquad (16.10)$$

The limit approach overestimates RR_{VaR} except for the case where $D = 0$ and $L \le V$.

The optimal contract for maximization of RR_L is again given by $L = L_{max}$. As discussed before, this contract will be suboptimal for the VaR and incite regulatory capital arbitrage.

Cover approach. A second and economically more reasonable interpretation of the limit approach is the cover approach which is based on the maximum compensation paid by the contract. The risk reduction as given by the simple measure changes to

$$RR_C(D, L) = L - D - P \qquad (16.11)$$

The cover approach gives the true reduction in VaR for $L \le V$ and overestimates it for $L > V$.

Even though the cover approach gives the correct risk reduction for $L \leq V$, the optimal contract is again given by $L = L_{\max}$. Hence, the cover approach also leads to regulatory capital arbitrage.

Adjusted cover approach. To alleviate the overestimation of the risk reduction for contracts with $L > V$ as well as the distortion of incentives regarding the optimal contract choice, we propose to use an exogenous upper bound on the risk reduction in the cover approach. We refer to this alternative as the adjusted cover approach. The risk reduction is given by

$$RR_{AC} = \gamma_{AC}(\max\{\min[L, V_{reg}] - D, 0\} - P) \tag{16.12}$$

where V_{reg} is an upper bound that is meant to prevent too high choices of the limit L. Naturally, the ideal value for V_{reg} would be the gross VaR, V, of the empirical loss distribution of the respective financial institution. However, this value is usually not known to the regulators. For practical reasons, the bound should furthermore be based on some industry-wide calibrated factor. An alternative would thus be the VaR_{gross} of the operational risk loss distribution of an industry-wide data pool.

Examples for such databases are the Loss Data Collection Exercise (LDCE) conducted by the Basel Committee or the ORX data base of the Operational Riskdata eXchange Association.[14] To approximate the true VaR of the financial institution as closely as possible, the bound should be scaled by a revenue factor to account for the size of the financial institution. Additionally, due to the level of detail available in the ORX database, different bounds can be used for different business lines, allowing the considerations of more sophisticated products than "all-risk" insurances.

For $\gamma_{AC} = 1$, the relationship between the risk reduction implied by the adjusted cover approach, RR_{AC}, and RR_{VaR} is

$$RR_{AC}(D, L) \begin{cases} = RR_{VaR} & \text{for } D \geq \max\{V, V_{reg}\} \text{ or } L < \min\{V, V_{reg}\} \\ > RR_{VaR} & \text{for } D < V_{reg} \text{ and } L > V \text{ if } V < V_{reg} \\ < RR_{VaR} & \text{for } D < V \text{ and } L > V_{reg} \text{ if } V_{reg} < V \end{cases} \tag{16.13}$$

For $V = V_{reg}$, the adjusted cover approach gives the true risk reduction for all contracts. If the regulatory VaR is larger than the VaR of the financial institution (i.e., for $V_{reg} > V$), there is still overestimation for $D < V_{reg}$ and $L > V$. If the regulatory bound V_{reg} is smaller than V, the simple measure underestimates the true risk reduction RR_{VaR} for $D < V$ and $L > V_{reg}$.

The optimal contract that maximizes RR_{AC} is given by $L = V_{reg}$. Whether there are incentives for capital arbitrage now depends on the relation between V_{reg} and V. In the ideal case of $V = V_{reg}$, the risk measures RR_{VaR} and RR_{AC} and thus also the contracts that maximize the risk reduction coincide, and there is no regulatory capital arbitrage. If the regulatory value at risk underestimates the VaR of the financial institution (i.e., if $V_{reg} < V$), the financial institution is incited to choose a contract with a lower limit as compared to the optimal one. Nevertheless, no regulatory capital arbitrage arises because the adjusted cover approach correctly reflects the risk reduction achieved by the insurance contract. The only case in which regulatory capital arbitrage still is incited is the case $V_{reg} > V$, where the financial institution chooses a limit L which is too large, and where the risk reduction achieved by this contract is overestimated by the adjusted cover approach.

16.4.3 Preliminary Assessment of the Simple Measures

The risk reduction as calculated by the simple measures depends on the contract characteristics D and L and on the price of the insurance only. The true risk reduction, however, additionally depends on the firm-specific quantile V of the gross loss distribution. There is thus no simple measure (with the exception of the adjusted cover approach for which $V_{reg} = V$ by chance) that always reflects the true risk reduction. For contracts with a too-high deductible or limit, the simple measures tend to overestimate the true risk reduction. In particular, they still give a positive risk reduction even for $D > V - P$, where the true risk reduction is negative. This problem is amplified by the fact that all measures except the premium approach A and the adjusted cover approach favor contracts with $L > V$ and thus also with a high-deductible D.

The optimal insurance contract is given by $L = V$ if the risk reduction is measured correctly, which coincides with the optimal contract as chosen by a simple measure only for the adjusted cover approach when $V_{reg} = V$ by chance. For the premium approach B, the cover approach, and the limit approach, the optimal choice is rather given by the maximal possible limit, which is larger than the optimal limit. The risk reduction achieved by the seemingly optimal contracts as calculated by the simple measures overestimates the true risk reducation, so that there is an incentive for regulatory arbitrage. For the adjusted cover approach, it depends on V_{reg} whether the limit is too low or too high and whether the true risk reduction is under- or overestimated. The premium approach A is the only simple measure for which the regulatory preferred contract with $L = V$ is, among all other contracts, optimal, but it does not give any guidance on which contract to choose, either.

16.5 MONTE CARLO SIMULATION

The relative performance of the simple measures with regard to the approximation of the VaR and the amount of regulatory arbitrage depends on the characteristics of the insurance contract, on firm-specific characteristics as well as on the choice of the pricing function. We thus do a Monte Carlo simulation to assess how severe the differences are in a realistic setup.

16.5.1 Setup

We do a Monte Carlo simulation with 500,000 paths both under the physical measure (for risk measurement) and under the risk-neutral measure (for pricing). The initial capital used for buying insurance is set to US$10,000.[15] A sensitivity analysis shows that there are no systematic differences in the results if we vary this amount.

The parameters of the loss distribution are taken from Lewis and Lantsman (2005) and are based on 91 unauthorized trading losses from the OpVaR operational risk database by OpVantage. The relevant parameters of the severity and the frequency distributions are $\mu = 10.41, \sigma = 2.14$ and $\lambda = 0.2$ for the physical measure. For this parametrization, the average individual loss size is US$327,682, and the VaR_{gross} for the 99% quantile is approximately US$ 1.1 million. The risk-neutral measure differs from the physical measure due to the market price of risk for jump size risk, and we increase the parameter μ by a factor of $\kappa = 1.067$, which corresponds to an increase of the expected loss size by a factor of 2.

We consider six different contracts. The contract specifications are given in Table 16.1. Contracts 1 and 2 cover the lowest and the middle part of the loss distribution, respectively. Contract 4 gives the largest reduction of the VaR. The other three contracts are optimal for the cover approach and the limit approach (contract 6, where we have set the maximal limit equal to the highest loss in the Monte Carlo simulation), the adjusted cover approach with $V_{reg} = 0.75\,V$ (contract 3), and the adjusted cover approach with $V_{reg} = 2.5\,V$ (contract 5).

For all contracts, either D or L is given, while the other parameter is chosen such that the initial price of each contract is US$10,000. Note that the parameters depend on which pricing approach is used. We have calibrated the parameters δ, β, and θ of the premium principles such that the truly optimal contract 4 is identical under all pricing approaches.[16]

TABLE 16.1 Contract Specifications

		Contract 1 D = 0	Contract 2 D = E[X]	Contract 3 L = 0.75 V	Contract 4 L = V	Contract 5 L = 2.5 V	Contract 6 L = maximum
Risk-	D	0	64	489	680	1,796	43,912
Neutral	L	84	195	838	1,117	2,793	253,070
Pricing	C	84	131	349	438	998	209,158
Expected	D	0	64	501	680	1,688	26,452
Value	L	47	159	838	1,117	2,793	253,070
Principle	C	47	95	337	438	1,105	226,618
Variance	D	0	64	477	680	1,958	207,718
Principle	L	95	217	838	1,117	2,793	253,070
	C	95	153	361	438	835	45,352
Esscher	D	0	64	468	679	2,101	251,179
Principle	L	98	228	838	1,117	2,793	253,070
	C	98	164	370	438	692	1,890

The table gives the deductible, limit, and cover for six different insurance contracts and for several pricing functions. The premium principles are calibrated such that contract 4 is identical for all choices of the pricing function.

16.5.2 Results

The subsequent assessment of the simple measures follows the two criteria established in Sections 16.1 and 16.4. First, we briefly review the contract specifications and show how different the optimal contract choices for the various risk measures are and in how far they incite regulatory arbitrage. Since according to our theoretical analysis in Section 16.3 none of the simple measures correctly reflects the true statistical risk reduction RR_{VaR}, we then analyze the structural differences and the absolute size of the deviations between the true regulatory risk reduction, RR_{VaR}, and the risk reduction implied by the simple measures—first without considering any scaling factors. The final question is, then, whether there exists a simple scaling factor that converts the risk reduction implied by the simple measures into the true statistical risk reduction RR_{VaR}.

Contract Characteristics and Regulatory Capital Arbitrage Table 16.1 gives the contract specifications for the different pricing approaches. The optimal contracts for the maximization of the risk reduction implied by the simple measures (contracts 3, 5, and 6) differ from the optimal contract for reduction of the VaR (contract 4), except for the premium principle A, for which all contracts are optimal. With the exception of the adjusted cover approach with $V_{reg1} < V$, the simple measures imply deductibles and limits that are much larger than the truly optimal ones.

Table 16.2 gives the risk reductions for the six contracts and for the different risk measures. For contract 6, which is optimal under the limit approach and the cover approach, the true VaR even increases, while the simple measures predict a (significant) risk reduction. These simple measures thus clearly incite regulatory arbitrage. From a regulatory perspective, they have a counterproductive effect and should therefore not be used to approximate the risk-mitigating impact of insurances in a regulatory framework. The premium approach, however, does not incite regulatory arbitrage but does not help in finding the optimal contract either.

The performance of the adjusted cover approach depends on the choice of V_{reg}. For $V_{reg} < V$, the seemingly optimal contract (contract 3) has a limit that is too low. But even if the contract is suboptimal, the risk reduction as implied by the simple measure coincides with the true risk reduction. For $V_{reg} > V$ (which results in contract 5), however, the true risk reducation is negative, and the simple measure incites regulatory arbitrage.

Besides the precise choice of the optimal contract, the simple measures also distort the assessment and ranking of insurance contracts in general. While contracts with $D > V - P$ are the least effective from a regulatory point of view, all simple measures with the exception of the premium approach A and the adjusted cover approach with $V_{reg} < V$ favor exactly these contracts. Thus, only the premium approach A and the adjusted cover approach with $V_{reg} < V$ satisfy the condition of no incentive for regulatory capital arbitrage.

Structural Differences between the Simple Measures and RR_{VaR} Figure 16.1 shows the risk reduction per unit of insurance premium as a function of the deductible. The contracts are priced by risk-neutral pricing with a premium for jump size risk only. For now, the scaling factors of the simple measures are assumed to equal 1.

First, we look at the risk reduction as measured by the benchmark measure VaR. As implied by Equation 16.7 RR_{VaR} increases in D until $L = V$ and decreases afterward. For all contracts with $D > V$, the risk reduction per unit of premium is -1.

None of the simple measures correctly reflects the true risk reduction RR_{VaR} for all contract specifications. The risk reduction per unit of insurance premium implied by the premium approach A equals 1 independent of the contract characteristics, while the risk reduction implied by the premium approach B increases monotonically and converges toward 1. Both premium approaches clearly underestimate RR_{VaR} for $L \leq V$ and overestimate it for $D > V$.

TABLE 16.2 Risk Reduction for Different Contracts and Different Risk Measures

	Contract 1 $D = 0$	Contract 2 $D = E[X]$	Contract 3 $L = 0.75\,V$	Contract 4 $L = V$	Contract 5 $L = 2.5\,V$	Contract 6 $L = $ maximum
Risk reduction per unit of premium measured by VaR						
Risk-neutral pricing	7.5	12.3	33.9	42.8	−1.0	−1.0
Expected value principle	3.8	8.6	32.7	42.8	−1.0	−1.0
Variance principle	8.5	14.4	35.1	42.8	−1.0	−1.0
Esscher principle	8.9	15.5	36.0	42.8	−1.0	−1.0
Risk reduction per unit of premium measured by premium approach A						
Risk-neutral pricing	1.0	1.0	1.0	1.0	1.0	1.0
Expected value principle	1.0	1.0	1.0	1.0	1.0	1.0
Variance principle	1.0	1.0	1.0	1.0	1.0	1.0
Esscher principle	1.0	1.0	1.0	1.0	1.0	1.0
Risk reduction per unit of premium measured by premium approach B						
Risk-neutral pricing	0.9	0.9	1.0	1.0	1.0	1.0
Expected value principle	0.8	0.9	1.0	1.0	1.0	1.0
Variance principle	0.9	1.0	1.0	1.0	1.0	1.0
Esscher principle	0.9	1.0	1.0	1.0	1.0	1.0
Risk reduction per unit of premium measured by limit approach						
Risk-neutral pricing	7.5	18.5	82.8	110.7	278.3	25,306.0
Expected value principle	3.8	14.9	82.8	110.7	278.3	25,306.0
Variance principle	8.5	20.7	82.8	110.7	278.3	25,306.0
Esscher principle	8.9	21.8	82.8	110.7	278.3	25,306.0

Risk reduction per unit of premium measured by cover approach					
Risk-neutral pricing	7.5	12.3	33.9	42.8	98.8	20,914.8
Expected value principle	3.8	8.6	32.7	42.8	109.5	22,665.7
Variance principle	8.5	14.4	35.1	42.8	82.5	4,538.6
Esscher principle	8.9	15.5	36.0	42.8	68.2	188.2

Risk reduction per unit of premium measured by adjusted cover approach with $V_{reg} = 0.75$ V					
Risk-neutral pricing	7.5	12.3	33.9	14.8	-1.0	-1.0
Expected value principle	3.8	8.6	32.7	14.8	-1.0	-1.0
Variance principle	8.5	14.4	35.1	14.8	-1.0	-1.0
Esscher principle	8.9	15.5	36.0	14.9	-1.0	-1.0

Risk reduction per unit of premium measured by adjusted cover approach with $V_{reg} = 2.5$ V					
Risk-neutral pricing	7.5	12.3	33.9	42.8	**98.8**	-1.0
Expected value principle	3.8	8.6	32.7	42.8	**109.5**	-1.0
Variance principle	8.5	14.4	35.1	42.8	**82.5**	-1.0
Esscher principle	8.9	15.5	36.0	42.8	**68.2**	-1.0

The table shows the risk reduction per unit of insurance premium achieved by the six contracts for various pricing functions and various risk measures. The bold numbers denote the risk reduction by the contracts that are optimal with respect to the risk measures considered.

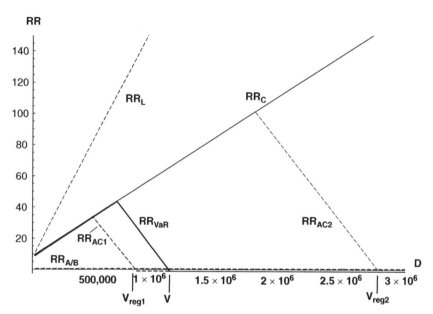

FIGURE 16.1 Risk Reduction per Unit of Insurance Premium
The figure shows the risk reduction per unit of insurance premium as a function of
the deductible D. The limit L is determined such that the price of the insurance
contract is equal to $10,000, where the price is determined by risk-neutral pricing.

The risk reduction per unit of insurance premium implied by the limit as
well as by the cover approach increases in D without bound. The limit approach overestimates the true risk reduction except for a deductible of zero.
For the cover approach, the risk reduction implied by the simple measure
equals RR_{VaR} for contracts with $L \leq V$ and overestimates it for the remaining contracts. While the overestimation goes to infinity for an increasing
deductible for both simple measures, it is nevertheless smaller for the cover
than for the limit approach.

For the adjusted cover approach, the risk reduction per unit of insurance premium implied by the simple measure increases until $L = V_{reg}$, then
decreases until $D = V_{reg}$, and is equal to -1 afterward. It coincides with the
true risk reduction for low and high values of the deductible. In between,
the adjusted cover approach underestimates the risk reduction if the portfolio is more risky than the average regulatory one (i.e., if $V > V_{reg}$), and it
overestimates the risk reduction if the portfolio is less risky than the average
one (i.e., if $V < V_{reg}$).

Scaling Factors The simple risk measures can be multiplied by scaling factors to bring the risk reduction they imply closer to the true risk reduction. These scaling factors can depend on the characteristics of the contracts such as the deductible, the limit, and the premium, but they should not depend on the (not easily observable) characteristics of the truly optimal contract. As becomes clear from Figure 16.1, such scaling factors do not exist for any of the simple measures.

Influence of Different Pricing Kernels The results remain qualitatively unchanged for different pricing kernels. The pricing kernels differ in particular with respect to the prices of very high losses, which are rather expensive for the Esscher principle, the variance principle, and a higher market price of jump size risk κ. This implies that the cover of contracts that pay off for high losses is reduced significantly as compared to the cover under the expected value principle and under the pricing kernel we have used up to now. Consequently, the risk reduction of these contracts is lower, too, while the risk reduction from contracts with a low deductible and limit increases as compared to the other principles. Furthermore, the deviations between the true risk reduction and the implied risk reduction are lower for contracts with payoffs for high losses.

To summarize, the simple measure that best complies with the two criteria established earlier is the adjusted cover approach with $V_{reg} < V$. Given a scaling factor of unity, it closest reflects the true reduction of the VaR independent of the specific contract characteristics. Furthermore, it is the only measure that does not incite regulatory arbitrage and that does not overestimate the true regulatory risk reduction for arbitrary contract characteristics. Among the remaining risk measures, the cover approach best reflects the true reduction in the VaR for contracts with $L < V$ while the premium approaches gives the smallest overestimation per unit of insurance premium for contracts with $D > V$.

16.6 POLICY IMPLICATIONS

For future policy implications, there are two important questions. The first is whether simple measures can and should be used to approximate the risk reduction achieved by operational risk insurance. This question needs to be answered separately for the case of (1) the AMA, for which the simple measures would only serve as approximations of the true statistical risk reduction, and (2) the basic indicator and the standardized approaches, in which operational risk insurance is not taken into account otherwise. The second question is which of the proposed simple measures should be chosen and what aspects need to be considered for practical implementation.

Based on the preceding analysis, the preferred measure from a regulatory point of view is the adjusted cover approach with $V_{reg} < V$. All other measures incite regulatory arbitrage or give an incorrect risk reduction. A bank already using the AMA, however, can achieve a higher regulatory capital relief by choosing the optimal contract for reducing its true VaR_{gross} and correctly calculating the statistical risk reduction. Hence, the simple adjusted cover approach constitutes no alternative for these banks.

The second part of the question is whether the simple measures should enable consideration of operational risk insurances in the context of the basic indicator and the standardized approaches. Given that insurance is (or even might only be) beneficial to banks and to the financial system as a whole, the restriction is that the simple measure should give the right incentives to banks and prevent regulatory arbitrage. Following the same line of argument as earlier, this leads to the adjusted cover approach with (preferably) $V_{reg} < V$. It is the only measure that prevents both overestimation of the true risk reduction and regulatory arbitrage.

The last question is the practicality of the implementation with respect to the calibration of the adjusted cover approach. An appropriate value for V_{reg} could be taken from the LDCE conducted by the Basel Committee or the ORX database. It would additionally provide a guideline for the choice of economically sensible insurance contracts if the institution itself lacks proprietary historical loss data. To further ensure that V_{reg} is as close as possible to the true VaR of the institution, V_{reg} should be scaled by a proxy for the size of the institution, such as the revenues (if possible for different business lines).

To conclude, the recommendation to allow the recognition of operational risk insurances in the context of the basic indicator and the standardized approaches hinges critically on the appropriate calibration of the value of V_{reg}. While a sufficiently precise calibration of V_{reg} may currently not be possible, this obstacle will probably be resolved in the coming years. In order to do so, the relationship between the frequency and severity of operational risk losses and firm characteristics should be further explored.

16.7 CONCLUSION

This chapter analyzes whether simple measures can serve as proxies for the risk reduction achieved by the use of operational risk insurance and potentially enable its recognition within the basic and standardized approach. The assessment of the simple measures is based on two criteria:

1. Good approximation of the correct risk reduction as measured by the regulatory benchmark measure VaR
2. No or only limited incentives for regulatory capital arbitrage

We show that the so-called adjusted cover approach proposed herein—given an appropriate calibration with $V_{reg} < V$—performs best with respect to approximating the true statistical risk reduction and exhibits the lowest incentives to engage in regulatory capital arbitrage. All other simple measures severely overestimate the true reduction of the VaR for at least some contract characteristics and—with the exception of the premium approach A—incite regulatory capital arbitrage.

Regarding future policy recommendations, we suggest the use of the adjusted cover approach with $V_{reg} < V$ as a proxy for the true risk reduction if the risk mitigation of operational risk insurance shall be considered within the basic and standardized approaches. All other simple measures severely overestimate the correct risk reduction as measured by the regulatory benchmark measure VaR for at least some contracts and incite regulatory capital arbitrage. The only practical constraint for the adjusted cover approach with $V_{reg} < V$ is a sufficiently precise calibration of the parameter V_{reg}, which seems not to be possible currently due to lack of detailed data on operational risk losses. From a regulatory point of view, the calibration of potential values for V_{reg} for different sizes of financial institutions as well as business lines should therefore become a focus of further research.

NOTES

1. Evidence for positive value creation has been found for example in a study by Kuritzkes and Ziff (2004).
2. All proofs of the propositions in this chapter are available upon request.
3. For an extensive analysis of models used for quantification of operational risk, see Cruz (2002).
4. Delbaen and Haezendonck (1989) characterize the set of equivalent probability measures that preserve the structure of the underlying compound Poisson process. For further derivations, see also Muermann (2001, 2003).
5. For a fundamental overview of available premiums principles and their applications, see Goovaerts, de Vylder, and Haezendonck (1984). The premium principles considered in our chapter are appropriate for thin to moderate fat-tailed distributions like the lognormal distribution used in our setup.

6. The pricing kernel is increasing in C and—for the contracts we consider—nondecreasing in X, so that it is relatively more expensive to insure large losses than small losses. For a formal derivation, see Delbaen and Haezendonck (1989).

7. The pricing kernel is a nondecreasing and strictly convex function of X and puts an increasingly higher probability mass on high loss realizations X under the risk-neutral measure. For a derivation and detailed discussion of the Esscher Principle, see Bühlmann (1980, 1983) and Goovaerts et al. (1984). For an application in an option pricing framework, see Gerber and Shiu (1994).

8. For an analog analysis based on the expected shortfall, we refer to Brandts (2006).

9. As, for example, shown by Jones (2000) in the context of credit risk, a distortion of incentives due to regulatory rules can actually increase the risk profile of a financial institution by inciting the choice of loans whose regulatory cost of capital is smaller than their true cost.

10. The risk reduction depends on how much the q-quantile of the net loss distribution is reduced. Since a decrease in losses above the q-quantile does not change the VaR, the limit L should not be above the q-quantile V, and investors should only reduce losses equal to V or below. If they reduce all losses between V and y<V to the level y, the new q-quantile is y, and the risk reducation is V-y-P. A reduction of losses below y again does not have any impact on the new quantile. Investors will thus use the whole premium for risk reduction in the interval from y to V. The lower-level y is just equal to the deductible D and follows from the fixed premium P.

11. In the text, we ignore any adjustments due to counterparty credit risk, for example. For a model incorporating residual risks, such as payment uncertainty and liquidity risk, which are required in an appropriate model according to the Basel Committee, see Brandts (2004).

12. An appropriate practical choice for the limit L is either the highest previously observed loss or the highest limit the insurer is willing to offer.

13. In the literature, a second formulation of the form $RR_L = L$ has been proposed, which we do not consider since it ignores the cost of insurance.

14. Founding members include 22 major private and commercial banks throughout Europe and internationally active U.S. and Canadian banks.

15. This corresponds approximately to the fair premiums that Lewis and Lantsman (2005) calculate for unauthorized trading policies. Actual prices are not available due to confidentiality reasons.

16. The assumption of a single loading for different contract characteristics corresponds to the formulation of the premium calculation principles in Section 16.3. If the loading would be different for each contract, the valuation would implicitly take additional characteristics into account that are not inherent in the formulation of the premium calculation principles. The fact that we observe different ratios between the premium and the expected loss under the physical measure for different levels of deductibles, as, for example, shown by Froot (2001), rather reflects the use of more sophisticated premium calculation principles than the expected value principle but does not imply a variable loading for the expected premium principle.

REFERENCES

Brandts, S. 2004. Operational risk and insurance: Quantitative and qualitative aspects. Working paper, University of Frankfurt, Frankfurt.

Brandts, S. 2006. Essays on risk management and insurance. Ph.D. diss., University of Frankfurt, Frankfurt.

Bühlmann, H. 1980. An economic premium principle. *Astin Bulletin* 11, no. 1:52–60.

Bühlmann, H. 1984. The general economic premium principle. *Astin Bulletin* 14, no. 1:13–21.

Cruz, M. 2002. *Modeling, measuring and hedging operational risk.* New York: John Wiley & Sons.

Delbaen, F., and J. Haezendonck. 1989. A martingale approach to premium calculation principles in an arbitrage-free market. *Insurance: Mathematics and Economics* 8, no. 4:269–277.

European Commission. 2002. Working document of the Commission Services on Capital Requirements for Credit Institutions and Investment Firms. Brussels: European Commission.

Froot, K. 2001. The market for catastrophe risk: A clinical examination. *Journal of Financial Economics* 60, nos. 2–3:529–571.

Gerber, H., and E. Shiu. 1994. Option pricing by Esscher transforms. *Transactions of the Society of Actuaries* 46, no. 2:99–140.

Goovaerts, M., F. deVylder, and J. Haezendonck. 1984. *Insurance premiums.* Amsterdam: North Holland.

Joint Forum. 2003. *Operational risk transfer across financial sectors.* Basel, Switzerland: Basel Committee on Banking Supervision.

Jones, D. 2000. Emerging problems with the Basel Accord: Regulatory capital arbitrage and related issues. *Journal of Banking & Finance* 24, nos. 1–2:35–58.

Kuritzkes, A., and B. Ziff. 2004. Operational Risk: New approaches to measurement and modeling. *MMC Viewpoint* 18, no. 2:1–9.

Lewis, C., and Y. Lantsman. 2005. What is a fair price to transfer the risk of unauthorized trading? A case study on pricing operational risk. Working paper, Fitch Risk Management, Greenwich, CT.

Matten, C. 2000. *Managing bank capital.* Chichester, UK: John Wiley & Sons.

Muermann, A. 2001. Valuation in integrated financial and insurance markets. Working paper, Vienna University, Vienna, Austria.

Muermann, A. 2003. Actuarially consistent valuation of catastrophe derivatives. Working paper, Vienna University, Vienna, Austria.

Risk Management Group. 2001. *The regulatory treatment of operational risk.* Basel, Switzerland: Basel Committee on Banking Supervision.

Risk Management Group. 2006. *International convergence of capital measurement and capital standards: A revised framework.* Basel, Switzerland: Basel Committee on Banking Supervision.

Working Group of the Insurance Companies. 2001. *Insurance of operational risk under the New Basel Capital Accord.* Basel, Switzerland: Author.

Issues in Operational Risk Regulation and the Fund Industry

CHAPTER 17

Toward an Economic and Regulatory Benchmarking Indicator for Banking Systems

John L. Simpson, John Evans, and Jennifer Westaway

ABSTRACT

This chapter expands a basic benchmark model for systemic regulatory capital introduced by Simpson and Evans (2005). The approach extends control for country risk factors. The importance of underpinning a modern banking system with low levels of country risk through a sound legal framework and financial infrastructure is reiterated. While an international central bank function is not proposed, it is maintained that policymakers will be able to apply an improved benchmark of systemic regulatory capital to ensure their banking system remains internationally competitive. Regulators may be able to use the model to revise the capital adequacy of banks within systems.

17.1 INTRODUCTION

Banking systems play a key role in global trade and in the economic health of countries. Banking markets are also important components of stock markets. At a fundamental level, banks provide the activity for the borrowing and lending of funds and the transfer of ownership of claims within the financial system of a country (Tunstall 2005). From an international perspective, banks provide the mechanism for the transfer of funds across national borders, thus facilitating global trade. As a consequence, financial markets have become more integrated and thus susceptible to cross-border volatilities, which can undermine economic stability. Country risk, with its financial, economic, and political components, influences the performance of economies and their banking and financial systems (see, e.g., Simpson 2007).

17.2 IMPORTANCE OF A SOUND LEGAL FRAMEWORK

Banks are subject to considerable legal regulation, particularly in the area of capital adequacy. As suggested in this chapter, the amount of regulation can impact a bank's performance profile. Countries with advanced levels of legal regulation and capital adequacy implementation in their banking systems are more likely to have lower levels of country risk. However, if regulation is equally stringent for both low- and high-risk banks, competitive positions are distorted. According to Smith (1992), it cannot be disputed that regulation is necessary to ensure the integrity of financial markets, by both preventing and deterring fraudulent and other illegal conduct by participants in the sector and by ensuring that banks implement adequate and effective risk management practices that address such risks as liquidity as well as efficiency.

It is, however, important to note that there are significant legal complexities in regulating financial markets, and they vary in impact on the banking sector. National banking regulatory laws are designed primarily to protect the integrity and financial stability of the local financial system, thus addressing the economic stability of the nation. Furthermore, such laws allow for private persons affected by improper conduct on the part of a bank to pursue legal redress in the form of compensation. The international picture is of course different from that of domestic banking. The recent collapse of the subprime mortgage market in the United States and the "rogue dealer" problem in equity futures markets in France demonstrates that systemic risk remains in international banking and financial markets.

This chapter identifies the concept of financial contagion through interdependence. In order to address this risk, there must be international legal cooperation between national regulators through the use of mutual arrangements. A number of countries have passed legislation addressing international cooperation, including the United States with the International Securities Enforcement Cooperation Act of 1990 (USA), the United Kingdom with the Financial Services Act of 1986, and Australia with the Mutual Assistance in Business Regulation Act of 1992. What is significant about the introduction of such legislation, however, is that while it identifies that cooperation is necessary, regulatory problems are created with respect to the identification and management of cross-border banking activities.

It is wrong to assume that cross-border misconduct is the only legal issue that needs to be addressed. National regulators of banking systems are by necessity primarily concerned that their banking system is fair, risk averse, and transparent, thus maintaining integrity. Most important, both domestically and internationally, is that legislators create a level playing field in terms of capital adequacy. Governments create the legislation that creates the legal regulatory framework under which their national regulators operate. However, national regulators cannot regulate their respective banking sectors without being impacted by international issues, which do not necessarily involve misconduct but may be the result of poor management or risk assessment practices. The legal framework in which national regulators operate must therefore include a comprehensive multilateral strategy that not only addresses bank safety at a national level but also systemic risk arising out of the interdependence of banks within and outside the domestic system.

In summary, the purpose and motivation for this chapter is to arrive at a benchmark for regulatory capital for a banking system, based on market returns with controls implemented for country risk and interdependence of banking systems. Such a benchmark can assist policymakers to ensure their banking systems are internationally competitive. Regulators could also use the benchmarks as guidelines for the honing of capital adequacy guidelines of banks within their systems.

The expanded model assumes that banking markets possess a reasonable degree of informational efficiency, that banking systems on average are at least adhering to similar risk-weighting mechanisms for the calculation of Tier 1 and Tier 2 capital, and that the most important business risk is market risk interacting internationally with country risk. Another assumption is that valuable and comprehensive information on which to base a regulatory capital benchmark is embedded in the values of banking system stock market indices.

17.3 LITERATURE ON STOCK MARKET RETURNS AND COUNTRY RISK

According to various authors (e.g., Bourke and Shanmuggam 1990; Simpson 2002), country risk is the risk that a country will be unable (economic and financial components) or unwilling (political components) to service its external debt. Due to the economic importance of banks, country risk is closely related to international banking risk. Because of the interdependence of the major international banks through interbank lines of credit and cross shareholdings, it is possible that the failure of one bank could lead to a chain reaction failure of other banks and eventually to widespread international financial instability (Simpson, Evans, and Di Mello, 2005).[1]

This risk is labeled systemic risk. Central bank functions, apart from those of implementing monetary and exchange rate policies, are directed to impose regulatory costs on banks in the form of capital adequacy as a safety valve for the prevention of the manifestation of systemic risk. Various authors have also established that there are strong relationships between stock markets and country risk. Banking markets are important components of stock markets, as recently demonstrated in the contagion arising out of the subprime mortgage market in the United States.

Studies such as those of Holthausen and Leftwich (1986), Hand, Holthausen, and Leftwich (1992), and Maltosky and Lianto (1995) argue that sovereign risk rating downgrades were informative to equity markets, but upgrades did not supply markets with new information. Cantor and Packer (1996) examined a sample of developed and emerging markets over the period 1987 to 1994 and found that sovereign risk ratings had a significant impact on bond yield spreads. Erb, Harvey, and Viskanta (1996) discuss the importance of an understanding of country risk for investors. They found that country risk measures are correlated with future equity returns but financial risk measures reflect greater information. They also found that country risk measures are also highly correlated with country equity valuation measures and that country equity value-oriented strategies generated higher returns. Diamonte, Liew, and Stevens (1996) used analysts' estimates of country risk to show that country risk represents a more important determinant of stock returns in emerging than in developed markets. They also found that over the past 10 years, country risk had decreased in emerging markets and increased in developed markets. They speculated that if that trend continued, the differential impacts of country risks in each of those markets would narrow.

Specifically in regard to the Asian currency crisis, Radelet and Sachs (1998) suggest that country/sovereign risk ratings agencies were too slow to react. When they did react, these authors suggest that their ratings intensified and prolonged the crisis.

Ferri, Liu, and Stiglitz (1999) argue that the ratings agencies behaved in a procyclical manner by upgrading country/sovereign risk ratings during boom times and downgrading them during crises. Hooper and Heaney (2001) studied regionalism, political risk, and capital market segmentation in international asset pricing. They conclude that multi-index models should be tested that incorporate a regional index, an economic development attribute, commodity factors, and a political risk variable in order to price securities more effectively.

Brooks, Faff, Hillier, and Hillier (2004) argue that equity market responses to country/sovereign risk ratings changes revealed significant responses following downgrades. Hooper, Hume, and Kim (2004) found that ratings agencies provided stock markets and foreign exchange markets in the United States with new tradable information. Ratings upgrades increased stock market returns and decreased volatility significantly. These authors also discovered significant asymmetric effects of ratings announcements where the market responses were greater in the case of ratings downgrades. However, Busse and Hefeker (2005) explored the connection among political risk, institutions, and foreign direct investment flows. They found that government stability, the absence of internal conflicts and ethnic tensions, basic democratic rights, and the ensuring of law and order are highly significant determinants of foreign investment flows.

The evidence is mixed, but most points to country/sovereign risk having a significant relationship with stock market returns. Because of the strong connection between country risk and international banking risk, it is likely that country risk will also have an effect on banking system returns. Thus, a country risk variable needs to be included in any new benchmarking model.

17.4 MARKET RISK AND ECONOMIC CAPITAL

Most financial economists, professional bankers, and banking regulators agree or at least accept that banks, because of their uniqueness and economic importance, require a degree of regulation in the form of regulatory capital. However, if regulation is too stringent, banking business incentive is destroyed. If too lenient, financial system safety, both domestic and international, is threatened (Simpson and Evans 2005).

According to Bessis (2002; cited in Simpson and Evans 2005), banking risk has involved the conceptualization of banking risks, such as market risk,[2] liquidity risk, credit risk, and operational risk. There are many issues involved in the measurement of market risk (Dowd 2002; cited in Simpson and Evans 2005). Should historical simulation or parametric value at risk (VaR) be used? If the latter, do we estimate with normally distributed profits and losses or with normally distributed arithmetic means? Do we estimate with lognormal VaR? How do we estimate expected tail loss? Clearly these are technical issues that require technical knowledge, expertise, and time if the analysis is to be at all worthwhile (Simpson and Evans 2005).

Bankers may also argue that there have been few bank burials over the past two decades, so why increase regulation and its associated costs? Of course a balanced view is required in this most important of financial and economic issues. Banks essentially borrow from the public and business unsecured at comparatively lower costs of funds than other financial intermediaries and corporate entities. They have, by definition, high debt to equity ratios. They do borrow short to lend long, treating core demand deposits as a long-term source of funds (Greenbaum and Thakor 1995). This is fine if the bank is perceived as being safe.

The concept of a social contract is of course underpinned by sound legal and financial infrastructure, as discussed in the previous sections. The perception of bank safety emanates not only from adherence to and enforcement of a strongly developed legal framework but also from the level of regulatory capital required. This safety valve is needed in the event of a bank run, the withdrawal of interbank lines of credit, or the losses that may arise due to poor credit risk management and assessment resulting in unsustainable levels of nonperforming loans. Governments and the public do not happily accept taxpayer-funded bailouts of troubled banks. Moreover, the moral hazard dilemma has proven to be a problem for banking systems where risk-taking banks write riskier business to improve expected returns. Shareholders need comfort in the face of higher regulatory costs. Banks of course are well aware that government bailout is available if they fail due to high bad and doubtful debt levels.

Bank regulators have in the past quite rightly focused on market risk (BIS 2002), but they have ignored the performance of banks in achieving optimal risk/return profiles. Regulators have also largely ignored the systemic risk[3] arising out of the interdependence of banks within and outside of systems, and they have failed to take country risk into account. A combination of all of these factors produces obvious threat of financial contagion.

A recent view of the regulators is that VaR models used to calculate regulatory capital, either formulated by the central bank or by the banks themselves with central bank approval, need to incorporate operational risk along with credit risk. The former risk largely arises out of bad luck or bad management. The question remains as to how accidents or natural disasters or management incompetence can be modeled, which could create more complexity in an already complicated framework. As mentioned, this chapter takes the view that operational risk and credit risk should be accepted as normal business risks for any corporation and should not require the holding of additional Tier 1 or Tier 2 capital. If markets are at least weak-form efficient, then market risk is the main risk that needs to be addressed. In addition, a less complex and fairer regulatory system would provide a disincentive for the practice of regulatory capital arbitrage by banks within systems.

Besides producing a tool for comparing systemic competitiveness, the notion of an appropriate theoretical level of a regulatory capital (i.e., a benchmark for appropriate systemic regulatory capital) also can produce a starting point for improving the formal regulation of banks within that system. The basis for this argument lies in the very strong relationship among the economic, financial, and political riskiness of countries and thus the riskiness of banks within those countries. Risk ratings agencies, such as Standard and Poor's and Moody's, provide country risk and international bank risk scores based on economic and financial data. Composite economic, financial, and political risk scores are provided by organizations such as the International Country Risk Guide (ICRG, 1995). There is a significantly high positive correlation between the risk scores of countries and the international banking risk scores of banks within those countries (Simpson 2002).[4]

This chapter is also motivated by a desire to simplify a complex framework that has been lacking in the historical one-size-fits-all approach to regulation. The central issues addressed are: How can systemic economic capital (the upper bound of expected negative returns for a bank system) be reasonably and easily calculated? How can regulators clearly gauge the performance characteristics of their banking systems compared to other bank systems? How can a system's economic capital be adjusted according to the risk/return profile, changes in country risk, and the degree of interdependence of its banking and financial system with other systems? Will that adjustment and resultant systemic benchmark be useful to regulators and policymakers to gauge comparative advantage and international competitiveness of bank systems? Can such a systemic model later be adapted to ascertain fair levels of regulatory capital for banks within financial systems?

To expand these issues, it is necessary to appreciate that it is a system, rather than a bank within a system, that is the starting point for analysis. In addition, a benchmark for comparison is proposed rather than legislation on systemic capital adequacy. A systemic capital adequacy benchmark would mean that a banking system or, rather, all banks within that system are holding a certain average percentage of their loan assets in prime liquid assets, such as deposits with the central bank or government securities with a short time to maturity. Thus, the underlying assumption must be that all banks within a system and internationally between systems are accurately valuing and thus risk weighting their loan and other assets in a conservative and uniform way.

17.5 SYSTEMIC EARNINGS AT RISK MODEL

According to Simpson and Evans (2005), the analysis first needs to capture the dispersion (volatility) of bank stock returns in a system over time. Volatility can be used as the unit for measuring systemic economic capital. The effect on the banking system of market risk can then be investigated. The distribution of bank stock index returns can be taken as a proxy for market random earnings over a short time period.

As noted earlier, the effect of credit risk of the banking system is not taken into account in this model because it is assumed that the distribution of earnings for the system will be highly asymmetrical, as is the case with earnings affected by credit risk in individual banks within the system. In any case, credit risk could be assumed to be part of the normal business risks of banking, as is operational risk and just as this is the case for other unregulated corporate entities. Over the centuries banks have evolved superior credit risk assessment and credit risk management skills in their prime function of lending money, and they do possess a comparative advantage in terms of narrowing the borrower/lender informational asymmetric gap.

One other drawback of earnings at risk models relates to the fact that trends of time series can themselves increase volatility if the series is time dependent. However, as explained in Simpson and Evans (2005), confidence intervals, assuming a normal distribution, are simply multiples of the downside volatility of the systemic earnings distribution. The upper bounds of negative deviations corresponding to the confidence intervals correspond to deviations from the mean of the distribution. The characteristic of loss distributions is that they have fat tails, which are the extreme sections of the distributions. The fat tails indicate that large systemic losses, although unlikely because their probabilities remain low, still have some likelihood of occurrence that is not negligible. The fatness of the tail refers to the nonzero probabilities over the long end of the distributions.

The essence of a systemic earnings at risk model is that economic capital can be taken as the amount that losses of earnings in a system are unlikely to exceed. The problem here is that a uniform confidence level guideline for all systems needs to be set by regulatory authorities so that comparisons are meaningful. Thus, the first step in the construction of the model is to provide for the calculation of a systemic benchmark for economic capital, taking the foregoing factors into account and especially setting appropriate standard confidence levels across bank systems.

17.6 INTERNATIONAL COMPARATIVE ADVANTAGE IN BANKING SYSTEMS

As discussed, when implementing techniques based on confidence levels, there is a need for a benchmark for the bank systems involved. When there is a tight confidence interval, the earnings at risk (or the upper bound of systemic losses of earnings) could be so high that bank transactions in and between systems would soon become limited by authorizations or not feasible at all. If globally competing systems use different confidence intervals in the same model, such internationally regulated systems would not operate on equal terms.

Tighter confidence intervals will reduce the volume of transactions in that system relative to another system and reduce the volume of business. Other systems would have comparative advantage. Regulators and policymakers in a system must be aware of this loss of international banking competitiveness as much as they are aware of the need for adequate regulatory capital for safety-valve reasons for banks within systems.

Addressing all risks results in the problem of overregulation and complexity with the current and proposed regulation. The measuring of international competitiveness of bank systems becomes an onerous task due to this complexity and because of country differences and banking system interdependence. A more straightforward model to be used for systemic benchmarking is desirable.

17.7 MODEL AND METHODOLOGY

As explained in Simpson and Evans (2005), after providing the machinery to estimate a system's benchmark economic capital, the expanded model takes into account the performance of and the correlation between the performances of different systems after controlling for country risk in each bank system. Country risk scores are included in the calculation of returns because the country has a strong relationship with the quality of the system's legal framework and financial infrastructure.

As mentioned, normal business risks (namely credit risk and operations risk) are assumed to be immediately reflected in the banking market data. This is in accordance with the efficient market hypothesis originally put forward by Fama (1976; cited in Simpson and Evans 2005). Market risk is referred to in portfolio theory by Markowitz (1952; cited in Simpson and Evans 2005). This component of total risk is unavoidable and thus is undiversifiable and is measured by a beta, which originally described the strength of the relationship between the returns of a security and the returns of the overall market.

A lower value of beta (say less than 1) for a bank system does not always mean low total riskiness of that system. The beta captures the market risk of the banking system. The other component of total risk in portfolio theory is unsystematic risk or, in the case of our example, bank system–specific or banking system idiosyncratic risk. This risk is avoidable through diversification, a common bank risk management practice.

The model also controls for the measurable part of country risk. Country risk can be proxied by composite risk scores for economic, financial, and political risk components from major risk ratings agencies such as the ICRG. Therefore, the country risk contribution to systemic returns will be an improvement of explanatory power. This reduces the size of the error term the balance of which remains as unsystematic or diversifiable risk.

Using entirely market-generated data in the returns of a banking system index and the risk-free rate applicable in the country of that system as well as the beta for that system, a bank system performance indicator (adapted from the performance index for securities by Treynor 1965)[5] is formulated. It describes a system's level of market risk and risk/return performance.

Models for a single banking system, two interacting bank systems, and more than two interacting systems can be developed. The data can be embodied in a final number to be used as an indicator of the overall economic and financial health of a banking system, and comparison can be made with the health of other systems. In addition, the level of economic capital for a bank system can be modified by the banking system performance indicator (BI) to arrive at a systemic benchmark level of capital adequacy.

17.8 ECONOMIC AND REGULATORY CAPITAL MODEL

The expansion, based on the original model, is described next.

17.8.1 Systemic Economic Capital

Readers are advised to review the section on systemic earnings at risk. The first step is to calculate economic capital for each bank system by applying confidence intervals to a distribution of bank stock index returns. Here random returns are generated between best- and worst-case scenarios for a bank system over some historical period, confidence levels are applied, and the upper bound of losses or negative returns is identified.

17.8.2 Market Risk for a Single Banking System

After economic capital is estimated, reversion is made to an entire distribution of random excess returns between best- and worst-case scenarios over the same period. The market risk (beta) can then be calculated using a basic market model. Market models for each of the bank systems that are being compared are analyzed to arrive at respective betas.

$$R_{i_t} = \frac{P_{i_t} - P_{i_{t-1}}}{P_{i_{t-1}}} \tag{17.1}$$

where $\quad R_{i_t}$ = return in the banking index for banking system (i) at time t

$P_{i_t}, P_{i_{t-1}}$ = values of the banking system (i) index at times t and t–1

$$R_{m_{i_t}} = \frac{P_{m_{i_t}} - P_{m_{i_{t-1}}}}{P_{m_{i_{t-1}}}} \tag{17.2}$$

where $\quad R_{m_{i_t}}$ = return on the stock market index for the country of banking system (i) at time t

$P_{m_{i_t}}, P_{m_{i_{t-1}}}$ = values of the stock market index for the country of banking system (i) at times t and t–1.

In a basic market model,

$$R_{i_t} = \alpha_{i_t} + \beta_{i_t}(R_{m_{i_t}}) + e_{i_t} \tag{17.3}$$

In this model, part of the error term is comprised of other factors that impact bank system returns, and some of these factors will be reflected in country risk scores. The model can thus be respecified for measurable components of country risk in economic, financial, and political risk scores to take these factors into account to explain a greater proportion of the returns variable. This process reduces the size of the error.

$$R_{i_t} = \alpha_{i_t} + \beta_{1_{i_t}}(R_{m_t}) + \beta_{2_{i_2}}(\Delta CR_{i_t}) + e_{i_t} \tag{17.4}$$

where α_{i_t} = regression intercept for banking system (i) at time t

$\beta_{1_{i_t}}$ = regression coefficient or measure of market risk for banking system (i) at time t and where $\beta_i > 0$

$\beta_{2_{i_t}}$ = coefficient for the change in country risk in banking system
(i) at time t

ΔCR_{i_t} = change in the country risk score in banking system (i) at
time t and where $\beta_{i_2} > 0$

e_{i_t} = residual or error term for banking system (i) at time t

Positive betas are assumed.[6] The banking system and change in country
risk betas will measure how closely the banking industry and the influence
of country risk on that system has followed the movements of the stock
market in the country of that banking system on average over long periods
of time. The market risk beta is calculated using past performance in the case
of the banking system and historical risk scores in the case of country risk.[7]

17.8.3 Performance in a Single Banking System

As adapted from Treynor (1965; see footnote 13 on Treynor's index), the
performance for a single system is:

$$BI_{i_t} = \left[\frac{R_{i_t} - R_{f_{i_t}}}{\beta_{i_t}} \right] \tag{17.5}$$

where BI_{i_t} = banking system performance indicator for a bank system (i)
at time t

R_{i_t} = return of the bank share price index for banking system (i) at
time t

$R_{f_{i_t}}$ = risk-free rate for country of banking system (i) at time t

β_{i_t} = average of the market risk and country risk coefficients (betas)
for banking system (i) at time t and where $\beta_i > 0$

17.8.4 Interdependence of Two Bank Systems

$$y_{i_{jt}} = X_{ij_t} \rho BI_{i_{jt}} \tag{17.6}$$

where $y_{i_{jt}}$ = interdependence measure of banking system (i) when it in-
teracts with bank system (j) at time t

X_{ij_t} = average weighting reflecting the ratio of the market capitalization of banking system (i) to the market capitalization of
bank system (i) plus that of banking system (j) at time t

$\rho BI_{i_{jt}}$ = correlation between the bank system performances of banking systems (i) and (j) at time t

17.8.5 Regulatory Capital for a Banking System Interacting with One Other Bank System

$$RC_{i_t} = (EC_{i_t} - BI_{i_t}) + y_{i_{j_t}} \qquad (17.7)$$

where RC_{i_t} = regulatory capital of banking system (i) at time t
       EC_{i_t} = economic capital of banking system (i) at time t

Note: Banking system performance (BI) is a reward that needs to be deducted from economic capital to reduce regulatory capital. Interdependence (y) is a penalty that needs to be added to economic capital to increase regulatory capital. In an environment where few banking systems interact with the system being benchmarked, the greater interdependence (the greater the threat of financial contagion), the greater the systemic risk in that system.

17.8.6 Interdependence in a Model for a Banking System Interacting with More than One Other Banking System

$$y_{i_{1-n_t}} = (X_{i1_t}\rho BI_{i1_t} + X_{i2_t}\rho BI_{i2_t} + X_{i3_t}\rho BI_{i3_t} + \dots X_{in_t}\rho BI_{in_t})/n$$
$$(17.8)$$

where $y_{i_{1-n_t}}$ = banking system (i) interacting with (1 to n) banking systems at time t

$X_{i_{1-n}}$ = average weighting; it is the average ratio of market capitalization of banking system (i) over the market capitalization of banking system (i) plus that of banking systems (1 to n) at time t

$\rho BI_{i1}, \rho BI_{i2},$
$\rho BI_{i3} \dots \rho BI_{in}$ = correlations of performance indicators for banking system (i) against those for banking systems 1 to n at time t (Recall these performance indicators have been adjusted for country risk because of the controlling for this factor in the returns model.)

n = number of banking systems that interact with banking system (i)

17.8.7 Regulatory Capital for a Banking System Interacting with More than One Other Banking System

$$RC_{i_{1-n_t}} = (EC_{i_t} - BI_{i_t}) + y_{i_{1-n_t}} \qquad (17.9)$$

where $RC_{i_{1-n_t}}$ = regulatory capital for banking system (i) interacting with banking systems $1-n$ at time t

17.9 DISCUSSION

The economic capital for any banking system is a worst-case scenario for losses for that system. In the model presented (see Table 17.1), economic capital for a banking system is adjusted down according to performance (with control for country risk in that banking system) and up in accordance with the degree of interdependence with other banking systems to arrive at an appropriate level of regulatory capital for that system.

Note: Regulatory capital for ease of explanation for each system is assumed to be no greater than 8%.

When the model is expanded to contain more than two country banking systems, average weighted correlation coefficients between banking systems are considered and Equation 17.7 can be applied. The weighting is in accordance with market capitalization of banking systems. A system with a higher average weighted correlation coefficient for performance will receive a higher upward adjustment of economic capital and therefore regulatory capital, as a penalty for increased systemic risk due to higher interdependence of that system with the other systems.

For example, if bank system (i) interacted with more than one other banking system with a weighted average performance correlation with the other systems of say 0.25%, then the regulatory capital for (i) should be increased by 0.25%. If the weighted average performance correlation for another bank system (j) interacting with these other banking systems was lower at 0.04%, then the upward adjustment to capital adequacy would be less at 0.04%, as there is lower systemic risk (interdependence) involved with bank system (j).

17.10 CONCLUSION

The purpose of this chapter is to provide an improvement to the systemic benchmarking model for regulatory capital proposed by Simpson and Evans

TABLE 17.1 Steps for the Calculation of Systemic Regulatory Capital (Hypothetical Data)

Steps for calculating systemic regulatory capital of banking system (*i*) interacting only with banking system (*j*)	System (*i*)	System (*j*)	Comment 1	Comment 2	Note
1. Economic capital	9%	8%	The upper bound of expected losses (negative returns) are higher for system (*i*)).		
2. System returns	13%	7%	Banking system (*i*) is performing better in terms of returns than system (*j*).	Assume calculated from **Equation 17.4** in an equation that includes and controls for changes in country risk ratings.	
3. Risk free rate	9%	3%	Interest rate levels are higher in system (*i*).		
4. Returns margin	4%	4%	Assume for ease of analysis that both systems have a similar margin of returns above the risk-free rate.		
5. Beta	1.25	.75	Equations 17.1, 17.2, 17.3, and 17.4.	In terms of market risk and country risk, system (*i*) is riskier than the stock market in the country of system (*i*) while system (*j*) is less risky than the stock market in the country of system (*j*).	

(Continued)

TABLE 17.1 *(Continued)*

Steps for calculating systemic regulatory capital of banking system (i) interacting only with banking system (j)	System (i)	System (j)	Comment 1	Comment 2	Note
6. Performance indicator	$4/1.25 = 3.2$	$4/.75 = 5.3$	Banking system (j) has performed better than banking system (i) in terms of risk for a given level of return.	Equations 17.4 and 17.5	Note interdependence of banking systems. Equations 17.6 and 17.7.
7. Regulatory capital	$(9.00 - 3.20) + 0.25 = 6.05\%$	$(8.00 - 5.30) + 0.25 = 2.95\%$	System (j) is penalized less (has a lower level of regulatory capital) because (j) has lower economic capital (lower systemic losses) and better risk/return performance.	Equations 17.8 and 17.9.	Assume weighted correlation of banking system performances for (i) and (j) is 0.25 as calculated from Equation 17.5.

(2005). The assumptions of the model are that market risks and country risks (and the interaction of these risks between banking systems) are the most important risks to consider when bank markets are at least weak-form efficient. It is also assumed that banking systems have at least adopted Basel Accord capital adequacy guidelines and that banks within those systems are risk weighting and valuing their assets in a similar way. Normal business risks for all financial systems in credit risk and operations risk, for example, are assumed to be nonexistent.

This chapter reiterates the importance of a sound legal framework and developed financial and legal infrastructures. The aim of the chapter is to assist policymakers by providing an uncomplicated benchmark measure of systemic regulatory capital so that they may move toward a level playing field in bank systems where better-performing banking systems are not penalized to the detriment of international competitiveness. Such a bank system benchmark might also assist regulators in fine-tuning the capital adequacy requirements for banks within banking systems. All concerned need to be ever vigilant in relation to the control of systemic risk, especially in the light of recent international spillover effects in the U.S. subprime market and mortgage insurance market and in the equities futures market in the case of Société Générale.

NOTES

1. Authors such as Oort (1990) have maintained that it is due to the capital adequacy provisions of the Basel Accord being adopted by the major banking systems that systemic risk and widespread bank failures can and have been avoided.
2. According to theory (Markowitz 1952), the terms "market risk" and "systematic risk" are synonymous.
3. Systemic risk is also the risk of contagion in financial markets and arises out of interdependence or strong interrelationships between banking systems and banks within financial systems. Sell (2001) discusses the common factors in relation to financial crises in Brazil and Russia. These seemingly unrelated economies had in common large U.S. dollar debt from western banks.
4. Simpson (2002) provided a model of risk score replication of some the major risk ratings agencies for country risk as well as international banking risk. Findings were that economic forces (trade performance and external debt data) were the principal drivers of international banking risk scores by the major risk ratings organizations.
5. Treynor's performance index was applied to securities and used a risky asset's beta as the risk index rather than its standard deviation, as used by Sharpe (1966). The security's beta is the covariance of a security return and the market

portfolio return divided by the variance of the market portfolio. The numerator was the difference between the security's return and the risk-free rate.

6. This is because the higher the market risk, the greater the expected returns. In our analysis, the beta provides a measure of how risky a banking system is in relation to the overall market. Recall we are comparing a banking stock price index in a country banking system to an overall stock market index in the same country.

7. Examples of betas include: A banking system with a beta of 1.0 has tended to closely follow the overall stock market in that system over long periods of time. If the beta is greater than 1, it will mean, in this analysis, that the banking system is riskier than the system's overall market. When the beta is less than 1, the banking system is less risky than the overall market for that system.

REFERENCES

Bessis, J. 2002. *Risk management in banking.* Chichester, UK: John Wiley & Sons.

Bourke, P., and B. Shanmugam. 1990. In *Risk and international lending*, P. Bourke (Ed.), Sydney, Australia: Addison-Wesley.

Brooks, R., R. D. Faff, and J. Hillier. 2004. The national market impact of sovereign rating changes. *Journal of Banking and Finance* 28, no. 1:233–250.

Busse, M., and C. Hefeker. 2005. Political risk, institutions and foreign direct investment. HWWA Discussion Paper 315. Hamburg Institute of International Economics. http://ssrn.com/abstract=704283.

Bank for International Settlements. 2002. The New Basel Capital Accord. Consultative Document, Basel Committee on Banking Supervision, Basel, Switzerland.

Cantor, R., and F. Packer. 1996. Determinants and impact of sovereign credit ratings. *FRBNY Economic Policy Review* 2, no. 2:37–54.

Diamonte, R., J. M. Liew, and R. L. Stevens. 1996. Political risk in emerging and developed markets. *Financial Analysts Journal* 52, no. 3:71–76.

Dowd, K. 2002. *Measuring MR.* Chichester, UK: John Wiley & Sons.

Erb, C. B., C. R. Harvey, and T. E. Viskanta. 1996. Political risk, economic risk and financial risk. Fuqua School of Business Working Paper 9606, Duke University. http://ssrn.com/abstract=7437.

Fama, E. F. 1976. Efficient capital markets: A Review of theory and empirical work. *Journal of Financial Economics* 3, no. 4:361–377.

Ferri, G., L. Liu, and J. Stiglitz. 1999. The procyclical role of rating agencies: Evidence from the East Asian crisis. *Economic Notes* 28, no. 3:335–355.

Greenbaum, S. I., and A. V. Thakor. 1995. *Contemporary financial intermediation.* Orlando, FL: Dryden Press.

Hand, J., R. Holthausen, and R. Leftwich. 1992. The effect of bond rating agency announcements on bond and stock prices. *Journal of Finance* 47, no. 2:733–752.

Holthausen, R. W., and R. Leftwich. 1986. The effect of bond rating changes on common stock prices. *Journal of Financial Economics* 17, no. 1:57–89.

Hooper, V. J., and R. Heaney. 2001. Regionalism, political risk and capital market segmentation in international asset pricing. Paper presented at the AFA New Orleans meetings. http://ssrn.com/abstract=255176.

Hooper, V. J., T. P. Hume, and S. J. Kim. 2004. Sovereign rating changes—Do they provide new information for stock markets? Working Paper, University of New South Wales. http://ssrn.com/abstract=685661.

Political Risk Services Group. 1995. *ICRG (International Country Risk Guide)*. www.icrgonline.com?page.aspx?=icrgmethods.

Maltosky, Z., and T. Lianto. 1995. The incremental information content of bond rating revisions: The Australian evidence. *Journal of Banking and Finance* 19, no. 5:891–902.

Markowitz, H. M. 1952. Portfolio selection. *Journal of Finance*, 6, no. 1:1–6.

Oort, C. J. 1990. Banks and the stability of the international financial system. *De Economist* 138, no. 4:37–46.

Radelet, S., and J. Sachs. 1998. The onset of the East Asian financial crisis. NBER working paper 6680. Cambridge, MA.

Sell, F. 2001. *Contagion in financial markets*. Edward Elgar. Cheltenham, UK.

Sharpe, W. F. 1966. Mutual fund performance. *Journal of Business* 39: 119–138.

Simpson, J. L. 2002. An empirical economic development based model of international banking risk and risk scoring. *Review of Development Economics* 6, no. 1.

Simpson, J. L. 2007. Expert political risk opinions and banking system returns: A revised banking market model. *American Review of Political Economy*, University of Washington, 5, no. 3:14–33.

Simpson, J. L., J. Evans, and L DiMello. 2005. Systemic Risk in the major Eurobanking markets: Evidence from inter-bank offered rates. *Global Finance Journal*, Craig School of Business, 16, no. 2.

Simpson, J. L., and J. Evans. 2005. Benchmarking of economic and regulatory capital for international banking systems. *Journal of Financial Regulation and Compliance* 13, no. 1:99–104.

Smith, A. H. 1992. The role of practitioners and self-regulatory organisations in the regulation of financial services. Paper presented to the 17th Annual Conference of the International Organization of the Securities Commission, Washington, DC.

Treynor, J. 1965. How to rate management investment funds. *Harvard Business Review* 43, no. 1:63–75.

Tunstall, I. 2005. *International securities regulation*. Sydney, Australia: Thomson Law Book Company.

CHAPTER 18

Operational Risk Disclosure in Financial Services Firms

Guy Ford, Maike Sundmacher, Nigel Finch, and Tyrone M. Carlin

ABSTRACT

Although there have been substantial developments in financial reporting over recent years, the reporting of risk in statutory reports is still very much evolving. This comes as no surprise, given numerous definitions and subsequent measures of risk. In the financial services sector, the industry standard for risk disclosure is value at risk (VaR), but this applies only to a relatively small proportion of financial service sector risk—this being market risk in trading activities. Although operational risk has been at the core of the collapse of a number of financial services firms over recent years, there are no formal reporting standards for operational risk. Further, the Basel Committee's requirements on operational risk disclosures are qualitative. This chapter examines the structure, form, consistency, and usefulness of risk disclosures by international banks, with a primary focus on operational risk disclosures. The information uses a large sample of international banking institutions. We find that the quantity and quality of operational risk disclosures vary significantly across institutions. The disclosures are predominantly descriptive and, in their current form, of little use to users of financial statements for the assessment and comparison of risk across institutions.

18.1 INTRODUCTION

Although there have been substantial developments in financial reporting over recent years, the reporting of risk in statutory reports is still very much in its infancy. This comes as no surprise, given the difficulties involved in standardizing the definition and measurement of risk. Users of financial statements have long known that risk is a key criterion for assessing balance sheet strength and earnings quality, but finding a consistent and meaningful definition for risk, and a methodology that integrates balance sheet risk with earnings quality, has proven elusive. Textbooks proclaim that shareholders are concerned only with market risks because risks unique to a firm can be diversified away, while creditors can draw on debt ratings to gauge the potential for default over a specific horizon, and these risks are appropriately priced in the cost of capital. Although these concepts may present some comfort, the growing number of firms reaching financial distress of recent years suggests there are significant risks not being adequately captured in the cost of capital, leading to pressure for firms to disclose risk more completely and meaningfully in their financial reports. This has particularly been the case in the financial services sector, where large undercapitalized risks threaten the safety and soundness of the financial system.

There have been some initiatives in risk reporting such as the Sarbanes-Oxley Act in the United States, the COSO project on fraudulent financial reporting, the European Union's Solvency II project for insurance companies, and the Basel Committee on Banking Supervision's (BCBS) capital guidelines for financial institutions. Notably, despite the significance of operational risk in explaining the collapse of a number of financial services firms (FSFs), there are no formal accounting standards requiring disclosures on operational risks, and the Basel Committee's requirements on risk disclosure (specifically, Pillar 3) are at best qualitative. This chapter examines the form and structure of operational risk disclosures in a sample of 65 large international banks, with focus on the consistency and meaningfulness of the disclosures of the banks in the sample. In one sense, this chapter represents an audit on the state of play with respect to disclosure practices on operational risk. In another, it represents our views on what should be disclosed to external stakeholders in FSFs: systematic data on the drivers of large losses in financial services firms that are related to operational risk, where such losses have the potential to erode significant portions of the capital base of an FSF.

In the financial services sector, regulatory requirements that determine the amount of capital that a deposit-taking institution must hold against the risk in its activities have evolved to become directly linked to the concept of a specified confidence level based on a predetermined solvency standard. This is set forth by the BCBS, which reports that the most important precedent for indexing capital requirements to measures of risk is the Market Risk Amendment to the Accord of 1988, which embodies a value-at-risk (VaR) methodology to relate capital to a target level of confidence (Bank for International Settlements [BIS] 2001a, p. 33). The VaR refers to the maximum likely loss from an exposure for a given time horizon and solvency standard. The problem with the VaR approach for determining capital requirements is that the measure carries the assumption of a neutral attitude toward risk, such that large losses (being capable of causing financial distress for the reporting entity) which occur with low probability are not penalized in capital requirements more than small losses with larger probability of occurrence. Yet it is the former that have been at the core of the collapse of a number of FSFs over recent years, such as Barings Bank and the Allied Irish Banks. In banking terminology, these losses arise from operational risks.

In the next section we review recent literature on risk disclosures in FSFs. Section 18.3 examines the specific disclosure requirements under the BCBS (Pillar 3) and sets the framework for our audit of disclosure practices in the banks in the sample. Section 18.4 presents our findings and an evaluation of these findings. Section 18.5 concludes and presents our views on what information should be disclosed to enable stakeholders to better understand the potential for losses related to operational risk.

18.2 RISK DISCLOSURE STUDIES

18.2.1 Accounting Perspective

Under generally accepted accounting principles, a general-purpose financial report has the objective of providing information about the financial position, financial performance, and cash flows of an entity that may be useful to a wide range of users in making economic decisions (Statement of Accounting Concepts [SAC] 2, para. 12).

It is widely known, however, that financial reports do not provide all the information that users may need to make informed economic decisions because they largely portray the effects of past events and do not necessarily provide important nonfinancial information (SAC 2, para. 13), such as customer satisfaction levels, product quality, and meaningful information of risk. With respect to the latter, although financial reports do require estimates of risk-adjusted values (such as impaired assets) and risk captured by contingencies (such as provisions and contingent liabilities), these assessments are somewhat naive and grounded in doctrines of conservatism. For example, financial statements do not include, nor do they attempt to convey, measures of asset volatility, either individually or jointly. Since 2001,

International Accounting Standards have been refined to include disclosures on the risk of financial instruments (IAS 39), although this is only part of the full risk situation faced by most reporting entities, and there remains no generally accepted methodology for the measurement and reporting of financial risks (Benston, Bromwich, Litan, and Wagenhofer 2006, p. 285), a fact that prevents meaningful comparison across reporting entities.

18.2.2 Regulatory Studies

The central player in setting the agenda for risk disclosures in FSFs is the Basel Committee on Banking Supervision. In a 1998 paper on enhancing bank transparency, the BCBS highlights the importance for creating effective supervisory frameworks that incentivize FSFs to provide timely and accurate risk-related information (BIS 1998). The framework draws on principles of market discipline, where, in theory, FSFs that provide poor disclosures of risk will be penalized by the market in terms of lower credit ratings and higher costs of capital.

The BCBS followed up the 1998 paper with three studies of disclosures on capital and risk-related issues such as capital structure, capital adequacy, and operational risk over the period 1999 to 2001, each of which generally found improvement in the volume and quality of operational risk–related disclosures in the sample set of FSFs. The first study covered a sample of 57 internationally active FCFs operating within Basel member countries (BIS 2001b). This study found that 63% of the sample institutions disclosed information about their major operational risk types, supplemented by identification and discussion of operational risk–related factors deemed significant by the BCBS. The second study reported an increase in the number of FSFs disclosing relevant operational risk–related information to 82%, although the number of FSFs in the sample dropped to 55 banks (BIS 2002). The third study, based on a sample of 54 FSFs, found that 91% of firms in the sample provided operational risk–related information (BIS 2003b). Notably, none of these studies provides specific information regarding the type and volumes of operational risk exposures faced by the sample institutions. This may be explained, in part, by the fact that regulations regarding operational risk disclosures were not formalized until 2001, when the BCBS published its first version of the framework now known as Basel II.

In 2004, the BCBS published a study on risk disclosure practices in the banking, insurance, and securities industries, with a focus on disclosures related to market, funding, liquidity, credit, and insurance risk (BIS 2004). Operational risk, as a specific risk category, was omitted from the study. At the time of writing, it appears that the BCBS has conducted no further studies on risk disclosures by FSFs.

18.2.3 Academic Studies

In a content-based study of 300 financial and nonfinancial firms in Canada, Lajili and Zeghal (2005) find limited usefulness in disclosures related to risk. The authors are particularly critical of the lack of quantitative information on risk in the disclosures of firms in the sample. Linsley and Shrives (2005) analyze risk-reporting procedures in public firms in the United Kingdom and find in a sentence-based analysis of 79 nonfinancial firms that risk disclosures are predominantly qualitative in nature and generally lacking in terms of the quality of content. In a study of risk disclosures in 9 banks in Canada and the United Kingdom, Linsley et al. (2006) find a positive correlation between bank size and the number of risk definitions contained in annual reports, but conclude overall that statements on risk are general in nature and of little value to users of financial statements. Linsley and Lawrence (2007) reach similar conclusions in a study of risk disclosures in the annual reports of 25 nonfinancial firms.

18.3 REGULATORY GUIDELINES ON RISK DISCLOSURE

In June 2006, the BCBS published a revised version of the "International Convergence of Capital Measurement and Capital Standards," more generally known as Basel II. In seeking to harmonize and standardize the measurement and management of capital in FSFs, the BCSB adopts a three-pillar approach.

The first pillar in the BCBS framework defines regulatory capital and the constituents of regulatory capital, and establishes guidelines for determining the minimum level of capital that FSFs should hold against credit, operational, and market risk exposures. In case of capital requirements for operational risk, the BCBS distinguishes among three approaches for determining capital requirements: (1) the basic indicator approach (BIA), (2) the standardized approach (SA), and (3) the advanced measurement approaches (AMA). These approaches increase in complexity and sophistication from the BIA to the AMA, with a general principle that FSFs that adopt more sophisticated approaches should face lower capital requirements, all else being equal. A proviso is that FSFs that wish to use the SA or AMA require regulatory approval, which will be granted only if the FSFs can demonstrate to the regulator that they have fulfilled a set of qualifying qualitative and quantitative criteria.[1] The second pillar outlines principles for supervisory authorities with respect to risk management guidance, supervisory transparency, and accountability. The third pillar focuses on standardized disclosure requirements for FSFs, in keeping with the broad concept of market discipline.

The most advanced approaches for measuring operational and credit risk provide FSFs with significant flexibility in their risk assessments and capital calculation methodologies. As such, the BCBS requires in the third pillar that FSFs disclose key information on their risk exposures and the potential for large unexpected losses. The BCBS asserts that disclosures based on a common framework provide an effective mechanism for informing markets about the exposure of an FSF to various risks as well as a vehicle for enabling comparison of risk across firms (BIS 2006, p. 226).

Pillar 3 consists of two parts. The first conveys the cornerstones of the disclosure requirements and addresses issues that may arise in the implementation of disclosure standards. The BCBS recommends that general risk-related information be produced on an annual basis, specific risk-related information be produced on a semiannual basis, and items susceptible to rapid change be produced on a quarterly basis. Interestingly, the BCBS recognizes the need for FSF to protect proprietary and confidential information, making provision that such information should only be provided at a more general level. The second part of Pillar 3 describes general and specific disclosure requirements developed by the BCBS in relation to an institution's capital position and exposure to major risk types.[2] Table 18.1 summarizes operational risk disclosure requirements recommended by the BCBS.

Disclosure requirements for operational risk under the BCBS guidelines are predominantly qualitative, with the exception being capital requirements for the approach under which an FSF qualifies. FSFs are required to provide general information on risk management strategies and processes, the structure and organization of the risk management function, the scope and nature of risk reporting/measurement systems, and policies for hedging and/or mitigating risk and monitoring hedge effectiveness. For specific qualitative operational risk disclosures, FSFs are required to outline the approach used for capital assessment for which the FSF qualifies. Those FSFs that qualify for the AMA approach for capital assessment are required to disclose additional information related to internal and external factors used in the measurement approach and to describe the use of insurance for the purpose of mitigating operational risk.

18.4 STUDY OF OPERATIONAL RISK DISCLOSURES

In this study we extract and analyze operational risk-related data from the 2004, 2005, and 2006 annual reports of 65 FSFs. The sample firms operate in various countries[3] and differ in both size and the nature of their core

TABLE 18.1 Operational Risk-Related Disclosure Requirements

Capital adequacy— quantitative disclosure	Operational risk capital requirement for the approach used by the bank

General qualitative disclosure requirements[a]	Description of risk management objectives and policies, including:
	  Strategies and processes
	  Structure and organization of the relevant risk management function
	  Scope and nature of risk reporting and/or measurement systems
	  Policies for hedging and/or mitigating risk and strategies
	  Processes for monitoring the continuing effectiveness of hedges/mitigants

Specific qualitative operational risk disclosures	The approach(es) for operational risk capital assessment for which the bank qualifies.
	For AMA banks:
	  A description of the AMA, including a discussion of relevant internal and external factors considered in the measurement approach; in case of partial use, scope and coverage of the different approaches used
	  A description of the use of insurance for the purpose of mitigating operational risk[b]

[a]The general qualitative disclosure requirement is compulsory for each individual risk type.
[b]This disclosure item is a compliance requirement for obtaining regulatory approval for capital relief due to insurance (BIS 2006, p. 155).

activities. Given the predominantly qualitative nature of information required under Pillar 3 of Basel II, we adopt a content-based analysis to examine the current state of disclosure quality and to identify most commonly disclosed items. Key findings are summarized in Table 18.2.

It can be observed from Table 18.2 that approximately 50% of FSFs in the sample disclose the approach used for measuring and allocating capital for operational risk. This is surprisingly small, given the BCBS Pillar 3 requirement that for specific qualitative operational risk disclosures, FSFs have to outline the approach used for capital assessment for which the FSF qualifies. It is also noteworthy that there has been only a marginal increase in the number of FSFs disclosing information in this segment. Our research shows that while some FSFs began to disclose such information in 2005 and 2006, others discontinued providing this information. Only one FSF in the sample 65 disclosed use of the BIA.

TABLE 18.2 Operational Risk-Related Disclosures: 2004–2006

	2004	% of Sample	2005	% of Sample	2006	% of Sample	Change: 2004 to 2006
Total banks disclosing Basel II approach	32	49.23%	31	47.69%	33	50.77%	3.13%
Banks opting for BIA	0	0.00%	0	0.00%	1	1.54%	100.00%
Banks opting for SA	8	12.31%	8	12.31%	10	15.38%	25.00%
Banks opting for AMA	24	36.92%	23	35.38%	22	33.85%	−8.33%
Use of risk transfer/ mitigation	24	36.92%	16	24.62%	17	26.15%	−29.17%
Decentralized operational risk management approach	30	46.15%	28	43.08%	24	36.92%	−20.00%
Use of key research indicators and early warning systems	26	40.00%	19	29.23%	25	38.46%	−3.85%
Self-assessments	28	43.08%	30	46.15%	28	43.08%	0.00%
Internal data collection and analysis	32	49.23%	31	47.69%	37	56.92%	15.63%
Use of external data	16	24.62%	15	23.08%	17	26.15%	6.25%
Information on measurement and management: total	37	56.92%	26	40.00%	32	49.23%	−13.51%
Focus on measurement	7	10.77%	10	15.38%	18	27.69%	157.14%
Focus on management	14	21.54%	11	16.92%	9	13.85%	−35.71%
Balanced focus	16	24.62%	5	7.69%	5	7.69%	−68.75%

We find the lack of disclosure in this area of concern. It is probable that the 50% of FSFs that did not disclose their approach for measuring and allocating capital for operational risk are either not attempting to meet BCBS guidelines or are using a lower-level methodology based around the BIA. We draw this conclusion on the basis that an FSF that discloses that it is using the BIA is essentially signaling to the market that it does not have either the data or capabilities to employ more sophisticated approaches for assessing its operational risk exposures, or it does not believe it approaches would receive approval from regulators. It could be the case that disclosing the use of the BIA presents a moral hazard in the sense that reporting such information would penalize the FSF in question, and it may be considered better to disclose nothing (or report that the FSF is working toward more sophisticated methodologies) rather than highlight a potential weakness in terms of resource deficiency. A similar argument could be put forward for the low number of FSFs reporting use of the SA, which in itself represents only a small increment in the sophistication of the methodology used for measuring operational risk. Despite these arguments, and perhaps somewhat troubling, we find no evidence in the data that banks that are not disclosing their approaches are being penalized by the market in terms of lower credit ratings or higher costs of capital. It seems that market discipline is failing in this regard.

In a similar vein, it is clear from the data in Table 18.2 that the number of FSFs providing specific data on operational risk management structures and data sources is declining over the period under examination. This is counterintuitive, given the increasing focus on disclosure in a number of BCBS documents; we would expect to observe an increase in the number of FSFs disclosing information related to operational risk. Again, this could be a sign of the potential moral hazard associated with signaling less sophisticated processes and data collection. Alternatively, this could represent FSFs moving cautiously on disclosure as various jurisdictions move closer to Basel II implementation dates. We observed in the course of this study that disclosures were of higher quality in larger FSFs in Europe and the United States. In the case of the latter, this is likely to reflect the fact that only large, internationally active banks are required to comply with the Basel II framework, while other FSFs are given an option to comply with the BCBS recommendations. In other jurisdictions, we observe no tendency for larger FSFs to provide higher-quality information than their smaller peers, suggesting that most FSFs are less concerned with market discipline considerations when given the option to comply with the BCBS requirements by their respective regulators.

In 2004, 37 FSFs provided information on their operational risk measurement systems, management methodologies, or both. Most of these FSFs provide general information on the structure of the overall risk management function and how it relates to the measurement and management of operational risks. In 2005, this figure had declined to 26, and in 2006, the figure was 32. Statements about the FSFs' operational risk management objectives generally focus on loss mitigation or prevention and the strengthening of risk awareness and culture. Information on models used to manage, measure, and allocate capital against operational risks is vague. Most FSFs, however, claim to use scenario analysis. This is expected, given that scenario analysis is a qualifying criterion for the use of the AMA (BIS 2006, p. 154). Other frequently mentioned models and tools include value-at-risk calculations, scorecard approaches, loss distribution approaches, and stress testing of results. Supporting information regarding the structure, nature, or underlying assumptions of these models is not disclosed. The description of the applied models is vague, if it exists at all. Some FSFs report that operational risk is managed "using best-practice approaches"—although definition, description, or data on these approaches is not disclosed. Further, in most cases there is no explanation on how the different tools interrelate, how they are used on a firm-wide level, and how they interact with and compare to tools used for other risk types.

We find that approximately half of the FSFs have implemented regular self-assessments for business units. The most commonly stated purpose is quality assurance. In most cases self-assessments are reported to be based on questionnaires that deal with the risk exposures and the quality of processes in business units. Little information is disclosed on the content of these questionnaires or how the results might be translated into operational risk management strategies. Although the BCBS recommends self-assessment techniques, it is difficult to make judgments on the usefulness of these questionnaires without some understanding of how the outcomes are processed and implemented within the FSF. Self-assessment might be viewed purely as a compliance exercise. One problem could be potential bias in the results, given that employees are assessing the risks in their business units, which in turn could result in higher capital charges and lower potential risk-adjusted returns—resulting in lower financial remuneration in the respective units. Again, moral hazard potentially mitigates information quality.

Approximately 40% of FSFs in the sample have implemented or are in the process of developing key risk indicators (KRIs) and/or early warning signs systems (EWSs). Again, little information is provided on the type of KRIs that are being developed and their effectiveness in managing operational risk. Some FSFs state that they use KRIs to analyze trends but fail to provide further information. It is possible that the majority of institutions are still in the process of identifying objective and forward-looking risk indicators that are suitable for their institution. Some FSFs report involvement in the KRI Library and Service—an initiative that seeks to exchange information on the development and usefulness of KRIs.

We find that approximately 50% of FSFs in the sample report the collection and use of internal operational loss data. The data are used predominantly to identify the frequency and severity of particular loss events. In some cases the FSF records losses that are deemed significantly large (i.e., that exceed an institutionally set threshold). While some FSFs provide the specific dollar amount that distinguishes between significant and nonsignificant losses, none provides justification for the amount set as threshold. Further, around 30% of FSFs in the sample report the use of external loss data, mostly provided by the Operational Riskdata eXchange Association (ORX). This figure is similar to the percentage of FSFs that report using the AMA for determining operational risk capital charges and reflects the fact that the use of internal and external loss data is required to use the AMA. Despite this requirement, some FSFs convey doubt by using external loss data given that operational risk losses are viewed as highly FSF-specific. Interestingly, this is also acknowledged by the BCBS (BIS 2003a, p. 22). Further, FSF are also required under Pillar 3 to provide information about risk mitigation policies and processes implemented to monitor the effectiveness of these techniques. We find that only 24 FSF in the sample in 2004 mention the use of operational risk mitigants or transfer techniques, with insurance being the most commonly quoted tool. By 2006, this figure had dropped to 17 firms in the sample.

Table 18.3 shows the percentage of economic capital allocated for operational risk in FSFs in the sample that disclosed such information.

The data show that only 18 FSFs in 2006 disclosed the proportion of total economic capital attributed to operational risk, and this proportion varies considerably across FSFs in a range of 3.90% to 28.48%. Out of the three major risk categories discussed in the Basel II framework, operational risk carries an average value of approximately 15%, behind credit risk (55%) and market risk (18%). The remainder represents economic capital allocated for "other" types of risk, although these risks are not disclosed.

18.5 CONCLUSION

Our study examines operational risk disclosures in 65 internationally active FSFs over each of the years 2004, 2005, and 2006. We use Pillar 3 of the Basel II capital adequacy framework as a benchmark for analysis of the volume and quality of disclosures in the sample set. We draw three main conclusions for our analysis. First, we observe that approximately half of the FSFs in the sample do not meet what we would consider to be basic requirements for operational risk disclosures under Pillar 3. This is surprising, given the increasing focus on operational risk and revised capital requirements in the global banking system. Second, for those FSFs that do

TABLE 18.3   Economic Capital for Operational Risk: 2004–2006

Total Economic Capital Bank	2004	2005	2006
Deutsche Bank (Germany)	15.94%	17.67%	24.00%
HVB (Germany)	14.50%	12.80%	10.00%
Commerzbank (Germany)	13.00%	13.76%	11.36%
ABN Amro (Netherlands)	17.00%	16.00%	10.00%
Barclays (UK)	7.29%	8.16%	22.88%
BBVA (Spain)	12.00%	11.00%	11.40%
Bank of Montreal (Canada)	N/I	12.00%	26.00%
Citigroup (USA)	14.09%	13.99%	12.38%
Credit Suisse (Switzerland)	16.76%	15.44%	10.77%
Danske Bank (Denmark)	10.34%	11.76%	N/I
DZ Bank (Germany)	13.43%	12.53%	9.08%
ING Bank (Netherlands)	11.84%	12.00%	10.69%
JP Morgan Chase (USA)	12.89%	12.56%	13.87%
National Bank of Canada (Canada)	23.50%	26.40%	28.48%
Nordea Bank (Sweden)	9.00%	9.00%	9.00%
Royal Bank of Canada (Canada)	13.00%	20.67%	19.22%
SEB (Sweden)	16.89%	8.62%	7.17%
Wachovia (USA)	26.00%	24.00%	24.00%
NordLB (Germany)	N/I	N/I	3.90%
Average	**14.56%**	**14.35%**	**14.68%**
Total number of disclosures	**17**	**18**	**18**

N/I: No information was provided.

disclose information in their annual reports, we observe a lack of consistency in the quantity and quality of disclosures—something we would not have expected as regulators in various jurisdictions move the FSFs under their purview closer to implementation of Basel II. Third, and most surprising, we find a general decline in the volume of disclosures in the FSFs in the sample in the period under review, with FSFs reducing their disclosures rather than increasing them in keeping with Pillar 3. We suspect that this may be attributed to concerns over signaling effects on the part of FSFs; less disclosure is better than revealing the use of less sophisticated capital measurement and allocation methodologies and risk reporting systems. This finding suggests that the foundation upon which Pillar 3 is built—market discipline—is failing to realize its intended outcomes.

Although we find little improvement in the quality of disclosures, we are less concerned with this outcome than might be considered the case. Operational risk is broadly defined by the Basel Committee as the risk of loss arising from inadequate or failed internal processes, people, and systems or from external events. Interestingly, while this definition includes legal risk, it excludes strategic and reputational risk. As a consequence, much operational risk measurement efforts in FSFs have centered on high-volume activities, such as transaction processing. However, losses related to these activities tend to be low in financial terms and are not likely to place strains on the capital base of the bank. An examination of the causes of large financial losses in FSFs over recent years that can be linked to operational risk shows that the actions of a single individual, or a small cohort of individuals, are often at play. A common factor has been unauthorized trading or the implementation (and misrepresentation) of large, undercapitalized positions. In the majority of these cases, individuals acted in response to the incentives set before them, as reflected in the structure of their remuneration schemes. This finding suggests that operational risk—of the form likely to result in significant losses to a bank—may have as its main source poorly structured incentive and remunerations schemes in FSFs. Although an FSF may establish policies, procedures, and internal controls in an attempt to mitigate excessive risk taking on the part of individuals, this may be of limited consequence if individuals are incentivized to take risky positions that are undercapitalized through gaming or misrepresentation.

We recommend that a systematic and ongoing investigation/risk audit of the remuneration schemes employed by FSFs, including the basis for the realization of bonuses (sales targets, profit targets, market share, etc.) should be required as part of an operational risk management strategy. It appears that in many FSFs, limited assessment of the risk-adjusted performance of individuals (and the implications for operational risk) is taken into consideration when goals are established in employee compensation schemes. It is well established in the psychology literature that the reference point (or hurdle), in terms of goals or performance benchmarks, will drive the risk attitude of individuals depending on whether they perceive themselves as operating below or above the reference point. We believe that a major seed of operational risk losses is the changing risk appetite of individuals (or teams) in response to perceived performance. Large losses in Barings, Allied Irish Bank, and recently, Société Générale are testimony to this fact.

NOTES

1. Those qualifying criteria are outlined in BIS 2006, pp. 148–154.
2. These include market, credit, operational, and interest rate risk.

3. The sample institutions have their major operations in the following countries: Australia, Belgium, Canada, China, Denmark, France, Germany, Ireland, Japan, Jordan, Netherlands, Scotland, Singapore, Spain, Sweden, Switzerland, United Kingdom, and United States.

REFERENCES

Bank for International Settlements. 1998. Enhancing bank transparency. Basel Committee on Banking Supervision, Basel, Switzerland.

Bank for International Settlements. 2001a. The internal ratings-based approach. Basel Committee on Banking Supervision, Basel, Switzerland.

Bank for International Settlements. 2001b. Public disclosures by banks: Results of the 1999 disclosure survey. Basel Committee on Banking Supervision, Basel, Switzerland.

Bank for International Settlements. 2002. Public disclosures by banks: Results of the 2000 disclosure survey. Basel Committee on Banking Supervision, Basel, Switzerland.

Bank for International Settlements. 2003a. Sound practices for the supervision and management of operational risk. Basel Committee on Banking Supervision, Basel, Switzerland.

Bank for International Settlements. 2003b. Public disclosures by banks: Results of the 2001 disclosure survey. Basel Committee on Banking Supervision, Basel, Switzerland.

Bank for International Settlements. 2004. Financial disclosure in the banking, insurance and securities sectors: Issues and analysis. Joint Forum, Basel Committee on Banking Supervision, Basel, Switzerland.

Bank for International Settlements. 2006. Basel II: International convergence of capital measurement and capital standards: A revised framework—comprehensive version. Basel Committee on Banking Supervision, Basel, Switzerland.

Benston, G. J., M. Bromwich, R. E. Litan, and A. Wagenhofer. 2006. *Worldwide financial reporting: The development and future of accounting standards.* New York: Oxford University Press.

IAS 39 *Financial Instruments: Recognition and Measurement.* Available at http://www.iasplus.com/standard/ias39.htm.

Lajili, K., and D. Zéghal. 2005. A content analysis of risk management disclosures in Canadian annual reports. *Canadian Journal of Administrative Sciences* 22, no. 2:125–142.

Linsley, P. M., and M. J. Lawrence. 2007. Risk reporting by the largest UK companies: Readability and lack of obfuscation. *Accounting, Auditing & Accountability Journal* 20, no. 4:620–627.

Linsley, P.M., and P. J. Shrives. 2005. Examining risk reporting in UK public companies. *Journal of Risk Finance* 6, no. 4:292–295.

Linsley, P. M., P. J. Shrives, and M. Crumpton. 2006. Risk disclosure: An exploratory study of UK and Canadian banks. *Journal of Banking Regulation* 7, no. 3/4: 268–282.

Operational Riskdata eXchange Association. 2008, April 21. www.orx.org.

Statement of Accounting Concepts SAC 2. *Objective of General Purpose Financial Reporting*. Available at http://reference.aasb.gov.au/public_docs/concept_statements/SAC2_8-90_2001V.pdf.

CHAPTER **19**

Operational Risks in Payment and Securities Settlement Systems: A Challenge for Operators and Regulators

Daniela Russo and Pietro Stecconi

ABSTRACT

This chapter discusses operational risks in clearing and settlement systems from a regulatory, economic, and policy perspective. It provides an overview of the regulatory approaches to operational risk and explains the implications of operational risk for the good functioning of payment and settlement systems. In particular, disruption to a nonsubstitutable system reintroduces trading frictions, with potentially severe implications for the markets supported by the stricken system; the costs might be expected to be most significant and widespread in the case of large-value systems supporting activity in financial markets. For instance, Klee (2007) shows in an empirical paper that operational incidents at the member level in Fedwire can affect trading conditions in

(*Continued*)

The authors wish to thank Corrado Baldinelli, of the Banca d'Italia, and Denis Beau, of the Bank for International Settlements, for their comments on the chapter; a special thank you to Susan Germain de Urday for her valuable editorial work. The views expressed therein are solely those of the authors and do not represent those of their respective institutions.

the Fed Funds market. Given the interdependencies among the different actors of the financial system, the containment of operational risks in settlement systems is an important component of the overall financial stability enhancement action. In this vein, the authors also examine a range of policy actions that can be considered by the relevant authorities to contain these risks, such as increasing coordination between overseers and supervisors, potential specific regulatory requirements (e.g., use of stress tests), and appropriate governance arrangements of system operators (i.e., incentives to adopt necessary but costly risk management measures).

19.1 INTRODUCTION

Systemically important payment systems (SIPS), securities settlement systems (SSSs), and central counterparties (CCPs) are key parts of the global financial infrastructure, since they are the providers of fundamental services for the financial system as a whole: final transfer of funds or exchange of a currency against another currency (SIPSs), mobilization of securities both on a free-of-payment and delivery versus payment basis (SSSs) and efficient management of counterparty risk on a multilateral basis (CCP).

The smooth functioning of these systems (hereinafter collectively referred to as PCSSs) is a necessary precondition for maintaining financial stability; because of the critical functions that PCSSs play in the global financial system and because they are in most cases operating in a monopolistic situation, they must work in a safe, reliable, secure, and efficient manner in any circumstance, without sustained periods of disruption.

Like any other financial infrastructure, PCSSs are exposed to operational risk; however, due to their inherently central position in the financial system, operational problems at a PCSS may easily hamper the control or even exacerbate other types of risk (e.g., market, liquidity, or credit risk) at a scale that could pose a systemic threat. In other words, operational problems at a PCSS might—both on an intraday and end-of-day basis—lead to unexpected liquidity distributions, cause settlement delays, or cause intermediaries to rely on their collateral for interbank/central bank transactions or transfer their positions at the CCP.

In a nutshell, severe and prolonged operational disruptions at a PCSS might easily provoke significant repercussions in other parts of the payment system and even affect the smooth functioning of the underlying monetary and financial markets, as the actual experience has shown several times.

Over time, the awareness of the relevance of the various forms of operational risk in PCSSs has grown, stimulated by the evolutionary factors of these systems: the increase of their technological complexity, the growing interdependency between the various components of payment systems, and the concentration of the payment and settlement activity at few global players. This reference framework has to be put in the context of the dramatic and rapid growth in the number and value of financial transactions over the last two decades, broadly exceeding the gross domestic product growth. This trend shows no sign of slowing down.

Traditionally, the toolbox for the operational risk management in financial institutions has basically included instruments such as sound corporate governance and adequacy of financial resources, effective internal and external controls, clear policies and procedures for reporting and making decisions, investments in human resources (training and recruitment), and, eventually, robust contingency plans and backup facilities.

In the case of PCSSs, more emphasis is given to ensuring the business continuity of their services more than on the availability of capital that could act as a financial buffer, should it be necessary to withstand the losses coming from severe operational problems; this is the result of the awareness that, at least in the short term, the "exiting" option is simply not viable in most circumstances for PCSSs. In this sense, when international standards on PCSSs deal with operational risk containment, they insist on the means to prevent operational problems more than on the financial capacity of the system's operator to absorb the resulting losses.

This chapter looks at operational risk from a basically institutional standpoint; first it provides an overview of the regulatory approaches to operational risk in PCSSs; then it addresses the implications of operational risk for the good functioning of SSSs and CCPs; finally it provides some suggestions for the debate on the policy and regulatory actions to be pursued.

19.2 OVERVIEW OF THE REGULATORY APPROACHES TO OPERATIONAL RISK IN PCSSs

It has been 20 years since the first sets of international standards in the payment and settlement field were issued: the 9 G-30 Recommendations on Securities Clearance and Settlement Systems (G-30 Recommendations; Group of Thirty 1988) and the Standards for Interbank Netting Schemes (the so-called Lamfalussy Standards; Bank for International Settlements [BIS] 1990). It is remarkable that in the G-30 report no recommendation deals with operational reliability or operational risk and that in the Lamfalussy report, although operational reliability is tackled by one of the policy principles, the term "operational risk" is never used.

At that time, consistently with what could be called a risk-based approach, public authorities and the private sector focused their priorities mostly on the containment of financial risks in PCSSs, whose relevance had been dramatically highlighted by episodes such as the 1987 crash of the equities markets and the failure of the Herstatt Bank. These circumstances showed that significant credit, liquidity, and legal risks could lurk in what, until then, had appeared purely operational processes, substantially risk free or at least perceived as such.

Moreover, public authorities and the private sector faced an urgent need to enhance the efficiency of PCSSs, which relied extensively on manual interventions in processes and a large use of paper-based or voice instructions. Awareness of the relevance of operational risk containment grew over time. Soon the issue of operational reliability became a greater part of the international standards on the safety and efficiency of PCSSs; for instance, one of the Eurosystem "Standards for the Use of EU Securities Settlement Systems in ESCB Credit Operations" (European Monetary Institute 1998) deals specifically with the operational reliability requirements of systems in euro area monetary policy operations, although these standards were issued from a user perspective, not as oversight indications.

The overall reference framework for the containment of operational risk in PCSSs is to be found in the principles/recommendations issued by central banks and securities commissions in the years 2001 to 2004, specifically the 2001 CPSS Core Principles on Systemically Important payment Systems,[1] the 2001 CPSS–International Organization of Securities Commissions (IOSCO) Recommendations on Securities Settlement Systems,[2] and the 2004 CPSS-IOSCO Recommendations for Central Counterparties.[3]

This set of policy indications shares the objective of ensuring in virtually any circumstance (thus implicitly excluding the business exiting option) the operational reliability of the systems they deal with, focusing on features such as security, scalability of capacity, availability of backup facilities, and timely completion of operational processes. In this framework, operational risk is defined as "the risk of deficiencies in information systems or internal controls, human errors, management failures, or disruptions from external events such as natural disasters resulting in unexpected losses."[4]

However, some differences among these principles are to be noted:

- As far as the issue of security is concerned, the Core Principles (CP) CP VII makes a specific reference to industry standards whereas Recommendations for SSSs and CCPs do not and seem to put less emphasis on this feature.

- With regard to operational reliability, CP VII makes a reference to the level of the services the system provides for, which should be documented in service-level agreements with participants. This latter indication is not mentioned in the relevant recommendation on SSSs and CCPs.
- Only the Recommendations for CCPs (issued after the September 11, 2001, attacks) tackle the critical issue of recovery time. CP VII and Recommendations on SSSs do not mention this requirement.
- Neither Recommendations on CCPs and SSSs deals specifically with secondary sites, whereas CP VII gives some discussion of these facilities, even for those of system participants.

Most of the differences are based on their issuance at different times, reflecting different degrees of awareness of the same problems. In this sense, for instance, the Recommendations on CCPs, issued after September 11, 2001, deal with the business continuity object more extensively than the Recommendations on SSSs. Other differences may depend on efficiency considerations, such as on the willingness of regulators/overseers not to pose unnecessary burdens on systems falling within their competence.

However, considering the growing interdependence among different systems it could make sense envisaging, at least in the field of operational risk, a common set of provisions for these core infrastructures of payment systems and financial markets—not forgetting to take into account the increasing presence of straight-through-processing mechanisms in the systems' design. Furthermore, more and more a significant portion of payments and securities transfers have become remarkably time critical, which places an increasing burden on the operational reliability of all the elements of a system. Payments to CLS and posting of margins at CCPs are examples.

Turning to the regulatory approach applied to intermediaries' operational risk, differences from the PCSSs' treatment seem to reflect that, whereas for most PCSSs exiting their business is not a viable solution, the same cannot hold for most intermediaries. The regulatory approach to operational risk at intermediaries includes concepts that may not necessarily be meaningful for PCSSs, such as the availability of economic capital as a financial buffer for operational events or transferring the risk in part or in whole to others.[5]

Table 19.1 provides for a brief comparison between the Recommendations CPSS-IOSCO for SCSSs and the Basel II framework.

Although very synthetic, Table 19.1 shows that the concerns of overseers and supervisors, as well as the tools to properly address those concerns, largely overlap. The main difference in the approaches lies in the fact that, unlike PCSSs, intermediaries subject to prudential regulation may rely on

TABLE 19.1 Comparison between CPSS-IOSCO Recommendations for SCSSs and the Basel II Framework

CPSS-IOSCO Recommendation 11	Capital Requirements Directive
Sources of operational risk arising in the clearing and settlement process should be identified and minimized through the development of appropriate systems, controls, and procedures.	Policies and processes to evaluate and manage the exposures to operational risk shall be implemented.
Risk is to be minimized through adequate management controls and sufficient (and sufficiently well qualified) personnel to ensure that procedures are implemented accordingly. Risks, operational policies and procedures, and systems should be reviewed periodically and after modifications to the system.	Includes a component on control/mitigation but allows intermediaries to identify the levels of acceptable risks within the overall operational risk framework.
Information systems are subject to independent audit. System operators who outsource operations should ensure that those operations meet the same standards as if they were provided directly by the system operator.	Article 4 (22) recognizes inadequate or failed internal processes as a source of operational risk. Annex V, No. 9, 13: "Contingency and business continuity plans shall be in place."

a diversified range of instruments for managing operational risks; the same ability is not foreseen within the oversight framework of PCSSs, whose only mission is, in most cases, to deliver their payment settlement guarantee system in the safest way. But the table shows more: that intermediaries are allowed to take "calculated" risks that PCSSs cannot. This can be explained partly by the fact that, unlike PCSSs, intermediaries are charged capital requirements for operational risk purposes.

19.3 IMPLICATIONS OF OPERATIONAL RISK FOR PAYMENT, CLEARING, AND SETTLEMENT SYSTEMS

A number of developments have highlighted the need for an enhanced focus on system resilience against operational shocks. First, in the wake of 9/11 and subsequent terrorist attacks around the world, central banks, as well as participants and infrastructure providers, have become acutely aware of the potential implications of large-scale operational disruptions. As a result, there has been a redoubled effort to ensure business continuity through, for example, backup sites for systemically important infrastructures. There has also been an effort to test operational resilience against market-wide shocks of a different nature, such as the potential impact of avian flu.

Second, increasing interoperability and interdependencies between systems might expand the channels of contagion arising from operational disruption at particular infrastructures, even in a world with multiple points of failure. Central banks are currently analyzing the implications of increasing system interdependencies. These also include operational environmental interdependencies that are significant in many countries, primarily because many payment and settlement systems depend on Society for Worldwide Interbank Financial Telecommunication (SWIFT) as a message carrier. SWIFT provides network services to a large number of large-value payment systems worldwide; supports a substantial, but smaller, number of CSDs and CCPs; and plays an important role in supporting several CSD-to-CSD links. This common reliance on SWIFT as well as several other key third-party providers significantly contributes to the interdependence of operational processes of payment systems and, to a lesser extent, securities clearing and settlement systems.

Third and perhaps most important, a continuing trend toward cross-border consolidation might call for increased resilience against operational shocks—in particular, if this consolidation establishes a single point of failure or interconnected and interoperable multiple points of failure. In fact, the provision of payment and settlement services is characterized by high fixed costs and low marginal costs—and hence increasing returns to scale—and network externalities. The traditional definition of a network externality is that the consumption of a good by one agent indirectly benefits others already consuming the good. In this context, the greater the volume of trade settling through a particular system, the greater the opportunities for netting and liquidity recycling. Together, these characteristics imply a tendency toward concentrated, perhaps monopoly, provision of payment and settlement services, which can lead to single-point-of-failure risks.

In other words, faced with a prolonged disruption (or frequent disruptions) to the operation of a single provider of payment and settlement services in a particular market, users will be unable to reroute volume readily to an alternative provider. Trades may then remain unsettled for a period, either implying direct losses (e.g., where the intended recipient of funds was relying on settlement, perhaps to meet a contingent obligation) or creating unintended credit or market exposures. Alternatively, users may seek workarounds, reverting to alternative, perhaps bilateral, settlement arrangements, with attendant costs and risks. More generally, disruption to a nonsubstitutable system reintroduces trading frictions, with implications for conditions in the underlying markets supported by the stricken system. Costs might be expected to be most significant in the case of large-value systems supporting activity in financial markets. While costs might be low for short periods of disruption in stable conditions, costs could be sizable if a disruption were to occur during stressed circumstances, when the disruption might exacerbate nervousness in already uncertain markets. And with growing interdependencies between systems, both domestically and across borders, channels for cross-system spill-over in the event of a disruption have increased. Such costs might not be fully internalized by a monopoly supplier in its investment in system resilience, which may imply a role for public intervention to impose system design and resilience standards commensurate with a system's critical role.

Some of these themes were also drawn out in analytical papers presented at the conference that the European Central Bank (ECB) and the Bank of England (BoE) jointly organized on November 12–13, 2007, the proceedings of which are available on the ECB's web site. Some of the research presented at that conference also focused on the implications of operational shocks for monetary policy and financial stability. For example, research by Elizabeth Klee (2007) of the Federal Reserve Bank of New York examined empirically the impact that operational problems at commercial banks in sending Fedwire payments have on the federal funds rate. It turned out that if a bank has an operational problem and cannot send funds over Fedwire, balances become temporarily trapped in one bank's reserve account, creating aggregate uncertainty of the level of balances available in the system. Such uncertainty can affect the federal funds market if banks seek to purchase funds in the market as they become more uncertain about end-of-day balances. Indeed, the deviation of the effective rate from the target rate is positive on days with possible operational problems would result in potentially higher aggregate uncertainty. In a nutshell, central banks are very much concerned with operational reliability as operational disruptions may affect monetary policy implementation.

There is further empirical evidence that the operational reliability of payment systems and market infrastructures is crucial for financial stability and the economy at large. At the ECB-BoE research conference, a paper by Andrea Gerali and Franco Passacantando focused on the implications of the loss of confidence in bank money during the Great Depression. While bank failures that took place in the Great Depression contributed to the contraction of the money supply, bank failures also reduced the acceptability of bank money as a payment medium. The wave of bank failures increased the risk of using bank money and thus induced a loss-of-trust effect. The resulting effects on payment services—that is, the increase in transaction costs—had an impact on consumption and investment.

19.3.1 Policy Challenges

While analysis suggests that the current regulatory and operational framework is equipped with tools to adequately monitor the operational risk, there are some specific challenges that operators, overseers and regulators must cope with. In particular, we would suggest that the next points deserve further consideration.

Ensuring Consistency between Different Sets of Regulatory Standards

As mentioned earlier, the existing sets of regulatory and oversight standards such as the CPSS Core Principles and the CPSS-IOSCO Recommendations for SSSs and CCPs were developed at different moments in time, reflecting different degrees of awareness of the same problems and also showing different levels of detail. For the sake of consistency and to reflect the increasing awareness of the need to address operational risks effectively, the existing regulations should be reviewed, updated, clarified, and refined in a number of aspects, such as business continuity and disaster recovery plans, the evaluation of the reliance on third parties, time criticality and maximum recovery time, second processing sites, and outsourcing of activities.[6]

Achieving Harmonized Regulatory Standards and Their Implementation across Different Markets

Cross-border groups are increasingly integrating several business functions across borders and legal entities. Similarly, infrastructures increasingly seize business opportunity by extending services to geographic markets outside their location or by developing new products outside the traditional market segments. On a global scale, one could assume that payments and financial transactions cross a complicated mix of legal, technological, and supervisory borders in going from one end user to the other; inefficiencies or problems at one of these borders may easily lead to widespread consequences. In this context, there is a need to ensure consistency among the requirements in different markets with a view to avoiding on the one hand unnecessary regulatory burden for global players or infrastructure and on the other hand regulatory arbitrage that can lead to concentration of providers in the least protected areas. Of course, any standards, such as the CPSS Core Principles or the CPSS-IOSCO Recommendations for SSSs and CCPs, are necessarily rather generic and leave some room for discretion when applied to a specific system. The existing assessment methodologies already aim at ensuring a high degree of consistency in implementing regulatory and oversight standards, but without rigorous coordination mechanisms between the various authorities involved, inconsistencies cannot be avoided.

Risk-Based Functional Approach   The payment, clearing, and settlement industries are in a process of change. For example, the roles of banks and nonbanks are becoming increasingly blurred which raises a number of questions regarding their regulatory treatment. The role of nonbanks in payment and settlement systems was also explored at the joint ECB-BoE conference. A research paper (Occasional Paper 76) produced by the ECB together with the Fed and presented at the conference concluded, among other things, that there is an increased need for cooperation among bank supervisors, regulators, and overseers. Moreover, as the provision of services for payments and securities transactions are typically organized in tiered structures, the repartition of roles between infrastructures on the one hand and intermediaries on the other hand is evolving. In particular, the role of critical participants in payment and securities infrastructure is increasing, and inconsistency in the regulation may lead to undesired shifts of business from infrastructures to their major participants. This will call for a functional approach for operational risk. As shown in ECB Occasional Paper 76, currently oversight and regulatory requirements address the same concerns but follow different approaches both in respect to the minimization of operational risk and with reference to outsourcing. These differences in approaches must not lead to major differences in the level of protection against operational risk, since the weakness of a system often coincides with the weakness of its weakest component (or participant). Note that the functional approach to mitigating operational risks does not necessarily mean that the same set of regulatory standards for controlling operational risks should be applied to both infrastructures and intermediaries. Rather, it means that regulation should result in the same level of protection from operational risks regardless of the institutional character of the services provider.

A related issue is to what extent systems need to be protected against operational risks. In other words, the challenge for overseers/regulators will be where to draw the limit of what overseers/regulators may request from stakeholders or systems. How far is too far? Will excessive requirements lead to shifts of transactions into less protected systems?

Growing Interdependencies   Financial globalization has led to greater complexity of the financial system and a growing number of interdependencies. Interdependencies arise when settlement flows, operational processes, and risk management procedures of one system, institution, or market are related to those of other systems, institutions, or markets. Other forms of interdependencies can arise also due to the transfer of operational risks across sectors through, for example, insurance policies. While interdependencies can improve the operational safety and efficiency of payment and settlement processes, they can also allow disruptions in operations to be passed on more easily and more quickly. It is crucial for central banks, supervisors, operators, and system participants to improve their understanding of the various interdependencies among payment and settlement systems, especially in order to ensure effective risk controls to contain the potential transmission of operational risk;[7] these issues have been addressed in a recent report by the Bank for International Settlements (2008).

Emergence of Globally Systemically Important Systems   The growing level of global integration and concentration implies that a number of globally systemically important institutions and infrastructure are emerging. In the field of payment systems, oversight at the national level distinguishes systems that are systemically important from those that are not systemically important. Some thought is now required to clarify whether a similar distinction is needed in view of the risks that globally systemically important systems post to the global financial system. There may be a need for a distinct and tailor-made regulatory treatment on the basis of the risk-based functional approach. Whether this would imply raising the bar for these globally systemically important entities should also be debated.

19.4 CONCLUSION

The overall picture described shows that the issue of containment of operational risks in PCSSs is heavily influenced by the assumption that for these systems the exiting option is, at least in the short run, not a viable one.[8] Moreover, the PCSSs' functioning is normally characterized by daily and even intraday deadlines, which, if not met, may easily turn into serious liquidity problems. Against this background, looking at the issue in a simplistic way, one could easily conclude that in PCSSs, operational risks cannot be only priced, or backed by enough financial resources, or transferred to third parties (insured). Given the peculiar nature of PCSSs and their position within the financial system, their operational risks must be effectively contained to the extent possible by the maintenance of efficiency conditions.

From a general perspective, it is clear that the first line of defense against operational risks lies with the systems operator's responsibility for the design, operation, and development of the system itself. Overseers are responsible for setting an appropriate regulatory framework and carrying out controls on the systems they oversee.

Containment of operational risks is thus a multifaceted issue where several factors come into play such as, *inter alia*, the trade-off between risk and efficiency, the coexistence of public interests and private profits, and the increasing blurring of differences between intermediaries and systems. In this respect we have already mentioned some issues where actions from overseers and supervisors could achieve significant progresses: cooperation and information sharing among them, adequate consideration of the massive recourse to outsourcing by systems and growing interdependencies among them, and so on; here we intend to draw the attention of system operators and overseers to issues that pertain not to the "external" economic context but to the level at which they "internalize" the containment of operational risks.

As far as systems operators are concerned a key question could be: Are the corporate governance arrangements (including the incentives for managers) of the system's operating company/entity appropriate to the effective containment of operational risks? As pointed out in the Core Principles and Recommendations, governance arrangements for PCSSs are in general extremely important, because the economies of scale that characterize their activities may impair the forces of competition that might otherwise be relied on to ensure that they operate safely and efficiently

The importance of governance[9] arrangements appears of particular relevance when the containment of operational risks is at stake. As already mentioned, one of the most difficult issues in addressing operational risks is that the probability of occurrence of an event can be quite low while the potential loss from such an event can be very high. Large amounts of money and human resources can be spent to reduce operational risks to very low levels. But because the effort by its very nature is basically a preventive maintenance, designed to insure against outcomes that cannot be precisely measured or predicted, it is hard to make a decision where one cannot be sure that the cost is worth the benefit. These are typically high-level decisions, for which senior managers should have the appropriate incentives, in particular when the company operates on a for-profit basis, as often happens for securities clearing and settlement systems. The extensive use of stress tests, the redundancy of and easy scalability of technological infrastructures, and the availability of secondary sites are only some examples of the measures usually recommended by international principles in terms of PCSSs' operational soundness.

Operational risks containment measures need to be effective so that the system's operational reliability is given a high-level priority in a corporate governance setting as well as in the ranking of incentives provided to the management of the operating company. This is particularly important when the latter operates on a for-profit basis and, thus, economic targets might conflict with the costs of the investments necessary to make the system operationally safer. In this situation, the company's corporate governance arrangements should be able to avoid that decisions are made to significant detriment of the operational risks containment target.

This last need appears particularly relevant in case of outsourcing of activities. In this case, the decision should be made after a careful examination of the potential implications of outsourcing the operational risks containment profile of the system's operating company, which ultimately retains the full responsibility for the functioning of the PCSS. Appropriate incentives for the operating company's management may prove quite useful to ensure they make decisions based on a balanced trade-off between risk containment and economic return.[10] Whatever model of corporate governance is used in a jurisdiction, PCSSs should adopt and ensure effective implementation of high corporate governance standards or best practices adopted by or recommended for companies in the jurisdiction in which they operate. Generally, this would imply that PCSSs at a minimum should adopt and implement the best practices recommended for listed companies (Russo, Hart, Malaguti, and Papathanassious 2004).

As far as systems overseers are concerned, this chapter has provided an array of issues to be considered in terms of consistency of regulation, growing interdependencies among different component of the financial system, need for coordination, emergence of global institutions, and need for an effective cooperation between systems overseers and banking supervisors. The very fact that some policy challenges are mentioned suggests how to go forward to fill the gaps.

Here key questions to ask systems overseers could be: Are oversight procedures and resources adequate to address effectively operational risks in PCSSs? Is the gap between official written standards and concrete oversight practices misleading for the industry?

If systems operators and their critical participants are called to an increasing commitment to tackle operational risks, overseers also should devote more and more resources to deal with these issues. Asymmetries in the effort to face risks by operators and overseers may lead to a suboptimal equilibrium. In this respect, it seems advisable that overseers ask themselves whether, for example, the skills they can rely on are sufficient, the flow of information they receive from the overseen entities is complete and adequately examined, and so on. This point seems particularly important, bearing in mind the complexity of the issues at stake. All the factors at play in shaping operational risks at PCSSs call for adequate oversight staff, in terms of both number and skills.

Furthermore, overseers could ask themselves whether it is necessary or advisable to make on-site inspections at the overseen companies (assuming that the legal framework grants this power to overseers). In our opinion, overseers should make such visits, considering that in general on-site inspections enable the gathering of a lot of information and verifying *de visu* how a company actually prevents or mitigates operational risks. The policy choice for overseers here could be whether to carry out the on-site inspections directly or rely on external auditors. To summarize, the containment of operational risks in PCSSs calls for a truly proactive attitude, both from system operators and overseers; this is, we think, the challenge they face in tackling operational risks effectively.

NOTES

1. Core Principle VII: The system should ensure a high degree of security and operational reliability and should have contingency arrangements for timely completion of daily processing.
2. Recommendation 11: Sources of operational risk arising in the clearing and settlement process should be identified and minimized through the development of appropriate systems, controls, and procedures. Systems should be reliable and secure, and have adequate, scalable capacity. Contingency plans and backup facilities should be established to allow for timely recovery of operations and completion of the settlement process.
3. Recommendation 8: A CCP should identify sources of operational risk and minimize them through the development of appropriate systems, controls, and procedures. Systems should be reliable and secure, and have adequate, scalable capacity. Business continuity plans should allow for timely recovery of operations and fulfilment of a CCP's obligations.
4. Core Principle VII: The system should ensure a high degree of security and operational reliability and should have contingency arrangements for timely completion of daily processing.
5. In this sense see Basel Committee on Banking Supervision (2003, p. 11) according to which "for example, insurance policies, particularly those with prompt and certain pay-out features, can be used to externalise the risk of 'low frequency, high severity' losses which may occur as a result of events such as third-party claims resulting from errors and omissions, physical loss of securities, employee or third-party fraud, and natural disasters."
6. This ensures consistency between the official practices and the practical evolution of central banks' oversight practices.
7. As the Joint Forum pointed out in its 2003 report, "it is incumbent upon supervisors to share information across sectors to most effectively keep pace with the level of risk transfer and to monitor the risk to the financial system and to specific firms."
8. In this sense, see also McPhail (2003).

9. For the importance of the internal governance arrangements at intermediaries in managing operational risks, see also CEBS (2006).
10. Within the Basel II, it is requested that the operational risk framework incorporate techniques for the allocation of operational risk capital to major business lines and that it creates incentive to improve the management of operational risk throughout the firm. (See Basel Committee 2006.)

REFERENCES

Bank for International Settlements. 1990. Report of the Committee on Interbank Netting Schemes of the Central Banks of the Group of Ten Countries. Basel, Switzerland.

Bank for International Settlements. 2001. Core principles for systemically important payment systems. Basel Committee on Banking Supervision, Basel, Switzerland.

Bank for International Settlements. 2003a. Operational risk transfer across financial sectors. Basel Committee on Banking Supervision, Basel, Switzerland.

Basel Committee on Banking Supervision. 2003b. Sound practices for the management and supervision of operational risk. Basel Committee on Banking Supervision, Basel, Switzerland.

Basel Committee on Banking Supervision. 2006. Observed range of practice in key elements of advanced measurement approaches. Basel Committee on Banking Supervision, Basel, Switzerland.

Bank for International Settlements. 2008. The interdependencies of payment and settlement systems. Basel Committee on Banking Supervision, Basel, Switzerland.

CEBS. 2006. Guidelines on the implementation, validation and assessment of advanced measurement (AMA) and internal ratings based (IRB) approaches. London: United Kingdom.

Committee on Payment and Settlement Systems and Technical Committee of the International Organization of Securities Commissions. 2001. Recommendations for securities settlement systems. Basel, Switzerland.

Committee on Payment and Settlement Systems and Technical Committee of the International Organization of Securities Commissions. 2004. Recommendations for central counterparties. Basel, Switzerland.

European Monetary Institute. 1998. Standards for the use of EU securities settlement systems in ESCB credit operations. Frankfurt, Germany.

Gerali, A., and F. Passacantando. 2007. The loss of confidence in bank money in the great depression. Presentation at the joint BoE/ECB Conference on Financial Stability, Frankfurt, Germany.

Group of Thirty. 1988. Clearance and settlement systems in the world's securities markets. Steering & Working Committees of the Securities Clearance and Settlement Study, Washington, DC.

Klee, E. 2007. Operational problems and aggregate uncertainty in the federal funds market. Finance and Economics Discussion Series, Divisions of Research & Statistics and Monetary Affairs, Federal Reserve Board, Washington, DC.

McPhail, K. 2003. Managing operational risk in payment, clearing and settlement systems. Working paper, Bank of Canada, Ottawa, Canada.

Russo, D., G. Caviglia, C. Papathanassiou, and S. Rosati. 2007. Prudential and oversight requirements for securities settlement. Occasional paper 76, European Central Bank, Frankfurt, Germany.

Russo, D., Hart, T., Malaguti, M.C. and Papathanassious, C. (2004) Governance of Securities Clearing and Settlement Systems. Occasional Paper, no. 21, European Central Bank, Frankfurt, Germany.

CHAPTER 20

Actual and Potential Use of Unregulated Financial Institutions for Transnational Crime

Carolyn Vernita Currie

ABSTRACT

The problems of hedge funds, mortgage brokers, and finance companies have several common themes: a lack of prudential supervision; an ability to evade anti–money-laundering legislation using cross-border transactions; regulators using a common escape clause of "natural market forces"; and benefits accruing to the originators. In view of the potential of these types of nonbank financial institutions (NBFIs) to generate systemic crisis by avoiding the new operating risk requirements of Basel II, the effectiveness of the new capital adequacy regime is now highly questionable. By offering a regulatory black hole, unregulated NBFIs appear to have become the home of the new transnational criminal.

20.1 HISTORY OF THE SUBPRIME CRISIS AND THE ROLE OF HEDGE FUNDS, FINANCE COMPANIES AND PLANNERS, AND MORTGAGE BROKERS

According to a recent analysis (Pennington 2007), the subprime mortgage crisis in the United States had its roots in operational risk (OR) problems.

Although credit risk played a significant role, Pennington (2007) defines subprime mortgages as loans to consumers with low credit scores at higher interest rates than prime credits.[1] She claims that the high rate of default made in the first eight months of the loan's life is not just due to bad credit risk factors but totally to OR factors such as:[2]

1. An influx of mortgage lenders during the period 2000 to 2006[3] due to high economic growth, overcapitalization of banks, low interest rates, and rising house prices. This led to deterioration in standards relating to documentation, disclosure of the true cost of the loans, and increasingly competitive loan products, such as low interest rates for two years (ARM or adjustable rate mortgages).
2. The growth of the secondary market, whereby mortgage lenders were quick to onsell their mortgages to investment banks to be securitized, which would later help spread the systemic risk.
3. Failure to price for volatility and risk leading to incorrect interest rate calculations.
4. Relationship problems intertwined with questionable corporate governance practices at the top of the firm making the primary transaction.
5. Staff hired with insufficient or no training, as the industry expanded quickly (finding of Walzak Risk Analysis quoted by Pennington 2007, p. 37).
6. Fraud was also an issue: "[E]ither from external parties such as brokers seeking to push loans through, or from borrowers who take advantage of the (meager) documentation and stressed system to tender fraudulent applications" (Pennington 2007, p. 37).
7. Unscrupulous underwriters, brokers, and financial planners who were incentivized and in some cases forced by their employers to push through questionable mortgage applications or originators who exaggerated the income of clients to allow them to qualify for the loan.[4]
8. Lack of diversification of the loan portfolios of the mortgage lenders.
9. Slack controls by the mortgage insurers, such as Fannie Mae and Freddie Mac.
10. Lack of stress testing models with an integrated risk management system, which could have softened the crisis through anticipation, hence setting risk management in process well before the crunch.

Although the government of the United States has put in place several measures to help the mortgage industry—namely mitigation programs to curb foreclosures—the fallout has spread globally through the investment banks that lent to and created the brokers, through the finance companies and hedge funds lending and investing in the subprime sector. Examples are Bear Stearns and Goldman Sachs—the former selling off large tranches of High-Grade Structured Credit Strategies Enhanced Leverage Funds, and other funds backed by subprime mortgages, which was insufficient to prevent the companies from being placed under an official rescue program. Many other international banks that were lending to mortgage lenders, finance companies investing in property, and hedge funds specializing in subprime mortgages have experienced a similar run on their share price. The Swiss bank UBS is closing its Dillon Road Capital Management hedge fund following a loss of US$123 million.

The long-delayed introduction of Basel II, introducing new credit and OR standards for banks, was caused by the very U.S. regulators who are now having to deal with the results of their own prevarications and stalling mechanisms. Until recently, the Federal Reserve after lobbying by the banking industry adopted the line that Basel II in its most advanced form was to be applied only to the largest four banks. As recently as June 2007, a senior U.S. regulator was reported as saying that "divergence between the U.S. plan to implement Basel II and the original version of the Accord being adopted internationally will not unfairly disadvantage American Banks" ("Basel II will not harm" 2007). Only one month later, a leading Reuters journalist (Atkins 2007) slammed Basel II for its regulatory deficiencies, loopholes, and black holes:

> *Shock losses at some of the world's biggest banks have left some people asking whether new global bank risk rules have failed their first test of fire. So as big banks line up to reveal massive losses on risky investments, critics are asking aloud whether the Basel accord rewrite—the biggest change to global banking rules in a generation—has failed before it has started. "Questions are being raised whether Basel II is out of touch with the markets," said analyst Luis Maglanoc at bank UniCredit in a recent note. Banks have been preparing for its implementation for years. Yet it appears that the Basel II framework has been limping behind the innovative power of the structured credit markets.*

Another major contributor to the accompanying fallout of the subprime crisis in the United States was the role of commission-based financial planners.

20.2 CURRENT PRUDENTIAL REGULATORY SYSTEM GOVERNING NBFIs

The resulting fallout from the subprime credit crisis on hedge funds, and the secondary effect on the whole mortgage lending and property finance industry, has revealed preexisting flaws in the regulatory models governing a country's financial system. That is, these NBFIs escape the regulatory controls such as the OR requirements of Basel II. Given this situation, it is not surprising that the subprime crisis spread, affecting the ability of property financiers to borrow in the wholesale market and thus spreading contagion in a secondary effect to related sectors. The principal role of hedge funds in this crisis merits examination.

20.3 ROLE OF HEDGE FUNDS

The term "hedge funds" lacks a precise definition. It commonly is used to identify:

- An entity that holds a pool of securities and perhaps other assets. In the United States, hedge funds do not register their securities offerings under the Securities Act and hence are not registered as an investment company under the Investment Company Act (SEC 2003). In Australia, the term refers to managed funds that use a wider range of financial instruments and investment strategies than traditional managed funds do, including the use of short selling and derivatives to create leverage, with the aim of generating positive returns regardless of overall performance (McNally, Chambers, and Thompson 2004, p. 57).
- An entity whose fee structure typically compensates the advisor based on a percentage of the hedge fund's capital gains and capital appreciation.
- An entity whose advisory personnel often invest significant amounts of their own money into the hedge funds that they manage.

Although similar to hedge funds, other unregistered pools of investments, including venture capital funds, private equity funds, and commodity pools, generally are not categorized as hedge funds. The investment goals of hedge funds vary among funds, but many seek to achieve a positive, absolute return rather than measuring their performance against a securities index or other benchmark.

Hedge funds utilize a number of different investment styles and strategies and invest in a wide variety of financial instruments. Hedge funds invest in equity and fixed income securities, currencies, over-the-counter derivatives, futures contracts, and other assets. Some hedge funds may take on substantial leverage, sell securities short, and employ certain hedging and arbitrage strategies. Hedge funds typically engage one or more broker-dealers to provide a variety of services, including trade clearance and settlement, financing, and custody services.

The Securities and Exchange Commission (SEC) in 2003 when reporting on "Implications of the Growth of Hedge Funds" concluded that investors in hedge fund assets, anticipated to exceed $1 trillion in the next 5 to 10 years,[5] suffered from a lack of information about these investment pools.

The growth in such funds has been fueled primarily by the increased interest of institutional investors, such as pension plans, endowments, and foundations, seeking to diversify their portfolios with investments in vehicles that feature absolute return strategies—flexible investment strategies that hedge fund advisors use to pursue positive returns in both declining and rising securities markets while generally attempting to protect investment principal. In addition, funds of hedge funds (FOHF), which invest substantially all of their assets in other hedge funds, have also fueled this growth.

The SEC study (2003, p. vii) commenced with a review of 65 hedge fund advisers (both registered and unregistered) managing approximately 650 different hedge funds with over $160 billion of assets. It focused on a number of key areas of concern: "including the recent increase in the number of hedge fund enforcement cases, the role that hedge funds play in our financial markets and the implications of the Commission's limited ability to obtain basic information about hedge funds." The study also examined the emergence of FOHFs that register under the Investment Company Act of 1940 and the Securities Act of 1933 so that they may offer and sell their securities in the public market. Finally, the study reviewed hedge fund disclosure and marketing practices, valuation practices, and conflicts of interest (SEC 2003, p. x).

The SEC concluded:

Hedge funds often provide markets and investors with substantial benefits. For example, based on our observations, many hedge funds take speculative, value-driven trading positions based on extensive research about the value of a security. These positions can enhance liquidity and contribute to market efficiency. In addition, hedge funds offer investors an important risk management tool by providing valuable portfolio diversification because hedge fund returns in many cases are not correlated to the broader debt and equity markets. (SEC 2003, p. xi)

However, the valuation practices were questioned:

The broad discretion that these advisers have to value assets and the lack of independent review over that activity gives rise to questions about whether some hedge funds' portfolio holdings are accurately valued. (SEC 2003, p. xi)

Other concerns of the SEC were the effect on systemic stability. Strategies that hedge fund managers may use include:

- **Global asset allocation,** which involves the use of research to exploit movements in different industry sectors, currencies, and stock markets. This strategy tends to be highly geared and uses derivatives.
- **Event driven,** which involves taking advantage of event- or transaction-specific situations, such as mergers, distressed debt, and natural disasters.
- **Relative value,** which exploits temporary arbitrage opportunities, such as where there are price differences in the shares of one company listed in two different markets.
- **Equity hedge,** whereby equity hedge managers buy undervalued securities and short sell overvalued securities.
- **Short selling,** whereby short sellers borrow, then sell, overvalued shares anticipating a decline whereupon the shares are bought back (SMH 2007).

The next section considers the contagion effects that could result from other unregulated NBFIs borrowing from and lending to both sophisticated and unsophisticated entities.

20.4 POTENTIAL FOR SYSTEMIC RISK AND CONTAGION FROM HEDGE FUNDS, MORTGAGE LENDERS, AND UNREGULATED FINANCE COMPANIES

Financial or systemic crises can be attributed to regulatory failure, which allow a shock, usually price volatility, to enter the financial system, raising systemic risk levels and lowering systemic efficiency. For instance, in 1987, failure to supervise banks' credit risk led to uncontrolled lending to entrepreneurs, margin loans, and property developments that resulted in several years of price instability and eventually bank failures in some OECD (Organization for Economic Cooperation and Development) nations. In 1997, the net result of a similar failure to supervise loans to emerging nations and lending within those nations impacted on all layers of the financial system. In the United States in 2002, regulatory failure of the corporate reporting of some large high-profile, nonfinancial institutions has resulted in international security price volatility. Hence we need a definition of the severity of regulatory failure that can precipitate financial crises. The Currie scale used herein is the author's own rating system: an arithmetic scale from 1 to 10 where the series represents an escalation in severity as follows (Currie 2002):

1. Volatile security and asset prices, resulting from failure by central banks to target inflation and prudently supervise the risk behavior of financial institutions.
2. Failure in major corporates and/or a minor bank and/or a major non-bank financial institutions.
3. Removal of funds from minor banks and/or nonbank financial institutions to major banks or to alternative investments, such as prime corporate securities.
4. Removal of funds from corporate securities to major banks, precipitating further volatility or at worst a stock market crash.
5. Removal of funds from major banks to government-guaranteed securities, such as postal savings accounts in Japan.
6. Flight to cash and or gold.
7. Contraction in lending leading to lower economic growth, disruption to savings and investment.
8. Failure in major nonfinancial institutions and failure in major nonbank financial institutions.
9. Failure in major banks.
10. All of the preceding points together with a currency crisis leading to rapid depreciation, rescheduling of external country debt, higher inflation, and negative economic growth.

Hedge funds appear to have contributed to the subprime crisis and its ongoing effects. To understand how and why, we need to appreciate the rate of growth of these funds and the attraction that they have offered to investors, which in 2007–2008 may have reversed, except for those funds that short sell. Australia has been relatively immune to subprime loans due to the strict application of Basel II capital adequacy to mortgage loans but has suffered fallouts in share values due to short selling and some notable financial collapses. Hence it is taken as a case study. The growth of these funds in Australia compared to overseas trends is illustrated by McNally's comparative study (2004, pp. 57–58). This shows that the pattern is similar. Global hedge funds both doubled in number from 1999 to 2004, which was mirrored in Australia. However, the assets under global management showed a 1,000% increase, while the Australian assets only doubled. Globally the number of funds grew from 500 to 1,000, while assets under managed increased from US$500 billion to US$10 billion. In Australia, the number of funds increased from 8 to 15, while assets controlled grew from US$48 billion to US$15 billion. The industry in Australia shows a high degree of concentration, evidenced by the top five hedge fund managers accounting for 47% of total funds under management, while the top 10 managers make up 66% of the market. Only a third had a track record of three years or more, with 7% to 10% ceasing operations each year.

The leverage of these funds[6] means that performance can be significantly higher than average but also highly variable, exposing such funds to severe diminutions in value when credit and market risk increase systemically. Returns compiled by McNally (2004, p. 62) are only for three years and encompass the effect of 9/11 in the United States. Australian hedge funds are at the top of the performance table. As pointed out by Dimensional Funds Managers, a U.S. firm whose portfolio management is directed out of the Chicago School of Economics based on the work of efficient market theorists such as Fama and French (Kun 1995),[7] the only true time frame to assess is over a 15-year period. In addition, the data in 2004 is hardly a representative sample (McNally 2003, p. 63).

The global meltdown effect on banks that had lent or invested in hedge funds affected by the subprime credit crisis scores a rating of 9/10 on the Currie scale described earlier. Major bank crashes have been averted by Federal Reserve intervention in providing liquidity through the discount window, lowering both the discount and overnight official cash rate, accepting subprime securities, specific liquidity lines, loosening rules governing the mortgage insurers, and "jawboning" (persuasion by talk rather than by legislation). This is evident by examining the series of events that led to such a ranking of this crisis, described in Table 20.1's timeline.

This timeline illustrates the failure of regulators to protect the financial system from the instability caused by incorrect operating risk controls, not by credit risk procedures, for all the reasons highlighted in Section 20.1.

20.5 LACK OF PROTECTION OF BORROWERS AND LENDERS EXPOSED BY THE SUBPRIME CREDIT CRISIS

The subprime crisis has affected average investors and corporations, which now face a variety of risks due to the inability of mortgage holders to pay. These exposures vary by legal entity. Some general exposures by entity type include:

- **Bank corporations.** The earnings reported by major banks are adversely affected by defaults on mortgages they issue and retain. Mortgage assets (receivables) are revalued based on estimates of collections from homeowners resulting in increased bad debt reserves and reducing

TABLE 20.1 Subprime Credit Crisis Timeline

2005: Boom ended August 2005. The booming housing market halted abruptly for many parts of the United States in late summer of 2005.

2006: Continued market slowdown. Prices are flat, home sales fall, resulting in inventory buildup. U.S. Home Construction Index is down over 40% as of mid-August 2006 compared to a year earlier.

2007: Home sales continue to fall. The plunge in existing-home sales is the steepest since 1989. In Q1/2007, S&P/Case-Shiller house price index records first year-over-year decline in nationwide house prices since 1991. The subprime mortgage industry collapses, and a surge of foreclosure activity (twice as bad as 2006). Rising interest rates threaten to depress prices further as problems in the subprime markets spread to the near-prime and prime mortgage markets. The U.S. Treasury secretary calls the bursting housing bubble "the most significant risk to our economy."

February–March: Subprime industry collapse; more than 25 subprime lenders declaring bankruptcy, announcing significant losses, or putting themselves up for sale.

April 2: New Century Financial, largest U.S. subprime lender, files for Chapter 11 bankruptcy.

July 19: Dow-Jones closes above 14,000 for the first time in its history.

August: Worldwide "credit crunch" as subprime mortgage-backed securities are discovered in portfolios of banks and hedge funds around the world, from BNP Paribas to Bank of China. Many lenders stop offering home equity loans and "stated income" loans. Federal Reserve injects about $100 billion into the money supply for banks to borrow at a low rate.

August 6: American Home Mortgage files for Chapter 11 bankruptcy.

August 7: Democratic presidential front-runner Hillary Clinton proposes a $1 billion bailout fund to help homeowners at risk for foreclosure.

August 16: Countrywide Financial Corporation, the biggest U.S. mortgage lender, narrowly avoids bankruptcy by taking out an emergency loan of $11 billion from a group of banks.

August 17: Federal Reserve lowers the discount rate by 50 basis points to 5.75% from 6.25%.

August 31: President Bush announces a limited bailout of U.S. homeowners unable to pay the rising costs of their debts. Ameriquest, once the largest subprime lender in the United States goes out of business.

September 1–3: Fed Economic Symposium in Jackson Hole, Wyoming, addresses the housing recession that jeopardizes U.S. growth. Several critics argue that the Fed should use regulation and interest rates to prevent asset-price bubbles, and blame former Fed chairman Alan Greenspan's low-interest-rate policies for stoking the U.S. housing boom and subsequent bust. Yale University economist Robert Shiller warns of possible home price declines of 50%.

(Continued)

TABLE 20.1 (*Continued*)

September 13:   British bank Northern Rock applies to the Bank of England for emergency funds caused by liquidity problems. Concerned customers withdraw an estimated £2 billion in three days.

September 14:   A run on the bank forms at the United Kingdom's Northern Rock bank precipitated by liquidity problems related to the subprime crisis.

September 17:   Former Fed chairman Alan Greenspan says, "we had a bubble in housing" and warns of "large double-digit declines" in home values "larger than most people expect."

September 18:   The Fed lowers interest rates by half a point (0.5%) in an attempt to limit damage to the economy from the housing and credit crises.

September 28:   Television finance personality Jim Cramer warns Americans on the *Today* show: "Don't you dare buy a home—you'll lose money," causing a furor among Realtors.

September 30:   Affected by the spiraling mortgage and credit crises, Internet banking pioneer NetBank goes bankrupt, the first FDIC-insured bank to fail since the savings and loan crisis. The Swiss bank UBS announces that it lost US$690 million in the third quarter.

October 5:   Merrill Lynch announces a US$5.5 billion loss as a consequence of the subprime crisis, which was revised to $8.4 billion on October 24, a sum that credit rating firm Standard & Poor's calls "startling."

October 15–17:   A consortium of U.S. banks backed by the U.S. government announces a "super fund" of $100 billion to purchase mortgage-backed securities whose mark-to-market value plummeted in the subprime collapse. Both Fed chairman Ben Bernanke and Treasury secretary Hank Paulson express alarm about the dangers posed by the bursting housing bubble; Paulson says "the housing decline is still unfolding and I view it as the most significant risk to our economy....The longer housing prices remain stagnant or fall, the greater the penalty to our future economic growth."

October 31:   Federal Reserve lowers the federal funds rate by 25 basis points to 4.5%.

November 1:   Federal Reserve injects $41 billion into the money supply for banks to borrow at a low rate. It is the largest single expansion by the Fed since $50.35 billion on September 19, 2001.

December 6:   President Bush announces a plan to voluntarily and temporarily freeze the mortgages of a limited number of mortgage debtors holding adjustable rate mortgages. He also asked members of Congress to pass legislation to modernize the Federal Housing Administration, to temporarily reform the tax code to help homeowners refinance during this time of housing market stress, and to pass funding to support mortgage counseling, as well as to pass legislation to reform government-sponsored enterprises (GSEs) like Freddie Mac and Fannie Mae.

TABLE 20.1   (*Continued*)

2008:

March 14:   Bear Stearns gets Fed funding as shares plummet.

March 16:   Bear Stearns gets acquired for $2 a share by JPMorgan Chase in a fire sale avoiding bankruptcy. The deal is backed by Federal Reserve providing up to $30 billion to cover possible Bear Stearn losses.

Adapted from http://en.wikipedia.org/wiki/Subprime_crisis_impact_timeline downloaded November 13, 2007.

earnings. Rapid or unexpected changes in mortgage asset valuation can lead to volatility in earnings and stock prices. The ability of lenders to predict future collections is a complex task subject to a multitude of variables.

■ **Mortgage lenders and real estate investment trusts.** These entities face similar risks to banks. In addition, they have business models with significant reliance on the ability to regularly secure new financing through CDOs (collateralized debt obligations) or commercial paper issuance secured by mortgages. Investors have become reluctant to fund such investments and are demanding higher interest rates. Such lenders are at increased risk of significant reductions in book value due to asset sales at unfavorable prices, and several have filed bankruptcy.

■ **Special purpose entities (SPEs), such as hedge funds.** Like corporations, SPEs are required to revalue their mortgage assets based on estimates of collection of mortgage payments. If this valuation falls below a certain level, or if cash flow falls below contractual levels, investors may have immediate rights to the mortgage asset collateral. This can also cause the rapid sale of assets at unfavorable prices. Other SPEs called special investment vehicles (SIVs) issue commercial paper and use the proceeds to purchase securitized assets, such as CDOs. These entities have been affected by mortgage asset devaluation. Several major SIVs are associated with large banks.

■ **Investors.** The stocks or bonds of the entities just discussed are affected by the lower earnings and uncertainty regarding the valuation of mortgage assets and related payment collection.

Only bank corporations are prudentially supervised—whereas other types of corporations in Australia are required only to register with the Australian Securities and Investments Commission (ASIC) and lodge reports as well as satisfy listing requirements if publicly owned with a large spread of investors numbering over 50. Therefore, the potential of a systemic crisis is huge for a significant portion of the small investment community. The U.S. regulatory model leaves financial system participants unprotected, in a similar manner, despite the fact that the SEC in 2003, as a result of its study of hedge funds, made recommendations regarding the operations of hedge fund advisers, funds of hedge funds, and hedge funds. These recommendations were never put in place. They were:

- Advisers be required to register as investment advisers under the Advisers Act, with strict disclosure requirements.
- Standards be introduced regarding valuation, suitability and fee disclosure issues relating to registered FOHFs.
- The SEC should consider permitting general solicitations in fund offerings to be limited to qualified purchasers.
- The staffs of the SEC and the NASD should monitor closely capital introduction services provided by brokers.
- Encourage unregulated industries to embrace and further develop best practices.
- The SEC should continue its efforts to improve investor education.

20.6 MECHANISMS FOR TRANSNATIONAL CRIME

In an effort to combat international organized crime, now known by the term "transnational crime," the United Nations in December 2000, after eight years of negotiation, opened for signature the Convention against Transnational Organised Crime (2001), also known as the Palermo Convention. Transnational crime was defined as including:

> *theft of cultural property, trafficking in arms, illegal gambling, smuggling of illegal migrants, trafficking in women and children for sexual slavery, extortion, violence against the judiciary and journalists, corruption of government and public officials, trafficking in radioactive material, trafficking in body parts, trafficking in endangered species, transnational auto theft, money laundering and computer related crime. (UN General Assembly 1994, p. 3)*

The Palermo treaty is supplemented by three protocols on trafficking in persons, smuggling of migrants, and trafficking in firearms and ammunition. It has been criticized by Schloenhardt (2005, p. 353) for failing in one of its main goals to establish a universal concept of organised crime: "the lack of a comprehensive definition of the term and the ambiguities arising from the elements of the organized criminal group definition will allow criminal organisations to continue to take advantage of the discrepancies between legal systems." Other criticisms are that extradition procedures are still faulty and the failure to recognize the root cause of organized crime: the demand side. A further fault is the lack of enforcement measures and a central authority: "it is still unclear how the signatories and the United Nations will respond to countries that fail to live up to expectations or that are found harbouring or collaborating with criminal organisations" (Schloenhardt 2005, p. 353).

So how and why can transnational crime continue to exist and why might it shelter behind hedge funds investing in subprime credits, or finance companies raising monies from the public for property investment, or in the specialized mortgage houses themselves?

20.6.1 Tax Havens

In a globalized marketplace, competition extends to the tax system, so that transactions with tax havens can often be used to avoid paying tax elsewhere (ATO, 2004, p. 2). A tax haven is defined by the OECD according to three criteria: none or only nominal taxes, lack of effective exchange of information, and lack of transparency. The OECD recognizes a total of 38 tax havens, three of which have committed to eliminating harmful tax practices. There are also countries that are not tax havens but by virtue of their bank secrecy arrangements may be exploited for tax haven purposes. Despite a number of treaties to reduce bank secrecy and tax havens, in particular the Financial Action Task Force, in 2002–2003, A\$3.8 billion (A\$5 billion in 2001–2002), flowed from Australia to tax havens (ATO 2004, p. 4). The fact that many of the hedge funds and other entities discussed in this chapter use tax havens as their corporate base means that the checks and balances on them to ensure they are not being used by transnational criminals is deficient. As can be seen from Table 20.2, 46.7% of funds are domiciled in the Caribbean, according to the Global Data Feeder. (The figure is higher for other DataFeeders.)

In Switzerland, bank secrecy is described as still "unassailable in the case of fiscal offences" (Chaikin 2005b). Despite the fact that Switzerland is seeking to protect its reputation as the world's leader in the management of offshore wealth by prohibiting its bankers from assisting in the flight of capital and tax evasion, the country still rates as a safe haven for illegally gotten

TABLE 20.2 Distribution of Funds

General	Global DataFeeder	Hedge Fund DataFeeder	Single Hedge Fund Manager DataFeeder	CTA DataFeeder
Number of reporting funds	6,096	5,246	3,001	850
Number of reporting management companies	2,182	1,670	1,197	512
Distribution				
Managers domiciled in USA	63.47%	62.10%	67.25%	67.97%
Managers domiciled in Europe	22.09%	22.40%	17.71%	21.09%
Managers domiciled in Caribbean	10.04%	10.90%	10.86%	7.23%
Managers domiciled in Rest of World	4.40%	4.61%	4.18%	3.71%
Funds domiciled in USA	34.81%	25.16%	31.86%	94.35%
Funds domiciled in Europe	14.78%	17.04%	9.03%	0.82%
Funds domiciled in Caribbean	46.87%	53.74%	53.75%	4.47%
Funds domiciled in rest of World	3.54%	4.06%	5.36%	0.35%

Source: www.barclayhedge.com

gains. In fact, as pointed out by Chaikin (2000), when grand corruption occurs and the dictator is overthrown,

> *this does not mean that the stolen monies will be recovered. Indeed, the modern experience is that dictators are able to keep their loot, which is deposited outside their country. The mobility of wealth prevents effective recovery of the assets and the sheer size of the stolen monies has major economic consequences for development.*

The use of tax havens by unregulated institutions involved in the subprime crisis, were used to conceal the true nature of the transactions.

20.6.2 Use of Corporate Groups and Nominee Companies

As pointed out by the OECD (2001), the misuse of corporate entities for transnational crime, such as money laundering, bribery and corruption, shielding assets from creditors, and illicit activities, has been on the increase.

The systemic side effects on financial stability have been evident in the subprime crisis, so that despite measures put in place to obtain beneficial ownership statistics, such use of corporate vehicles still occurs (OECD 2001, p. 3):

> *Money launderers exploit cash-based businesses and other legal vehicles to disguise the source of their illicit gains, bribe-givers and recipients conduct their illicit transactions through bank accounts opened under the names of corporations and foundations, and individuals hide or shield their wealth from tax authorities and other creditors through trusts and partnerships, to name a few examples.*

Mechanisms for obtaining beneficial ownership and control information fall into three types: up-front disclosure to the authorities, primary reliance on intermediaries, and primary reliance on investigative systems. Not all options are suitable for all jurisdictions; investigative systems only work, for instance, with adequate investigative mechanisms to effectively monitor compliance by corporate service providers, where there is a sufficient number of such providers with suitable experience and resources and where there is a strong enforcement mode with good transparency and governance mechanisms. Unfortunately, such methods of obtaining beneficial ownership have fallen far short of expectations. This can be seen in the case of nominee shareholders in Australia, let alone attempting to penetrate foreign nominees.

The original justification for nominee shareholdings was that it provided "an efficient mechanism for the administration of assets held on behalf of another person, and that it secured the financial privacy of persons who did not wish to appear on the company registry" (Chaikin 2005a). However, nominee companies can be used for illicit purposes, particularly money laundering. In Australia, the failure of the corporate regulator to trace powers and penetrate the Swiss nominees in *ASC v. Bank Leumi* has created a precedent that has undermined the strategic enforcement objective of detecting insider trading and other abusive market behavior (Chaikin 2006). All of these types of mechanisms have left any financial system that fails to prudently supervise all deposit-taking institutions, such as hedge funds, mortgage lenders, and finance companies specializing in property investment, open to abuse by transnational criminals.

20.6.3 Viewing the Subprime Crisis as a Special Case of Financial Statement Manipulation or a Failure of Operating Risk Systems

Another way of viewing the subprime crisis is as a special case of financial statement fraud, which is a failure of the operating risk systems in a bank to detect fraud being perpetuated on the bank. This is done to induce banks to lend money. The opportunity is created by the lack of regulation, standards, disclosure, adviser licensing and education detailed in Sections 20.6.2 and 20.6.3 above. Such a hypothesis fits neatly into the Albrechts' nine-factors "perfect fraud storm" theory (2004):

1. A booming economy (which neatly hides the fraud)
2. Moral decay
3. Misplaced executive incentives
4. Unachievable expectations of the market
5. Pressure of large borrowings
6. U.S. rules-based accounting
7. Opportunistic behavior of audit firms
8. Greed on the part of a wide variety of groups of people
9. Educator failures (Brennan and McGrath 2007, citing Albrecht et al. 2004)

Using Cressey's fraud triangle (1953), the motivation is easy to fill in: high commissions based on reported earnings and/or possibility of timely self-redemption given the high degree of manager/adviser investment. According to Brennan and McGrath (2007), other motivations include:

- Desire to increase or maintain share or unit prices
- The need to meet internal and external forecasts
- The desire to minimize tax liabilities
- The avoidance of debt covenant violations
- The desire to raise further debt and equity cheaply

The rationalization would be that originators of property finance companies, mortgage lenders, and hedge funds investing or exploiting the subprime credit market believe they are endowing their intelligence on creditors and investors in order to return to them above-normal profits (Brown and Goetzmann 2003).

The methods of committing financial statement fraud defined as "any intentional act or omission that results in materially misleading financial statements" (AICPA 1987) are fairly common. They can be categorized under four types:

1. Changing accounting methods
2. Altering managerial estimates
3. Improperly recognizing revenues and expenses
4. Overstating assets

In the Brennan et al. study (2007) of 14 companies that were subject to an official investigation, recording false sales was the most common method, motivated by meeting external forecasts, with mostly incumbent or new management discovering the fraud. In the case of the three types of companies singled out in this report—property financiers, mortgage lenders, and hedge funds—the conflict of interest that exists where management can be both an investor and creditor may preclude any discovery until the fraud has produced insolvency, with funds safely banked in a tax haven or bank secrecy haven.

A replication of the Brennan et al. (2007) study could be made asking the same six questions using their case study methodology: questions related to the perpetuators, the method, the motivation, the organizational factors, the mode by which it was detected, and the outcome. Such a study would only focus on the fraud under investigation and on the information regarding motives and methods on publicly available records, with perpetrators openly identified.

20.7 CONCLUSION: A REGULATORY BLACK HOLE AND A FIELD RIFE FOR FUTURE RESEARCH

Since the crisis, regulators have taken these actions:

- Open market operations to ensure member banks have access to funds (i.e., liquidity). These are effectively short-term loans to member banks collateralized by government securities.
- First, central banks have lowered the interest rates charged to member banks (called the discount rate in the United States) for short-term loans, thus providing access to funds for those entities with illiquid mortgage-backed assets. Second, the available funds stimulate the commercial paper market and general economic activity. Lenders and homeowners both may benefit from avoiding foreclosure, which is a costly and lengthy process. Some lenders have reached out to homeowners to provide more favorable mortgage terms (i.e., loan modification or refinancing). Homeowners have also been encouraged to contact their lenders to discuss alternatives.
- Reexamination of the credit rating process to encourage greater transparency to the risks involved with complex mortgage-backed securities and the entities that provide them.
- Regulatory action regarding lending practices, bankruptcy protection, tax policies, affordable housing, credit counseling, education, and the

licensing and qualifications of lenders. Basel II needs to be enforced in the United States in respect to all institutions.

■ Amendments to disclosure rules governing the nature, transparency, and regulatories required for the complex legal entities and securities involved in these transactions.

■ Media encouragement to promote investor education and awareness and public debate.

Early warning signals were evident as early as the 2003. For instance, in the annual report issued by Fairfax Financial Holdings Limited (2003), Prem Watsa raised concerns about securitized products:

> We have been concerned for some time about the risks in asset-backed bonds, particularly bonds that are backed by home equity loans, automobile loans or credit card debt (we own no asset-backed bonds). It seems to us that securitization (or the creation of these asset-backed bonds) eliminates the incentive for the originator of the loan to be credit sensitive. . . . With securitization, the dealer (almost) does not care as these loans can be laid off through securitization. Thus, the loss experienced on these loans after securitization will no longer be comparable to that experienced prior to securitization (called a "moral" hazard). . . . This is not a small problem. There is $1.0 trillion in asset-backed bonds outstanding as of December 31, 2003 in the U.S. . . . Who is buying these bonds? Insurance companies, money managers and banks—in the main—all reaching for yield given the excellent ratings for these bonds. What happens if we hit an air pocket?

Meanwhile www.MarketWatch has cited several economic analysts with Stifel Nicolaus claiming that the problem mortgages are not limited to the subprime niche. "The rapidly increasing scope and depth of the problems in the mortgage market suggest that the entire sector has plunged into a downward spiral similar to the subprime woes whereby each negative development feeds further deterioration." The analysts call it a "vicious cycle" and add that they "continue to believe conditions will get worse." Of the estimated US$1.3 trillion in subprime mortgages, 16% were in default as of October 2007, or approximately $200 billion. Considering that $500 billion in subprime mortgages will reset to higher rates over the next 12 months (placing additional pressure on homeowners) and the recent increases in the payment default rate cited by the Federal Reserve, direct loss exposure would likely exceed $200 billion. This figure may be increased significantly by Alt-A (or non-traditional mortgages) defaults. The impact will continue to fall most directly on homeowners and those retaining mortgage origination risk, primarily banks, mortgage lenders, or those funds and investors holding mortgage-backed securities.

What have we learned from this?

First, as the international financial system enters the third millennium, there is a need to resolve challenges, such as designing regulatory models that promote economic and social development for both emerging and advanced nations. The former are just coming to terms with bank supervision yet may be forced to cope with problems that advanced nations have still not successfully overcome, such as supervision of conglomerates, insurance companies, e-commerce, and transnational financial crime. Some consider that

> *correcting regulatory failure requires better regulation—which means setting more appropriate prudential and market conduct standards, improving surveillance and strengthening enforcement. Integrated regulation may help facilitate this process, but it does not, by itself, cause these changes to occur. (Carmichael 2002, p. 6)*

Second, failure in the United States to implement quickly the operating risk requirements of Basel II across all financial institutions can be blamed for the lack of quick regulatory action that could have averted this crisis.

Third, what may help is more research on regulatory failure, its definition, measurement, and causes, and attempts to validate the inputs into the new general theory of regulation developed by the author (Currie 2005), which is based on a taxonomy, a measurement method, and a scale. A more precise mathematical exposition of the Currie scale, together with research as to the exact types of functional relationships that exist between the components of the new general theory of regulation, would provide a guide to both national and international policymakers, such as the International Monetary Fund, in attempting to mold economies in the right direction for growth and stability.

A basis for such initial research would be a classification of regulatory models in advanced and emerging nations and then ongoing monitoring of the performance of financial institutions in order to verify the hypothesis that moving the regulatory model toward one with a strong enforcement mode with strong sanctions and compliance audits, but with weak discretionary and strong institutionalized protective measures, will achieve the desired goals of greater efficiency while maintaining systemic stability. This combined with studies to isolate regulatory black holes, to understand their potential for developing systemic crises, to determine whether they are the result of fraud or the failure to properly apply the carefully developed operating risk systems of Basel II, would also help solve the problems of transnational crime that help beggar nations.

NOTES

1. "Subprime lending" is a general term that refers to the practice of making loans to borrowers who do not qualify for market interest rates because of problems with their credit history or the ability to prove that they have enough income to support the monthly payment on the loan for which they are applying. A subprime loan is one that is offered at an interest rate higher than A-paper loans due to the increased risk. The value of U.S. subprime mortgages was estimated at $1.3 trillion as of March 2007, with over 7.5 million first-lien subprime mortgages outstanding. The estimated value of subprime adjustable-rate mortgages (ARM) resetting at higher interest rates is $500 billion for 2008. Source: http://en.wikipedia.org/wiki/2007_Subprime_mortgage_financial_crisis downloaded November 13, 2007.
2. This was highlighted in research published by risk consultants Algorithmics, based on information stored on its FIRST database (Pennington 2007, 36).
3. Ibid.
4. For instance, in one case a borrower reported earning US$6,000 per month as a teacher with neither the underwriter or loan officer questioning whether this was an annual salary or just a piece-rate payment.
5. Participants at the commission's May 14–15, 2003, Hedge Fund Roundtable estimated that there are approximately 6,000 hedge funds currently operating in the United States, with approximately $600 billion in assets under management. Other estimates vary greatly. The commission estimated in 1992, based on media reports, that there were approximately 400 hedge funds in existence.
6. Although according to Van Hedge Fund Advisors only 30% of all global funds at the end of 2003 used leverage, this may be disguised through the use of margin loans and FOHF.
7. See also: www.dfaus.com/library/bios/eugene_fama and www.dfaus.com/library/videos/thinkers_french/.

REFERENCES

AICPA. 1987. Report of the National Commission on Fraudulent Financial Reporting. National Commission on Fraudulent Financial Reporting (Treadway Commission), New York.

Albrecht, W. S., et al. 2004. Cited in N. M. Brennan and M. McGrath. 2007. Financial Statement Fraud; Some lessons from U.S. and European case studies. *Australian Accounting Review* 17, no. 2:51.

Albrecht, W. S., C. C. Albrecht, and C. O. Albrecht. 2004. Fraud and corporate executives: Agency, stewardship and broken trust. *Journal of Forensic Accounting* 5:109–130.

Atkins, T. 2007. Bank shocks cast doubts on new risk rules. Reuters, August 22. www.reuters.com.

ATO. 2004. Tax havens and tax administration. Australian Taxation Office, February. http://www.ato.gov.au/corporate/content.asp?doc=/content/46908. htm&page=36&H36

Basel II will not harm banks, says regulator. 2007. *Oprisk & Compliance* 8, no. 6:11.

Brown, Stephen J., and William N. Goetzmann. 2003. Hedge funds with style. *Journal of Portfolio Management* 29, no. 2:101–112.

Chaikin, D. 2000. Tracking the proceeds of organised crime—The Marcos case. Paper presented at the Transnational Crime Conference convened by the Australian Institute of Criminology in association with the Australian Federal Police and the Australian Customs Service, Canberra, March 9–10.

Chaikin, D. 2005a. Nominee shareholders: Legal, commercial and risk aspects, *Australian Journal of Corporate Law* 18, no. 3.

Chaikin, D. 2005b. Policy and fiscal effects of Swiss bank secrecy. *Revenue Law Journal* 15, no. 1:90.

Chaikin, D. 2006. Penetrating foreign nominees: A failure of strategic regulation? *Australian Journal of Corporate Law* 19, no. 2.

Cressey, D. R. 1953. *Other people's money: A study in the social psychology of embezzlement.* Glencoe, IL: The Free Press.

Currie, C. V. 2000. The optimum regulatory model for the next millennium—Lessons from international comparisons and the Australian-Asian experience. In *New financial architecture for the 21st century*, ed. B. Gup. Westport, CT: Quorum/Greenwood Books.

Currie, C. V. 2001. Is the Australian financial system prepared for the third millennium? In *Global business and economics review—Anthology 2001*, ed. D. Kantarelis. Worcester, MA: Business and Economics Society International.

Currie, C. V. 2002. Regulatory failure in emerging and advanced markets—Is there a difference? In *Global business and economics review—Anthology 2002*, ed. D. Kantarelis. Worcester, MA: Business and Economics Society International.

Currie, C. V. 2005. The need for a new theory of economic reform. *Journal of Socio-Economics.* 34, no. 4:425–443, 1053–5357.

Currie, C. V. 2006. A new theory of financial regulation: Predicting, measuring, and preventing financial crises. *Journal of Socio-Economics.* 35, no. 1:1–170.

Diamond, P. W., and P. H. Dybvig. 1983. Bank runs, deposit insurance, and liquidity. *Journal of Political Economy* 91, no. 3:401–419.

Eichengreen, B., and R. Portes. 1986. Debt and default in the 1930's: Causes and consequences. *European Economic Review* 30, no. 3:599–640.

Eichengreen, B., and R. Portes. 1987. The anatomy of financial crises. In *Threats to international financial stability*, ed. R. Portes and A. W. Swoboda. New York: Cambridge University Press.

Fairfax Financial Holdings Limited 2003 Annual Report, pp. 15–16. www.fairfax.ca/Assets/Downloads/040305ceo.pdf.

Flood, R. P., and P. M. Garber. 1982. Bubbles, runs and gold monetization. In *Crises in the economic and financial structure*, ed. P. Wachtel. Lanham., MD: Lexington Books.

Gup, B. 1995. *Targeting fraud.* Westport, CT: Quorum Books.

Kun, M. 1995. Coming full circle. GSB Chicago, March.

MarketWatch. Market in a downward spiral. Available at CBS.MarketWatch.com.

McNally, S., M. Chambers, and C. Thompson. 2004. *Financial Stability Review.*

Organization for Economic Cooperation and Development. 1991. *Systemic risks in securities markets.* Paris, France: Author.

Organization for Economic Cooperation and Development. 1992. *Banks under stress.* Paris, France: Author.

Organization for Economic Cooperation and Development. 2001. Behind the corporate veil—using corporate entities for illicit purposes. Paris, France: OECD Publications Service, 3.

Pennington, V. 2007. Bringing down the house. *Oprisk & Compliance* 8, no. 7:36–39.

Schloenhardt, A. 2005. Transnational organised crime and the international criminal court developments and debates. *University of Queensland Law Journal* 24, no. 1:93–122.

Securities and Exchange Commission. 2003. Implications of the growth of hedge funds. Report Commissioned by the United States Government of America, Washington, DC.

SMH. 2007. Understand hedge funds before investing. Business, *Money*, May 15.

UN General Assembly. 1994. Naples Political Declaration and Global Action Plan against Organised Transnational Crime. UNDocA/RES/49/159. December 23, 3.

CHAPTER 21

Case Studies in Hedge Fund Operational Risks: From Amaranth to Wood River

Keith H. Black

ABSTRACT

The majority of catastrophic losses experienced by hedge fund investors were in some part related to operational risks. While we cannot discount the role of market risk, operational risk is likely more detectable and more preventable. This chapter describes the debacles at Amaranth, Bayou, Lancer, and Wood River, with a focus on explaining the role of operational risks in these prominent hedge fund failures. Hedge funds that fail for operational reasons often have not submitted data to auditors or third-party pricing or risk management services. Investors who require the use of quality auditors and third-party risk management services may be able to reduce the probability and severity of financial losses due to hedge fund operational risk. A checklist of operational risk issues is included, which can be used as a vital part of the due diligence process.

21.1 INTRODUCTION

While the subject of hedge fund frauds and failures may be uncomfortable to discuss, these discussions are important to increase our understanding of how to prevent future occurrences. Many constituents may be harmed when a hedge fund fails. Clearly, we are concerned about the investors who have lost money during these failures. However, we must also consider the impact on the prime broker and the external partners of the hedge fund firm, including third-party marketers, funds-of-funds managers and investors, auditors, and administrators. Finally, there may be innocent employees and partners within the hedge fund firm who will lose not only financial assets but also their professional reputation, even though they may have not directly participated in the activities that led to the demise of the firm. The more quickly these risks are uncovered, the easier it may be to recover assets and prevent new investors from contributing to a failing fund.

21.2 MARKET RISK AND OPERATIONAL RISK

In this chapter we refer to the failure of a hedge fund as an event when nearly all of the assets under management are lost in some way. These losses are usually attributed to market risk and/or operational risk. A hedge fund can lose a significant portion of investor assets due to market risk, where the trading positions of the fund suffer a significant decline in value. This can happen very quickly during a time of great stress and volatility in the market, or over a longer period of time due to a change in market conditions or a failure of the fund's investment strategy.

A hedge fund can also lose assets through an operational failure. Kundro and Feffer (2004, 2005) estimate that 54% of hedge fund failures can be attributed, at least in part, to operational risks. Of the funds that failed due to operational failures, they estimate that 6% of occurrences were due to inadequate resources, 14% due to unauthorized trading and style drift, 30% from the theft of investor assets, and 41% from the misrepresentation of investments and performance. Further, they estimate that 38% of hedge fund failures had only investment risk, meaning that the operational controls were in place and effective. Surprisingly, 54% of hedge fund failures were due to operational risk while the final 8% of hedge fund debacles could be attributed to business risk or a combination of a number of different risks.

There has been a significant research focus on quantifying market risk, as models such as value at risk, scenario analysis, and portfolio stress testing enjoy significant popularity. Third-party services, such as RiskMetrics or MeasuRisk, have been developed to report and model the market risk of investment portfolios. Quantitative risk management of hedge fund investments is an extremely popular and effective way to reduce the probability and the size of investor losses due to adverse market events. Clearly, many investors spend a substantial amount of time modeling and managing market risk. However, only 38% of hedge fund failures are solely attributed to market risk. Unfortunately, investors may be spending much less time and effort on the detection of the operational risks that are present in 54% of hedge funds that presented their investors with catastrophic losses. If investors are not effectively measuring and monitoring the risks that lead directly to significant losses, there can be an opportunity to upgrade the effectiveness of the entire risk management process.

The combination of theft of investor assets and the erroneous reporting of portfolio composition, returns, and risks is responsible for at least as many hedge fund failures as market risk. However, the search for theft and fraudulent performance reporting has not been nearly as well developed or understood as the measurement and detection of market risk. The goal of a risk detection system is to be able to mitigate the risk in a timely fashion. For market risk, we would like to ask the manager to reduce the position size before the losses occur, or a fund-of-funds manager may make trades at the portfolio level to reduce market risks. In extreme cases, investors may choose to sell their interest in the fund in order to reduce their market risk. Ironically, the market risk failures of a fund may happen very quickly due to the speed at which financial markets prices can move during a time of crisis. Even if market risk can be detected, investors may not have time to request a return of their investments before the market has claimed significant losses.

Operational risks may operate more slowly. If investors are constantly searching for these risks, they may have the ability to redeem their fund interests months, or years, before the likely demise of the fund. Investors clearly have been successful if they receive a return of their investment and the fund later fails due to reasons predicted by their risk monitoring system. Clearly, then, the risk-monitoring focus of many hedge fund investors has been on market risk issues, and many have failed to see the entire risks of hedge fund investing, which include operational risk issues.

21.3 DUE DILIGENCE AND MANAGER TRANSPARENCY

Most investors understand the importance of performing a due diligence review before hiring a hedge fund manager. Many contributors to Parker (2000) present exhaustive checklists of the steps of performing due diligence on a hedge fund manager. These due diligence tasks typically focus on people and systems.

Before hiring a hedge fund manager, we need to determine that they are honest and highly qualified. Investors desire to hire fund managers with a significant educational background and professional experience at a reputable bank or trading firm. Allison and Schurr (2005) discuss the due diligence process. Control Risks Group is a firm that studies the personal backgrounds of hedge fund managers. These private investigators search public records and verify the history and career of each significant employee.

There are some surprisingly large instances of dishonesty among hedge fund managers. For example, Control Risks Group estimates that 80% of fund manager resumes include some misstatements or omissions. On average, 14% of these hedge fund investigations reveal some negative information, which can range from an overstatement of assets under management to the manager having been previously involved in litigation regarding financial fraud or unpaid bills. Investors would also like to make sure that the hedge fund manager is focused on the business and does not lead a reckless lifestyle. A current divorce proceeding, a significant side business, or a driving under the influence accusation are some red flags that may cause some investors to question the appropriateness of hiring this manager. Much of this due diligence work requires contacting the accountants, prime brokers, and administrators of the fund to verify the assets, returns, and trading activity in the portfolio.

However, not all investors are as serious about monitoring developments at the hedge fund firm after the investment has been made. Tran (2006) emphasizes the importance of the ongoing due diligence efforts. A significant red flag is the turnover of senior personnel within a hedge fund company. This may signal a conflict between the partners of the firm, which could be regarding trading philosophies, valuation and performance issues, or the unprofessional or unethical behavior of someone within the firm. Tran also demonstrates the importance of the hedge fund's auditor. The auditor should be a reputable, verifiable firm that can confirm the historical returns and current asset levels of the fund. During 2000, as many as 40% of hedge funds had no auditor. Funds with smaller assets under management are more likely to have unaudited financial statements. Tran states that the reported returns of audited funds are much more accurate than those of unaudited funds. Also, the probability of a fund liquidation is larger in funds that do not employ an auditing firm.

Transparency is an extremely important part of the due diligence process. A transparent hedge fund is one where an investor's questions are freely answered. Investors may request the disclosure of positions, position exposures, or return estimates on a weekly basis. An opaque fund will divulge little about its operations to investors beyond the reported monthly returns. While investors may want the fund to be transparent, hedge fund managers may have legitimate reasons to avoid sharing information with their investors. Transparency allows investors to be informed with their selection and retention of hedge fund managers and gives them important information that they can use to minimize the risks of their investment.

Hedge fund managers earn higher incomes when they attract larger assets under management and earn larger returns. The lack of transparency requested by some hedge fund managers is simply an attempt to protect their valuable franchise. If their trading strategy is lucrative yet easy to replicate, it is clear that they would not like to share their trading algorithms with investors, brokers, or accountants. Should one of these counterparties choose to replicate the strategy and make the same trades, the hedge fund manager may be significantly impacted. As other investors seek to make the same trades, the profitability of a hedge fund declines. As others replicate the trading strategy, hedge fund managers can lose their unique edge, as other fund managers may start to market a similar strategy. The impact on a given hedge fund can be even larger when the identity of the fund's largest positions is revealed to the market, especially when the fund has large positions in small-capitalization stocks or illiquid fixed income securities. When the market knows that a fund has large positions to liquidate, as occurred at Long Term Capital Management, these positions become much harder to exit, and the trading costs will soar. If the fund's short sales are revealed, this can limit the fund manager's ability to communicate with the management of the firm, cutting them off from a potentially valuable source of information.

Hedges (2005) states that full transparency may not be as valuable to investors as they might think. While the disclosure of all positions may seem like important information to investors, a current snapshot of holdings does not necessarily provide the information necessary to understand the risk exposures or the trading strategy of the hedge fund. In fact, the full disclosure of position data may be confusing to investors. An interesting compromise is for managers to disclose aggregated data about the fund's investment positions. Rather than revealing the specific securities, the fund would provide investors with summary data that calculates statistics that can be used to assess the risk of the fund. This data can range from the leverage and diversification of the fund, to the distribution of positions across various fixed income and equity sectors. The release of aggregated fund data assures fund managers that their position information is not revealed to the market. Similarly, investors can benefit, as the aggregated risk exposures of the fund provide a clearer understanding of the fund's risks than would be provided by full disclosure of the fund's holdings. It is important to note here that Hedges suggests that risk exposures are disclosed to investors directly by the fund manager. We will return to the importance of this point later in the chapter.

Hedges (2005) also describes how managed accounts, or separate accounts, can provide the safest and most transparent arrangement for investors. In a managed account, the assets managed by the hedge fund manager remain in the investor's account at a brokerage firm. Investors retain custody of the assets, so it is not possible for the fund manager to withdraw the funds. Given that the account belongs to investors, they have the ability to access account positions, balances, and performance in real time. This allows investors to see returns on a much more frequent basis, if desired, when compared to the monthly returns provided to most hedge fund investors. There will likely be no question about the valuation of the securities in the account, as the price of the positions will be determined by the custody bank or broker, not by the fund manager. Investors have the ultimate liquidity in a managed account, as the fund manager has no legal right to impose lockup periods or request that withdrawals are made at quarter-end with 60 days' notice.

Unfortunately, transparency is not the only area where manager and investor interests may come into conflict. Hedge fund managers want to maximize the dollar amount of management and incentive fees earned by their fund. Therefore, it is in their best interest to retain investors' assets for longer periods of time and to report the highest possible performance. However, whenever hedge fund managers earn high fees, this directly reduces the return to their investors. While the vast majority of hedge fund managers are honest and hardworking, these fee structures can tempt some managers to misstate performance, especially during a period of underperformance. When funds are chosen on the basis of risk-adjusted returns and incentive fees are paid on reported returns, some managers may manipulate reported returns to enhance their income or to maximize the probability of retaining investor assets. This gives managers the idea to report large gains quickly while reporting losses slowly. If losses are smoothed over a long period of time, the fund appears to have higher returns and lower volatility, which can assist in the retention of assets. Investors should be especially careful when the reported returns of a fund are far above those of funds with similar objectives. Additionally, investors should be concerned when a fund suddenly becomes less correlated to market risk factors or funds with similar investment objectives, which is likely when a fund is manipulating returns to avoid showing losses similar to or greater than those earned on similar investments.

21.4 FOUR RECENT FRAUDS HIGHLIGHT THE IMPORTANCE OF OPERATIONAL RISKS

21.4.1 Amaranth Advisors, LLC

Till (2007) gives an in-depth explanation of the causes of the collapse of Amaranth Advisors, which lost nearly $6 billion of its $9.2 billion in assets in September 2006. Amaranth started as a convertible bond arbitrage fund and later moved into the multistrategy space, where positions are placed in a number of markets, ideally with the goal of reducing the volatility of returns and lengthening the potential life span of a fund. While many multistrategy funds are carefully diversified over a variety of hedge fund trading strategies, Amaranth chose to place half of its positions in the energy markets.

The size of Amaranth's positions in the natural gas markets was likely due to their prior success in this market. Amaranth's energy trader, Brian Hunter, led a team that had made billions in profits in the natural gas market but had previously posted a month (May 2006) where their energy book had earned nearly $1 billion in losses. With monthly volatility often exceeding 10%, or daily volatility exceeding 2%, investors should have clearly understood the size of the risks in the fund, especially in the energy trading book.

The team had taken long positions in natural gas, primarily for the volatile winter months. While many of these positions were spread trades, hedged with short positions in other contract months, the natural gas market is so seasonal that these spreads have the potential to be extremely volatile. It appeared that the trades were designed to benefit from a shock to the natural gas market, similar to the profitable trades that Amaranth enjoyed in the wake of Hurricane Katrina's damage to natural gas facilities in the prior summer. While traditional value-at-risk analysis may not have predicted the full risk of the positions, scenario analysis of prior events of extreme weather and inventory disruptions in the natural gas market may have been able to better predict the magnitude of these losses.

Positions were placed both in the NYMEX futures market as well as the over-the-counter (OTC) market. The OTC market allowed large positions to be placed for winter natural gas many years into the future. Till estimates that the size of the OTC positions, especially in deferred years, may have been larger than the open interest in the NYMEX natural gas futures markets. Because these deferred markets are less liquid, the size of Amaranth's position and the small number of OTC dealers in this market made their position very illiquid. If Amaranth needed to exit these positions quickly, there would likely be a substantial price impact, which would cause losses for the fund.

What can we learn from this situation? While market risk clearly played a role, it is not clear that Amaranth would have met its demise if its position sizes were, perhaps, only 20% of the actual position size. A multistrategy fund should clearly not have 50% of its capital dedicated to one specific market or trade, especially if that fund holds itself out to be well diversified. Investors should watch for signs that the fund has concentrated positions, such as a volatility of monthly returns often exceeding 10%. Fund management should closely supervise all traders, even those star traders who have previously earned billions of dollars in profits. Risk managers at Amaranth may have allowed Hunter to take more risk than justified simply due to the size of his prior trading gains. The separation between Hunter and Amaranth may have also been a factor, as Hunter ran a small office in Alberta, Canada, far from Amaranth's Connecticut home. This could have made it difficult to understand the extent of Hunter's dealings, should he have chosen to conceal his positions. Finally, Hunter had a checkered past, which may have given some investors pause. In his prior career at Deutsche Bank, Hunter's trading privileges were said to have been revoked after a series of crippling losses on energy trades.

In July 2007, the Commodity Futures Trading Commission (CFTC) filed a civil enforcement action against Amaranth and Hunter, charging that the size and timing of their natural gas trades were manipulative of the NYMEX futures markets. The Federal Energy Regulatory Commission (FERC) has fined Hunter $30 million and Amaranth $200 million, in addition to the request to return profits of $59 million. In a surprising show of hubris, Hunter lashed out at the CFTC and the FERC, charging that these enforcement actions were interfering with his ability to raise assets for his new hedge fund, Solengo Capital. Kishan (2008) reports that Solengo Capital was purchased by Peak Ridge Capital. The Peak Ridge Commodity Volatility fund, now managed by Hunter and other former Amaranth employees, earned 103% from its November 2007 launch to March 2008. This level of return volatility, should it persist in the future, could predict more losses in Hunter's future.

While the managers at these other infamous funds have been charged criminally, it is not clear that Hunter or others at Amaranth will have similar legal issues. While they are subject to civil fines and litigation, a lack of respect for market liquidity and reasonable risk management and position sizes is, unfortunately, not a criminal offense.

21.4.2 Bayou Management, LLC

The details of the alleged fraud at Bayou Management, LLC, is described by several reporters (Eisinger 2005; MacDonald and Emshwiller 2005; MacDonald, Dugan, and Lucchetti 2005; Morgenson 2005) from the *New York Times* and the *Wall Street Journal*. Samuel Israel III claimed to manage a long-short equity fund with over $400 million in assets under management. Although there were many red flags that could have been seen during an initial due diligence review, the commitment to ongoing risk monitoring of the fund could have saved investors from this meltdown.

To start, Israel's fund should have failed any standard due diligence checklist if the investigators looked in the right places. Israel's resume overstated his position and his tenure at Leon Cooperman's Omega Advisors. While Israel claimed to have been a head trader at this large, well-respected hedge fund from 1992 to 1996, this turns out to have not been true. Reference checks found that Omega claimed that he was an employee for only 17 months in 1994 and 1995 and that he did not have trading authority at the fund. While Israel claimed that the Bayou had started in early 1997, it seems that the fund may have been started in late 1996. The later start date allowed Israel to conceal significant losses during the first several months of the fund's operations.

Tran's suggestions to check the auditor relationship would also have been helpful here. It is alleged that the chief financial officer of Bayou, Daniel Marino, was the principal of the firm's auditor, Richmond-Fairfield. While Bayou claimed that Grant Thornton was its auditor in 2002, the reputable auditor told the *Wall Street Journal* that it had ceased auditing Bayou's returns a few years earlier. Bayou was also an NASD registered broker-dealer, where all of Israel's trades were cleared by his own brokerage firm. For a fund that claimed to execute very frequent trades in the equity markets, earning a commission on a large number of trades may appear to some to be a conflict of interest.

While Israel claimed to earn profits through long and short positions and frequent trading in equity securities, there was not nearly enough trading volume in the fund's accounts in its last 18 months to justify claims that the fund was still following this strategy. Bayou may have initially traded in the manner that was disclosed to, and agreed on by, investors, but the trading slowed down significantly. What likely happened is that the fund had earned significant trading losses in the most recent two years of the fund. Marino's in-house auditing firm disclosed incorrect returns to investors in order to retain the assets and to continue earning the incentive fees on the erroneous profits. Bayou claimed to have managed $400 million in investor assets, but bank records only showed $160 million.

Some shrewd investors, such as Tremont, withdrew their assets when some of the red flags were revealed. This fund manager's redemption request was a result of finding significant differences between the reported returns of Bayou's onshore and offshore funds. When questioned, Israel gave a disappointing answer about reallocating profitable trades from one fund to the other in order to equalize performance. Tremont's ongoing due diligence process was very profitable, as it was able to withdraw assets before the demise of the fund.

As is often the case, the alleged fraud was perpetrated by Israel and Marino, without the knowledge of any of their employees. While Bayou had a board of directors, it seems that Israel and Marino constituted a quorum of the board. Unfortunately, the two voted to move $100 million in investor assets to a bank account in Israel's name. The state of Arizona was able to flag and seize this $100 million as the likely proceeds of financial fraud, but the remainder of investor assets remains unaccounted for.

In April 2008, Israel was sentenced to 20 years in jail after pleading guilty to securities fraud and conspiracy. He forfeited $100 million in assets and was required to pay an additional $300 million to investors to compensate them for over $450 million in losses. Previously, Marino and cofounder James Marquez were sentenced to nearly six years of combined sentences for their role in the fraud.

21.4.3 Lancer Group

The story of Lancer Group is chronicled in *Forbes* magazine by Condon (2005). It seems that Michael Lauer would have passed any type of preinvestment due diligence checks. Lauer had the pedigree that other hedge fund managers dream about, as he was a graduate of Columbia University and a six-time member of *Institutional Investor*'s all-star equity analyst team.

As at Bayou and Wood River, Lancer focused on trades in equity securities. This time, there was a mix of private and public shares, typically of very small-capitalization companies. Lauer's investors allowed him the personal discretion to value the restricted shares of these illiquid holdings. This violates one of the cardinal rules of operational risk management: Never allow a portfolio manager the ability to price his own positions, especially if his income depends on those valuations. If investors allow a portfolio manager to value his own holdings, the temptation to earn high incentive fees may overcome his naturally honest personality. The higher the valuation of the fund's securities, the higher the incentive fees earned by the fund. However, if the shares cannot be sold at the inflated price, the large incentive fees can quickly deplete the assets in the accounts. Over a three-year period, Lauer is reported to have earned management and incentive fees totaling $44 million. The fund raised $613 million in investor capital, net of redemptions. While Lancer valued the assets at $1.2 billion, at the end of the day, the fund actually held only $70 million.

Lauer declined to offer transparency to his investors, as he refused to identify the companies that were owned in the portfolio. As his fund was filled with large positions in illiquid shares, his hesitancy to reveal the names of his holdings could have been related to the large market impact that other traders could inflict on the value of Lancer's stocks.

Condon describes how Lancer allegedly purchased large stakes in unregistered shares. Financial theory tells us that unregistered shares should trade at an illiquidity discount when compared to the freely floating shares issued by the same firm. Lauer is said to have purchased 1.7 million unregistered shares in SMX at 23 cents per share. While the company had no operations, the fund valued the company at nearly $200 million in market capitalization. Hedge fund valuations are typically calculated at the end of each calendar month, using the last prices traded in each holding. Lancer, and other hedge funds, may participate in "window-dressing" by making trades that are designed to manipulate the month-end prices of large holdings. At the end of a month, Lauer was reported to have purchased 2,800 of the freely floating shares at $19.50 per share, a large premium to the price trading just minutes earlier. Later in the year, he purchased 1,000 as the last trade of the month, this time at $27. These small trades in the registered, tradable shares were used to mark all 5.7 million shares in the fund at a gain of 8,000% over the purchase price. Not only were the public shares not able to be sold at this price, but the restricted shares would likely trade at an even lower price.

Eisinger (2005a) describes the potential of similar window-dressing issues at JLF Asset Management. This hedge fund manager owns over 5% of four different publicly traded companies. Each of these companies increased in value by 3% to 8% in the final minutes of August 2005, when the Russell 2000 increased by only 2% in the entire day. Although the article did not access the trading records of the hedge fund, the circumstantial evidence seems to have many similarities to Lancer.

Unfortunately, PricewaterhouseCoopers (PwC), which served as Lancer's auditor, eventually published an audit verifying these valuations. The firm asked for full appraisals on 10 companies yet only received 4. Those four appraisals were written by a biased party who may have had an ownership stake or a financial interest in the target companies. In the end, the audit stated that most of the fund value was based on unrealized gains, with prices based on the manager valuation. PwC does not seem to have questioned the ultimate valuation of the target companies, leaving investors to decide from the auditor's language whether Lauer's valuations were warranted.

Because investors gave Lauer discretion in valuing the shares, he may have legally been able to do so, even at these extremely high prices. However, Lancer may have perpetrated one illegal activity. Condon explains that Lancer did not file a Form 13D on 15 companies, which the Securities and Exchange Commission (SEC) requires whenever an investor owns greater than a 5% stake in a firm. Had he filed these 13D reports as required, careful investors may have been able to understand the significant illiquidity risk in the fund.

In February 2008, Michael Lauer and four other defendants were charged with securities fraud and other crimes that could lead to prison sentences of up to 25 years. The indictment alleges that two of the auditors were providing false valuations and had financial interests in the companies that they were valuing for Lancer's fund.

21.4.4 Wood River Capital Management

The alleged losses at Wood River Capital Management are described by Cantrell (2005). Wood River was a $265 million equity hedge fund. The offering memorandum given to investors stated that "individual long positions would typically be capped at 10 percent of the portfolio." It seems that Wood River failed due to unauthorized trading, as the most significant losses in the fund came from one stock that was over 80% of the fund's value. Of course, this large concentration is contrary to the offering memorandum, which investors relied on when making their decision to allocate assets to the fund. Taking concentrated positions is not illegal when it is specifically allowed in the offering memorandum. However, trading in excess of the risk limits provided to investors may likely subject Wood River to civil liabilities for the trading losses.

Wood River's trading losses were incurred in Endwave, a small-capitalization stock that declined in value from $54 to $14 per share between July and October of 2005. Investing over 80% of the firm's capital in a stock that declines 75% is a significant market risk event that could lead to significant losses and likely liquidation of any fund. It is important here to note the interaction of market risk and operational risk in this case. Clearly, a 75% decline in the value of one stock is the definition of market risk. This fund failure would be solely attributed to market risk should Wood River's initial position in the stock have been less than the self-imposed 10% limit. However, when the size of the position exceeded the 10% holdings limit, this became an operational risk issue, as the increase in the size of the position was unauthorized by the investors. The portfolio manager informed investors that the fund was being audited, but that was not true. Clearly, an audit by a reputable firm could have uncovered this concentrated position, perhaps before the losses were incurred. Wood River did not file the required SEC disclosures when holding over 5% of the shares of a publicly traded company.

An interesting loser in this fund was Lehman Brothers, the firm's prime broker. Lehman stated that Wood River placed an order to buy $20 million in Endwave shares. When Lehman executed the trade, Wood River is alleged to have not settled the trade as promised, leaving Lehman responsible to pay the seller of the shares. Unfortunately, Endwave shares dropped quickly, leaving Lehman Brothers with an $8 million loss.

The portfolio manager of Wood River, John Whittier, was sentenced to three years in prison in October 2007 and forfeited assets of over

$5.5 million. Whittier pleaded guilty to securities fraud that caused the loss of $88 million in investor capital.

21.5   RED FLAGS IN THE HEDGE FUND INDUSTRY

Bollen and Krepeley (2005) offer a proposal to the SEC to build a quantitative system that can flag the hedge funds that may have the highest potential for operational risk failures. This time-series model searches for asymmetric serial correlation in returns. Hedge fund managers can maximize their incentive fees or attempt to cover trading losses when they are quick to report large gains and slow to report smaller losses. Only 4% of funds in their sample show this return pattern. This finding can quickly focus the due diligence efforts of the overworked SEC on a relatively small corner of the hedge fund universe.

Once the investigator has found this smaller sample, a more comprehensive look at the risk of each individual fund is undertaken. Funds may legitimately show this return pattern if their holdings typically contain purchased options. For funds that fail the quantitative screen, the presence of additional red flags can be a very strong signal that this could be a fund with a significant probability of operational failure. Funds that seem to be misrepresenting their returns will exhibit an asymmetric smoothing of returns, where they are quick to report gains but smooth losses over an extended period of time.

One of the most important risk factors found by Bollen and Krepeley is the presence of a significant volatility of investor cash flows. Funds that raise a large amount of assets may have problems investing at a higher scale, while funds with significant withdrawals may have other investors who have discovered issues that made them uncomfortable with the risks of the fund. Funds with large withdrawals may be tempted to misrepresent returns in order to prevent other investors from exiting the fund.

21.6   PROPOSAL FOR PARTIAL TRANSPARENCY

What policy prescription can we propose as a result of these recent hedge fund failures and our focus on operational risk? If full transparency is not offered by hedge fund managers or valued by investors, perhaps it is best that investors not demand complete knowledge of the fund's positions and trading strategies. It is recommended that investors access a system of partial transparency that searches for clues that betray both the operational and market risks of a hedge fund.

It is imperative that the partial transparency system be provided by a third-party valuation or software firm. This firm would have an expertise in financial modeling and would have strict controls on the confidentiality of its data and the trading behavior of its employees. The data input to this system *must* be provided to the aggregating firm directly by the hedge fund's custodial banks and prime brokers. Given that we are dealing with operational risk, we need an independent verification of assets, positions, and returns. Otherwise, if we relied on fund managers to provide the inputs to the system, as proposed by Hedges (2005), they could provide fraudulent positions nearly as easily as they provide fraudulent returns to their investors, which would render our operational risk system ineffective.

The inputs into the market risk system are well known and have been documented by the many contributors to Parker (2000). With the position data provided by all parties in custody of the assets of the hedge fund, the aggregator will calculate the risk exposures. The report to investors or regulators would contain only aggregated data, thus protecting the valuable position level data of the fund.

The market risk report would contain these statistics:

- Total investor capital (assets under management)
- Total dollar value of positions, which can be used to calculate leverage
- Total notional value of positions for derivatives
- The total size of long and short positions in each exchange traded market:
  - Stocks, options, and futures
- The total size of long and short positions in each OTC and restricted liquidity market:
  - Options, swaps, fixed income securities, restricted stock, venture capital
- The net exposures to market risk factors:
  - Beta, duration, convexity, yield curve risk, volatility, equity multiples, and so on.
  - Range and average market capitalization of equity securities
  - Credit rating distribution of fixed income securities
  - Sector distribution of futures, options and equity securities
- Liquidity statistics:
  - Total dollar value traded in the fund each time period
  - Total dollar value traded as a percent of total volume in that security
  - Size of each position as a portion of average volume
  - Percent of each issue owned
  - Diversification statistics
  - Size of the largest position

- Size of the average position
- Number of positions owned

The inputs into the operational risk system may be less obvious or well known:

- Total investor capital (assets under management)
- Investor cash flows minus contributions to and withdrawals from the fund
- Change in trading volume
- Change in types of instruments traded
- Relationship of returns of the fund to other funds in the same trading style
- Source of and process for valuing OTC positions
- Estimate of performance, with marks directly from brokers or pricing services
  - At month end, to match to the manager's return estimate
  - At a random midmonth date, to detect window dressing

It is easy to see the application of the market risk statistics. If leverage, position sizes, or factor risks are too large, investors can ask the manager to reduce the position. Alternatively, managers can implement their own hedging strategy or investors can search for a manager with a more comfortable risk profile. The liquidity statistics are important, as they feed directly into the operational risks of valuation. For example, the liquidity statistics could have detected that Wood River's Endwave position was larger than that allowed by investors. These statistics could have also detected the failure of Lancer and Wood River to file the 13D forms required by the SEC.

The application of the operational risk statistics directly follow from the case studies of recent hedge fund frauds. Bollen and Krepely (2005) show the importance of the volatility of assets under management. A rapid decline in assets may show the misappropriation of investor funds. We would hope that the sooner this activity is revealed, the greater the probability of recovering a significant portion of the investor funds. If Bayou overstated its assets under management (AUM), this misrepresentation would be revealed on the operational risk report. If managers are misstating the amount of AUM, they may also be untruthful in other areas. AUM is an important issue, as many large investors are unable to commit assets to a fund until the manager has reached critical mass. The requirement of a large asset base, perhaps over $100 million AUM, can ensure that the institutional investor will not control the majority of the fund's assets, but also that the fund manager has significant experience trading with this asset size. Trading larger blocks of securities can be much more complicated than the experience of trading in a smaller account.

We could also see how Bayou's significant decline in trading volume may have revealed that the fund was planning on liquidating many months before over $100 million was moved into the fund manager's personal account. The midmonth return estimate would be effective at valuing Lancer's positions at closer to their true market value rather than the manipulated value at the closing minute of each month. A change in trading volume and the types of instruments traded can show the potential for style drift or the preparations for the liquidation of the fund or the theft of investor assets.

Bayou, Wood River, and Lancer typically stated that they traded equity securities. Exchange traded securities, such as stocks, futures, and options, have little model risk or valuation risk. Once the exchange sets the closing price for the day, it is easy to apply that price to the positions within any investment account. Tran (2006) shows the difficulty of valuing securities that are not exchange traded. Given that hedge funds enjoy earning the return premiums of holding illiquid securities, these difficult-to-value positions are becoming an even larger portion of hedge fund holdings. Consider the wide range of fixed income securities, including convertible bonds, junk and distressed bonds, and mortgage-backed securities. Because many of these bonds are issued in small sizes, the trading volume may be very low. If weeks, or months, pass since the last trade of a specific security, the issue can be difficult to value, even by an honest and intelligent analyst. Not only are these issues illiquid, but they can be subject to significant model risk, as the pricing process can require estimates of volatility, correlation, credit spreads, and mortgage prepayment rates. Even soliciting broker quotes can be problematic, as brokers may provide a wide range of prices, especially for securities with wide bid-offer spreads. Valuation becomes even more imprecise for complex OTC derivatives or private equity positions. OTC positions, such as those in the natural gas market traded by Amaranth, are subject to illiquidity and pricing risk. Extremely large positions in an illiquid market are subject to significant market impact costs should fund managers be forced to exit those positions quickly. Market impact costs increase rapidly when positions are revealed to the market, which can occur when a fund is forced to exit positions due to investor redemptions, market losses, or a reduction in leverage required by the prime broker.

21.7 CONCLUSION

Most hedge fund investors are familiar with the methods and data required to calculate the market risk of a fund. However, not all hedge funds provide the transparency required to calculate these statistics. Even if investors could get accurate market risk statistics, much less attention has been paid to the detection and prevention of operational risk.

When managers do not provide complete transparency, investors should be pleased to have the opportunity to purchase reports on market risk and operational risk that have been aggregated from information provided directly by the fund's brokers and custodians. Investors who are able to see complete risk information may have the opportunity to request and receive a redemption of their investment months or years before the fund might fail due to these risks.

Finally, if this concept becomes more popular, hedge fund managers who consent to partial transparency may be seen as a less risky option. Tran (2006) states that the funds that provide audited returns report more accurate returns and have a lower probability of failure. Perhaps funds that consent to partial transparency will have similar statistics, as investors would view these funds as the ones that have nothing to hide—even if they refuse to reveal the specific investments in their portfolio.

REFERENCES

Allison, K., and S. Schurr. 2005. On the trail of crooked hedge funds. *Financial Times*, March 8, www.ft.com/cms/s/0/545f1000-8f77-11d9-af70-00000e2511 c8.html?nclick_check=1.

Bollen, N. P., and V. Krepely. 2005. Red flags for fraud in the hedge fund industry. Working paper, Vanderbilt University, Nashville, TN.

Cantrell, A. 2005. Wood River woes run deep. CNN/Money, October 11. http:// money.cnn.com/2005/10/11/markets/wood_river/index.htm

Condon, Bernard. 2005. A prickly hedge. *Forbes*, www.forbes.com/global/2005/ 1226/096A.html.

Eisinger, J. 2005. Lifting the curtains on hedge-fund window dressing. *Wall Street Journal*, September 7.

Eisinger, J. 2005. Scandals from afar: Bayou case and others won't hurt. *Wall Street Journal*.

Hedges, J. R. IV. 2005. Hedge fund transparency. *European Journal of Finance* 11, (5):411–417.

Hutchings, W. 2008. US charges Lancer Hedge Fund managers with fraud. *Financial News*, February 20, www.efinancialnews.com/homepage/content/2449849712.

Kishan, S. 2008. Brian Hunter fund delivers 40% return after demise of Amaranth. *Bloomberg*, April, 11. www.bloomberg.com/apps/news?pid=newsarchive& sid=am1N_.ddy5eU.

Kundro, C., and S. Feffer. 2004. Valuation issues and operational risk in hedge funds. *Capco* White paper, New York.

Kundro, C., and S. Feffer. 2005. Understanding and mitigating operational risk in hedge fund investments. *Capco* White Paper. New York.

McDonald, I., and J. R. Emshwiller. 2005. Did Bayou bet with con artists? *Wall Street Journal,* September 2, C1.

McDonald, I., I. G. Dugan, and A. Luchetti. 2005. Hedge-fund havoc: Missing cash and a principal's suicide note. *Wall Street Journal,* August 29, A1.

Morgenson, G. 2005. Clues to a hedge fund's collapse. *New York Times,* September 17. www.nytimes.com/2005/09/17/business/17bayou.html.

Reynolds Parker V., Ed. 2000. *Managing hedge fund risk.* London: Risk Books.

Siegel, A. 2008. Bayou "mastermind" gets 20-year sentence. *Investment News,* April, 15. www.investmentnews.com/apps/pbcs.dll/article?AID=/20080415/REG/838266685/-1/BreakingNews04.

Till, H. 2006. EDHEC comments on the Amaranth Case: Early lessons from the debacle. EDHEC Risk and Asset Management Research Centre, Nice, France.

Tran, V. Q. 2006. *Evaluating hedge fund performance.* Hoboken, NJ: John Wiley & Sons.

U.S. Department of Justice. 2007 Hedge fund manager sentenced to 3 years in prison for $88 million securities fraud scheme. http://media-newswire.com/release_1056258.html.

CHAPTER 22

A Risk of Ruin Approach for Evaluating Commodity Trading Advisors

Greg N. Gregoriou and Fabrice Douglas Rouah

ABSTRACT

Loss of investor capital through gambler's ruin represents the worst possible outcome for investors in commodity trading advisors (CTAs). Investors that choose CTAs with a high risk of ruin might be exposing themselves to operational risk, since those CTAs may be straying from their stated investment objectives and assuming large amounts of risk, or may be too preoccupied with running daily operations and raising investor capital to focus on their investments. While the manager screening and selection process usually involves quantitative analysis that focuses on alpha, the Sharpe ratio, and other measures, the risk of ruin of a CTA and the optimal leverage that the CTA is using are rarely examined. In this chapter, we examine drivers of the risk of ruin and show that CTAs that chase high returns and incur high volatility are at increased risk of ruin. We also show that the risk of ruin is asymmetrical with returns, so that investors are punished with a high risk of ruin when returns deteriorate but are not necessarily rewarded with a decreased risk of ruin when returns improve.

The views expressed by the authors in this chapter are their own and do not necessarily represent the views of State Street Corporation or of any of its subsidiaries or affiliates.

22.1   INTRODUCTION

The managed futures industry has been increasing progressively during the last 10 years, due in part to higher global market volatility. In volatile markets or during bear markets, investors turn to managed futures to balance and provide downside protection in traditional stock and bond investment portfolios. It is well known that stocks and bonds alone are not able to provide portfolio diversification as efficiently as when alternative investments are included. As pointed out by Diz (2001), adding alternative investments such as managed futures into traditional investment portfolios increases diversification, decreases risk, and improves portfolio returns. Investors opting to add CTAs into their portfolios frequently allocate only a small fraction of their assets (Georgiev 2001). In view of their low to negative correlation to stock, bond, and currency markets, CTAs can provide positive net returns during volatile and down markets.

One operational risk faced by investors is that the CTAs they select may take on undue risk and that the investor capital will be lost through overly aggressive investing, excessive use of leverage, or carelessness. Hence, investors want to avoid CTAs whose risk of ruin is high. This is especially important for hedge funds and CTAs, since these funds are often illiquid and impose long lock-up periods on capital and infrequent redemptions. Traditionally, when potential investors or fund managers weigh performance against risk, they are indirectly implying risk of capital loss or risk of ruin, but probabilities of ruin are rarely calculated. The risk of ruin does not measure manager skill, nor can it help the fund manager trade efficiently. It does, however, provide an estimate of the probability that a fund manager will lose a given amount of investor capital. Most investors select CTAs by examining historical performance, by running regression models, by picking the previous year's winners, and by conducting various screening tests such as on-site visits prior to investing. Calculating the worst possible outcome, namely the risk of ruin, is rarely done.

Another operational risk faced by investors is that of a CTA straying from its initial targeted leverage and taking on excessive leverage, because performance is eroding, because the CTA is not devoting enough time to screen investments and to conduct research and perform due diligence, because the CTA is preoccupied with running daily operations, or because of laziness or greed. As Diz (2003) highlights, a 1% increase in leverage is associated with a 0.27% increase in returns, so CTAs with eroding performance may have the incentive to take on additional leverage in an attempt to bolster returns. Gregoriou et al. (2005), however, show that high leverage is associated with decreased survival time. Hence, CTAs may be tempted to increase leverage to magnify returns but will incur higher risk and experience quicker deaths than CTAs that are more cautious in their use of leverage. This is especially important given the finding by Brown, Goetzmann, and Park (2001) that CTAs show shorter survival times than hedge funds.

22.2 DATA

The data set consists of 133 live CTAs taken from the Barclay Trading Group (BAR) database. We use monthly returns net of all management and performance fees, spanning the period from January 1, 1997, to September 30, 2007. The period selected covers the extreme market events of the Asian currency crisis of October 1997, the Russian ruble crisis of August 1998, the NASDAQ bubble of 2000, the terrorist attacks of September 2001, and the subprime loan crisis of August 2007. Using a longer time horizon would have increased the sample size only slightly. The BAR database separates CTAs into four subcategories: Currency, Diversified, Financial, and Stock index. In our analyses we also focus on the largest 50 CTAs, defined in terms of ending assets under management at September 30, 2007.

22.3 METHODOLOGY

22.3.1 Risk of Ruin

Although the risk of ruin is frequently calculated in gambling and in games, it is rarely used as a screening tool for fund managers. The risk of ruin can provide investors with an estimate of the worst-case scenario for investing, namely the probability of losing one's entire initial capital. The risk of ruin cannot help an investor determine whether a CTA manages a portfolio of futures efficiently—that task is better suited to data envelopment analysis (Gregoriou and Zhu 2005). The risk of ruin of a CTA can be defined in terms of the probability of losing money on each trade, summed over an infinite amount of trades. It is calculated assuming that the trades are independent and occur over an infinite horizon and that the probability of ruin will be attained if the CTA trades continually. We reproduce the next equations for the risk of ruin from Vince (1990).

$$\text{Risk of Ruin} = \left(\frac{1-P}{P}\right)^{U} \quad \text{with} \quad P = \tfrac{1}{2}(1 + Z/A) \tag{22.1}$$

where

$$A = \sqrt{\left(\frac{\text{Average Win}}{\text{Stake in Dollars}}\right)^2 \times PW + \left(\frac{\text{Average Loss}}{\text{Stake in Dollars}}\right)^2 \times (1 - PW)}$$

$$Z = \left|\frac{\text{Average Win}}{\text{Stake in Dollars}}\right| \times PW - \left|\frac{\text{Average Loss}}{\text{Stake in Dollars}}\right| \times (1 - PW)$$

PW = probability of winning on any trade

$U = G/A$

G = Percent of account depletion that defines ruin

Hence, if $G = 0.30$, then 30% of the account must be depleted in order for the investor to be ruined. The case $G = 1$ corresponds to the depletion of the entire initial capital.

To investigate the relationship between the risk of ruin and CTA investment traits such as returns, volatility, and leverage, we run the next regression on the estimated risk of ruin.

$$y_i = \alpha + \beta_1\sigma_i + \beta_2 L_i + \beta_3 L_i^2 + \beta_4 DD_i + \beta_5 r_i$$
$$+ \beta_6 r_i^2 + \beta_7 \log(AUM_i) + \varepsilon_i \qquad (22.2)$$

where, for the ith CTA,

σ_i = annualized volatility
L_i = leverage
DD_i = maximum drawdown
r_i = annualized compounded return
$\log(AUM_i)$ = logarithm of ending assets under management
ε_i = error term

The dependent variable, y_i, is the risk of ruin with $G = 0.20$. We include squared values of leverage and returns since a visual inspection of plots between risk of ruin and these two variables suggest a parabolic relationship. We also use nonparametric local regression (Loess) to investigate the univariate relationship between the risk of ruin and explanatory variables.

22.3.2 Optimal Leverage and Risk of Ruin

In this study, leverage is defined as a multiplier on monthly net returns. Optimal leverage is that value of the multiplier that produces the highest geometric average of monthly returns. It is called the "Optimalf" by Vince (1990). Leverage below unity implies that the CTA is maintaining a portion of the investor capital as a reserve, whereas leverage above unity implies that the CTA is borrowing funds to boost performance. The optimal amount of leverage is therefore the multiplier required to generate the greatest amount of final capital for the investor during a given time period.

A CTA leveraged at the optimal amount will usually have a maximum drawdown of approximately 50%, which is not acceptable to most investors. Optimal leverage will yield the greatest final wealth, but this wealth may never be attained since a large drawdown would force many CTAs to liquidate their positions prior to the terminal date. If the CTA experiences a drawdown significantly larger than its historical drawdown, the CTA may find it optimal to close its positions before the terminal wealth is reached. To obtain the optimal leverage, we use a numerical search algorithm that maximizes the geometric average. For additional information about the optimal leverage factor, see Vince (1990).

22.4 RESULTS

Descriptive statistics on the 133 CTAs in our sample appear in Table 22.1. The risk of ruin of 20% of capital is 19.2% on average, while the optimal leverage is slightly above 5%. The largest CTA had ending assets of over $32 billion, while the smallest, barely over $100,000. The performance of the cohort is good and the volatility is not unreasonably high.

In Table 22.2 we present statistics on the top 50 CTAs in the database, including annualized compounded return and standard deviation, optimal leverage, risk of ruin (with $G = 0.20$), ending millions under management, Sharpe ratio, and maximum drawdown. The results indicate that CTA 50 has the greatest risk of initial capital loss (risk of ruin). For that CTA, there is a 52.5% probability that the capital loss will exceed 20%. Twelve CTAs are tied with the lowest probability of 1%, and six of those are in the top 10 CTAs in terms of ending assets under management greater than $1.9 billion. One possible explanation is the inverse relationship between size and risk. Large CTAs are concerned with capital preservation, and hence adopt more

TABLE 22.1 Descriptive Statistics for the Entire Sample

Variable	Mean	Std Dev	Median	Min	Max
Risk of 20% Ruin (%)	19.2	23.6	10.4	1	100
Optimal Leverage (%)	5.4	9.1	3.4	−4.9	66.9
Ending Assets ($M)	647	3,035	49.7	0.1	32,844
Annualized Return (%)	10.9	6.0	10.4	−5.8	28.8
Annualized Std Dev (%)	19.8	10.0	17.5	1.6	58.8
Sharpe Ratio	0.19	0.49	0.25	1.00	0.99
Maximum Drawdown (%)	29.4	16.9	26.1	1.3	90.9

TABLE 22.2 Summary Statistics for 50 Largest CTAs

CTA	Annualized Return	Annualized Std Dev	Optimal Leverage	Risk of Ruin of 20%	Ending Millions	Sharpe Ratio	Maximum Drawdown
1	10.0	8.7	11.8	1.0	32,844	0.7	14.2
2	7.5	13.1	4.8	5.1	8,532	0.2	15.1
3	10.9	13.8	5.2	3.4	8,244	0.5	16.8
4	6.1	5.3	30.0	1.0	2,738	0.4	4.2
5	17.0	18.0	5.9	3.5	2,684	0.7	18.0
6	7.9	8.9	9.1	1.0	2,404	0.4	12.4
7	26.9	32.2	2.5	15.3	2,154	0.6	41.2
8	15.7	14.5	8.5	1.0	1,962	0.8	9.4
9	15.3	13.1	7.8	1.0	1,942	0.9	19.4
10	10.4	9.0	13.2	1.0	1,861	0.7	10.8
11	15.4	13.8	9.6	1.0	1,600	0.8	11.5
12	7.3	16.1	2.6	17.2	1,548	0.1	23.3
13	9.9	9.5	10.7	1.0	1,472	0.6	11.1
14	11.2	14.8	4.8	3.3	1,160	0.5	18.7
15	4.3	15.1	1.7	17.4	1,038	−1.0	27.6
16	12.5	14.4	5.3	2.0	1,026	0.6	17.2
17	8.3	13.2	4.8	4.7	1,018	0.3	15.8
18	9.5	13.5	4.8	4.3	953	0.4	16.8
19	7.9	16.2	3.0	15.9	847	0.2	23.7
20	20.5	22.7	4.8	5.3	547	0.7	36.5
21	9.5	11.1	8.3	1.0	542	0.5	11.9
22	5.2	8.6	7.0	1.2	542	0.1	14.9
23	12.8	35.6	1.1	48.2	493	0.1	47.1
24	9.8	13.5	5.8	2.8	380	0.4	16.5
25	7.2	15.6	2.9	12.1	380	0.1	26.0
26	9.3	18.4	2.9	16.7	373	0.2	29.3
27	13.8	18.4	4.5	7.3	360	0.5	20.2
28	13.8	14.9	8.8	1.0	351	0.6	16.9
29	8.8	17.2	3.1	13.9	345	0.2	25.4
30	15.4	23.2	2.9	14.8	332	0.4	32.1
31	14.2	17.2	4.8	5.7	266	0.6	20.1
32	10.3	22.4	2.0	28.1	251	0.2	30.5
33	15.9	18.5	4.6	6.2	233	0.6	21.6
34	9.3	18.2	2.8	16.5	204	0.2	29.1
35	20.8	23.7	3.5	10.1	199	0.7	19.9
36	11.8	23.5	2.1	27.3	178	0.2	45.6
37	17.1	36.6	1.3	45.9	178	0.2	63.8
38	17.8	18.3	7.8	1.1	176	0.7	17.2
39	9.4	17.5	3.5	6.0	165	0.2	23.6

TABLE 22.2 (*Continued*)

CTA	Annualized Return	Annualized Std Dev	Optimal Leverage	Risk of Ruin of 20%	Ending Millions	Sharpe Ratio	Maximum Drawdown
40	10.4	24.0	1.9	27.8	164	0.2	27.1
41	4.0	17.9	1.3	41.8	152	−1.0	26.9
42	15.9	14.6	4.0	1.0	151	0.8	24.4
43	12.7	19.6	2.9	10.7	147	0.4	41.1
44	10.7	26.9	1.5	37.5	143	0.1	28.2
45	17.4	17.7	3.7	1.2	139	0.7	26.0
46	14.2	14.9	9.1	1.0	131	0.7	14.4
47	16.4	25.3	2.7	19.1	130	0.4	27.2
48	7.2	23.0	1.4	39.3	126	0.0	39.3
49	10.4	9.0	13.1	1.0	114	0.7	6.1
50	7.9	27.5	1.1	52.5	112	0.0	43.6
Average	11.9	17.6	5.5	12.1	1,681	0.4	23.6

conservative investment strategies and take on less risk, while small CTAs need to post high returns to attract investor capital. This is reflected in a lower standard deviation and lower risk of ruin for large CTAs. The opposite is true for small CTAs.

Table 22.3 presents the Spearman correlations on risk of ruin (with $G = 0.20$) and the variables under consideration. The results are in line with what can be expected for ruin probabilities. The risk of ruin decreases with increasing size, performance, and optimal leverage but increases with volatility and maximum drawdown. CTAs with low Sharpe ratios also have a high risk of ruin. Hence, CTAs that take on undue risk are especially prone to losing capital. As long as leverage is optimal, the use of leverage

TABLE 22.3 Spearman Correlations

	Leverage	AUM	Returns	Volatility	SR	DD
Ruin	−0.95***	−0.33***	0.01	0.76***	−0.62***	0.84***
Leverage	1	0.36***	−0.05	−0.79***	0.60***	−0.90***
AUM		1	0.18**	−0.18**	0.39***	−0.37***
Returns			1	0.56***	0.65***	0.22**
Volatility				1	−0.14*	0.83***
SR					1	−0.42***

***, ***, * denote a correlation significant at the 1%, 5%, and 10% level, respectively.

TABLE 22.4 Regression of Risk of Ruin

Variable	Model 1	Model 2	Model 3	Model 4	Model 5	Model 6	Model 7
Intercept	−9.55***	35.88***	−12.00***	26.73***	31.44***	13.06***	14.64***
Standard Deviation	1.42***					1.79***	2.12***
Leverage		−4.36***				−0.27	
Leverage Squared		0.06***				0.01	
Maximum Drawdown			1.04***			0.18	
Monthly Return				−5.93***		−4.35***	−4.58***
Monthly Return Squared				0.22***		0.08***	0.08***
Log(AUM)					−3.44***	0.40	
Adjusted R-squared	0.39	0.39	0.61	0.30	0.15	0.82	0.82

***, ***, * denote a coefficient significant at the 1%, 5%, and 10% level, respectively.

decreases the risk of ruin. In that sense, leverage is not risky but beneficial. As expected, volatility is positively correlated with returns and maximum drawdown. High-volatility CTAs earn high returns but can also experience large drawdowns.

Table 22.4 presents the results of a series of regression models that use the risk of ruin as a dependent variable, and the variables in Table 22.1. The variables are first examined univariately and then jointly in Model 6. Model 7 retains only those variables in Model 6 that are significant at the 1% level or less. In these analyses we use squared values for returns and leverage, since these variables exhibit a parabolic relationship with the risk of ruin.

Models 1 through 5 indicate that all the variables are significantly related to the risk of ruin, when the variables are examined univariately. In multiple regression (Model 6), only returns and volatility remain significant predictors; the other variables drop out. The final model (Model 7) shows that these variables are strongly related to returns and volatility. CTAs will experience an increase of 212 basis points (bps) in their risk of ruin when their volatility jumps by 100 bps. They will experience a decrease in their risk of ruin when their returns increase, but this decrease will be mitigated in CTAs whose returns are already high. Suppose, for example, that two CTAs each have an annualized volatility of 20%, and that one CTA posts a 5% annualized return while the other posts a 15% annualized return.

An increase of 100 bps in the first CTA's returns (from 5% to 6%) will decrease its risk of ruin by 370 bps, since

$$\left[14.64 + 2.12(20) - 4.58(6) + 0.08(6^2)\right]$$
$$- \left[14.64 + 2.12(20) - 4.58(5) + 0.08(5^2)\right] = -3.70$$

Similarly, the second CTA will experience a decrease of only 210 bps in risk of ruin when its returns increase from 15% to 16%. Hence, poorly performing CTAs have the greatest incentive to bolster returns and avoid capital deterioration through risk of ruin.

The results in Table 22.4 point to returns and volatility being the strongest predictors for the risk of ruin. To examine this relationship more closely, we perform nonparametric local regression of risk of ruin on returns and volatility separately, using as a dependent variable the risk of ruin using $G = 0.10, 0.20, 0.50,$ and 1.00. Figure 22.1 presents a plot of predicted values from the nonparametric regression of ruin on volatility. The graph shows a strong linear and positive relationship between the risk of ruin and volatility. This relationship is particularly strong for low risk of ruin. For example, for funds with 40% volatility, the risk of losing 10% of initial

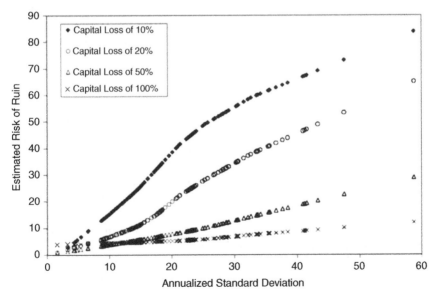

FIGURE 22.1 Nonparametric Regression of Risk of Ruin on Returns Volatility

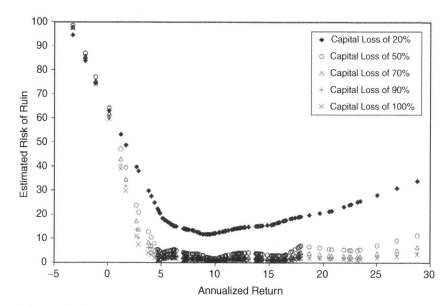

FIGURE 22.2 Nonparametric Regression of Risk of Ruin on Returns

capital is roughly 70%, while the risk of losing 20% of initial capital is roughly 45%. For higher values of risk of ruin, however, the relationship is weak. The risk of losing all initial capital ($G = 1$) is under 10%, regardless of the CTA's volatility. Hence, while low volatility might be a favorable signal that the risk of losing small amounts of capital is small, the signal is weak when large ruins are involved. Unfortunately, low-volatility CTAs cannot be expected to protect investors against the risk of losing large amounts of capital, only against small amounts.

The results of the nonparametric regression of risk of ruin on annualized returns are presented in Figure 22.2 and tell a different story. For small capital ruin ($G = 0.20$), the relationship is convex, so that the lowest risk of ruin occurs among CTAs that post annualized returns of roughly 10%. For large capital ruins ($G \geq 0.50$), however, the relationship is kinked at an annualized return of 5%. Hence, for large capital ruin, the exposure of investors to the risk of ruin is similar to holding a put option on ruin, with a "strike" of roughly 5%. When returns are above 5%, the risk of ruin is always below 10%, but when returns fall below 5%, the risk of ruin increases dramatically, and in a linear fashion. This suggests that an annualized return of 5% acts as a threshold for large ruin. As long as the CTA can earn this return, investors are protected from ruin. When returns fall below 5%, however, the put option is exercised and investors become heavily exposed to the risk of ruin. The asymmetrical relationship between risk of ruin and returns implies that investors are punished with an increased risk of ruin when returns fall but are not rewarded with a decrease in risk of ruin when returns recover.

22.5 CONCLUSION

Loss of capital represents the worst operational event for investors into CTAs. In this chapter, we demonstrate that the risk of ruin is a screening tool that pension funds, institutional investors, fund-of-funds managers, and high-net-worth individuals can use to select CTAs that are likely to avoid losing their capital through negligence or incompetence. Both measures are nonparametric and can complement existing quantitative measures to help widen the picture of CTA performance appraisal. While leverage is often thought of as risky, in this chapter we show that CTAs using an optimal amount of leverage actually face a decrease in the risk of ruin. We also demonstrate that the risk of ruin is strongly related to returns and volatility. Low volatility protects investors against the risk of ruin, but only for small losses in capital. Low volatility does not appear to protect investors again the loss of most or all of their capital. We also find an asymmetrical relationship between the risk of ruin and returns that resembles a put option on the risk of ruin.

ACKNOWLEDGMENTS

We thank Richard Oberuc Sr. at Laporte Asset Allocation System/ Dynaporte.

REFERENCES

Brown, S. J., W. N. Goetzmann, and J. Park. 2001. Careers and survival: Competition and risk in the hedge fund and CTA industry. *Journal of Finance* 56, no. 5: 1869–1886.

Diz, F. 1999. "How do CTAs' return Distribution characteristics affect their likelihood of survival?" *Journal of Alternative Investments* 2, no. 2:37–41.

Diz, F. 2001. Are investors overinvested in equities? *Derivatives Quarterly* 7, no. 3:59–62.

Diz, F. 2003. Commodity trading advisors' leverage and reported margin-to-equity ratios. *Journal of Futures Markets* 23, no. 10:1003–1017.

Georgiev, G. 2001. Benefits of commodity investment. Working paper, Isenberg School of Management, University of Massachusetts, Amherst, MA.

Gregoriou, G. N., G. Hübner, N. Papageorgiou, and F. Rouah. 2005. Survival of commodity trading advisors: 1990–2003. *Journal of Futures Markets* 25, no. 8:795–816.

Gregoriou, G. N., and J. Zhu. 2005. *Data envelopment analysis: Evaluating hedge funds and CTAs.* Hoboken, NJ: John Wiley & Sons.

Vince, R. 1990. *Portfolio management formulas.* Hoboken, NJ: John Wiley & Sons.

CHAPTER 23

Identifying and Mitigating Valuation Risk in Hedge Fund Investments

Meredith A. Jones

ABSTRACT

Portfolio valuation and pricing can be a significant issue for hedge funds, from both a strategy execution and an operational standpoint. There have been several instances where failure to thoughtfully value a portfolio has ultimately led to a hedge fund's untimely demise. This chapter attempts to shed light on the operational issues surrounding hedge fund valuation and pricing. It includes a discussion of the operational risks involved in valuation and pricing, separates operational valuation from strategy-related valuation issues, discusses which strategies are more susceptible to operational valuation risk, and specifies what investors can do to discover and mitigate these risks.

23.1 INTRODUCTION

When evaluating or investing in hedge funds, it is important to consider both strategy risks and operational risks. For most, evaluating the strategy risks involved in making hedge fund investments has become second nature. However, the importance of and skills required for evaluating the operational risks involved with hedge fund investing have only begun getting the same attention in recent years. Operational risk, however, cannot be ignored. In fact, a 2005 EDHEC white paper attributed fully 50% of hedge fund failures to operational issues alone. Certain widely known hedge fund failures, such as Beacon Hill, Lancer Management Group, Bayou Fund, and Integral Investment Management, give credence to how critical the operations of a fund can be to its ultimate success or failure (Giraud 2005). With all of the funds just listed, faulty or fraudulent valuation and pricing procedures ultimately led to the failure of the fund and investor losses of hundreds of millions, highlighting the need for investors to understand valuation and pricing risks, and how to investigate and mitigate those risks effectively.

23.2   WHAT IS OPERATIONAL VALUATION RISK?

When calculating the value of any hedge fund investment, the underlying holdings must be appropriately priced. With some types of investments, such as equities or bonds, this is a straightforward process, involving the accepted, widely known, and easily verified market prices. Other instruments, such as mortgage-backed securities, Private Investment in Public Equities (PIPES), debt instruments, Regulation D investments, warrants, asset-backed securities, and other instruments that do not have readily observable prices, may require complex modeling, outside price quotes, or subjective input from various parties (including but not limited to the fund management) to obtain a current value. It is in this valuation process where significant operational risk can be introduced.

Before continuing, it is important to distinguish between the investment risk of valuation and the operational valuation risk. As any investor knows, past performance is not necessarily indicative of future results, and all investments can deteriorate in value. However, actual losses on investments, although they decrease the value of a fund, do not constitute operational valuation losses. Take, for example, a fund that holds 100 shares of IBM at $100 per share. If the share price of IBM slips to $90 per share, the fund will post a $1,000 loss. These losses could be attributed to poor stock selection by the manager (skill), a broad market move, or chance but would not be attributed to poor valuation practices. Now take the same manager, who also holds a position in XYZ Corp., a publicly held company, through a PIPE or Regulation D investment. If the position in XYZ Corp. is held at cost, one might assume that the valuation risk is zero. However, when exiting the position, the manager, who owns a significant amount of the float and whose total number of shares far exceeds the total daily trading value of the company, posts a loss when the market is flooded by shares without a corresponding increase in demand. By not accounting for these issues in their marking with a liquidity discount or other mechanism, the manager has arbitrarily valued the position higher than its actual value. Further, if that manager has sole discretion over the value of this position, with no independent verification, and can mark based on his judgment alone, then there is not an appropriate control over the valuation of the position. If the manager had losses in another portion of the portfolio, he or she could arbitrarily mark this position up to make up for those losses. Both of these instances represent valuation risk. In the first instance, even though there are some inherent valuation risks involved in this strategy, the manager also exercised poor valuation risk control on a strategy level by not accounting for the percent of float and the daily trading volume. In the second instance, the manager opens up to valuation risk by not having sufficient controls in place to guarantee the integrity of the fund valuation.

23.3   VALUATION RISK: STRATEGY RELATED

As demonstrated, there are two primary kinds of valuation risk, some the natural result of certain investment strategies, which we will examine first, and others that result from poor valuation controls within a fund or fund management company, which we will discuss in Section 23.3.

Valuation risk can be a natural result of certain strategies that do not lend themselves to black-and-white valuation procedures. One way to understand strategy-related valuation risk may be to look at three managers who all employ the same basic strategy and the differences in valuation practice between them. Let us take three Regulation D securities managers as an example where each fund invests in private securities of public companies.

Fund A has a portfolio of Regulation D investments and provides monthly net asset values (NAVs) to investors. The valuation policy that Fund A employs is to determine the total potential profit for each deal booked and spread that profit equally over the expected duration of the deal. Therefore, if a position was booked in at a 25% discount to market value of the stock, with a five-month expected holding period, Fund A would book an unrealized 5% gain in each of the next five months. Fund A's valuation risk is quite high, since the 5% unrealized gains booked each month are rather arbitrary and do not consider the actual price that may be booked on liquidation nor how long that liquidation may actually take, which can further impact returns. The returns for Fund A may appear very smooth, as long as deal flow remains strong and the markets favorable. Additional investors are likely to be attracted to the steady gains and may be in for a nasty surprise if deal flow slows or if liquidity dries up. For example, let us assume the position just mentioned takes an additional 10 months to liquidate after the initial expected 5-month duration "maturation." During this time, the market sells off (think the "tech wreck" that occurred in 2001), and the position must be liquidated in a bearish environment where the fundamentals of the company have changed. At this point, the 25% gains that were booked are given back and then some, resulting in a disproportionately large, and perhaps surprising, loss.

Fund B also has a portfolio of Regulation D investments and provides monthly NAVs to investors. The valuation policy of Fund B is different from Fund A in that Fund B takes 10% of the expected gain in the first month (2.5% in our example) and then holds the position at that value until the actual liquidation occurs. In this example, Fund B is slightly more conservative than Fund A, but still allows for an initial unrealized gain and then holds the position steady until liquidation. While Fund B has not taken large, unrealized gains arbitrarily, holding the positions at a steady value regardless of market movements can artificially smooth returns as well. When actually liquidating the position, the fund may experience disproportionately large losses related wholly to its valuation policies and their independence of market input.

Fund C's portfolio of Regulation D investments is marked still differently. This manager holds all positions at cost or market, whichever is lower, until actual liquidation. This fund has the lowest valuation risk, with little smoothing of returns or arbitrary inflation of valuation. Any losses due to a change in market environment would be gradual and easier to explain based on the strategy and instruments involved.

As you can see, the options are many and varied for pricing a portfolio of investments that are hard to value, thinly traded, or less liquid, even for fairly straightforward transactions within those strategies. If additional instruments, such as warrants, resets, or collateral obligations, were included in any of the sample funds discussed, the complexity of and manager input into valuation would increase, requiring more diligence on the part of potential investors.

Reg D investments are not the only asset class that introduces an element of valuation risk into a hedge fund investment. Table 23.1 provides an indicative but not exhaustive list of instruments that are more susceptible to valuation risk related to strategy and instruments employed. If investors choose funds that employ these instruments, additional due diligence and ongoing monitoring are required to assess the valuation risk inherent with these instruments and the strategies that utilize them.

Additional guidance on hard-to-value securities is provided by the Financial Accounting Standards Board (FASB), which in November 2007 implemented FAS 157, the fair-value measurement standard. FAS 157 provides guidelines for valuing assets and making disclosures on those assets

TABLE 23.1 Indicative List of Instruments where Valuation Risk Is Inherently Present

---

Nano-cap stocks
Futures
Debt instruments
PIPES
Reg D securities
Warrants
Real estate
Private equity
Asset backed securities
Mortgage-backed securities
Certain option instruments
Convertible bonds
Swaps
Micro-cap stocks
Interest rate forwards

---

by breaking them into one of three levels. Level 1 assets have observable market prices; Level 2 assets do not have observable prices but have inputs that are based on observable prices; and Level 3 assets have no observable price and one or more inputs that do not have observable prices. Reviewing the documentation around FAS 157 can familiarize investors with the types of instruments that may require more diligence and transparency from their hedge fund managers and samples of how those valuations and disclosures might be appropriately made.

23.4   VALUATION RISK: CONTROL RELATED

In addition to valuation risk introduced by certain strategies and instruments, investors must also consider the valuation risk that is caused by a lack of appropriate pricing controls within a fund. Loosely defined, highly subjective, and nonexistent valuation policies can open the door to fraud and fund failure. There have been a number of cases in recent years where a lack of operational controls surrounding the valuation process have resulted in large-scale fraud. A perfect example of this occurred in 2002 when the Securities and Exchange Commission (SEC) filed suit against Conrad P. Seghers and James R. Dickey, alleging that their firm, Integral Investment Management and related funds, had engaged in fraudulent valuation practices. The suit alleges that Signers and Dickey raised more than $71.6 million from approximately 30 investors based on fraudulent fund valuations, which were reported to both current and potential investors.

In short, the strategy that Signers and Dickey employed involved transferring money to a third party, Same M. El Biro, for trading and management using a system that Biro had allegedly developed. From June through November 2000, although 90% of the funds were held in cash, the fund reported gains to their administrator, which in turn reported the results to investors. According to SEC records, the fund asset value was overstated by an average of 20% each of the six months. Table 23.2 details the actual, and perhaps shocking, discrepancies between actual value and stated value.

From March through June 2001, despite Biro informing Signers that the broker-dealer for the account had made a number of errors that prevented accurate valuations, Signers continued to provide fund asset values to investors and prospects. These NAVs were overstated by an average of nearly 46%. Table 23.3 details even more aggressive valuations by Signers, in sharp contrast to the actual asset values.

So, what went wrong? The valuation process broke down because the fund manager, Signers, exclusively controlled the valuation and NAV calculations for the fund, with no independent verification from the administrator. This was fully disclosed to investors in the fund, but at that time, the practice was fairly standard and investors did not have the focus on operational issues such as valuation that they should have today.

Other funds have taken valuation control and fraud even further. The Bayou Group LLC, for example, operated an elaborate Ponzi scheme from 1998 through 2005 that involved funneling commissions from trades placed

TABLE 23.2 Discrepancies between Actual and Stated Value

Statement Date	Funds' Asset Value Reported by Signers to Investors	Funds' Asset Value Calculated Using Reports by Brokers and Banks to Signers	Amount Signers Overstated to Investors	Percent Overstated
6/30/2000	$30,803,908.74	$22,334,733.83	$8,469,174.91	38%
7/31/2000	$35,798,145.28	$30,589,132.96	$5,209,012.32	17%
8/31/2000	$39,571,680.37	$34,252,256.61	$5,319,423.76	16%
9/30/2000	$39,324,430.97	$33,953,941.26	$5,370,489.71	16%
10/31/2000	$35,680,662.52	$29,885,476.69	$5,795,185.83	19%
11/30/2000	$46,448,585.52	$41,041,764.30	$5,406,821.22	13%

Source: Securities and Exchange Commission v. Conrad P. Signers and James R. Dickey

TABLE 23.3 Valuations by Signers in Contrast to Asset Values

Statement Date	Funds' Asset Value Reported by Signers to Investors	Funds' Asset Value Calculated Using Reports by Brokers and Banks to Signers	Actual Asset Value (Correcting for Broker's Errors)	Amount Signers Overstated to Investors	Percent Overstated
3/31/2001	$69,837,817.94	$60,039,724.55	$47,234,137.05	$22,603,680.89	48%
4/30/2001	$69,181,990.53	$57,164,081.70	$47,499,831.70	$21,682,158.83	46%
5/31/2001	$71,555,919.52	$38,948,100.82	$48,103,600.82	$23,452,318.70	49%
6/30/2001	$70,886,740.54	$41,303,631.85	$50,780,381.85	$20,106,358.69	40%

Source: Securities and Exchange Commission v. Conrad P. Signers and James R. Dickey

through the firm's internal broker-dealer back into the fund to hide losses while simultaneously raising capital from new investors to continue the illusion of success. Bayou went a step further, however, even creating a fictitious auditing firm, Richmond-Fairfield, to hide trading losses and preserve the fund's fabricated NAVs.

Michael Lauer, of Lancer Management Group, used the valuation leeway he had in thinly traded penny stocks employed by his trading strategy to inflate fund and position valuations, combining both operational pricing risk, resulting from strategy, with operational valuation risk, resulting from having poor controls, to defraud investors out of capital. As can be seen, a lack of appropriate controls on the valuation procedures, including independent input and review, can quickly spell disaster for all involved.

23.5 EVALUATING AND MITIGATING VALUATION RISK

Given the potential problems that can arise from poor valuation procedures, it is incumbent on investors to make a thorough review of pricing and valuation procedures prior to making an investment. Furthermore, periodic reviews of procedures should be conducted after an investment has been made to ensure that the fund continues to comply with those practices.

To determine the level of strategy-related valuation risk that may exist in the fund, investors should first and foremost be fully aware of all of the assets that the manager is allowed to use within the fund and the instruments that the manager has historically chosen to use. Getting this information is critical to determining the level of additional investigation into the fund's assets and valuation policies as well as what should be watched on an ongoing basis. For example, many offering documents give fund managers wide latitude in the assets that the fund may buy and sell. Looking at the historical use of these assets can provide guidance toward which assets are actually employed and which have been listed for more theoretical purposes. For example, a long/short equity fund may have generally invested in, not surprisingly, equities, but at one point in the fund's history invested in a PIPE transaction. Determining that these disparate assets have been bought and sold at the beginning of the process can help an investor determine if appropriate valuation procedures were used and what plans may be in store to employ these assets (and price them) in the future. That way, there are no surprises should the investor find a PIPE in the fund in the future, and he or she will know exactly how the manager intends to value the asset.

Once the instruments that are or may be used by the fund have been determined, it is important to get a detailed description for how these assets are valued within the fund. For some instruments, such as publicly traded stocks and bonds, the answer may be as simple as a mark-to-market transaction. For more complex, thinly traded, or illiquid securities, the valuation policy will be more complex and will likely require additional digging on the part of the investor. Every investor should get a full write-up of valuation policies and be prepared to ask additional questions to further vet the process. Sample questions might include: If a manager invests in mortgage-backed securities, for example, do they mark at bid, ask, or mid? Whatever the answer, what is the justification for the policy, and does the manager consider it to be a conservative or aggressive approach? Do other managers that employ the same strategy use similar valuation practices? What steps could the manager take, if any, to further ensure the fair valuation of the portfolio? The investor might also ask the manager to explain how market movements (including broad market, sector, interest rates, energy prices, etc.) may impact, positively or negatively, the prices established by the manager. Would a drying of liquidity or a credit crunch impact the portfolio and, if so, have any valuation allowances been made for that?

In talking to the manager during the due diligence process, the investor might look for certain cues that could trigger additional valuation-related questions. Six cues are described.

1. Realized versus unrealized gains. A larger percentage of unrealized gains may signal a more illiquid portfolio, which should trigger additional questions about valuation models and liquidity discounts, if applicable.
2. Annual turnover can provide a good indication of the liquidity of the instruments in the fund. Again, less liquid assets generally require more diligence into the valuation models and policies.
3. Side pockets, past or present, should always trigger additional questions about valuation since side pockets by definition contain hard-to-value securities. The percent of the overall portfolio represented by the side pocket, how long it has existed, how the side pocket is being valued, the expected liquidation date, and expectations to engage in similar arrangements in the future should all be explored.
4. The use of models to price all or a portion of the portfolio. If a model is used, how was it created? Has it been independently tested and verified?
5. The existence of or lack of an independent pricing service, which is often provided by the administrator for offshore funds and prime brokers for U.S.-domiciled funds. Does the administrator or other third party have direct access to all brokerage and bank accounts? Do they generate and send all account statements directly to investors? If the fund does not have an independent pricing service, why not?

6. Experience of the back-office team should be a concern when looking at harder-to-value portfolios. Do the chief financial officer (CFO) and other back-office team members have relevant experience to assist in pricing decisions and valuation policies? For example, in an asset-backed lending fund, the credit and loan experience of those valuing the portfolio is crucial, and when valuing mortgage-backed securities, there will be some professional judgment required, even if FAS 157 guidelines are strictly followed. In addition to knowledge and practical experience, is the CFO experienced enough to confidently stand up to the portfolio manager, if necessary?

In recent years, multiple organizations have encouraged better valuation policies by establishing best practice and fair value guidelines. As previously mentioned, FAS 157, which went into effect on November 15, 2007, gives guidance for valuing and disclosing hard-to-value assets. In addition, two hedge fund industry groups, the Alternative Investment Management Association (AIMA) and the Managed Funds Association (MFA), have released sound practice guides for hedge fund valuation. The recommendations are fairly similar and are summarized and synthesized in the next section.

23.6   SUMMARY AND SYNTHESIS OF SOUND PRACTICE GUIDELINES FOR FUND VALUATION FROM AIMA AND THE MFA

The following is a list of guidelines for fund valuation from the Alternative Investment Management Association and the Managed Funds Association.

1. Establish pricing and valuation guidelines prior to fund launch, producing a valuation policy document. This pricing document should define roles within the valuation process, establish the frequency of NAV calculation and the sources for pricing data, as well as escalation procedures. Furthermore, the guidelines should be realistic. An independent valuation service provider should be able to implement the valuation policy document guidelines.

2. Create a segregation of valuation duties, employing an independent valuation service provider if possible, and otherwise avoiding conflicts of interest by establishing robust controls between the front and back office. To the extent practicable, the investment manager should not be involved in valuing assets.

3. Oversight of the valuation process should rest with the governing body of the fund.
4. Those who calculate, determine, and produce the NAV should be named in the offering documents, with special disclosures around any involvement by the investment manager.
5. Administrators should produce and mail NAVs directly to end investors, with any NAVs produced by the investment manager duly noted.
6. The independent valuation service provider should apply the valuation guidelines uniformly. Any deviations should be approved by the governing body of the fund. Where the fund manager must be involved in valuing assets, full documentation should be provided to any independent valuation service providers to support the valuation.
7. Valuations should be checked against a primary and secondary price source. If broker quotes are used, multiple quotes should be used and the sources of quotes should be consistent. Broker quotes should be obtained by the independent valuation service provider without intervention by fund management.
8. Hedge funds should establish procedures for obtaining confirmations and periodic reconciliations of over-the-counter derivatives with counterparties.
9. The use of pricing models must be approved by the fund's governing body and should be appropriately vetted. If a fund manager's models are used, they should be independently tested.
10. Any use of side pockets should be approved by the fund's governing body. Side pockets should be disclosed to all investors and should be employed consistently by the fund.
11. Hedge funds should adopt appropriate "fair value" accounting standards and periodically close the books, consistent with appropriate accounting principles. The hedge fund should further make provisions for the recordation of all financial and nonfinancial assets and liabilities and should review the allocation of income and expense to end investors. Periodic audits and reviews should be conducted.

One way that hedge fund investors can mitigate valuation risk is to invest only in funds that follow the industry recommended best practices and follow FAS 157 accounting guidelines. Finally, if investors do not feel comfortable establishing that the valuation practices of a particular manager are fair and reasonable, they should look into hiring external firms that specialize in valuation to assist in the evaluation process.

Once an investment has been made, an investor's work is not done. In order to maintain confidence in the manager's valuation practices, the investor should continue to verify that policies are applied consistently and uniformly. This may be as simple as requesting portfolio positions and verifying adherence to stated pricing policies with the help of a Bloomberg terminal or may involve sitting with the portfolio manager and walking through each position in the portfolio on a periodic basis. Again, various valuation firms can assist in the ongoing monitoring process if the investor does not have the time or relevant financial experience.

23.7 CONCLUSION

Valuation of a fund is a critical process. Without appropriate valuations, investors cannot determine if a fund is or remains an appropriate investment, or whether to subscribe, redeem, or add additional funds. Given the existence of hard-to-value securities in a variety of hedge fund strategies, it is essential for any investor to thoroughly review the valuation procedures employed by a fund to protect against strategy valuation risk and operational valuation risk, which in the most extreme cases can lead to fund fraud and failure. Whether an investor chooses to complete valuation due diligence internally or outsource the process is governed by the time and experience that an investor has to devote to the process. Whatever route is chosen, the key is for investors to understand that valuation risk is real, that it can potentially wipe out an investor's capital, and that due diligence is required.

REFERENCES

Alternative Investment Management Association Ltd. 2007. *AIMA's guide to sound practices for hedge fund valuation.* London: Author.
EDHEC. 2005. Mitigating hedge funds' operational risk: Benefits and limitations of managed account platforms. White paper. Nice, France.
Financial Accounting Standards Board. 2007. *Summary of Statement No. 157.* www.fasb.org/st/summary/stsum157.shtml.
Giraud, J. 2005. Mitigating hedge funds' operational risks: Benefits and limitations of managed account platforms. Working Paper, Edhec Risk and Asset Management Research Centre, Nice, France.
Managed Funds Association. 2007. *Sound practices for hedge fund managers.* Washington, DC: Author.
Securities and Exchange Commission v. Michael Lauer, Lancer Management Group, LLC, and Lancer Management Group II, LLC, Defendants, and Lancer Offshore, Inc., Lancer Partners, LP, OmniFund, Ltd., LSPV, Inc., and LSPV, LLC, July 8, 2003, Relief Defendants. Case No. 03-80612-CIV-ZLOCH. United States District Court for the Southern District of Florida.

Securities and Exchange Commission v. Samer El Bizri, Conrad P. Seghers, and James Dickey, Integral Hedging LP, Integral Arbitrage LP, and Integration Equity LP, February 8, 2002. Case No. CV 02-01251 MMM (FMOx). United States District Court for the Central District of California.

Securities and Exchange Commission v. Samuel Israel III; Daniel E. Marino; Bayou Management, LLC; Bayou Accredited Fund, LLC; Bayou Affiliates Fund, LLC; Bayou No Leverage Fund, LLC; and Bayou Superfund, LLC, September 29, 2005. Civil Action No. 05-CIV-8376. United States District Court for the Southern District of New York.

Index

Printed and bound by CPI Group (UK) Ltd, Croydon, CR0 4YY

23/04/2025

14661010-0001